Sharon Harner

DIAGNOSIS AND REMEDIATION OF THE DISABLED READER

Second Edition

ELDON E. EKWALL
The University of Texas at El Paso

JAMES L. SHANKER
California State University, Hayward

ALLYN AND BACON, INC.
Boston   London   Sydney   Toronto

Eldon E. Ekwall
dedicates this book to
John H. Renner, M.D.

James L. Shanker
dedicates this book to
his most important teachers,
his parents,
Jack and Ida Shanker

Library of Congress Cataloging in Publication Data

Ekwall, Eldon E.
  Diagnosis and remediation of the disabled reader.

  Includes bibliographies and index.
    1. Reading disability. 2. Reading—Ability testing.
  3. Reading—Remedial teaching. I. Shanker, James L.
  II. Title.
  LB1050.5.E37 1983   428.4′2   82-18177
  ISBN 0-205-07931-8

Printed in the United States of America
10 9 8 7 6 5 4 3 2 1   88 87 86 85 84 83

Contents

Preface

This book is designed to be used by students who are taking their first course in diagnosis and/or remediation of reading disabilities. It was also written for practicing teachers who want to broaden their knowledge and skills in diagnostic and remedial techniques. We have assumed that anyone reading this material will have a basic knowledge of the teaching of reading as taught in a reading foundations course. However, because of the diversity of the subject matter and the manner in which foundation courses are often taught, we have in a number of places defined the terminology necessary to develop a general background for the discussion of major concepts.

This book begins with a chapter on the reasons why pupils fail in reading. In this case we are operating under the premise that to be an effective diagnostician, as well as an effective remedial reading teacher, it is often helpful to have a broad knowledge of causal factors in reading disabilities. A number of factors have a significant correlation with reading disabilities but do not appear to exhibit a direct causal relationship. We have discussed these as well, since there is still much to learn in this ever-changing subject and to ignore any factors relating to reading would, in effect, be educating you for obsolescence.

Chapter 2 contains a discussion of some operational procedures of which we believe all reading specialists should become aware. Portions of Chapter 2 are expanded on in later chapters; the added emphasis should serve to alert you to the importance of these topics.

Chapter 3 contains a framework for the examination of educational problems in reading diagnosis and remediation. Chapters 4 through 8 discuss diagnosis and remediation under the categories of educational, psychological, sociological, and physical factors. Chapter 9 is devoted to the diagnosis and treatment of severe learning disabilities. You will note that each of these chapters is broken down into Diagnosis and Remediation sections. A new chapter (Chapter 13) has been added to help the reading teacher make the most efficient diagnosis possible using only those tests and evaluative instruments that may change the course of reading instruction for disabled readers. Tests recommended in each area of possible weaknesses are also given.

The remaining chapters deal with additional diagnostic and remedial techniques and administrative procedures with which the reading specialist should become familiar. Chapter 17 covers the interpretation of tests and research results in relation to reading. If you have not had a course in educational research or educational statistics, you may wish to read Chapter 17 first. Included at the end of the book are appendices containing material that you should find helpful in your day-to-day work with disabled readers.

ACKNOWLEDGEMENTS

We would like to thank a number of people who have in some way contributed to the completion of this book. First we would like to thank Cheryl Milner, who served as research assistant for the second edition. We are grateful to Mable Chew and Lilia Lavender who helped with the typing of the manuscript during its various stages of production. Our appreciation is also extended to Naomi Maupin, Ann Holly, Wedge Johnson, Karen Sheffield, Susan May, and Pam Round, who spent many hours helping document certain information. We would also like to thank Dr. Don Swink for his help in the preparation of the section on vision. Our appreciation is also extended to Roger De Santi, University of New Orleans; Richard Allington, SUNY, Albany; Norman Koch, Western Oregon State College; Eunice Askov, Penn State University; and Hal B. Dreyer, Mankato State University who reviewed the manuscript and contributed many scholarly suggestions. We would also like to thank the many fine graduate students who have taken our courses in diagnosis and remedial reading, who along with our own teachers, Dr. Ruth Strang and Dr. George Sherman, have helped us learn what we hope we have been able to communicate to the reader in this book. Our deepest appreciation is also extended to Wilson Wayne Grant, M.D., who has worked closely with one of the authors over the years and who has been unusually successful in diagnosing and treating severely disabled readers. Dr. Grant has written Chapter 9 on severe learning disabilities. We also extend our appreciation to Susan Middleton of Bywater Production Services who spent many long hours in carefully editing the final manuscript. James Shanker would like to thank his wife Susan and his sons Kenneth and Michael for their support and assistance. And finally, Eldon Ekwall would like to extend his most sincere gratitude to Carol Ann for her kindness and encouragement during a very sad part of his life.

To the Teacher

This is a textbook designed to be used in a first course in diagnosis and/or remediation of reading disabilities. It is designed for either advanced undergraduates or graduate students who have had at least one course in the foundations of reading instruction.

You will note that Chapters 4 through 9 contain a section on diagnosis (Part A) and a section on remediation (Part B). If your institution offers separate courses in diagnosis and remediation, this format should facilitate the assignment of readings to supplement classroom activities. On the other hand, if diagnosis and remediation are combined into the same course, the student should read Parts A and B of these chapters.

We have yet to find a textbook concerning diagnosis and/or remediation of reading difficulties that presents various topics in the order in which we wish to present them in our classes. In this text we have presented the topics in what we believe to be a logical sequence for a student's learning needs. However, some professors may wish to cover certain topics in a somewhat different sequence. For example, you may wish to cover the administration and scoring of informal reading inventories before Chapter 11. This should present no problems.

Many students have expressed the concern that books presenting a constant deluge of research and a long list of references to each research study are ineffective. We have tried to make this book scholarly enough to maintain the faith and respect of both the student and professor; also, we have tried to avoid listing many references to research that is commonly known or readily available to anyone with access to a library. Yet where issues are controversial or where the research is meager, we have tried to reference each study.

It is our hope that you will find the overall format stimulating and the material rewarding.

1

Reasons for Failure in Reading

This chapter contains a discussion of the various factors that contribute to, or are related to, disability in reading. At this point no attempt will be made to discuss diagnostic and remedial procedures for various causal factors. The purpose of this chapter is to give an overview of these factors and the relative prevalence of each factor, so that appropriate diagnostic and remedial procedures can then be devised.

It is fascinating to see the pieces of a diagnostic puzzle begin to take shape through the process of interviewing, collecting background data, and testing. It is also extremely rewarding to see the progress of a disabled reader as the information derived from the diagnostic process is implemented in the teaching program. However, regardless of the thoroughness of the diagnostic process, you are likely to see few positive results unless it is followed by a remedial program based on the results of the original diagnosis. Likewise, a remedial program that is not based on the results of a thorough diagnosis is likely to fail. Since a child is constantly growing and changing, it is imperative that diagnosis and remediation be a continuous process.

Since reading diagnosis and remediation can seldom be separated for practical purposes, it becomes imperative that the reading specialist be well trained in both areas. As a practicing or future reading specialist you must know what kinds of problems to look for and what to do about these problems when they are found to exist. Most of the diagnostic-remedial process for the reader deals with problems that could be classified under four major categories. These categories are illustrated in Figure 1–1.

As a reading specialist, your primary concern is the diagnosis and remediation of educational factors. However, a study of the problems related to reading disability should also make you more aware of various causal fac-

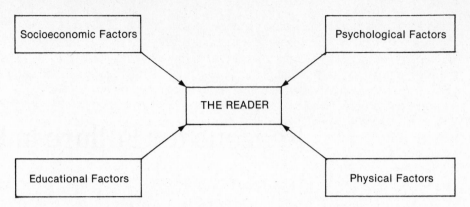

FIGURE 1-1.   Factors that influence the reader.

tors that are often different from those that appear obvious when a diagnosis is made. In many cases, even though remedial procedures are instituted for a particular student, they are of less value than they might have been if some precautions had been taken to alleviate conditions or factors that caused the reading disability in the first place. Perhaps it should be emphasized at this point that there are also many factors that seem to have a close relationship to reading disability but cannot be established as having direct causal relationships. Since this textbook is not directed solely for the training of reading "technicians," it seems important to stress more than the "how to" of test administration and the "how to" of certain remedial techniques. Testing methods and materials, as well as teaching methods and materials, are constantly being updated and revised. To teach only those used at this time without examining other important aspects of reading would, in effect, be educating for obsolescence. There is still much to learn in the field of remedial reading and although many problems are ambiguous we cannot simply ignore them as being of little importance.

A monumental study done by Helen Robinson (1946) and described in her book entitled *Why Pupils Fail in Reading* is perhaps the best known, and has contributed more to our knowledge about the reasons for pupil failure in reading than any other research effort. Because it was a landmark study, the results of Robinson's work will be summarized in the remainder of this chapter. Her findings will also be compared with those of more recent studies. Keep in mind, however, that it is seldom possible to determine the exact percentage of poor readers whose reading disability stems from a particular anomaly as Robinson did in her research. This is true because we know that reading difficulties are often the result of multiple problems, or in many cases multiple problems are present that tend to mask the retarding effect of any one problem. Because of this problem many studies only report the percentage of retarded or disabled readers versus the percentage of normal readers who have exhibited certain anomalies. Other studies simply report whether there is a significant difference in the mean number of disabled readers versus the mean number of normal readers who exhibit certain anomalies. The term *disabled reader* has often been used to describe readers who are not reading well as measured by a combination of reading test scores compared to their potential as measured by intelligence tests. Or the term *disabled readers* may simply mean those students who are reading below the level of most students in their class. A more thorough definition of the term *disabled reader* and its implications for the remedial reading program is contained in Chapter 14, for either those students who have a serious discrepancy between their reading ability and their reading potential or those students who are not able to deal effectively with the reading materials used for instruction in their classrooms. In Robinson's study those students who were below nine years of age and who had a reading grade level 0.9 years below their mental age and chronological age were accepted for study. Those students who were nine years or older and had an average reading grade two years or more below their mental and chronological ages were also accepted for further study.

In conducting her study Robinson planned three steps. The first step was to summarize the literature concerning pupil failure, and with the aid of various specialists an attempt was made to evaluate the information found in the literature. The second step in Robinson's study was to identify and evaluate the causal factors in a group of severely disabled readers. The third and final step in Robinson's study was to present significant conclusions concerning causal factors and to discuss various problems needing further study.

In conducting her study Robinson enlisted the aid of various specialists. Included in this group were a social worker, a neurologist, a psychiatrist, three ophthalmologists, an otolaryngologist, an endocrinologist, a speech specialist, a reading specialist, and Professor Robinson, who acted as psychologist and reading specialist. Thirty severely disabled readers with Binet IQs between 85 and 137 were examined by each of the various specialists. Following the examinations all specialists met to present their findings. An intensive remedial program was then begun with twenty-two of the original thirty cases. During the remedial program an attempt was made to determine the "potency" of each of the possible causes listed as anomalies in the original diagnosis of each pupil.

In the initial diagnosis a number of factors were found in Robinson's group of disabled readers. At the conclusion of the remedial program Robinson's group again met to discuss the various anomalies that were considered to be probable causes of pupils' failure. Some of these factors were later determined to have had little or no impairing effect on the reading ability of the group. This information is summarized in Table 1–1.

TABLE 1-1.   Percentage of anomalies considered to be important versus probable causes in Helen Robinson's study.

	Percentage of anomalies considered important	Percentage of anomalies considered to be probable causes
1. Visual difficulty	63.6	50.0
2. Neurological difficulty	22.7	18.1
3. Auditory difficulty	13.6	9.1
4. Speech or discrimination difficulty	27.3	18.1
5. General physical difficulty	9.1	4.5
6. Endocrine disturbance	22.7	9.1
7. Emotional maladjustment	40.9	31.8
8. Social problems	63.6	54.5
9. School methods	22.7	18.1

As you will note, the percentages of agreement between anomalies considered important and those considered to be probable causes are not the same. This, of course, indicates that the group did not believe that certain anomalies, even though definitely present, were necessarily contributors.

Although the number of pupils examined in Robinson's study was relatively small, the study had a number of outstanding features, some of which have been lacking in more recent studies. For example, every pupil was thoroughly examined by specialists in every area considered important to reading success or failure. Robinson was then able to carry on a remedial program and follow the progress of each student. Where necessary, students were even removed from their home environments and placed in a special school to determine whether home environmental conditions were causal factors in the pupils' failure. The social worker was able to visit homes to get a first-hand look at the students' environment. Additionally there were several specialists working in certain fields to check on any biases that any one tester might possess.

Reasons for pupils' failure are classified under the four major categories previously mentioned plus a fifth category that is a combination of all four. These categories will be discussed in the following order:

1.   Physical factors
2.   Psychological factors
3.   Socioeconomic factors
4.   Educational factors
5.   Combinations of the four major categories listed above

PHYSICAL FACTORS

The Eyes and Seeing

Robinson's initial analysis indicated that 63.6 percent of the pupils had some sort of visual difficulty. However, in the final analysis the specialists concluded that sight difficulties were the cause of reading retardation in only 50 percent of the cases.

It is almost impossible to find any substantial amount of agreement among the researchers concerning exact percentages of disabled readers who exhibit seeing difficulties. It would appear, however, that Robinson's study is in general agreement with others who have studied seeing problems. For example, Howard Coleman (1968), examined eighty-seven children in grades one to six who had severe deficits in the reading and/or language arts areas. He reported that approximately 50 percent of these children had either sight or visual-perceptual dysfunctions. Of the 50 percent mentioned, Coleman reported that 19.5 percent of the group had refractive errors and 30 percent had visual-perceptual dysfunctions. Many researchers also agree with the position taken by Thomas Eames (1962), who states,

> One child might be greatly handicapped by a visual defect while another might perceive adequately on the basis of very poor retinal images. Statistically, it has been shown that defective visual acuity is not much more frequent among reading failures than among non-failures, although individual cases occur in which failure is definitely the result of impaired vision. Such cases are greatly benefitted by glasses if the poor vision is due to refractive error (eyes out of focus) but glasses are of no benefit when the visual deficiency is of amblyopic (insensitivity) nature. The mere existence of low acuity is to be regarded as a possible but not invariable cause of poor reading.

There is some disagreement among various researchers concerning the types of seeing problems responsible for reading disability. Certain types of eye and seeing problems do, however, tend to appear to be more closely related to reading disability than others. Chapter 8 contains a detailed discussion of these problems.

Auditory Difficulties

In discussing auditory difficulties it is necessary to make a distinction between auditory acuity and auditory discrimination. *Auditory acuity* refers to the ability to hear various frequencies at various intensities of loudness (measured in decibels). *Auditory discrimination* refers to the ability to hear major or slight differences in sounds.

It is somewhat difficult to interpret Robinson's percentages in these categories because difficulties in these areas were viewed somewhat differently than at the present time. One reason for this is that we now have better tests of auditory discrimination than were available to Robinson and her researchers. Robinson lumped speech and discrimination difficulties together. Each of these will be discussed separately.

Auditory Acuity.   Robinson reports that inadequate auditory acuity was an anomaly considered to be a cause of reading difficulty in 9 percent of her reading disability cases. However, Robinson also states that her study reinforces the general opinion that insufficient auditory acuity is relatively unimportant as a cause of severe reading disabilities. It would be difficult, however, to determine whether Robinson's 9 percent figure would be valid for disabled readers in general, since most researchers have tended to study auditory difficulties as a whole rather than isolate auditory acuity and study it as a separate factor.

Guy Bond, Miles Tinker, and Barbara Wasson (1979) report that various research studies disagree on the number of children with serious hearing losses. This disagreement occurs because of the different measurement techniques used and the lack of clear standards for determining what constitutes a hearing impairment. Nonetheless, Bond, Tinker, and Wasson estimate that approximately 5 percent of the total population of school children have serious hearing losses. They also believe that many additional children have a slight hearing loss that may develop into a serious impairment if not treated early.

Studies tend to show that there are more cases of impaired auditory acuity among groups of disabled readers than among groups of average or good readers. However, even though the differences are sometimes statistically significant the fact that a child has impaired auditory acuity is not necessarily predictive that the child will become a disabled reader.

It appears that hearing losses in the high frequency ranges are more likely to result in reading impairment than hearing losses in the middle or low frequency ranges. It also appears that boys tend to experience loss in the high ranges more often than girls. The fact that the percentage of women teachers in the primary grades is much higher than the percentage of men teachers also makes a loss of acuity in the high frequency range more detrimental since women's voices tend to range closer to the high frequencies.

In summary, it appears that although inadequate auditory acuity as a whole is seldom responsible for failure in reading it may be an important factor in some isolated cases, especially if very severe and if not detected soon enough. There is general agreement that a test for auditory acuity should be included as part of a thorough diagnosis of a disabled reader. Recommendations with respect to testing in this area follow the discussion of auditory discrimination in Chapter 8.

Auditory Discrimination. Robinson combined the categories of speech, general auditory discrimination, and memory span for sounds into a category called "Speech or Discrimination Difficulty." She reported that these factors were contributing anomalies in 18 percent of her severely disabled readers. However, she believed that dyslalia (a speech impairment due to a defect in the speech organs) was responsible for 14 of the 18 percent and that only the remaining 4 percent were caused by inadequate auditory discrimination or inadequate memory span.

It should be emphasized at this point that inadequate memory span is seldom studied in conjunction with inadequate auditory discrimination, however, both are often considered to be important factors in the diagnosis of disabled readers. As mentioned previously, better instruments have also been developed for the purpose of measuring impairment in both of these areas.

It should also be emphasized that children's auditory discrimination skills improve considerably as they progress through the primary grades. Bertha Thompson (1963), conducted a longitudinal study of auditory discrimination in a group of 105 children. She concluded that "inaccurate discriminative ability is more characteristic of first grade entrants than accurate ability. The reverse is true at the end of the second grade." (p. 377) Thompson also reported that at the end of the second grade approximately 24 percent of the students had inaccurate auditory discrimination ability. Approximately half (12 percent) of this group were classified as poor readers. Thompson's view of the relationship between auditory discrimination and reading is representative of a number of researchers. She states, "This again points toward the importance of adequacy in auditory discrimination to success in primary reading. However, it definitely reveals that other factors are important in reading disability." (p. 377)

Reid Lyon (1977) has reviewed the research in this area and has concluded that the evidence does *not* support the view that auditory discrimination ability is necessary for later success in reading. This remains a controversial issue which will be discussed more fully in Chapter 8.

As stated earlier, several tests of auditory memory have been developed since Robinson completed her study; these will also be discussed in Chapter 8. Little is known concerning the relationship between auditory memory and reading. Various studies indicate that a larger percentage of disabled readers have impaired auditory memory span or ability to sequence than do good readers. The mystery that remains, however, is what to do about this problem since the training of auditory memory per se seldom seems to have any appreciable effect on children's reading ability.

Speech. Robinson reported that speech problems were considered to be probable causes of reading failure in 14 percent of her cases. This is in general agreement with a number of studies reported by Thomas Eames (1950) and Bond, Tinker, and Wasson (1979), although the above-mentioned authors stated that some studies showed that the number of students with speech defects was no higher among disabled readers than in a normal population.

There is some feeling that certain neurological dysfunctions contribute to inadequacy in speech as well as reading and therefore there is a tendency to view the reading disability as stemming from the speech problem when in reality both result from the neurological dysfunction. Some researchers also believe that emotional reactions caused from defective speech may, in turn, contribute to reading disability. Eames (1950) states that certain broad generalizations may be drawn concerning the relationships that exist between reading and speech. These are as follows:

1. Neurological lesions in the language centers or their interconnections may impair both speech and reading.
2. Failure or inadequacy of auditory association and discrimination may predispose to either speech or reading trouble.
3. Speech defects occur in a certain proportion of reading failures and vice versa.
4. Emotional reactions to speech difficulties may impair reading.
5. Oral reading is more difficult for a person with a speech defect. (p. 53)

Laterality, Mixed Dominance, and Directional Confusion

Before beginning a discussion of the topics of laterality, mixed dominance, and directional confusion, it would be helpful to first define these terms as they are commonly used. The definitions that follow are those of Alice Cohen and Gerald G. Glass (1968), as derived from Albert Harris (1958).

Lateral Dominance refers to the preference or superiority of one side of the body over the other (hand, eye, foot) in performing motor tasks. Right lateral dominance would indicate preference for the right hand, eye, and foot.

Laterality is another term for lateral dominance.

Consistent Dominance refers to the preferential use of one hand, eye, or foot.

Mixed or Incomplete (hand, eye, or foot) Dominance exists when the individual does not show a consistent preference for one (eye, hand, or foot).

Mixed Dominance without specific reference to hand, eye, or foot includes both crossed dominance (see below) and mixed dominance.

Crossed Dominance exists when the dominant hand and dominant eye are on opposite sides.

Visual Motor Consistency occurs when the subject's dominant hand, eye, and foot are on the same side of the body.

Directional Confusion refers to knowledge of left and right. "Knowledge of Left and Right" is demonstrated by the subject in response to questions such as, "show me your right hand, left eye" etc. (This is distinguished from actual use of the dominant hand, eye, or foot in performance tasks.) (p. 343)[1]

[1]Reprinted by permission of the authors and the International Reading Association.

Robinson did not attempt to determine what percentage, if any, of her disabled readers' problems resulted from mixed dominance or difficulties with laterality. She stated that tests for mixed dominance were given but that the specialists cooperating in her study did not know how to interpret their findings.

The research on the relationship of laterality, mixed dominance, and directional confusion to reading is voluminous. From all of this, however, there are still no clear-cut answers as to what we should test for and what we can do about these problems when they are found to exist. Some of the proponents of various approaches to the remediation of problems in this area have been very vociferous and consequently, in our opinion, have oversold the value of remedial materials and techniques in this area. Studies such as those of E. Shearer (1968), Steven Forness (1968), and R. J. Capobianco (1967) are in general agreement with the findings of Cohen and Glass (1968) who studied 120 subjects in the first and fourth grades. Half of their sample were defined as "good" readers and half were defined as "poor" readers. Their statistical analysis revealed the following relationships as being significant:

1. *Knowledge of left and right and reading ability in the first grade.* Good readers were more likely to be "normal" and poor readers were more likely to be "hesitant" or "confused" in their knowledge of left and right.
2. *Hand dominance and reading ability in first grade.* Good readers were more likely to have a dominant hand and poor readers were more likely to have mixed-hand dominance.
3. *Knowledge of left and right between first and fourth grade children.* There were significantly more first grade children who were hesitant or confused in their knowledge of left and right than fourth grade children. There were significantly more fourth grade children who were normal in their knowledge of left and right than first graders.
4. *Knowledge of left and right and hand dominance.* Right handed children were more likely to have knowledge of left and right. Left handed and mixed children were more likely to be hesitant or confused in their knowledge of left and right.

However, no significance was found between fourth graders' reading ability and knowledge of left and right. The same was true for hand dominance. The reader may be most concerned with the factor of *crossed dominance.* This factor is what most people are referring to when the area of laterality is discussed. No significant relationship was found between crossed dominance and reading ability in the total population studied. (p. 345)[2]

Similar findings were reported by Albert Harris (1979) in a review of recent research.

As stated earlier Robinson's researchers administered tests for lateral dominance, but did not feel that they knew how to interpret their findings. These researchers were simply being conservative in their beliefs. Very little more is known today regarding the accurate interpretation of findings such

[2]Reprinted by permission of the authors and the International Reading Association.

as those reported by Cohen and Glass. Until more is known regarding effective remedial procedures for these areas that will, in turn, improve children's reading ability, a diagnosis for laterality, mixed dominance, and directional confusion seems to be of dubious value.

Neurological Problems

Laterality, mixed dominance, and directional confusion could be quite properly, and often are, classified as neurological dysfunctions. They are separated here from the general heading of neurological problems for purposes of clarifying the discussion of these factors. General neurological problems also include an array of dysfunctions related to difficulties in reading. It is believed that neurological dysfunctions may stem from genetic mutations and that certain characteristics are also heritable. A further cause of neurological dysfunctions is brain injury.

Robinson and her researchers believed that neurological difficulties were an important anomaly in 22.7 percent of her retarded readers, and they were considered as a probable cause in 18.1 percent of these cases. It would be difficult to determine whether these percentages would apply to disabled readers in general, since the term *neurological difficulty* is interpreted so broadly. Furthermore, some authorities also feel that neurological difficulties can only be accurately diagnosed by a neurologist; therefore, the results of a number of studies of so-called neurologically impaired disabled readers may be contaminated by other factors. A further problem exists in that many children exhibit symptoms of neurological dysfunction and yet read perfectly well. Che Kan Leong (1980) pointed out:

> The field of cerebral mechanisms underlying reading disabilities is vast, complex and touches on many disciplines: psychology, neurology, language and education. Partly because of this complexity and the interrelatedness of the workings of the brain, the findings are less than conclusive. (p. 198)

Children classified as dyslexic or alexic[3] are usually categorized under the general heading of neurological difficulties. Robinson believed, as have many others since, that children are often classified as alexic or dyslexic when in reality they do not exhibit the symptoms of the typically dyslexic or alexic child. This again complicates any attempt to determine the percentage of disabled readers who have neurological difficulties.

The fact does remain that a certain proportion of disabled readers do have neurological difficulties but that neurological difficulties probably account for a small percentage of the actual causes of reading disability.

[3]The term *dyslexic* refers to a condition of severe reading disability. Some authors have stated that it is related to neurological dysfunctions and others simply define the term as a condition in which a student is severely disabled in reading for no apparent reason. (For a more thorough discussion of this term and of severe reading disability, see Chapter 9.)

However, as Barbara Bateman (1974), has stressed, the fact that a student is classified as having a minimal brain dysfunction (MBD) does not help in the diagnosis of the child's reading problem. A student who is an extremely disabled reader ultimately must be taught to read regardless of how we label his or her condition.

Other Physical Factors

Researchers who have studied other physical factors than those discussed previously have often concluded that glandular disturbances contribute to reading disabilities. Robinson and her researchers believed that endocrine disturbances were anomalies important in 40.9 percent of her reading disability cases. They did, however, conclude that endocrine disturbances were the actual causes in only 9.1 percent of her cases. This still, of course, represents a rather high figure and makes glandular disturbances an important factor in reading difficulties. Robinson also stressed the point that when endocrine disturbances were present they not only retarded progress in learning but also tended to interfere with progress in other areas such as orthoptic treatment, social adjustment, and physical well-being. She stated that although this anomaly was less frequent in occurrence it did have a marked influence on certain cases.

Other researchers, such as Donald E. P. Smith (1958), and Lyman Cavanaugh (1948), have also concluded that glandular disturbances are an extremely important factor in contributing to reading disability. Cavanaugh studied 660 children and concluded that 18 percent had rather serious thyroid deficiencies that could contribute to disability in learning. Smith believed that treatment for endocrine disturbances could, in some cases, yield promising to dramatic results.

Other physical factors often listed as either causal or concomitant are malnutrition, poor dentition, allergies, infected tonsils and/or adenoids, vitamin deficiencies, and susceptibility to colds. However, among these disorders Robinson found that only malnutrition could be considered a causal factor. She believed that although various physical disorders are often present in cases of reading disability they are seldom the actual cause of reading disability.

PSYCHOLOGICAL FACTORS

A number of studies have been conducted to determine the relationship of various psychological factors to reading disability. Among the psychological factors often studied are various emotional problems, intelligence, and self-concept. It should be stressed that all of these factors are, no doubt, highly interrelated, so that it becomes difficult if not impossible to completely separate them for isolated study.

Emotional Problems

In researching emotional problems the question that most often arises is whether reading disability is caused by emotional problems or whether reading disability results in emotional problems. It appears that each tends to contribute to the other with reading disability causing emotional problems more often than emotional problems causing reading disability.

Robinson reported that 40.9 percent of her disabled readers had a significant degree of emotional maladjustment, but she believed that it was an anomaly that caused reading failure in only 31.8 percent of her cases. Robinson's reported percentages in this category probably vary more from those reported in other studies than do her percentages for any of the other categories. Gates (1941) reported that 75 percent of the disabled readers studied by him showed personality maladjustment; Gates believed that in about 25 percent of these (or about 19 percent of the total group of disabled readers) the emotional maladjustment was a contributing cause of reading disability. Albert Harris and Edward Sipay (1980) report that of several hundred cases of reading disability seen in the Queens College Educational Clinic during a fifteen-year period, close to 100 percent showed some kind of maladjustment. Harris and Sipay report that emotional maladjustment was a causal factor in about 50 percent of the cases in this group. Harris and Sipay also report on a study by Eve Malmquist (1967). Malmquist's examination of 399 Swedish children indicated that nervous traits were probably contributing causes of reading failure in 23 percent of the disabled readers.

It is evident that there is wide disagreement not only about the percentage of disabled readers we might expect to have emotional problems, but also about the contribution of emotional maladjustment as a causal factor in reading failure. The important point, however, is that the disabled reader who comes to the educational diagnostician or to the remedial reading teacher is likely to exhibit some sort of emotional maladjustment. For this reason proper diagnosis and remediation for emotional problems must be considered a necessary part of a remedial reading program.

Intelligence

A number of research studies have been conducted to determine the relationship between achievement and intelligence. Albert Harris (1972) has pointed out that

> the relation between intelligence and reading is low to moderate at the beginning level, but increases as children get older. . . . As the nature of the reading task becomes more one of comprehension and interpretation, intelligence becomes a stronger determining factor. (p. 42)

Harris decries the use of group intelligence tests, suggesting that the non-verbal tests are unfair to disabled readers and poor measures of the abilities required for successful reading development. Harris believes that an individual verbal intelligence test, such as the Stanford-Binet or the Revised Wechsler Intelligence Scale for Children, is the best available device for estimating a child's potential to read with comprehension.

In spite of the fact that literally thousands of studies have been conducted on intelligence tests, it is not clear how useful such instruments are in diagnosing reading difficulties. For example, a study by Louise Ames and Richard Walker (1964) sought to determine whether fifth-grade reading achievement could be predicted from WISC IQ scores administered at the kindergarten level. In their conclusions Ames and Walker stated that they believed that the usefulness of their reported findings did not lie in their employment for predicting fifth-grade reading scores. Rather, they offered the suggestion that individual subject characteristics other than either general intelligence or specific reading skills contributed to individual differences in reading at the above-average level as well as below average.

George and Evelyn Spache (1977) expressed a similar viewpoint:

> . . . Research studies of school beginners show that intelligence test results are not highly predictive of early reading success. If pupils are arranged in the order of their reading test scores after a period of training, the order just does not neatly parallel a ranking based on mental age or intelligence quotient. Only the extreme cases, the very superior and the mentally retarded pupils, tend to agree in their ranks in reading and intelligence. The degree of reading success for most pupils is determined not by their exact level or rank in intelligence but by other more influential factors. (pp. 156–157)

It seems evident then that we should not place a great deal of faith in IQ scores as predictors of potential reading ability. However, as Spache and Spache point out, the IQ is a fairly good predictor of reading ability for children with extremely high IQs or for children who are mentally retarded. Most researchers agree that children with very low IQs are at a considerable disadvantage in learning to read; therefore, a low IQ is often an important hindering factor. For this reason it is often helpful to administer an individual intelligence test as part of the normal diagnostic procedure with a disabled reader. An important point to remember, however, is that many children with low IQs become good readers and many children with medium and high IQs become disabled readers. Therefore, the IQ should only be considered in conjunction with other factors.

Some estimates have been made regarding the percentage of disabled readers whose problem stemmed from having a low IQ. The authors believe, however, that any percentage figure based on IQ alone is misleading because of the interaction of low IQ with a multitude of other factors such as home environment and teaching methods.

Self-Concept

The self-concept and its close relationship with teacher expectation is a psychological factor that should not be overlooked in the diagnosis of a disabled reader. Studies such as those of William Padelford (1969), and Maxine Cohn and Donald Kornelly (1970) have shown that a significant positive relationship does exist between reading achievement and self-concept. Padelford found that this relationship exists regardless of ethnic group, socioeconomic level, or sex. Cohn and Kornelly indicate that a program of remediation for a low self-concept can produce positive achievement in reading.

Monte Smith (1979) found that the combination of word knowledge performance, math performance and family socioeconomic status (SES) was a significant predictor of self-concept. Interestingly, Smith also found that learning-disabled students from high SES families possessed lower self-concepts than their counterparts from low SES families.

Little is known regarding the percentage of disabled readers whose problems are directly related to the possession of a low self-concept. However, we do know the problem exists, and as Frances Pryor (1975) states, "Changing a poor reader's self-concept by bolstering his feelings about himself is perhaps the first step toward improving the academic problem." (p. 359) For this reason this factor should not be overlooked in the diagnosis and remediation of the reader.

SOCIOECONOMIC FACTORS

Robinson reported that maladjusted homes or poor interfamily relationships were found to be contributing causes in 54.5 percent of her cases studied. As she stated, this percentage was somewhat higher than those reported in other studies. Robinson believed that we often underestimate the importance of this factor. In her study a social worker was especially diligent in obtaining information from parents concerning difficulties and problems. Robinson apparently believed that, because information concerning interfamily relationships and other related factors are somewhat difficult to obtain, the percentages of these factors that appear as causal factors in reading disability are often unrealistically low.

Socioeconomic factors are usually so closely related that it would be impossible to list any specific percentage of reading disability cases resulting from any one isolated factor. Factors often studied, however, are presence of the father in the home (or broken homes), ethnic background and its social relationships, economic level, dialect, presence of books or stimulating reading materials in the home, sibling relationships, and parent-sibling relationships.

Martin Deutsch (1967) studied family relationships including broken homes where the father was not present in the home. Deutsch stated that "intact homes are more crowded than broken ones, although the children from the intact homes do better in scholastic achievement. . . . Apparently, *who* lives in the home is more important than *how many*." (p. 104)

Ethnic background and its social ramifications are also important influences on reading achievement. For example, the United States Commission on Civil Rights (1971) reported as follows:

> The Commission found, on the basis of information provided by school principals, that from 50 to 70 percent of Mexican American and black students in the fourth, eighth, and twelfth grades are reading below the level expected for the grade to which they are assigned. In contrast, only 25 to 34 percent of all Anglo youngsters in these grades are reading below grade level. This approaches a two to one ratio of below average reading achievement for students of minority groups. (p. 24)

Of course, ethnic background is in many cases related to economic level. Many studies have shown that the overall reading level of children from poor communities, regardless of ethnicity, is often far below that of children from more affluent communities.

Nila Banton Smith (1974) has suggested that three of the characteristics of disadvantaged readers that are basic contributing factors to reading difficulties are low self-concept, impoverished environment, and poor health.

The problem of dialect and its relationship to reading difficulties has received considerable attention. Researchers and writers such as S. Alan Cohen and Thelma Cooper (1972) have stressed, however, that dialectal differences of the urban disadvantaged reader are not a hindering factor in learning to read. Studies by Richard Rystrom (1968) and W. Labov (1969) have tended to confirm Cohen and Cooper's beliefs. Rystrom (1972) stated:

> There is virtually no evidence to indicate that dialect is causally related to reading failures. . . . Any regional or social dialect is, so far as has been determined, an equally effective vehicle for learning to read as any other regional or social dialect.

Studies dealing with the relationship of reading ability and such factors as the number of books found in the home or between reading ability and the amount of time children's parents spend reading are of little value in furnishing us with information concerning the contribution of these factors to reading achievement. The problem, of course, lies in the fact that the number of books found in a home or the amount of time that parents spend reading is so often related to a host of other factors. Among these factors are education, occupation, and economic level of the parents. Perhaps about all we can say with any certainty is that there appears to be a group of other socioeconomic factors that interact to influence reading ability.

Social relationships between siblings and/or between parents and siblings are another social factor that appears to be worthy of consideration in a thorough diagnosis. However, definite information on the percentage of reading disability cases caused by interfamily relationships is sadly lacking due to the complexities involved in their identification.

Language Factors

Inadequate language development is undoubtedly a factor in reading failure. Unfortunately, we are unable to determine specifically the extent to which language difficulties affect reading performance. Nor are useful instruments currently available for diagnosing language problems per se. In order to be useful, such a test must not only identify specific language weaknesses but also provide information for prescriptive instruction to remediate the difficulties.

A relatively new test, *The Test of Language Development* (TOLD) (Newcomer and Hammill, 1977), does enable the diagnostician to evaluate children's expressive and receptive competencies in the areas of phonology, semantics and syntax. This standardized test is sufficiently reliable and valid. It is not a lengthy test and it yields a comparative index of the child's language abilities. The TOLD is not designed to provide direct information for prescriptive instruction. As the authors point out:

> The results yielded by the TOLD will focus attention upon the specific areas of language in which the child is unable to perform as well as his peers do. In effect, the results will identify his primary linguistic deficits. However, before a remedial program is planned, it will be necessary to determine through informal assessment, including criterion-referenced testing, and possibly diagnostic teaching, the specific skills within an area which are in need of remediation. (Test Manual, p. 16)

The TOLD is intended for use with most children between the ages of 4-0 and 8-11. A companion test, *The Test of Early Language Development* (TELD) (Hresko, Reid and Hammill, 1981) was designed for use with children between the ages of 3-0 and 7-11 who possess more severe language difficulties or who are less proficient in English.

Harris and Sipay (1980) believe the most significant aspects of language are the child's (1) vocabulary, (2) understanding of sentence structure, and (3) clarity of pronunciation. Emerald Dechant (1981) adds a fourth factor, listening comprehension.

This is an emerging and exciting area of research in the field of reading. Recent theories, supporting research, and recommendations for instruction in language skills will be presented in Chapter 7.

EDUCATIONAL FACTORS

Robinson mentioned a number of school factors or conditions that she and others believed often influenced or were conducive to reading failure. Among these factors were teachers' personalities, methods of teaching reading, school policy on promotions, materials available, and class size. In her final analysis Robinson believed that school methods were a probable contributing causal factor in 18.1 percent of the cases she studied. She admitted, however, that there are so many factors involved in assessing educational factors that any definite conclusion is nearly impossible.

It is our opinion that Robinson's figure in this case is not representative of the total percentage of reading failures caused by educational factors. If one views educational factors contributing to reading disability as strictly those that are so bad that many children within any classroom fail to learn, then perhaps Robinson's figure would be representative of the situation that exists in general. However, many experts agree with John Manning[4] who expressed the viewpoint that more than 90 percent of our reading failures could or should be blamed on poor teaching. Since only approximately 2 percent of our students experience learning disabilities so severe as to require the services of a specialist, it seems logical that near perfect teaching would result in a failure rate of no more than this 2 percent.

S. Jay Samuels (1970) expresses the opinion that instruction in reading is quite likely to be less than adequate. He states,

> It is this author's contention that the assumption of adequate instruction is probably false in numerous instances because at the present time a complete analysis of the skills which must be mastered in the process of learning to read has not been made. Without a complete analysis of each of the subskills and concepts which must be mastered in the process of learning to read, it is difficult to understand how any instruction can be considered adequate. In the absence of a complete analysis of skills necessary for reading, there is a danger that the teacher may omit teaching important skills because she does not realize they are essential; or falsely assuming that certain skills have already been mastered, she may not teach them; or she may teach nonessential skills believing they are important. (p. 267)

Gerald Duffy and Lonnie McIntyre (1981) found that even highly rated first- and second-grade teachers do not necessarily provide quality instruction. The teachers studied were rated by peers and supervisors as "good teachers," yet the researchers found that they almost never provided structured lessons or direct assistance to students during reading instruction.

As one can see, the problems in assessing educational factors as a cause of reading failures are so complex that any stated percentage is, at

[4]From a speech given by John Manning at the University of Kansas, Summer, 1969.

best, an educated guess. The fact remains, however, that educational factors should not be overlooked in the diagnostic procedure.

Recent research in the area of teacher behavior and its effects on students' reading performance has begun to shed some light on this matter. Christopher Clark (1979) identified five different approaches to research on teaching designed to answer the question, What makes a good teacher? Jere Brophy (1979a) reviewed much of the recent research in this area and summarized some of the major findings in an occasional paper written for the Institute for Research on Teaching (IRT) at Michigan State University. The IRT was established in 1976 by the National Institute of Education and has received over $6 million in grants to serve as a center for research on teaching, a forum for communication, and a training program for researchers. Some of the findings of IRT researchers will be included in the review of selected studies on teacher effectiveness that follows. Particular attention will be given to findings that relate teachers' instructional behaviors to students' reading achievement.

In 1976 the California state legislature directed the superintendent of public instruction to analyze selected schools to identify the educational factors that accounted for the distinction between unusually high-performing schools and unusually low-performing schools, as determined by standard tests of school achievement. The selected schools were comparable in social and demographic factors and varied only according to pupil attainment. The result was the *California School Effectiveness Study* (1977). This study found that factors *other* than those traditionally assumed to account for pupil achievement, such as family income and parents' occupational status, were significant determinants of pupil success. These other factors included:

1. *Staff characteristics.* Higher-achieving schools had principals who were more effective and involved, used aides significantly more for *non-instructional* tasks, and had central office administration that was rated higher by teachers in the areas of instructional leadership and allocation of materials and resources.
2. *Measures of contact between students and staff.* Teachers at higher-achieving schools did *not* report spending more instructional time on reading and language development.
3. *Instructional and organizational characteristics.* Students in higher-achieving schools "were perceived to be happier, more engaged in their work, and less disruptive, restless, or bored." (p. 8) Teachers at higher-achieving schools placed more emphasis on students' academic performance, divided their classes into several groups (rather than providing "individualized" instruction), and participated in a reading program that was more stable or less subject to change.

Marjorie Powell (1979) reported on the six-year Beginning Teacher Evaluation Study, also conducted in California. Some of the findings of this study included:

1.   The greater the proportion of time that students are engaged in their work (on-task), the more they learn.
2.   Some teachers were more effective than others in keeping their students on-task.
3.   Some teachers were more effective than others in providing their students with instructional tasks that led to a high success rate.
4.   The more total time spent in reading instruction, the more students learned in that area. (This finding contradicts the findings of the School Effectiveness Study.)
5.   Some teachers placed greater emphasis than others on "academics" and had higher expectations for students. The teachers with the high standards produced students with higher achievement.
6.   In higher-achieving classrooms, teachers and students demonstrated greater respect for each other and worked in a more cooperative atmosphere.

Wilbur Brookover and Lawrence Lezotte (1979) found that emphasis on the "basics" is one of the major differences between improving and declining schools. The staffs of improving schools emphasize basic reading objectives, devote more time toward achieving these objectives and believe that *all* of their students can master basic skills. Brookover and Lezotte also found that improving schools have principals who are assertive in their instructional leadership and take responsibility for evaluating student performance.

Jane Stallings and others (1978) compared classes with high gains in reading to those with low gains at the secondary school level. The authors stressed the importance of a structured program with clear expectations for pupils and minimal time wasted during instruction. It was found that in high-gain classrooms, teachers assisted students more with written assignments than with verbal directions that students were to follow on their own. Also, these teachers varied the activities, closely monitored seatwork, and provided supportive feedback to students.

In summarizing the recent research that evaluates the effect of teaching behaviors on pupil achievement, Jere Brophy (1979*b*) concluded:

1.   Teachers make a difference. Some teachers produce more learning in their students than others.
2.   Teacher expectations for student learning are an important factor.
3.   Effective teachers possess the skills needed to successfully organize and conduct instruction. They are good classroom managers.

4. Effective teachers provide a maximum amount of instruction on critical skills, with minimal time wasted.
5. Students who receive a great deal of direct instruction in a structured curriculum have the highest achievement.

We wish to point out that all studies do not support the generalizations we have noted above. However, a significant amount of research is emerging to support some basic principles of teaching that are consistent with our philosophy. We hope that as you read the remaining chapters in this book, you will bear in mind that all diagnostic and remedial procedures must fit within a framework of sound principles of instruction. For example, even the best techniques for remediating a specific reading difficulty will fail if the teacher does not set high expectations for the learner, maintain the students' task attention and provide direct instruction in a well-managed environment. Some important operational procedures for the diagnostic-remedial teacher are discussed in detail in Chapter 2.

PHYSICAL, PSYCHOLOGICAL, SOCIOECONOMIC, AND EDUCATIONAL FACTOR COMBINATIONS

During the past two decades a number of combinational factors have been reported as having a moderate to high degree of relationship to reading. Robinson mentioned a number of these factors in her study, but did not study most of them in detail because of their unwieldy nature and/or because not enough was known about them at the time to study their exact contribution as causal factors to reading disability. Although we now know somewhat more about some of these factors, only a meager amount of information is available regarding the exact role that these factors play in reading failure. Therefore, in the discussion that follows some of these factors will be discussed, but no attempt will be made to designate any specific percentage of disabled readers who possess these problems, nor will any attempt be made to designate the percentage of disabled readers whose problems originated from these factors.

The Relationship of Intelligence to Organic and Functional Etiological Factors

Stanley Krippner (1968) studied the etiological factors in reading disability of the academically talented in comparison to that of pupils of average and slow learning ability. Organic disorders referred to disorders in the central nervous system or in the endocrine system, whereas functional disorders were those arising from social, emotional, educational, or cultural handicaps.

Krippner reported that the academically talented group demonstrated significantly less organic etiology as a major factor and significantly more functional etiology as a major factor than either the average or slow-learning group.

Krippner reported that many of the pupils seen in his reading center did not improve even under intensive remediation. He states,

> Tutoring in reading is a process of sinking shafts into sand if the basic physiological foundations for learning do not exist. Satisfactory auditory discrimination must be present before a child can memorize whole words. A child must know the difference between his right and his left hand before he can master the difference between such words as "was" and "saw."
>
> Once the bases of perception and symbol-making have been established, the academically talented child who is a poor reader shares many of the same remedial needs as other children with neurological inadequacies. He needs to improve his visual discrimination of letters and to improve his ability to blend phonemes into words. (pp. 277–278)

Krippner also states that "the customary skills of abstract thinking and conceptualization which most academically talented children possess cannot be relied on if emotional disturbance, brain injury, or disturbed neurological organization is present." (p. 278) Krippner also stresses the fact that because a child has relatively high intelligence does not mean that reading problems will be overcome automatically. Furthermore, children of varying intelligence levels demonstrated different modes of learning.

The Relationship of Visual-Motor Perceptions to Reading Disability

A number of studies have dealt with the relationship between visual-motor perception and reading disability. Typical of the results of many of these studies is one conducted by Ernest Schellenberg (1962), who studied thirty-six matched pairs of disabled and adequate third-grade readers. Schellenberg used the Marianne Frostig Developmental Test of Visual Perception, the E. Koppitz scoring method of the Bender Visual-Motor Gestalt, and the deviation measurements of the Bender Gestalt to measure visual-motor perception. He also used the Silent Reading Diagnostic Tests of the Developmental Reading Tests to measure word perception. Schellenberg found that the Silent Reading Diagnostic Tests significantly differentiated the disabled and adequate readers. However, the distribution scores on the Developmental Test of Visual Perception failed to differentiate disabled from adequate readers. Also, the Bender figures drawn for the Bender Visual-Motor Gestalt Test did not differentiate disabled from adequate readers. This test did, however, show differences between matched pairs of girls when the Bender figures were measured to the nearest sixteenth of an inch. Schellenberg concluded that tests such as the Silent Reading Diagnostic Test have greater usefulness at the third-grade level than nonverbal perception tests.

Earl Heath, Patricia Cook and Nancy O'Dell (1976) conducted a study to test their belief that "smooth, coordinated ocular-motor control is closely related to efficient reading performance." (p. 435) They found that ocular control could be improved and that the Bender program was superior to two other methods studied. They reported that the students who received the Bender treatment "approached the level of significance in reading gain" (p. 443). However, an examination of the reading gain scores reveals that the Bender group results were *not* significantly higher than the other perceptual groups. The Bender group did score significantly higher than the control group on the reading measure. However, the control group received no treatment whatever, while the Bender group received ten weeks of treatment plus additional assistance from the parents. It is reasonable to assume that any form of instruction combined with parental involvement would produce some improvement in students' reading scores. This study might justify the belief that the Bender program improves ocular-motor control, but based on the data presented by the researchers, one cannot properly conclude that this program had a significant effect on the students' reading performance.

Barbara K. Keough (1974) reviewed the research conducted to determine the effects of vision-training programs on academic readiness and remediation of learning difficulties. She concluded that the value of such programs was questionable due to inadequate methodology in the research.

Jean Harber (1979) investigated the relationship of four perceptual and perceptual-motor skills—visual perception, visual-perceptual integration, sound blending, and visual closure—to two measures of reading achievement. She found that deficits in these perceptual skills were not highly related to reading performance in learning-disabled students. She suggested that such skills may not necessarily be requisite for success in reading. It may be that a number of difficulties commonly assumed to be related to reading disability are neither related nor important to remediate. Nicholas Aliotti (1980) found that letter reversal errors were a common developmental characteristic of many children.

Although certain items of the visual-motor perception tests may relate to reading disabilities they appear to be of dubious value in the actual diagnosis of disabled readers. It would probably be more profitable to simply determine whether a child recognizes words and to examine the kinds of errors made when words are miscalled. Remediation would then be directed at obvious problems rather than requiring the disabled reader to spend a great deal of time in nonword perceptual training. Nonword perceptual training seems to be of little or no value in reading. Studies usually indicate that children receiving this type of training consequently perform better on perceptual tests but fail to reach a higher level of reading achievement.

The Relationship Between Teacher Expectations and Self-Concept

A number of researchers and writers during the past decade have placed a growing emphasis on the relationship between teacher expectations and student performance growing from students' self-concepts. Among those who have studied these relationships are James M. Palardy (1968), Dale L. Carter (1970), and Robert Rosenthal and Lenore Jacobson (1966). Palardy studied the effects of teacher attitudes on the achievement of first-grade boys and girls. He found that, when first-grade teachers reported that they believed that boys are far less successful in learning to read than girls, then the boys in these teachers' classes did achieve significantly less than boys in classes where teachers believed that boys are just as successful as girls.

Carter studied the effect of teacher expectations on the self-esteem and academic performance of seventh-grade students. He found that teacher expectations are in part determined by cumulative records and that these expectations significantly affect students' level of confidence and scholastic potential.

In a series of extensive studies Rosenthal obtained similar results and also found that teacher expectations even affect children's measured IQs.

Results such as these leave little doubt that students' self-concepts and attitudes are often adversely affected by teacher expectations and that teacher expectation can be a major factor in reading disabilities.

Reading Disability Is Usually a Result of Multiple Factors

We have attempted to list the various factors shown by research to be responsible for reading disabilities among school-age children. It should be stressed, however, that seldom is any child's reading disability a result of any single factor. The cases studied in detail by Robinson and her group showed that nearly every student's reading disability was considered to be a result of multiple factors rather than any one single factor. In a discussion of learning disabilities, Jules Abrams (1970) states,

> There is no one single etiology for all learning disabilities. Rather, learning problems can be caused by any number of a multiplicity of factors, all of which may be highly interrelated. Unfortunately, all too often the child who is experiencing learning disorders is approached with a unitary orientation so that extremely important aspects of his unique learning problem may very well be ignored. The tendency of each professional discipline to view the entire problem "through its own window of specialization" often obscures vital factors which may contribute to, or at least exacerbate, the basic difficulty. It is just as invalid to conceive of one cure, one panacea, applied randomly to all types of learning disorders. (p. 299)

Margaret Early (1969) also cautions us to be aware of multiple factors in reading diagnosis as well as in future research. She states,

> Causes of reading disability are multiple. All research points to this conclusion, either directly as in Robinson's study, or indirectly by the very inconclusiveness of studies related to single factors. Future research should be concerned with broad studies, centered in schools rather than clinics involving both retarded and able readers, to determine the interactions among causative factors. Of the physical, emotional, mental, environmental, social, and educational factors that may affect reading ability, what combinations produce results?
>
> Three implications for the classroom teacher, in addition to those already mentioned are as follows:
>
> 1. Insight into the causes of reading failure requires study of all phases of the learner: his health, home and family, personality, experience background and learning abilities, including detailed evaluation of the complex of skills that constitute reading. Adequate study of many of these facets is beyond the teacher, or reading clinician, or psychologist. Each of these persons needs to know when to make referrals when his diagnostic tools prove inadequate.
> 2. Since causation is multiple, remediation must also use many approaches. A single method of attack may be detrimental as well as useless.
> 3. As research in causation is tentative, so is diagnosis of individual cases. As hunches are confirmed or rejected by new insights, plans for treatment must also be changed. Diagnosis of the complex process of reading is continuous. (pp. 61–62)

SUMMARY

A student's ability or inability to read is affected by a number of factors. These factors might be classified as socioeconomic, psychological, educational, and physical. A monumental study was done by Helen Robinson a number of years ago. In her study Robinson employed the services of a number of specialists in fields that relate to reading disabilities. Robinson and her group attempted to determine the kind and number of problems that each of her cases possessed. Through subsequent study they then attempted to determine which problems were causal factors in each student's reading disability. The various causal factors listed by Robinson, as well as the percentage of students who have reading disabilities caused by these factors, are generally in agreement with more recent studies.

There are, of course, many causes of reading disabilities, and many of these cannot be completely isolated since they often appear in conjunction with other factors believed to contribute to problems in reading. The disabled reader is likely to possess combinations of physical, psychological, socioeconomic, and educational problems, all of which contribute to reading difficulties.

A number of research studies have shown that certain problems such as those of a visual-perceptual nature may be related to, if not direct causal factors of, reading disability. Many studies, however, have also shown that remediation of this type of problem has little or no direct effect on a student's ability to read.

Other more recent studies have shown that problems other than those studied by Robinson may also affect students' ability to read. For example, there appears to be a relationship between socioeconomic level, visual and auditory discrimination, and modality shifting. There is also believed to be a relationship between syntactic competence and reading disability. To date, however, little concrete research has been done that will help the remedial reading teacher diagnose and remediate these problems even when they are known to exist.

One of the most important points to be learned from Robinson's and subsequent studies is that students' reading disabilities are not usually the result of any single factor. The remedial reading teacher should be especially careful to keep this in mind in both diagnostic and remedial work. The practitioner must also be careful not to be consumed by the search for the specific cause or causes of a student's reading disability. Attention to this area should not be so great as to detract from your efforts to correct the reading problem.

REFERENCES

Abrams, Jules C. "Learning Disabilities—A Complex Phenomenon," *Reading Teacher.* Vol. 23, (January, 1970), 299–303.

Aliotti, Nicholas C. "Tendency to Mirror-Image on a Visual Memory Test," *Academic Therapy.* Vol. 15, (January, 1980), 261–267.

Ames, Louise B., and Walker, Richard N. "Prediction of Later Reading Ability from Kindergarten Rorschach and IQ Scores," *Journal of Educational Psychology.* Vol. 55, (December, 1964), 309–313.

Bateman, Barbara. "Educational Implications of Minimal Brain Dysfunction," *Reading Teacher.* Vol. 27, (April, 1974), 662–668.

Bond, Guy L.; Tinker, Miles A.; and Wasson, Barbara B. *Reading Difficulties: Their Diagnosis and Correction.* 4th ed., Englewood Cliffs, N.J.: Prentice-Hall, 1979.

Brookover, Wilbur B., and Lezotte, Lawrence W. *Changes in School Characteristics Coincident with Changes in Student Achievement.* East Lansing, Mich.: Institute for Research on Teaching, 1979.

Brophy, Jere E. *Teacher Behavior and Its Effects.* East Lansing, Mich.: Institute for Research on Teaching, 1979a.

Brophy, Jere E. *Advances in Teacher Effectiveness Research.* East Lansing, Mich.: Institute for Research on Teaching, 1979b.

California School Effectiveness Study—The First Year: 1974–75. Sacramento, Calif.: California State Department of Education, 1977.

REFERENCES

Capobianco, R. J. "Ocular-Manual Laterality and Reading Achievement in Children with Special Learning Disabilities," *American Educational Research Journal.* Vol. 4, (March, 1967), 133–138.

Carter, Dale L. "The Effect of Teacher Expectations on the Self-Esteem and Academic Performance of Seventh Grade Students," Doctoral dissertation, University of Tennessee, 1970.

Cavanaugh, Lyman. "Reading Behavior with Regard for Endocrine Imbalances," Thirteenth Yearbook of the Claremont College Reading Conference, Claremont, California, 1948, pp. 95–102.

Clark, Christopher. *Five Faces of Research on Teaching.* East Lansing, Mich.: The Institute for Research on Teaching, 1979.

Cohen, Alice, and Glass, Gerald G. "Lateral Dominance and Reading Ability," *Reading Teacher.* Vol. 21, (January, 1968), 343–348.

Cohen, S. Alan, and Cooper, Thelma. "Seven Fallacies: Reading Retardation and the Urban Disadvantaged Beginning Reader," *Reading Teacher.* Vol. 26, (October, 1972), 38–45.

Cohn, Maxine, and Kornelly, Donald. "For Better Reading—A More Positive Self-Image," *Elementary School Journal.* Vol. 70, (January, 1970), 199–201.

Coleman, Howard M. "Visual Perception and Reading Dysfunction," *Journal of Learning Disabilities.* Vol. 1, (February, 1968), 116–123.

Dechant, Emerald. *Diagnosis and Remediation of Reading Disabilities.* Englewood Cliffs, N.J.: Prentice-Hall, 1981.

Deutsch, Martin, et al. *The Disadvantaged Child.* New York: Basic Books, 1967.

Duffy, Gerald, and McIntyre, Lonnie. *A Qualitative Analysis of How Various Primary Grade Teachers Employ the Structured Learning Component of the Direct Instructional Model When Teaching Reading.* East Lansing, Mich.: Institute for Research on Teaching, 1981.

Eames, Thomas H. "The Relationship of Reading and Speech Difficulties," *Journal of Educational Psychology.* Vol. 51, (January, 1950), 51–55.

Eames, Thomas H. "Physical Factors in Reading," *Reading Teacher.* Vol. 15, (May, 1962), 427–432.

Early, Margaret J. *Reading Disabilities: Selections on Identification and Treatment.* Edited by Harold Newman. Indianapolis: Odyssey Press, 1969.

Forness, Steven R. "Lateral Dominance in Retarded Readers with Signs of Brain Dysfunction," Doctoral dissertation, University of California, Los Angeles, 1968.

Gates, Arthur J. "The Role of Personality Maladjustment and Remedial Reading," *Journal of Generic Psychology.* Vol. 59, (1941), 77–83.

Harber, Jean R. "Are Perceptual Skills Necessary for Success in Reading? Which Ones?" *Reading Horizons.* Vol. 20, (Fall, 1979), 7–15.

Harris, Albert J. *Harris Tests of Lateral Dominance—Manual of Directions.* 3d ed., New York: Psychological Corporation, 1958.

Harris, Albert J. *Readings on Reading Instruction.* Edited by Albert J. Harris and Edward R. Sipay. 2d ed., New York: David McKay, 1972.

Harris, Albert J. "Lateral Dominance and Reading Disability," *Journal of Learning Disabilities.* Vol. 12, (May, 1979), 57–63.

Harris, Albert J., and Sipay, Edward R. *How to Increase Reading Ability.* 7th ed., New York: Longman, 1980.

Heath, Earl J.; Cook, Patricia; and O'Dell, Nancy. "Eye Exercises and Reading Efficiency," *Academic Therapy.* Vol. 11, (Summer, 1976), 435–445.

Hresko, Wayne P.; Reid, D. Kim; and Hammill, Donald D. *The Test of Early Language Development.* Austin, Texas: Pro-Ed, 1981.

Keough, Barbara K. "Optometric Vision Training Programs for Children with Learning Disabilities: Review of Issues and Research," *Journal of Learning Disabilities.* Vol. 7, (April, 1974), 219–231.

Krippner, Stanley. "Etiological Factors in Reading Disability of the Academically Talented in Comparison to Pupils of Average and Slow Learning Ability," *Journal of Educational Research.* Vol. 61, (February, 1968), 275–279.

Labov, W. "The Logic of Non-Standard Dialectic." Edited by James E. Alatis. School of Languages and Linguistics Monograph Series, 1969.

Leong, Che Kan. "Laterality and Reading Proficiency in Children," *Reading Research Quarterly.* Vol. 15, (1980), 185–202.

Lyon, Reid. "Auditory-Perceptual Training: The State of the Art," *Journal of Learning Disabilities.* Vol. 10, (November, 1977), 564–572.

Malmquist, Eve. *Reading and Writing Disabilities in Children: Diagnosis and Remedial Methods.* Lund, Sweden: Gleerup, 1967.

Newcomer, Phyllis L., and Hammill, D. *The Test of Language Development.* Austin, Texas: Pro-Ed, 1977.

Padelford, William B. "The Influence of Socioeconomic Level, Sex, and Ethnic Background upon the Relationship Between Reading Achievement and Self-Concept," Doctoral dissertation, University of California, Los Angeles, 1969.

Palardy, James M. "The Effect of Teachers' Beliefs on the Achievement in Reading of First-Grade Boys," Doctoral dissertation, Ohio State University, 1968.

Powell, Marjorie. "New Evidence for Old Truths," *Educational Leadership.* Vol. 37, (October, 1979), 49–51.

Pryor, Frances. "Poor Reading—Lack of Self Esteem?" *Reading Teacher.* Vol. 28, (January, 1975), 358–359.

Robinson, Helen. *Why Pupils Fail in Reading.* Chicago: University of Chicago Press, 1946.

Rosenthal, Robert, and Jacobson, Lenore. "Teachers' Expectancies: Determinants of Pupils' IQ Gains," *Psychological Reports.* Vol. 19, (August, 1966), 115–118.

Rystrom, Richard. "Effects of Standard Dialect Training on Negro First Graders Being Taught to Read," *Report Project No. 81–053.* U.S. Dept. of HEW, 1968.

Rystrom, Richard. "Dialect Differences and Initial Reading Instruction." Address given at National Council of Teachers of English Conference, November, 1972.

Samuels, S. Jay. "Research-Reading Disability," *Reading Teacher.* Vol. 24, (December, 1970), 267 + .

Schellenberg, Ernest D. "A Study of the Relationship Between Visual Motor Perception and Reading Disabilities of Third Grade Pupils," Doctoral dissertation, University of Southern California, 1962.

Shearer, E. "Physical Skills and Reading Backwardness," *Educational Research.* Vol. 10, (June, 1968), 197–206.

Smith, Donald E. P. "A New Theory of Physiological Basis of Reading Disability," *Reading for Effective Living.* Conference Proceedings of the International Reading Association. Newark, Del.: International Reading Association, Yearbook No. 3 (1958), 119–121.

Smith, Monte D. "Prediction of Self-Concept among Learning Disabled Children," *Journal of Learning Disabilities.* Vol. 12, (December, 1979), 664–669.

REFERENCES

Smith, Nila B. "Some Basic Factors in Reading Difficulties of the Disadvantaged," *Reading Improvement.* Vol. 11, (Fall, 1974), 3–9.

Spache, George D., and Spache, Evelyn B. *Reading in the Elementary School.* 4th ed., Boston: Allyn and Bacon, 1977.

Stallings, Jane; Cory, R.; Fairweather, J.; and Needles, M. *A Study of Basic Reading Skills Taught in Secondary Schools.* Palo Alto, Calif.: Stanford Research Institute, 1978.

Thompson, Bertha B. "A Longitudinal Study of Auditory Discrimination," *Journal of Educational Research.* Vol. 56, (March, 1963), 376–378.

United States Commission on Civil Rights. *The Unfinished Education.* Washington, D.C.: Government Printing Office, October, 1971.

2

Some Important Operational
Procedures

The experienced diagnostician and teacher have usually discovered that there are certain operational procedures that, if applied, tend to make their jobs easier and the results of their labor more successful. These are sometimes discovered while working with children over a period of years, and sometimes they are learned through the professional literature and by taking courses in reading diagnosis and remediation. The first part of this chapter contains a discussion of some important operational procedures for the diagnostician. This is followed by a list of important operational procedures for the teacher. The chapter then concludes with a discussion of some common reasons for failure in the diagnostic-remedial process.

IMPORTANT OPERATIONAL PROCEDURES FOR THE DIAGNOSTICIAN

The following operational procedures will be discussed in this section:

1. Know the amount of diagnosis necessary before remediation is begun.
2. Make sure the test information is accurately communicated.
3. Gather enough initial diagnostic information to begin a program of remediation, but make sure the program remains flexible.
4. Do not do unnecessary testing but gather enough information to serve as a data base for measuring improvement.
5. Do not be overly concerned about the repetition involved in the teaching of a few skills already known by the child.
6. Diagnosis for a disabled reader should involve more than an appraisal of educational factors.

7. Make the diagnosis as efficient as possible.
8. Test in a situation that is analogous to actual reading.
9. Major decisions concerning the welfare of a child should be based on known facts.
10. Become aware of the strong points and limitations of group standardized, individual standardized, and informal measuring instruments.

Know the Amount of Diagnosis Necessary Before Remediation Is Begun

One of the operational procedures facing personnel in the field of reading is whether it is better to do a great deal of diagnosis before remediation is begun or whether it is better to do only enough diagnosis to initiate remediation and then continue the diagnosis while teaching.

Proponents of a system of doing a great deal of diagnosis before beginning remedial procedures often argue that their method of operation is better because more information is available for planning a program of remediation. They also state that time may not be wasted in doing unnecessary remediation and that a thorough initial diagnosis provides a basis for measuring progress. They also believe that children with similar difficulties can be located and grouped for more efficient instruction.

Those who oppose doing a great deal of initial diagnosis before beginning remediation argue that children tend to become discouraged if too much initial testing is done. Proponents of this view also believe that diagnosis continued during remediation deals with the problem as the child sees it and that when the diagnosis is continuous the remedial program is likely to be flexible.

We would suggest that the best method of operation lies somewhere between the two extremes, with the observation of certain precautions. Some of these precautions are explained in the following.

Make Sure Test Information Is Accurately Communicated

If the person doing the diagnostic work also carries out the remedial procedures, there is seldom cause for concern; however, a plan that is sometimes used in larger school systems is to employ a number of full-time diagnosticians. These people spend their entire day doing diagnostic work. After each child is diagnosed, they then write prescriptive procedures in accordance with their diagnosis. Where this type of procedure is in operation, the normal problems are often compounded because of the difficulty in accurately relaying diagnostic information to the person charged with carrying out the remedial procedures.

Anyone who has read psychological testing reports or reports from educational diagnosticians would probably agree that frequently these reports leave you wondering what has really been prescribed as treatment. Because of this problem of communication, many people feel that the person who will eventually do the remediation should also do the diagnostic testing. A typical example of what happens in the communication of test results is illustrated by the following excerpt from a test report: "Dwight exhibits problems with lateral dominance and would probably benefit from procedures to correct this problem."

A group of experienced remedial reading teachers were asked to explain what they would do with this information. Following are some of the answers:

Teacher 1: "I would have him practice pacing his reading with his hand, using a left-to-right motion."
Teacher 2: "I would start him on the Frostig program."
Teacher 3: "Research shows that there is no relationship between lateral dominance and reading, so I would ignore it."

At this point no attempt will be made to evaluate the teachers' responses, but it is evident that each teacher interpreted the information differently. Such is often the case when one teacher attempts to interpret what another has written.

Another problem with test reports is that they often use such statements as, "Dwight has difficulty with the initial consonant blends." This statement is too vague to be of any real significance. For example, one might then ask the following questions: Does he have difficulty with all blends? Does he not know the phonemes represented by various graphemes? Or does he lack the ability to blend various initial consonant blends with word families or phonograms? In this case the person doing the remediation would still have to do further diagnosis before meaningful teaching could begin. On the other hand, if the person who did the testing also did the remedial procedures with the same child, then there would be no communication problem.

Gather Enough Initial Diagnostic Information to Begin a Program of Remediation, but Make Sure the Program Remains Flexible

A major problem that sometimes occurs is that the program of remediation becomes set or inflexible and is not changed according to the changing needs of the child. For example, a child who is slightly nervous or who is reading at a frustration reading level is likely to make a number of substitutions for basic sight words. A child who does make substitutions for some basic sight words may in fact really know these sight words when the words are tested in isolation. The problem would then be to determine why the substitutions were made. However, if the original diagnosis indicated that the child should have instruction on the basic sight words, then that child is very likely to have to sit through a great deal of instruction that is not really needed. This situation occurs more often when the original diagnosis is done by someone other than the person doing the remediation. It is also more likely to occur when one child is placed with other pupils who indicate similar weaknesses.

Do Not Do Unnecessary Testing, but Gather Enough Information to Serve as a Data Base for Measuring Improvement

In determining initial versus ending performance in a remedial program, consider such factors as (1) progression in reading-grade placement, (2) various phoneme-grapheme relationships learned, and (3) number of basic sight words learned. It would, of course, be very difficult to accurately determine whether the child had actually learned from day-to-day if there was no accurately determined base or beginning point.

Attempting to measure progress without some base point is somewhat like the situation of parents who are told how much their child has grown. This growth is often very difficult for the parents to notice since they are in daily contact with the child. The visiting relative, however, who has not seen the child for a year is very much aware of the child's growth. The parents may also get out last year's blanket sleeper as cold weather approaches and find that it is now too small for the child. The size of the child when it did fit the sleeper versus a year later when it was tried on is analogous to a beginning and ending measurement of the reading skills. That is, we become much more aware of growth from a beginning-to-ending period than we do when we are exposed to a child's daily growth in reading skills.

Since many remedial reading programs are supported by some sort of special funding, accountability becomes extremely important. Often the very existence of remedial reading programs is dependent on the demonstration of success with the pupils with whom you are working. When such a situation occurs, no choice remains but to attempt to show improvement in students from the beginning to the end of the program.

It should be emphasized, however, that certain precautions should be observed in doing the initial testing. A very common and often deserved criticism of remedial reading programs is that a great deal of testing is done and then little time is left for remediation. One school system, with which we are familiar, tests children who are candidates for the remedial reading program for about one-fourth of the school year before any remedial work is done. These children often become even more discouraged about their reading than they were in a normal classroom situation. This is, of course, true by the nature of the testing itself. In order to find a child's IQ or frustration reading level, the child must be taken up to a level of questioning or reading that is extremely difficult. This, of course, often results in discouragement, feelings of inadequacy, and consequently a loss of rapport between the child and the tester.

If the person who has done the initial testing with the child is also the same person who will later be doing remedial work with the child, it is often difficult to re-establish the good rapport that may have been lost during the testing periods. For this reason alone it would seem that only a minimal amount of initial testing would be desirable.

A highly skilled tester can usually administer a test in such a manner that almost any child will appear to enjoy the test. Some children are also delighted to be excused from the classroom to participate in a testing program. When such is the case, it is less damaging to the self-confidence of the children than when they are forced to participate. The tester should, however, remember that most children soon tire of any activity in which they are not entirely successful, and in a test situation complete success for the child is nearly always lacking.

Do Not Be Overly Concerned about the Repetition Involved in the Teaching of a Few Skills Already Known by the Child

It is quite natural for a remedial reading teacher to begin remedial work with some help being given in the comprehension skills even though the teacher may know that the child's diagnosed problem is in word-attack skills. Some teachers would logically argue that this time would be wasted since it does not focus on the exact needs of the child. If the time in which the child is to be tutored by the remedial reading teacher is severely limited, this argument would be somewhat valid.

A number of research studies such as those of Joseph Lillich (1968) and Keith Dolan (1964) have shown, however, that the guidance and counseling aspects or establishing of rapport with a disabled reader is just as important as teaching reading skills per se. It would then appear that some time in working with a skill in which the child was somewhat more adept may in fact not be harmful and that the benefits from the improved relationship between the disabled reader and the teacher may far outweigh the fact that there is some repetition of materials. Furthermore, it seems doubtful that any class can claim efficiency to such a degree that there is never repetition of known facts even if repetition *was* completely undesirable.

Diagnosis for a Disabled Reader Should Involve More Than an Appraisal of Educational Factors

A teacher who has a student who has developed a minor problem with some phase of the reading skills, such as learning certain initial consonant sounds, may only be interested in locating and correcting that particular problem. The student may have failed to learn certain initial consonant sounds because a day or two of school was missed; the student may not have been listening closely when those consonant sounds were initially taught; or the student may have simply required more time and drill to learn them. When a student only misses an occasional concept, the teacher is not usually concerned with factors other than the educational problem itself. In the case of a somewhat severely disabled reader, however, a diagnosis should involve more than an appraisal of educational factors.

One of the major reasons that school personnel are faced with as many seriously disabled readers as they are is that teachers often fail to locate and correct incipient reading problems while they are still in an easily correctable stage. However, the reasons for failure to learn are often more complicated than those mentioned previously, for example, absence from school or failure to listen closely on one occasion. When failure to learn stems from other causes, often more serious, even a teacher who is well trained in locating and correcting incipient reading problems may find certain students who do not learn. When this is the case, a much more thorough diagnosis involving more than educational factors is necessary.

When a child fails to learn in a normal educational setting, somewhat more complicated causes of the learning disability such as physical, psychological, or socioeducational factors may be responsible. Each of these factors, of course, can be broken down into a number of subfactors or subcategories that may contribute to, or in some cases result from, a reading disability. The essential point for the reading diagnostician to remember is that what often appears as a problem may be only a symptom of a more difficult and involved problem.

Make the Diagnosis as Efficient as Possible

A diagnosis should be as thorough as necessary, but should not extend beyond what is required. The problem of the reading diagnostician, of course, is to determine just what is and is not necessary. Although this is often somewhat difficult, there are some very definite guidelines that the experienced diagnostician will soon learn to follow.

One of the most common problems leading to inefficient diagnosis is that the diagnostician falls into the habit of giving the same diagnostic tests to each student regardless of the apparent problem or problems. This can often lead to inefficiency as well as inadequate diagnosis. In some cases, certain phases of commonly used diagnostic procedures can easily be omitted. When this is the case, a great deal of time can be saved. For example, you may note that a child who is in the fifth or sixth grade reads orally very poorly. For a child such as this, a somewhat logical approach would be to diagnose a number of questionable areas such as initial, ending, and medial consonants sounds, consonant clusters, vowel, vowel-team and special letter combination sounds, vowel rules, and structural analysis skills. However, if the student can read the words on the Pronunciation of Quick Survey Words test of the Ekwall Reading Inventory (Ekwall, 1979), you can automatically eliminate testing in each of the above-mentioned areas because a child weak in these areas would not be able to read long nonsense words. There are also other areas where certain commonly administered tests may be omitted for certain children, such as visual screening tests for a child who has recently been examined by an optometrist or an ophthalmologist, or IQ tests for a child who definitely demonstrates an ability to learn.

Just as it is easy to fall into the habit of using tests that are not needed, it is also easy to omit tests or further checks that may be indicated in some instances. The reading diagnostician should continually examine the methods of diagnosis by asking such questions as: Am I giving this test only because I am in the habit of doing so? Are there more efficient methods of locating problems than I am now using? Is the information I seek already available in the child's cumulative records? Will the cause of the child's disability also affect future attempts at remediation?

Test in a Situation That Is Analogous to Actual Reading

A serious problem with group diagnostic tests is that they often do not measure reading skills in a situation that is analogous to actual reading. This is also a criticism of some individually administered tests. Research by Eldon E. Ekwall (1973) has indicated that many types of tests do not measure what they purport to measure. It appears that only in some areas such as comprehension and vocabulary can reading diagnosticians feel fairly sure that they are really measuring what the tests purport to measure when group tests are used. The implications are also quite clear that if you really want to measure certain reading skills, you must use an individually administered test.

Typical examples of the type of group tests that often give misleading information are tests for basic sight words and tests for phonics skills. One of the coauthors once taught an evening reading class to a group of elementary and secondary teachers in the school district in which these teachers were employed. After discussing ways of testing for knowledge of the basic sight words, one ninth-grade teacher of a group of extremely poor readers asked the writer to administer a group basic sight word test in his class. In taking this test the student is required to underline or circle one of a choice of four words that is the same as a word pronounced aloud by the person administering the test. There were approximately thirty students in the class who took the test. Each student was tested on 220 words or, in other words, had to underline or circle 220 words from a choice of 880 words. This meant that 220×30 or 6600 choices were made. When these tests were corrected, only six errors were found. Certainly this many mistakes would be expected on the basis of clerical errors alone.

Next, several consultants sat down individually with students and asked each of them to simply pronounce each of the 220 basic sight words on the test. This time many students missed from twenty-five to fifty words each. The results in this case are quite typical of those obtained when you try to test in a situation that is not analogous to actual reading. It is, of course, much easier to pick one word pronounced by a tester from a choice of four than to see the same word and then pronounce it. The latter case is, however, what you must do when you read orally. As you can see, what we wanted to know was which students did not know which words. Administration of the test to a group simply did not give us this information.

As in the case just illustrated, most group tests require students to choose one of several answers as a correct choice. This is simply not what a student does when reading and, therefore, in most cases does not tell us what we want to know.

Group phonics tests also present problems typical of the problem encountered in the basic sight word test. For example, in testing initial consonant sounds a test may call for a student to circle one of four letters that represents the same sound as the beginning sound of a word pronounced by the teacher. Here again, it is easier to circle one of four letters (for example d, p, b, c) that represents the beginning sound in the word dog than it is to see a d and pronounce the "d" phoneme, which is what a student must do when reading a new word beginning with d.

Authors of tests often claim that since the kinds of group tests mentioned above have a high correlation with individual tests they are therefore a valid instrument for diagnosis. You must keep in mind, however, that a high correlation between two tests only means that those students who scored high on the group test also scored high on the individual test. This would usually happen whenever two highly related skills are tested and the results of two groups scores are correlated.

This type of information may be useful to the reading specialist who wishes to survey a group of students to determine which ones are most seriously deficient in the skills tested. For example, in the test for initial consonant sounds mentioned above, students who fail this test would be demonstrating that they are extremely weak in phonics skills. Students who pass this test may or may not have mastered their initial consonant sounds. In other words, passing this test would be a necessary but not sufficient condition for mastery of this skill. This is because the test described measures only low-level phonics knowledge. A more complete discussion of the levels of phonics knowledge will be included in Chapter 5. For now, the diagnostician should bear in mind that, in order to evaluate a student's ability to apply phonics skills in the act of reading, the testing must be conducted individually.

This is not meant to imply that all individual tests are good. A number of individual tests contain subtests designed to measure certain skills that do not require the student to use the same skills in taking the test that are required in the act of reading. Chapters 4 through 6 address the testing of various educational factors in reading. Problems encountered in test construction and administration are covered in considerable depth in those chapters. The essential point for the reading diagnostician to keep in mind from the foregoing discussion is that, in order to obtain the information needed for prescriptive instruction, testing must be done in a situation that is analogous to actual reading.

Major Decisions Concerning the Welfare of a Child Should Be
Based on Known Facts

Most of us who have worked in the public schools have at some time heard about or witnessed a case of a child suddenly "taking hold" or "blooming" after having been a poor student. Even the best of teachers, psychologists, or diagnosticians are unable, in many cases, to predict whether this sort of thing will happen to a child. The important point to remember, however, is to leave the door open to the possibility of such an occurrence.

Any major decisions for prolonged remedial work that will remove a child from the normal learning environment should be based on the opinions of several people and the results of several tests. A psychologist, for example, who examines a child for as long as several hours may develop some excellent insights about a child; yet this same person may lack a great deal of information that has been available to the child's classroom teacher, the principal, or the child's parents. We once heard an elementary principal say, "When the school psychologist works with one of our children for several hours and then writes his report, it often tells us that now *he* knows as much about the child as we did when the psychologist started testing." This statement should not be taken to discredit the work of the school psychologist, but it does illustrate the previous point that no individual can hope to gain enough information about a student in an hour or two to make decisions that will often affect the student's entire life.

School personnel who are involved with making decisions concerning intensive remedial work or assignment to special classes should develop procedures for placement of students. A diagnostic-referral procedure, such as that outlined in Figure 2-1, will enable school personnel to place children according to the best information that can be derived from all sources.

The Non-Discrimination on the Basis of Handicap Act (Public Law 93-112, Section 504) and the Education for All Handicapped Children Act (Public Law 94-142) have had a significant impact on the services provided to disabled readers. This federal legislation includes a number of provisions that now by law affect all handicapped students between the ages of three

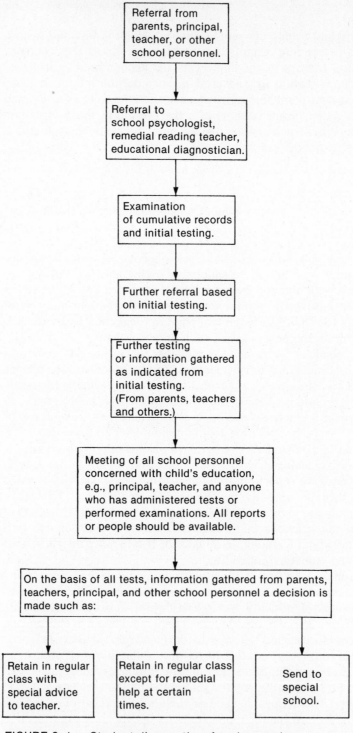

FIGURE 2-1. Student diagnostic-referral procedure.

and twenty-one.[1] The term *handicapped children* includes students who have "specific learning disabilities." Within this category are included disabled readers. These students must receive a "free, appropriate public education" designed to meet their special needs.

For each handicapped student an Individualized Education Program (IEP) must be developed. The teacher, one or both parents, the child (where appropriate), a representative of the public school other than the child's teacher (usually the school principal), and other individuals (such as the reading specialist, speech teacher, and school psychologist) all participate in the development of the IEP.

According to P.L. 94–142, Section 121a.346, the IEP for each child must include:

1. a statement of the child's present levels of educational performance;
2. a statement of annual goals, including short term instructional objectives;
3. a statement of the specific special education and related services to be provided to the child, and the extent to which the child will be able to participate in regular educational programs;
4. the projected dates for initiation of services and the anticipated duration of the services; and
5. appropriate objective criteria and evaluation procedures and schedules for determining, on at least an annual basis, whether the short term instructional objectives are being achieved.

The reading specialist should be aware of certain additional specifications of the federal legislation. Section 121a.550 describes the mandate for the Least Restrictive Environment (Mainstreaming).

Each public agency shall insure:

1. that to the maximum extent appropriate handicapped children . . . are educated with children who are not handicapped, and
2. that special classes, separate schooling or other removal of handicapped children from the regular educational environment occurs only when the nature or severity of the handicap is such that education in regular classes with the use of supplementary aids and services cannot be achieved satisfactorily.

The student's parents must approve the IEP and consent to the placement of the student. They must also approve all changes in the program and have the right to pursue an impartial due-process hearing if they are dissatisfied. Assessment of the student must be conducted by a team that includes at least one teacher or other specialist with knowledge of the area of disability.

---

[1]For additional information on this legislation, we refer you to *The Rights of Parents and the Responsibilities of Schools*, compiled by James G. Meade (Cambridge, Mass.: Educators Publishing Service, 1978).

Since a high percentage of specific learning disabilities are reading difficulties, the reading specialist should anticipate frequent participation in IEP assessment. The law mandates that no *single* procedure may be used to determine a student's placement or program.

Become Aware of the Strong Points and Limitations of Group Standardized, Individual Standardized, and Informal Measuring Instruments

The reading diagnostician should make every effort to become familiar with as many tests as possible. This is not to say that any one person will or should continually change the tests that are commonly used in diagnosis; however, the diagnostician should continually search for newer and better tests and methods of testing. The process of examining new tests and test procedures is certain to be excellent in-service training in itself. For example, the authors of tests are not likely to stress the weaknesses inherent in their own material; however, they are likely to explain why certain techniques or procedures they use are better than others. This explanation in itself will often enable the diagnostician to better evaluate tests and testing procedures.

The strong points of various group and individual tests and testing techniques are discussed in considerable detail in later chapters. There are, however, some inherent weaknesses and strong points in certain types of testing that are of such importance to personnel concerned with reading that they should receive special emphasis at this point.

Group Standardized Tests.   Group standardized tests are perhaps more misused than any other type of tests on the market today. Some of this misuse can be attributed to the users of the tests, but certainly some of the blame also lies with the authors who have a tendency to overstate the test's value for some purposes.

The most flagrant misuse of group standardized tests is, no doubt, in using them to make final decisions about individual students. Although the publishers of group achievement tests often claim that their tests have considerable individual diagnostic value, it is doubtful that this claim can be substantiated in most cases. For any individual, group test scores are often so unreliable that it would be difficult to place any real confidence in their results. One of the coauthors administered a nationally used reading achievement test designed for grades four through six to a class of college students. The students, however, were not given the questions but were instructed to mark the answer sheets at random. One of the subtests on this test purports to measure children's reading vocabulary in science. The class of college students scored from a low grade level of 2.5 to a high grade level of 6.5 on this subtest. Remember, of course, that this was a situation similar to one in which none of the students could read at all! The grade placement of the students on the entire test ranged from 2.9 to 4.3, which also makes it evident that individual students' total reading scores varied too much to place any credence in them for individual grade placement. The problem here results from the high guess factor that may be inherent in these tests. Another problem with group standardized tests is their relative unreliability for individual students. Most experienced teachers have noticed with puzzlement that some students score *lower* on the posttest than the pretest. Surely these students did not lose learning over the course of the year. Such deviations balance out when group data are examined, but this fact is of little consolation to the parents or teacher of the individual student. While working as a specialist with groups of extremely low-achieving students, one of the coauthors discovered another weakness in using group standardized tests. The students were pre- and posttested with levels of a test that corresponded to the students' grade placement. Unfortunately, the norms of the test did not extend low enough to reflect the performance of some of the older readers (for example, sixth graders reading at or below a first-grade level). Even though these students may have grown a year or more in ability, this was not reflected in the testing, since they still had not reached the low end of the norms on this particular test. This was especially distressing because the amount of future funding for this special program was based on the students' growth as demonstrated by scores on this test.

Yet another inherent weakness of group tests is that they cannot test many of the reading skills in a situation that is analogous to actual reading. This point was discussed in more detail earlier in this chapter. Reading skills such as vocabulary and comprehension are, however, more amenable to testing with group tests.

Some of the strong points of group standardized tests are that they are useful for measuring overall class achievement during a specified period of time. If one examines the subtests rather carefully, they can also be useful in determining whether overall areas, such as the study skills, are receiving adequate attention in the curriculum. Another important point in favor of using group tests is that they are less time consuming to administer. Group standardized tests also allow school personnel to compare the achievement of their students with that of the nation as a whole or the norm group on which the test was originally standardized. Finally, group tests can be useful for the *initial* screening of students for the remedial reading program. Many specially funded programs require that only those students who score below the 50th percentile on a standardized achievement test may be served by the program. Group tests will enable you to quickly determine which students qualify. Also, many reading specialists are assigned to schools with many more problem readers than can be served directly. By using group test data these reading specialists can select those students with the greatest apparent need

for individual diagnostic evaluation. If instead the reading specialist randomly selected students for diagnosis or relied only on teacher referral, then too
much time would be spent diagnosing an unnecessarily large number of
students.

Individual Standardized Tests.   Individual standardized tests are less misused than group standardized tests for several reasons. To begin with, the
people who find a need to use individual standardized tests, such as the Durrell Analysis of Reading Difficulty, (Durrell and Catterson, 1980) are usually
more experienced in test administration and are therefore better informed
about the strong points and limitations of various tests. Individual standardized tests are also more difficult to administer than group standardized
tests. For this reason they are likely to be given only when needed, in contrast
to group tests, which are often given simply because it is "test time."
    Individual standardized tests can be given in a situation that is analo-
gous to actual reading and thus have a tremendous advantage over group
standardized tests. For example, you can simply ask a child to read orally
while you mark the kinds of mistakes made, or the child can be asked to simply pronounce basic sight words. Individual standardized tests also have the
advantage of being standardized, which will enable you to compare a child's
reading abilities with those of other children of the same age and/or grade
level. A further advantage of individual standardized tests is that the tester
can easily omit certain subtests that may not be relevant to a certain student.
    Perhaps the greatest disadvantage of individual standardized tests is
that they are time consuming to administer. In many cases they are somewhat difficult for a classroom teacher to administer and, therefore, do or
should require some special training. This could, however, be interpreted as
a blessing in disguise.

Informal Measuring Instruments.   Informal measuring instruments such as
word lists, informal reading inventories, decoding-skill inventories, and cloze
passages are also valuable diagnostic tools. Often these instruments are
readily adaptable to the materials within the classroom. By using the standard criteria for the informal reading inventory or cloze procedure, the
teacher can rather quickly and easily determine whether a certain student
can read a certain book at the "instructional" or "free" reading level. The
teacher can also use these procedures to determine whether a new textbook
is written at a proper reading level for the students. The use of word lists
from a book commonly used in the school will also enable teachers to make a
rapid check on a student's ability to deal with the vocabulary load in that
book. Decoding-skill inventories can be an invaluable tool for determining a
specific phonics or structural analysis skills a student needs to learn. Often
these inventories are criterion referenced so that the diagnostician may com-

pare the student's performance to the accepted criterion for mastery of the particular skills.

Informal measuring instruments have several rather serious disadvantages. They must be used by someone who can understand and use the standard criteria for their application or they are no better than simply listening to a child read and then guessing at the child's grade level. Although the procedure for using them is rather simple, they are still somewhat difficult to construct. For example, it is a tremendous task to find questions that measure more than simple recall of facts for use in an informal reading inventory. It is also difficult and time consuming to construct and check cloze passages to use for measuring a student's ability to read a certain book or to construct tests that properly measure phonics and structural analysis skills. Other specific advantages and disadvantages of using informal measuring instruments are discussed in detail in Chapter 11.

IMPORTANT OPERATIONAL PROCEDURES FOR THE TEACHER

As experience is gained in working with disabled readers, the reading teacher is likely to find that some techniques work especially well with some students and yet seem somewhat less successful with others. One of the characteristics of a successful teacher is the ability to determine whether a certain teaching procedure is producing the desired results with a particular student. When a certain teaching procedure does not produce the desired results, the experienced teacher will alter the approach. Certain teaching procedures have, however, proven to be consistently successful with almost all students regardless of such factors as their specific reading problems, age, grade, or sex. It is imperative that the remedial reading teacher become aware of these teaching procedures and make every effort to implement them. Some of these important procedures are as follows:

1. Select a remedial reading program that is highly individualized.
2. Start at the child's level.
3. Start with the child's strongest area.
4. Provide an opportunity for success for the child.
5. Make the disabled reader aware of the progress that has been made.
6. Make the learning process meaningful to the child.
7. Use materials appropriate to the needs of the child.
8. Continue the diagnosis while you teach.
9. Be alert to pick up any clues given by the child.
10. Capitalize on the motivation that the child may already possess.
11. Maintain a relaxed attitude.
12. Do not be too authoritative.
13. Have confidence in the child's ability to learn.

14. Direct the child toward self-instruction.
15. Begin each period with a summary of what you intend to do and why you intend to do it and end each period with a summary of what you did and why you did it.
16. Provide for a follow-up program.

Select a Remedial Reading Program That Is Highly Individualized

Terms such as *a well-balanced program* or *a well-rounded program* sound good and are appropriate for a developmental reading program, but they do not describe the type of reading program that is desirable in remedial reading. In most cases the remedial reading program must be highly individualized and directed toward correcting certain individual reading deficiencies rather than giving a child a well-rounded program. By "individualized" we do not mean that instruction must necessarily occur on a one-to-one basis. Generally, in the school setting the remedial reading teacher is able to group students according to their skill needs.

Many children in remedial reading classes are simply retarded a year or more in almost all of their reading skills; however, a large percentage of children are behind a year or more only in certain areas of reading. For those students who are lacking only in certain reading skills it would prove inefficient to provide a remedial program that covered all reading skills. These children can be brought up to reading grade level much more rapidly by receiving an intensive instructional program only in the skills in which they are deficient. One might think of a child's progression in developmental reading as the steps or rungs on a ladder or as a continuum of skills with each step representing the accomplishment of a certain skill such as learning the initial consonant sounds, the initial consonant blends, or the short vowel sounds. Whenever a child fails to learn one of these important skills, a step is omitted from the ladder or continuum of skills. The task of the corrective or remedial reading teacher is to fill in these omitted steps or rungs in the ladder or continuum of reading skills rather than to build a whole new ladder. For this reason the remedial reading teacher must be very specific in the diagnosis and then specific in the remediation given for noted weaknesses in order to provide for efficient use of both teacher and student time.

Start at the Child's Level

The educational cliché, "start where the child is," has special relevance for the remedial reading teacher who may get a child who is advanced in some areas and extremely disabled in others. As mentioned previously, a thorough diagnosis is a prerequisite for beginning the remedial program. The diagnosis must not only include the area or areas in which the child is deficient, but for the sake of efficiency should report the level of each skill in which the child is deficient. For example, it is not enough to say that John is a fourth grader who is deficient in comprehension skills; the diagnostic report should also state the level at which he does comprehend. Likewise, a student who is having difficulty with consonant blends should be reported as deficient in knowledge of the *bl, fl, pl,* etc., blends and not simply as "having trouble with consonant blends." In both cases the teacher will be able to begin at the child's level of achievement if the diagnostic report is precise. An important point of which both the remedial teacher and classroom teacher must be cognizant is that the disabled reader must not merely begin to make normal progress, but must also progress at a faster than normal rate in order to catch up with children of a normal age-grade level.

Start with the Child's Strongest Area

Most readers, whether disabled or not, have at least one area in which they are strong or in which they are somewhat more competent than others. The strength may be in a certain area of reading itself, for example, knowledge of initial consonant blends, or it may be in an area such as mathematics. Because of the extreme importance of establishing proper rapport with a disabled reader, it often works well to begin remedial work by focusing on the strong area. This will allow the disabled reader to experience initial success and thus create an atmosphere in which the child can enjoy working on the reading problem. To continue work in an area in which the disabled reader is already competent would, of course, be inefficient in terms of both student and teacher time; however, the value to be gained from improving the initial attitude of the child will usually outweigh the fact that certain material in the beginning stages is repetitious.

Provide an Opportunity for Success for the Child

Most teachers realize the importance of providing lessons in which children can experience considerable success. This concept has usually been stressed in various methods courses and in psychology courses as well. In remedial reading, however, providing an opportunity for success for the child is even more crucial and deserves special emphasis. The reason for this special emphasis is that the child who ultimately comes to the remedial reading teacher has already experienced a series of failures that led to the disability. In spite of good teaching or at least a proper attitude on the part of the disabled reader's classroom reading teacher, the disabled reader is almost certain to have experienced less success than most children in the classroom.

Since the disabled reader has usually experienced considerable failures, the student's overall attitude toward learning will often need to be reoriented. This reorientation may be changed somewhat by "educational engineering," in which the teacher consistently arranges for situations to occur in which the child is able to succeed; two examples are winning a word game or doing a series of easy exercises in which the child gets 100 percent correct. Some children, however, may need more than normal success to change their attitude. The teacher may find, for example, that the reorientation process will require not only constant success, but counseling as well. A typical counseling procedure is described in Chapter 7.

Make the Disabled Reader Aware of the Progress That Has Been Made

Disabled readers need to be aware of their progress. To simply say, "You're doing better," is often not sufficient to convince children that you are actually helping them. Just as students' physical growth is not clearly noticeable to them, neither is their growth in reading. If you really wanted a child to believe that physical growth was occurring, you might mark a line on the wall when the child was measured and label it: "Jane's height on February 20, 19__." A year later you could measure Jane and mark another line to show her year's growth. Most children would accept such evidence as proof that they were growing.

The remedial reading teacher can, and should, use measurements that are just as concrete as the line on the wall. One excellent method of demonstrating students' progress is to code all of the errors that they make in reading materials at and slightly above their grade level. These coded errors can then be tallied as shown in Figure 2–2.

After the students have improved in their reading, they can read the same material while the teacher again codes the various types of errors. The students can then be shown the reduction in each type of error from the first to the second reading. Tape recordings of the first and second readings are also an excellent way to demonstrate improvement to students. Tape recordings in conjunction with coded series of reading passages are, of course, still better.

Students who make a number of errors on basic sight words or phrases can be given cards with the known words or phrases on them. As the students learn new words or phrases, they can receive new cards. In this way the students can easily watch their basic sight vocabulary grow. The teacher could also elect to take cards from the students as they master words and phrases. In this way the students see their stacks of cards gradually disappear until their basic sight vocabulary "troubles" are gone.

In phonics or structural analysis the teacher could simply check or circle the elements not known and show these checklists to the students. As the

TYPES OF ERRORS
(Indicate number of each type)

First Trial		Second Trial	Percent of Increase (+) or Decrease (−)
6	Omissions	2	− 66⅔
2	Insertions	0	− 100
14	Partial mispronunciations	7	− 50
0	Gross mispronunciations	0	—
2	Substitutions	0	− 100
8	Repetitions	2	− 75
3	Inversions	0	− 100
0	Aid	0	—
6	Self-corrected errors	0	− 100

CHARACTERISTICS OF THE READER
(Indicate with checkmark)

First Trial		Second Trial
✓	Poor word-analysis skills	0
✓	Head movement	0
✓	Finger pointing	0
✓	Disregard for punctuation	0
✓	Loss of place	0
✓	Overuse of phonics	0
✓	Does not read in natural voice tones	0
✓	Poor enunciation	0
✓	Word-by-word reading	0
✓	Poor phrasing	0
✓	Lack of expression	0
✓	Pauses	0

Student _James Wilson_   Teacher _Anne Updike_

Date _9/23_   School _Lincoln Elementary_

FIGURE 2–2.   Coded errors of a student's oral reading.

students learn various elements, they could then erase the checkmarks or circles.

By seeing actual growth in their reading skills, students are more likely to be motivated. Also, students who are aware of their progress are more likely to take an active interest in increasing their rate of progress.

Make the Learning Process Meaningful to the Child

A college student was working with a disabled reader on a phonics problem. The disabled reader was in the fourth grade, but was reading on a first-grade level. After learning several initial consonant blends and several phonograms, the child was given an opportunity to form some new words by blending the initial consonant blends with the phonograms. After forming several new words, the child exclaimed, "Hey, this helps you figure out new words!" Perhaps one would be critical of the college student for not explaining why the blends and phonograms were being taught, but one must certainly be critical of the child's former teachers who had allowed the child to progress to the fourth grade without really ever knowing why he should learn his phonics lessons. It is evident that this child simply perceived phonics as a subject or an activity completely different and unrelated to reading.

Children, until they reach the junior high level or beyond, will seldom question why they are being taught various concepts and subject matter. However, the fact that they do not question why it is being taught does not mean that they believe in the necessity of learning it; in fact the attitude that children often demonstrate makes it a certainty that they do not.

Most children, just as adults, when told that they must learn the basic sight words because they account for over half of the words they will ever need to read, can understand the importance of thoroughly learning them. Children also understand, if told, that they must do comprehension exercises to help them understand what they are reading so that they can get more out of their science and social studies books. Likewise, children need to be shown how learning the various word-attack skills helps them unlock new words.

Use Materials Appropriate to the Needs of the Child

The reading program in many classrooms is dictated by the kinds of materials found within each classroom. This sort of situation is not desirable even in a developmental reading program, but it is completely intolerable in remedial reading. Excellent reading materials are no better than poor materials if they are not appropriate to the needs of the learner. Many remedial reading programs have failed because an untrained teacher simply gave the disabled reader "more of the same."

The remedial reading teacher must remember that referred students are, for the most part, disabled only in certain areas and that the weak areas must receive special attention. For example, a readily available book designed to improve a child's comprehension skills is of little value to a child who is experiencing problems with word-attack skills.

Teachers and administrators should be extra cautious when buying materials to be used in remedial reading. Some materials attempt to do too many things to be really worthwhile in any one area of difficulty. For example, materials that attempt to enrich vocabulary, improve comprehension, and improve word-attack skills in each lesson are likely to be of questionable value in remedial reading since a child is more likely to need an intensive saturation in one area rather than a well-rounded program of teaching each of these three skills. Educational research has also shown that many of the devices designed to speed up reading are of questionable value in developmental reading and may very well be detrimental to a disabled reader. In most cases there is simply no valid reason for using them. Materials appropriate for the remedial reading classroom should contain lessons that are designed to remedy specific reading difficulties. Chapter 16 contains considerable information on the selection and evaluation of materials for remedial and/or corrective reading.

Continue the Diagnosis While You Teach

A student who is being tested will often fail to perform as well as would be expected in the more relaxed, day-to-day reading situation. If this happens, there is of course the danger that the student while being tested will fail certain items that were actually known. The student might then be channeled into remedial work that is unnecessary. For example, after testing a child, you may discover that a number of phonic elements and basic sight words were missed. The student may also have missed a number of comprehension questions. You are likely to find that later in a normal classroom atmosphere the student will know some of the phonic elements and basic sight words and may improve a great deal on comprehension.

Improvement in these areas is often accounted for by the difference in stress or performance criteria between testing and actual reading. The prevalence of such cases emphasizes the need for continual diagnosis during the remediation period.

Be Alert to Pick Up Any Clues Given by the Child

Regardless of how thoroughly a disabled reader may be tested in the beginning, you will find many opportunities to expand on the initial diagnosis while you work. It is most important that you develop an alertness to significant clues that children may give concerning their reading disability. Some clues may lead you to change your initial diagnosis, while others will allow you to expand on or confirm the original diagnosis. Following are some clues that were dropped by children who were being taught by university students:

Casey: "Sometimes Mom makes me study in the evening for five minutes and sometimes she makes me study for three or four hours. It just depends on what kind of a mood she's in."

Casey's mother was divorced and was working full time in the daytime and dated quite often at night. Casey did his homework if his mother supervised it; however, she often simply ignored him and did not really concern herself with whether it was done. Sometimes she would tell him that he had to read for three hours for punishment. Most importantly, Casey did not know what to expect and had developed some poor work habits as a result of his mother's erratic behavior. Since reading was used as punishment, he had come to view reading as something to be done only when you are bad.

Counseling sessions with Casey's mother helped her to see the need to be more consistent. She also was made aware of the negative feelings that Casey was developing toward reading because it was used as punishment.

Jeffrey: "Sometimes I can see a word and sometimes I can't."

Jeffrey's eyes had been tested by the school nurse earlier in the year. She had reported that Jeffrey had normal vision. This clue, however, led the teacher to refer Jeffrey, through his parents, to an eye doctor who discovered that he was farsighted (had poor nearpoint vision). Glasses were prescribed and his vision and reading both improved.

Tim: "Dad doesn't read and he gets along fine."

Tim's father was a truck driver who spent a great deal of time away from home. Tim had indicated that he would like to be like his dad and he had never seen him sit down and read. During an ensuing conference with Tim's mother and father, the teacher found that both of Tim's parents read a great deal. Tim was later brought into the conference. Tim's father explained that his job depended on the ability to read. For example, he had to read road maps and road signs and a considerable amount of paperwork connected with his work, such as delivery instructions and Interstate Commerce Commission regulations. Tim's father also told Tim that when he stayed in motels at night he often read a book each night. This conference proved well worthwhile and improved Tim's attitude toward reading.

Clues such as those listed above often lead the teacher to examine certain aspects of a child's reading problem that might otherwise go unnoticed. The remedial reading teacher who is alert to such clues will often be able to add considerable worthwhile information to the original diagnosis.

Capitalize on the Motivation That the Child May Already Possess

Most children have at least one thing that seems to interest them somewhat more than others. The remedial reading teacher who is able to determine that area of interest can often capitalize on it in reading. For example, Kurt came to the reading center after being referred by his classroom teacher. After his teacher at the reading center had talked with him at length, she found that he had seldom, if ever, read at home or for that matter he had seldom read anything that his teachers had not required him to read. After several work sessions with Kurt, the teacher at the reading center discovered that he was very interested in airplanes. His father was an Air Force pilot and had taught him to identify a great many commercial as well as Air Force planes. The teacher asked Kurt if he would be interested in reading if he could find some books about airplanes. He said that he thought he might. For several succeeding sessions Kurt and his teacher searched the library for books about airplanes and flying in general. Kurt found eleven books that he expressed an interest in reading. By the end of the semester Kurt had read eight of the eleven books and had asked several times if his teacher knew where he could find some more books on the subject.

Other teachers have been successful in getting students interested in reading about various occupations in which the students were extremely interested. Still others have motivated students to read by showing them how and why reading is a necessary part of occupations in which the student someday hoped to work. Teachers are often successful in motivating students in an area in which they previously had no interest. However, this extrinsic interest is often much more difficult to generate than intrinsic interests or motivation that the student may already possess.

Maintain a Relaxed Attitude

Children often come to remedial reading possessing feelings of hostility. Many of these children have failed for a number of years and can see no reason why the special class in reading should be any different. As adults, we often forget how it feels to experience constant failure. For example, imagine what kind of an attitude you might have toward a college statistics course if you were in it for the third time after either having failed it or after receiving the lowest grades in the class the first two times. Certainly you would not bounce exuberantly into the class asking, "When do we get started?"

When a child comes to remedial reading possessing a negative or hostile attitude, it becomes very easy for this same attitude to be transferred to the teacher working with the child. The remedial reading teacher must, however, learn to not take such an attitude too seriously. You must mantain a relaxed attitude and teach the child that you will accept mistakes and that the child need have no fear of correction from you. Once the child sees that there is no reason to possess a hostile attitude, the hostility will usually disappear.

One of the coauthors worked with a young boy who almost always came to remedial reading with a negative attitude. In fact, in all honesty, it was very difficult for the author to maintain a pleasant attitude toward the child. During the course of the year the child's reading improved considerably, but the child's overall attitude remained pretty much the same. At the end of several years, the author happened to revisit the school and met this same boy walking back to his classroom from an outside recess period. The boy exclaimed, "Say, you're the guy who helped me learn how to read. You know that sure helped me!" This, coming from what was probably the most hostile student the author had ever taught, is an excellent example of a child whose only defense against failure and all things connected with it was a hostile attitude.

Do Not Be Too Authoritative

As mentioned previously, the remedial reading teacher must maintain a relaxed attitude. Maintaining such an attitude should also preclude becoming too authoritarian in the remedial reading classroom. This is not to say that the teacher should not be firm in demanding certain standards of work and behavior, but merely that the remedial reading teacher's job should not be that of disciplinarian or authoritarian in the eyes of the child. Studies such as those of Sarah D. Muller and Charles H. Madsen, Jr. (1970), James Gardner and Grayce Ransom (1968), and Richard Cheatham (1968) would indicate that the counseling aspects of teaching remedial reading are just as important as the teaching of reading per se. The teacher who is too authoritative would, of course, soon become an ineffective counselor.

The teacher must strive to maintain a climate in the remedial reading classroom where students can express their fears and resentments. Students should be spared unnecessary sermons on why they should try harder. Instead, the remedial reading teacher can help students to develop motivation and self-direction by providing the success that derives from effective instruction.

Have Confidence in the Child's Ability to Learn

The remedial reading teacher must not only have confidence in the student's ability to learn but also transfer this belief to the child. A study by J. Michael Palardy (1969) demonstrated that what the teacher believes regarding students' abilities can significantly affect final student achievement. Palardy also indicated that teachers can either positively or negatively influence students' self-concepts, which in turn influence achievement.

The remedial reading teacher must be cognizant of this type of research and constantly strive to maintain a positive attitude toward each student's ability to learn. Perhaps the best way to develop this attitude is through careful record keeping as described under the earlier section entitled, "Make the Disabled Reader Aware of the Progress That Has Been Made." Such procedures will allow both teacher and student to see the student's week-by-week progress and thus give both of them the needed confidence in the child's ability to learn.

Direct the Child Toward Self-Instruction

Although the specific instruction that students receive in a remedial reading classroom is almost always certain to be of considerable benefit, the amount that students learn on their own is often of equal or greater importance. This is, no doubt, true of almost any class that students attend, regardless of the subject matter involved. The learning that takes place within the classroom is, of course, of greater importance in the beginning, but it only serves as a stepping stone to the broadening of one's knowledge. One might say that the classroom learning points students in the direction from which they then proceed to expand and broaden their knowledge. This is especially true in remedial reading. Often the amount of time available for special tutoring sessions is severely limited due to the lack of an adequate teaching staff. Because of these factors, the remedial reading teacher must direct the students toward self-instruction.

Self-instruction may take many different forms depending on the age-grade level of the student, the nature of the reading disability, and a host of other factors. For example, a teacher may diagnose a child as having a very limited sight vocabulary and as a result may spend many hours teaching words that should have been learned as the student progressed through the grades. Such effort, however, can be futile if the child does not begin to read independently to gain continual exposure to the new words learned during the remedial sessions. Our work at the reading clinics at the University of Texas at El Paso and California State University, Hayward, has shown that even the brightest child needs many exposures to a word before it becomes a sight word.

Richard Allington (1980) examined the amount of actual reading assigned to students during classroom reading instruction. He found that good readers read on average more than twice as many words per session as poor readers in first- and second-grade classrooms. In addition, the poor readers had fewer opportunities to read silently, and their oral reading errors were more often treated out of context.

Elsewhere in this book we stress the importance of substantial practice *in the act of reading.* We believe that one of the major contributors to students' reading difficulties is their limited exposure to reading in context. Though this fact may appear obvious, it bears repeating here. The implication for the remedial reading teacher is clear: The single most important form of self-instruction for the student is to spend as much time as possible in the act of reading.

In the area of comprehension and study skills children can be taught to improve themselves by applying study techniques such as SQ3R (see Chapter 6) to reading their science and social studies lessons. They can also be taught the use of full and half signals such as "in the first place," "secondly," and "and then," which will enable their comprehension to improve while reading on their own.

Begin Each Period with a Summary of What You Intend to Do and Why You Intend to Do It, and End Each Period with a Summary of What You Did and Why You Did It

As parents, most of us have at some time or another asked our children what they learned at school today. An all too common answer to this question is, "Oh nothing." As teachers most of us also realize that the "Oh nothing" statement is probably incorrect. What you must remember, however, is that the "Oh nothing" represents the child's perception of what was learned. For the purpose of stimulating or motivating a child to want to learn you must be cognizant of how the child feels about it. If you are successful in convincing the child that learning is in fact taking place, chances are the child will take a more active interest in what is being taught.

In order to avoid the "Oh nothing" response, you should brief the child at the beginning of the session on what is to be learned. Then, at the end of the remedial session, you and the student should review what has been learned and why it was learned. If you follow this procedure, you will find an overall improvement in the children's attitude toward learning, and, in addition, you are likely to improve your public relations program with the parents of the children you teach.

Provide for a Follow-Up Program

Remedial reading programs in which the disabled readers have been kept for a considerable length of time have tended to be more successful than those that have only brought children in for short periods of time. This is especially true where some sort of follow-up program was not instituted for children who were terminated from short-term remedial reading programs.

Bruce Balow (1965) reported on a study of three groups of disabled readers, some of whom were given assistance during a follow-up period. He states,

> Continuing growth seems to depend upon continued attention to the problem. While the second and third groups received additional remedial assistance throughout the follow-up period, few of the pupils in Sample I had any further special help. Sample I pupils did not lose the reading skill they had acquired during the time in the clinic, but neither did they continue to develop on their own. Quite in contrast is the continuing progress of the second and third groups. Given far less intensive, but nonetheless supportive, help over the follow-up period, these pupils continued to develop in reading at a pace more rapid than that preceding intensive tutoring. Rate of growth over the follow-up period was approximately 75 percent of normal growth. (p. 585)

Balow indicates that, unfortunate as it may seem, short-term intensive programs have not been successful, although children are helped somewhat during the course of instruction. He believes that reading disability should probably be considered a relatively chronic illness needing long-term treatment.

Similar results were reported by Theodore A. Buerger (1968), who also did a follow-up study of remedial reading instruction. In his conclusions Buerger stated, "What is needed after a rather intensive remedial period is provision for supportive reading assistance during the follow-up period." (p. 333)

E. Shearer (1967), studying the long-term effects of remedial reading instruction, also concluded that children do make gains in remedial reading and that these gains can be preserved if follow-up remedial help is given.

The activities of the follow-up program in most cases will closely parallel the period of more intensive remediation. Some teachers prefer to cut the time allotted to each remedial session, while others prefer to keep the length of remedial sessions the same but have the child come to class less often.

REASONS FOR FAILURE IN THE DIAGNOSTIC-REMEDIAL PROCESS

Certain factors, if allowed to interfere, can seriously impede the diagnostic-remedial process. Educational diagnosticians and/or remedial teachers should constantly examine their own diagnostic-remedial procedures to insure that certain influencing factors are not adversely affecting either their diagnostic or remedial procedures. Some common reasons for failure in the diagnostic-remedial process are as follows:

1. Too much time is spent on the diagnosis so that no time is left for remediation.
2. Sometimes the data are inadequate.
3. Some single causes of reading disability are overemphasized.
4. Sometimes the diagnosis is determined by one person and the remedial work is done by another.
5. Some diagnosticians come up with the same factors time after time.
6. We sometimes diagnose and work on factors that do not help children's reading.
7. Previous bias may exert an undue influence.

Too Much Time Is Spent on the Diagnosis So That No Time Is Left for Remediation

The problem of spending so much time on diagnosis that little or no time is left for remediation is more prevalent than many people working in remedial reading realize. In some schools the initial testing system for admitting a child to remedial reading and then the initial diagnosis once the student en-

ters the remedial reading program may take up nearly one-half of the first semester of school. Even though the child may not be directly involved in testing
every day, the admittance procedure often becomes so involved that the child
loses out on valuable remedial time. School personnel who deal with disabled
readers should attempt to simplify procedures for initial diagnosis as much
as possible in order to avoid unnecessary testing. For some children certain
tests that are given as routine procedure for all students may be omitted. For
example, routine hearing tests could probably be omitted for children whose
problem is in an area such as reading comprehension. Likewise, individual
intelligence tests may often be omitted if the child is to be admitted to the remedial reading program regardless of the outcome of the test. Chances are
the type of instruction given will not be influenced by the child's IQ even if it
were extremely high or extremely low. In most cases a good remedial reading
teacher would simply use those methods or procedures that proved successful with the child.

Another problem in this area is that people involved in reading simply
become curious about certain children's abilities and administer tests to
satisfy their own curiosity. The remedial reading teacher should be able to
justify the administration of all tests given a child on the basis that the test
results will ultimately help the child. Curiosity is healthy, and much good research and practical knowledge stem from it. However, unless some justifi-
able research is involved, the point should again be stressed that children
should not be subjected to unnecessary testing. The remedial reading teacher should also remember that a great deal of useful information, such as how
children learn, their success in mastering certain concepts, and their reasons for failure, will be uncovered in working with children on a day-to-day
basis.

Sometimes the Data Are Inadequate

Although the diagnostic-remedial process can easily be hampered by the collection of too much unnecessary data, it can just as easily be hampered when
the data collected are inadequate. Some children are simply referred to the
remedial reading teacher who then immediately begins work on specific
problems. Operating in this fashion can often be inefficient and wasteful of
the teacher's, as well as the child's, time.

Data are often readily available that could help the remedial reading
teacher plan a more effective program. For example, many children are not
successful in learning phonics through the application of a great many rules;
therefore, some of these children come to remedial reading with a deficiency
in phonics knowledge. In some cases children may even come to the remedial
reading teacher in the fourth grade with a deficiency in phonics knowledge
after having completed three years of intensive "rule type" phonics. If the remedial reading teacher is not aware of a child's inability to learn phonics

through this type of approach, the child may continue to be exposed to more of the same. On the other hand, a short interview with the child's former teachers, or in some cases, a check of the child's cumulative folder would make this information readily available to the remedial reading teacher and thus avoid duplication of the same type of efforts. Another example of data that may be readily available is information on the child's physical condition that could adversely affect the child's reading. A short interview with the child's parents can often provide information that will be helpful in planning the remedial program.

Some Single Causes of Reading Disability Are Overemphasized

Unfortunately some diagnosticians and remedial reading teachers become extremely interested in some particular aspect of reading and consequently have a tendency to overemphasize that aspect in their diagnoses and remedial work. This may happen as the result of the reading of a journal article on the subject, a report for a class, a speech at a professional meeting, and so forth. No professional person would deny the value of any of these activities; however, you should guard against becoming so involved in diagnosis in any specific area that other important deficiencies are overlooked.

Other areas that often receive undue emphasis are the learning of vowel rules, syllable principles, and accent generalizations. The remedial reading teacher should remember that the learning of any of these is merely a means to an end, that end being the ability to properly attack and pronounce an unfamiliar word. If a child can already pronounce words on or above grade level, or if the child can readily pronounce difficult nonsense words, there is little reason to learn the vowel rules, syllable principles, or accent generalizations as word-attack skills.

The diagnostician and remedial reading teacher may do well to constantly ask themselves such questions as: Do I consistently find myself teaching the same thing regardless of the original diagnosis? Do my diagnoses indicate that I constantly prescribe the same remediation? Do I use only one or two tests with which I am familiar that may tend to give me the same results each time? Do other diagnosticians concur with my findings and recommendations? Would the total number of disabled readers I have diagnosed show approximately the same percentage of reading problems in each category as reputable studies have indicated are the causes of reading disability?

Sometimes the Diagnosis Is Determined by One Person and the Remedial Work Is Done by Another

When a diagnosis is done by one person and turned over to another for remediation, communication problems often arise. Communication concerning reading deficiencies is sometimes difficult because of semantic differences in reading terminology. Helen Robinson (1970) states,

> Examples of differences in terms and labels may be found by comparing articles dealing with reading in almost any publication. In learning to read, a child may be expected to identify words, discriminate words, recognize words, or perceive words. (p. 78)

Unless the reading diagnostician has the ability to accurately communicate the diagnosis to the person who will be carrying out the remedial procedures, the child is quite likely to receive inadequate or unnecessary help.

Most of the problems encountered in the area of communication between the diagnostician and teacher are a result of a lack of preciseness. For example, a part of one diagnostician's report read as follows: "This child should be provided with help in word-attack skills." Such a statement is of little value to a teacher since there are so many word-attack skills. Even if the statement was narrowed to any one word-attack skill such as phonics, the diagnostician should still be exact in describing what the child needs. For example, a report that reads as follows would provide much more direction for immediate remedial help:

> This child should be provided with help in learning the initial consonant blends, *bl, pl, fl,* and *pr.* He should then be given help in learning to blend them with various phonograms.

Another problem encountered when the diagnosis is done by one person and then turned over to another is that children who are exposed to a strange person in a testing situation often fail to perform up to their normal standards. When this happens, the person doing the remedial work will, of course, find discrepancies in the original diagnosis, which will in turn lead to an inefficient diagnostic-remedial procedure.

Some Diagnosticians Come Up with the Same Factors Time after Time

Most educational diagnosticians tend to rely on certain tests with which they have become familiar through continued use. The use of the same test or tests time after time can be beneficial in that the tester becomes more efficient in the diagnostic process. Efficiency in administration of tests is of little value, however, if the diagnostician fails to diagnose certain important causal factors and continually comes up with the same recommendations for remediation time after time.

Unfortunately, in reading psychologists' and educational diagnosticians' reports, we often find that nearly all reports even on different students diagnosed by one person contain the same recommendations. The reports on various students diagnosed by another person may contain different types of recommendations but again often contain the same recommendations for all students. All of you dealing with the diagnosis of disabled readers should continually evaluate your findings and recommendations to determine whether they are generally in line with educational studies showing various causal factors and the percent of time you might expect each to occur. Research by J. F. Vinsonhaler (1979) examined three types of agreement in reading diagnosis: group agreement, intraclinician agreement, and interclinician agreement. Vinsonhaler found that reading clinicians do not agree very well with themselves or with other clinicians.

We Sometimes Diagnose and Work on Factors That Do Not Help Children's Reading

In most cases there is little value in diagnosing factors for which we either do not expect to provide remediation or for which remediation has not proven effective in the past. For example, Donald Hammill, Libby Goodman, and J. Lee Wiederholt (1974) summarized the research in the areas of eye-motor coordination and visual perception. They concluded that readers with visual-perception problems, such as eye-motor coordination, discrimination of figure-ground, and position in space, were not helped by training in these areas per se. Therefore, unless these tests can be justified strictly for research purposes, there seems to be little if any value in their routine administration in the public schools. Jean Harber (1979) found that the skills of visual perception, visual-perceptual integration, sound blending, and visual closure were not highly related to reading performance in learning disabled children. Therefore, the remedial reading teacher must question the value of instruction designed to remedy weaknesses in these areas.

A child who has difficulty in discriminating a "b" from a "d" may, for example, also score low on Frostig's (1966) *Developmental Test of Visual Perception* subtest "Position in Space." However, simply having the child read or write the letters of the alphabet will quickly enable the diagnostician to determine whether the child is making letter reversals. If letter reversals are occurring, research evidence suggests two possible approaches; either the problem should be ignored, since the child will likely outgrow it; or, if remedial procedures are employed, it is more logical to work on the b and d problem directly, rather than to do the types of exercises recommended by Frostig when children obtain a poor score on the "Position in Space" subtest. In doing the type of remediation recommended by Frostig you can only hope that the remediation will transfer to the b and d reversal problem.

The remedial reading teacher and/or educational diagnostician should continually examine their diagnostic procedures to determine whether unnecessary testing is being done in terms of what is being provided in the remedial program. Care should also be taken to provide adequate diagnosis for any suspected areas of difficulty for which remediation has proven effective.

Previous Bias May Exert an Undue Influence

Few, if any, of us would deny that we are somewhat biased on matters such as politics, religion, and certain beliefs concerning education. We must, however, continually examine our own beliefs and practices to determine whether they are exerting an unhealthy influence in diagnosing and treating reading disabilities. It is all too easy, for example, to simply ignore research that indicates that our beliefs may be wrong and look for research that tends to confirm any bias that we may possess.

Reading personnel should constantly guard against developing attitudes that are likely to be detrimental to their diagnostic or remedial procedures. While serving as a reading consultant in the public schools, one of the coauthors encountered a reading teacher with very little formal training in the teaching of reading. The teacher was using procedures that were far from being in line with procedures that have proven their worth in the past. Still, this teacher insisted that his ideas and methods were successful. A subsequent check of the standardized test scores of this teacher's classes during the four previous years indicated that his pupils' class average had dropped about ten percentile points each year during the time he had taught them. There was certainly no doubt that his own personal bias concerning methodology was adversely affecting his pupils.

Experimentation should be encouraged, and when certain procedures prove successful they should be adopted. On the other hand, when test results or experience proves that procedures are detrimental to the welfare of students, those procedures should be revised.

SUMMARY

Through a combination of research and experience remedial reading teachers have found that certain procedures can make their remedial reading programs more effective. It is important to know which operational procedures have been successful and which have lacked success in the diagnostic process. Some of these have been discussed in this chapter. It is also important to know which procedures have been successful in the remedial process. These have also been discussed in this chapter. Quite often remedial reading programs have failed to achieve the kind of results that have been expected from students. The information presented in this chapter should help remedial reading teachers avoid the same mistakes.

REFERENCES

Allington, Richard L. *Poor Readers Don't Get to Read Much.* East Lansing, Mich.: Institute for Research on Teaching, 1980.

Balow, Bruce. "The Long Term Effect of Remedial Reading Instruction," *Reading Teacher.* Vol. 18, (April, 1965), 581–586.

Buerger, Theodore A. "A Follow-up of Remedial Reading Instruction." *Reading Teacher.* Vol. 21, (January, 1968), 329–334.

Cheatham, Richard Beauregard. "A Study of the Effects of Group Counseling on the Self-Concept and on the Reading Efficiency of Low-achieving Readers in a Public Intermediate School," Doctoral dissertation, The American University, 1968.

Dolan, Keith G. "Effects of Individual Counseling on Selected Test Scores for Delayed Readers," *Personnel and Guidance Journal.* Vol. 42, (May, 1964), 914–919.

Durrell, Donald D., and Catterson, Jane H. *Durrell Analysis of Reading Difficulty.* New York: Psychological Corporation, 1980.

Ekwall, Eldon E. "An Analysis of Children's Test Scores When Tested with Individually Administered Diagnostic Tests and When Tested with Group Administered Diagnostic Tests," *Final Research Report.* University of Texas at El Paso, University Research Institute, 1973.

Ekwall, Eldon E. *Ekwall Reading Inventory.* Boston: Allyn and Bacon, 1979.

Frostig, Marianne. *Developmental Test of Visual Perception.* Palo Alto: Consulting Psychologists Press, 1966.

Gardner, James, and Ransom, Grayce. "Academic Reorientation: A Counseling Approach to Remedial Readers," *Reading Teacher.* Vol. 21, (March, 1968), 529–536.

Hammill, Donald; Goodman, Libby; and Wiederholt, J. Lee. "Visual-Motor Processes: Can We Train Them?" *Reading Teacher.* Vol. 27, (February, 1974), 469–478.

Harber, Jean. "Are Perceptual Skills Necessary for Success in Reading? Which Ones?" *Reading Horizons.* Vol. 20, (Fall, 1979), 7–15.

Lillich, Joseph M. "Comparison of Achievement in Special Reading Classes Using Guidance, Skill-Content and Combination Approaches," Paper presented at International Reading Association Conference, Boston, Massachusetts, April, 1968, pp. 1–11.

Muller, Sarah D., and Madsen, Charles H., Jr. "Group Desensitization for Anxious Children with Reading Problems," *Psychology in the Schools.* Vol. 7, (April, 1970), 184–189.

Palardy, J. Michael. "For Johnny's Reading Sake," *Reading Teacher.* Vol. 22, (May, 1969), 720–721.

Robinson, Helen. "Significant Unsolved Problems in Reading," *Reading Teacher.* Vol. 14, (November, 1970), 77–82.

Shearer, E. "The Long-Term Effects of Remedial Education," *Educational Research.* Vol. 9, (June, 1967), 219–222.

Vinsonhaler, J. F. *The Consistency of Reading Diagnosis.* East Lansing, Mich.: Institute for Research on Teaching, 1979.

3

A Framework for the Diagnosis and Teaching of Educational Factors

The first purpose of this chapter is to develop a framework for the diagnosis and remediation of educational factors in reading. The second purpose is to illustrate a scope and sequence of the commonly taught reading skills to enable the teacher to determine which reading skills students should have mastered at various stages in their progression through the grades. This is then followed by a discussion that is intended to clarify the usage of materials for diagnosis, teaching, or reinforcement.

Many definitions for the act of reading have been proposed over the years. Many of these are very similar to the following: reading is the act of interpreting, by the reader, what was written by the author. This definition, although somewhat useful for theoretical purposes in discussing the act of reading, is not concrete enough to be meaningful for the remedial teacher in the diagnosis and remediation of educational factors. For the purpose of diagnosis and remediation of educational factors you might want to think of reading as a process of recognizing words and of understanding words and ideas.

We often hear beginning teachers make such statements as, "I have a student in my class who is a good oral reader, but can't seem to understand what he reads." Still others will say, "One of my students can really understand what she reads, but she just can't seem to say all of the words." When hearing this type of statement we are reminded of the story of the man who was raised in a Spanish-speaking community. He spoke both Spanish and English but only learned to read and write English. During the process of learning to read he never seemed to have learned to "sound out" words, or as we would say in reading, he didn't learn sound-symbol correspondence. During his college years he began to date a young lady from Mexico City. One Christmas vacation when the young lady went home, she sent the young man a letter written in Spanish. Since the young man had only learned to speak Spanish, he could not read the letter. He solved the problem, however, by getting one of his friends to help him. His friend could not speak Spanish, but he could pronounce the words since Spanish is a phonemic language and his friend had a good knowledge of sound-symbol relationships. The essential point here was that neither one of the young men could "read" the letter. One of them could pronounce the words and one of them could understand the words and ideas, but it took both of them to "read" the letter.

Reading, then, as stated previously, is a process of recognizing words and understanding words and ideas. What the beginning teachers mentioned earlier meant was that certain students in their classes were either poor in their knowledge of sight words or word attack or they were poor in their comprehension of words and ideas. A lack of knowledge in either area would make a student a poor reader.

The scope of the reading skills as discussed thus far would be illustrated as shown in Figure 3–1. "Recognizing words" is usually broken down into two subdivisions. These two subdivisions are "sight words" and "word-attack skills." Here then are two situations for a reader who must recognize words. The reader will either have come in contact with a word enough times so that it is instantly recognized, or, if it is not instantly recognized, the reader must apply one or more of the word-attack skills in order to determine how to recognize and thus say or think that word.

If the word is one that the reader has come in contact with a number of times before and it is recognized instantly, it is considered a sight word. The number of sight words in any one reader's storehouse of words will, of

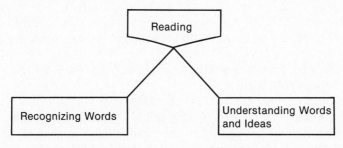

FIGURE 3–1.   Two basic categories of reading skills.

course, vary with such factors as the amount of previous reading the student has done, the student's grade level, and the student's intelligence. For example, the word *and* will become a known sight word for most readers shortly after they begin to read because of its high utility in the English language. On the other hand, the word *sextant* would not become a sight word for most readers until much later in their life.

The term *sight vocabulary* is often used by authors and reading specialists to refer to the total stock of words that are recognized by a student by sight. In this case they would not be concerned with whether the student knew the meaning of the word but only with whether the word was recognized and pronounced instantly. Some words may be in students' "recognition" vocabularies but not in their "meaning" vocabularies, and vice versa. Still other authors reserve the word *vocabulary* strictly for "word meaning." When the term *vocabulary building* is used, most authors are referring to the building of a word-meaning vocabulary at which time the word may or may not also be learned as a sight word. In this book the term *sight vocabulary* means the same as "sight words," i.e., simple word recognition. The term *vocabulary* used by itself indicates "meaning vocabulary."

Under the "sight word" category are two subcategories. These are "basic sight words" and "other sight words." The term *basic sight word* usually refers to a certain list of *high-utility words* (words that appear most often in print) compiled by writers and researchers in the field of reading. Examples of some of these are the Dolch List (1955), the Harris-Jacobson List (1973), and the Durr List (1973). The term *basic sight word* is also used to simply indicate that a certain word is one of high utility that should be known as a sight word and should, therefore, not require the application of word-analysis or word-attack skills.

Listed under "sight words" is another category called "other sight words." This category includes all words known instantly or known without the use of word-attack skills. The number of other sight words would, of course, vary from reader to reader and would vary within any one reader through continual contact with new words time after time. For example, a word such as *establish* might require the application of word-attack skills for quite a number of times in which a student encounters it, but it would eventually become a sight word. It would then be classified here as one of the "other sight words." That is, it would be known instantly by the student, but it would not be of such high utility that it would appear on someone's list as a "basic sight word."

The scope of the reading skills as explained this far would now be illustrated as indicated in Figure 3–2.

As stated earlier, the other subcategory of "recognizing words" is "word-attack skills" or "word-analysis skills." When a reader does not have instant recognition of a word, then the reader must apply one or more of these word-attack skills. The subcategories of "word-attack skills" are usual-

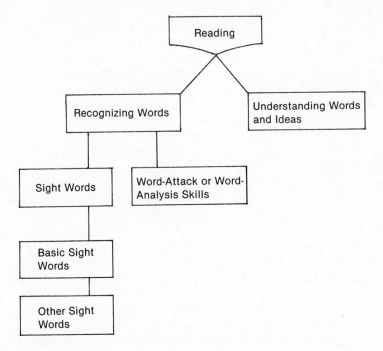

FIGURE 3–2.   A partial breakdown of the skill of recognizing words.

ly referred to as "configuration clues," "context clues," "phonics," "structural analysis," dictionary skills," and parts of the "study skills." Configuration clues refers to the hints a student receives by the overall shape or configuration of a word. The configuration of a word is influenced by such factors as length (*elephant* versus *bed*), use of capital and lower-case letters (*BED* versus *bed*), use of extenders and descenders (*l, b,* versus *p, j*), and use of double letters (*look* versus *have*). Context clues refers to the clues a student receives from a word by the way it is used in the context of a sentence. (The old car rattled as the farmer drove down the country ____ [road].) Another kind of context clue that is often useful to beginning readers is the picture context clue. It tells the reader what the word might be, based on a picture illustrating the reading passage. Phonics usually refers to the sound-symbol relationships between the small, usually nonmeaning-bearing, parts of words. This would include learning the sounds represented by consonants, consonant blends, consonant digraphs, vowels, vowel teams, and special letter combinations. Phonics also includes the knowledge of phonetic generalizations, e.g., rules governing vowel sounds. Syllabication principles are also often considered a phonics skill, although they are more appropriately listed under the category of "structural analysis." Structural analysis is similar to phonics: however, the term as commonly used refers to larger parts of words that bear meaning, such as root words, suffixes, prefixes, word endings, apostrophe + s to show possession, contractions, and compound words. Sometimes, the term *structural analysis* is used to refer to the student's ability to *derive meaning* from word *parts*. Although this is an important skill that may serve to broaden a student's meaning vocabulary, such knowledge does not contribute directly to decoding ability. The dictionary skills, of course, apply to a number of abilities, such as alphabetizing of letters and words, locating a specific word, using guide words, and interpreting preferred spellings. Some of the study skills are also helpful in word analysis, such as the ability to find a word in an encyclopedia and/or dictionary. With the addition of the subcategories of "word-attack" or "word-analysis" skills the scope of the reading skills would now be illustrated as in Figure 3–3.

Note the use of the broken line from the end of the listing of "word-attack skills" to "study skills." The broken line indicates that only a part of the study skills would be considered a subcategory of "word-attack skills" and that the relationship would not be so direct as in the case of the other five subcategories. The ability to use the encyclopedia would contribute to, or could be considered, a word-attack skill, but many of the other study skills would not necessarily be related to the ability to attack words.

The problem of deriving subcategories to illustrate the skills required for understanding words and ideas, or what is usually referred to as comprehension, is much more complicated and less clear-cut than the area of word-attack or word-analysis skills. Research to date has generally shown that investigators are not able to accurately differentiate more than about two or three broad factors. According to George and Evelyn Spache (1977) the factors influencing comprehension may be arranged in three broad categories:

1. those inherent in the material being read,
2. the characteristics of the reader, and
3. the influences dependent upon the manner of reading.   (p. 447)

Within these categories Spache and Spache include these as prominent factors: vocabulary knowledge; the structure and style of the material being read; the ability to use reasoning processes; the beliefs, attitudes, and prejudices of the reader; the purposes of the reader; and the rate of reading.

Most commonly used measures of reading achievement only attempt to measure two broad categories of comprehension—vocabulary and reading comprehension. It would appear, then, that one would be justified in categorizing the subskills of comprehension as "vocabulary development" and "other comprehension skills."

Thomas Barrett (1967) suggests that the cognitive dimension for comprehension categories might be classified as: "(a) literal meaning, (b) inference, (c) evaluation, and (d) appreciation." (p. 21) Literal meaning, as

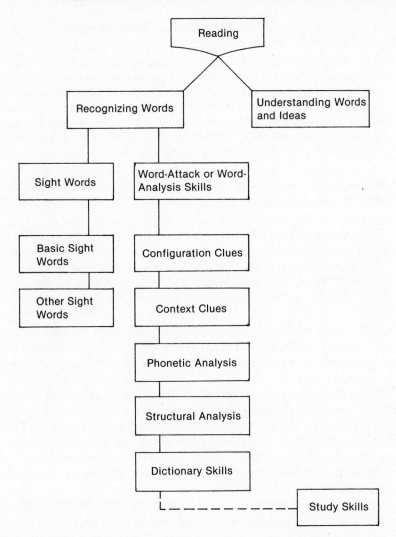

FIGURE 3-3.   A breakdown of the skill of recognizing words.

defined by Barrett, would be concerned with ideas and information explicitly stated in a reading selection. The first of these in terms of pupil behavior would be "recognition" and the second of these would be "recall." Inference, as Barrett states, occurs when the student "uses the ideas and information explicitly stated in the selection, his intuition, and his personal experience as a basis for conjectures and hypotheses." (p. 22)

In explaining his concept of evaluation Barrett states,

> Purposes for reading and teachers' questions, in this instance, require responses by the student which indicate that he has arrived at a judgment by comparing ideas presented in the selection with external criteria provided by the teacher, other authorities or written sources, or with internal criteria provided by the reader's experiences, knowledge, or values. In essence, evaluation deals with judgments and focuses on qualities or correctness, worthwhileness, or appropriateness, feasibility, and validity. (p. 22)

Barrett's last category of appreciation would involve all of the other mentioned levels of thought but would go beyond them. Barrett states,

> Appreciation, as used here, calls for the student to be emotionally and aesthetically sensitive to the written work and to have a reaction to its psychological and artistic elements. For example, when a student verbalizes his feelings about part or all of a reading selection in terms of excitement, fear, dislike, or boredom, he is functioning at the appreciational level. (p. 23)

It should be kept in mind that Barrett's taxonomy of skills for comprehension are only suggested and could not necessarily be defended in terms of factoral analysis studies dealing with concretely measured categories. They do, however, add meaning to our goals for viewing and teaching these skills.

Barrett's categories placed under the category of "other comprehension skills" would then appear as in Figure 3–4.

In addition to the subskills of comprehension mentioned by Barrett a number of authors have listed other categories such as the abilities to see "main ideas," see "important details," see "the author's purpose," develop "mental images," see "a sequence of ideas," and see "the author's organization."

Note the broken line from "appreciation" to "study skills." This again indicates that the study skills have a relationship to, or contribute to, reading comprehension. This relationship is, however, less direct than the relationship between comprehension and the other subcategories previously mentioned.

Perhaps this breakdown of the comprehension skills is not justified on the basis of research. We believe, however, that it is helpful to examine, in at least this much detail, what we have commonly believed to be some of the other subskills of comprehension.

The relationships that are shown to exist in Figure 3–4 no doubt grossly oversimplify the reading act. For example, we know that the purpose and/or state of mind that a student might possess previous to reading a passage can greatly affect the student's comprehension. These might be considered psychological factors, and this should be shown in the comprehension part of

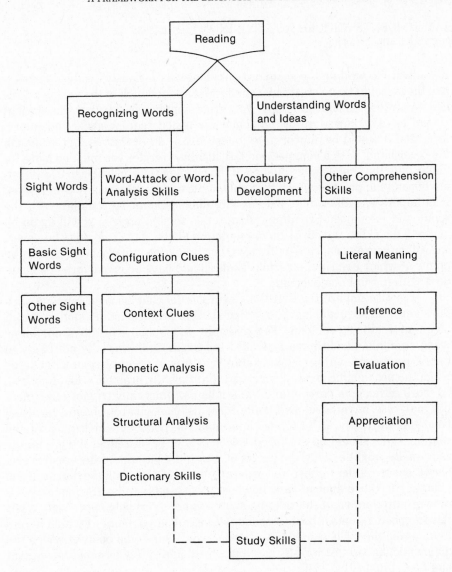

FIGURE 3–4. Scope of the reading skills.

Figure 3–4. There are, however, so many factors of this nature that it would be virtually impossible to illustrate them in a diagram. Furthermore, at the present time, we do not know how to measure many of these complex factors that are known to exist. Figure 3–4 then represents those relationships that are generally known to exist and the educational factors in reading that, to some extent, can be measured.

COMPETENCIES THAT STUDENTS SHOULD ACHIEVE IN THEIR PROGRESSION THROUGH THE GRADES

If you were to wait until a secondary student was seriously disabled in reading, there would be no need to be concerned about which of the various skills should be tested. That is to say, you could simply assume that the student should have mastered all of the commonly tested reading skills and, therefore, that it would be appropriate to test any or all of the reading skills. On the other hand, with a younger and less disabled reader you must be more familiar with the scope and sequence of the reading skills in order to avoid testing beyond the point at which that student should have normally progressed. It is imperative, then, that the reading diagnostician be familiar with the scope and sequence of reading skills. In this section reference will again be made to the skills and subskills presented in Figure 3–4. This time, however, we will be more concerned with a further breakdown of these skills and the points at which each of the various skills should have been mastered by a student with normal achievement.

It is also imperative that the classroom teacher become familiar with the scope and sequence of the reading skills in order to locate students with incipient reading problems. For example, a teacher who does not know when students should have mastered the basic sight words is not likely to notice a student with a mild disability in this area until somewhat later when the problem becomes obvious. At that time the problem will, of course, be more difficult to correct and the student will not only be more disabled, but may also have developed concurrent psychological problems resulting from this difficulty. In order to determine the point at which each of the reading skills should be mastered, seven sets of basal readers[1] were analyzed. As one might expect, the points at which the authors of the various series of basal readers chose to introduce each of the skills varied to some extent. For the diagnostician, however, these minor disagreements as to time of introduction of the reading skills are not extremely important. What the diagnostician must be concerned with is the latest point at which all authors agree the skills should have been taught. This is the point at which the diagnostician can test for any particular skill and safely assume the student has been taught that skill.

An important point for the diagnostician to keep in mind is that some of the reading skills should definitely be mastered and others will be extended and refined ad infinitum. For example, the basic sight words should definitely be known by average students by the middle of their third year in school.

---

[1]Publishers whose books were analyzed were the latest editions of the following: Allyn and Bacon, The Economy Company, Ginn and Company, Harper and Row, Houghton Mifflin, Macmillan Publishing Company, and Scott, Foresman and Company.

On the other hand, a student's knowledge of other sight words will continue to expand. Likewise, there is no point at which one can assume the comprehension skills are completely mastered. The ability to make inferences from a paragraph, for example, probably continues to improve as our vocabulary and background of experiences continue to expand. Skills that are extended and refined rather than completely mastered should then be learned by the student and should also be tested; however, keep in mind that a student who continues to learn will also continue to improve in the ability to use these skills. In the breakdown of the reading skills in Figure 3-5 you will note the use of single and cross-hatched lines, which appear under various grade levels (see key). The level at which either of these appears is opposite the listing of that skill or subskill and indicates the general point at which you could assume that the skill had been taught and likewise the point at which you could logically assume the student should have mastered (in some cases) or should have a knowledge of the use of that skill. In interpreting the chart you should keep in mind that the designation of grade level serves only as a general guideline. Also, in using the scope and sequence chart several precautions need to be observed. First, you should not consider any one skill that appears on the chart to necessarily be prerequisite to a child's learning to read. For example, knowledge of vowel rules might only be necessary if a child cannot pronounce various short and long vowel sounds and if the child needs this skill to decode. The learning of vowel rules is only a means to an end. If the child can pronounce various vowel sounds and combinations of vowels and vowel controlling letters, then there is no need for the child to master that skill. Many very good adult readers can pronounce almost any word or syllable; however, it would be very difficult for many of these same adults to give the vowel sounds in isolation. Furthermore, knowledge of vowel sounds is neither necessary nor helpful for all readers. Many readers are able to decode effectively using other word-attack skills. Therefore, we are only "reporting" the information in Figure 3-5. We shall evaluate the relative importance of the various skills in succeeding chapters.

It should again be emphasized that Figure 3-5 does not attempt to point to a specific time when the skill should be taught. The points of time illustrated represent the stage at which all of the basal reader programs examined agree each skill should be known.

A final but very important consideration is that there are often considerably different levels of development of a certain skill. For example, a child may be able to recognize and circle one of four phonemes that is the same as the initial sound heard in a word pronounced by a tester. However, the child may not be able to pronounce the same phoneme in a strange word when it is encountered in the act of reading. This would, of course, be the level of competency necessary in actual reading. This point will be emphasized again in later chapters as methods of testing for various competencies are discussed.

FIGURE 3–5.   Competencies that students should achieve in their progression through the grades.

SKILL

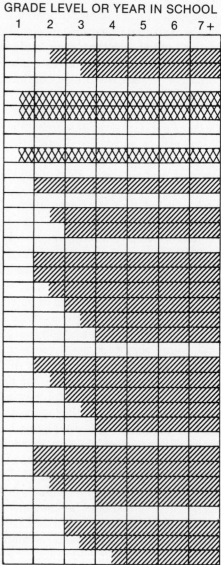

GRADE LEVEL OR YEAR IN SCHOOL
1   2   3   4   5   6   7+

Knowledge of Dolch Basic Sight Words (or similar)
   First Half
   Second Half
Other Sight Words
Configuration Clues[a]
   (Word length, capital letters, double letters and letter height)
Context Clues
   (Pictures and words)
Phonic Analysis
   Single initial consonants
      (all but soft *c* and *g*)
      soft *c*
      soft *g*
   Initial consonant blends
      bl, br, fl, fr, gr, st, tr, cl, cr,
      dr, pr, sl, sp
      pl, gl, sk, sm
      sn, thr, sw, wr
      tw, sch, sc, squ, str, spl, spr, scr
      shr, dw
   Ending consonant blends
      st
      ld, nd, ng
      nk, nt
      ft, mp
      lt
   Consonant Digraphs
      sh, th (three, this), wh (which, who),
      ch (church)
      ck, ng
      gh, ph
   Silent Consonants
      kn, gh(t), wr
      mb
      gn

  Skill firmly established   ⬡⬡⬡⬡ Skill extended and refined, but has been introduced

[a]The use of configuration clues is taught in grade one, but older students continue to use and improve in this skill as their knowledge of structural analysis increases.

(cont.)

FIGURE 3–5. (cont.)

SKILL	1	2	3	4	5	6	7+
Short Vowel Sounds							
a, e, i, o, u		▨	▨	▨	▨	▨	▨
Long Vowel Sounds							
a, e, i, o, u			▨	▨	▨	▨	▨
Vowel Teams and Special Letter combinations							
ay, ee			▨	▨	▨	▨	▨
oo (book), oo (moon), ea (each),							
ea (bread), oe, ai, oa, ow (cow),							
ow (snow), ir, ur, or, ar, aw, ou, er							
oi, oy, al, au, ew							
Rules for Y sound							
at end of multi-syllable word			▨	▨	▨	▨	▨
at end of single syllable word			▨	▨	▨	▨	▨
Vowel Rules For Open and Closed Syllables							
Contractions							
didn't, won't, can't, isn't, don't		▨	▨	▨	▨	▨	▨
let's, it's, that's, wasn't, hadn't, I'll,		▨					
I'm, he's		▨					
we'll, I've, he'll, hasn't, haven't,			▨	▨	▨	▨	▨
we're, you're, what's, there's, she's,			▨	▨	▨	▨	▨
they'd, she'll, here's, ain't, couldn't,			▨	▨	▨	▨	▨
they're, you'll, she'd, weren't, I'd,			▨	▨	▨	▨	▨
you've, you'd, we'd, anybody'd, there'll,			▨	▨	▨	▨	▨
we've, who'll, he'd, who'd, doesn't,			▨	▨	▨	▨	▨
where's, they've, they'll			▨	▨	▨	▨	▨
aren't, wouldn't		▨	▨				
Possessives							
Accent Rules[b]							
1. In two syllable words the first is usually accented.				▨	▨	▨	▨
2. In inflected or derived forms the primary accent usually falls on or within the root word.				▨	▨	▨	▨
3. If two vowels are together in the last syllable of a word it may be a clue to an accented final syllable.					▨	▨	▨
4. If there are two unlike consonants within a word, the syllable before the double consonants is usually accented.					▨	▨	▨

Column header: GRADE LEVEL OR YEAR IN SCHOOL

[b] At present no definitive research is available as to which accent generalizations are of high enough utility to make them worthwhile to teach. The four listed here are believed to be quite consistent and also of high utility.

(cont.)

FIGURE 3–5. (cont.)

SKILL

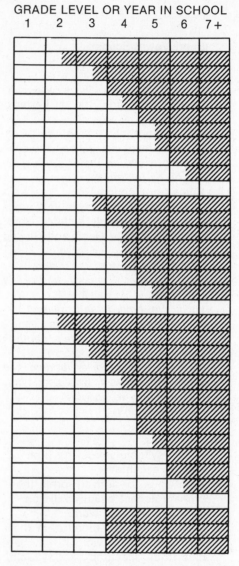

GRADE LEVEL OR YEAR IN SCHOOL
1   2   3   4   5   6   7+

Prefixes (recognition only)[c]
- *a*
- *un, re*
- *dis*
- *in, per, pre, al, be, de, con*
- *im, under, mid*
- *for, ex, over, ad, sub, photo, en,*
- *com, pro, non, fore, anti, out*
- *auto, mis, trans*
- *inter, self, tele, counter, ab*

Prefixes (meaning only)
- *re* (back or again), *un* (not)
- *pre* (before, prior to)
- *ex* (out, forth, from)
- *de* (from, away, from off)
- *dis* (apart, away from), *in* (into), *in* (not)
- *en* (in, to make, put into), *sub* (under)
- *com* (with, together)

Suffixes (recognition only)
- *ly*
- *est, er*
- *y, less*
- *fully, self, en, full, ness, ily, ty*
- *an, ier, some, ish*
- *ern, ite, ion, able, ment, ology, ous,*
- *or, ward, al, th, ious, ese, hood, ship,*
- *ist, ure, ive, ible, age*
- *ity, ation, ant, ian, ent*
- *ance, ence, ic, ical, ling, eer, ery,*
- *ey, most, wise*
- *ary*

Syllable Principles
1. When two like consonants stand between two vowels the word is usually divided between the consonants.

[c]The prefixes *un* and *re* should be known by the middle of the third year in school. From that point on, the student should continue to extend and refine his or her knowledge of prefixes. This extension and refinement would continue throughout his or her elementary and high school years. The same is true of the suffixes such as *est* and *er* which should be known by the end of the second year of school but would be extended and refined throughout the student's elementary and high school years. (The authors suggest that "known" in this case only means that the student recognizes the prefix and/or suffix, but that he or she not be required to know its meaning.)

(cont.)

FIGURE 3–5. (cont.)

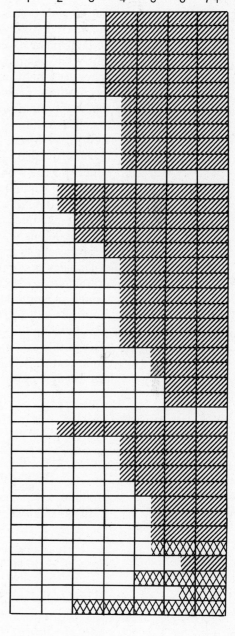

GRADE LEVEL OR YEAR IN SCHOOL
1   2   3   4   5   6   7+

2. When two unlike consonants stand between two vowels the word is usually divided between the consonants.
3. When a word ends in a consonant and *le*, the consonant usually begins the last syllable.
4. Divide between compound words.
5. Prefixes and suffixes are usually separate syllables.
6. Do not divide letters in consonant blends and consonant digraphs.

Dictionary Skills
Alphabet in order
Alphabetizing letters
Alphabetizing words to first letter
Alphabetizing words to second letter
Estimating location of a word
Alphabetizing words to third letter
Using guide words
Interpreting symbols
Interpreting accent and stress
Selecting word meaning from context
Interpreting pronunciation key
Using cross reference
First and second spellings
Word origin
Parts of speech

Study Skills
Table of Contents
Index
Glossary
Encyclopedia (Find topic)
Encyclopedia (Use index volume)
Encyclopedia (Use cross-reference)
Almanac
Telephone Directory
Interpret tables
Library card index
Read maps
Read graphs, charts, and diagrams
Skimming

CLASSIFICATION OF DIAGNOSTIC, TEACHING, AND REINFORCEMENT ACTIVITIES

The diagnostician and remedial reading teacher should keep in mind that there is a distinct difference between diagnosis, teaching, and reinforcement activities. For example, one would not expect a student to "learn" anything new while completing a page in a workbook that requires the student to use concepts taught in a previous lesson. One would, however, expect to "reinforce" these previously taught concepts so that the student would become thoroughly familiar with their use and thus be less likely to forget them. On the other hand, a page in a programmed textbook would be likely to teach, as well as reinforce, various concepts. Most testing is done so that the teacher can learn more about the student, but testing, as such, has no immediate benefit to the student unless the answers are provided to the questions on which the student is being tested.

The double-column listing that follows illustrates the three categories (testing examples or diagnosis, teaching, and reinforcement or practice) and some activities that might be associated with each. As you examine the various suggestions in the following chapters for remediation of various reading skills, keep these three categories in mind. That is, do not expect a straight practice exercise to teach or do not expect a teaching exercise to test, although examination of student performance on reinforcement or practice materials will provide some diagnostic information.

In using the diagnostic, teaching, and reinforcement materials that appear in this text as well as in other textbooks and commercially or teacher-made materials you should consider your overall instructional purpose and use the appropriate materials to accomplish this purpose.

Testing and diagnostic materials	*What they are designed to accomplish*
Examples	
1. Basic sight-word lists	Provides the teacher with diagnostic information on the basic sight-word knowledge of the student. The *student learns little or nothing unless the teacher pronounces each word as it is missed.*

Testing and diagnostic materials	*What they are designed to accomplish*
Examples	
2. Cloze technique for assessing student's level of reading comprehension (see Chapter 11)	If used only for finding a percentage score of right and wrong answers to determine grade placement, little or no teaching is done. If the exercises are discussed after the student has completed them, some teaching and possibly some reinforcement takes place.
3. Informal reading inventories	Provides the teacher with an overall grade placement and considerable information on specific weaknesses. Little teaching is accomplished other than when aid is given when a word is unknown.
Teaching materials	
1. Material held in the hands of students and explained by the teacher	This is a typical teaching situation. If it is material that is being reviewed, then it may teach *and* reinforce. Unless the teacher provides for some type of feedback, little or no diagnostic information will be derived.
2. Preparation of a language experience chart or story	Provides the teacher with an opportunity to teach the student to decode new words. The student receives ample reinforcement as the dictated story is reread. Provides some diagnosis of the student's language and oral reading skills.

Testing and diagnostic materials	What they are designed to accomplish

Teaching materials

3. Worksheets used in conjunction with a tape recorder

If the directions on the audiotape provide for instruction on how to do the worksheets, and then give the student the answers and provide an opportunity for the student to correct any that are wrong, this would teach and reinforce. If provisions are made for the teacher to see which answers were missed, some diagnosis may also take place.

Reinforcement materials

1. Worksheets

Most worksheets only provide for reinforcement of concepts that have already been learned but which need to be mastered more thoroughly.

2. Reading games

Most games *do not* teach since they require that nothing new be learned in order to play the game, e.g., recalling and using previously learned material. If properly constructed, games will provide reinforcement. Games in which one pupil competes with another may teach, for example, if one pupil creates words from initial consonants or consonant blends and phonograms or uses words in sentences in which the other pupil learns the meaning from context.

3. Practicing words or phrases from flash cards

This can provide excellent reinforcement of sight vocabulary, if the words or phrases were previously introduced by the teacher.

SUMMARY

In order to begin doing diagnosis work in the field of reading the remedial reading teacher must have a thorough knowledge of the scope and sequence of the reading skills. The teacher must not only understand what needs to be diagnosed in terms of educational problems, but must also know when to expect each student to have mastered each of the reading skills.

In doing diagnostic work it should be kept in mind that we have identified certain skills that are definitely necessary for a student to learn to read. On the other hand, there are some areas in which skills have been identified as being helpful to some readers in learning to read, but these same skills are often not known by some very excellent readers. In other words, some of the reading skills are only a means to an end, and if the student has already reached the end there is little or no use in diagnosing the skills that supposedly lead to that end.

We have also discussed the classification of diagnostic, teaching, and reinforcement activities.

REFERENCES

Barrett, Thomas C., ed. *The Evaluation of Children's Reading Achievement. Perspectives in Reading No. 8.* Newark, Del.: International Reading Association, 1967.

Dolch, Edward W. *Methods in Reading.* Champaign, Ill.: Garrard Publishing Co., 1955.

Durr, William K. "Computer Study of High Frequency Words in Popular Trade Juveniles," *Reading Teacher.* Vol. 27, (October, 1973), 37–42.

Harris, Albert J., and Jacobson, Milton D. "Basic Vocabulary for Beginning Reading," *Reading Teacher.* Vol. 26, (January, 1973), 392–395.

Spache, George D., and Spache, Evelyn B. *Reading in the Elementary School.* 4th ed., Boston: Allyn and Bacon, 1977.

4

Diagnosis and Remediation of Educational Factors: *Letter Knowledge and Sight Words*

One purpose of this chapter is to examine the need for, and methods of, testing for letter knowledge and knowledge of sight words and basic sight words. A second purpose is to examine some of the pros and cons of each method. A third purpose is to discuss some ways of teaching letter knowledge, sight words, and basic sight words.

Part A: DIAGNOSIS

ALPHABET KNOWLEDGE

A number of research studies have shown that letter knowledge is not necessarily a prerequisite for learning to read. On the other hand, numerous studies have also shown that children who begin their schooling with a knowledge of the ABC's are more likely to become better readers than children who lack this knowledge. For some time this was taken to mean that letter knowledge was helpful or necessary in learning to read. Diane Chisholm and June Knafle (1978) found that first-grade pupils who knew letter names were able to learn words in significantly fewer trials than their counterparts who did not know letter names. Olga Speer and George Lamb (1976) found that the *speed* of letter-name recognition was the critical factor. Most authorities believe, however, that knowledge of the ABC's, for entering school-age children, is simply indicative of a host of factors that are often conducive to learning to read. Among these factors are a natural potential for learning to read, educational level of parents, and good reading environment at home.

It should be stressed, however, that children who reach the middle or upper elementary grades without a thorough knowledge of the alphabet are quite likely to be disabled readers. It should also be stressed that, although children *can* learn to read without being able to identify the name of each letter, it becomes a difficult task in most classrooms simply because of communication problems. Furthermore, children who cannot distinguish a *b* from a *d* or a *q* from a *p* are likely to encounter a great deal of difficulty in learning to read. For these reasons a check on children's knowledge of the alphabet should be included as a regular part of the diagnostic procedure.

Beginning teachers and inexperienced diagnosticians are likely to take it for granted that children in the middle and upper grade levels possess a thorough knowledge of the alphabet. Testing at this level soon reveals, however, that a rather large percentage of disabled readers still experience difficulty in this area. Since the diagnosis for alphabet knowledge is so quick and simple, it should be included as one of the beginning procedures.

One procedure that is relatively easy is to put the letters of the alphabet on two cards approximately 5 in. × 8 in. Put the lower-case alphabet on one card and the upper-case alphabet on the other. On one side of the card you may wish to type the letters with a primary typewriter or print them by hand. On side two of the card you can then reproduce what is on side one plus any directions you may wish to look at while the child looks at side one. It is also better to put the letters in random order since some children will have learned the alphabet song or will have simply learned the alphabet in order which would in turn make it appear as though they know letters that in reality they do not know.

Another procedure that you may wish to use instead of or in addition to that described above is to ask the child to write the alphabet. After the child finishes you may wish to ask the child to write any omitted letters or any that he or she appeared to have difficulty with while writing them.

Flash cards with one letter on each card also work well for testing alphabet knowledge. Some disabled readers prefer to work with flash cards since they tend to have an aversion to a typical reading-type situation in which the letters are printed on a line. In either case it will be necessary to note letters with which the student has difficulty. The best way to do this is to always present the letters in the same (not alphabetical) order and tape record the testing. The tape can be played back later to compare the student's responses to a prepared record sheet that lists the letters in the same order as they were presented to the student.

Some children will have a great deal of difficulty with many, or nearly all, letters. When this is the case, you should then proceed to the next easiest task in alphabet knowledge. This involves having the child identify letters as you call them. The 5 in. × 8 in. card will work well for this, or you may wish to arrange flash cards so the child can see at least five to ten of them at a time. A few extremely disabled readers will not even be able to accomplish this task. When this is the case, you may wish to determine whether the child is able to match letters, which is a task still easier than identifying them when their names are called.

The *Durrell Analysis of Reading Difficulty* (Durrell and Catterson, 1980) contains a series of eight readiness-level tests, called the Prereading Phonics Abilities Inventories. These tests include Syntax Matching (measuring students' awareness of separate words in spoken sentences), Identifying Letter Names in Spoken Words, Identifying Phonemes in Spoken Words, Naming Letters—Lower Case and Upper Case, Writing Letters—from Dictation and from Copy, and Identifying Letters Named. If this test is available for your use, you may wish to use it instead of constructing your own materials. The *Sipay Word Analysis Tests* (Sipay, 1974) also contains tests for alphabet knowledge.

SIGHT-WORD KNOWLEDGE

Sometimes the words *sight vocabulary* are used to refer to overall sight-word knowledge. And, although the term *sight vocabulary* is a proper one, in this case it should be stressed that this discussion will be concerned only with instant recognition of words and not with meaning vocabulary. The difference between "sight words" and "basic sight words" was discussed in Chapter 3. However, it should again be stressed that the terms are not being used interchangeably. *Sight words* refer to all words any one reader can recognize instantly, while *basic sight words* refer to a designated list of words, usually of high utility, that appear on someone's list. Any word if read enough times can become a sight word, and thus each of us possesses a different sight vocabulary depending on such factors as our occupation, reading interests, and ability to remember. However, anyone reading above middle third-grade level would have the same basic sight-word vocabulary since we would instantly recognize all of the commonly designated high-utility words.

Because of the difference in meaning of the terms *sight-word vocabulary* and *basic sight-word vocabulary*, techniques for diagnosis of each will be discussed separately. In testing for sight-word knowledge we usually use a sampling of words referred to as a *graded sight-word list*, while in testing for basic sight-word knowledge we usually test the entire population of words on a designated list. The following discussion explains the need for, and methods of testing for, knowledge of basic sight words.

A number of researchers and writers have studied the utility of various words (Curtis, 1938; Hockett, 1938; Stone, 1939, 1941). Although these studies are seldom in exact agreement because of the differences in the materials they choose to study, they are in general agreement concerning the percentage of total running words[1] that are accounted for by certain numbers of words. Table 4–1 shows a general summary of the results of these studies. In interpreting these figures you should keep in mind that the percent of total running words for each specific number of words is likely to be slightly higher for beginning reading materials and slightly lower for adult reading materials.

Words such as I, the, and, and make up the highest-utility words and appear so often in reading matter that it is imperative that children know these as sight words. As Table 4–1 also shows, even in learning only approximately 200 words a child is likely to have mastered considerably more than one-half of the words he or she is likely to encounter in reading. As you will also note, the percentage of utility begins to drop off rather rapidly after a child has learned the 500 words most used in reading. For this reason most basic sight-word lists contain from two hundred to five hundred words.

The importance of learning to read and spell high-utility words was emphasized by Richard Madden (1959) in a study of low- and high-utility words. Madden pointed out that in spelling there is very little value in attempting to teach students to spell words of lower utility until they have completely mastered all of the words of high utility. To illustrate this futility Madden states that a child in grade five with only 5 percent misspellings in a random sample

TABLE 4–1.   The percentage of total running words in reading materials accounted for by various numbers of words.

Number of words	Percentage of total running words
3	8 —12
10	20 —25
100	60 —65
200	66 —70
500	75 —80
1000	83 —85
1500	87 —88
2000	89 —90
3000	91 —92
5000	92.5—93.5

[1]Total running words are all the words that appear in a particular selection.

of the first 500 words in frequency will make more errors in writing than if the child misspells all 600 words in the commonly designated list for grade five. The same concept is, of course, true for reading.

In a more recent study of the high-frequency words in popular juvenile trade books, William Durr (1973) found that ten words were of such high frequency, in the eighty books studied, that a young reader could expect to meet one of the ten words in nearly every four words read. Durr further stated that the 188 high-frequency words he listed, although making up only 6 percent of all the different words found, would make up nearly 70 percent of the running words in print in the eighty library books he studied.

Studies such as those mentioned above illustrate the importance of learning certain "core" or "basic" sight words instantly so that no word-analysis skills are required when a student encounters them in print. Furthermore, many of these high-utility words are not phonetically regular and do not lend themselves to phonic word attack. Glen Gagon (1966) quotes Arthur Heilman as saying that approximately 35 percent of the usual primary reading vocabulary is phonetically regular. We have analyzed other basic sight-word lists and find them to be from 30 to 77 percent phonetically regular depending on the number of phonic rules applied.

A discussion of how to test for knowledge of basic sight words may at first appear so elementary that it would seem that almost anyone could, and would, be likely to find this an easy task. During the past several years, however, we have researched several different methods and found the results obtained differ considerably depending on the method employed. There has also been considerable controversy over whether basic sight words should be tested in or out of context.

Many people assume that children know more basic sight words, which are often referred to as *service words*, when they are used in context than when they are not used in context. However, there seems to be little evidence that the context setting of most service words is such that it is of great value in helping the student with word identification. H. Alan Robinson (1963), in a study of techniques of word identification, found that only about one-seventh of 1 percent of the words he studied were identified by students through context clues alone. Even when context, configuration, and phonic and structural elements in initial and final positions were all used together, students only scored 3.93 correct out of twenty-two possible responses.

We have also heard reading specialists say it is not fair to the child to test a word out of context. First of all, we might say, "What is fair?" Even if the context were a valuable aid in word identification some of the time, you would not want a child to get a word right in one situation and not know the same word at another time when it was not used in as meaningful a context. What seems unfair to the child then, is to test the child on a word in meaningful context and later find that the child does not really know the word when it is not in a meaningful context. If testing words in isolation is more difficult, then you should test them that way since you are more likely to discover words that may later prove difficult for the child. Again, remember that basic sight words appear so often that children cannot afford to miss or be unsure of any of them. In reality, testing a word in a meaningful context may be depriving them of the opportunity to learn it. This should not be construed to mean, however, that we are necessarily suggesting that basic sight words be "taught" in isolation. The issue of teaching basic sight vocabulary in isolation versus in context will be discussed in the remediation section of this chapter.

One of the points stressed in Chapter 2 was that you should always try to test in a situation that is analogous to actually reading. This principle is extremely important in the case of basic sight words. A common mistake that is often made by beginning reading teachers is thinking that they can use a group test to assess children's knowledge of basic sight words. A group test often used for this purpose is the Dolch Basic Sight Word Test (Dolch, 1942). In using it the teacher gives each student a sheet of paper that has numbers down the left-hand column of the page. Opposite each number are four words. The teacher calls out one of the four words, and each child is expected to underline or circle the word that is the same as the one called by the teacher. One of the problems with this type of test is that even if a child did not know any of the words he or she would be likely to get one-fourth of them right by simply guessing. A second problem with this type of test is that it is not analogous to actually reading; i.e., underlining a word when you hear it is much easier then seeing a word and saying it. Our experience has shown that many children who get almost every word right on this type of test will miss from twenty-five to fifty words when they are required to take a test in which they are to look at words and say them. Because of these problems it seems logical to conclude that any attempt to assess children's basic sight word knowledge with a group test is of little value.

The problem then becomes one of how to best test the child in a one-to-one situation. This, of course, is not difficult, but even here there are some important considerations. One can simply give a child a list of words and ask the child to read them while the examiner marks the right and wrong responses on a similar list. We have found, however, in trying this method with children in our university reading centers, that disabled readers often get tense when confronted with a long list of words and will, in turn, make more errors than if the words are presented one at a time on flash cards. A further problem with the former method is that it is difficult to control the length of exposure that the child has to each word. What happens, in reality, is that this often becomes a word-analysis test where the child has time to apply various word-attack skills to each word. This can be prevented to some extent by using a card and sliding it over each word after the child has been exposed to the word for about one second. This, however, is difficult to judge and some children resent having you cover the word if it is difficult for them.

We have also found that many students learn the sight words only in isolation and are unable to correctly pronounce these same words when reading a passage orally. This is the major reason for testing, and later teaching, the sight word phrases. The phrases seem to build a bridge between isolated pronunciation and contextual reading.

What follows is what we have determined to be the most practical and efficient method for teachers and/or diagnosticians to use to evaluate students' knowledge of basic sight vocabulary.

The examiner will need the following materials:

1. A tape recorder.
2. Prepared scoring lists (or protocols) for the assessment of basic sight words and phrases. Copies of the scoring lists for *both* words and phrases are necessary for each student tested.
3. Prepared flash cards, arranged in the same order as the word lists.

The examiner turns on the tape recorder and places the microphone on the table where the testing takes place. The examiner then lifts off twenty to thirty words from the ordered stack. These are flashed individually to the student at a rate of *one second or less* per flash card. Since the examiner's purpose is to test *instant* sight-word recognition, it is critical for the words to be flashed quickly enough to prevent the student from sounding them out.

The examiner's attention should be focused on flashing the cards, not on the student's responses. Do *not* separate the cards into "right" and "wrong" piles, since this may serve to distract the examiner, upset the student, and confuse the order of the flash cards. Continue flashing the cards until the student does not respond to ten consecutive words, or otherwise indicates an inability to successfully complete the test. If the student appears to be pronouncing most of the words correctly, continue the procedure until all cards are flashed.

To complete the scoring procedure, the examiner rewinds the audio tape, selects the appropriate prepared list, and indicates by marking + or − whether the student correctly or incorrectly pronounced each word. (The scoring procedure is usually completed after the student has left the testing site.) In scoring, *only the first response counts.* Having mastered a word, the student recognizes it instantly. If the student hesitates, the flashed word is not known by *sight.*

The same procedure is repeated for the testing and scoring of sight word phrases. The examiner may allow up to two seconds per phrase when flashing the cards. Each sight-word test takes approximately six minutes to administer and score.

By examining the prepared lists the examiner can determine specifically which basic sight words and phrases have not been mastered by the student. These can then be taught without having to misuse instructional time teaching words or phrases that are already known.

The criterion for mastery of the total list is 90 percent. If the student attains this level, the examiner should not feel that it is necessary to teach the few words or phrases that may have been missed. It is reasonable to expect that a few words be mispronounced due to the speed of the test.

The examiner must use judgment in evaluating a student's performance on the sight-word tests. Young children may have greater difficulty with a speed of one word per second, although ultimately it is essential that the words be recognized at this rate. Similarly, students with speech difficulties may need an adjustment in the rate of flashing.

The examiner must be sure that the student is not excessively nervous and that the setting is conducive to the student's best performance. It is suggested that this assessment procedure be presented as a kind of game or fun activity. Paraprofessionals may be trained to conduct this testing. The sight-word tests may be repeated periodically while instruction is taking place, in order to check students' progress.

There has been debate among reading experts about which sight-word list to use. A number of investigators have suggested that the Dolch list is outdated, and therefore no longer appropriate. Lillie Pope (1975), for example, has offered a newer list of Sight Words for the Seventies. Robert Hillerich (1974) questions not the datedness, but rather the appropriateness, of the Dolch list. On the other hand, John Mangieri and Michael Kahn (1977), A. J. Lowe and John Foilman (1974), and Jerry Johns (1974) all agree that the Dolch list remains as relevant for today's students as for those of the 1930s.

We believe that it really does not matter which of the many basic word lists are used for testing and teaching basic sight vocabulary. Almost all contain the same high-frequency words. For example, excluding nouns that Dolch listed separately, there is an 88 percent overlap between the words on the Durr list (1973) and the older Dolch list. Basic sight words do not go in and out of fashion. What does matter is that the teacher provides effective instruction to enable students to master the basic sight words taught.

The modified Dolch list that follows includes the 220 Dolch words reordered according to frequency of occurrence as found in the Durr list. The 220 individual words are then divided into eleven sublists of twenty words each for ease of scoring and instruction.

The list is presented based on the assumption that all students will not master all the words. It is therefore reasonable to begin by teaching the words that appear most often.

The phrase list is compiled so that each word from the isolated words list is presented in a phrase. Only seventeen new words are added to complete phrases. These are nouns that are all drawn from the preprimer level of a popular basal series.

The lists are presented as facsimiles of the scoring sheets you may use in following the procedure outlined above.

INDICUAL DIAGNOSIS OF DOLCH WORDS
INDIVIDUAL DIAGNOSIS OF DOLCH WORDS
(Listed in Descending Order of Frequencies)

Pre [/220] Post [/220]

LIST I	Pre	Post
1. the		
2. to		
3. and		
4. he		
5. a		
6. I		
7. you		
8. it		
9. of		
10. in		
11. was		
12. said		
13. his		
14. that		
15. she		
16. for		
17. on		
18. they		
19. but		
20. had		
*	/20	/20

LIST II	Pre	Post
1. at		
2. him		
3. with		
4. up		
5. all		
6. look		
7. is		
8. her		
9. there		
10. some		
11. out		
12. as		
13. be		
14. have		
15. go		
16. we		
17. am		
18. then		
19. little		
20. down		
*	/20	/20

LIST III	Pre	Post
1. do		
2. can		
3. could		
4. when		
5. did		
6. what		
7. so		
8. see		
9. not		
10. were		
11. get		
12. them		
13. like		
14. one		
15. this		
16. my		
17. would		
18. me		
19. will		
20. yes		
*	/20	/20

LIST IV	Pre	Post
1. big		
2. went		
3. are		
4. come		
5. if		
6. now		
7. long		
8. no		
9. came		
10. ask		
11. very		
12. an		
13. over		
14. your		
15. its		
16. ride		
17. into		
18. just		
19. blue		
20. red		
*	/20	/20

*Number of words read correctly.

LIST V

	Pre	Post
1. from		
2. good		
3. any		
4. about		
5. around		
6. want		
7. don't		
8. how		
9. know		
10. right		
11. put		
12. too		
13. got		
14. take		
15. where		
16. every		
17. pretty		
18. jump		
19. green		
20. four		
*	/20	/20

LIST VI

	Pre	Post
1. away		
2. old		
3. by		
4. their		
5. here		
6. saw		
7. call		
8. after		
9. well		
10. think		
11. ran		
12. let		
13. help		
14. make		
15. going		
16. sleep		
17. brown		
18. yellow		
19. five		
20. six		
*	/20	/20

LIST VII

	Pre	Post
1. walk		
2. two		
3. or		
4. before		
5. eat		
6. again		
7. play		
8. who		
9. been		
10. may		
11. stop		
12. off		
13. never		
14. seven		
15. eight		
16. cold		
17. today		
18. fly		
19. myself		
20. round		
*	/20	/20

LIST VIII

	Pre	Post
1. tell		
2. much		
3. keep		
4. give		
5. work		
6. first		
7. try		
8. new		
9. must		
10. start		
11. black		
12. white		
13. ten		
14. does		
15. bring		
16. goes		
17. write		
18. always		
19. drink		
20. once		
*	/20	/20

*Number of words read correctly.

LIST IX

	Pre	Post
1. soon		
2. made		
3. run		
4. gave		
5. open		
6. has		
7. find		
8. only		
9. us		
10. three		
11. our		
12. better		
13. hold		
14. buy		
15. funny		
16. warm		
17. ate		
18. full		
19. those		
20. done		
*	/20	/20

LIST X

	Pre	Post
1. use		
2. fast		
3. say		
4. light		
5. pick		
6. hurt		
7. pull		
8. cut		
9. kind		
10. both		
11. sit		
12. which		
13. fall		
14. carry		
15. small		
16. under		
17. read		
18. why		
19. own		
20. found		
*	/20	/20

LIST XI

	Pre	Post
1. wash		
2. show		
3. hot		
4. because		
5. far		
6. live		
7. draw		
8. clean		
9. grow		
10. best		
11. upon		
12. these		
13. sing		
14. together		
15. please		
16. thank		
17. wish		
18. many		
19. shall		
20. laugh		
*	/20	/20

SCORE

LIST	Pre	Post
I		
II		
III		
IV		
V		
VI		
VII		
VIII		
IX		
X		
XI		
TOTAL		

*Number of words read correctly.

INDIVIDUAL DIAGNOSIS OF SIGHT WORD PHRASES

Pre [/143] Post [/143]

LIST I	Pre	Post
1. he had to		
2. she said that		
3. to the		
4. you and I		
5. but they said		
6. on a		
7. for his		
8. of that		
9. that was in		
10. it was		
*	/10	/10

LIST II	Pre	Post
1. look at him		
2. as little		
3. at all		
4. I have a		
5. have some		
6. there is		
7. down there		
8. then we have		
9. to go		
10. to be there		
11. look up		
12. look at her		
13. we go out		
14. I am		
*	/14	/14

LIST III	Pre	Post
1. look at me		
2. can you		
3. a little one		
4. you will see		
5. what is that		
6. my *cat*		
7. I will get		
8. when did he		
9. like this		
10. get them		
11. so you will see		
12. I could		
13. we were		
14. would not		
15. yes, I do		
*	/15	/15

LIST IV	Pre	Post
1. a big ride		
2. went into		
3. if I ask		
4. come over with		
5. they went		
6. I am very		
7. there are blue		
8. a long *book*		
9. an *apple*		
10. your red *book*		
11. its *name*		
12. they came		
13. just now		
*	/13	/13

*Number of phrases read correctly.

LIST V

	Pre	Post
1. I take every		
2. the four green		
3. they don't want		
4. right around		
5. a good jump		
6. a pretty *rabbit*		
7. I know how		
8. where can I		
9. the *duck* got		
10. it is about		
11. don't put any		
12. take from		
13. too little		
*	/13	/13

LIST VI

	Pre	Post
1. ran away		
2. let me help		
3. going to sleep		
4. five yellow *ducks*		
5. the old *turtle*		
6. by their *mother*		
7. call after six		
8. the brown *rabbit*		
9. I am well		
10. will think		
11. will make		
12. you saw		
13. here it is		
*	/13	/13

LIST VII

	Pre	Post
1. we eat		
2. two may walk		
3. on or off		
4. before seven		
5. today is cold		
6. play by myself		
7. don't stop		
8. it is round		
9. who is eight		
10. have never been		
11. can fly again		
*	/11	/11

LIST VIII

	Pre	Post
1. black and white		
2. start a new		
3. must try once		
4. don't keep much		
5. it does go		
6. always drink *milk*		
7. will bring ten		
8. *Lad* goes		
9. write and tell		
10. work is first		
11. can give it		
*	/11	/11

*Number of phrases read correctly.

LIST IX

	Pre	Post
1. open and find		
2. *Jill* ate the		
3. those are done		
4. is funny		
5. buy us three		
6. this is only		
7. gave a warm		
8. soon we ate		
9. had a full		
10. run and hold		
11. made a big		
12. it is better		
13. our *duck*		
*	/13	/13

LIST X

	Pre	Post
1. sit with both		
2. you use it		
3. carry a small		
4. the cut hurt		
5. the fast *car*		
6. then the light		
7. which will fall		
8. pull it in		
9. had found		
10. under here		
11. be kind		
12. pick it up		
13. *Bill* can read		
14. my own *bed*		
15. why is it		
16. I can say		
*	/16	/16

LIST XI

	Pre	Post
1. wash in hot		
2. because it is		
3. grow best		
4. once upon		
5. sing and laugh		
6. please thank		
7. we draw these		
8. shall we show		
9. the wish is		
10. we clean		
11. they live		
12. too far		
13. all together		
14. many *turtles*		
*	/14	/14

SCORE

LIST	Pre	Post
I		
II		
III		
IV		
V		
VI		
VII		
VIII		
IX		
X		
XI		
TOTAL		

*Number of phrases read correctly.

QUICK CHECK FOR BASIC SIGHT WORD KNOWLEDGE

The *Quick Check for Basic Sight Word Knowledge*[2] may be used as a quick way to test students' knowledge of basic sight words. The test consists of thirty-six words taken from Eldon E. Ekwall's basic sight word list. It may be given to students whom you suspect are deficient in their knowledge of basic sight words. It was developed by giving Ekwall's basic sight word list to 500

ANSWER SHEET

Name: _____   Date: _____

School: _____   Tester: _____

Directions: After the student reads the words from flash cards, mark those read correctly with a plus (+) and those read incorrectly with a minus (−) or write in the word substituted. If the student says he or she does not know an answer then mark it with a (?) and consider it an error.
(IF A STUDENT MISSES ANY WORDS ON THIS TEST THEN HE OR SHE SHOULD BE GIVEN THE FULL LIST OF BASIC SIGHT WORDS).

1. I _____		19. pretty _____
2. the _____		20. again _____
3. you _____		21. thank _____
4. down _____		22. only _____
5. here _____		23. well _____
6. he _____		24. first _____
7. fly _____		25. thing _____
8. help _____		26. any _____
9. this _____		27. also _____
10. happy _____		28. while _____
11. tree _____		29. should _____
12. his _____		30. upon _____
13. hot _____		31. sure _____
14. end _____		32. always _____
15. ride _____		33. than _____
16. saw _____		34. present _____
17. light _____		35. such _____
18. sat _____		36. hurt _____

FIGURE 4–1.   Quick Check for Basic Sight Word Knowledge.

[2]Reprinted by permission of Charles E. Merrill Publishers, adapted from: Ekwall, Eldon E., *Locating and Correcting Reading Difficulties* (3rd ed). Columbus, Ohio: Charles E. Merrill, 1981, pp. 205–207.

students in grades two through six. One hundred students were tested at each of these five grade levels. A computer analysis then listed in ascending order of difficulty the words most often missed. From this list approximately every eighth word was taken, so that the words at the beginning are the easiest and the words at the end are the most difficult. We suggest that you administer this test in the same manner as that described previously. A student who misses even one word on this test should then be given the entire basic sight word list.

Sight Words in General

Graded word lists are usually used to assess children's knowledge of sight words in general or reading level in relation to word knowledge. In doing this it is also possible in many cases to make a close estimation of a child's overall reading level. These tests are also useful for placing students for further testing in informal reading inventories. A number of graded word lists are available; however, one that we have found to be useful is the San Diego Quick Assessment List. A description of the list, directions for its use, and the list itself follow:[3]

PP	Primer	1	2
see	you	road	our
play	come	live	please
me	not	thank	myself
at	with	when	town
run	jump	bigger	early
go	help	how	send
and	is	always	wide
look	work	night	believe
can	are	spring	quietly
here	this	today	carefully

3	4	5	6
city	decided	scanty	bridge
middle	served	business	commercial
moment	amazed	develop	abolish
frightened	silent	considered	trucker
exclaimed	wrecked	discussed	apparatus
several	improved	behaved	elementary
lonely	certainly	splendid	comment
drew	entered	acquainted	necessity
since	realized	escaped	gallery
straight	interrupted	grim	relativity

[3]La Pray, Margaret, and Ross, Ramon. "The Graded Word List: Quick Gauge of Reading Ability." *Journal of Reading*, Vol. 12 (January, 1969), 305–307. (Reprinted with permission of the authors and the International Reading Association.)

7	8	9	10	11
amber	capacious	conscientious	zany	galore
dominion	limitation	isolation	jerkin	rotunda
sundry	pretext	molecule	nausea	capitalism
capillary	intrigue	ritual	gratuitous	prevaricate
impetuous	delusion	momentous	linear	risible
blight	immaculate	vulnerable	inept	exonerate
wrest	ascent	kinship	legality	superannuate
enumerate	acrid	conservatism	aspen	luxuriate
daunted	binocular	jaunty	amnesty	piebald
condescend	embankment	inventive	barometer	crunch

Administration

1. Type out each list of ten words on index cards.
2. Begin with a card that is at least two years below the student's grade-level assignment.
3. Ask the student to read the words aloud to you. If he misreads any on the list, drop to easier lists until he makes no errors. This indicates the base level.
4. Write down all incorrect responses, or use diacritical marks on your copy of the test. For example, *lonely* might be read and recorded as *lovely*. *Apparatus* might be recorded as *a per' a tus*.
5. Encourage the student to read words he does not know so that you can identify the techniques he uses for word identification.
6. Have the student read from increasingly difficult lists until he misses at least three words.

Analysis

1. The list in which a student misses no more than one of the ten words is the level at which he can read independently. Two errors indicate his instructional level. Three or more errors identify the level at which reading material will be too difficult for him.
2. An analysis of a student's errors is useful. Among those which occur with greatest frequency are the following:

Error	Example
reversal	*ton* for *not*
consonant	*now* for *how*
consonant clusters	*state* for *straight*
short vowel	*cane* for *can*
long vowel	*wid* for *wide*
prefix	*inproved* for *improved*
suffix	*improve* for *improved*
miscellaneous	(accent, omission of)

3. As with other reading tasks, teacher observation of student behavior is essential. Such things as posture, facial expression, and voice quality may signal restlessness, lack of assurance, or frustration while reading.

Other sources of graded word lists are the *Botel Reading Inventory* (Botel, 1978), the *Diagnostic Reading Scales* (Spache, 1981), the *Slosson Oral Reading Test* (Slosson, 1963), and the *Wide Range Achievement Test* (Jastak and Jastak, 1978).

Graded word lists may also be constructed from basal readers or from social studies and science books. These can be helpful in assessing children's sight-word knowledge in materials in which they are likely to be placed. When constructing your own graded word lists you should expect children to know approximately 95 percent of the words at their instructional level.

In using graded sight-word lists you should keep their limitations in mind. For example, remember that you are only sampling a few words at each level as an overall estimate of a child's ability to pronounce words at that level. A child who is very good at word-attack skills may tend to correctly pronounce quite a few words that are not in his or her sight vocabulary. You should, however, be able to determine whether this is happening, to some extent, based on the time and ease with which the child responds to each word. You should also keep in mind that many children are disabled in reading because of their inability to comprehend what they read. For this type of child the graded word list is quite likely to be inaccurate in terms of placement level.

Part B: REMEDIATION

This part of the chapter will present techniques for teaching sight words in general and basic sight words. There is no separate section devoted exclusively to teaching letter knowledge. Many of the techniques and principles that apply to the teaching of sight words are also useful in teaching the alphabet. It should also be emphasized that the techniques for teaching sight words as a remedial procedure differ very little from those used in teaching sight words in a developmental program. Quite often, in fact, the same techniques and materials are used. For that reason many of the suggested procedures and materials will be the same as those commonly used in many developmental programs. There are, however, a few specialized procedures for children who exhibit severe difficulties in learning. These procedures will also be discussed in this part of Chapter 4.

SOME BASIC PRINCIPLES AND TECHNIQUES

In teaching any sight word, one of the most basic things to remember is that, for any normal child without problems in reading, a word is not likely to become a sight word until the child has encountered the word many times. Studies have tended to disagree on how many times it takes a child to learn a word well enough so that it is instantly known. However, we do know that before most words are instantly recognized a student must encounter them a number of times (probably a minimum of around twenty for most words). The number of exposures would, of course, depend on such factors as the potential of the child for word-learning tasks, the meaning or relevance of the word for a child, the configuration of the word, and the context in which it is used. The important point, however, is that in teaching any word you must arrange for the child to come into contact with the word many times before expecting the child to recognize it instantly.

One of the most important questions that must be addressed in teaching basic sight vocabulary is, Will students learn these words most easily if they are taught in isolation or in context? Kathryn Hampton (1979) compared the effectiveness of two methods of teaching basic sight vocabulary to fourth- and fifth-grade remedial readers. In the first method the words were taught in isolation. In the second method the words were presented in a combination approach consisting of words in isolation, words in phrases, and words in sentences. The results favored the isolated approach; that is, students learned to *pronounce* more words when the words were taught in isolation.

Research conducted by Linnea Ehri and Lee Wilce (1980) found that there are multiple aspects of the basic sight words to be learned by beginning readers. First graders were able to *pronounce* the words faster and more accurately when they were practiced in isolation. However, the students learned more about the *syntactic/semantic* (meaning) identities of the words when they were practiced in sentence context. The researchers concluded that perhaps the best approach is to provide both types of word-reading practice.

A similar controversy centers around the role of pictures in learning new words. The focal-attention theory proposed by S. Jay Samuels suggests that words should be learned in isolation, and that picture and context clues actually deter the acquisition of sight vocabulary because they enable the child to identify the word without focusing on its graphic features. A number of studies support this hypothesis, including those reported by Harry Singer, S. Jay Samuels, and Jean Spiroff (1973–1974) and Samuels (1977). However, Marshall Arlin, Mary Scott, and Janet Webster (1978–1979) dissent. They concluded from their research that pictures presented with words facilitate rather than hinder learning. Singer (1980) suggested that methodological and analytical flaws in the research conducted by Arlin and colleagues made their results questionable. Arlene Strikwerda (1976) found that pictures neither aided nor interfered with the learning of sight words by first-grade children, if the time of exposure to pictures was limited.

Such controversy among researchers provides little help to the practitioner who must decide daily which approach to use. Our recommendation, which will become evident in the suggestions that follow, is to use a *combination* approach.

One of the first problems often encountered is how to group remedial students for instruction on basic sight words. One very effective solution is to buy a number of different colored 3 in. × 5 in. (or smaller) cards. Designate a color to each of the levels on the basic sight word lists shown earlier in this chapter, for example, green for list one, pink for list two, etc. After the tests are completed, the teacher should have little difficulty organizing groups according to the students' performance. The teacher may wish to write each word or phrase missed on a separate card color coded according to level. Children are then given these cards, which they file in junior-sized shoe boxes by color. It is usually most efficient to teach students in groups by level. Thus, the teacher may ask that all students with pink cards bring their cards with them when they come to the group for instruction.

TEACHING SIGHT WORDS IN GENERAL

There are many ways to teach a new word to a student or to a group of students; however, a method somewhat similar to the following will often prove successful:

1. Write a sentence on the chalkboard in which the new word to be introduced is used in a meaningful context. Underline the word.
2. Let students read the sentence and attempt to say the new word using context clues along with other word-attack skills. If you are introducing a new story that students are to read, it is especially important that you not tell them each new word in advance, as this deprives them of the opportunity to apply word-attack skills themselves.
3. Discuss the meaning of the word or how it is often used in talking and writing. Try to tie it to something in their background of experiences. If possible, attempt to illustrate the word with a picture or some concrete object.
4. Write the word as students watch. Ask them to look for certain configuration clues such as double letters, extenders, and descenders. Also ask them to look for any well-known phonograms or word families, e.g., *ill, ant, ake,* but do not call attention to little words in big or longer words.
5. Ask students to write the word themselves and to be sure and say the word while they write it. Research done by the Socony-Vacuum Oil Co. showed that people tend to remember about 90 percent of what they say

as they do a thing, 70 percent of what they say as they talk, 50 percent of what they see and hear, and only 10 to 20 percent of what they simply read or hear.

6.   Have students make up and write sentences in which the word is used in context. Have them read these sentences to each other and discuss them as they are read.

TEACHING BASIC SIGHT VOCABULARY

In order to learn basic sight vocabulary, remedial readers frequently require a systematic and intensive approach. The following techniques have proven effective not only in our university clinics but also in remedial and developmental classrooms. Usually, formal, systematic instruction does not begin until students have completed a primer level reader. If, by the end of third grade, students have not mastered the lists of basic sight words and phrases, then specific, direct instruction is imperative.

When teaching children individually or in small groups, introduce the words a few at a time. The number of words to be learned per week will vary from student to student. Success, however, is critical. *It is better to learn fewer words well.* The students should see mastery as a challenging goal. Often the students themselves can best determine the number of new words to be learned at a time. If in doubt, begin with five words.

When presenting sight words, always be sure that the student is *looking at the word,* not at you. If possible, the teacher should try to spend a few minutes with the student individually when presenting the words for the first time. The following sample represents a thorough approach. Usually not all of the steps noted are necessary.

Teacher: (Hold up flash card.) "Look at this word. The word is *the*." (Use it in a sentence.) "I am *the* teacher. Say the word."
Student: "The."
    T: "Good. Now say it five times."
    S: "The, the, the, the, the."
    T: "Outstanding. Now say it really loud."
    S: "The."
    T: "No, that's not loud enough. Let me hear you say it really loud."
    S: "The."
    T: "Here, I'll show you. THE!"
    S: (chuckle) "THE!"
    T: "Fantastic. Now let me hear you whisper it."
    S: (whispering) "The."
    T: "Excellent. Now close your eyes. Can you see the word on your eyelids?"

S: "Yup."
T: "Spell it."
S: "t–h–e."
T: "Good. Now describe the word. What does it look like?"
S: "Well, it's kinda small."
T: "How are you going to remember it?"
S: "Uh, it has two letters that stick up."
T: "Terrific! Now, what's going to happen to you if you forget this word?"
S: "I don't know. What?"
T: "I'm going to kill you!" (chuckle)
S: "Oh."

Humor aside, the previous dialogue included some of the critical factors in the learning of sight words: the student's attention is focused on the word, the student visualizes the word, and strong reinforcement is provided.

Each new word should be presented using the "overlearning" procedure: 1, 2; 1, 2, 3; 1, 2, 3, 4; 1, 2, 3, 4, 5. For example, the, to; the, to, and; the, to, and, he; etc. If, after all the new words have been presented, the student still has difficulty pronouncing them quickly, the following steps may be taken:

1.   Have the student trace the word, write it on paper, or use chalk or magic slates.
2.   Have the student repeat the word each time it is written.
3.   Have the student write the word without looking at the flash card; then compare the two.

Other tactile-kinesthetic approaches may be used. These are described more fully in a later section of this chapter.

As many of the procedures as necessary should be repeated for each new word. For many students it is sufficient to show them the word, use it in a sentence, and provide brief reinforcement. For a very few students even the heroic procedures yield only intermittent success.

Immediate follow-up (lots of practice) is essential for the student to remember the new words. Some suggestions:

1.   Create "study buddies." Match learners in the classroom with fellow students who have mastered the words. Take time to teach the "tutors" how to effectively reinforce new words. Provide a big reward to both tutor and learner once the learner has attained the goal.
2.   Provide reinforcement games for students to use on their own or with their study buddies. Games may be open-ended game boards or developed by levels according to the sublists. Specific suggestions for written exercises and games are provided later in this chapter.

3. Provide charts, graphs, and other devices for students to display their progress. These serve as excellent motivators, especially since students are competing with themselves rather than each other.
4. Use your imagination. Have students dramatize phrases, build a sight-word "cave," practice words while lining up, read sight-word "plays," etc.

It is important for the teacher to provide regular posttests on sublists to establish mastery. Remember to mix the flash cards to be sure that students have not merely memorized the words by order. The following technique may be used for posttesting: If the student says the word or phrase correctly on the test, put a star or sticker on the back. The word or phrase is not mastered until five stars are accumulated. If at any time the word is missed on a test, all of the previous stars are removed and the process must begin again. This is painful but important. If teachers would do this, students would not forget words in the future that were previously learned. *"Mastery" means the student will know the word instantly forever!*

When twenty-five words are mastered, the student qualifies for "time trials." Using a stopwatch the teacher tests the students and graphs and displays the results. By flashing the cards more slowly in the beginning trials, the teacher can insure that improvement will be demonstrated on the graphs.

To be certain that mastery of individual words translates to recognition of words in the reading act, *it is important to repeat the entire procedure for the sight word phrases on completion of each sublist of words.* Thus, the teacher would teach word list I, followed by phrase list I, word list II, phrase list II, and so on. Once the phrases have been mastered for each sublist, students should practice reading these phrases embedded in complete sentences or brief stories, which may be teacher constructed. In addition, students will, of course, need generous exposure to low-level trade books.

Although the procedures outlined above may appear to be difficult to employ, we have seen many teachers in both classrooms and clinics utilize these techniques successfully. With enthusiasm and dedication this potentially dull and tedious—though critical—phase of instruction can become richly rewarding for both teachers and students. Progress on the lists is continuous and demonstrable, and the immediate, direct effect on the students' reading behavior is most satisfying.

THE USE OF THE LANGUAGE-EXPERIENCE APPROACH

Some severely disabled readers will know hardly any words at all. In this case it is difficult to follow the procedures explained above. When this occurs, the methods used in the language-experience approach are often quite successful. Furthermore, the language-experience approach, in its latter stages, can also be used with great success with average or better readers. In using the language-experience approach with a group of disabled readers a method similar to the following may be used:

1. Discuss some event of great interest. After discussing the event ask students if they would like to write a story about it.
2. As students dictate the story, write it on chart paper using the following methods:
    a.   Use manuscript or cursive writing—whichever is common to the age-grade level of the group with whom you are working.
    b.   Use a heavy writing instrument such as a felt-tip pen.
    c.   Use the language of the students and do not attempt to alter it.
    d.   Make sure students see the words as they are being written.
    e.   Try to adhere to the one important event and follow a sequence of events.
    f.   Use one-line sentences for severely disabled readers and gradually increase sentence length as improvement is noted.
    g.   In beginning each new sentence emphasize the fact that you start on the left and proceed to the right.
    h.   Emphasize the return sweep from the end of one sentence to the beginning of the next.
3. After the story has been completed, reread it as a choral exercise. Either you or a child may point to each word as it is read. It is important that the word being read is the same one being pointed to.
4. Have individual children take turns rereading the story sentence by sentence.
5. Duplicate the story on a large piece of tagboard and have students cut it into sentence strips. These can then be put in a pocket chart to form the original story. Go back to the original chart when necessary. Also let students rearrange the sentences to form a different order of events in the story.
6. After students have read the story over many times, you may wish to cut the tagboard sentences up into words and let students form the original sentences and new sentences.
7. As more stories are dictated and read and as students build a larger sight vocabulary, you may wish to duplicate stories on ditto paper and give each individual student a copy to be cut up into sentences and/or words for building varying story order and new sentences.
8. As students' reading ability grows, you should begin to let each student write and illustrate his or her own stories. These can be bound into booklets with attractive covers on them indicating the "author" of each book. Students should then begin to read each other's books.
9. A great deal of emphasis should always be placed on rereading materials that were written earlier, as children require a great many expo-

sures to each word before it becomes a sight word. After sight vocabularies begin to grow considerably, students can begin to read library or trade books.

When using the language-experience approach with an individual student you may wish to use a process somewhat similar to the following:

1. As with a group, find some event of interest to the student and ask the student to record the event on paper.
2. As the student dictates the events, you should write them on a piece of paper with the student seated so that the words can be observed as they are written. The same methods listed in steps 2 (a) through (h) above for a group should be observed, except the writing may be done on 8½″ × 11″ paper with a pencil or felt-tip pen.
3. After the story has been completed, you may wish to type it on a pica or primary-size typewriter as appropriate to the grade level of the student. (For third grade and above use regular pica type.)
4. Have the student reread the story, with either you or the student (if able to do it properly) pointing to each word as it is read. Depending on the ability of the student at this stage, the story may be reread sentence by sentence in varying order.
5. Let the student illustrate the story or apply stickers, pictures, or other decoration. Finally, the story should be placed in a booklet to be kept and reviewed each time you meet.
6. You may wish to duplicate the typewritten copies of these stories so that students can cut them up and rearrange first the sentences and later the words within each sentence.
7. Bind groups of experience stories into booklets with illustrated covers and encourage all students to exchange and read each other's booklets.
8. Gradually encourage the student to branch out into the reading of trade books.[4]

The language-experience approach is especially appropriate for disabled readers because it is immediately meaningful to them—they are writing about events in their own lives and using their own speaking vocabularies. Another advantage is that it develops a feeling of security and success and keeps pace with their development. It also gives meaning to their reading be-

[4]For a more detailed explanation of this approach see the following sources: Hall, Mary Anne. *Teaching Reading as a Language Experience.* 3rd ed., Columbus, Ohio: Charles E. Merrill, 1981. Lee, Dorris M., and Allen, R. V. *Learning to Read through Experience.* 2d ed., Englewood Cliffs, New Jersey: Prentice-Hall, Inc., 1966. Stauffer, Russell G. *The Language Experience Approach to the Teaching of Reading.* 2d ed., New York: Harper & Row, 1980. Veatch, Jeannette; Sawicki, F.; Elliott, G.; Flake, E.; and Blakey, J. *Key Words to Reading.* 2d ed., Columbus, Ohio: Charles E. Merrill, 1979.

cause students learn to associate printed stories with their own experiences from having seen their own experiences transferred into print.

Although the language-experience approach offers a number of advantages for beginning or disabled readers, there are also some disadvantages of which the teacher should be aware. For example, there is no step-by-step teacher's manual, and an inexperienced or untrained teacher is likely to fail to present a complete program. That is, the teacher may fail to use certain high-utility words enough times. Or, the teacher may fail to diagnose specific problems with various word-analysis skills. There may also be difficulty in transferring the students from reading material written by students to that written by adult authors. Most of the problems encountered in using the language-experience approach can, however, be overcome if the teacher is well trained and aware of the problems that are likely to come up when using this approach.

THE USE OF THE TACHISTOSCOPE

As stated earlier, words should be taught in both isolation and context; however, a tachistoscopic presentation of words is also helpful for some students. Such an approach may be especially useful with words that are easily confused. For example, for the student who confuses words such as *that* and *them* or *what* and *when,* a few sessions with a tachistoscopic presentation of these words mixed in with other more familiar combinations can be extremely helpful.

The use of the tachistoscope and controlled reading devices tended to fall into disrepute during the 1960s because a number of studies showed that tachistoscopic presentations of gradually widening spans of numbers and phrases did not contribute appreciably to reading speed. Furthermore, studies indicated that hand pacing in a book was equal to, or in some cases, more effective than controlled reading devices. This kind of research information should not, however, be interpreted as meaning that the tachistoscope has no value whatever in a reading program. The same is true for controlled reading devices. Although often expensive, they can serve as excellent motivating devices and are useful in helping children overcome problems with habitual repetitions.

A tachistoscopic presentation of phrases can also be of considerable value in helping children learn sight words. When using either words or phrases, a good technique to use is to let several children work together and yell out the words and phrases as they appear on the screen or the window of a hand-held tachistoscope. Although this is a noisy technique, it is one in which most children love to participate. As with any other reading activity most of the words (95 percent or more) should be previously known by the students.

TABLE 4-2.   Factors affecting use of the tachistoscope.

Successful	*Less successful*
Elementary school students (grades 1-6).	*Older students of high school or college level.*
1. Tachistoscope was used for giving multiple exposures of words or phrases or to get children to attend to the configuration of words.	1. Tachistoscope was used to attempt to widen vision span and thus increase reading speed.
2. Students had follow-up activity writing words or words and phrases after each lesson.	2. There was no written follow-up.
3. Children yelled out or read words and phrases aloud.	3. Reading was usually done silently.
4. Tachistoscope was used by someone who believed in its effectiveness. (This factor would, of course, tend to make any device or material often appear to be superior.)	4. Tachistoscope was used as just another device.

We have contrasted various factors (Table 4-2) that we believe have tended to separate studies reporting successful results with the use of the tachistoscope from those reporting less success.

It should be stressed that the factors noted only represent a general trend toward the more successful versus the less successful use of the tachistoscope. It should, however, be useful in establishing guidelines for the use of the tachistoscope in your own remedial program.

ADDITIONAL RESEARCH FINDINGS

Several studies have provided some important information on how students learn words and/or letters, which is important in using the tachistoscope and other learning devices. For example, Joanna Williams, Ellen Blumberg, and David Williams (1970) studied cues used in visual word recognition. They concluded, as did several previous researchers, that the overall shape of a word, or word "configuration," may not be as important for beginning readers in word recognition as is simple knowledge of first and last letters. They found that beginning readers used initial letters as an important clue in word recognition and that ending letters also provided an important clue. They did, however, state that older or adult readers tended to use a different method of word recognition strategy that would perhaps depend more on overall configuration. These authors' research indicates that, for younger readers, it may be highly important to discuss beginning and ending letter differences in words that are unknown, or in words with similar configurations that are often confused.

Richard Allington (1973) studied the use of color cues to focus attention in discrimination, visual memory, and paired-associate tasks. He found that discrimination, visual memory, and paired-associate tasks all improved on letter-like figures when maximum color was added and then taken away. The results of his study also indicated that the vanishing color was superior to a method in which no color was added at all or to a method in which maximum color was added and remained. Mark Goodman and Bert Cundick (1976) obtained similar results. These studies may indicate that it would be helpful to some students to learn letters and/or words if they were first presented with a strong color cue in order to focus their attention. It may also be helpful to add color cues to words that have similar configurations such as *though* and *through, county* and *country,* and *when* and *what* in order to help students distinguish between these words when they are confused.

A study done by Joanna Williams (1969) also indicates that some methods of teaching letters or letter discrimination are apparently more effective than others. She concluded that too much time is often spent in copying and tracing. She suggested that more time be devoted to discrimination training that involves comparison of letters with their transformations. It should be stressed, however, that Williams's recommendations were based on children's initial problems in kindergarten or first grade and may not necessarily apply to older students.

Charles Hargis and Edward Gickling (1978) found that the imagery level of basic sight words appears to be an important factor in the rate of learning and retention of the words. Low-imagery words are more difficult to recall than are high-imagery words and therefore require more repetition.

A study by Ernest Adams (1970) indicated that when words were introduced via a tape recording (referred to as *response familiarization*) before they were introduced visually, they were learned more easily. Adams also found that words of high meaningfulness were easier to learn than words of low meaningfulness. This evidently means that words should always be in a student's listening-speaking vocabulary before they are introduced in their printed form. Most reading specialists are aware of this but perhaps often fail to take it into consideration when teaching. However, in Adams's study even basic sight words (which were probably already in students' speaking-listening vocabulary) were learned more easily when students were familiarized with words by hearing them before seeing them.

WRITTEN EXERCISES AND GAMES

There are many different types of written exercises that are helpful in teaching sight words. However, in using any type of written exercise with disabled readers it should be kept in mind that certain students are likely to experience a great deal of failure if they are simply left to these types of exercises on their own. When using written exercises with disabled readers it is helpful to have a teacher's aide or a student tutor work closely with the student to help the student with difficult words and to provide for immediate feedback and correction. It is also helpful to tape record written exercises so that the student can listen to the material if unable to read all of the words. The tape recorder can also provide immediate feedback to the student by providing the answers after each question. Most important of all, the teacher must remember that written exercises and games serve only to reinforce or supplement previous instruction. Such activities must never be used as a substitute for directed teaching. Similarly, activities such as those described below do not take the place of substantial practice in the act of reading, which is essential for sight-word mastery.

Examples of Written Exercises and Games

There are many different types of written exercises that are helpful in teaching sight words. Some examples of these are as follows:

1. Have students fill in the blanks in sentences from a choice of sight words that are often confused as in the following example:
   a. Jim _____ he could run faster than Ann. (though, thought, through)
2. Have students write sentences using as many sight words as they can from a list of about ten sight words in the same sentence. Have students underline all sight words used. (See example below)

   (*Sample list*)

   go   him
   not   am
   she   will
   with   when
   from   after

   a. When I go after him, she will not be with me.

3. Make students aware of context and teach them to read up to the word and slightly beyond and then attempt to get the word from a combination of context and beginning and/or ending phonemes. This is a good way to give practice on words that present a great deal of difficulty.
   a. Fred liked his new t_____r very much. (teacher)
   b. Amy found a b_____r way to do the job. (better)

4. Have students draw pictures of scenes that represent certain words such as *wash, throw,* and *run.* Be sure to "label" each scene.

5. Give students lists of words and several different colored crayons or pencils. Give them directions as follows:

    a. "Use your yellow pencil to circle all of the things that are alive."
    b. "Use your red pencil to circle all of the words that show action."
    c. "Use your blue pencil to circle all of the words that could be used to describe something."

    (*Sample list*)

cow	throw
the	did
when	go
dog	run
pretty	man
ugly	brown

    This is a good scanning exercise to be done in x number of seconds (depending, of course, on the age of the students and the length of the list).

6. Give students envelopes containing about ten words on cards. Place a pocket chart in the front of the room and then give directions such as the following:

    a. "Place any cards in the pocket chart that tell (a) what we eat, (b) where we go in the morning, (c) what you like to do, etc."

    (*Sample list*)

home	food
table	work
chair	apple
room	have
school	pie

These are but a few examples of the many types of exercises that can be devised for the remediation of difficulties with sight words. Games are also beneficial in teaching sight words. They have the added benefit of presenting the reading task in a new dimension in which the child has not experienced failure.

Mary Kolb (1977) found that a game approach was as effective as worksheets in the reinforcement of basic sight words taught to first and second graders. Not surprisingly, the students showed a significant preference for the games compared to the traditional reinforcement approach. Some examples of games for teaching sight words follow:

Head-Chair Game.   Line up chairs and designate the chair on one end as the "head chair." Students then occupy the chairs. The teacher then flashes words to the student in the head chair. The student in the head chair continues to occupy that chair until a word is missed. After missing a word, the student goes to the end of the line and everyone moves up one chair. The idea, of course, is to see who can stay in the head chair.

Sight-word Bee.   Use the same rules as you would for a spelling bee, but instead of spelling words have students say words as they are flashed.

Sight-word Hunt.   Two or more students are blindfolded while other students hide sight-word cards around the room. When the signal is given, the blindfolded students remove the blindfolds and begin to hunt the sight-word cards. After the hunt is completed students must say all of the words on the cards they have found in order to keep them. The one who has the most cards after saying the words is the winner.

What Word?   Fill the pocket chart with sight words. Let children take turns trying to answer questions such as: "What word tells a number?" "What word is a color?" "What word begins with the p sound?" etc. Either the teacher or students can make up the questions.

These are only a sample of the many types of games that are effective for teaching sight words. Many commonly played games can be adapted to be played using sight words, for example, Bingo, rummy, checkers, etc. Appendix C also contains a listing of commercial programs, games, and other materials useful in teaching sight words and basic sight words.

THE USE OF THE TAPE RECORDER

One of the best aids a teacher can have for teaching sight words is the tape recorder. Although Chapter 16 deals with the topic of using the tape recorder in reading, we would also like to illustrate several of its many uses in teaching sight words in this chapter. One of the values of the tape recorder, of course, is that it never gets bored or tired with simple tasks. It is also a great motivator for children, and can provide for homework activities to extend the lessons carried on in the regular classroom. Following are some specific ways in which the tape recorder can be used in teaching sight words:

1.   Write words a student has missed in sentences and give the student the list of sentences. The tape recorder script to accompany the student's list would be as follows:
"Read sentence number one. (*Pause.*) Now let's check to see if you got it right. It says, 'John and Bill were going to go fishing.' Read it once more to be sure you have it right. (*Pause.*) Now read sentence number two. . . ."

2.   Give the student a list of sight words with each word numbered. The tape-recorded script to accompany the student's list would be as follows:

"I will say number one and then wait two seconds and then say the word by number one. You are to try to say the word before I say it. Be sure to listen each time to see if you got it right. Number one (*two-second pause*) 'at,' number two (*two-second pause*) 'go,' number three. . . ."

3.   Make up a group of eight sight words—one on each card. Number the cards on the back from one through eight. The tape-recorded script to accompany the cards would be as follows:

"Lay the cards out in front of you in two rows. Place four cards in each row. Turn the tape recorder off until you have done this. (*Four-second pause.*) As the words are called, pick up the word and place it on a pile in front of you. Place the second card over the first card, the third card over the second and so on. Here are the words: 'go' (five), 'do' (five), 'of' (four), 'from' (four), 'went' (three), 'want' (three), 'had' (three), 'have' (three). Now turn the pile of cards over and check to see if they are numbered from one to eight with one on top and eight on the bottom. If they are not in that order, change them so that they are in that order. Turn the tape recorder off until you have done this. (*Four-second pause.*) If they were all in the right order you knew all of the words and you may rewind the tape and put the tape and the cards away. If they were not in the right order then turn the cards over and pick each one up and say it after me. Ready 'go,' 'do,' 'of,' 'from,' 'went,' 'want,' 'had,' 'have.' Now rewind the tape and begin again."

This exercise is completely self-correcting with the number system, and, as you will note, students who miss words are given a chance to learn the word by hearing and saying it, and they are automatically channeled back into the same exercise again and again until they learn all of the words. The numbers after the words the first time through represent the number of seconds you should pause before giving the next word. Keep in mind that the student needs a slightly longer pause on the first words than on the last because the student has more words from which to discriminate. The words must be called in the same order as they are numbered on the back. Also note the four-second pause after the instructions to turn the tape recorder off. In recording the directions you should not stop the recorder but simply pause for four seconds. This is just about the right amount of time for the student to respond to the directions when the student hears it and *does* have to shut it off.

Again, these are but a few of the many ways in which the tape recorder can be used in teaching basic sight words. Trial and experience will bring to mind many more ideas.

Another type of instrument that is useful in teaching letters, sight words, or phrases is the electronic card reader such as the Language Master® shown in Figure 4–2. The Language Master is a device used for recording and playback of a strip of audio tape attached to the bottom of a card. These cards are available in various sizes. They are available in either blank or prepared form. The device contains a built-in microphone and a "Student-Instructor" switch. When the switch is set on "Student" mode, the student can pronounce a word written on a card while pressing the record button. This will record the student's voice on the tape. The student can then insert the card again and listen to the word as the student pronounced it. When using a prepared card, the student can set the selector switch to "Instructor" mode and again insert the card. This time a voice will pronounce the

FIGURE 4–2.   The Language Master® card reader/recorder.

Reproduced by permission of the Bell & Howell, Audio Visual Products Division, 7100 McCormick Road, Chicago, Illinois 60645. (The "Language Master" is a registered trademark of the Bell & Howell Co.)

word written on the card. The student then has an opportunity to compare, and correct if necessary, the response in accordance with the one pronounced by the instructor.

Since blank cards are available, this and similar instruments allow the teacher to record on cards those words, letters, phonemes, phrases, etc., missed by a particular student. This, of course, allows the student to work alone and correct errors, thus making the program highly individualized. Prepared cards also come in many forms from which the teacher can select and assign those needed by a certain student.

CHILDREN WITH ESPECIALLY DIFFICULT LEARNING PROBLEMS

Children who do not learn by normal sight or auditory approaches are sometimes quite successful when taught by use of a kinesthetic approach. The kinesthetic approach is described in detail by Grace Fernald (1943); however, since the publication of the text by Fernald a number of variations of her original method have been used. In teaching words using the kinesthetic approach the procedure is usually somewhat like that described as following.[5]

1. Show the child a word and pronounce it for the child. The word may be written on the chalkboard, on a large sheet of paper, or on a flash card approximately 3″ high by 9″ wide. Wherever it is written, the letters should usually be about two inches high. A very broad felt-tip marking pen works well for writing on tagboard flashcards. It may be written either in manuscript or cursive writing. The one chosen is usually that with which the child is most familiar or the one presently being used in school.

2. Ask the child to trace the word while saying it. The child should say each part of the word while tracing that part; however the word should not be sounded out letter by letter. It is also important that the child's finger or fingers contact the surface of the paper or tagboard at all times while the child is tracing the word. Some teachers have children use only their index finger. We would suggest, however, that you have the child use the middle and index fingers at the same time as though they, both together, were one large pencil or piece of chalk. The child should continue this tracing until you are relatively sure the child knows the word.

3. Then ask the child to write the word while looking at the original copy. When the child writes the word, it should also be written in letters that

[5]For a thorough explanation of the Fernald Technique that is similar to this see Chapter 9.

are about two inches high. The child should also be directed to say each word part as it is being written.

4. In the final step of this procedure, tell the child to write the word again, but this time from memory. Also tell the child to say the word again as it is written.

In using the kinesthetic approach some teachers prefer to have the child write the words in sand or in salt sprinkled in a container such as a shoebox lid. Another approach that works well is to lay paper over a piece of window screen and then write the words with a crayon. This has the advantage of leaving a series of raised areas on the paper that the child can actually feel when tracing.

For children who have a great deal of difficulty with some words or letters you may wish to cut letters or words out of sandpaper so that they are easily felt. The same effect can also be achieved by using felt material or by forming letters or words with white glue and then sprinkling them with salt or sand. When dry, these have a texture that can easily be felt.

The kinesthetic approach has an advantage over other forms of instruction in that it combines the sense of touch (tactile) and kinesthesia (muscle and/or body movement perception) with the normal auditory and visual modes of learning. The disadvantage, on the other hand, of using this approach is that it is time consuming. Studies have not shown the kinesthetic approach to be superior to other modes of learning for groups of children as a whole. Its superiority is evident only for those children who are not successful with a traditional approach.

Frequently, children who have difficulty learning the letters of the alphabet or sight words are identified as suffering from perceptual disorders or learning disabilities. Teachers should be cautious in forming such conclusions. Sandra Moyer and Phyllis Newcomer (1977), in reviewing research studies related to reversals, found that reversals are often a result of the child's unfamiliarity with directionality as it relates to letter discrimination, not of a perceptual disorder. Richard Allington, Kathleen Gormley, and Sharon Truex (1976) sought to determine whether poor readers exhibited perceptual confusions in words of high frequency, low discriminability, and low meaningfulness (basic sight words). They concluded that a visual perceptual deficit is unlikely to be a major factor in reading disability. Thomas Kampwirth and Marion Bates (1980) reviewed twenty-two studies conducted with children under ten years of age that compared auditory and visual preferences with visual and auditory methods of teaching words. After examining the research on the "modalities preference" approach, the writers concluded that there is little research supporting the efficacy of matching children's auditory and visual preferred modalities to teaching approaches.

They stated:

> Indeed, with this sort of evidence available, one is hard pressed to justify the continued reliance on this supposed "truth" in the learning disabilities field, that teaching according to preferred modalities, however measured, will lead to greater success than doing the opposite. . . . Obviously, it is imperative that we look much more closely at this idea than we have done in the past. (p. 604)

These issues will be examined in depth in Chapters 9 and 10.

SUMMARY

Although it is possible to learn to read without complete letter knowledge, most teachers would agree that letter knowledge is an important part of learning to read. However, reading teachers often feel that any student above the first-grade level will automatically know the alphabet. Such is often not the case even for older students, and a part of the diagnostic procedure should include testing for letter knowledge.

An extremely important part of the diagnostic procedure is the testing of sight-word knowledge, including basic sight words. Students can never expect to become fluent readers until they have mastered the basic sight words or the high-utility words that appear so often in print. Basic sight words and phrases should be tested using flash cards so that you can be assured that students have "instant" recognition of these words. Sight-word knowledge in general is usually determined by using a graded list of words that samples representative sight words at each grade level.

We have reviewed pertinent research on letter and word learning and presented some general and specific techniques for teaching letter knowledge and sight words. Among these are methods for teaching sight words in general, a systematic procedure for teaching basic sight vocabulary, the language-experience approach, the use of the tachistoscope, the Fernald Technique, and methods of using the tape recorder as a teaching device.

REFERENCES

Adams, Ernest L. "Influence of Meaningfulness and Familiarization Training on Basic Sight Vocabulary Learning with First-Graders," Doctoral dissertation, Michigan State University, 1970.

Allington, Richard L. "An Evaluation of the Use of Color Cues to Focus Attention in Discrimination and Paired-Associate Learning," *Reading Research Quarterly.* Vol. 10, No. 2, (1974–1975), 244–247.

REFERENCES

Allington, Richard L.; Gormley, Kathleen; and Truex, Sharon. "Poor and Normal Readers' Achievement on Visual Tasks Involving High Frequency, Low Discriminability Words," *Journal of Learning Disabilities.* Vol. 9, No. 1, (May, 1976), 292–296.

Arlin, Marshall; Scott, Mary; and Webster, Janet. "The Effects of Pictures on Rate of Learning Sight Words: A Critique of the Focal Attention Hypothesis," *Reading Research Quarterly.* Vol. 14, No. 4, (1978–1979), 645–660.

Botel, Morton. *Botel Reading Inventory.* Chicago: Follett, 1978.

Chisholm, Diane, and Knafle, June. "Letter-Name Knowledge as a Prerequisite to Learning to Read," *Reading Improvement.* Vol. 15, (Spring, 1978), 2–7.

Curtis, H. M. "Wide Reading for Beginners," *Journal of Educational Research.* Vol. 32, (December, 1938), 255–262.

Dolch, Edward W. *Basic Sight Word Test.* Champaign, Ill.: Garrard Press, 1942.

Durr, William K. "Computer Study of High Frequency Words in Popular Trade Juveniles," *Reading Teacher.* Vol. 27, (October, 1973), 37–42.

Durrell, Donald D., and Catterson, Jane H. *Durrell Analysis of Reading Difficulty.* New York: Psychological Corporation, 1980.

Ehri, Linnea C., and Wilce, Lee S. "Do Beginners Learn to Read Function Words Better in Sentences or in Lists?" *Reading Research Quarterly.* Vol. 15, No. 4, (1980), 451–476.

Fernald, Grace. *Remedial Techniques in Basic School Subjects.* New York: McGraw-Hill, 1943.

Gagon, Glen. "Modern Research and Word Perception," *Education.* Vol. 86, (April, 1966), 464–472.

Goodman, Mark D., and Cundick, Bert P. "Learning Rates with Black and Colored Letters," *Journal of Learning Disabilities.* Vol. 9, No. 4, (November, 1976), 600–602.

Hampton, Kathryn. "An Investigation of the Effectiveness of Two Methods of Teaching Basic Sight Vocabulary," Master's thesis, California State University, Hayward, 1979.

Hargis, Charles H., and Gickling, Edward E. "The Function of Imagery in Word Recognition Development," *Reading Teacher.* Vol. 31, (May, 1978), 870–873.

Hillerich, Robert L. "Word Lists—Getting It All Together," *Reading Teacher.* Vol. 27, (January, 1974), 353–360.

Hockett, J. A. "Comparative Analysis of the Vocabularies of Twenty-Nine Second-Grade Readers," *Journal of Educational Research.* Vol. 31, (May, 1938), 665–671.

Jastak, J. F., and Jastak, S. R. *Wide Range Achievement Test.* Wilmington, Del.: Guidance Associates, 1978.

Johns, Jerry L. *Some Comparisons Between the Dolch Basic Sight Vocabulary and the Word List for the 1970's,* U.S. Educational Resources Information Center, ERIC Document ED 098 541, 1974.

Kampwirth, Thomas J., and Bates, Marion. "Modality Preference and Teaching Method: A Review of the Research," *Academic Therapy.* Vol. 15, No. 5, (May, 1980), 597–605.

Kolb, Mary C. "A Game Activity Approach Versus a Traditional Approach in the Reinforcement of Sight Words Taught to First and Second Graders," Master's thesis, California State University, Hayward, 1977.

Lowe, A. J., and Foilman, John. "Comparison of the Dolch List with Other Lists," *Reading Teacher.* Vol. 28, (October, 1974), 40–44.

Madden, Richard. *Language Arts Notes—Number 11.* New York: World Book Co., 1959.

Mangieri, John N., and Kahn, Michael S. "Is the Dolch List of 220 Basic Sight Words Irrelevant?" *Reading Teacher,* Vol. 30, (March, 1977), 649–651.

Moyer, Sandra B., and Newcomer, Phyllis L. "Reversals in Reading: Diagnosis and Remediation," *Exceptional Children.* Vol. 43, No. 7, (April, 1977), 424–429.

Pope, Lillie. "Sight Words for the Seventies," *Academic Therapy.* Vol. 10, (Spring, 1975), 285–289.

Robinson, H. Alan. "A Study of the Techniques of Word Identification," *Reading Teacher.* Vol. 16, (January, 1963), 238–242.

Samuels, S. Jay. "Can Pictures Distract Students from the Printed Word: A Rebuttal," *Journal of Reading Behavior.* Vol. 9, (Winter, 1977), 361–364.

Sipay, Edward R. *Sipay Word Analysis Tests.* Cambridge, Mass.: Educators Publishing Service, 1974.

Singer, Harry. "Sight Word Learning with and Without Pictures: A Critique of Arlin, Scott and Webster's Research," *Reading Research Quarterly.* Vol. 15, No. 2, (1980), 290–298.

Singer, Harry; Samuels, S. Jay; and Spiroff, Jean. "The Effect of Pictures and Contextual Conditions on Learning Responses to Printed Words," *Reading Research Quarterly.* Vol. 9, No. 4, (1973–1974), 555–567.

Slosson, Richard L. *Slosson Oral Reading Test.* East Aurora, N.Y.: Slosson Educational Publications, 1963.

Spache, George. *Diagnostic Reading Scales.* 3rd ed., Monterey, Calif.: California Test Bureau, 1981.

Speer, Olga B., and Lamb, George S. "First Grade Reading Ability and Fluency in Naming Verbal Symbols," *Reading Teacher.* Vol. 29, (March, 1976), 572–576.

Stone, Clarence R. "Most Important 150 Words for Beginning Reading," *Educational Method.* Vol. 18, (January, 1939), 192–195.

Stone, Clarence R. "Vocabularies of Twenty Preprimers," *Elementary School Journal.* Vol. 41, (February, 1941), 423–429.

Strikwerda, Arlene W. "The Effect of Pictorial Stimuli on the Instruction of Sight Words to First Graders," Master's thesis, California State University, Hayward, 1976.

Williams, Joanna P. "Training Kindergarten Children to Discriminate Letter-like Forms," *American Educational Research Journal.* Vol. 6, (November, 1969), 501–514.

Williams, Joanna P.; Blumberg, Ellen L.; and Williams, David V. "Cues Used in Visual Word Recognition," *Journal of Educational Psychology.* Vol. 61, (August, 1970), 310–315.

5

Diagnosis and Remediation of Educational Factors: *Word-Analysis Skills*

The first part of this chapter contains a discussion and examples of the problems involved in various types of testing for word-analysis skills. This is followed by a description of some of the more commonly used commercial tests and surveys along with a discussion of their strengths and weaknesses. A method of constructing your own phonics survey is then described along with the rationale for use of the El Paso Phonics Survey that appears in Appendix A. The remainder of the chapter deals with specific methods of diagnosing and remediating reading difficulties in other word-analysis skills.

Part A: DIAGNOSIS

PHONICS AND STRUCTURAL ANALYSIS

Before making a decision about which test to use in the area of phonics and structural analysis, you must decide how you are going to use the information obtained. For example, if you plan to group a number of children who are simply labeled "weak" in overall phonics knowledge, chances are a *group* diagnostic test would suffice for your needs. On the other hand, if you intend to teach to students' specific weaknesses, for example, lack of knowledge of the initial consonant sounds *p, f,* and *g,* and consonant blends *fl, gr,* and *pl,* you will need to administer an *individual* diagnostic test.

Many educators have been under the impression that they can accurately diagnose an individual's specific weaknesses with a group diagnostic test. Research in the El Paso Reading Center has shown that this is not so (Ekwall, 1973). Once again, you should keep in mind the testing principle stated earlier; i.e., test in a situation that is analogous to actual reading. In other words, the test should require that the student perform the task being tested in the same manner as the student will be required to do when he or she reads. When a student takes a group diagnostic test, it is impossible by the nature of the test for the student to respond to the answers, in most cases, in a way that is analogous to actually reading. For example, in taking a group diagnostic test the student is usually given directions somewhat similar to the following:

> "Write the beginning sound you hear in the following words: Number one, *need*, number two, *teach*, etc."

The student in this case is to write an *n* in blank number one and a *t* in blank number two. A second set of directions for group testing for knowledge of the "n" and "t" sounds might be as follows:

> "On your papers are four letters. Circle the beginning sound you hear in the following words. The first word is *need*. The second word is *teach*, etc."

In this case the students' answer sheets would be similar to the following:

1.   p f n d
2.   g t h r

At first glance both tests may appear to be valid; however, on examining them more closely you will realize that hearing the words *need* and *teach* and writing *n* and *t* in a blank or hearing *need* and *teach* and circling their beginning sounds from a choice of four letters is simply not the same skill as is required for seeing the *n* and *t* graphemes and responding with the "n" and "t" phonemes. Extensive research in the El Paso Reading Center has shown that the item-by-item agreement on items missed on various group and individual-type tests is extremely low and that group diagnostic tests do not diagnose accurately enough for prescriptive teaching. Since remedial reading is usually a process of filling in the gaps in a student's reading skills, prescriptive teaching is a necessity. And in most cases remedial reading teachers will need to give individual diagnostic tests in order to accurately diagnose and remediate specific problems students are experiencing in phonics and structural analysis. In all fairness to the authors and publishers of group diagnostic tests it should also be stated that much of the teaching of phonics and structural analysis is done by simply grouping those children with the lowest overall scores and teaching them practically everything covered on the test. In a situation where a teacher is dealing with a large number of children in a group, this approach, although somewhat inefficient in terms of the students' time, is quite efficient in terms of the teacher's time. And, if this type of teaching is to be done, a group diagnostic test will serve the purpose; that is, it will generally pinpoint those students who are extremely poor in word-attack skills from those who are at a medium or higher level. In some cases this information may be valuable in making *initial* determinations about students' word-attack skills. The examiner may, for example, use a group-test format to identify the students who are most deficient in word-attack skills so that those students may then be given individual tests to identify specific weaknesses for prescriptive instruction.

Although it would seem that testing phonics knowledge is an easy task, this is not necessarily the case. For example, listed below are some commonly used methods of assessing children's phonics knowledge and what we believe to be the shortcomings of each method.

Method 1: Children are shown letters, e.g., *a, b, c,* and told to give the sounds of these letters. First of all, although perhaps a minor point, the letters do not "have" sounds, they represent sounds, and we should ask the child to tell us the sounds that these letters stand for. One of the major problems with this method, however, is in determining whether a certain sound given is correct. In playing tape recordings of children taking this type of test in our classes we find that the agreement among the scorers is so low that this method, although appearing somewhat valid, cannot in reality be at all valid since it is not even reliable. That is, the scorers do not agree on which answers are right and which are wrong. This type of test then lacks interscorer reliability. The main problem among the scorers is that they do not "hear" the same thing. For example, they cannot agree on whether they hear "er" or "ruh" for the "r" sound. Another problem with this method is that some children who know their sounds in the context of a word do not know the sounds in isolation. Testing sounds in isolation would yield irrelevant information in such cases.

Method 2: Children are given a piece of paper on which four letters, blends, etc., appear by each number. They are told to circle or underline the letter, blend, etc., that begins or ends or has the same middle sound as a word pronounced by the tester. The problem with this type of test, as stated earlier, is that hearing a word and circling a sound heard in it is not the same as actual reading. Furthermore, if there are four possible choices on each question, the student has a one-fourth chance of guessing the correct answer. There is a fairly high correlation between being able to do this and actually attacking a new word, and thus those children who are good at this task will probably be good at attacking words and vice versa; however, this type of test, as shown by our research, is simply not accurate enough for prescriptive teaching purposes.

Method 3:   Children are given a sheet of paper with a blank by each number. They are then instructed to write down the beginning sound, beginning blend, vowel sounds, etc., heard in a word pronounced by the tester. This method has the same weaknesses as those described in method 2. That is, it is not analogous to actual word attack in reading.

Method 4:   Children are shown nonsense words that contain the initial consonants, blends, vowels, etc., to be tested. For example in testing for knowledge of the "p" sound a child may be given the nonsense word *pide*. For some children this presents major problems. In order to pronounce the nonsense word *pide* they would have to know the following:

a. The long and/or short vowel sound for "i";

b. The "d" sound;

c. The vowel rule stating that when there is a vowel-consonant-final *e* the first vowel is usually long and the *e* is silent.

In addition, the student must possess the ability to *blend* the various phonemes together. As you can see, all of the knowledge listed in (a), (b), and (c) above are equal to, or more difficult than, simple knowledge of the "p" sound. Therefore, if the child does not respond, you would not really know if it was because the child did not know the "p" sound or if, in reality, the child had no knowledge of one, two, or all three areas listed in (a), (b), and (c) above or inability to blend the letters. It should also be kept in mind that vowel sounds and/or vowel rules are usually taught somewhat later than initial consonant sounds. Therefore, many children having difficulty with initial consonant sounds are likely to experience even more problems with vowel sounds and/or vowel rules. A final problem with this method is that many students simply resist reading nonsense words. These students, even when told that the words are not "real words," have difficulty pronouncing nonsense syllables. It may be that for these pupils pronunciation of nonsense words represents a task that is more difficult than reading real words.

Method 5:   Children are given a list of real words, each beginning with a specific initial consonant, blend, etc., to be tested. The problem here, of course, is that if the words are already in the child's sight vocabulary, it is not a test of word-attack skills at all. And, if the words are not in the child's sight vocabulary, many of the same problems encountered in using method 4 are also encountered here.

In order to understand why the foregoing methods are inadequate for diagnosing phonics weaknesses, it may be helpful to think of the testing and teaching of phonics skills as occurring at three stages: low-level skills, high-level skills, and blending skills.

A student who masters low-level skills is able to recognize the correct letter(s) when the sound is provided. In this situation the student is going from sound to symbol, which is the easiest phonics task. Methods 2 and 3 above will adequately test for this ability. However, in order for a student to utilize phonics as an aid to decoding, he or she must go from symbol to sound, a more difficult skill. When reading, the student first sees the letter(s) or symbol(s) and then must think of the associated sound. This can be thought of as high-level phonics. Methods 1, 4, and 5 above purport to test this level; however, there are a number of testing problems that were noted in our discussion of these methods.

Successful application of phonics skills requires not only high-level skills but also blending ability; that is, the student must blend the sounds or phonemes together to pronounce the whole word. Methods 4 and 5 above attempt to do this but do not sufficiently control the exposure of new skills or prevent recognition of the whole word by sight. Later in this chapter we will present an alternative method for testing the various phonics elements that will enable you to accurately diagnose specific phonics weaknesses.

Some Commercially Published Tests and Surveys: Their Strengths and Weaknesses

In this section a number of tests are described in detail, along with their strengths and weaknesses. The purpose of the somewhat lengthy descriptions is to make the user aware of the common shortcomings of some of our most popular reading diagnostic tests. The information gained in this section should also help you in critically analyzing other reading tests that are now on the market or in analyzing those that are likely to appear in the future.

The *Botel Reading Inventory* (Botel, 1978) contains a Decoding Test, a Spelling Placement Test, a Word Recognition Test, and a Word Opposites Test. The latter two tests have two forms each and are designed for use as reading placement tests. The Decoding Test includes twelve subtests:

1.   "Letter Naming"
2.   "Beginning Consonant Sound/Letter Awareness"
3.   "Rhyme Sound/Letter Pattern Awareness"
4–12. "Decoding Syllable/Spelling Patterns"

The first three decoding tests are administered as group tests; the remaining decoding tests are individually administered.

On the "Letter Naming" subtest the students identify by circling the letters named by the examiner. On the "Beginning Consonant Sound/Letter Awareness" subtest the students circle or underline words that begin with the same sound as pairs read by the examiner. This format is similar to that noted in method 2 above and has the same advantages and disadvantages. The test does provide a measure of low-level phonics ability, but evaluates only ten beginning single consonant sounds. High-level skills and blending are not measured.

The "Rhyme Sound/Letter Pattern Awareness" subtest uses the same group format and measures the students' ability to recognize ten rhyming patterns or ending phonograms, such as *-ed, -ake,* and *-ot.*

The individually administered "Decoding Syllable/Spelling Patterns" subtests consist of nine lists of ten words each, grouped according to spelling patterns. The student is to read the words on the lists aloud until two or more errors (80 percent correct) are made on one of the lists. These tests are essentially a series of sight-word tests of increasing difficulty much like method 5 above. If a student misses a word, there is no way of determining whether the error was caused by the student's failure to decode the beginning sound, vowel sound, or ending sound or by an inability to blend the various sounds together.

The last three lists contain multisyllable words, and in these cases we would have to add structural-analysis weaknesses to the list of possible reasons why a student might fail to pronounce a word correctly.

The last list is perhaps the most useful of the entire test. It contains a number of difficult nonsense words such as *pegflitting* and *quidderish.* Although the author of the test does not point it out, it is quite logical to assume that a student who can pronounce these words has an adequate knowledge of single consonant sounds, consonant blends and digraphs, vowel rules, structural analysis, and to some extent accent generalizations. This test is, therefore, useful as a quick screening device; in other words, if a student can pronounce the words on this list, the above-mentioned skills would not need to be tested, thus saving a considerable amount of time in the diagnosis of certain students.

In short, the *Botel Reading Inventory*, although somewhat time consuming to administer, does not provide the examiner with the kind of information required to plan prescriptive instruction.

The *Diagnostic Reading Scales* (DRS) (Spache, 1981) contains twelve word-analysis and phonics tests to supplement a series of graded reading passages. We believe that the word-analysis and phonics tests are vastly improved over the eight subtests that appeared in the earlier (1972) edition. Apparently, Spache has responded resourcefully to criticism of the earlier subtests.

The twelve subtests of the DRS are as follows:

Test 1:   Initial Consonants. In this subtest, the student is to read aloud nine one-syllable real words and thirteen one-syllable nonsense words that begin with a consonant. Words such as *bam, cam*, and *dam* are used. Although the use of nonsense words may present a problem for some students (as we pointed out previously in our discussion of method 4), in order to accurately test for higher-level phonics skills some use of nonsense words is inevitable. In this subtest Spache provides a good mixture of real and nonsense words. In this way, the examiner can determine whether only nonsense word items were missed and can, at the same time, be sure that the student is not recognizing all the words by sight.

Test 2:   Final Consonants. Using a similar format, this test evaluates a student's ability to pronounce (go from symbol to sound) fifteen different final consonants in one-syllable words.

Test 3:   Consonant Digraphs. Similar to tests 1 and 2, this test measures a student's ability to pronounce various consonant digraphs in both initial and final positions. This test will be somewhat more difficult for students because a variety of beginning and ending parts are used to complete the syllables in which the consonant digraphs appear. However, Spache wisely cautions the examiner to "disregard mispronunciations of vowels and consonants appearing with the digraphs."

Test 4:   Consonant Blends. Similar to test three.

Test 5:   Initial Consonant Substitution. This test measures the student's ability to substitute beginning consonant sounds and is a good measure of a student's ability to do simple blending. The sample items present a one-syllable word, then the ending phonogram of the word, then a new word with the substituted consonant, as follows:

        dark   ark   bark

The student is given three trials with this format, then is asked to perform the substitution task on items that are presented as follows:

    c   bake

The student must pronounce *bake* and *cake*, though the examiner may provide additional aid if necessary. A similar subtest in the earlier edition was criticized for being too difficult for primary children. This new test represents a considerable improvement. However, it would appear to be most effective (i.e., least confusing) to present all items in the same way as the sample items are presented. Or the test items might be presented as follows:

    bake   cake

There is reason to believe, based on our experience testing students on initial-consonant substitution tasks, that the *c   bake* format represents a formidable visual task for the student—one that may interfere with measuring the decoding skill, which is the purpose of the test.

Test 6:   Initial Consonant Sounds Recognized Auditorily. In this test the student names the letter that begins the word pronounced by the examiner. This is similar to method 3 described previously and measures only low-level phonics ability (sound to symbol). Our criticism of this test is not so much with the format but rather with its placement. It would seem logical to place this test before test 1 since it evaluates a lower-level, or prerequisite, skill. Otherwise, the author should point out that this test will only be necessary for students who failed test 1. And, since any student who fails test 1 will be likely to fail tests 2 through 5, it would again make most sense to place test 6 before test 1.

Test 7:   Auditory Discrimination. This test uses the common format of having the student identify identical and contrasting pairs of words that are pronounced by the examiner; for example, *end–end* and *bin–pin*. The placement of this test is even more puzzling than the previous one. Auditory discrimination is a prephonics skill that requires no visual skill whatever. Surely this test should be the first given in the battery or instructions should be given to skip this test for students who attain mastery on any of the other tests.

Test 8:   Short and Long Vowel Sounds. This test consists of sixteen one-syllable word pairs with one word in each pair having a short vowel sound and the other a long vowel sound; for example, *red–ride*. Some of the words are real words and some are nonsense words. Vowel-sound abilities are perhaps the most difficult of all phonics skills to test accurately. This test has the virtue of requiring the student to read words rather than recite rules. Some of the problems mentioned under method 4 appear because the student must read words that contain a number of different consonants, consonant blends, and consonant digraphs. However, it is probably reasonable to assume that students will master these skills prior to learning short and long vowel patterns.

Test 9:   Vowels with *r*. In this test the student pronounces ten words that contain the *r*-controlled vowel pattern.

Test 10:   Vowel Diphthongs and Digraphs. In this test the student pronounces thirty real and nonsense words that contain common vowel digraphs and diphthongs.

Test 11:   Common Syllables or Phonograms. In this test the student pronounces thirty-four common syllables or phonograms that occur frequently in primary reading materials, such as *tion, atch,* and *ile.* For some reason, in this test the syllables appear in isolation, instead of in real or nonsense words as in previous tests. Also, it would seem that this test is misplaced since the skill tested is probably easier than those evaluated on tests 9 and 10.

Test 12:   Blending. This test consist of ten nonsense words divided into phonograms, such as *gr–ell–on.* The student is asked to pronounce each word element and then blend them into one word. The student is evaluated on the ability to blend the elements rather than on the ability to pronounce the phonograms. This test, undoubtedly, does test the ability to blend. It would seem reasonable, however, to present words with fewer and easier phonograms. Even though the pronunciation of the phonograms is not to be taken into account in the scoring, it is likely that students will be frustrated by this aspect of the task and fail to demonstrate blending skill that may in fact exist.

As noted earlier the new DRS subtests are significantly improved over those in the earlier edition. Most diagnosticians will find these tests to be useful in the evaluation of various phonics skills. Since the author continues to present the tests in a puzzling order, we would recommend that the examiner simply alter the order of administration.

The *Durrell Analysis of Reading Difficulty* (3rd edition) (Durrell and Catterson, 1980) does not contain enough depth in phonics testing to plan prescriptive instruction. The "Identifying Sounds in Words" subtest provides for evaluation, similar to method 2, of low-level phonics skills. These include only seven beginning consonants, eight beginning blends and digraphs, five ending consonants, and nine items where the student must identify both beginning and ending sounds. The "Sounds in Isolation" subtest tests sixteen beginning consonants, sixteen consonant blends and digraphs, and twenty phonograms. This testing is done in isolation and, therefore, suffers from the problems mentioned in method 1. Perhaps the real value of the *Durrell Analysis of Reading Difficulty* is in the training it can provide the diagnostician on what to observe in students' reading abilities. Once this has been learned, however, many diagnosticians and teachers will find that the administration of the various subtests is too time consuming for the diagnostic information that it provides.

The *Gates-McKillop-Horowitz Reading Diagnostic Tests* (2nd edition) (Gates, McKillop, and Horowitz, 1981) contains a series of nine tests designed to evaluate a student's word-attack skills. The order of these subtests is as follows: "Syllabication," "Recognizing and Blending Common Word Parts," "Reading Words," "Giving Letter Sounds," "Naming Capital Letters," "Naming Lower Case Letters," "Vowels," "Auditory Blending," and "Auditory Discrimination."

In giving the "Syllabication" subtest, the student is shown a series of seventeen nonsense words, such as *rivlob*, and *acdengist* and told to pronounce them. This test purports to measure the student's "ability to combine syllables into words." However, the nonsense words are quite difficult, and in order to pronounce them the student must also have mastered phoneme-grapheme correspondence and structural analysis. Therefore, it would seem more appropriate to use this test as a quick screening device to determine which students possess adequate phonics and structural-analysis skills to eliminate further testing in these areas. This is the same recommendation that we made for the last test in the Botel battery.

The "Recognizing and Blending Common Word Parts" subtest tests the student's ability to pronounce nonsense words such as *spack* and *twable*. If the student cannot pronounce the word, he or she is then shown each part separately, for example, *sp* and *ack*. After pronouncing each part, the student attempts to blend the parts into a whole word. This subtest will provide a gross measure of the student's knowledge of blends, digraphs, diphthongs, and phonograms or word families, as well as the student's ability to blend these word parts. However, the presentation of various beginning sounds with a variety of ending sounds makes the task somewhat difficult. The blending skill itself could be better measured if only one or two ending phonograms were used. As the test is presently constructed, a student may miss an item, and the examiner will find it difficult to determine whether the error results from an inability to blend or from a failure to recognize the beginning or ending sounds. The authors do provide a scoring system for evaluating the student's performance on the various subtasks, and this should aid the careful examiner.

The "Reading Words" subtest requires the student to read fifteen one-syllable nonsense words, such as *rus* and *soat*. The authors wisely caution that "some children have difficulty handling a [nonsense word] task, and poor performance may not indicate poor phonetic skills." With this caution in mind, it does appear that this subtest provides a gross measure of a student's ability to apply phonic analysis to isolated words.

The "Giving Letter Sounds" subtest, as the name implies, is a test for the letter sounds of the consonants and vowels. Each sound is tested in isolation. All consonants are presented along with ten vowels and vowel combinations, and the results should be thorough enough for prescriptive teaching. However, since the sounds are tested in isolation, this subtest suffers from the problems described in method 1. The inclusion of the vowels is somewhat unusual, and the child is expected to provide more than one sound where appropriate. It does not seem reasonable to ask a child to give long and short sounds for vowels in isolation, let alone provide alternate sounds for the *ea* digraph. What we should be concerned with is not the child's ability to produce from memory the vowel sounds in isolation, but rather the child's ability to apply the correct sound in the context of reading words.

The subtests for "Naming Capital Letters" and "Naming Lower Case Letters" require the child to say the name of each of the letters.

The "Vowels" subtest follows the format described in method 2. This test will evaluate the student's ability to recognize (sound to symbol) the long and short vowel sounds. As pointed out earlier, this low-level skill is not the same as that required of the student when reading.

In the "Auditory Blending" subtest the examiner reads word parts to the child, such as *b–ox* and the child is to pronounce the whole word, *box*. Auditory blending ability is considered a prerequisite to the skill required in blending while reading.

The "Auditory Discrimination" subtest is administered by having the student sit with his or her back to the examiner while the examiner reads a number of pairs of words. The student is to say whether the words are the same or different. This subtest should serve as a sufficient screening device for auditory discrimination.

The various subtests of the *Gates-McKillop-Horowitz Reading Diagnostic Tests* evaluate a range of prereading and word-attack skills. The authors suggest that the examiner compare the student's test performance on various subtests. Some of the tests could be constructed differently, and the examiner may have difficulty planning prescriptive instruction based on the results of the subtests. Nonetheless, this individually administered inventory does provide useful information to the reading diagnostician.

The *Phonics Knowledge Survey* (Durkin and Meshover, 1964) is designed to test a number of phonics word-attack skills. It contains fifteen subtests designed to test knowledge of letter names, letter sounds, vowel sounds, vowel rules, soft and hard *c* and *g* sounds and rules, sounds and rules for *y*, consonant blends, consonant digraphs, diphthongs, *r*-controlled vowels, sounds of *qu*, *oo*, *x*, and silent consonants, and some syllabication principles. Both consonant and vowel sounds are tested in isolation, and thus this part of the test presents those problems explained in method 1. Vowel rules are tested in the context of nonsense words. This seems feasible since students should not be required to know or recite the rules if they can apply them in attacking a strange word. (It is only when they cannot apply the rules and sounds that they need to learn the sounds and rules.) This same method is applied to knowledge of the soft and hard sounds of *c* and *g* which again seems logical. Knowledge of the sounds and rules for *y* are tested in the same manner in words such as *yad, bly, adsy,* and *fyth.* Consonant blends and digraphs, diphthongs, *r*-controlled vowels, and the sounds of *qu, oo, x,* and silent consonants are all tested in isolation. This again presents some problems as mentioned in method 1. This is even more pronounced in testing silent consonants, which are extremely difficult, even for good readers, when shown in isolation. The test for syllable rules appears to be effective since it also requires the student to divide nonsense words into syllables. The division of words into syllables is done to help the student in knowing which vowels appear in open and closed syllables; therefore, this test requires that the student perform a task that would be required in the act of reading. The syllabication test fails, however, to test what is perhaps the most helpful of all syllabication principles—that prefixes and suffixes form separate syllables.

The *Sipay Word Analysis Tests* (SWAT) (Sipay, 1974) are a series of seventeen subtests, administered individually, to test students' knowledge of word-analysis skills. The subtests are as follows: "Survey Test," "Letter Names (Lower-Case and Upper-Case)," "Symbol-Sound Association: Single Letters (Sounds and Words)," "Substitution: Single Letters (Initial Consonants, Final Consonants, and Medial Vowels)," "Consonant-Vowel-Consonant Trigrams," "Initial Consonant Blends and Digraphs (Blends, Digraphs and Triple Clusters)," "Final Consonant Blends and Digraphs (Blends and Digraphs)," "Vowel Combinations (Most Common and Consistent Vowel Digraphs, Most Common and Consistent Diphthongs, More Common Vowel Combinations That Usually Represent One of Two Sounds, Less Common Vowel Combinations That May Represent One of Two Sounds)," "Open Syllable Generalization," "Final Silent *e* Generalization," "Vowel Versatility," "Vowels + *r* (Single Vowel + *r*, Two Vowels + *r*, Single Vowel + *r* + Silent *e*)," "Silent Consonants," "Vowel Sounds of *y*," "Visual Analysis (Monosyllabic Words, Root Words and Affixes, Syllabication)," "Visual Blending (Component Elements into Syllables, Syllables into Words)," and "Contractions."

Each of the SWAT subtests has four components: a "mini-manual," a set of test cards (approximately 57 mm × 90 mm), an answer sheet, and an individual report form. The mini-manuals provide general information on the subtest, what skills are measured, how to administer and score it, how to analyze and interpret the results, and suggestions for follow-up testing. The test cards are used to present the stimuli to the student. The answer sheets are used for recording the student's responses and to allow the examiner to make a more detailed analysis of the learner's performance. The individual report forms are used by the examiner to summarize and report his or her findings.

Because of the length of this test each subtest will not be analyzed in this section. However, it should be noted that the author of this test recognized that word-attack skills generally cannot be tested in a group situation and took considerable care to construct a test that will allow the student to perform on each subtest in a situation such as the student would be likely to encounter in actually reading. He also did considerable research in order to find which graphemes were of high enough utility to make them worthwhile testing. This test should yield results that are accurate enough for exact prescriptive teaching.

One feature of the test that some teachers may find undesirable is that they are required to handle a great many cards while administering the various subtests. However, this is also an advantage since it takes the test materials out of the traditional setting and puts them into a context that a student is more likely to perceive as a game or fun type of activity.

The *Stanford Diagnostic Reading Test* (Karlsen, Madden, and Gardner, 1976) is a group diagnostic tests in four levels, with two parallel forms (A and B) at each level. The Red Level is intended for use at the end of grade one, in grade two, and with low-achieving students in grade three and above. It evaluates auditory discrimination, the basic phonics skills, auditory vocabulary, word recognition, and comprehension of short sentences and paragraphs. The Green Level is intended for use in grades three and four and with low-achieving students in grade five and above. It evaluates auditory discrimination, phonetic and structural analysis, auditory vocabulary, and literal and inferential comprehension. The Brown Level is intended for use in grades five through eight and with low-achieving high school students. It evaluates phonetic and structural analysis, auditory vocabulary, literal and inferential comprehension, and reading rate. The Blue Level was published in 1974. It is also called the SDRT Level III. It is intended for use with high school and community-college students. It evaluates phonetic and structural analysis, reading vocabulary, literal and inferential comprehension, reading rate, and scanning and skimming.

This battery offers both content-referenced and norm-referenced scores and is well constructed and standardized. Administration of this test should enable a teacher to determine appropriate placements for students; that is, which ones are good, fair, or poor readers. However, by its nature (it is group administered) it is possible to evaluate only low-level skills using this test. Thus, the test provides only a gross measure of a few word-attack skills and does not provide sufficient information for prescriptive teaching as would be required for remedial readers.

The *Woodcock Reading Mastery Tests* (Woodcock, 1973) are a series of five tests designed for individual administration. They are for use for kindergarten to grade twelve. One of the five tests is designed to test word-attack skills. Two alternate forms of the battery are available. The author of this test states,

> This battery of tests is particularly useful for clinical or research purposes and in any situation for which precise measures of reading achievement are desired. Raw scores can be converted to traditional normative scores including grade scores, age scores, percentile ranks and standard scores. Primary interpretative emphasis, however, is directed toward using the specially designed Mastery Scale which predicts the individual's relative success with reading tasks at different levels of difficulty. Separate norms are available for boys and girls in addition to total group norms. An innovative feature is the provision of SES (socioeconomic status) adjusted norms based on communities having SES characteristics similar to the local community. (Page 1, *Teacher's Manual*.)
>
> The Word Attack Skill Test contains 50 items which measure the subject's ability to identify nonsense words through application of phonic and structural analysis skills. Items are arranged in order of difficulty. At the lower end of the test the nonsense words are simple consonant-vowel or consonant-vowel-consonant combinations such as "dee" and "lat." Multisyllable words such as "ipdan" and "depnonlel" are presented at the upper end of the test. Represented within the set of nonsense words are most consonant and vowel sounds, common prefixes and suffixes, and frequently appearing irregular spellings of vowels and consonants ("ph" for "f" and "igh" for long "i"). (Page 3, *Teacher's Manual*.)

This test has the advantage of being rather easy to administer and is contained in an easel type notebook that is functional. The student who is able to read all of the nonsense words would, no doubt, have adequate word-attack skills. However, as described earlier in method 4, the use of nonsense words presents a number of problems. If the student does not respond, the tester does not really know whether the student does not know the initial consonant, the medial vowel, the ending consonant, etc., or whether the student does not know how to blend. For this reason the only "precise measurement" that can be obtained is whether the student does or does not possess adequate word-attack skills. This test would not be adequate for prescriptive teaching of specific phonemes.

Constructing Your Own Test or Using the El Paso Phonics Survey

Before choosing or constructing a test for phoneme-grapheme relationships you should first examine the research on which graphemes are of high enough utility or which represent a specific sound or phoneme to a degree that makes them worthwhile testing and teaching. For example, Lou Burmeister (1968), in examining the 17,310 words from a study by P. R. Hanna and others (1966), found that the vowel pair *ie* appeared 156 times. In those 156 words the *ie* grapheme represented six different phonemes as heard in the following words (p. 448):

Word	Frequency	Percent
thief	56	35.9
Lassie	30	19.2
die	26	16.7
patient	23	14.7
cashier	17	10.9
friend	4	2.6

The "ie" sound heard in the word *thief* accounted for 35.9 percent of the total words, the "ie" sound heard in *Lassie* accounted for 19.2 percent of the total words, etc. As you can see, however, it would not be practical for a teacher to try to teach students all six of the "ie" variations. For this reason decisions need to be made concerning which graphemes are of high enough utility to make them worthwhile teaching, based on such factors as the percent of time that vowel combinations represent certain phonemes, frequency of appearance in children's literature, etc. Oswald and Ekwall (1971) have developed a list of phonic elements that are recommended to be tested and taught to children in grades one through three and to older disabled readers. These are the graphemes tested in the El Paso Phonics Survey shown in Appendix A. In that survey you will note that some graphemes represent two phonemes. Where it is recommended that both be taught, it is because both sounds are approximately equal in utility.

There is a way of testing for the various phonic elements that establishes a situation that is nearly analogous to actual reading and that does not possess the innate disadvantages of the methods used in many commercial tests. An example of this type of test along with complete directions for its administration is shown in Appendix A. The procedure for constructing such a test and the rationale for its use are as follows:

1.   Choose about three small stimulus words that are usually known by children in their early reading. The words should contain only one syllable and should begin with a vowel. Ekwall suggests the following three words:

      in
      up
      am

Print these words on three cards to be used as flash cards or print them all on one larger card or at the top of the stimulus sheet that the student will see.

2. Place each initial consonant, consonant blend, or consonant digraph before one of these small words to form a nonsense word. The element to be tested and the stimulus word should precede the nonsense word on the same line as follows:

    a. m   in   min
    b. t   up   tup
    c. p   am   pam
    d. s   up   sup
    e. pl   up   plup
    f. ch   am   cham
    g. qu   am   quam

    The use of at least three stimulus words will enable you to form nonsense words with any combination of initial consonants, blends, and digraphs.

3. In constructing the test be sure to place about eight to twelve of the easier consonants first, e.g., the following: *p, n, s, t, r, m, b,* and *d.* These are later used in nonsense words to test for vowel knowledge.

4. Combine each vowel, vowel team (vowel digraphs and diphthongs), and special letter combinations (*r-, l-,* and *w*-controlled vowels, etc.) with one or two of the easier consonants listed above to form a nonsense word as shown below:

    a. a   bam
    b. i   mip
    c. o   tope
    d. a   mape
    e. oi   poi

    Be careful to construct long-vowel and short-vowel nonsense words that do not violate common vowel rules. For example, put short vowels between two consonants to conform to the cvc pattern in which we expect the vowel to be short. Put the long vowels in a pattern of cv final *e* or cv[1] in which we would expect the vowel to be long.

The procedure for administering the test using this method is as follows:

1. Make sure that all children to be tested know the three stimulus words so they can say them without any hesitation. Before administering the test always show the student these words and ask the student to pro-

---

[1]Although there are some exceptions to the rule that vowels are usually long in the cv pattern in "words" (it is not a good rule when dealing with syllables), many more words do have the long vowel sound in this pattern, e.g., *go, me, he,* and *she.* A few exceptions are *do* and *the* when *the* is pronounced with a schwa sound at the end.

nounce them. If the student does not know one or more of them, teach them to the student and have the student come back at a later date when he or she has learned them thoroughly.

2.   Have the student respond to each line by saying the *name* of the letter or letters (not the letter(s) sound), the small stimulus word, and then the nonsense word. It is important that the student say all three exactly as outlined here.

3.   In the vowel section the student should respond by saying the name of the vowel and then the nonsense word. Before administering the vowel section you should, of course, make sure that the student knows the initial consonant letter sounds chosen to combine with the vowels, vowel teams, and special letter combinations. If the student does not respond, you can feel assured that it is because of a lack of knowledge of the vowel sound rather than a lack of knowledge of the rest of the word.

Administering a test of this nature is not at all difficult, and the results will be gratifying. You will also find this type of test to be highly reliable. Some of the reasons for, and advantages of, using this type of test are as follows:

1.   It places the testing in a situation that is analogous to actual reading. That is, the student has to react as he or she would in reading, to "decode" words rather than "encode" them as one does in spelling. Also, sounds are not tested in isolation when this method is used.

2.   Although nonsense words are used, you can presume that the student will know all of the word but the element being tested. This way if the student fails to respond properly, you can be reasonably sure it is because the student does not know the element being tested and not some other part of the word. In a few instances students will fail to respond because they do not know how to blend. If you find that a student does not respond, then you can easily check to see if blending is a problem by having the student give the sounds in isolation. If the student can give them in isolation, you can assume that blending is a problem. If the student cannot do that, you can assume that he or she does not know the letter sounds.

3.   The student is not being tested on words that may already be in his or her sight vocabulary; therefore, if the student responds correctly, you are assured that he or she does know the element being tested.

4.   When the student responds, it is not at all difficult to determine whether the response is correct or incorrect. Eldon E. Ekwall has demonstrated this with fifty or more teachers when testing a child and has gotten 100 percent agreement on all answers. When testing sounds in isolation one seldom gets 100 percent agreement from fifty teachers on any answer. It should be stressed that you should not attempt to test students until all of the stimulus words are known.

The format of the El Paso Phonics Survey does pose four possible problems. The first is the use of nonsense words. As we noted earlier, some students seem to have particular difficulty decoding nonsense words. Patricia Cunningham (1976) reported the results of an investigation in which the decoding abilities of thirty second graders were measured by two pronunciation tasks, one a real-word task, the other a nonsense-word task. The results of this study suggest that nonsense-word pronunciation tasks may not be valid indicators of a reader's decoding ability. As an alternative Cunningham recommended either using real words that the reader has probably heard but that are not likely to be in his or her sight vocabulary, or using syllables that form real words with space between, such as *de   mand* and *ob   ject*. Albert Harris and Edward Sipay (1980) suggest:

> Two points should be considered. First, it is probably easier to decode words that are in your listening vocabulary because you have a model against which your response can be compared. Second, words in context are easier to decode than words in isolation because additional cues are available. These two points lead to the conclusion that a test employing nonsense words in isolation probably requires a higher degree of decoding ability than is necessary for decoding real words in context. On such tests, therefore, one may be willing to accept a mastery level below that which might be desirable if real words were used. (p. 240)

However, Harris and Sipay state:

> It also should be noted that (1) a real word that is not in a child's vocabulary is probably as much a "nonsense" word as an artificially contrived word; (2) not all words a reader encounters will be in his or her vocabulary, and thus a high level of decoding ability is desirable; (3) alternate probable pronunciations should be accepted (e.g., *gof* = /gof/ or / guv/); and (4) nonsense words should use acceptable English spelling patterns. The latter can be accomplished by using only syllables from real words. (p. 240)

Harris and Sipay alluded to a second possible difficulty—the testing of phonics skills out of context. Here again, the student may be penalized relative to his or her performance on a test where context clues may be utilized. However, to insure that only phonics skills are being measured diagnosticians must not allow the student to use other clues to decode an unknown word. A third problem relates to the test length and the possibility that the student will tire or become frustrated. Here the examiner must use judgment, try to present the test as a fun activity, and be alert to the student's behavior.

A final possible problem in using the El Paso Phonics Survey relates to the requirement that the student give the letter name instead of the sound. Many teachers assume that this will pose undue difficulty for the student. In fact, once the student understands what is expected, he or she will pronounce the letter name and blend the parts of the nonsense word as easily as if the letter sound were first pronounced. By having the student pronounce the letter name, problems of interscorer reliability that often arise with letter sounds will be avoided. We recommend the format of the El Paso Phonics Test, not because it is without problems, but rather because this approach is the best of the available options.

We would also caution the diagnostician to use judgment when planning instruction based on the results of any phonics test. The student's performance on a variety of reading tasks should be considered. The examiner should not assume that, just because a student fails to pass certain items on a phonics test, instruction on these items is necessarily indicated. For instance, many students may have difficulty pronouncing all of the vowel patterns correctly. Yet an analysis of the oral reading performance of these students may show that they can successfully decode real words in which these vowel patterns occur. Similarly, these students may demonstrate sufficient comprehension of material read silently that contains words in which these vowel patterns are present. In this case further instruction on these vowel patterns would not be justified. What we are concerned with is the student's ability to use certain phonic skills *when necessary* to decode unknown words. If the student is able to decode successfully using context clues and beginning letter-sound associations with an ample sight vocabulary, instructional efforts might well be directed to other areas of need. Since it is possible to decode words in context even when all of the vowels have been removed, diagnosticians must be especially careful when prescribing instruction on the letter-sound correspondences of various vowels and vowel combinations.

A complete diagnosis for a disabled reader's knowledge of phonics skills usually includes testing for weaknesses in consonants, consonant blends and digraphs, and various vowel sounds. Frequently such testing also includes an evaluation of the student's ability to pronounce representative phonograms or word families. Thorough testing in this area can easily consume one-half hour of time. And after all of this time the diagnostician may find that the disabled reader is really not weak in phonics ability at all.

For students who have adequate phonics word-attack skills the examiner can save a great deal of time by simply administering a group of long nonsense words such as those in the Quick Survey Word List found in the *Ekwall Reading Inventory* (Ekwall, 1979). These are words such as *pramminciling* and *twayfrall*. Similar word lists are found in the *Botel Reading Inventory* and the *Gates-McKillop-Horowitz Reading Diagnostics Tests*, as previously noted. If the student is able to pronounce these words, there is really no need to test in the areas of phonics mentioned above or, for that matter, in the area of structural analysis. You should keep in mind that the learning of vowel rules, syllable principles, and so on, is simply a means to an end. If the student is able to decode new words, then there is no need for him or her to be able to "tell" you the vowel rules or syllable principles. Indeed, in this case, there is no need for the student to pronounce vowel or consonant sounds in isolation. For example, many students in reading methods courses can pronounce almost any word, but they have long since forgotten, or never knew, how they learned to do so. For this reason, we would recommend that students above the third-grade level (where most of these skills should have been mastered) be given a list of nonsense words at the beginning of the diagnostic procedure to determine whether they possess a knowledge of the various phonics word-attack skills. If, however, after attempting one or two of these words it becomes obvious that the student cannot pronounce them, the examiner should put the list aside and conduct further diagnosis to determine the specific phonics skills in which the student is weak.

Vowel Rules or Principles and Accent Generalizations

Research during the past decade has shown that some of the vowel rules formerly taught are, in reality, of very little value. As a result most textbooks are beginning to reflect this change. Although some research has been done on word accent, there is still very little definitive information to guide us in selecting worthwhile generalizations for teaching.

In testing for knowledge in these areas you should again remember to devise or use a test that is analogous to what the student does when the student is actually reading. For example, in testing for knowledge of various vowel rules you should ask the student to respond to a nonsense word such as *rup* rather than have the student recite the rule. (A single vowel in a closed syllable usually has the short sound.) Many students are able to recite rules that they are unable to apply, and conversely, many students seem to have learned or developed a "sixth sense" for the application of rules that they cannot recite. What the teacher should remember in testing, once again, is that various rules and generalizations are a means to an end. And, if a student can already apply the rule or generalization, he or she has achieved that end and there is little or no value in discussing or teaching the means to the end.

Vowel Rules.   In the discussion of vowel rules that follows, the most useful rules will be listed, and then a method or methods of testing for knowledge of the rule will be presented.

1.   In *words* containing a single vowel letter that appears at the end of the word, the vowel letter usually has the long vowel sound. (Note that this rule refers to words and not just syllables. There is a similar rule for single vowel letters at the end of syllables—see number 2 below).

Testing: Write several nonsense words with this pattern (such as those that follow) and say to the student, "If these were real words, how would you say them?"

sho

bri

na

Note that it is assumed the student will know the "sh," "br," and "n" sounds as well as short and long vowel sounds. If not, it would not normally be appropriate to test for vowel rule knowledge anyway.

2.   In syllables containing a single vowel letter that appears at the end of the syllable, the vowel letter may have either the long or short vowel sound. Try the long sound first. (Note that this is the same rule as in number 1 above. Here, however, the reference is to all syllables rather than syllables that are words.)

Testing: Use the same test as in number 1 above. When teaching this rule be sure to stress that the student should be flexible; i.e., try the short vowel sound if the long one does not form a word that is in the student's speaking-listening vocabulary.

3.   A single vowel in a syllable usually has the short vowel sound if it is not the last letter or is not followed by *r, w,* or *l*.

Testing: Write several nonsense words with this pattern (such as those that follow) and say to the student, "If these were real words, how would you say them?"

pid

pud

lat

4.   Vowels followed by *r* usually have a sound that is neither long nor short.

Testing: The directions for this would be the same as in number 3. Use nonsense words such as the following:

bur

ber   } All rhyme with fur

bir

bor   (bore)

dar   (rhymes with star)

5.   A *y* at the beginning of a word has the "y" consonant sound, *y* at the end of a single syllable word, when preceded by a consonant, usually has the long "i" sound, and *y* at the end of a multisyllable word, when preceded by a consonant, usually has the long "e" sound. (Some people hear it as short "i.")

Testing: The directions for this would be the same as in number 3. Use nonsense words such as the following:

cly

fory

       mippy

       yint

       yand

6.   In words ending with vowel-consonant-silent *e* the *e* is silent and the first vowel may be either long or short. Try the long sound first.

    Testing: The directions for this would be the same as in number 3. Use nonsense words such as the following:

           tete

           papt

           mide

In teaching this rule you should also stress that the student should be flexible; i.e., try the short vowel sound if the long one does not form a word in his or her speaking-listening vocabulary. It has been demonstrated that students who are taught to be flexible in attacking words when applying rules such as this become more adept at using word-attack skills than those who are not taught this flexibility.

7.   When *ai, ay, ea, ee,* and *oa* are found together, the first vowel is usually long and the second is usually silent.

    Testing: This would normally be tested under the vowels, vowel teams, and special letter combinations section of the test described earlier in the chapter and shown in Appendix A. The directions would again be the same as in number 3. Use nonsense words such at the following:

           dea

           dee

           boap

8.   The vowel pair *ow* may have either the sound heard in *cow* or the sound heard in *crow*.

    Testing: This would also normally be tested under the vowels, vowel teams, and special letter combinations section of the test described earlier in the chapter; otherwise, show the student a nonsense word such as *fow* and say, "If this were a real word, how would you say it?" If the student says it so it rhymes with *cow* then say, "Yes, and how else could we say it?" The student should then pronounce it so it then rhymes with *crow* if the student knows both common pronunciations. If not, then you would need to teach whichever one the student did not give you.

9.   When *au, aw, ou, oi,* and *oy* are found together, they usually blend to form a diphthong.

    Testing: This would also normally be tested under the vowels, vowel teams, and special letter combinations section of the test described in Appendix A. If not, handle the testing the same as described in number 3.

10. The "oo" sound is either long as in *moon* or short as in *book.*
    Testing: This is the same situation and can be handled the same as *ow* described in number 8 above.
11. If *a* is the only vowel in a syllable and is followed by *l* or *w*, then the *a* will usually be neither long nor short.
    Testing: This is the same situation and can be handled the same as the *r* control rule listed in number 4 above.

Accent Generalizations.   Accent generalizations are of less importance for a disabled reader than the learning of vowel rules. This is partially true because a student who properly attacks a new word that is in his or her speaking-listening vocabulary, but not in his or her sight vocabulary, is likely to get the right accent without any knowledge of accent generalizations. Although some guidance as to which accent generalizations to teach has been given by a study done by Carol Winkley (1966), information is still lacking concerning the utility of various accent generalizations. For these reasons the testing of a disabled reader's knowledge of accent generalizations is probably not worthwhile.

Contractions

An area of structural analysis that often causes problems for children is the learning of contractions. The method of testing them should be very similar to that of basic sight words, i.e., simply give the student a list of them and ask the student to first read the contractions and then tell what two words each contraction stands for. In scoring each contraction keep in mind that it is important that a student know each contraction since contractions appear so often in print. Although it is less important, the student should also know what two words each contraction stands for. Table 5–1 is a list of contractions, taken from five commonly used sets of basal readers, that may be used for testing purposes. Although many of the following contractions do not appear on basic sight word lists, at least one of the two words from which these contractions were derived does appear on these lists. Because writing styles vary a great deal, it would be difficult to find an "average" utility value for these words. However, it is known that contractions do cause some students considerable difficulty, and for those students who experience these difficulties remedial exercises with contractions improve their reading. Note that following each contraction is a grade-level designation. This designation represents the point at which you might expect most students to know that contraction. Remember, however, that the grade-level designations are only guidelines.

TABLE 5–1.   When contractions are known.

Word	Grade level	Word	Grade level
let's	2.9	wouldn't	3.5
didn't	2.9	she'll	3.5
it's	2.9	here's	3.5
won't	2.9	ain't	3.9
that's	2.9	couldn't	3.9
can't	2.9	they're	3.9
wasn't	2.9	they'd	3.9
isn't	2.9	you'll	4.5
hadn't	2.9	she'd	4.5
don't	3.5	weren't	4.5
I'll	3.5	I'd	4.5
we'll	3.5	you've	4.5
I've	3.5	you'd	4.5
he'll	3.5	we'd	4.5
hasn't	3.5	anybody'd	4.5
haven't	3.5	there'll	4.5
aren't	3.5	we've	4.5
I'm	3.5	who'll	4.5
he's	3.5	he'd	4.5
we're	3.5	who'd	4.5
you're	3.5	doesn't	4.5
what's	3.5	where's	4.5
there's	3.5	they've	4.5
she's	3.5	they'll	4.5

Inflectional Endings

Inflectional endings include -s and -es, 's, -d and -ed, -ing, -er, and -est. These are suffixes that indicate a change in number or tense, possessive, comparison, present participle, or third-person singular verbs. Sometimes -y and -ly are also considered to be inflectional endings. These word parts are introduced at the beginning of the reading program, and students must learn to recognize them in order to decode successfully. You may test for inflectional endings by placing the following word list in front of the student:

bake	*pale*	*slow*
baker	paler	slower
baked	paling	slowest
bakes	palest	slows

Simply say to the student: "Read these words. I will read the first one in each column." Then observe to see if the student can pronounce each word with the added ending. It is acceptable to use real words in this case since you are not concerned with the student's ability to pronounce the base word, but rather with his or her ability to recognize and correctly pronounce the added inflectional ending.

Affixes

The term *structural analysis* is used to refer to two quite different processes. Sometimes the term refers to a student's ability to derive *meaning* from word parts. Although this skill may serve to broaden a student's meaning vocabulary, such knowledge does not contribute directly to decoding ability. We are concerned here with structural analysis as a tool to aid the student in analyzing (decoding) multisyllable words. This distinction is particularly important in diagnosing prefix and suffix knowledge.

Studies such as that by Russell Stauffer (1969, pp. 348–351) suggest that the diagnostician not be concerned with the *meaning* of any suffixes and of only fifteen prefixes, based on the consistency of these meanings each time they are used. The fifteen prefixes suggested include *in-* and *de-*. The prefix *in-* means "input," "into" or "not." The prefix *de-* means "from," "away from" or "off." It is doubtful that knowledge of the meanings of even these "consistent" prefixes will aid the student in understanding words such as *intense*, *decode*, *defeat*, or many others.

However, a high percentage of the words that students will encounter as their reading level increases contains prefixes, suffixes, or both. Usually these affixes are easily recognizable and have consistently regular pronunciations. The student who can learn to *recognize* and *pronounce* these word parts will be greatly assisted in decoding the "big" words that are frequently troublesome.

Experts disagree about which prefixes and suffixes should be tested and how they should be tested and taught. The following tests present ten of the most common prefixes and nine of the most common suffixes. These affixes are presented in an attempt to provide a consensus and an appropriate scope for testing and teaching these critical skills. Our experience has shown that students who master these affixes have little difficulty in transferring this skill to other structural parts. Specific teaching procedures will be presented in the remediation section of this chapter.

There are three simple tests that you can give to evaluate a student's ability to recognize and pronounce prefixes and suffixes. The first two use the same format and rationale as the test for inflectional endings presented in the previous section.

Prefix Test.   Place the following word list in front of the student:

play	mote	form
replay	remote	conform
display	promote	inform
misplay	demote	deform

take	tend	pack
retake	intend	unpack
intake	contend	prepack
mistake	extend	repack
	distend	
	pretend	

Say to the student: "Read these words. I will read the first one in each column." Then observe to see if the student can pronounce each base with the added prefix. Some of the prefixes are tested more than once. Thus you can judge if the student consistently misses this word part. If the student misses any of the items, you must determine whether the failure resulted from the student's inability to pronounce the prefix, blend the prefix with the base, or both. This will determine the remedial approach that you will employ. The same procedure is used for the suffix test that follows.

Suffix Test.   Place the following word list in front of the student:

joy	invent	base	elect
joyous	inventive	basement	election
joyful	inventable	baseness	elective
joyless		baseless	

The third test requires the student to pronounce two-syllable words containing one common affix. On this test the examiner does not pronounce the base word, so the task is significantly more difficult for the student than the two previous tests.

Affix Test.   Place the following word list in front of the student:

uncall	treeness
proclaim	sunning
indeem	bookful
demark	raytion
prestrain	darkous

Say to the student: "Read as many of these words as you can. Some are not real words." In this case, the student must use all three steps of decoding through structural analysis: (1) separating the word parts; (2) pronouncing the word parts; and (3) blending the separate parts to pronounce the whole word. If the student fails to pronounce the base word correctly, this suggests that the student lacks sufficient word recognition or phonics ability, which is prerequisite to decoding through structural analysis.

Syllabication Principles

The testing and teaching of syllabication is the most controversial area of structural analysis. Many authorities believe that syllabication should not be taught at all. We agree, however, with Patrick Groff (1981) who, after reviewing the literature, concluded:

> The number of studies that support the teaching of syllables for word recognition stands in contrast to those that advise against this kind of teaching. It is difficult, in fact, to find empirical data to support the contentions that the successful decoding of words is not related to syllabication skills, that the syllable is too complex a phenomenon to be used by children for word recognition, or that it is impossible for a child to work out the pronunciation of a word through an analysis of the sound of its syllables. (p. 662)

Part of the problem results from an adherence by many experts and practitioners to syllabication instruction that is based on dictionary word divisions. Diagnosticians should not be concerned with the student's ability to identify the *specific* points in words where syllable division takes place according to the dictionary. This skill, often called *end-of-line division*, is frequently tested. Unfortunately, it is not useful for decoding purposes. Indeed, the only time that this skill is required is when one is engaged in formal writing and there is no dictionary at hand. To further complicate the matter, dictionaries do not always agree on where words should be divided. Groff states:

> The syllabication taught children for learning to read should not be traditional dictionary syllabication. Despite the fact that dictionary syllabication has often been recommended to teachers, its rules are not based on linguistic research but rather on the arbitrary decisions of typesetters from the early days. Dictionary syllabication rules have little to do with the actual sound patterns of syllables, are often impossible to apply because they are inconsistent, and are not truly useable by children for word recognition. . . . (p. 663)

In order to apply most of the dictionary syllabication rules that are taught, the reader must first pronounce the word to be divided. Since you are seeking to help the student do precisely the opposite—that is, learn to divide the word for aid in pronunciation—you must use another approach.

First determine if the student can *hear* the separate parts (syllables) of words. Then test to find out if the student can proceed through the following *decoding* steps: (1) separate the word parts (this is a visual task); (2) pronounce the word parts (usually a base word with the addition of an inflectional ending and/or one or two affixes); and (3) blend the separate parts to pronounce the whole word.

This process is analogous to that of phonic analysis on words of one syllable. With phonic analysis the student separates, pronounces, and blends individual sounds or phonemes. With structural analysis (of which syllabication is a key component), the student separates, pronounces, and blends larger units or syllables.

In order to test a student's ability to hear the separate parts (syllables) of words, you need only give the following direction and ask the student to listen carefully: "I am going to say some words. Tell me how many syllables or parts you hear in each word." Then pronounce a series of words containing one to four syllables, such as *cowboy*, *intention*, *steam*, *disagreement*, and *randomly*. The words should be pronounced slowly and clearly, without, however, exaggerating the syllable divisions in the words. After only a few words it will be easy to determine whether the student possesses sufficient auditory understanding of syllabication. This skill is not, of course, what is required of a student when decoding. It is, however, a necessary prerequisite. The student who fails on this test will require instruction at this level before proceeding to the next step.

One way to evaluate the student's ability to use syllabication as a decoding tool is to observe the student's performance when reading orally material that contains a number of multisyllabic words. If the student does not attack these words at all or merely gives the appropriate beginning sound and then guesses wildly, he or she will likely need instruction in syllabication.

To test for knowledge of specific syllable principles you may give the student some nonsense words or long words that are not likely to be in the student's sight vocabulary and ask the student to draw lines separating the syllables. Below is a list of some of the most commonly taught and generally accepted syllable principles, as well as words you can use to test students' knowledge of these principles.

1. When two consonants stand between two vowels, the word is usually divided between the consonants, e.g., *dag-ger* and *cir-cus*.

    botnap

    daggal

    In some of the newer materials words are divided after the double consonant, e.g., *dagg-er*. It should be remembered that in reading we are usually teaching syllabication as a means of word attack. Therefore, you should also accept a division after double consonants as correct even though the dictionary would not show the division in that way.

2.   When one consonant stands between two vowels, try dividing first so
      that the consonant goes with the second vowel, e.g., *pa-per* and *mo-tor*.
      Students should be taught that flexibility is required in using this rule,
      e.g., if this does not place the vowel in a pattern to give a word in the
      student's speaking-listening vocabulary, then the student should divide
      it so that the consonant goes with the first vowel as in *riv-er* and *lev-er*.

      lador

      mafel

3.   When a word ends in a consonant and *le*, the consonant usually begins
      the last syllable, e.g., *ta-ble* and *hum-ble*.

      nable

      frable

      (The "le" sound is usually heard as "ul.")

4.   Compound words are usually divided between word parts and between
      syllables in these parts, e.g., *hen-house* and *po-lice-man*.

      cowperson

      dogthrower

5.   Prefixes and suffixes usually form separate syllables.

      rebaseness

      distendable

As indicated above, principles 1 and 2 have many exceptions. When evaluating students' performance on these items you should be most concerned with
whether the student divided the word at an *appropriate* place, not whether
the student divided the word precisely according to the rule. For example, in
the real word *basket*, a student could appropriately divide the word as
ba-sket, bas-ket, or *bask-et* and still end up with pronounceable units. However, the following divisions would be clearly unacceptable: *b-asket* or
baske-t.

Another way to test a student's ability to syllabicate is to present the
student with a list of real words that are sufficiently difficult that the student
would be unlikely to recognize them as sight words. Such a list of words
follows:

automotive	premeditate
displacement	imperfection
conformation	unreasonable
remarkable	misplaying
impeachable	complicated

By observing the student's attempts to decode these words, the examiner
should be able to determine whether the student has difficulty (1) dividing the
words into appropriate (pronounceable) units; (2) pronouncing the parts; (3)

blending the parts into whole words; or (4) some combination of all three difficulties.

Two additional facts bear mentioning. First, the goal here, much as with instruction in phonics for smaller words, is to give the student sufficient word-attack skills to be able to use them, together with context, to decode unfamiliar words *in the act of reading*. If the student possess some ability to use context, it is seldom necessary for the student to arrive at a "perfect" pronunciation through phonics or structural analysis. Second, all of the word-attack skills will be insufficient if the student has a severely limited vocabulary. New words that the student decodes must be at least minimally recognizable to the student in order for the student to arrive at the correct pronunciation.

These facts were well illustrated by a student named Tony. When his teacher presented multisyllabic words to Tony in list form, he had great difficulty pronouncing them in spite of excellent direct instruction. However, when the teacher presented the same words in sentences, Tony was able to decode them with but a moment's hesitation. For example, when presented the word *engagement* in isolation, Tony read *en-gag-uh-ment*. Yet when reading the sentence, *The boy gave his girl an engagement ring*, Tony pronounced the word correctly. In this case, Tony had sufficient vocabulary knowledge for context to assist him in combination with his structural-analysis skills. Incidentally, after substantial practice in the act of reading, "big" words like *engagement* became easily recognizable sight words for Tony.

The example of Tony serves not only as a conclusion to this section but also as an introduction to the next section.

CONTEXT CLUES

Research such as that done by Alan Robinson (1963) on context clues indicates that a student would be able to attack an unfamiliar word with the use of context clues alone only a small percentage of the time. However, when a student uses context clues, it is usually in conjunction with phonics or structural analysis. For example, a student may often read up to an unfamiliar word, sound the first letter, and then, using the clues gained from both, say the word. (He saw the man who was coming h__ __ __ [home].) Or, the student may read up to a word and pronounce the first syllable. (When the dis__ __ __ __ __ was determined, they stopped the measurement [distance].) The use of context clues is one of the most important word-attack skills a student can possess. Paul Burns and Leo Schell (1975) suggest that "the use of context may well be the major skill which distinguishes connected meaningful reading from reading of word lists." (p. 90) They quote Nita Wyatt's observation that "the good reader uses context to predict what an unknown word may be *before* the analysis process or *as* the process begins." (p. 90)

Beginning teachers often make the mistake of thinking that children will automatically learn to use context clues without any instruction in their use. Many children do seem to use both picture clues as well as written context clues almost innately; however, some children, especially those who become disabled readers, need specific instruction in this important skill.

For teaching purposes context clues are often categorized according to type such as "summary clues," "experience clues," and "synonym or definition clues" as explained by Ruth Strang, McCullough, and Traxler (1967). However, for testing purposes this is not necessary.

In constructing exercises for testing you should obtain several short paragraphs written at varying grade levels, e.g., first, third, and fifth grade. Be sure not to employ materials commonly used, such as well-known graded reading inventories, as many children will have already been given these reading passages or are quite likely to encounter them later. Type or print the passage on one side of a 5″ × 8″ card and leave out several words. Passages written for first or second graders should be typed with primary type or printed in letters of at least an equivalent size or larger. Words chosen to be omitted should be those for which few or no substitutions could be made in the context in which they are used. They should also be words that could easily be derived from the context if the student is able to use context clues. Where words are omitted, you should substitute Xs or dashes for each letter in the word. This also gives the student a clue as to word length, which again is analogous to the clues that he or she would have in actually reading. On the back of the card you may wish to include the directions you will give the student, along with the reading passage and answers to be supplied in each of the blanks.

The front of the card might appear as in Figure 5–1; the back of the card would then appear as in Figure 5–2.

The testing of context clues in this manner should not be confused with the *cloze* technique, which is a method of testing students' comprehension—explained in Chapter 6. In using the standard *cloze* procedure every fifth word is omitted and a standard-sized line is left for each omitted word on which the student is to write the word that he or she thinks was omitted. In using the procedure described above there are no standards in terms of number of words to be omitted or percentage of right and wrong answers. Your judgment of the student's ability to supply oral answers in the reading passages used for context clues will be based on your opinion of how well the student does in relation to other average readers of the same grade level.

If students are unable to use context clues when they read, they should be tested on their ability to use them orally. For example, you may wish to simply read a sentence leaving out a word and then ask the student what word might be used where the blank appeared in oral context. Students who

Fred had a pet cat.

Its name xxx Jiffy.

Jiffy liked xx run xxx play.

Jiffy xxx not like Fred's dog.

And, Fred's dog xxx not xxxx Jiffy.

FIGURE 5–1.

Read this story. Some of the words have been left out.

When a word was left out some x's were put in its place.

As you read the story try to say the words that you think

belong in the story where the x's are.

Fred had a pet dog.

Its name was Jiffy.

Jiffy liked to run and play.

Jiffy did not like Fred's dog.

And, Fred's dog did not like Jiffy.

FIGURE 5–2.

are able to do considerably better on oral context clues than on written context clues may be lacking so severely in word-recognition skills that they are
unable to concentrate their efforts on the use of context clues. On the other
hand, those students who do no better in oral exercises using context clues
than they did in written exercises are usually simply unaware of the value
and use of context clues and need to be taught how to make use of this im-

portant word-attack skill. The teacher should also be aware that sufficient oral vocabulary and the ability to use speech effectively are essential prerequisites for teaching context clues. A child who says "me go" or "her does that" is not ready to profit from instruction in context clues.

An alternative or additional procedure for assessing a student's ability to use context clues is to ask the student to read orally from material where he or she will make about five to ten errors per page. While the student reads, note whether miscalled words are logical replacements; that is, does the student rely on context clues when other word-attack skills are inadequate? As the difficulty of the material increases, the student's ability to derive meaning from context naturally decreases. Because this is a potentially frustrating task for the student, you should be sure to keep this part of the evaluation brief.

The diagnostician should bear in mind that students' difficulties with context clues may be reflected in two opposite behaviors. Many students fail to use context clues adequately and appear to read word by word. A common example of this type of problem is the student who reads the sentence, *The boy went into the house,* as, *The . . . boy . . . went . . . into . . . the . . . horse.* This student apparently overrelies on graphic information at the expense of meaning clues. At the other extreme are students who overrely on context. These students may appear to be reading fluently, but, in fact, what they read may not be what was written. Such a student might read the sentence given above as, *The boy went into the garage.* Both forms of context-clue difficulties are detrimental to the students' reading ability.

Paul Burns and Leo Schell (1975) listed several common traits associated with *not* using context clues. These include:

1.   Stops when meeting an unknown word;
2.   Overrelies on other skills, such as configuration and beginning/ending sounds;
3.   Practices less effective analysis techniques, such as relying on signals from the teacher or on picture clues.

EFFICIENCY SKILLS

Some students may have mastered the decoding skills of phonic, structural, and contextual analysis and possess an adequate sight vocabulary yet still have difficulty reading fluently. Most often these students lack the ability to read with appropriate speed, accuracy, or both. They may try to read material too quickly and thus inaccurately, or their reading rate may be unusually slow. They may lack the ability to read with proper phrasing or expression. Some of these students consistently ignore punctuation; some persist in finger pointing or subvocalizing when reading silently. We consider students who have these difficulties and others like them to have problems with "efficiency skills." Somehow, in the process of learning to read, these students failed to put together the various pieces of the puzzle of reading. Often these students have merely picked up faulty habits along the way that have persisted. Unfortunately, teachers do not always realize that these students have efficiency problems that can be remedied with a host of appropriate and effective procedures. Sometimes teachers will continue to drill these students on phonics or basic sight words, which may only make the problem worse.

In the remediation section of this chapter we will offer specific methods for assisting students who have difficulty reading efficiently. Usually no specific diagnosis is necessary to spot these problems. Teachers who have carefully observed their students when reading and who have conducted a thorough enough diagnosis to eliminate other decoding-skill problems may reasonably assume that these students will benefit from techniques designed to overcome reading-efficiency difficulties. However, a specific procedure for assessing students' reading-efficiency skills follows.

The examiner should have the student read passages orally at two different levels—one at a comfort or independent reading level and a second at the instructional level. As the student reads, the examiner should complete transcriptions on copies of the passages (as described in Chapter 11) and evaluate the student's performance in the following areas:

1. *Speed*—Did the student read too fast, causing unnecessary word-recognition errors, or was the reading speed too slow for acceptable comprehension and adequate rate of learning?
2. *Phrasing*—Was the phrasing appropriate, or did the student read word by word or with other inappropriate phrasing?
3. *Punctuation*—Were punctuation cues followed, or did the student ignore or misinterpret punctuation marks?
4. *Accuracy*—Did the student correctly pronounce the words in the selection, or were words miscalled due to excessive speed or poor phrasing? If omissions, repetitions, insertions, or substitutions occurred, were these the result of poor decoding skills, efficiency problems, or both? (See Chapter 11 for a discussion of techniques for remediating problems of omissions, repetitions, or substitutions.)

The following efficiency-skill weaknesses may be observed by the examiner while the student is reading silently: lip movements, finger pointing, or head movements. An examination of the student's performance on the basic sight words tests (described in Chapter 4) will also provide a clue to efficiency skills. A student whose performance is significantly better on the test of basic sight words in isolation than in phrases is likely to have a problem with efficiency skills.

CONFIGURATION CLUES

Some authorities believe that it is helpful for beginning and/or disabled readers to receive instruction in the use of configuration clues. We would simply suggest that in your day-to-day teaching procedures you note whether the student is confusing words of similar configuration and whether the student seems to be aware of differences in words with extenders and descenders, capital and lower-case letters, and with double letters.

Where it is apparent the student is not fully aware of these differences, remediation as described in Part B of this chapter (under the heading "Configuration Clues") would be appropriate.

DICTIONARY SKILLS

Although few would argue the importance of a thorough knowledge of the use of the dictionary for students from the middle elementary grades through their adult lives, the lack of knowledge of dictionary skills is not a serious problem for disabled readers. Most of the basic word-analysis skills are, or should be, achieved by the time most students begin to work with the dictionary. Furthermore, only a very small percentage of one's total meaning vocabulary is achieved through the use of the dictionary. Therefore, for seriously disabled readers it is not recommended that a test for knowledge of dictionary skills even be included in the initial diagnosis. For older, less disabled readers, however, you may wish to take inventory of their ability to use the dictionary.

Part B: REMEDIATION

The whole-word approach or sight approach to the learning of words is rapid at first; but as students begin to encounter many new words, they usually find that they must use some method of word analysis or word attack. In most cases a student attacks new words by using a combination of several methods such as phonics, structural analysis, configuration, and context clues. Many readers become disabled because they have not developed one or more of these word-attack skills. Before beginning work on the remediation of a student's word-attack skills you should first determine whether the student is lacking in only one area of word-attack skills or whether he or she needs to "start from scratch" and learn how to use all of the skills mentioned above.

There are several ways of teaching the various word-attack skills. For example, some commercial programs present a great many rules for long and short vowel sounds, vowel combinations, syllabication, etc. Students are taught these rules and are expected to memorize the rules as well as their application. Other programs present lists of graphemes for which the students are to learn their phoneme equivalent either in isolation or when blended with a familiar phonogram. In this type of program few rules are taught. An attempt is simply made to get the student to the automatic response level. Before beginning a specific program of remediation you should also attempt to discover what type of word-attack program each student has had. If, for example, a student has been through a rule-oriented phonics program and failed to learn, it may be more productive if the student is instructed in techniques that do not require learning and application of a great many rules. On the other hand, a student who has been taught using a program in which few, if any, rules are taught can often benefit by learning certain worthwhile rules and/or principles.

Most students are unable to describe the type of program they have been through and are also unaware of the publisher of the materials from which they have been taught. However, if they are asked whether they ever had a book in which there were stories about Tag and Dot and Jim, or Baby Sally or Dick and Jane they can usually tell you with little hesitation. For this reason we would suggest that a part of your diagnostic kit contain a list of characters from the most common basal readers and supplementary readers or phonics programs used in your state. This can easily be compiled by looking through the various materials commonly used in your state or from areas from which you receive transfer students. You will, of course, need to be somewhat familiar with the type of word-attack program presented in each series.

In teaching word-attack skills in remedial reading you should consider that students who are deficient in their ability to attack new words may have gotten that way because they were not able to learn by the method used by their regular classroom teacher. An eclectic approach to word-analysis skills may have been used, and a student predisposed to learning through any one approach may not have gotten enough instruction in that one approach. On the other hand, the student's classroom teacher may have used a rule-oriented program, as mentioned previously, from which some students experience success, yet from which some are doomed to almost certain failure if not exposed to other methods.

In beginning a program of word-attack skills with a new student you should first attempt to discover whether the student is immediately successful with whatever approach you choose in the beginning. If you then discover that the student is still not successful, be prepared to switch to another approach. You should also examine your own methods of teaching from time to time to insure that you are not wedded to any one approach. The use of any one approach that seems best to you may often be beneficial in teaching developmental reading. However, being a one-approach teacher in remedial reading is highly undesirable.

PHONICS AND STRUCTURAL ANALYSIS

Many of the activities that follow appear to be simple testing situations if they are not followed up with correctional procedures when a student fails to respond correctly. Remedial reading if done properly is, of course, a highly individualized procedure. When the student responds incorrectly on either written or oral exercises, he or she should be corrected immediately so as not to reinforce a wrong response. These correctional procedures can either be carried out by the teacher while the student works or they can be done by a teacher's aide or by an older student who is familiar with the material and who can, in turn, immediately correct any wrong answers.

It is essential for the remedial teacher to recognize that substantial direct instruction will usually be required for remedial readers to master the various word-attack skills. The teacher must demonstrate the skill to be learned, present the subtasks in a systematic way, and assist the student in practicing the new skill *before* resorting to seatwork or other reinforcement material that will help the student to practice the skill. We also strongly recommend that teachers provide sentences or stories for students to read as they are learning each new skill so that they can immediately apply their new knowledge in the act of reading. We want students to rely on context clues as they are learning phonics and structural analysis skills. We also want to be sure that students understand that the purpose of our instruction is to aid them in decoding so that they can obtain *meaning* from printed words.

Phonic Elements

The term *phonic elements* is often used to define various letter combinations and the sounds they represent. We have chosen to use the term rather than use *phoneme* for sounds and *grapheme* for its written equivalent in this case because some letter combinations (phonic elements) consist of more than one phoneme and consequently more than one grapheme.

There are, of course, many methods that can be used in teaching the various elements. One typical procedure is as follows:

1. Developing awareness of hearing the sound:
   1.1. Say, "Listen to these words. Each of them begins with the 'bl' sound. Circle the *bl* on each word on your paper as you hear the sound. *Blow—blue—blunder*, etc."

2.   Developing awareness of seeing the sound:
        2.1. Tell the student to circle all of the words in a passage that begin
        with *bl*.
3.   Providing practice in saying words with the "bl" sound:
        3.1. Pronounce each word and have students pronounce it after you.

                blow
                blue
                blunder
                bleed
                blast

4.   Providing practice in blending the "bl" sound with common word fam-
        ilies or phonograms:
        4.1. Teach or use several phonograms with which students are already
        familiar such as *ock* and *ush*. Put the *bl* in one column, the phono-
        gram in a second column, and the two combined in a third column
        as follows:

                bl   ock   block
                bl   ack   black
                bl   ur   blur
                bl   under   blunder

        Instruct the student to say *bl* (the two letters and not the sound)
        and then the phonogram (this time sound represented by the letters
        in the phonogram) and then the word formed by the two.
        4.2   Another similar exercise that works well and gives practice in
        blending is to place the letters and words as follows:

                bl   <u>fl</u>ock   (block)
                bl   <u>la</u>ck   (black)
                bl   <u>fu</u>r   (blur)
                bl   <u>th</u>under   (blunder)

        Instruct the student to say *bl*, then the middle word, and then take
        off the underlined letters from the middle column word and re-
        place it or them with *bl* and say the new word that is formed. If
        students cannot do this mentally, have them write the complete
        word shown in column 3 above.
5.   Asking the student to make a list of some words that begin with *bl*. If
        this is too difficult for the student, provide him or her with a list of some
        phonograms from which some *bl* words can be formed. Ask the student
        to say each word as he or she writes it.
6.   Providing practice in reading *bl* words. Either present a paragraph or
        story that has a number of *bl* words in it or write a paragraph using the
        bl blend in a number of words.

        The above procedure takes the student through the critical steps in
learning a new phonic element. Steps 1, 2, and 3 help the student to recognize
the association between the letter(s) and sound that you are teaching. This

provides the foundation for the low-level phonics knowledge (sound to symbol) that we described in the diagnosis section of this chapter. Steps 4 and 5 teach the student high-level phonics (symbol to sound) and blending ability, which are required to apply phonics as a decoding tool. Step 6 not only reinforces the previous learning but also gives the student an opportunity to apply the skill in the act of reading.

One important factor to remember in teaching any phonic element is that you should not expect to teach it and then assume the student has full recall and use of it from then on. To begin with, remember that you are likely to have received the student because he or she did not learn at a normal rate or through whatever methods the classroom teacher used initially. Furthermore, it takes many exposures to a word before it becomes a known sight word. It is unlikely that a student can learn a certain phonic element without some initial teaching and then repeated exposures to that element in various types of written and/or oral exercises.

When teaching a group of students to listen for, and become aware of, sounds in words you can increase participation by giving everyone three cards on which are printed the numbers 1, 2, and 3 and/or the words *beginning, middle*, and *end* on the reverse side of the card. As you say words, have each student respond by holding up the appropriate card. For example, in teaching a lesson on the 'n' sound you might say, "I am going to say some words, some of which have the 'n' sound in them. If you hear it at the beginning of the word, hold up your number 1 card. If you hear it in the middle of the word, hold up your number 2 card. And if you hear it at the end of the word, hold up your number 3 card. Some words may have more than one 'n' sound in them. If you hear the 'n' sound at the beginning and middle, then hold up both your number 1 and 2 cards," etc. This type of exercise will quickly enable you to evaluate which students are learning to recognize the "n" sound and which are not. When only calling on one student there is often a tendency to overlook other students who do not respond.

The activity just described is an example of an *every pupil response technique* (EPRT). Such techniques are very effective. They not only increase the number of student responses but also tend to improve the on-task time of all students, who know that they must be prepared to respond at all times. This way less time is wasted and the learning rate for all pupils increases. In addition, as previously noted, EPRT enables the teacher to conduct diagnosis while teaching. Other examples of EPRT include:

1. *Yes-no cards*—to provide group response to "yes-no" or "right-wrong" questions. For example, the teacher might say, "I am going to read some words that start with the 'b' sound and some that start with other sounds. If the word I read starts with the 'b' sound, hold up your 'yes' card. If it starts with another sound, hold up your 'no' card. Does everybody understand? Good. Ready? *ball, tree, house, bat, Bill, dig*," etc.

2. *Thumbs up, thumbs down*—the same as yes-no cards; thumbs up indicates "yes," thumbs down indicates "no."

3. *Open eyes, close eyes*—the same as above; this method has the added advantage of eliminating the possibility that students will mimic the responses of others.

4. *1, 2, 3 . . .*—to provide a group repetition response. For example, the teacher might say, "Printed on this chart are a number of words that begin and end with sounds you know, so I know you will be able to read them. Say each word on the signal as I point to it. Ready? . . ." As the teacher points to each word, he or she says: "1, 2, 3. . . ." The students then read the word quickly. After the list is read in order, the teacher may use the pointer to point to words quickly in random order. Students enjoy the speed and challenge of this technique and it provides excellent practice.

Note that the first three techniques listed above are appropriate for practicing low-level (recognition) phonics tasks, while the last method may be used to have students practice high-level (production) skills, blending skills, or both.

Some other types of exercises for practicing phonics skills follow. Most of these should only be used after direct instruction has taken place.

1. Omit letters from a word used in context and give several choices to be filled in. This usually encourages the student to try several sounds in order to arrive at the correct answer.

   1.1. Cindy and Dwight like to go ____ishing.

   (g, f, b, h)

   1.2. Sam forgot his ____ooks at school.

   (d, p, b, q)

   1.3. Paul did a goo____ job of washing the car.

   (d, p, b, g)

2. Give each student an envelope with several cards in it. On the front and back of each card print one letter. For example, each student might have five cards, each of which has one of the following letters: *c, f, g, h,* and *d.* As you say words, have students hold up the card that has a letter representing the sound they hear at the beginning, middle, and end of various words. Do this same type of exercise having students hold up various vowel letters and vowel pairs that they hear in words.

3. Have students write and read their own and other students' alliterative-type stories. For example, a junior high student's paragraph illustrating the use of *f* read as follows:

   Once in a fir forest there were four fast fireflies. The four fireflies like to fly forward and backward. Once on the fourth of February the four fireflies flew fast forward and then fast backward into a flaming fire. Now there are not four fireflies in the fir forest.

4. Have students scan the newspaper and circle or underline learned phonic elements. Discuss the words found.

5. Start a "thing box" in which you simply put many miscellaneous articles such as a ball, book, bike (toy), toothbrush, tank, dress (doll), and drum. Have boxes labeled b, d, t, etc. As students pick up each article, they say the name of the article, listen for the initial sound, and then sort the items into their respective boxes. This type of exercise can be made self-corrective by using a label maker to put the correct beginning letter on the bottom of each item.

6. The same type of exercise described in number 5 above can be done using a file folder in which an envelope is glued or taped to one inside fold. This envelope can contain many pictures representing various initial consonants, blends, digraphs, vowels, etc. On the other side of the inside fold make pockets by cutting out pieces of tagboard and taping them on the sides and bottom. Students then take pictures out of the envelope and sort them into the proper pockets. This exercise can also be made self-correcting by writing the correct letter (grapheme) on the back of the pictures. A file folder done in this manner to teach vowel sounds is illustrated in Figure 5-3.

7. Tell the students to put an X in front of each word in the list on the right that has the same beginning sound as the thing shown in the picture on the left.

```
_____ dog
_____ from
_____ fright
_____ glow
_____ free
```

8. "Say the words below and listen for the long or short vowel sound in each word. Write long in the blank after the word if you hear the long vowel sound in the word and short if you hear the short vowel sound in the word."

bid	_____	he	_____
make	_____	lake	_____
up	_____	three	_____

Another similar exercise calls for the student to say each word and mark the long and short vowels over each vowel letter using the breve (⌣) and macron (—).

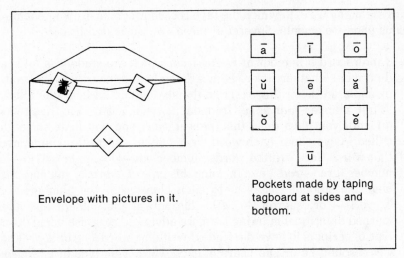

Envelope with pictures in it.

Pockets made by taping tagboard at sides and bottom.

FIGURE 5–3.   File folder for vowel sounds.

9. "Say each of the following words to yourself and listen for the vowel sound. Then write the words from the top list under the word that has the same vowel sound."

Spain	came	mood
freight	Mike	piece
ate	each	trial
me	ran	Sue
blue	meat	sleigh

too	line	tree	lake	cat
_____	_____	_____	_____	_____
_____	_____	_____	_____	_____
_____	_____	_____	_____	_____

10. "Find the vowel sound that is heard in each blank by looking at the key word preceding each sentence. Then find the correct word from the list that has that vowel sound in it." (Help the student with the stimulus words to the left of the numbers if he or she does not know them before beginning the exercise.)

let—hop—lid—lake—lad—like

(Ed)   1. Father _____ me go with him.
(cat) 2. The small _____ went with his mother.
(cake) 3. We went to the _____ to go fishing.
(it)   4. Father put the _____ on the pot.
(kite) 5. I _____ to go fishing.
(top) 6. Can you _____ over the fence?

There are many ways in which the tape recorder can be used in teaching the various phonic elements. Several of these are illustrated below.

11. Tape record a number of words from which the student is to listen to determine whether he or she hears the long or short vowel sound. For example, in doing this exercise the student would hear the following: "First, number your paper from one to twenty. Turn the tape recorder off until you have done this (*pause*). Now you will hear some words called. As you hear each word write *long* or *short* after the number of that word. Here are the words: number one—*dog*, number two—*lake*, number three—*rod*," etc. In doing this type of exercise you may wish to have the student simply mark each blank after the numbers with a breve (⌣) or macron (—). (Do this only if the student has already learned diacritical marking.) A more advanced exercise using the same type of script is to have the student write the word *long* or *short* and the vowel sound he or she hears in each word. This type of exercise can also be done with initial consonants, consonant digraphs, etc.

One major advantage of the tape recorder is that it can act as a self-correcting device for various types of exercises. This is illustrated below:

12. Each student is given a sheet of paper prepared as follows:
     1. d f g t   f r   b n
     2. t c v w   p l s n
     3. etc.
   The tape recorder script would be as follows: "On your paper are numbers, and after each number are four letters, a space, and then four more letters. Now you will hear some words called. You are to circle the letter you hear at the beginning of each word from the first group of four letters and the letter you hear at the end of the word from the second set of letters by each number. Here are the words. Be sure to listen carefully. Number one—*din*, number two—*camps*," etc. "Now we will check your work. The first word was *din*. You should have circled the *d* from the first group of letters and the *n* from the second group of letters. Circle these two letters now if you did not get them right the first time. The second word was *camps*. You should have circled the *c* from the first group of letters and the *s* from the second group of letters. Circle the two letters now if you did not get them right the first time. The third word was . . ." etc.

When using the tape recorder keep in mind that almost any type of material that you could check as a class exercise can be checked by the tape recorder. Although it takes a little more time to record these exercises in the beginning, it will certainly save much time in the long run.

Blending

Many students learn the various consonant and vowel sounds in isolation or are able to give the sounds in isolation but are unable to blend various sounds together to form words. The inexperienced teacher who tests sounds in isolation may be led to believe some students have no problem with sounds when, in reality, their inability to blend known sounds may be as disabling as not knowing the sounds at all. The importance of the blending skill in the word-attack process cannot be overstressed. A study by Jill Whaley and Michael Kibby (1980) found that word synthesis (blending) was related to beginning reading achievement regardless of the reading strategy employed by the students. Research by Wanda Homen (1977) determined that blending skill was equally predictive of first graders' reading success as knowledge of letter names.

If the testing procedure described in Part A of this chapter is followed, students' ability to blend will be tested along with their knowledge of grapheme-phoneme relationships. In another article, Jill Whaley (1975) presents some excellent procedures for the direct teaching of blending skills. These include:

1. Teach the child to use his or her voice to "slide" through the sounds of unfamiliar words. The teacher tells the student to say the sound when the teacher points to a letter and continue saying the sound until the teacher's finger points to the next letter. After some practice at this, the finger pointing is eliminated and the child is told to read through a word as if the teacher were still pointing to it.

2. Use analogies between blending and other activities, such as skating. The teacher may place large letters on the floor and have the child "skate" from one to another while saying the letter sounds out loud. Or, the teacher may have the student "stretch" a rubber band between words.

3. Provide kinesthetic reinforcement by tapping the child near the shoulder for the beginning sound and lower down the arm for subsequent sounds while the teacher pronounces the word. Then the teacher says the whole word while sliding a hand the length of the student's arm. The student may then practice the exercise by using one of his or her own hands on the other arm.

4. Use scrabble squares or other movable letters, which may be gradually moved apart while a word is sounded slowly, then brought back together as the whole word is pronounced. Again, after the teacher demonstrates, the child may move the letters.

5. Tell the child to form his or her mouth in preparation for saying the beginning sound of a syllable, but then to say the following vowel instead. "Such a technique would seem to force the child to think ahead and be

prepared for the second sound rather than concentrating solely on the first sound, thus eliminating an undesirable stuttering, letter by letter work attack."   (p. 100)

The following exercises may be assigned for additional assistance to students who have blending difficulties:

1. After students have learned to hear beginning, middle, and ending sounds, they can begin blending using the technique called *double substitution*. In using this technique you should start by using an oral presentation, for example:

    1.1. "What word begins like *down* and ends like *hog*?" (*dog*)
    1.2. "What word begins like *dig* and ends like *log*?" (*dog*)
    1.3. "What word has two letters that begin like *white* and end like *hen*?" (*when*)

    After considerable practice using an oral presentation you may wish to give students word lists and directions as follows:

    "Using the beginning sound from the word in the first column and the ending sound from the word in the second column write a new word in the blank in the third column. Say the word as you write it."

    Initial consonants
    1. can   2. bar   3. _____ (car)
    1. name   2. go   3. _____ (no)
    1. to   2. lake   3. _____ (take)
    etc.

    Initial consonant blends
    1. from   2. crank   3. _____ (Frank)
    1. stair   2. land   3. _____ (stand)
    1. plum   2. clay   3. _____ (play)
    etc.

    Initial consonant digraphs
    1. champ   2. blew   3. _____ (chew)
    1. wheel   2. gale   3. _____ (whale)
    1. thin   2. sing   3. _____ (thing)
    etc.

2. Put several initial consonants, blends, or digraphs on the chalkboard in a column. To the right of these put several familiar phonograms (see example below).

        ch op
        sl ap

Tell students that you will quickly point to a beginning consonant or blend on the left and then to one of the phonograms on the right. They are to say the word formed by the combination of the two. This exercise works well with three to four students. You should use your hand and sweep across from the initial sound to the phonogram very rapidly. Do not hesitate to use combinations that form nonsense words.

3. "Read the questions below. Letters are missing from the beginning of each word. Write the missing letters in the blank using one of the sets from the row at the top to answer the question."

    br   cr   dr   fr   gr   pr   tr   bl   cl   fl   pl   thr

1. What do you do when you are thirsty?   _____ink
2. What do you do when you get bigger?   _____ow
3. What does a baseball pitcher do?   _____ow
4. What does a rooster do?   _____ow
5. What does the wind do?   _____ow
6. What do you do at recess time?   _____ay

Rules for Hard and Soft *C* and *G*

Most reading specialists agree that students are more likely to learn and remember rules, generalizations, and/or principles governing sounds when they have been learned inductively or by the discovery technique. The rule, as generally stated, governing the hard and soft sounds of *c* and *g* is as follows: When *c* and *g* are followed by *e, i,* or *y,* they usually retain their soft sounds; if they are followed by any other letter, they usually retain their hard sounds. In teaching this rule or generalization to a student or to a group of students the procedure would be as follows. (Only *c* is illustrated; however, *g* would be done in the same manner.)

1. Discuss the fact that the letter *c* stands for more than one sound.
2. Discuss the fact that rules can usually be applied that help us to remember which sound to use in various situations.
3. Suggest that a list be made to examine a number of *c* words to see if students can make up their own rule.
4. Have students think of a number of *c* words while you list them on the chalkboard. Examples might be as follows:

can	came	cry
cent	cycle	cog
cigar	century	color
cancer	cut	certain
come	curve	cavity
cell	city	circus

5.   Have students reread all the words to determine how many different sounds the *c* represents. (In this exercise the answer should be two—the "k" sound as in *cut* and the "s" sound as in *cell.*

6.   Group all words under the following two headings:

k-sound	s-sound
can	cent
cancer	cigar
come	cell
came	cycle
cut	century
curve	city
cry	certain
cog	circus
color	cancer
cavity	
circus	

7.   At this point after some discussion students will usually come up with the correct generalization. Do not rush them. Also, if necessary, find more words to make sure that all parts of the rule are covered.

8.   Provide practice in applying the rule by giving students a list of *c* words and letting them mark a *k* or *s* over, or after, each *c* to indicate the correct sound according to the rule, e.g.,

       s
      cent   or   cent   s

      k
      came   came   k

      etc.

9.   Provide practice in applying the rule in the act of reading by having students read short sentences or stories containing words with the "c" sounds.

The rules governing the various "y" sounds may be taught the same way. This same technique also works well with most other generalizations of fairly high utility.

R Control Rule

The *r* control rule can easily be taught using a technique similar to that described above concerning the rules for hard and soft *c* and *g*. A typical procedure would be as follows:

1.   Discuss the fact that when *r* follows a vowel it usually "controls" or modifies the sound of the vowel.

2. Again, discuss the fact that rules can usually be made to help remember various r-controlled vowel sounds.

3. List a number of words in which r follows a vowel, e.g.:

fir	brother	cur	bird
fur	corn	torn	Ford
far	scorn	morning	herd
jar	happier	mar	

4. Categorize the different sounds:

"ar" as in car	"or" as in corn	"er" as in herd
far	scorn	fir
jar	torn	fur
mar	morning	brother
	Ford	happier
		cur
		bird

5. Let students make up a generalization, e.g., *ir, ur,* and *er* usually have the sound heard in *herd. Ar* usually has the sound heard in *car.* And, *or* usually has the sound heard in *corn.*

6. Give students a chance to practice using their newly gained knowledge, e.g., give exercises such as the following:

    6.1. Write the correct vowel plus r in the blanks below.
    I ate breakfast this m__ __ning.
    Many animals are covered with f__ __.
    Father came home in a new c__ __.
    etc.

7. Give students an opportunity to practice the skill in the act of reading by having them read short sentences or stories containing words with r-controlled vowels.

Vowel Rules and Accent Generalizations

As stated earlier, learning various vowel rules can be of considerable benefit to a disabled reader. However, the commonly taught accent generalizations are of less utility. First of all, there is insufficient research regarding which accent generalizations are of high enough utility to make them worthwhile teaching. Secondly, we need to consider *why* we teach accent generalizations. When students encounter words that are in their speaking-listening vocabularies, but not in their sight vocabularies, they will have to apply one or more word-attack skills to determine that word. For example, a student may not know the word *cabin* in the sentence, *The Smiths went to their cabin by the lake.* After applying the necessary word-attack skills, the student would be left with accenting the word as *cab-in'* or *cab'-in.* With the help of context clues, the student would be quite likely to accent it properly if *cabin* was in the student's speaking-listening vocabulary since there are only two choices to begin with. It is only when words are not in a student's speaking-listening vocabulary that accents really becomes useful. Since most disabled readers' reading levels are likely to be one or more years behind their speaking-listening vocabularies, they have less need for learning accent generalizations than a normal reader does. It is only when their reading level approaches a normal level that this need becomes more apparent.

One of the problems that teachers and students encounter when learning the various vowel rules is the many exceptions to the stated rules. Teachers can alleviate this problem somewhat in the beginning by using words that do follow the rules. However, students will discover that there are many exceptions, and they should be taught to be flexible in their approach to word attack. For example, the vowel rule, "When a vowel comes at the end of a syllable, it is usually long," should be taught as, "When a vowel comes at the end of a syllable, try the long sound first." Even when exceptions appear, students usually accept this fact quite well if you simply explain to them that rules and generalizations have been derived to fit our complex language. Had it been possible to design a language to fit a set of existing rules, it would have been different.

The initial procedure for the introduction of vowel rules can be done somewhat the same as the procedure explained for teaching the hard and soft *c* and *g* sounds, i.e., by use of the discovery technique. In introducing the vowel rules, however, you may wish to introduce a word list, prepared prior to the lesson, from which your students can then derive various rules and/or generalizations. This word list should contain only words that are not exceptions to the rule or principle being taught. In the initial introduction use words that are already familiar to most students.

After the various vowel rules have been introduced, provide students with the opportunity to practice the application of the material they have learned. Just as you would not expect most students to learn a new word well enough for it to become a sight word after one or two exposures, you should not expect students to learn the application of a particular vowel rule from only applying it one or two times.

Word Families, or Phonograms

The teaching of word families, or phonograms, to disabled readers is often very beneficial. The practice of "looking for little words in big words" has usually been discouraged because the pronunciation of the little word often changes when it becomes part of a longer word. Phonograms, however, tend to have fairly consistent pronunciations from one word to another. Phonograms are also extremely useful in teaching blending of initial consonants, blends, and digraphs.

One technique you may want to use in teaching word families is to simply call students' attention to the fact that there are certain clusters of letters that tend to have similar sounds from one word to another. Students can compile lists of the common phonograms, and these can be used in exercises such as the following:

1. "See how many words you can make by combining the list of initial consonants or consonant clusters on the left and the word families on the right."

br	ell
b	ank
sh	all
cr	anch
c	eak

2. Have students make, or you can make, a flash card for each phonogram with which they have difficulty. Pair students for study using exercises as described above. Also have students test each other on their own and other students' phonogram lists or groups of flash cards.

The teacher may also prepare simple sentences or short stories that frequently repeat a few phonograms. A number of supplementary readers are available from publishers that do the same thing. Teachers should also consider using the so-called linguistic readers that present word families a few at a time and with much repetition.

Contractions

Contractions often present difficulties for normal as well as disabled readers. Although a lack of knowledge of contractions alone will not cause a student to become a disabled reader, it can be an important factor in the overall error pattern. One of the major reasons that students encounter difficulties with contractions is that their oral language is often less formal than what is found on the printed page. Therefore, students find a discrepancy between what might seem natural to say and what they actually read. Many contracted forms that are apparent in students' oral language are seldom seen in print and, therefore, are simply not seen often enough to be thoroughly learned.

The teaching of contractions then becomes a matter, for most teachers, of providing for multiple exposures to each contraction and insuring that each trial is practiced correctly. The procedures outlined in Chapter 4 for teaching basic sight words will work equally well for contractions. Since contractions are common in oral language, the tape recorder can also be used as a device for reinforcement of contractions. Some examples follow:

1.   Give students sheets of paper, with numbers, in which two to four contractions appear to the right of each number, for example:
        1.1. they've   they're   they'd
        1.2. wouldn't   would've
        Tape record sentences and have students circle the contraction they hear in the sentences, e.g., in numbers 1 and 2 above the sentences would be as follows:
        1.3. The boys said they'd rather not go.
        1.4. We would've gone if they would have asked us.
2.   Do the same type of exercise as shown above, only give students sentences in which the contracted word is blank. Students are to pick the correct contraction from a choice of several to make the sentence read correctly.
3.   Give students numbered lists of contractions and have them write the two contracted words beside the contraction. Use a tape recorder to correct each answer immediately after it has been done. The students' papers would appear as follows:
        3.1. I've _____
        3.2. Haven't _____
        etc.
        The tape recorder script would be as follows: "Write the two words that stand for the contraction in the blank in number one. (*Beep.*) The contraction is *I've* and the two words it stands for are *I have.* Now do number two. (*Beep.*) The contraction is *haven't* and the two words are *have not.* Now do number three," etc. (The "beep" is a signal to turn off the tape recorder.)

Possessives

Possessives usually present few problems for students; however, a few disabled readers tend to confuse them with contractions, i.e., when pronouncing words with possessive endings they attempt to contract the word in some manner. Disabled readers can usually correct this problem rather easily if they are simply told that whenever the apostrophe is followed by, or comes after, *s* it means that the word is simply pronounced as though the apostrophe were not there. A few practice sentences or phrases including contractions or possessives will be helpful in reinforcing students' learning.

For example:

1. Jim's hat was lost.
2. I'd like to go.
3. Sam lost Frank's watch.
4. The boys found Frank's watch.
5. The boys said they'd like to go.

Inflectional Endings

To recognize and correctly pronounce inflectional endings the student must learn to apply structural analysis. The student must be able to identify word parts, visually separate the word parts, pronounce the word parts, and then blend the parts together to form the whole word. The following procedure will teach students to do this with the inflectional endings -s, -ed, and -ing. The same procedures may be used with other inflectional endings:[2]

Step I: Identify word parts
1. Review the following base words to be sure that students can pro-nounce them: *clean, born, cover, dress*
2. Write the following word lists on the chalkboard:

   look   asks
   looks   works
   looked   called
   looking   asking
             calls
             worked
             calling
             asked
             working

3. Direct the students' attention to the first list. Say: "How are these words alike?"
4. Circle the base word *look*:

   look   s
   look   ed
   look   ing

   Say: "How are these words different?"

---

[2] We are indebted to Cheryl Milner, principal, Hayward, California Unified School District, and William Radulovich, reading specialist, San Ramon Valley, California Unified School District, for their assistance in developing and field testing specific procedures for teaching structural analysis skills.

5. Write these headings across the chalkboard:

    <u>s</u>   <u>ed</u>   <u>ing</u>

6. Direct the students' attention to the second list. Say: "These words have some of the same endings you saw on the word *look*. Which column would you place the word *asks* under?"

7. Repeat number 6 with the other words in the second list.

Step II: Separate word parts
(*Note:* This step is optional. If students appear to have little difficulty separating the word parts, you may move to step III.)

1. Review the base words *turn* and *help*.

2. Give each student a page or large card that has the following words printed on it in boxes approximately 3″ × 4″: *turned, helping, helps, turns, turning, helped.* Also give each student an envelope and a pair of scissors.

3. Say: "The words on this paper each have one of the three word endings we have been studying."

4. Write the endings on the chalkboard: *s, ed, ing.*

5. Write the word *turned* on the chalkboard. Say: "Find the word *turned* on your paper. Cut it out." Check to be certain that students cut out the correct word. Say: "Which ending does this word have?" Then say, "Cut off the *ed*." Then say, "What is left?" Then say, "Excellent. Put the word *turn* and the ending *ed* in your envelope."

6. Repeat number 5 for the other words.

Step III: Blend word parts
(This step is also optional, and will not be necessary for all students.)

1. Direct the students to place their word parts face up in front of them. Make certain all cards are face up and right side up.

2. Say: "Find the word *turn*. Find the ending *ed*. Put the parts together. What is the word?" Then say, "If you take away the *ed*, what is left?" Then say, "If you take away *turn*, what is left?" Then say, "What is the whole word?"

3. Repeat number 2 for the other words.

4. Ask each student to read the words on his or her table aloud.

In order to reinforce this skill, the students will need ample practice in reading whole words that contain these inflectional endings and in reading sentences or stories that contain these words. A list of words, sample sentences, and a story for practicing the *-s, -ed,* and *-ing* endings follow:

walks   watering
watered   plays

playing	started
starts	opening
opened	waits
waiting	walking
walked	waters

She turns and helps the girls.
She turned and helped the girl.
She is turning and helping the girl.
Mother knows when the family eats, plays, and sleeps.
The family likes being mothered.
The family will be eating, playing, and sleeping here.
He opens the doors for his friends.
He opened the door and called his friend.
He is opening the door and calling his friend.
Bob stops and looks up and down the streets.
Bob looked before he crossed the street.
Bob is looking before crossing the street.
Sis likes trees, walks, and dogs.
Sis watered and walked the dog.
Sis will be watering and walking my dog.
Sam waits and thinks about how many days it takes.
Sam played while he waited.
Sam is waiting and thinking about the day.

A Long Camping Trip

It all started when I came home from camp. I was walking home from the bus stop. As I turned down my street I saw some friends a block away. I called hello, but they acted like they did not hear me.

I was feeling a little sad as I opened the doors to our house. I needed a snack, so I went to find mom and get some nuts and apples. When I saw her I laughed and said, "Here I am!" Mom seemed not to hear or see me. I started yelling. I jumped up and down. It was no use. She just went on cooking. "She does not look the same as before," I thought.

I walked out the back door. First my friends, and now my mother! What had I done? Was no one glad to see me? The trees were blowing, and the birds were singing, but I felt like crying as I climbed a tall tree near the gate.

I started thinking. My dog Rags would be happy to see me! I jumped from the tree and ran to find Rags. He would be in my room sleeping. I ran up the steps. When I walked into my room I was shocked to find it filled with trunks, junk, and all kinds of odds and ends.

Just then my little sister Kate ran up the stairs. To my surprise she walked right by me too. She looked to be about five years too old to be little Kate! As I walked down stairs I saw the date in the hall, July 16, 1988. But this is only 1983!

The steps outlined above may seem unnecessarily long and tedious for teaching three relatively simple endings. In fact, it will not be possible to go through all of the steps with most students in one session. However, we are persuaded that, if the structural analysis skills are initially taught thoroughly and carefully, reteaching will not be required, and subsequent skills can be taught more rapidly.

Affixes

As explained in the section on testing students' knowledge in this area, instruction should focus on pronunciation of affixes and not on meaning. The procedures you may use to teach prefixes and suffixes are identical to those outlined above for inflectional endings. The remedial reading teacher will find that for those students who have mastered basic sight vocabulary and phonics skills, effective teaching of structural analysis will result in dramatic improvement in their decoding ability.

Listed below are a series of words and sentences that may be used to teach the prefixes re- and un- following the steps previously outlined. The teacher may use similar lists and sentences, as well as stories, to teach and reinforce the other prefixes and suffixes tested in Part A of this chapter.

For teaching:

unclean	reclaim
reclean	uncover
unborn	recover
reborn	undress
uncap	redress
recap	untouch
unclaim	retouch

For practice:

redone	unfair
undone	renew
recall	unjust
unbroken	repay
refresh	unplug
redo	unseen
relay	untrue

The weather announcer will repeat the report on our pleasant weather at six o'clock.

My dog will refuse to unclench his teeth and release the stick after I throw it.

Unlace and remove your shoes, unzip your coat, and relax until dinner is ready.

Unless we repair the old chair, it will be unsafe, and we will be unable to sit in it.

Please remind me to unload the washer after we return from the store.

Bob was feeling a little uncertain and very uneasy about trying out for the class play.

They had to unwind the ropes and release the sails as a wind came up in order to return the boat to the dock.

It would be unwise to unfasten the ribbon and unwrap the present before the party.

You must review the story and rewrite this paper before I retest you.

As he began to unsaddle his horse and unpack the saddlebags, the sheriff said, "I regret having to lock you up, Sam, but I can't let you get revenge for your brother's death."

Listed below are some commonly used exercises that are also intended to assist students with prefixes and suffixes:

1. Have students underline all the affixes they can find in a newspaper article. Compile a list of the ones found. Discuss each affix and then compile a master list of all the different affixes found for a period of time.

2. Do the same thing as described in number 1 above, but furnish the students with lists of affixed words.

3. Give students one or more root words such as *do* and have a contest to see who can make the most variations of the word. For example:
   a. undo
   b. doing
   c. doer
   d. redo
   etc.

4. Have each student make flash cards for any affixes with which he or she has trouble. On one side of the flash card write the affix and several words illustrating its use. On the other side of the card write a sentence using the affix on a word in a sentence.

Syllabication

Students who have learned to identify, separate, pronounce and blend affixes in whole words will already have mastered the ability to decode most two- and three-syllable words, such as *payment* and *promotion*. The only words that will remain difficult for them to decode are words that are not in their listening vocabularies (i.e., words that are not recognized by students when the teacher pronounces them) and unusually long or difficult words. There is nothing the teacher can do to assist students to "decode" words in the former category. Instruction must focus on methods of increasing the students' meaning vocabularies before students will be able to "read" words that they do not presently recognize. However, there are six syllabication generalizations that students may learn that will help them to decode difficult words as long as they recognize these words when they hear them. Examples of long words for which the generalizations may apply are *decompression, craftsmanship, unreasonable,* and *composition.*

The six generalizations, in order of application, are:

1. Look for prefixes or suffixes.
2. Look for a known base or root word.
3. Read to the end of the sentence. Think of a word with the parts that you know that makes sense.
4. If necessary, try different divisions of the base word to form syllables.
5. Try different sounds, syllables, and accents until you form a word that makes sense.
6. If you still can't figure the word out, use a dictionary.

These guidelines are not perfect; however, our experience leads us to conclude that they are the most helpful of available generalizations. The first three are the most effective and usually will be sufficient to unlock the unknown word. If the base or root word is a difficult word, as in *investigate,* the fourth and fifth steps probably represent the best guidelines that a student can use. Here's why: Using the word *investigate,* we will assume that (1) the student will "recognize" it if he or she gets close enough with decoding skills; (2) the student has used step 1 and can pronounce *in* and *ate* or *gate;* steps 2 and 3 were not helpful and the student is stuck on the *vesti* or *vestig* part of the word. One traditional syllabication rule tells the student to divide between two consonants; however, another rule says do not divide between consonant blends. A third rule tells students to treat consonant blends as though they were a single letter and divide before the blend when the blend stands between two vowels. The student who is able to remember these rules and identify the consonant blend (both of which are doubtful under the circumstances) is likely to end up thoroughly confused and no closer to decoding *investigate.* In any case it does not matter, for the student may be able to decode the word if he or she divides it before the *s,* between the *s* and the *t,* or after the *t.* Incidentally, trying to decode the word by analyzing the vowel sounds will probably prove as frustrating for the student as trying to apply syllabication rules that do not work.

Thus, we provide steps 4 and 5, which tell the student to try different divisions of sounds, syllables, and accents in hopes of arriving at the proper pronunciation. These steps are similar to the one rule offered by Shirley Rosati (1973), who wryly suggested: "Either divide before or between consonants or don't."

When all else fails, there is step 6. If the teacher observes students following this step too often, either the students are not satisfactorily applying the previous steps or they are being expected to read material that is too difficult for them.

The best way to teach the syllabication steps we have listed is to first model the use of the steps yourself while students observe. Select a few difficult words, put them in sentences, and demonstrate for students how you would go through the steps one at a time to decode the "unknown" word in a sentence. Do this with enough words to go through the various steps using a different number of steps each time to arrive at the pronunciation. Always go through the steps in order. You want to convince students that the first three steps, in order, are the most helpful. Reassure students that this system works and that with practice they will learn to read "great, big" words with little difficulty. Of course, you must be sure that students have mastered the prerequisite skills of phonic analysis, basic sight word mastery, and mastery of prefixes, suffixes, and inflectional endings. The students must also have some ability to use context clues as an aid to decoding.

After you have demonstrated the syllabication strategy, provide students with sentences that they may use to apply the steps themselves; guide their work if necessary. It is a good idea to list the steps on a chart and have the students memorize the steps so that they will *use* them. If they are able to decode the words quickly, so much the better. If they are not, then you want them to use a systematic approach. For students who have severe difficulties with multisyllabic words the strategy usually consists of one glance and panic. You will be showing them a concrete, systematic, and helpful approach to decoding these most challenging words.

Following your demonstration of the steps and the students' attempts to use the strategy with multisyllabic words in sentences, all that remains is for the students to apply the skills continually in the act of reading. You must persuade students at this level that they will need to read *a lot* for their new word-attack skills to become automatic.

A list of sentences follows that you may use to teach and practice the syllabication steps. These are difficult sentences, since most contain more than one multisyllabic word. If these prove too difficult for your students initially, then we would recommend that you prepare more sentences like the first and third.

The amplifier made the music louder.
The archaeologist studied the bones of the dinosaur and the other artifacts
     found near the caves.
Sara is a kind, compassionate person.
The twelve contributors contributed five hundred dollars to the charity.
That delicatessen has delicious potato salad.
After the explosion there was an evacuation of the building.
The horizontal lines on the television screen make it impossible to see the
     picture.

The intricate puzzle is very frustrating.
The hurricane did substantial damage to our neighborhood.
The barometric pressure is falling rapidly.

CONTEXT CLUES

Context clues are a very important word-attack skill, as well as an important means of vocabulary development. Although basal reader teacher's manuals tend to thoroughly teach the use of this skill today, many readers in the past were seldom given any instruction in the use of context clues. Even today, however, many disabled readers have failed to learn to use context as a word-attack skill. Evidently, teachers sometimes believe that the use of context is so obvious that students are likely to learn this skill with little or no instruction. This, of course, is simply not true. Many readers need a considerable amount of instruction and a great deal of practice in using this skill. Susanna Pflaum and Ernest Pascarella (1980) reported on a study that found learning-disabled students whose initial instructional level was at or above grade two benefited significantly from instruction in the use of context clues. Eunice Askov and Karlyn Kamm (1976) found that students in grades three, four, and five who were taught a classification of context clues, such as cause-effect and direct description, demonstrated improved reading performance.

One of the first and most important techniques for teaching context clues is simply to talk with students about the use of context clues. For example, many disabled readers do not have any idea that a word could often be attacked by the use of the context. Some students apparently figure it out for themselves, but the disabled reader often seems less adept at reaching these conclusions without some help.

The following general techniques will assist students in using context clues to decode unknown words:

1. Have students preread material silently before reading orally. Discuss troublesome vocabulary.
2. Set purposes for reading. Stress accuracy in reading, not speed.
3. Use short, easy selections. Have students stop frequently to explain what they have read in their own words.
4. Use high-interest material, including student-authored language-experience stories.
5. Encourage students to read *past* unknown words to the end of the sentence and then to come back. Research indicates that words that come after are often more helpful than those that come before unknown words.

6.   Have students scan for important words. Have them guess the content and then read to see if the guess was accurate.

7.   Encourage practice in the act of reading. There is no better technique for students to learn to read for meaning. Provide time, appropriate materials, the proper setting, and encouragement for sustained silent reading.

Other types of ideas and exercises are listed below:

1.   The tape recorder can be used to advantage in first making students aware of context clues in oral exercises. Note: Wait five seconds after reading each sentence. The script would be as follows:
"I am going to read a short story. Once in a while I will leave out a word. Where a word is left out or omitted you will hear a beep sound. When you hear the beep, try to fill in the word that belongs there before I give the answer. Here is the story.
    "Once Jack and Jim were going to _____ fishing. (*go*) First they dug _____ worms. (*some*) Then they took. . . . " etc.

2.   Give students sentences with words left blank. For every blank give the student several choices of words that might belong in the blanks. For example:
    2.1 Mary was _____ to visit her Uncle George.
        (*they - going - did - being*)
    2.2. Frank's dog did _____ like cats.
        (*that - give - not - be*)

3.   Give students sentences such as those listed in number 2 above but give only the first letter of the missing word. For example:
    3.1. Mary was g_____ to visit her Uncle George.
    3.2. Frank's dog did n_____ like cats.

4.   Give students sentences such as those listed in number 2 above but do not give any clues as to what word or words might be used in the blanks. After students have completed the blanks, have each student read his or her sentence and hold a discussion about the appropriateness of the words chosen.

5.   Use cloze passages where approximately every eighth to tenth word is omitted. Ask students to fill in the blanks. After students have completed the exercise, hold a discussion about what words were used in each blank. Research in the use of this technique has generally shown that this type of exercise has very little value without the discussion that follows, so do not omit that part. An example of a cloze passage follows:
    5.1. George was going to visit _____ Grandpa and Grandma. He _____ going to go on an airplane. His father _____ with him to buy his ticket. The clerk _____ the desk asked George _____ he wanted to . . . , etc.

Context clues aid the student not only in word attack but also in comprehension. For this reason, additional suggestions for using the cloze procedure as a teaching technique (number 5 above) will be included in the next chapter.

A WORD-ATTACK STRATEGY

Thus far in this chapter we have described techniques and procedures for diagnosing and remediating the following word-analysis skills: phonics, structural analysis, and context clues. In the previous chapter, we discussed testing and teaching letter knowledge and sight words. If you have been successful in your instruction to this point, you will have provided students with the necessary tools to decode. It is possible, however, for students to overrely on one or more of these skills or to apply the wrong skill in certain situations. Also, your students will need to learn to use their skills in situations where you will not be present to assist them. Therefore, you can help your students by teaching them a word-attack strategy. This strategy will assist students in incorporating the various decoding skills when they meet unfamiliar words in the act of reading.

The strategy consists of four simple steps. The steps are similar to those that were presented for syllabication in the previous section; however, these steps are more appropriate for readers in the earlier decoding stages. You may wish to present the following on a chart:

When you come to a word you don't know:
1. Say the beginning sound.
2. Read the rest of the sentence. THINK.
3. Say the parts that you know. GUESS.
4. Ask someone or skip it and go on.

These steps may appear obvious to the teacher; however, the remedial student frequently lacks a systematic approach to decoding and will likely benefit from applying the four steps. The first step—applying initial letter-sound associations—is the one step that most students will do automatically. We know from research and experience that beginning sounds are often the most helpful. The second step requires the student to use context clues *before* applying additional phonics or structural analysis. Most often the combination of initial letter sounds and context will result in correct identification of the unknown word. It seems reasonable to ask the student to use context clues before resorting to less helpful word-analysis techniques. Also, step 2 requires the student to read to the end of the sentence to take advantage of the context clues that may come after the unknown word.

If the student still has not decoded the word, step 3 instructs the student to apply other word-analysis clues, such as ending sounds, vowel sounds, or structural analysis. Depending on the level of instruction, the teacher may wish to be more specific at this step. The student is encouraged to guess, if necessary, so as not to spend too much time trying to decode a single unknown word. The last step encourages the student to ask for help or continue reading if all else fails. It is quite possible that context clues picked up in reading further will permit the student to identify the unknown word.

If students must resort to step 4 often, then the material is too difficult and the student should be given easier material to read. Similarly, if the student encounters more than one unknown word in a single sentence, the strategy is likely to break down, indicating that the material is too difficult.

To teach the strategy to students, the teacher should follow the same steps outlined for teaching the syllabication generalizations presented in the previous section. That is:

1. Present the steps, using a written chart that students can remember and refer to.
2. Model use of the steps yourself with sample sentences.
3. Reassure students that the strategy "works."
4. Provide students with sentences that they may use to apply the steps as you provide guidance.
5. Insure that students use the steps as they practice in the act of reading.

At the end of this paragraph is a list of sentences that you may use to teach, and give students practice in, the four-step strategy. The numbers after each sentence indicate which steps are *likely* to assist students. It is not possible to determine exactly which steps will help students. Some students will recognize "unknown" words as sight words. Others will use only one or two steps. Some may not succeed at all. The teacher will need to provide other examples for students based on their specific knowledge of the students' needs.

1. The *light* is red. (1, 2)
2. I will *take* you there. (1, 2)
3. I cannot *remember* your name. (1, 2, 3)
4. I like *chocolate* cake. (1, 2, 3)
5. The *cat* is my pet. (1, 2)
6. The *hamster* is my pet. (1, 2, 3)
7. The *armadillo* is my pet. (1, 2, 3, 4?)

EFFICIENCY SKILLS

In Part A of this chapter we pointed out that some students master decoding skills but fail to read efficiently. These students may possess faulty reading habits, such as inappropriate reading rate, inaccurate reading, improper phrasing or expression, inability to recognize punctuation, lip movements, finger pointing, and head movements. This section contains a number of general suggestions as well as specific procedures for remediating these difficulties.

General Suggestions

1. Make sure that the decoding skills of basic sight vocabulary, phonics, structural analysis and contextual analysis have been mastered. If not, provide remedial instruction in these areas.
2. Take time to discuss with students the specific nature of their efficiency skill problems and suggest general approaches to solving them. It is often helpful to tape record the student while he or she is reading orally, then play back the recording while the student is listening, so the student can become aware of the specific problem.
3. Do not expect students to read efficiently material that is above the students' meaning-vocabulary level. Generally, use *easy* materials that encourage students to read in great quantity.
4. Encourage wide reading from a *variety* of materials. In addition to the necessary practice this provides, students can be directed to read different types of materials at different speeds and for different purposes, such as pleasure, information, instruction, and so forth.

To remediate problems with reading rate, accuracy, phrasing, or expression we recommend that teachers use a variety of oral reading methods, not because oral reading is the goal, but because it often helps students to identify and correct specific reading difficulties. Oral reading is most effective if it is done in a one-to-one fashion or with very small groups so that students participate as much as possible in the oral reading activities. In using these methods, it is important for the teacher to stress to students that oral reading is only one way of reading and that this practice will ultimately lead the student to greater ability in silent reading. Also, oral reading practice is not being substituted for silent reading. Rather, it is presented to give students additional experience with the printed word.

Betty Anderson (1981), Claire Ashby-Davis (1981), and Albert Harris (1981) among others have described three different oral reading techniques and reviewed the research evidence that supports their use. These techniques are (1) the neurological impress method, (2) echo reading or imitative reading, and (3) repeated readings.

The neurological impress method (NIM) was developed by R. G. Heckelman who first described its value in 1966. The method, which has some variations, generally consists of having the student and teacher (or other adult) read the same material out loud at the same time. Initially, the instructor reads slightly louder and faster than the student. The instructor points to the words as they are read and directs his or her voice into the student's ear. Sentences or passages may be reread to achieve fluency. A variation that we have found to be particularly effective is for the instructor to use easy material and read slightly behind the student. In this case the teacher's voice is like an instant echo of the student's, serving to reinforce the student's word recognition. (This is not to be confused with echo reading, which will be described presently.) When using this variation of NIM, the instructor can usually anticipate which words a student will miss in a particular selection and pronounce these ahead of the student to minimize the student's failure and discouragement.

When using NIM, specific correction is seldom, if ever, offered. Nor is questioning or testing of the content provided. As the student's ability improves, he or she may take over the finger movements and more challenging materials may be read. Advocates of NIM recommend that it be used for up to fifteen minutes daily for a total time of eight to twelve hours. Usually students show progress after only a few sessions; the method should be discontinued after four hours if the student fails to respond positively.

In echo reading the instructor reads first and the student then repeats or echoes what the instructor read. Material can be read in either phrases or sentences, and finger pointing is utilized in this method also. A common variation uses recorded texts that students may first listen to straight through while following the written text and then read along with the recording. An advantage of this method is that an instructor need not be present for the student to participate. On the other hand, this variation lacks the immediacy and psychological force of the teacher's presence. At present there are a number of high-interest, low vocabulary "read along" materials available that appear in varying formats with accompanying records, tapes, or slides. Students seem to enjoy these, and, if used properly, they can be beneficial. The teacher must be sure that students *can* read the materials and that they stay on-task and *do* read when they are supposed to.

Repeated readings is a method that has been suggested by S. Jay Samuels (1979). In this method, students are given selections to read that consist of from fifty to 200 words. The student is instructed to practice the selection and then is timed, after which reading rate and number of errors are recorded on a chart. While the teacher is checking other students, the student rereads the material along with a recording of the text. The rereading may be done over and over. When the student feels ready, another test is given. When the student achieves a rate of eighty-five words per minute, another selection is provided. Comprehension checks may also take place. Graphing the student's results serves as a positive motivator for continued progress.

We believe that the repeated-readings method is excellent, but we would add one caution. Our experience has led us to conclude that a primary cause of efficiency or fluency difficulties is that remedial students often try to read too fast. For most students (excepting overanalytical readers) it is helpful to first encourage them to read accurately and then work to improve their speed. This is analogous to learning to play a musical instrument such as the guitar. Initially, the budding musician should concentrate on picking the notes cleanly. Speed will come later.

To this end we have developed a technique that has been used successfully at the California State University, Hayward Reading Clinic, which we call *precision reading*. This adaptation of other fluency techniques first emphasizes accuracy, then speed. While the student reads, the evaluator (the teacher, another adult, or another student) records the student's accuracy sentence by sentence. A form is prepared to record the student's reading efficiency. The form has spaces to indicate the beginning and ending page numbers of the material read, the total number of *sentences* read, the number of sentences read perfectly, and the number of sentences read with one or more errors. At the beginning the student is given relatively easy material to read and reads a set number of sentences, such as twenty-five. The evaluator records the student's accuracy on each sentence, so that on completion a fraction of correct sentences out of the total is derived; for example, 20/25. This would indicate that the student read twenty sentences perfectly and made one or more errors on five of the sentences. The fraction is then changed to a percentage—in this case, 80 percent accuracy—and the percentage figure is graphed daily. The students enjoy seeing their performance graphed, and this serves as a powerful motivator for continued progress. It is important to select material where the accuracy rate is unlikely to drop below 75 percent. Also, the teacher may select different material for the student to read each day. However, it is helpful if the passage is chosen at least one day in advance so that the student can begin practicing the material in advance as part of his or her homework. As the student improves and begins to read consistently at or near 100 percent accuracy, the teacher may provide more difficult material or add the factor of speed. To do the latter, you may have the student read as many sentences as possible within a prescribed period of time, as long as the accuracy rate does not drop below, say, 90 percent. Then the number of sentences read perfectly would be graphed daily.

Additional suggestions for oral reading activities are listed below:

1. The teacher and student may take turns reading the material out loud by alternating paragraphs, sentences, or lines.
2. The student may preread silently first, note difficult vocabulary, and review the vocabulary with the teacher; then the student and teacher may read together.
3. The teacher may provide choral reading activities for small groups of students.

4. The teacher may provide plays for students to read. A number of kits are available with simple two-, three-, or four-person plays; or teachers and students may write their own plays.
5. Many students enjoy relaxed paired reading. A student and a friend select two copies of a good book and then take turns reading it out loud together.
6. Younger students may read selections using puppets.
7. Older students enjoy participating in reader's theater activities.
8. The teacher may provide a reinforcer, such as clicking a counter or putting a chip in a bank, each time the student reads a sentence perfectly.
9. The teacher may use favorite games such as tic-tac-toe, hangman, and dots to "score" reading accuracy. For example, a student reads while the other records a part for the hangman if the student who is reading makes an error. (Numbers 8 and 9 are variations of the precision-reading method described above.)
10. The use of controlled readers or reading pacers is *not* recommended unless great care is taken to guard against the frustration that is likely to occur when the student is unable to keep up with the machine.

The audio tape recorder may also serve as an excellent device for students to practice oral reading. The teacher might set up a "recording studio" in the classroom. In addition to the tape recorder the teacher will need a microphone and cassette tapes for the students. If possible, provide a cassette for each student. The cassettes may be hung on a pegboard for easy access. The tape recorder may be used for commercially prepared read-along materials. The following activities may also be provided:

1. The student may read orally into the tape recorder, play back the tape, and
    a. listen to the recording noting errors; or
    b. read along silently; or
    c. read along with his or her own voice orally.
2. The teacher or another person may read a selection into the tape recorder, the student may play it back as above, or the teacher may make purposeful errors or exhibit poor efficiency skills, such as inadequate phrasing, excessive speed, ignoring punctuation, etc. The student would evaluate the teacher's performance and try to apply this to his or her own reading.
3. Two or more students may read into a tape recorder together, using some of the above techniques.
4. The student may use the Language Master® or equivalent machine to practice phrase or sentence reading. (For a description of the Language Master®, see Chapter 4, section entitled "The Use of the Tape Recorder.")

The following procedures may be used with students who are having difficulty with phrasing.

1. Have students practice reading phrase flash cards. Dolch phrases are commercially available or you may make your own (see Chapter 4). Chart the student's progress.
2. Tachistoscopic devices may be used with phrases.
3. Type up material with words separated in phrase units. Have the student practice reading this out loud.
4. Use vertical marks to indicate the phrases in written material. Phrases may be divided at any appropriate place.
5. Use other oral reading techniques noted above.

Students who habitually ignore punctuation are bound to have difficulties in reading efficiently. The teacher should not assume that students have been taught the function of common punctuation marks. You may use the tape recorder to help the student become aware of the problem and then teach the uses of the period, comma, question mark, quotation marks, apostrophe, and colon. Some specific suggestions follow:

1. Prepare a paragraph with no punctuation marks. Have the student try to read it. Then you and the student together punctuate and read the selection.
2. Use short written paragraphs to demonstrate how punctuation affects the pitch and stress of your voice. Have the student repeat and then re-read the paragraphs.
3. Use guides—three counts for periods, two for commas.
4. Use an overhead projector with paragraphs without punctuation. Together fill in appropriate marks and read.
5. Dictate to the student simple paragraphs. The student provides the punctuation, in part, by the inflections of your voice.
6. Use the language-experience approach and leave out all punctuation marks from the student's dictated story. Then have the student fill them in.
7. Provide cards with words or phrases and cards with punctuation marks. Have the student arrange them properly.

There are a number of silent reading difficulties that reflect poor efficiency skills. These include: lip movements, finger pointing, head movements, and skipping unfamiliar words. Procedures for remediating these difficulties follow:

1. Lip Movements
   a. Have the student place a finger against his or her lips when reading silently.

b.   Have the student place a small piece of paper between his or her lips when reading silently.

c.   Temporarily reduce the amount of oral reading.

d.   Discuss with the student the importance of forming mental pictures when reading. Explain that it is not necessary to "say" each word.

2.   Finger Pointing

a.   Have the student's eyes checked if you suspect a vision problem.

b.   Have the student use a marker *temporarily*.

c.   Provide practice in phrase reading.

d.   Provide practice in reading from charts and the chalkboard where finger pointing is impossible.

e.   Have the student use both hands to hold the book.

f.   Use material with large, clear print.

3.   Head Movements

a.   Have the student place elbows on the table and index fingers against his or her temples.

b.   Demonstrate how to use the eyes to scan a page while the head remains stationary.

4.   Skipping Unfamiliar Words

a.   Have the student read orally first, then silently.

b.   Increase vocabulary instruction before silent reading.

c.   Use easier material.

d.   Deemphasize speed. Stress the importance of reading each word accurately.

e.   Make sure the student has mastered the basic decoding skills.

f.   Teach the word-attack strategy presented in the previous section.

g.   Teach the student how to use the glossary and dictionary in emergencies.

CONFIGURATION CLUES

Although the use of configuration clues is an important skill in word analysis, very little concrete information exists on effective ways of teaching students to become more aware of it. Most of the research tends to show that methods that have traditionally been used are of little value. For example, many textbooks on reading have suggested that lines be drawn around words printed in lower case to show contrasting shapes as in the words   what   and   when   . However, research by Gabrielle Marchbanks and Harry Levin (1965), as well as others, has shown that in actual practice this technique has very little value. The problem probably lies in the fact that so many words have exactly the same shape when outlined. If this technique has any value at all, it would probably be for the student who constantly confuses two somewhat similar words. This technique might then be used to emphasize slight differences in the configuration of only those two words at a time.

We also know that words printed in lower case tend to be easier to read than words printed in upper case, when the lower half of the word is masked. Thus, we would be led to believe that using the lower-case alphabet in beginning reading would be more effective. However, even this argument does not tend to be supported by the research. In actuality it does not seem to make any difference in students' overall reading achievement when they are instructed in lower case, upper case, or as in normally done, by combining the two.

Occasionally, a student will have considerable difficulty with words such as *though, through,* and *thought.* Where this is the case, it seems somewhat effective to point out differences such as the "t" sound and the *t* letter at the end of *thought* and the *r* in *through.* You also improve students' ability to note configuration in teaching word families—phonograms—such as *all* and *ate.* Generally speaking, however, unless a student is confusing two similar words such as *county* and *country,* you could probably spend your time on more effective methods of word attack than dwelling on configuration clues.

DICTIONARY SKILLS

As stated in Part A of this chapter, students do not become seriously disabled readers from a lack of knowledge of dictionary skills. This is not to belittle the importance of thoroughly learning the use of the dictionary. However, from the standpoint of economy of time the remedial reading teacher will probably spend most of his or her time in remediating problems that have a more immediate effect on most students' reading.

There are numerous filmstrips, workbooks, etc., that effectively cover the teaching of dictionary skills. Because of these factors, we have not included discussion of the teaching of the dictionary skills. A list of sources for teaching the dictionary skills is shown in Appendix C.

SUMMARY

For the teacher who has no experience in the testing of word-attack skills the problem of assessing the students' knowledge in this area may seem quite simple. On the other hand, the experienced diagnostician, who is familiar with an array of tests in this area, will know that there are many different ways of testing word-attack skills. Research has shown that, although the correlations between any two of these tests may be rather high, one is not likely to obtain item-by-item agreement on particular skills or phonemes when using one test as contrasted with another. If the remedial reading teacher is to do exact diagnostic teaching on the basis of test results, it will be necessary to examine the type of test to be used to make sure it tests students' word-attack skills in a situation comparable to the act of reading.

A number of tests that contain subtests for word-attack skills have been discussed in this chapter. The beginning teacher and even the experienced diagnostician would do well to familiarize themselves with a number of these tests. In many cases it will be better to use a combination of subtests from several different test batteries. You may also feel that in many cases testing materials can be constructed that will be as good as, and in may cases more appropriate than, some of the commercial materials that are presently being marketed.

In Part B of this chapter a thorough description of procedures for teaching and reinforcing each of the word-attack skills was presented.

REFERENCES

Anderson, Betty. "The Missing Ingredient: Fluent Oral Reading," *Elementary School Journal.* Vol. 81, (January, 1981), 173–177.

Ashby-Davis, Claire. "A Review of Three Techniques for Use with Remedial Readers," *Reading Teacher.* Vol. 34, (February, 1981), 534–538.

Askov, Eunice N., and Kamm, Karlyn. "Context Clues: Should We Teach Children to Use a Classification System in Reading?" *Journal of Educational Research.* Vol. 69, (May, 1976), 341–344.

Botel, Morton. *Botel Reading Inventory.* Chicago: Follett, 1978.

Burmeister, Lou. "Vowel Pairs," *Reading Teacher.* Vol. 21, (February, 1968), 445–542.

Burns, Paul C., and Schell, Leo M. "Instructional Strategies for Teaching Usage of Context Clues," *Reading World.* Vol. 15, (December, 1975), 89–96.

Cunningham, Patricia M. "Can Decoding Skills Be Validly Assessed Using a Nonsense-Word Pronunciation Task?" *Reading Improvement.* Vol. 13, (Winter, 1976), 247–248.

Durkin, Dolores, and Meshover, Leonard. *Phonics Knowledge Survey.* New York: Teachers College Press, 1964.

Durrell, Donald D., and Catterson, Jane H. *Durrell Analysis of Reading Difficulty.* 3rd ed., New York: Psychological Corporation, 1980.

Ekwall, Eldon E. "An Analysis of Children's Test Scores When Tested with Individually Administered Diagnostic Tests and When Tested with Group Administration Tests," Final Research Report, University Research Institute, University of Texas at El Paso, 1973.

Ekwall, Eldon E. *Ekwall Reading Inventory.* Boston: Allyn and Bacon, 1979.

Ekwall, Eldon E., and Oswald, Lowell D. *Rx Reading Program.* Glenview, Ill.: Psychotechnics, 1971.

Gates, Arthur I.; McKillop, Anne S.; and Horowitz, Elizabeth C. *Gates-McKillop-Horowitz Reading Diagnostic Tests.* 2nd ed., New York: Teachers College Press, 1981.

Groff, Patrick. "Teaching Reading by Syllables," *Reading Teacher.* Vol. 34, (March, 1981), 659–664.

Hanna, P. R.; Hanna, Jean S.; Holdges, R. G.; and Rudorf, E. H., Jr. *Phoneme-Grapheme Correspondence as Cues to Spelling Improvement.* Washington, D.C.: Office of Education, United States Department of Health, Education, and Welfare, 1966.

Harris, Albert J. "What Is New in Remedial Reading?" *Reading Teacher.* Vol. 34, (January, 1981), 405–410.

Harris, Albert J., and Sipay, Edward R. *How to Increase Reading Ability.* 7th ed., New York: Longman, 1980. Copyright 1940, 1947, © 1956, 1961, 1975, and 1980 by Longman, Inc. Copyright renewed 1968 and 1975 by Albert J. Harris. Reprinted by permission of Longman, Inc., New York.

Heckelman, R. G. "Using the Neurological Impress Remedial Technique," *Academic Therapy Quarterly.* Vol. 1, (1966), 235–239.

Hislop, Margaret J., and King, Ethel M. "Application of Phonic Generalizations by Beginning Readers," *Journal of Educational Research.* Vol. 56, (May–June, 1973), 405–412.

Homen, Wanda J. "Predicting First Grade Reading Success with a Test in Letter-Sounds and Synthesis," Master's thesis, California State University, Hayward, 1977.

Karlsen, Bjorn; Madden, Richard; and Gardner, Eric F. *Stanford Diagnostic Reading Test.* New York: Harcourt Brace Jovanovich, 1976.

Marchbanks, Gabrielle, and Levin, Harry. "Cues by Which Children Recognize Words," *Journal of Educational Psychology.* Vol. 56, (April, 1965), 57–61.

Pflaum, Susanna W., and Pascarella, Ernest T. "Interactive Effects of Prior Reading Achievement and Training in Context on the Reading of Learning-Disabled Children," *Reading Research Quarterly.* Vol. 16, (1980), 138–158.

Robinson, H. Alan. "A Study of the Techniques of Word Identification," *Reading Teacher.* Vol. 16, (January, 1963), 238–242.

Rosati, Shirley. "Emancipate Syllabication," *Reading Teacher.* Vol. 26, (January, 1973), 397–398.

Samuels, S. Jay. "The Method of Repeated Readings," *Reading Teacher.* Vol. 32, (January, 1979), 403–406.

Sipay, Edward R. *Sipay Word Analysis Tests.* Cambridge, Mass.: Educators Publishing Service, 1974.

Spache, George D. *Diagnostic Reading Scales.* Monterey, Calif.: CTB/McGraw-Hill, 1981.

Stauffer, Russell G. *Teaching Reading as a Thinking Process.* New York: Harper & Row, 1969.

Strang, Ruth; McCullough, Constance M.; and Traxler, Arthur E. *The Improvement of Reading.* 4th. ed., New York: McGraw-Hill, 1967.

Whaley, Jill W., "Closing the Blending Gap," *Reading World.* Vol. 15, (December, 1975), 97–100. Reprinted by permission of The College Reading Association and Jill W. Whaley.

Whaley, Jill W., and Kibby, Michael W. "Word Synthesis and Beginning Reading Achievement," *Journal of Educational Research.* Vol. 73, (January–February, 1980), 132–138.

Winkley, Carol. "Which Accent Generalizations Are Worth Teaching," *Reading Teacher.* Vol. 20, (December, 1966), 219–224.

Woodcock, Richard W. *Woodcock Reading Mastery Tests.* Circle Pines, Minn.: American Guidance Service, 1973.

6

Diagnosis and Remediation
of Educational Factors:
Comprehension, Vocabulary
Development, and Study Skills

One purpose of this chapter is to discuss methods of, as well as limitations of, diagnosing students' reading comprehension and vocabulary
development. The first section on diagnosis contains a general description of commonly used methods of diagnosing general comprehension
and vocabulary development. Following this general section specific
suggestions are given for diagnosing difficulties with comprehension.
Another purpose of this chapter is to identify methods of diagnosing
those study skills that are likely to contribute to students' failure in
school. The last purpose of Chapter 6 is to discuss some practical methods for dealing with students who are disabled in these areas.

Part A: DIAGNOSIS

THE NATURE OF COMPREHENSION

Over the years reading-methods textbooks and basal reader teacher's manuals have often listed a host of different comprehension skills that students
should supposedly master during their progression through the grades. Some
examples of skills commonly listed are: the abilities to note and grasp details,
main ideas, and the author's purpose; the ability to underline or note key

words, the ability to make generalizations; and the ability to predict outcomes. As mentioned in Chapter 3, however, research in the area of reading comprehension does not support the theory that these skills actually exist as separate entities. A statistical technique that is often used to attempt to locate or measure separate variables is factor analysis. If separate comprehension abilities actually exist, then through the technique of factor analysis one should be able to identify each of these separate factors. Once these factors are located and identified, one can then devise tests over each factor or skill and administer these subtests to groups of students. If, in reality, the factors are measurable entities, one would expect to obtain rather low correlations among these various factors or entities. That is, one would expect students to exhibit strengths in some factors, and weaknesses in others. For example, musical ability and mathematical ability are not highly related. If tests were given to ten students measuring their abilities in each area, one would be quite likely to find that there was really very little relationship between the two or, in other words, some students who were extremely talented in music might do quite poorly in math and vice versa. This would produce a low correlation. One would, of course, obtain a high correlation if all of the students who were talented in music were also talented in mathematics and if all of the students who did poorly in music also did poorly in mathematics.

Research such as that done by Donald Spearritt (1972) has shown that we can identify a word or vocabulary factor as a separate entity from other comprehension skills, but all other factors tend to correlate highly and thus fall into what one might quite practically describe as a big conglomeration termed *other comprehension skills* or simply *comprehension*. Spearritt was able to locate three other comprehension skills in addition to word knowledge, through the process of factor analysis. He found, however, that these three factors correlated so highly that it was doubtful if they could be considered as separate entities.

According to George Spache (1981a),

> . . . No factor analysis of reading tests has yet shown that different types of thinking are really assessed by [the] various types of questions. The components of the reading act appear to be vocabulary difficulty, relationships among ideas, and inductive and deductive reasoning, not the types of ideas identified by labeling questions such as main ideas, details, conclusions, inferences, and the like. (p. 209)

Perhaps Isidore Levine (1970) is nearly correct in his explanation of differences that exist in the ability of one person versus another to comprehend a reading passage. Levine contends that most people who comprehend well in a certain subject do so because of their wide reading and experience in that area and not because of their ability to "unravel paragraph complexities." Levine states,

> We can conclude that the ability to select main ideas and supporting details in a paragraph is not a skill that can be developed and transferred from subject to subject. A grasp of the concepts and data in a body of knowledge is assured when one has perused thousands of paragraphs in that subject. (p. 675)

We agree with Levine that major differences in comprehension probably can be accounted for by the experience factor. On the other hand, certain disabled readers who consistently have difficulty with reading comprehension, even though they comprehend well in an oral presentation, can usually benefit from specific instruction in comprehension skills. It should also be noted that Levine implies that knowledge of vocabulary will improve comprehension. For some students this is probably true, but there is evidence to show that this would not necessarily be true for all students.

Morton Wiener and Ward Cromer (1967) have proposed a "difference" model and "disruption" model for students having difficulties in their reading. Unlike Levine, Wiener and Cromer contend that students who might be categorized in the difference model have reading difficulties because of a difference in the way material is written and the student's normal mode of responding. Students classified in the disruption model would be likely to possess emotional and psychological barriers that interfere with the reading process.

Cromer (1970) conducted a study to validate his theory of the difference model. He took two groups of junior college students who exhibited poor comprehension skills. One group was classified as "deficit" because of their low scores in vocabulary. The other students were in the "difference"-model group. These students had normal scores on vocabulary. Reading materials were rewritten and organized differently to make phrasing and sentence patterns more apparent. These materials were then presented to both groups. When this was done the performance of students in the difference group was as high as that of good readers of a comparable grade level. However, the deficit students' reading performance remained low. Cromer's experiment lends credence to his theory that students classified in his difference model might be helped by either having the materials changed to meet their needs or by instructing or changing the students' mode of response in reading the materials.

Michael Strange (1980) describes the present debate among experts as a disagreement about whether reading comprehension is a bottom-up or top-down process. Proponents of the bottom-up or text-driven position argue that "the page brings more information to the reader than the reader brings to the page." (p. 392) Those who believe in the top-down or concept-driven model take the other point of view: "When someone is reading s/he has a good deal of prior knowledge about the world and this prior knowledge is used to make good guesses about the nature (relationships, episodes, characters, etc.) of the text." (p. 392) Strange suggests that a third conceptualization, an interactive model, properly describes the process as both concept and text driven, where the reader and the text work together to elicit meaning.

An additional concept, known as *schema theory*, is also being explored at the present time. Studies have shown that individuals' presuppositions, or "schemata," about the meaning of a passage can have a strong influence on comprehension. Indeed, some readers may not accept text information that conflicts with their presuppositions. Schema theory is related to the top-down or concept-driven model, although the assumption is made that schemata are adaptable or changeable. Tom Nicholson and Robert Imlach (1981) studied the inferences that children make when answering questions about narrative stories and found that both text data and background knowledge competed for priority in question answering. The results tended to provide more support for a text-driven or bottom-up view, however. A crosscultural study conducted by Margaret Steffensen, Chitra Joag-Dev, and Richard Anderson (1979) was interpreted as showing opposite results, favoring the influence of prior knowledge of the content on comprehension. In this study, subjects from the United States and India read letters and answered questions about an American and an Indian wedding. The subjects read the native passage more rapidly and with better comprehension. The researchers concluded that the reader's schemata greatly influenced their understanding of the written material.

Teachers can expect to see more conflicting results from research as concepts and research methods continue to develop in this complex field. While a clear direction has not yet emerged for the diagnostician, the continued interest in comprehension research should eventually help all teachers to better understand this most essential component of the reading act.

From a testing standpoint, based on what we know about comprehension at this time, it does not seem justified to attempt to diagnose a student's comprehension abilities beyond separating them into one category of word or vocabulary knowledge and another category of other comprehension in general.

METHODS OF DIAGNOSIS FOR GENERAL COMPREHENSION LEVEL

Traditionally used methods of diagnosing students' level of comprehension could be divided into five main categories. These categories would be group standardized tests, individual standardized tests, informal reading inventories, informal recall procedures, and the cloze procedure. The cloze procedure, however, as a somewhat standardized technique, is somewhat newer than either of the first four mentioned categories. A sixth method gaining popularity is that of the analysis of sentence meaning from its structure, sometimes referred to as *deep structure.*

Group Standardized Achievement and Diagnostic Tests

The use of standardized tests is by far the most commonly used method for diagnosis in group situations. Although they have some major disadvantages, standardized tests do have several advantages that have tended to make them popular. One advantage of group standardized tests is that they are quite efficient in terms of teacher time. They also have the advantage of being standardized so that you can compare the performance of a group of students with that of other students. It has been repeatedly mentioned in earlier chapters that one criterion for any reading test should be that it measures reading skills in a situation that is analogous to actually reading. Although it is nearly impossible to do this with tests of word-attack or word-recognition skills in a group situation, it does appear feasible to test reading comprehension with groups of students since this can be done in a situation nearly analogous to actually reading. Another often-claimed advantage of group standardized tests is that they are usually written by "experts." On the other hand, a number of critics have pointed out that certain standardized tests, although well known and much used, contain many questions that tend to make them of dubious value.

Most group standardized tests do not attempt to classify various subskills of general reading comprehension beyond one category of vocabulary knowledge and another category usually referred to as comprehension. This is somewhat confusing, however, since vocabulary knowledge itself is such an important factor in general reading comprehension. It is important to emphasize that when test writers purport to measure vocabulary *and* comprehension, what they really mean is that they are attempting to measure vocabulary knowledge and *other* comprehension skills. Both of their categories collectively measure "general comprehension" or what has been referred to in the scope of the reading skills, shown in Chapter 3, as "Recognizing and Understanding Ideas."

As mentioned above, most group standardized tests do not attempt to categorize the subskills of vocabulary and comprehension. The *Stanford Diagnostic Reading Test* (Karlsen, Madden, and Gardner, 1976) does, however, break reading comprehension down into two categories called "literal" and "inferential." The authors have provided norms for each of these two subcategories. However, because of the fill-in format of items it is difficult to believe that they can actually measure these categories accurately. A separate subtest is also provided for vocabulary. Within the category called "comprehension" most test authors have tried to devise questions that supposedly measure the student's ability to make inferences, remember important details, understand the author's purpose, see a sequence of events, etc. A careful reading of the questions on some of even the best-known group standardized tests will often cause the well-trained reading specialist to become disenchanted. For example, in reading the passages and then reading the questions pertaining to these passages it soon becomes obvious that some generalizations the student is expected to make could not possibly be made from the information presented in the material itself. Success with a particular question of this nature may then depend entirely on the student's background of experiences. For more information on this and other problems with group standardized tests consult the article by Howard F. Livingston (1972) entitled, "What the Reading Test Doesn't Test—Reading." In that article Livingston discusses, in much more detail, some of the problems encountered with group standardized tests.

As stated earlier, nearly all group standardized tests lump the various types of questions mentioned above into a broad category of "comprehension," from which you would only get a grade-level score.

One of the disadvantages of group standardized tests is that they will not allow the teacher to check on total recall in most cases, since the student is usually able to look back over the material and find answers to the questions that he or she encounters at the end of the reading passage. However, the most serious problem encountered with group standardized tests, as far as disabled readers are concerned, is that students can often simply guess at all answers and yet make a somewhat respectable score. To illustrate this problem to students who are beginning their first course in reading, we have often given them the machine-scorable answer sheet for the intermediate battery (grades four to six) of a nationally known reading test and instructed them to randomly mark their answers. In this case they do not even see the test questions. This would be similar to a situation in which every student was a complete nonreader. When all answers are marked, the class members are given the answers and their grade-level scores are then computed. Invariably the class average is from 3.2 to 3.5, with individual subtest scores ranging as high as 6.5. On seeing these kind of results one can see the futility of attempting to derive any meaningful grade-level scores for extremely disabled readers. Perhaps a good rule to follow in interpreting individuals' test scores on group standardized tests is to simply ignore any score at or below what could be achieved by chance.

In summary one might look at some ways in which group standardized tests might be useful and some ways in which they should not be used. Some ways in which they might be used are as follows:

1.   To measure the achievement of a group from the beginning to the end of a remedial period. However, even then you must keep in mind that for those students who cannot read at all, or for those who are severely disabled, you are not likely to obtain an accurate beginning measurement, and thus the full extent of student gains will not be shown.

2.   To measure overall class or group weaknesses in certain areas, e.g., general vocabulary, study skills, or social science vocabulary, which should, in turn, point to specific areas for upgrading the instructional program. This may, however, have little relevance for the remedial program.
3.   To look at the specific types of questions that any one student or small group of students are missing.
4.   To initiate a beginning point in the diagnosis of individuals.

Some ways in which group standardized tests should not be used are as follows:

1.   For grade placement of disabled readers or in making any major decision concerning the welfare of a single student based on a grade-placement score.
2.   For judgment of the amount of gain in overall reading ability, for a single student, from the beginning to the end of an instructional period.

In summary, you should use a great deal of caution in interpreting the results of group standardized tests before making judgments concerning individual students unless you are simply examining the types of questions on which a student was, and was not, successful or unless the tests serve as a beginning point for a more thorough diagnosis.

Appendix B lists some commonly used group standardized reading tests, the grade levels for which they are appropriate, and the skills that each test purports to measure.

Individual Standardized Reading Tests

Individual standardized reading tests have been popular with reading specialists for many years. They have the disadvantage of being more time consuming to administer, but while administering the test the teacher has the distinct advantage of being able to observe various characteristics displayed by the reader. Individual standardized tests are also available for measuring oral as well as silent reading. This is also an advantage over group standardized tests, which, of course, are limited to the measurement of students' *silent* reading ability.

The *Durrell Analysis of Reading Difficulty* (Durrell and Catterson, 1980), which is well known among reading specialists, contains subtests for both oral and silent reading. In the oral reading subtest the student reads a series of graded passages. After each passage the student answers literal comprehension questions about what was read. Norms for oral reading are based primarily on reading speed and only secondarily on comprehension ability. These norms are intended to provide an estimate of the child's instructional reading level. In the silent reading passages the student is merely told to read the passage and to try to remember what was read. The score sheet or record booklet contains an exact reproduction of each passage, phrase by phrase or idea by idea. After reading the passage the student is told to tell all that he or she can remember about the story. The examiner then records the unaided memories on the score sheet. The student is later asked specific questions about memories that were not voluntarily recalled. These memories are also recorded but are not included in determining the norm scored. Norms are based on time of reading and the amount of recall and are intended to provide an estimate of the student's independent reading level. Suggestions are also given for evaluating students' imagery in silent reading; however, the term is not carefully defined, and the examiner is given neither criteria for measurement nor directions for diagnostic application.

Leo Schell and Robert Jennings (1981) have criticized a number of aspects of the Durrell inventory. They believe that the somewhat unique method of evaluating silent reading has a number of drawbacks and that comprehension would be better measured using traditional examiner-asked questions. Durrell and Catterson, the authors of the Durrell inventory, stress the importance of observing and recording students' strengths and weaknesses. We feel that if the emphasis is placed on these aspects of the diagnostic process, the Durrell inventory can serve as an excellent instrument for training diagnosticians.

The *Diagnostic Reading Scales* (revised 1981 edition) by George D. Spache (1981b) is another well-known individual standardized reading test. The DRS contains a special bound test book or student reading book, an examiner's manual and a consumable examiner's record book. Three sets of word-recognition lists are used for placing students for further testing of oral and silent reading to determine three reading levels for each student: an instructional level, an independent level, and a potential level. Spache defines the instructional level as a measure of oral reading and comprehension that indicates appropriate basal-reader placement. The independent level is defined as a measure of silent reading ability and is said to designate the highest level for supplemental instruction or recreational reading. The potential level is a measure of auditory comprehension that suggests the upper limit of a students' present capability. Spache's use of the terms *instructional level* and *independent level* is quite different from that of most experts in the field and in contrast with the standards of traditional informal reading inventories (IRIs) (see the next section). Normally we expect that students' independent levels will be lower than their instructional levels. With Spache's test the opposite is usually the case. Although Spache offers justification for his approach, most test reviewers and practitioners have found that the Diagnostic Reading Scales (DRS) inflate students' scores relative to other measures and typical basal-reader placements.

The DRS contains two sets of reading passages (a total of 22 selections) graded from 1.4 to 7.5 grade level. This is in contrast to some of the commercially published IRIs that contain four sets of comparable passages at each grade level for ease and flexibility of administration. The Durrell battery described above contains one set each for oral and silent reading. Since Spache's passages are used for oral, silent, and potential level reading assessment, the examiner may find that the DRS, like the Durrell battery, contains an insufficient number of passages for pre- and posttest evaluation. Although Spache (1981*a*) claims that "I have added a third series of parallel, equated reading selections in the latest revision to meet this situation" (p. 211), a third set of passages cannot be found in the new edition of the DRS.

In spite of the criticisms noted above and others, the DRS is widely used and can be an effective instrument for observing and evaluating individual students' comprehension strengths and weaknesses.

Another type of individual standardized reading test is the *Gilmore Oral Reading Test* (Gilmore and Gilmore, 1968), which, as its name implies, measures oral reading. It contains a subtest for oral reading comprehension and the norms provide for interpretation in terms of grade-level score, a stanine score, and a general rating for the actual grade level of the student being tested. The general rating for a student would be "poor," "below average," "average," or "superior." In administering this test the student is told to read carefully because he or she will be asked some questions about each story after it is read. There are five comprehension questions concerning each paragraph, and the authors present some guidance in interpreting the answers to questions designed to test the student's ability to comprehend beyond simply the recall level.

This type of test can be very useful, especially for the beginning reading diagnostician, since it provides norms and gives other criteria by which to judge the adequacy of a student's reading. The norm group was also fairly large for a test of this nature. The authors report that the performance ratings for their scores were based on a distribution of scores of 4455 pupils from six school systems in various locations throughout the United States.

It should be stressed that certain individual diagnostic tests, although standardized for certain subtests, do not necessarily contain norms or standardized information for grading either silent or oral reading comprehension. For example, although Durrell and Catterson present comprehension norms for their silent reading subtest in the *Durrell Analysis of Reading Difficulty*, it should be noted that no comprehension norms are presented for the oral reading subtest. For that subtest, norms are based essentially on time. The *Gray Oral Reading Tests* (Gray, 1967) also provide questions to be asked of students after reading each passage. It should again be noted, however, that the norms for this test are based on time and number of oral errors and that comprehension was not considered in the norming.

Informal Reading Inventories

Informal reading inventories (IRIs) have become quite popular as a measure of students' comprehension abilities during the past twenty years and especially during the past decade. Part of the reason for this is that there are now many more well-qualified reading specialists than formerly. Another reason for the popularity of informal reading inventories is increased mistrust of group standardized test results, which at one time were more or less the standard by which most pupils' reading was judged.

Informal reading inventories are usually constructed from materials that students will be expected to use in the course of their normal instruction, or they are written at specific grade levels using one of the better-known readability formulas as the criterion for difficulty. Usually two or more reading passages are written or found for each grade level. The student then alternates from silent to oral reading at each grade level and is asked from about four to ten comprehension questions over each reading passage.

When constructing IRIs teachers usually attempt to devise questions that cover main ideas, important details, vocabulary, and inferences. There is a more-or-less standard set of criteria for judging adequate performance on the comprehension section of IRIs; however, there is still some disagreement among authorities on the exact percentage necessary for placement at the "Free or Independent," "Instructional," and "Frustration" reading levels.

Informal reading inventories are often advantageous since they may be constructed from the actual material from which a student is likely to be instructed. This puts the student in a situation in which he or she is dealing with vocabulary, concepts, and syntax that are truly illustrative of his or her instructional needs. On the other hand, it is difficult to find passages that are representative of a book as a whole. It is also difficult to write good comprehension questions concerning the material once it is found. A further difficulty encountered by teachers and diagnosticians is the accurate interpretation of the adequacy of inferential-type questions. Any one teacher may feel that he or she is accurately interpreting a student's answers; however, when the rating is compared with that of several other people, a rather large discrepancy is often found to exist.

Leo Schell and Gerald Hanna (1981) have pointed out that, at present, commercially published IRIs do not accurately assess the various *subskills* of comprehension because the IRIs:

> (1) fail to demonstrate objective classifications of questions, (2) neglect to provide and to demonstrate comparable scores across subskill categories, (3) fail to provide evidence of uniform passage dependence and passage independence of questions across categories of comprehension, and (4) fail to provide reliable subskill scales and evidence thereof. (p. 267)

Schell and Hanna noted, however, that each of these deficiencies could be corrected with more careful construction of commercial IRIs.

In spite of their limitations informal reading inventories have become, and will probably continue to be, one of the most useful instruments that the reading diagnostician may possess. Chapter 11 is devoted to the construction and use of informal reading inventories and the cloze procedure. For this reason we will not discuss either of these methods of measuring reading comprehension in great detail in this chapter.

Informal Recall Procedures

Although not often publicized by this term, *informal recall procedures* have largely been used as a measure of students' comprehension for as long as reading has been taught. This procedure may take the form of a teacher asking a student a number of questions from a teacher's manual or "off the top of the teacher's head" after the student has read a passage. Sometimes the teacher may simply ask the student to tell about what was read. One of the major disadvantages of this system is that there are no criteria by which to judge the adequacy of an answer. Teachers can often compare one student's answers against those of other students in the class, but even this is often misleading if the teacher has a low-ability group, a high-ability group, or teaches in a community with an extremely low or high socioeconomic level, which, in turn, usually influences overall achievement. Although this procedure has some advantages for the classroom teacher, it usually has limited usefulness for the reading diagnostician.

The Cloze Procedure

The cloze procedure is a technique whereby every nth word is omitted from a reading passage, and a blank is then left in place of each omitted word. The student is given the passage and told to fill in the blanks with proper words to fit the context of the sentences from which they were omitted. Many authorities in the field of reading believe this technique to be one of the better measures of reading comprehension. They contend that filling in the blanks requires a deeper comprehension of a reading passage than could generally be measured with oral or written questions or with multiple-choice-type questions. In fact, anyone who doubts the fact that a thorough comprehension of a reading passage is required in order to obtain a high score on a mutilated passage has but to try one.

A great deal of research has been done in an attempt to develop a standardized procedure for building and scoring cloze passages. Much of this research concerned itself with developing specific percentages of correct responses that would be equivalent to a student's free or independent, instructional, and frustration reading levels. By comparing students' scores on cloze passages with those of the same passages in multiple-choice form (and in some cases administered as informal reading inventories) researchers such as John Bormuth (1967) and Earl Rankin and Joseph Culhane (1969) have developed what is now generally recognized as a standardized procedure for the percentage of words to be omitted as well as the percentage of correct responses corresponding to the three reading levels mentioned above. Most of the percentages have been developed on the basis of leaving out every fifth word and replacing each word with blanks of equal length. Based on the omission of one word in five, the percentage of correct responses equivalent to the commonly recognized reading levels are as follows:

57 percent plus = free or independent reading level
44 to 56 percent = instructional reading level
43 percent minus = frustration reading level

Cloze passages have the advantage of group-type tests in that they can be administered to more than one student at a time. When used with a plastic overlay to check the answers they are also quite easy to score and interpret. See Chapter 11 for details of the construction, use, and scoring of cloze passages.

Sentence Structure or Deep Structure

Very little formal research has been done on the use of the recovery of sentence structure as a measure of students' comprehension. Herbert Simons (1971), for example, believes that through linguistic theory and psycholinguistic research better comprehension tests may emerge. As Simons points out, transformational grammar is the theory of the inherent structure of natural language. It includes a study of the way words are put together to form sentences, the meanings of which vary according to the way in which they are strung together. Simons stresses the point that comprehension cannot take place without the recovery of the original underlying relationships in a reading passage.

Simons suggests several methods of using knowledge of sentence structure as a measure of comprehension. One of these methods would be to determine which two of three sentences is a paraphrase of another, as in the following example:

a.   He painted the red house.
b.   He painted the house red.
c.   He painted the house that was red.   (p. 359)

Another method of recovering sentence structure suggested by Simons is the filling in of blanks to make sentences having the same meaning, as follows:

1. For the girl to leave is what the boy would like.
   What the _____ would like is for the _____ to leave.
2. He painted the house that was red.
   He painted the _____ _____.
3. The girl asked the boy when to leave.
   The girl asked the boy when _____ should leave.   (p. 359)

A third method suggested by Simons would be to simply have students paraphrase what was read. In order to do this, of course, one would have to have very objective scoring criteria. Simons's suggestions seem to hold a great deal of promise for research in the area of construction of comprehension tests and could be adapted, to some extent, by reading specialists in their day-to-day diagnostic procedures.

DIAGNOSIS FOR VOCABULARY KNOWLEDGE

Some of the most commonly used methods of testing for vocabulary knowledge include the use of group standardized tests, the vocabulary section of individual standardized reading tests, the vocabulary section of individual intelligence tests, informal questioning, and informal reading inventories.

Group Standardized Tests

Group standardized tests have traditionally been popular as a measure of both group and individual vocabulary development. As in the case of general comprehension, group standardized tests are easy to administer and are generally efficient in terms of teacher time. Most of the other advantages, as well as disadvantages, discussed in using group standardized tests as a measure of general comprehension also apply when using them as a measure of vocabulary development. However, most critics of group standardized tests have tended to be less critical in reviewing the vocabulary sections of these tests than in reviewing questions dealing with its general comprehension. Perhaps this is simply because questions designed to measure vocabulary knowledge are inherently easier to construct.

Most group standardized tests report vocabulary development in terms of grade-level placement. See Appendix B for a listing of a number of commonly used group standardized tests containing vocabulary subtests, publishers, and grade levels for which they are appropriate.

Some ways in which you may wish to use group standardized tests in vocabulary measurement are as follows:

1. To measure the overall vocabulary development of a group.
2. To compare a group's vocabulary development with its general comprehension development.
3. To find particular areas of weakness or strength, such as mathematics or social studies vocabulary.
4. To establish a beginning point in examining the vocabulary of an individual, providing he or she scores above the level that could be achieved by chance.
5. To measure overall class achievement from the beginning to end of an instructional period, providing that most of the group scores are high enough in the beginning to be above the level that could be achieved by chance.

Avoid using group standardized vocabulary tests for the following:

1. To determine grade placement of disabled readers or to make any major decision concerning the welfare of a student.
2. To judge the amount of gain in vocabulary development, for a single student, from the beginning to the end of an instructional period, especially where the initial score is low enough so that it could have been achieved by chance.

In using group standardized tests you should keep in mind that you are not only measuring students' knowledge of words but also their ability to read the words being tested and, in most tests, a number of other words and synonyms. The fact that a student does not score high on a group standardized test does not necessarily mean that he or she has a low listening or speaking vocabulary.

The Vocabulary Sections of Individual Standardized Reading Tests

Certain individual standardized tests, such as the *Durrell Analysis of Reading Difficulty*, contain subtests for diagnosing individual students' oral word knowledge. In the Durrell battery, this subtest is called the "Listening Vocabulary" test. In this case, reading word knowledge is not measured, but rather knowledge of word meanings is evaluated when students hear the words read to them. The authors of the Durrell battery suggest that oral vocabulary knowledge may be thought of as a good indicator of reading capacity. In taking the subtest, the student looks at three pictures, such as a clock, an elephant and a rainbow. The examiner explains to the student that the first picture is for words about time, the second for words that mean "big," and the third for words about color. The examiner then reads a series of words, such as *red, large,* and *century,* while the student points to the appropriate picture. The Durrell battery has the further advantage of testing the student's ability to *read* these same words in another subtest, so that the examiner may have a clue as to whether word recognition weaknesses are a function of vocabulary deficiencies. The tests are constructed to minimize learning transfer between the two subtests.

The Vocabulary Sections of Individual Intelligence Tests

The vocabulary sections of certain individual intelligence tests, such as the *Wechsler Intelligence Scale for Children—Revised (WISC-R),* (Wechsler, 1974), the *Wechsler Adult Intelligence Scale (WAIS)* (Wechsler, 1955), and the *Stanford-Binet Intelligence Scale* (Terman and Merrill, 1972) can also be useful in assessing children's oral vocabularies. The *WISC-R* and *WAIS* both contain a vocabulary subtest from which a raw score is obtained. This raw score can then be converted to a scaled score from which interpretations can be made in terms of IQ, percentile rating, grade equivalent, etc. (See Figure 17–1, Chapter 17.) The Stanford-Binet also contains a subtest for the measurement of oral vocabulary from which it is also possible to derive a mental age and thus a grade equivalent. The real value of tests of oral vocabulary, or any of the three intelligence tests mentioned in this section, is to determine whether there is a discrepancy between a student's oral and reading vocabularies. When test results reveal a normal, or near normal, reading vocabulary for a student, very little would be gained by administering these tests. On the other hand, for the student who achieves a low reading-vocabulary score, the information obtained from an oral vocabulary test can be useful in determining whether the difficulty lies in a low oral or overall vocabulary.

Informal Questioning

The use of informal questioning can be a very valuable tool in determining whether a student is having difficulty with the vocabulary of a reading passage. You need only say, "What did the word _____ mean in this passage?" There is no need to prepare well thought out questions prior to the student's reading the passage as is necessary for assessing general comprehension. In informal questioning you also have the opportunity to delve further into questionable answers, which, of course, enables you to place further confidence in the validity of your assessment. The major problem with informal questioning, as with any method of informal assessment, is that there are no standards with which you can compare the answers you obtain, other than the answers given by other students. Where a teacher is working with very bright or very dull students, this sometimes presents a problem.

Informal Reading Inventories

Informal reading inventories (IRIs) can also be used in assessing vocabulary knowledge and have the same advantages and disadvantages as informal questioning techniques. However, because informal reading inventories are prepared in advance, they are more likely to contain a vocabulary more representative of a particular book or grade level.

A SUGGESTED SEQUENCE FOR DIAGNOSIS OF READING COMPREHENSION AND VOCABULARY DEVELOPMENT

Most diagnosticians would include an assessment for vocabulary knowledge as a part of a general diagnosis for general reading comprehension. Our heading, "reading comprehension *and* vocabulary development," is used to note the fact that vocabulary development has been included as a part of this suggested sequence.

As a starting point for the diagnostician there are generally two situations—one in which a fairly recent (six months or less) group achievement or diagnostic test score is available and one in which no group scores are available. In a situation in which group achievement or diagnostic test scores are available for a student, these scores can serve as a guideline for further diagnosis. Where these scores are available, there will be several possibilities:

1.   Average-to-high vocabulary and average-to-high comprehension
2.   Average-to-high vocabulary and low comprehension
3.   Low vocabulary and low comprehension
4.   Low vocabulary and average-to-high comprehension

In situation 1 in which a student has an average-to-high score (in other words at grade level or above) in both vocabulary and comprehension, you can feel fairly certain that overall comprehension (vocabulary and comprehension) is not a contributing factor to the reading difficulty. As mentioned previously it is possible to score within approximately six months to one year of grade level on some tests by simply guessing; however, the chances of a student achieving a score at grade level or above on the entire battery are remote. In addition to this information you may wish to verify the group score using an informal reading inventory. This will also provide for a check on the student's comprehension while reading orally and will enable you to verify the group achievement test scores on vocabulary and comprehension. Although the informal reading inventory would not be a necessity, major decisions concerning the welfare of a student should not be made on the basis of one test score. Furthermore, the time spent in giving the informal reading inventory will not be wasted since valuable information can be obtained, while giving it, on problems the student may have in the area of word-attack skills.

Situation 2, in which a student achieves an average-to-high vocabulary score and a low comprehension score on group achievement or diagnostic tests, is fairly common. Scores of this nature are common when students have problems with units larger than single words. The problem, of course, is to determine the level at which comprehension actually does break down. Since most group achievement or group diagnostic tests use reading passages of several paragraphs, you can feel fairly sure the difficulty will be with units of two to three paragraphs or, quite likely, a paragraph or less. Since the group test score indicates a difficulty with silent reading, you should also check to see if the student has the same problem when reading orally. Since an informal reading inventory will allow you to check on all of these things, it can be used at this point. In giving the IRI note the level at which comprehension breaks down and then give the student individual sentences to read and ask the student to paraphrase them for you. This can be done on both the oral and silent passages; i.e., have the student read sentences from oral passages aloud and then paraphrase them and then have the student read sentences from silent passages silently and paraphrase them also. If the student seems to comprehend sentence units but has difficulty with entire paragraphs, he or she is likely to need remediation in the understanding of larger units. While administering the IRI you can also ask informal questions on the vocabulary of the reading passages and verify the results of the vocabulary score obtained on the group test.

A student who does not understand sentence units will need further diagnosis. During oral reading, note whether the student phrases properly or whether phrase units seem to have little meaning. Also note whether the student is aware of punctuation marks or whether he or she ignores punctuation and thus fails to phrase properly.

Another factor that affects group achievement and group diagnostic test scores is the student's reading speed since these tests are timed. It may be necessary to check certain students' reading rates to see if they fall considerably below the norm for their grade levels. This can be done with the "Oral Reading" subtest of the *Durrell Analysis of Reading Difficulty,* or it can be done by simply giving a student a timed reading test. The time can then be checked against that of normal readers. Albert Harris and Edward Sipay (1980) present an excellent set of norms in their book entitled *How to Increase Reading Ability.*

For students with average-to-high vocabulary scores and low comprehension scores it is often helpful to administer a listening comprehension test. This will tell you, to some extent, whether the student's problem is the mechanics of reading or whether the student is having difficulty remembering facts and restructuring a sequence of events. The student who cannot do appreciably better in comprehending a passage read orally to him or her will need remediation concerned with restructuring events, remembering details by forming visual images, etc. On the other hand, the student who does well in listening comprehension but poorly on reading comprehension will likely need help with the mechanics of reading. For example, some students do not comprehend well because they lack an adequate sight vocabulary. Consequently, while reading, so much effort is spent on word attack that overall comprehension suffers. For the listening comprehension test you may wish to use a test such as the "Listening Comprehension" subtest of the *Durrell Analysis of Reading Difficulty* or use IRI passages and apply the criteria as described in Chapter 11.

In situation 3, in which a student receives a low vocabulary and a low comprehension score the possibilities of causation are increased over situation 2. In this case you might first wish to determine whether the student's problem is actually one of comprehension or whether the comprehension score is symptomatic of a problem in word-attack skills; i.e., a student cannot achieve a high comprehension score if he or she is not able to read the words in a reading passage. As a first step, then, you may wish to administer a word pronunciation test such as the *San Diego Quick Assessment* list described in Chapter 4, or the word pronunciation section of the *Wide Range Achievement Test* to determine the student's approximate grade level in terms of word pronunciation ability. If a serious problem is indicated here, very little can be done with overall comprehension until remediation is provided for the difficulty with word attack.

If the problem is not in the area of word attack, you may then wish to determine whether the student has an adequate oral vocabulary. If the results of the *WISC* or *WAIS* (the *WISC* is for ages 5–15 and *WAIS* is for ages 16 +) or Stanford-Binet are available, these can be checked. If they are not available, you may wish to administer an oral vocabulary test.

If the student's problem is not in the area of word attack or oral vocabulary, you would proceed much the same as in situation 2; i.e., administer an IRI, check for problems at the paragraph, sentence, and phrase level, and check for the student's knowledge of the vocabulary used in each passage. Also check the possibility that lack of speed was a factor contributing to poor performance on the group test. If you do not have an IRI available or do not feel proficient in their use, you may wish to administer the "Oral and Silent Reading" subtests of the *Durrell Analysis of Reading Difficulty*. If you choose to use the "Silent Reading" subtest of the Durrell, however, we would recommend that it be supplemented with a few questions concerning vocabulary and interpretation that measure beyond the simple recall level.

As in situation 2, it may prove helpful to administer a listening comprehension test for the same reasons as described there. In a case where a student has a low vocabulary and a low comprehension score, you may also wish to check the results of previously given individual IQ tests, or administer one yourself if you are qualified, to determine if the student is experiencing problems with both areas because of mental deficiency. As in any mental testing program, however, you should not let a slightly low IQ score influence your expectations for a student since there are many students with low IQs who read perfectly well. It serves little purpose to administer an IQ test if the remedial procedures will remain the same regardless of the outcome.

Situation 4, in which a student scores low on the vocabulary section and average to high on the comprehension section of group achievement and diagnostic tests, is somewhat less common than the first three situations. Your first step in this case might be to determine whether the student has a low oral vocabulary. This could be done, as described previously, by checking the subtest scores of the *WISC* or *WAIS* or Stanford-Binet, if available, or by administering an oral vocabulary subtest. If the student's oral vocabulary is low, chances are his or her reading vocabulary will not improve unless remediation is provided in that area first.

If the student's oral vocabulary is adequate, i.e., above the level of the reading vocabulary, you may wish to verify the results of the group vocabulary test using an IRI with informal questions concerning the vocabulary. If the reading vocabulary (in terms of meaning) is low, you will need to provide remediation in word meaning and provide for wide reading experiences.

In cases where there are no recent group achievement tests or group diagnostic tests to serve as a guideline for beginning diagnostic procedures, the procedure would normally follow a somewhat standard pattern. A good beginning point would be to administer a word pronunciation test such as the *San Diego Quick Assessment* or the "Word Pronunciation" subtest of the *Wide Range Achievement Test*. A student who is considerably below grade level on this type of test is not likely to improve in comprehension until he or she receives remediation for word-analysis difficulties.

If the student is found to be somewhere near grade level on the word pronunciation test, then the diagnosis should continue. At this point you may wish to use an informal reading inventory, or you can use an oral reading test such as the *Gilmore Oral Reading Test*. If you choose one of these oral reading tests, you should also give a silent reading test. As mentioned previously, the *Durrell Analysis of Reading Difficulty* contains a normed subtest for silent reading comprehension, but you should supplement it with vocabulary and inference-type questions since the norms only provide for "memories" or literal recall.

In administering either an IRI or a combination of the other silent and oral tests be careful to note whether the student is having a great deal of trouble with vocabulary. If it is evident that the student is encountering vocabulary problems, you would probably want to administer an oral vocabulary subtest or check the student's scores on the vocabulary subtest of the *WISC, WAIS,* or Stanford-Binet if they are available. The student who scores low on oral vocabulary will need remediation in that area before you can expect reading vocabulary to improve to any great degree. However, the two can certainly be remediated and probably should be remediated simultaneously. If the student's oral vocabulary is extremely low, you may wish to check on previously administered IQ tests, or administer an individual IQ test, to determine whether the student has an extremely low IQ and thus reduced potential for learning. However, the vocabulary subtest itself is a good measure of reading potential, and very little is gained, in many cases, by administering an entire IQ test. The student whose oral vocabulary is considerably higher than his or her reading vocabulary would need work in improving his or her understanding of written words, which, as mentioned previously, should include broad reading experiences.

If the student's vocabulary proves adequate, the diagnosis should begin to focus on other comprehension problems. Check to see if the student has difficulty only with passages longer than a paragraph or whether the student experiences difficulty even at the paragraph level. If the student experiences difficulty with paragraphs, check to see whether he or she can read and understand single sentences. As mentioned previously this should be done in both oral and silent reading by having the student paraphrase each sentence after it is read.

If the student cannot comprehend sentences adequately, check the phrasing as the student reads orally to determine whether comprehension of the phrase enables the student to use the correct intonation, pitch, and stress. Also attempt to determine whether a lack of knowledge of punctuation is interfering with proper phrasing. Look for pauses before words that should be sight words. Students who have to expend a great deal of effort in analyzing words in a passage are not likely to comprehend well. If frequent pauses before many words are noted, the student will need to build up a larger sight vocabulary before comprehension will improve to any great extent.

For the student who seems to possess an adequate reading vocabulary but inadequate comprehension, a listening comprehension test can be of considerable help in the diagnosis. Students who cannot comprehend well on either type of test will need help in skills such as structuring events and developing visual images. On the other hand, students who do well on listening comprehension tests but poorly on reading comprehension usually have difficulty in areas such as sight-word knowledge, word attack, punctuation, or some combination of the three.

DIAGNOSIS OF STUDENTS' KNOWLEDGE OF STUDY SKILLS

There are a number of study skills that are of considerable importance to the student in developing a background for working in an academic setting. Any student who did not develop most of these skills would be somewhat handicapped in the elementary grades and would be even more handicapped in high school. However, the failure to develop adequate study skills is not likely to cause a student to become a disabled reader even though it may cause the same student to fail in an academic setting. The end result is, of course, the same. For this reason the diagnosis of an older student who is doing poorly in school work should include an analysis of the student's study skills.

Diagnosis in the area of study skills is relatively easy since most of the skills involved can easily be tested using a group informal inventory. Some commonly listed study skills and methods of assessing students' ability to use these skills are as follows:

Skill	*Method of assessment*
1. Using table of contents	Using students' textbooks ask questions such as, "What chapter contains a discussion of wild animals?" "On what page does Chapter 10 begin?"
2. Using index	Using students' textbooks ask questions such as, "On what page would you find information on the topic of polar bears?"
3. Using glossary	Using students' textbooks ask questions such as, "What does your book say the word *armature* means?"
4. Using encyclopedia	Ask questions such as, "On what page of what volume would you find information on the life of Abraham Lincoln?" "What other topics would you look under to find more information on Lincoln?"
5. Using almanac	Ask questions such as, "What city has the largest population in the world?"
6. Using telephone directory	Ask questions such as "What is the telephone number for Amos Abrams?" "List the telephone numbers for three companies that sell firewood."
7. Using library card index	Use questions such as, "How many cards have a listing for the book, *World War Two Airplanes?*" "What does the Author Card include?" "What does the Subject Card include?" "What does the Title Card include?" "What is the call number of the book, *Hitler?*"
8. Learning to skim	Using a newspaper give timed exercises for finding such things as an article on atomic energy or auto accidents; or using students' textbooks give timed exercises in finding a certain date, sentence, etc., in a specific chapter.
9–12. Learning to read maps, graphs, tables, and diagrams	Use students' textbooks to derive questions. This will be more meaningful than questions commonly asked on standardized achievement tests.

Skill	*Method of assessment*
13. Learning to take notes	Play a short tape recording of a lecture or radio program on a subject in which the students are interested and ask them to take notes.
14. Using time to good advantage	Use a time analysis sheet (see "Methods of Remediating Deficiencies in Study Skills," later in chapter).

Part B: REMEDIATION

METHODS OF REMEDIATING GENERAL COMPREHENSION DIFFICULTIES

There seems to be some question as to whether general comprehension is actually amenable to teaching. That is, some people believe that teaching comprehension skills per se does very little to increase the comprehension abilities of students. They would contend that given the ability to attack and thus "say" words properly a student's comprehension will depend almost entirely on his or her background of experience with the subject. Others contend that unless a student has an average or higher IQ he or she will not be able to learn the higher-level comprehension skills. Although it would be foolish to contend that background of experience is not of great importance, you do not have to examine the research in reading too extensively to find that significant gains in comprehension have been achieved by students who have participated in certain programs designed to improve their comprehension. And, as Helen Caskey (1970) reports in a discussion of the research on the relationship between comprehension abilities and IQ, "it appears that if the pupil has skills adequate for dealing with the material at his level, a higher level of comprehension is dependent not so much upon intellectual ability as it is upon the kind of instructional assistance that is given him." (p. 651)

Dolores Durkin (1978–1979) reported on an observational study that was conducted to determine whether elementary school teachers provide instruction in reading comprehension and, if so, how much time is allotted to this task. Durkin selected middle- and upper-grade classrooms on the assumption that more instruction in comprehension would likely be found at this level. Observations were conducted during both reading and social studies periods by Durkin and two assistants for a total of 300 class hours. Of her findings, Durkin writes:

> Major findings included the fact that almost no comprehension instruction was found. The attention that did go to comprehension focused on assessment,

which was carried on through teacher questions. Instruction other than that for comprehension was also rare. It could not be concluded, therefore, that teachers neglect comprehension because they are busy teaching phonics, structural analysis, or word meanings. What they do attend to are written assignments. As a result, time spent on giving, completing, and checking assignments consumed a large part of the observed periods. Sizeable amounts of time also went to activities categorized as "Transition" and "Non-instruction."(p. 481)

Carol Hodges (1980) responded to Durkin by suggesting that a broader definition of comprehension instruction would yield different results. Instead of the less than 1 percent of the observation time that Durkin found accounted for instruction, Hodges's analysis with the broader definition found that 23 percent of the time was spent in comprehension instruction.

Regardless of which definition of instruction is applied, the findings of Durkin's research are distressing. It does not matter which of the various methodologies of teaching comprehension are used if substantial direct instruction is not provided to students.

If you assume that comprehension skills can be taught with teacher-directed instruction, then the next logical question is, What kinds of programs and/or techniques are needed to successfully develop students' comprehension skills? Leo Schell (1972) indicates that regardless of the type of program involved you cannot expect it to succeed unless it is carried out on a long-term basis. Schell suggests, for example, that ten minutes once a week for ten weeks will not accomplish it. He suggests that a reasonable minimal amount of time in which you could expect to see comprehension growth would be one in which the student received nothing less than three lessons per week for ten weeks. He further suggests that the student will continue to need periodic reinforcement of the instruction after the termination of the formal lessons.

There are a number of techniques that have proven their effectiveness; however, isolating any one or any small group of these as being better than others has not been successfully done. Furthermore, because of the complexity of the skills involved in comprehension and the array of instructional techniques and background of experience to which most students are likely to have been exposed, it seems improbable that any one method or small group of combined methods would be successful with all, or even most, students. In the material that follows, however, you will find a discussion and concrete illustrations of techniques that have proven their worth or that show promising possibilities for further development.

Interesting Materials

One of the most important things to remember in beginning a program of remediation with a student is to use material that is familiar and interesting. Most students have one or two hobbies or at least one or two subjects that tend to interest them. J. Harlan Shores (1968) points out that the most important factors in speed and comprehension are those factors that relate the reader to the material that is being read. Shores mentions, for example, the student's background of experience with the material, interest in the field, purpose for reading the material, and mental set for reading it. Shores also points out that students who are familiar with material in a certain field of interest are more likely to be familiar with the phraseology used by the author. Through interest inventories and interviews you can quite easily find the kind of things that are of interest to students at a particular time. Another technique for placing students in materials of interest to them is to simply display many books at their reading level and let them browse until they find something that they want to read. Steven Asher, Shelley Hymel, and Allan Wigfield (1978) found that children perform better on high-interest than on low-interest passages. They concluded that interest seems to have a direct effect on reading comprehension. Although the finding applied to both boys and girls, the researchers found that boys were more strongly affected. In a finding that conflicts with results of most research in this area, Kathleen Stevens (1980) concluded that high-interest materials had a significantly positive effect on the reading comprehension of higher-ability students only. The reading comprehension of lower- and middle-ability students was not affected by the interest level of the material in this study. Donald Neville and Rudolph Hoffman (1981) reported that reading comprehension increased when stories were written to include the name of the reader and names of people and places familiar to the reader. The results of this study suggest not only the importance of interest on comprehension, but also the potential value of language-experience activities.

Questioning

It is sometimes difficult to separate the process of diagnosis from remediation in reading since in some cases they appear to be one and the same. For example, the technique of questioning appears to be one of the best methods we have found for teaching comprehension. Although effective, this technique could be improved if teachers would ask more questions beyond the simple recall level. Frank Guszak (1967), for example, found that over half the questions asked by teachers he observed dealt with recall of facts. Other researchers have found that 10 percent or less of teachers' questions required students to use interpretative skills. Caskey suggests that teachers attempt to cure themselves and their students of the "right-answer syndrome," i.e., the idea that there is a correct answer that must exactly correspond with the material in the text. She suggests that teachers often condition pupils to respond with the "right answer" to the point that they are afraid to attempt to answer questions that call for them to speculate. Robert Willford

(1968) reported that researchers with whom he worked had a great deal of success asking negative-type questions. As an example he states:

> Watch a five or six year old. You put a picture up and you say, "Okay, what can you do with a horse?" Out of a group of 10, five of them have had an experience. The others don't know what you can do with a horse. We turn it completely around and say, "What can't you do with a horse?" You ought to see the differences in responses we get. Every child can tell you what you *can't* do with a horse. "What can't you do?" "Well you can't take a horse to bed with you." Someone else might say, "You can too if you live in a barn." This kid never thought about this. So now we find, what can you do with a horse? You can take a horse to bed with you if you live in a barn. You can flip the thing over by using a negative question as a stimulus to get a variety of answers. Kids love to do this. You may get more conversation of a single picture than any single thing you can do. (p. 103)

Linda Gambrell (1980) presents evidence to suggest that one of the critical aspects of questioning is to allow "think-time." She suggests that teachers allow a minimum of five seconds to elapse after posing a question to permit students to think about a response. Think-time should also be provided after a student responds to stimulate higher-level thinking. Gambrell believes that students verbalize in spurts and need extra time to process information to higher levels. She is persuaded that providing think-time is difficult but that teachers can be trained to do this and will find the results most gratifying.

James D. Riley (1979) believes that teachers' responses may be as important as the questions themselves. He suggests that teachers carefully observe student responses, try to guess what underlies these responses, make students aware that their statements and thoughts are valued, and then assist students to generalize or expand on their responses.

Signal Words

Teaching students to become aware of signal words can do a great deal to help them understand and follow a sequence of ideas or events. Some authors classify certain signal words as full signals and others as half signals. Words such as, *first, second, third,* or *one, two,* and *three* are full signals; words such as *then, after, that,* and *furthermore* are half signals. Note the use of full signals in the paragraph below:

> *First,* I would like to recommend Mr. Edwards for this position. *Second,* I would like to elaborate on some of his accomplishments during his tenure in his former position. *Third,* I would like to discuss some of his fine qualities as a husband and a father.

Note the use of half signals in the following paragraph:

> When hybrid corn first came on the market most farmers ignored it. *Then* they began to note the increased yields obtained by the farmers who used it. *After* that it was not long until nearly every farmer planted it. *Now* it would be almost impossible to find a farmer who plants anything but hybrid seed corn.

Often there is a mixture of half and full signals in books such as those written in the social studies field. And, sometimes authors make points or lead the reader through a series of events or ideas without the use of any formal signals. They are, however, used consistently enough to make students aware of the value of recognizing them. In teaching students to become aware of signal words you can simply use the students' own textbooks as a source of material. In the initial stages you will need to read each unit paragraph by paragraph and count signals as you go.

Structured Comprehension

For the student who has difficulty at the paragraph or sentence level a technique called "structured comprehension," described by Marvin Cohn (1969), works extremely well. For this technique Cohn suggests choosing factual-type material that is just difficult enough to be beyond the comprehension level of the students who will be reading it. Cohn suggests that students read the first sentence and then answer the question, "Do I know what this sentence means?" This forces each reader to be an active participant rather than a passive reader. If the reader does not understand all or part of the sentence, he or she is to ask the teacher or a peer as many questions as are necessary to fully comprehend the meaning. After all student questions have been answered, the teacher then asks one or more questions about the sentence. The students are to write the answer to each question asked by the teacher. This, of course, again forces all students to actively participate. After all answers are written, the question is then discussed and answers are checked. Cohn also points out that when answers are written the student cannot rationalize that a mental answer was right. He emphasizes the point that in the beginning you should stress literal meaning more than relationships. He suggests asking for the antecedent of every pronoun, the meaning of figurative expressions, and any new or uncommon vocabulary words. After the teacher has begun to set a pattern for questioning, the students should begin to use the same type of question in their search for meaning. Cohn stresses the fact that the book should remain open during the entire process. After ten questions have been answered, each student scores his or her own paper and compares it with those done previously.

Request Procedure

A technique somewhat similar to structured comprehension is one called the "request procedure" as described by Anthony Manzo (1969). In using the request procedure the teacher begins by telling the student to ask the kind of questions pertaining to each sentence that the student thinks the teacher might ask. The student is also told that each question is to be answered as fully and as honestly as possible and that it is considered unfair for the teacher to pretend not to know the answer to try to draw out the student and that it is also unfair for the student to say, "I don't know," since the student should at least explain why he or she cannot answer the question.

The game begins by having the teacher and student both read the first sentences silently. The teacher then closes his or her book and the student ask questions concerning the content of the sentence. Then the student closes his or her book and the teacher asks questions about the material. The teacher should attempt to be a model for good questions, i.e., using thought-provoking questions that call for reasoning rather than strictly factual recall. After several sentences have been read, the teacher should ask questions that call for integration and evaluation of sentences read previously. Questioning is to continue until the teacher feels the student can answer the questions, "What do you think will happen in the rest of the selection?" "Why?" Manzo (1969) recommends specific types of questions as follows:

1. Questions for which there is an *immediate reference*, e.g., "What was the second word in the sentence?" or "What did John call his dog?"
2. Questions which relate to *common knowledge* and for which answers can be reasonably expected, e.g., "What kind of animal has been associated with the name Lassie?"
3. Questions for which the teacher does not expect a "correct" response, but for which he can provide *related information*, e.g., "Do you happen to know how many varieties of dogs there are? . . . well I just happen to . . ."
4. Questions for which neither the teacher nor the selection is likely to supply a "right" answer but which are nonetheless worth pondering or discussing; "I wonder why some animals make better pets than do others?"
5. Questions of a *personalized type* which only the student can answer, e.g., "Would you like to have a pet?", "Why?", "How did the different members of your family react to your first pet?"
6. Questions which are answerable, but are not answered by the selection being analyzed; *further reference* is needed, e.g., "I wonder what is the average height and weight of a collie?"
7. Questions requiring *translation*. Translation questions frequently call upon students to change words, ideas, and pictures into a different symbolic form, e.g., translation from one level of abstraction to another, from one symbolic form to another, from one verbal form to another. "In a few

words, how would you summarize what happened to Lassie?" "What is happening in this picture?" "What do you suppose the ex-convict meant by 'up at the big house'?"   (p. 126)[1]

SQ3R

One of the most effective aids to comprehension that has ever been devised is the SQ3R technique. It was first described by Francis Robinson (1941), and since that time a number of variations have been devised. None of the variations, however, seems to have proven any more successful than Robinson's original technique. SQ3R stands for "survey, question, read, recite and review." This method is best adapted to material in which subject headings are used such as are commonly found in social studies and science books. In brief form the technique a student would use in reading a chapter or unit would be as follows:

Survey: The student reads any introductory sentences that appear at the beginning of the chapter and then all boldface headings, captions under pictures, and questions at the end of the chapter. (Students who first use this technique should be timed to make sure they *only* survey. They have a tendency to simply read the material as they have been doing, if they are not put under some time pressure. A period of two to three minutes is usually sufficient; however, time will depend on the age and proficiency of the readers and the length of the chapter.)

Question: Each heading is turned into a question. For example, the heading in a science book might read, "Iron is an important metal." This might then be changed to, "Why is iron an important metal?" (When students first begin to use this technique you should help them devise questions. One way to do this is to develop a list of common beginnings for questions such as, "When did," "Why are," "Why did," and "Why is.")

Read: Students then read down to the next boldface heading to find the answer to the question.

Recite: After reading down to the next boldface heading the student looks up from the book and attempts to answer the question. When students are first learning this technique, this can be done orally as a class procedure. After they have had a chance to practice, they should recite silently to

[1]Reprinted by permission of the author and the International Reading Association.

themselves. If a student cannot answer a question, he or she should read the material under that boldface heading again.

Review: After the entire chapter has been read, students go back and read only the questions derived from the boldface headings and see if they can answer them. If any questions cannot be answered, they would read the material under that question again.

Considerable thought about the nature of the material is required in order for the student to be able to change the boldface headings into questions. This technique also forces the student to actively seek answers to each question while reading. Some students find this method to be extremely rewarding, just as some find it to be rather burdensome. In teaching this method you should actually go through a number of chapters with students until they become adept at devising questions and following the other outlined procedures. You will find this technique to be generally suitable for students at the junior high school level and above.

Cloze Procedure

The use of cloze procedure as a teaching technique is becoming more useful as teachers uncover more and better ways to use it. Some past attempts to use this technique as a teaching procedure have ended in failure. Subsequent research on the cloze procedure has shown, however, that it cannot successfully be used as a teaching device in the same manner in which it is used as a testing device. For example, as a standard test procedure most teachers omit every fifth word. Therefore, there is no selection of specific types of words in the beginning stages. Passages in which every fifth word is deleted are extremely difficult for some students and, furthermore, the omission of certain words makes it almost impossible for the student to reconstruct the original passage. Also, as mentioned earlier, when used as a testing procedure, synonyms are not counted as correct answers.

Several authors have suggested important modifications of the cloze technique. Among the most important modifications is the necessity of discussing why certain answers either are or are not correct. J. Wesley Schneyer (1965) made this important point a number of years ago when he stated that merely giving a student blanks to fill in without a discussion of why certain words would and would not be correct is like a method of teaching comprehension in which a pupil reads a passage and then answers questions calling for knowledge of word meaning, main ideas, and conclusions. Schneyer emphasizes that a student in checking which answers *are* correct and incorrect may never learn *why* they are correct or incorrect. Schneyer says, "The reasons for the appropriate responses must be verbalized." (p.178)

Lea McGee (1981) conducted a study suggesting that cloze passages should initially be constructed so that deletions are easily supplied with correct words. Others have recommended that aural practice with the cloze procedure be provided prior to written work. Materials from which cloze passages are developed should be of high interest and not require excessive knowledge apart from the students' experiences.

Leo Schell (1972) and Robert Bortnick and Genevieve Lopardo (1973) have offered additional specific suggestions for using the cloze procedure as a teaching technique. Some of these suggestions are as follows:

1. In the beginning stages use a multiple-choice format rather than simply leaving blanks and forcing the reader to come up with answers on his or her own. As the student gains confidence and the ability to make correct choices, you can then gradually switch to the standard format of simply deleting words altogether.
2. In the beginning delete only selected words such as nouns and verbs and do not be concerned about deleting every fifth or even every tenth word.
3. After students have been allowed time to read a paragraph silently, read it aloud, sentence by sentence. Students can then offer suggestions on what might fit in the blanks. Semantically and syntactically correct answers should be accepted, but students should be asked to justify their answers. In doing this you may wish to compare the original passage with students' answers.
4. As students improve in their ability to read multilated passages you should increase the difficulty of the material. This can be done by using material of a higher reading level to begin with, by omitting a larger percentage of the words, or both.

Illustrating Paragraph Structure

The drawing of various-sized rectangles to illustrate paragraphs showing the relationship between main ideas and important details is a technique that incorporates writing with reading. This is somewhat similar to having students underline key sentences and/or words but gives students a better overall understanding of the relationships that exist among sentences. In using this technique, main idea sentences are represented by rectangles that are slightly larger than sentences that represent important details. For example, note the following paragraph and the corresponding illustration (Figure 6–1).

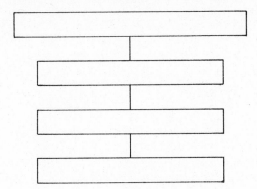

FIGURE 6–1.

Meadowlarks are wonderful birds. They sing pretty songs. They are very beautiful. And, they destroy insects that would harm our gardens.

The large rectangle at the top of Figure 6–1 represents the main idea sentence, i.e., "Meadowlarks are wonderful birds," and each of the three supporting detail sentences are illustrated below it.

In using this system to teach paragraph structure you should start out by explaining that various-sized rectangles represent main ideas and important details, and then have students write their own paragraphs to fit various structural patterns. Students seem to find it easier in the beginning to write paragraphs of their own to fit a specific pattern than to analyze the structure of someone else's paragraph. This also has the added advantage of helping students to improve their ability to write well-structured paragraphs, and for some to understand what defines a paragraph. To use this as a method of instruction we would suggest the following procedure:

1. Introduce the idea as explained above.
2. Draw a simple structural form and have students work in small groups to write a paragraph to fit the form.
3. Change the structure by putting the main idea at the end and then have students rewrite their paragraphs to fit the new form.
4. Illustrate different forms, e.g., where there is a main idea sentence at the beginning, then several important detail sentences, and finally a summary sentence. (See Figure 6–2.)
5. Provide students with well-written paragraphs that clearly show main idea and important detail sentences; have students illustrate them. Gradually increase the difficulty of the patterns.
6. When students are both writing their own and illustrating others' paragraphs, be sure to discuss their responses and allow them to justify

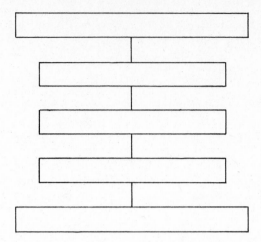

FIGURE 6-2.

what they write or draw. Be sure to accept reasonable alternatives. The important point is not necessarily that all students agree on how a paragraph form should be drawn, but it is important that students be able to justify their own illustrations.

7. As you work with differing forms, have students illustrate each new form and place it on a chart showing various forms. Use different colors to differentiate the main idea rectangles from the important detail rectangles on the permanent models.

8. Students also enjoy naming different forms; e.g., one group of students named the one shown in Figure 6-1 "the natural," and the one with a larger rectangle at both the beginning and the end (Figure 6-2) was called "the double natural."

In using this method of instruction you should remember that all paragraphs do not have a main idea sentence. It is very frustrating for students if they do not realize this in the early stages of looking for a structural pattern in paragraphs written by others. There are also paragraphs that have the main idea somewhere near the middle, and still others that have two main ideas with supporting detail sentences for only one of the two.

Alternative Procedures for Teaching Main Idea

It is frequently helpful to provide students with a specific strategy for finding the main idea of a paragraph or selection. If students have mastered the prerequisite skills of decoding the words, understanding the vocabulary, and remembering and understanding the details of the paragraph, the following steps will assist them in finding the main idea:[2]

1.   Read the paragraph.
2.   Study and restate each sentence in your own words.
3.   Ask yourself what one thing most of the sentences were about.
4.   Find or state the main idea.
5.   Check your answer.

The last step is very important, though somewhat tedious for students initially. To "check your answer," students will need to review *each* sentence and ask themselves: "Does this sentence tell about or support the main idea?"

In order to teach this strategy, the teacher should:

1.   Introduce the steps.
2.   Demonstrate or model the use of the steps for the students with a sample paragraph that all students can follow, such as a paragraph written on a large chart.
3.   Provide a substantial amount of guided practice. This can be accomplished by giving the students a series of short paragraphs and going through each step together.
4.   Provide independent practice for the students only after they have demonstrated an ability to complete the steps under teacher guidance.
5.   Provide review as needed.

Each of the teaching steps listed above is important for students to master this skill. To introduce the steps, the teacher might present the strategy on a chart for students to view. The teacher would then tell the students that he or she is about to show them how the steps work. It is then critical for the teacher to *show* the students by thinking out loud as the steps are demonstrated. Next, the teacher works *with* the students as the steps are practiced together on sample paragraphs. This is a good time for students to interact as they discuss their interpretations of sentences and main ideas. The independent practice and later review will enable students to cement the new skill if the previous instruction was effective. A similar strategy and teaching steps may be utilized to teach other specific comprehension skills, such as sequence, cause and effect, and predicting outcomes.

David Moore and John Readence (1980) suggest that teachers can use "parallel lessons" to teach main idea. These lessons progressively develop

[2]This strategy and these teaching steps were developed by Cheryl Milner, principal, Hayward, California Unified School District.

students' comprehension abilities by moving from the concrete to the abstract and from the simple to the complex.

Moore and Readence would begin by providing pictures for students to view. Students locate the main idea of the picture and its supporting details after the teacher has modeled the task and provided multiple-choice samples. The next step is listening, in which the teacher reads a passage aloud or has the students listen to a recorded tape. Again the teacher first demonstrates and then tells the students to find the main idea. The next step is group oral reading, such as choral reading, reader's theater, or play reading. As before, the teacher models, provides a multiple-choice task, and then students determine the main idea. Finally, the steps are applied to silent reading.

Phrase Training

There is a growing body of research to indicate that certain types of phrase training can be helpful in a program designed to improve students' comprehension. For example, Rollin Steiner, Morton Wiener, and Ward Cromer (1971) compared a group of fifth-grade poor readers with a group of good readers. Steiner stated that as contrasted with good readers, the poor readers failed to utilize syntactic and contextual cues in materials. He believed that poor readers tend to treat words as unrelated items in a series. Other researchers, such as John Downing (1969), have reported that children in their early stages of reading development encounter the same problems, i.e., they see little relationship between words and phrases in relationship to meaning.

Experimental studies in the past using the tachistoscope for training in reading skills have tended to indicate that at least some training is of very little value. It appears, however, that certain types of training can be especially helpful to the comprehension process. For example, Bruce Amble (1966) used a series of phrase-training films to provide tachistoscopic-type practice in phrase reading with a group of fifth- and sixth-grade students. Students using the phrase-training filmstrips made significant gains in comprehension over a control group that did not use the phrase-training films. Amble suggested several reasons why his students may have made more progress than students in other programs who have been instructed using a tachistoscopic technique. These reasons are as follows:

1. Students in Amble's group were at the elementary school level rather than at the high school or adult level as had often been the case where tachistoscopic training had not been successful.
2. Students were trained using meaningful phrases rather than abstract symbols or numbers or even letters.
3. Practice trials were increased to over 5000 rather than the average of around 1000 in former studies.

The case for phrase training is also supported by Leo Schell (1972) who quotes Carl Lefevre as saying that students must learn to master clause markers such as *if, that,* and *now.* Lefevre said, "Reading clause markers quickly and accurately . . . is a first requirement of effective comprehension of meaning." (p. 423)

In phrase training students should also be taught the meaning of punctuation marks and how these influence the intonation, stress, and pitch of the reader. This can be illustrated by tape recording the oral reading of a student who phrases properly versus a student who does not read punctuation marks properly and thus fails to phrase correctly. Play the tape recording and then discuss why it is easier to derive meaning from material when the phrasing is accurate. Also construct exercises in which commas are omitted and show how the meaning of a phrase can often be influenced by the placement or omission of a comma.

Figures of Speech

Some students, especially those who are bilingual or who have meager language backgrounds, have difficulty with figures of speech. For these students it is often necessary to spend considerable time in discussing what is meant by commonly used figures of speech such as, "She was very upset," "She's sitting on top of the world," or "He's sitting on a gold mine." The problem, in the case of many students, is that they do not use these figures of speech in their conversations with their families at home and have not had a chance to hear them often enough elsewhere to know what they mean. There are no fast or sure cures for this problem but you should note whether disabled readers come from bilingual or non-English-speaking homes. For these students you will need to provide more opportunities for conversation time with their peers who do come from English-speaking homes. In most cases the free interchange of conversation with other students in various school settings will do more to improve their language backgrounds than the remedial teacher has time for or is trained to do. However, if you use a highlighting pen or some other method of marking figures of speech in materials commonly used for remediation, you will quickly and easily be able to locate them and prepare students for their meanings before they read them.

Mental Imagery

Peter Wolff and Joel Levin (1972) have demonstrated the importance of visual imagery in reading. In several studies they have shown that when students are told to develop a mental image of a scene or of word pairs they were able to remember details of the scene or the word pairs better than students who did not use this technique. They also stressed the fact that good readers seem to possess a greater innate ability to form mental images. Wolff and Levin also point out, however, that in line with the theories of Piaget, younger children (in the first grade or younger age-grade level equivalent) cannot generate mental images as well as older children without the aid of a picture or a concrete object. Research done prior to that of Levin and Wolff also demonstrated that children from low socioeconomic levels were not able to develop visual images as well as children from middle or upper socioeconomic levels.

Sandra Steingart and Marvin Glock (1979) found that students instructed in the use of mental imagery recalled significantly more correct text relations, had better recall, and a higher level of inference ability than students instructed with a repetition technique. Ellen D. Gagné and David Memory (1978) found that general comprehension was better for students who were told to form a mental image than for students who read the same passages after being told to read carefully.

There is also some evidence to indicate that those students who seem to be adept at developing mental images also tend to read more for pleasure, especially in the area of fiction. In order to enjoy certain fictional sequences one would, of course, have to develop some mental image of the scene. It should also be noted that if a student is able to develop a mental image of a sequence of events, it will later aid recall. There is also evidence that some students tend to be "image thinkers." It is not known whether this trait is inherited or developed; however, most authorities believe it is amenable to training.

One of the easiest methods of developing mental imagery is through listening to short descriptions. For disabled readers listening exercises are especially helpful since students can concentrate on developing a mental image rather than expending all of their energies on word-attack skills. Read or play tape-recorded short descriptive passages and then ask students to illustrate what they heard. In the beginning you may wish to have students close their eyes as they listen. After the illustrations have been completed, ask students to compare them. At this time note important features that should have been completed and also any completely misleading details that are not justified based on the description. As students improve in illustrating scenes from descriptions they hear, have them read and illustrate short descriptive passages. Then discuss these using the original reading passage as a check on the accuracy of the illustrations.

Following Directions

The ability to follow directions is an important comprehension skill. It is also one that is amenable to teaching, as shown by Clarence Calder, Jr. and Suleiman Zalatimo (1970), who designed a program in which twenty-six fourth-grade pupils participated for a period of thirty-six weeks. The twenty-six pupils received the same language arts program as a group of twenty-four pupils in a control group, but were requested to do work in "instructional booklets" that were designed to teach the skill of following directions as related to science, mathematics, art, social studies, and arts and crafts. Students in the experimental group did significantly better on a written test of following directions at the end of the experimental program.

Exercises for teaching the ability to follow directions are simple to devise, and most students find them amusing and challenging to do. Some examples of exercises and materials that are helpful in developing this skill are as follows:

1. Have students write directions for getting from one place in the schoolroom to another. Then have a student (or students) read these written directions to see if they end up in the right place. For those who do not achieve success, analyze what went wrong.
2. Have students read directions for drawing a certain design, and then attempt to draw it or draw it as they read. Show the correctly drawn design on the back of the direction sheet and analyze any obvious errors.
3. Have students work in pairs and assemble model cars and airplanes using the directions enclosed in the kits.
4. Have students practice following directions for paper folding. (There are several books written on the subject of *origami* that both illustrate and give written directions.)

Sequence of Events

Learning to place a sequence of events in the correct order is a skill that is important in reading social studies and science materials. Exercises for improving students' skills in this area can easily be devised by cutting short stories into paragraphs or by cutting paragraphs up into individual sentences. Exercises can also be made self-correcting by numbering the sentences or paragraphs on the back so that when the student has arranged all parts in what he or she thinks is a logical order, the student only has to turn them over to check the accuracy of the arrangement. Workbook exercises designed to give students practice in this skill have traditionally presented a story and then a series of events that the student is to place in a logical order by placing numbers by each event. The problem with this type of exercise is that after completing most of the work the student may find he or she has left out one or more events at or near the beginning. This, of course, necessitates erasing all the numbers. This can be avoided by cutting up the workbook pages into individual exercises and placing each one in an envelope. The events can then be arranged in sequential order and, if in doing the exercise the student discovers an event was omitted at the beginning, he or she only has to slide it into its proper place. When using this system each exercise can also be used many times.

When devising exercises for giving students practice in sequencing events properly you may want to begin by using only three or four short sentences for a paragraph as follows:

They saw many animals.
Soon Cindy was tired and wanted to go home.
Cindy and her father went to the zoo.
One of the animals was an elephant.

In the beginning stages of instruction discuss why a certain paragraph, such as the one illustrated above, could only be sequenced in one way. Also discuss any other logical sequences if they exist. After students become adept at sequencing sentences in paragraphs, they can begin work on longer exercises such as sequencing paragraphs into stories. In devising exercises of this nature be sure to use stories or paragraphs that definitely show a sequence of events that can be properly sequenced through careful reasoning. Comic strips work well as beginning exercises since most of them contain clues to their logical sequence.

Use of Pictures or Objects

The use of pictures and/or cartoons is often a good beginning point in helping students develop the higher-level comprehension skills such as making interpretations and evaluations. Since the stimulus in a picture is continuously present, it is somewhat easier for students, in the beginning stages, to make evaluations than it is for them to make somewhat similar evaluations for written materials. The suggestions that follow are similar to part of the parallel-lessons procedure that Moore and Readence developed, which was described in a previous section of this chapter.

As students look at a cartoon for example you can ask such questions as, "Why do you think the artist showed the president looking so mean?" "Does he usually look this way?" "Would you have shown him this way if you had been drawing the cartoon?" "What effect is this likely to have on the people who read it?" After students have begun to give answers that indicate they are beginning to understand interpretative and evaluative questions, you can then switch to short reading passages and use questions that call for the same types of skills used in interpreting and evaluating the pictures.

Pictures also work well as a beginning point in teaching students to make inferences; e.g., in a picture of a high snow-capped mountain you might ask questions such as, "What do you think the weather is like at the top?" "Why?" "Do you think anyone lives at the top of this mountain?" "Why?"

From working with pictures you can proceed to simple paragraphs such as the following:

Norma put on her bathing suit.
She sat down beside the pool.
The water was very still.
She soon moved under the umbrella.

Ask questions such as, "What kind of a day do you think it was?" "Why?" "Were there other people in the pool?" "How do you know?" One important point that should be stressed here is that the use of pictures to accompany written prose does not, in most cases, improve comprehension. In a review of the research S. Jay Samuels (1970) found that the use of pictures tended to interfere with the acquisition of a sight vocabulary when children are learning to read and that pictures did not facilitate comprehension. He did, however, find that pictures depicting multiethnic groups resulted in a positive change of students' attitude toward the ethnic groups that were depicted.

Stephen Elliot and James Carroll (1980) reported on research that suggests that manipulation of objects may assist students in comprehending what they read. Elliot and Carroll recommend the use of a "story board" to accompany children's reading. After the student completes a sentence, he or she manipulates objects on the board to provide a concrete demonstration of what was read. It is suggested that this active involvement on the part of the reader will not only increase the student's comprehension but also serve as a visual check of the reader's understanding.

Other Methods for Remediating Comprehension Difficulties

Linda Henderson and James Shanker (1978) reported on the use of interpretive dramatics activities in place of basal-reader workbooks to develop the comprehension skills of recognition and recall of details, sequencing of events, and generalizing the main idea. They found that the comprehension of second-grade students was significantly higher in all three areas, as measured by written tests, when using the interpretive dramatics activities. In addition, the pupils strongly preferred this approach. The method, which took no longer than the workbook activities to complete, consisted of (1) a pre-drama discussion to determine the number of characters and identify roles, (2) acting out of the story with no or minimal props, and (3) discussion to determine whether the critical elements of the story were portrayed. Since all children were required to participate in the acting out of each story, most stories were dramatized more than once. Additional findings included an increased interest in the stories by the students who would later act them out and spontaneous dramatization of stories by children after pleasure reading at the classroom library center. The increased comprehension of the students after interpretative dramatics activities might be explained by a number of factors. These include: (1) the fact that students might read more carefully knowing that they would later have to act out the story, (2) increased motivation; and (3) the reinforcing effect of the dramatizations.

Samuel Perez (1981) recommends a method that he calls the "retelling technique," in which students are asked to elaborate on what was read by retelling a story in their own words. The teacher's role is to prompt responses, practice active listening, and wait patiently without interrupting the student's retelling.

A number of researchers, such as Walter Kintsch and Ely Kozminsky (1977), have reported studies that show a strong correlation between comprehension after reading and after listening. Based on such findings and the logical assumption that it is easier for remedial readers to understand material when it is read to them than when they do the reading, many teachers have found that planned exercises in listening can be highly beneficial. Of course, it is essential for students to later transfer these skills to the reading act.

James Christie (1980) is one of a number of writers who recommends the use of sentence-combining activities to promote reading comprehension. Originally, sentence-combining exercises were used to improve students' writing skills. However, Warren Combs (1977) suggests that this approach will improve students' reading comprehension by helping them understand complex syntactic structures. Sentence combining involves changing simple sentences into complex sentences by using signal words, such as *that, what,* and *because.* For example:

1. Bob did not know SOMETHING.
    His cat escaped. (that)
    He forgot to close the door. (because)
2. Bob did not know that his cat escaped because he forgot to close the door.

Combs's article provides specific suggestions for teachers who wish to develop their own sentence-combining exercises. Or, teachers may use commercially prepared activities. (See Horst and Rosenberger, 1981; Strong, 1973.)

One of the most effective means of increasing students' comprehension is by getting them to do a great deal of free or recreational reading. Wide reading usually results in an increase in students' vocabularies as well as in their general knowledge of their environment. Although some students will need instruction in certain aspects of comprehension such as following directions or seeing a sequence of events, there is no substitute for time spent in simply practicing the art of reading. Perhaps an analogy to sports is appropriate. Athletes never make "all-American" by sitting on the bench listening to the coach tell them how they should play. Likewise, students will never become expert readers by listening to the teacher tell them how they should read. Once the basics are mastered, the secret is to read, read, read.

There are many commercial materials designed to aid students in developing comprehension skills. Most of these, however, tend to be books or kits that provide reading materials at various levels of difficulty with accompanying questions. There is still a dearth of material actually designed to show the student "how" to comprehend. You will find a listing of programs for teaching comprehension, the level for which they are appropriate, and the publishers of the materials in Appendix C.

METHODS OF REMEDIATING VOCABULARY DEFICIENCIES

There are many ways of remediating vocabulary deficiencies, but there is no substitute for wide reading. Many students in remedial reading will be unable to read widely in the beginning stages, and others, if they could, would not. However, as you begin a program of remediation in vocabulary skills you should always attempt, as soon as possible, to encourage students to read as much as possible on their own. Since the meanings of many words can be learned through context and through repeated exposure, it is not necessary to "teach" every new word. In reality, only a very small percentage of the total meaning vocabulary of adults is achieved through specific vocabulary instruction or through the use of the dictionary.

Another important point to remember in starting a program of vocabulary development is to try to break the habit that many students will have developed of skipping unknown words. Not only disabled readers, but most people have this habit to some extent. For example, most remember a number of times when they have learned a new word either from a discussion of its meaning or by looking it up in the dictionary. They then found that during the next few weeks they came across the word a number of times in their reading. Common sense, of course, tells them that they did not just "happen" to read the new word for the first few times during the weeks following learning it, but that it had probably appeared many times before when they merely did not notice it. The problem, of course, is that many people train themselves *not* to notice new words because it is much more convenient. You can help break this habit in disabled readers by simply talking about it and by calling their attention to new words. You can call their attention to new words by using games and contests. For example, you can give several disabled readers the same reading passage and see who can find the most words that other students will not know the meaning of. Or you can have students read short passages and look up the meaning of any words they do not know. Then, after reading the passage, let other students give the students who read the passage an oral quiz on the meanings of various words found in the passage. Another method of calling attention to new words is to have students carry a pack of 3″ × 5″ cards with them. Each time they find a new vocabulary word, they are to write the word on one of the cards. They should also write the original sentence in which it was found and then look it up in the dictionary and write its definition and a new sentence using it in the same context as the original sentence. At the end of the week have each student discuss new words he or she has learned with several other students.

The important point to remember in doing activities such as those described above is that the number of new words learned is not so important as the fact that you are helping students break the habit of skipping unknown vocabulary words. And, the development of an awareness to word meaning is an important first step in vocabulary building.

A large part of everyone's vocabulary is developed through both oral and written context. Although the exact meaning of a word often cannot be derived from the context, the sheer volume of words that one hears and reads in context insures that many words will be repeated in context enough times so that word meanings gradually become known. Many students will realize that word meanings can, to some extent, be derived by noting their use in context. However, some students need specific instruction and reinforcement in the use of context clues as an aid to word meaning.

Kenneth Dulin (1970) states that students often expect words to have a specific meaning based on the way they occur in a sentence. As an example he uses the following excerpt from Lewis Carroll's *Jabberwocky*: "Twas brillig, and the slithy toves did gyre and gimble in the wabe." (p. 440) Using this material, or normal narrative-type reading passages with words omitted, the teacher can help students become aware of what Dulin refers to here as "expectancy clues" by discussing various possibilities for replacement of words used by Carroll or possibilities for the meanings of words omitted in normal narrative-type reading passages.

Dulin (1970) and Ruth Strang, Constance McCullough, and Arthur Traxler (1961) have listed a number of categories that may be used for classifying context clues for teaching purposes. For remedial purposes, however, you should focus on only the most obvious types and not become overly concerned with categorization. Both of these two sources, however, contain an excellent discussion of the subject and would be of considerable value to a teacher with little knowledge or experience in the teaching of context clues.

In the beginning stages of instruction in the use of context clues you should use sentences that contain obvious clues to word meaning, e.g., "It had been dry for some time, but now it is very *humid*." Ask questions such as, "What do you think *humid* means?" "How did you figure it out?" and "Are we often able to do this with other words?" After students have become somewhat adept at deriving the meaning of obvious context clues, you should then use their own textbooks for instruction. The use of students' textbooks will give them a feeling of the immediacy of application of the skill. Find a certain paragraph that contains one or more new words, and have students read silently and find these words. Then discuss the possible meanings of these words based on the way they were used and the position they occupy in the sentence. The teaching of the use of context clues should be a long-term effort, i.e., should continue on a somewhat regular basis for a long period of time. Even after the formal teaching has been completed, exercises should be designed from time to time to reinforce use of the skill.

The use of the dictionary should be taught to any student who is at a third- to fourth-grade level or above and is not adept at its use. You should keep in mind, however, that only a rather small percentage of one's total vocabulary is developed through its use. Furthermore, it is usually only effective if used in conjunction with other techniques. For example, in a school where one of us worked as a reading consultant we once checked several classes who had just had an hour of work on word meaning with the dictionary. Immediately following the one-hour period students were checked to see what percentage of the word meanings they had retained. These students were able to accurately recall the meanings of only about 20 percent of the words.

After conducting research designed to investigate the relative effectiveness of four techniques for teaching word meanings, Joan Gipe (1978–1979) concluded:

> Findings were interpreted as supportive of vocabulary instruction, which includes using new words in sentences that provide examples of appropriate usage of the new word within the context of familiar events. Associating new words with familiar synonyms was also supported. Use of category labels and dictionary practice was not strongly supported. (p. 624)

Some other specific types of exercises and activities for vocabulary development are as follows:

1. Make charts showing new words learned. Immediately below each word show how the new word was used in context the first time it was encountered. Review each chart regularly and have students use words on the chart in a sentence. Continue to review until words have been thoroughly learned.
2. When studying any new word, emphasize the meaning as well as the ability to recognize it. One of the best ways to determine whether students know words is to have them use them in sentences different from the ones in which they were originally encountered.
3. Set aside specific time for word study. Words should also be studied whenever they appear, but setting aside a specific time for study will help make students more aware of new words when they appear.

4.   Encourage students to try to think of synonyms and antonyms for new words as they are encountered. Work with crossword puzzles will help increase students' knowledge of synonyms.

5.   Make certain that students know how to use the glossaries in each of their textbooks. Provide practice exercises in using the glossary, and discuss word meanings as they are found.

Many authorities recommend that teachers teach students the meanings of prefixes and suffixes and provide practice in their use to aid students in developing their vocabularies. Unfortunately, very few affixes have meanings that are sufficiently consistent to serve as aids to word meaning when words appear in isolation. As Albert Harris and Edward Sipay (1980) point out:

> It takes a fairly high level of mental ability to understand a generalized meaning and apply it correctly in particular situations, so as to be able to utilize a knowledge of words roots, prefixes and suffixes effectively in attacking the meaning of unknown words. Such a level is probably not reached by the average student below the ninth- or tenth-grade level. In the elementary grades, only the brightest pupils are likely to be able to profit from such instruction. Try, for example, to work out the meaning of *conspicuous* from the common meanings of its morphemes (together-look-full of). (p. 466)

Therefore, we do not recommend that teachers spend valuable instruction time on the teaching of the meanings of prefixes and suffixes to remedial readers.

Commercial materials are available for vocabulary development alone, as well as for the development of vocabulary and general comprehension. Listings of these materials, the levels for which they are appropriate, and the publishers of these materials are included in Appendix C.

METHODS OF REMEDIATING DEFICIENCIES IN STUDY SKILLS

From the list of study skills previously discussed in this chapter, we have found the inability to use time to good advantage to be the most seriously disabling factor in contributing to students' academic failure. While serving as a consultant at the high school level, one of us noticed that many students were referred for having a reading problem that contributed to failure in the subject taught by the teacher making the referral. A fairly large percentage of these students were, in reality, seriously disabled in reading. On the other hand, on testing many of these students it was discovered that they often possessed the reading ability to deal with the reading matter in their textbooks but they simply never read. On being interviewed, these students' usual response as to why they did not read was that they did not have time.

Most of them, of course, had a great deal of time, but the important point was that they perceived themselves as not having enough time. In order to determine how students spent their time, they were asked to fill in a form with listings for each half-hour time period throughout the day. As they went through a typical day they would fill in the blanks showing exactly what they did during each time period. The form had time periods shown up to midnight. After the students had gone through a typical day, we would then go over it and discuss possible time periods when they could read and study. Such information is often shocking to students. They often do not realize that such long periods of time are spent in "going home," "watching TV," etc. You will find this type of form especially useful with junior high and high school students.

Procedures for remediating difficulties with other study skills will not be presented since most of these procedures are intuitive for the average teacher. Furthermore, the level of teaching the other study skills, such as "skimming" and "map reading," depend to a large extent on the grade level and specific materials in which students are working. Commercial materials are also available for teaching the various study skills. Appendix C contains a listing of some of these materials, the companies that publish them, and the levels for which they are appropriate.

SUMMARY

A number of studies have been conducted during the past decade to help teachers understand more about the nature of reading comprehension. Although this research has helped somewhat, in reality very little is still known about the true nature of reading comprehension. This includes how to test it as well as how to teach it. Most researchers have not been successful in identifying various subskills if, in reality, they do exist. In most studies researchers have only been able to identify a vocabulary or word-knowledge factor and one other broad factor simply labeled as "comprehension."

Although researchers are not able to identify subcategories of the comprehension skills they are still somewhat sure that with observation, teachers can identify such weaknesses as the inability to obtain important details, the inability to derive main ideas, and the inability to make inferences. However, when doing this, teachers are still not sure that they are actually observing any one specific skill. Joel Levin, Peter Wolff, and others appear to have been successful in illustrating that students who have the ability to form mental images are able to learn better than those students who are not. This ability appears to be amenable to training. M. Wiener and W. Cromer have also been successful in identifying readers who are not able to read materials that are written in a "different" format from that which they are used to responding to. There also appears to be some hope of remediating students whose reading comprehension suffers because of this "difference" difficulty. This may be done by changing students' response patterns.

Although researchers have not been successful in identifying the subskills of comprehension, we do know that when students who have extremely poor comprehension are given intensive training in this area their reading comprehension does improve. Therefore, although we are not able to identify various subskills, you can still be successful, in many cases, in improving students' reading comprehension. In this chapter a number of tests for reading comprehension have been reviewed and a number of suggestions have been given that have proved their worth in teaching this complicated skill.

REFERENCES

Amble, Bruce R. "Phrase Reading Training and Reading Achievement of School Children," *Reading Teacher.* Vol. 20, (December, 1966), 210–215.

Asher, Steven R.; Hymel, Shelley; and Wigfield, Allan. "Influence of Topic Interest on Children's Reading Comprehension," *Journal of Reading Behavior.* Vol. 10, (Spring, 1978), 35–47.

Bormuth, John R. "Comparable Cloze and Multiple-Choice Comprehension Test Scores," *Journal of Reading.* Vol. 10, (February, 1967), 291–299.

Bortnick, Robert, and Lopardo, Genevieve S. "An Instructional Application of the Cloze Procedure," *Journal of Reading.* Vol. 16, (January, 1973), 296–300.

Calder, Clarence R., Jr., and Zalatimo, Suleiman D. "Improving Children's Ability to Follow Directions," *Reading Teacher.* Vol. 24, (December, 1970), 227–231 +.

Caskey, Helen J. "Guidelines for Teaching Comprehension," *Reading Teacher.* Vol. 23, (April, 1970), 649–654.

Christie, James F. "Syntax: A Key to Reading Comprehension," *Reading Improvement.* Vol. 17, (Winter, 1980), 313–317.

Cohn, Marvin L. "Structured Comprehension," *Reading Teacher.* Vol. 22, (February, 1969), pp. 440–444 +.

Combs, Warren. "Sentence-Combining Practice Aids Reading Comprehension," *Journal of Reading.* Vol. 21, (October, 1977), 18–24.

Cromer, Ward. "The Difference Model: A New Explanation for Some Reading Difficulties," *Journal of Educational Psychology.* Vol. 61, No. 6, Part 1 (December, 1970), 471–483.

Downing, John. "How Children Think about Reading," *Reading Teacher.* Vol. 23, (December, 1969), 217–230.

Dulin, Kenneth L. "Using Context Clues in Word Recognition and Comprehension," *Reading Teacher.* Vol. 23, (February, 1970), 440–445 +.

Durkin, Dolores. "What Classroom Observations Reveal about Reading Comprehension Instruction," *Reading Research Quarterly.* Vol. 14, (1978–1979), 481–533.

Durrell, Donald D., and Catterson, Jane H. *Durrell Analysis of Reading Difficulty.* New York: Psychological Corporation, 1980.

Elliot, Stephen N., and Carroll, James L. "Strategies to Help Children Remember What They Read," *Reading Improvement.* Vol. 17, (Winter, 1980), 272–277.

Gagné, Ellen D., and Memory, David. "Instructional Events and Comprehension: Generalization Across Passages," *Journal of Reading Behavior.* Vol. 10, (Winter, 1978), 321–335.

Gambrell, Linda B. "Think-Time: Implications for Reading Instruction," *Reading Teacher.* Vol. 32, (February, 1980), 534–537.

Gilmore, John V., and Gilmore, Eunice C. *Gilmore Oral Reading Test.* New York: Harcourt, Brace & World, 1968.

Gipe, Joan. "Investigating Techniques for Teaching Word Meanings," *Reading Research Quarterly.* Vol. 14, (1978–1979), 624–644.

Gray, William S. *Gray Oral Reading Tests.* Edited by Helen M. Robinson. Revised ed., Indianapolis: Bobbs-Merrill, 1967.

Guszak, Frank. "Teacher Questioning and Reading," *Reading Teacher.* Vol. 21, (December, 1967), 227–234.

Harris, Albert J., and Sipay, Edward R. *How to Increase Reading Ability.* 7th ed., New York: Longman, 1980. Copyright 1940, 1947, © 1956, 1961, 1970, 1975, and 1980 by Longman, Inc. Copyright renewed 1968 and 1975 by Albert J. Harris. Reprinted by permission of Longman, Inc., New York.

Henderson, Linda C., and Shanker, James L. "The Use of Interpretive Dramatics Versus Basal Reader Workbooks for Developing Comprehension Skills," *Reading World.* Vol. 17, (March, 1978), 239–243.

Hodges, Carol A. "Commentary: Toward a Broader Definition of Comprehension Instruction," *Reading Research Quarterly.* Vol. 15, (1980), 299–306.

Horst, William H., and Rosenberger, Debbie A. *Sentence Combining.* Evanston, Ill.: McDougal, Littell & Company, 1981.

Karlsen, Bjorn; Madden, Richard; and Gardner, Eric F. *Stanford Diagnostic Reading Test.* New York: Harcourt Brace Jovanovich, 1976.

Kintsch, Walter, and Kozminsky, Ely. "Summarizing Stories after Reading and Listening," *Journal of Educational Research.* Vol. 69, (1977), 491–499.

Levine, Isidore. "The Fallacy of Reading Comprehension Skills," *Elementary English.* Vol. 47, (May, 1970), 672–677.

Livingston, Howard F. "What the Reading Test Doesn't Test—Reading," *Journal of Reading.* Vol. 15, (March, 1972), 402–410.

McGee, Lea M. "Effects of the Cloze Procedure on Good and Poor Readers' Comprehension," *Journal of Reading Behavior.* Vol. 13, (Summer, 1981), 145–156.

Manzo, Anthony V. "The Request Procedure," *Journal of Reading.* Vol. 13, (November, 1969), 123–126 + .

Moore, David W., and Readence, John B. "Processing Main Ideas Through Parallel Lesson Transfer," *Journal of Reading.* Vol. 23, (April, 1980), 589–593.

Neville, Donald D., and Hoffman, Rudolph R. "The Effect of Personalized Stories on the Cloze Comprehension of Seventh Grade Retarded Readers," *Journal of Reading.* Vol. 24, (March, 1981), 475–478.

Nicholson, Tom, and Imlach, Robert. "Where Do Their Answers Come From? A Study of the Inferences Which Children Make When Answering Questions about Narrative Stories," *Journal of Reading Behavior.* Vol. 13, (Summer, 1981), 111–129.

Perez, Samuel A. "Effective Approaches for Improving the Reading Comprehension of Problem Readers," *Reading Horizons.* Vol. 22, (Fall, 1981), 57–65.

Rankin, Earl F., and Culhane, Joseph W. "Comparable Cloze and Multiple-Choice Comprehension Test Scores," *Journal of Reading.* Vol. 13, (December, 1969), 193–198.

Riley, James D. "Teachers' Responses Are as Important as the Questions They Ask," *Reading Teacher.* Vol. 32, (February, 1979), 534–537.

Robinson, Francis P. *Effective Study.* New York: Harper & Row, 1941.

Samuels, S. Jay. "Effects of Pictures on Learning to Read, Comprehension and Attitudes," *Review of Educational Research.* Vol. 40, (June, 1970), 397–407.

Schell, Leo M. "Promising Possibilities for Improving Comprehension," *Journal of Reading.* Vol. 15, (March, 1972), 415–424.

Schell, Leo M., and Hanna, Gerald S. "Can Informal Reading Inventories Reveal Strengths and Weaknesses in Comprehension Subskills?" *Reading Teacher.* Vol. 35, (December, 1981), 263–268.

Schell, Leo M., and Jennings, Robert E. "Test Review: Durrell Analysis of Reading Difficulty (3rd Edition)," *Reading Teacher.* Vol. 35, (November, 1981), 204–210.

Schneyer, J. Wesley. "Use of the Cloze Procedure for Improving Reading Comprehension," *Reading Teacher.* Vol. 19, (December, 1965), 174–179.

Shores, J. Harlan. "Dimensions of Reading Speed and Comprehension," *Elementary English.* Vol. 45, (January, 1968), 23–28.

Simons, Herbert. "Reading Comprehension: The Need for a New Perspective," *Reading Research Quarterly.* Vol. 6, (Spring, 1971), 338–362.

Spache, George D. *Diagnosing and Correcting Reading Disabilities.* 2d ed., Boston: Allyn and Bacon, 1981a.

Spache, George D. *Diagnostic Reading Scales (Revised Edition).* Monterey, Calif.: CTB/McGraw-Hill, 1981b.

Spearritt, Donald. "Identification of Subskills of Reading Comprehension by Maximum Likelihood Factor Analysis," *Reading Research Quarterly.* Vol. 8, (Fall, 1972), 92–111.

Steffensen, Margaret S.; Joag-Dev, Chitra; and Anderson, Richard C. "A Cross-Cultural Perspective on Reading Comprehension," *Reading Research Quarterly.* Vol. 15, (1979), 10–29.

Steiner, Rollin; Wiener, Morton; and Cromer, Ward. "Comprehension Training and Identification for Poor and Good Readers," *Journal of Educational Psychology.* Vol. 62, (December, 1971), 506–513.

Steingart, Sandra Koser, and Glock, Marvin D. "Imagery and the Recall of Connected Discourse," *Reading Research Quarterly.* Vol. 15, (1979), 66–83.

Stevens, Kathleen. "The Effect of Topic Interest on the Reading Comprehension of Higher Ability Students," *Journal of Education Research.* Vol. 73, (July–August, 1980), 365–368.

Strang, Ruth; McCullough, Constance M.; and Traxler, Arthur E. *The Improvement of Reading.* New York: McGraw-Hill, 1961.

Strange, Michael. "Instructional Implications of a Conceptual Theory of Reading Comprehension," *Reading Teacher.* Vol. 33, (January, 1980), 391–397.

Strong, William. *Sentence Combining.* New York: Random House, 1973.

Terman, Lewis, and Merrill, Maud A. *Stanford-Binet Intelligence Scale.* Revised edition, Boston: Houghton Mifflin, 1972.

Wechsler, David. *Wechsler Adult Intelligence Scale.* New York: Psychological Corporation, 1955.

Wechsler, David. *Wechsler Intelligence Scale for Children—Revised.* New York: Psychological Corporation, 1974.

Wiener, Morton, and Cromer, Ward. "Reading and Reading Difficulty," *Harvard Educational Review.* Vol. 37, (Fall, 1967), 620–643.

Willford, Robert. "Comprehension: What Reading's All About," *Grade Teacher.* Vol. 85, (March, 1968), 99–103.

Wolff, Peter, and Levin, Joel R. "Role of Overt Activity in Children's Imagery Production," Report from the Project on Variables and Processes in Cognitive Learning in Program 1, Conditions and Processes of Learning, Wisconsin Research and Development Center for Cognitive Learning, University of Wisconsin, 1972.

7

Diagnosis and Remediation of Psychological and Sociological Problems

The first purpose of this chapter is to present information on the importance of, and nature of, diagnosis for psychological and sociological problems that the disabled reader may possess; a second purpose is to discuss some specific diagnostic procedures, and the last purpose is to present some techniques for dealing with problems in this area.

Part A: DIAGNOSIS

AN OVERVIEW OF PSYCHOLOGICAL AND SOCIOLOGICAL PROBLEMS

The psychological and sociological problems with which teachers and diagnosticians are concerned in reading are so often entwined that it is difficult to deal with one and not the other. For this reason, in this chapter no attempt will be made to deal with the diagnosis and remediation of psychological and sociological difficulties as separate entities. However, it will be obvious at times that certain discussions will deal with one much more than the other.

One of the major problems you face in diagnosing psychological problems is whether certain apparent emotional problems are the causes or effects of reading disabilities. As mentioned in Chapter 1, Arthur Gates

(1941) believed that 75 percent of the students who came to remedial reading were likely to have a concomitant personality maladjustment. He also estimated that one-fourth of these, or about 18.75 percent of the total group, would have developed a reading disability as a result of the personality maladjustment. On the other hand, Helen Robinson (1946) believed that emotional maladjustment was present in 40.9 percent of her disabled readers and that it was a contributing factor in 31.8 percent of the cases. Robinson also believed that social problems were present in 63.6 percent of her cases and that these social problems were a disabling factor in 54.5 percent of her cases. Exact agreement in this area is, of course, quite unlikely because of the nature of the measuring instruments. Stanley Krippner (1968) also studied various etiological factors in reading disability and stated, "Almost all children with reading disabilities have some degree of emotional disturbance, generally as a result of their academic frustration." (p. 277) Krippner also concluded, "Rarely is one etiological factor responsible for a reading problem. . . . Isolating the major factor was extremely subjective in many instances and the multifactor causation of reading disabilities became apparent to the clinicians involved in this study." (p. 277)

From the standpoint of remediation of psychosocial (combinations of emotional and social) problems it usually does not matter whether the psychosocial problem was a cause or result of a reading disability. You will simply need to recognize that it exists and that you will need to deal with it.

John B. Fotheringham and Dorothy Creal (1980) concluded, after a review of the literature and as a result of their own studies, that "the major influence on the differences in academic achievement among children is the family" (p. 316). Although you as educators cannot realistically hope to solve all of the problems that affect children when they are not in school, you should do everything within your power to improve the psychosocial aspects of students' learning. Studies such as those of D. Lawrence (1971) have shown that the counseling aspects of remedial reading are just as important as remediation of specific reading skills. Lawrence divided a group of disabled readers into four subgroups. One group received remedial reading only, a second group received remedial reading plus counseling, a third group received counseling only, and a fourth group served as a control group who received no treatment. At the end of a six-month period the group that had received only counseling had made significantly greater gains than any of the other groups except the one that had received both counseling and remedial reading. Lawrence also stated that the type of counseling received by the students in his program could have been done by any intelligent, sympathetic layperson with only brief instruction in his techniques.

An important caution must be noted at this point. Teachers, reading specialists, and clinicians must be especially careful to avoid playing amateur psychologist. The techniques described in the following pages can be effective even if you lack sophisticated psychological training. However, you must remember that your primary role is to assist remedial students with their educational problems. As will hopefully be clear, the techniques presented are merely a part of sound instructional procedures. Put another way, effective reading instruction not only improves the student's reading ability but also improves the student's feelings of self-worth.

IDENTIFYING PSYCHOSOCIAL PROBLEMS

A number of techniques have been suggested for identifying students with psychosocial problems. It should be stressed, however, that most of these methods are somewhat unreliable. Furthermore, as Lawrence indicated in his study, some of the students in his groups did not display any of the so-called typical signs of emotional disturbance and yet seemed to benefit from the counseling. In spite of their shortcomings, some of the methods you may wish to use are teacher observation, interviews, introspective and retrospective reports, projective techniques, personality inventories, and referrals to the school psychologist or counselor.

Teacher Observation

Although observation of a student during day-to-day activities is a simple technique, it can often be valuable. The advantage of teacher observation is that it is not a "one-shot affair" as are some of the commonly used tests and inventories. Through the use of guided observation you have the opportunity to watch students in many situations that may cause stress. For example, you may observe the student's attitude relative to coming to the remedial class, the student's attitude toward the peer group, the student's work habits, or the student's ability to concentrate for a sustained period of time. Since the school psychologist would be likely to work with the student for only a short period of time, these traits would be difficult for the psychologist to observe. The use of guided observation also has an advantage over the use of surveys or inventories for the same reason; i.e., you are not merely taking a sample of a student's feelings at any one particular period of time.

The use of teacher observation also has some distinct disadvantages. One of these is the bias of the teacher; i.e., we are often prone to see what we expect to see and ignore those characteristics that are not in keeping with our expectations. Another major problem with teacher observation is that some students who are apparently somewhat emotionally disturbed display no outward signs of this disturbance. Some psychologists also claim that to be effective an observer must be highly trained.

The characteristics most commonly listed as indicative of some degree of emotional disturbance are that the student:

1. Fails to sustain interest and effort.
2. Does not work well with other students.
3. Is hostile toward adults.
4. Has withdrawal tendencies.
5. Is overly dependent.
6. Has low self-esteem.
7. Cannot sit quietly.
8. Has a fear of failure in group situations.
9. Is nervous.
10. Refuses to read orally.
11. Has a strong desire for attention from teacher.
12. Prefers to play alone.
13. Has difficulty in separation of important from unimportant aspects of assignments.
14. Prefers routine over new activities and assignments.
15. Brags and continually seeks approval for accomplishments.
16. Lacks initiative.
17. Has a tendency to be impulsive in oral reading, i.e., skipping unknown words and miscalling words without analyzing them.
18. Exhibits nail biting.

In using an observation checklist such as this it should be stressed that any conclusions or referrals for psychological help should be based on the observation of a cluster of these tendencies rather than on the observation of one or two. Yet it should be noted that most students, even though they do possess some degree of emotional disturbance, would not be likely to display all or even most of these symptoms.

Interviews

Interviews are advantageous because the skilled interviewer can often gain a great deal of information in a relatively short period of time. Another important advantage of the interview is that it will allow you to immediately delve further into any area that appears to have diagnostic significance. Certain answers a student may give either on written reports or in oral conversation often prove to be more than superficial when pursued by a skilled interviewer. For example, the interviewer can quickly gain a great deal of insight into a student's self-confidence by pursuing remarks such as, "I don't think I can do that."

The use of open-ended questions in the interview can also give a great deal of insight as to how the student perceives his or her own reading ability. One important step in the remedial process is to get the student to accurately perceive and verbalize the reading problem. Through open-ended questions such as, "What do you think about your reading?" you can quickly determine the accuracy of the student's perception of the reading problem. Chapter 12 is devoted exclusively to the development of the techniques of interviewing.

Introspective and Retrospective Reports

Ruth Strang (1969) lists several kinds of introspective and/or retrospective reporting methods that we have found to be especially effective with older students. One of these is the reading autobiography. The reading autobiography may be either oral or written and, as its name implies, is a biography of the student's life experiences in reading. As Strang indicates, the amount of information you are able to obtain will, to some extent, depend on the amount and types of questions asked. For example, when asking the student to write the reading autobiography you may want to provide a list of questions to be answered, such as, Did you learn to read before starting school? Do you read materials other than those assigned at school? How many books have you read in your lifetime? Do other members of your family read a great deal? How do you feel about your reading? When did you first realize you had a reading problem? What were some things you especially liked about reading? The kinds of questions illustrated here are, of course, designed to encourage discussion of the student's feelings toward reading and reading-related subjects. You may also wish to include more questions that assess other factors such as the kinds of material the student likes to read, and the student's use of the school and public library.

Some students will respond quite freely to a completely unstructured type of reading autobiography. In using the unstructured type of autobiography you can merely ask the student to write everything that is important about his or her life as a reader, with no time limit or guiding questions.

Another technique suggested by Strang is the use of retrospective questioning following reading or reading-related tasks. For example, immediately following a student's reading of a story you might ask questions such as, Did you like that story? How did you feel when you were reading it? If you wish to get information concerning *how* the student reads, then you may wish to expand on your questioning by asking such things as, What did you do when you came to a word you did not know? When you paused at the word *government* and then understood it, what did you do? How did you remember all of the details?

Another introspective-retrospective technique is the use of short student essays on reading tasks. Subjects for the essays may vary according to the area in which you feel you need more information. For example, if you feel the student does not work well with others, you might ask for a short essay entitled, "Working with Groups at School"; or for the student who continually disturbs others you might ask for a short essay entitled, "My Behavior at School." When using this technique you should be sure that the student does not perceive the writing of the essay as punishment. This can often be done by explaining to the student that you will be able to provide more assistance with reading if you know more about how the student writes. Writing short essays also serves as a good catharsis for students who have strong feelings that they are hesitant to express orally.

Projective Techniques

Projective techniques have been used by psychologists and psychiatrists for years; however, most of the techniques used by them require rather extensive training and should not be attempted by someone who is not well-versed in their use. These techniques include the use of such instruments as the *House-Tree-Person Projective Technique* (Buck and Jolles, 1955), the *Draw-a-Person Quality Scale* (Wagner and Schubert, 1955), the *Thematic Appercep- tion Test* (Murray, 1951), and the *Rorschach* (Rorschach, 1960). There are, however, other projective techniques that can be used by someone with less training. One of these is the use of incomplete sentences. Although the interpretation of this type of instrument is somewhat difficult, it often uncovers obvious areas for further exploration. See Figure 7–1 for an example of this type of instrument and the results that were obtained by giving it to a sixth-grade student.

It does not take an expert to spot some potentially important information derived from this student. She is evidently upset about her parent's divorce (10, 26) and appears to be somewhat insecure (3, 8). It is also highly apparent that she has a negative attitude toward reading and her reading class (9, 13, 15, 18, 20, 23, 24, 25). There is also a suggestion of a physical problem with her eyes (1, 5, 11).

Another projective technique that often provides useful information for the remedial reading teacher is the use of wishes. In using this technique the student is simply asked, "If you had three wishes, what would you wish for?" The three sets of examples shown below reveal the type of responses you might expect from this technique.

Student A:
1. I would wish my family would be happy.
2. I would wish I would get good grades at school.
3. I would wish we were still living in Louisiana.

Sentence Completion   Reading Center
Date: February 19, 19__   Grade: 6th   Name: Nancy _____   Age: 11 years
Directions: On each line below add words to make a good sentence. Each time tell what you think. There are no wrong answers, and no right answers. Write the first thing you think of. Work quickly.

1. When I read _my eyes get dizzy_

2. I don't like to read when _I'm having fun._

3. I wish I could _Live forever_

4. I seem to understand what I read best when _I wan't to read_

5. When I read, my eyes _hurt._

6. I like to read when _I feel like Reading_

7. School is ~~Okay~~ _Alright_

8. The most important thing to me _is Life_

9. I don't understand what I read when _I feel Sick_

10. My father _Is divorced from my Mom_

11. When I read words seem _mixed together_

12. My family _is Great!_

13. When I have to read _I ~~felt mad~~ feel mad_

14. I can't seem to _Get together with some people_

15. New words _seem Very different like a new word_

16. The easiest thing I read _is Baby Books_

17. My mother _Loves dogs_

18. When I read, my body _feels like a ~~Big~~ block of ice_

19. Teachers seem to _get meaner & Nicer_

20. Reading classes always seem _terrible_

21. Other classes are always _great_

22. The hardest thing I read _is colledge work_

23. When I read, my mind _almost fal\s apart_

24. I would read more if _I liked reading_

25. Compared to reading, TV is _much Better_

26. I wish my parents _would go back together_

27. I am afraid _of gangsters_

FIGURE 7–1.   Sentence completion exercise. (Written by Eldon E. Ekwall and Everett E. Davis.)

Student B:
1. I would like to have a new ten-speed bicycle.
2. I would like to have lots of money.
3. My third wish would be that I could have all the wishes I wanted.

Student C:
1. I would wish my Mom didn't have to work so hard.
2. I would wish I could read better.
3. I would wish I was the smartest person in the whole world.

The wishes shown above are all verbatim responses of three disabled readers who visited the El Paso Reading Center. Although responses such as these must be interpreted with some caution, they do help provide more information about these students. For example, because of the responses given by Student A, further questioning was done that revealed that his father and mother were in the process of getting a divorce and he was very anxious about the outcome in terms of where he would live, etc. He was also being berated by both parents for making poor grades in reading, social studies, and science. And, he had a desire to go back to the past when his family lived in Louisiana, at which time life for him was understandably happier.

The responses of Student B are less revealing than for either of the other two students. His wishes did, however, reveal that the school situation, including his low grades and his inability to read, was not uppermost in his mind. Students often have a desire to please adults by telling them what they perceive the adult wants to hear. This student, however, was not overly concerned with pleasing anyone other than himself. This student also had a very high IQ, as shown from his school records. Later work with this student revealed that he did not really perceive himself as having a reading disability.

Student C was the only child in the family and was often left in the care of a maid because his mother and father both worked. He realized he was a very poor reader and had a strong desire to improve. His classroom teacher revealed that his peer group had sometimes poked fun at him for not being able to read well in class.

Although the three-wish technique often fails to reveal anything of significant value, it is not time consuming and is usually perceived as an enjoyable experience by the student making the wishes. The responses you receive are not likely to be especially revealing by themselves; however, they often lead to further, more meaningful diagnosis.

Another technique similar to the three wishes is to ask the student, "What would you do if you had a million dollars?" This tends to solicit similar responses to those elicited by using the three-wishes technique. You may want to try this in addition to the three wishes.

Other types of projective techniques are the use of student drawings and illustrated picture stories. We would suggest, however, that unless you have had extensive training in the interpretation of student drawings you would be better off not to attempt to use this technique. First of all, the natural artistic ability of students varies a great deal. Secondly, minor recent events in the student's life may greatly influence the drawings. And thirdly, the interpretation of students' drawings often tells more about the interpreter than the student!

Personality Inventories

Through numerous research studies a number of personality variables have been shown to have a relationship to reading. Some of these variables and the researchers who found them are as follows:

David Bell (1969)—Poor Readers' Characteristics:

1.   Negative attitude or lack of acquiescence to authority (important among Caucasians)
2.   Passivity
3.   Aggression
4.   Excitability
5.   Impulsivity

R. J. Brunkan and F. Shen (1966)—Low Rate Ineffective Readers' Characteristics:

1.   Preferred to follow rather than lead
2.   Tendency to be passive
3.   Need for constant reassurance

Glen Chronister (1964)—Significant Correlations Between Reading and Personality for the Following Variables:

1.   Self-reliance (in other words, good readers were more self-reliant and poor readers less self-reliant)
2.   Personal worth
3.   Personal freedom
4.   Feeling of belonging
5.   Freedom from withdrawal tendencies
6.   Freedom from nervous symptoms
7.   Social standards

8. Social skills
9. Freedom from antisocial tendencies
10. Family relations
11. School relations
12. Community relations
13. Cooperation
14. Friendliness
15. Integrity
16. Leadership responsibility

Chronister also studied these relationships for boys and girls separately. All correlations between reading and these variables were statistically significant for the boys ($p < .01$), but only freedom from nervous symptoms was significant ($p < .01$) for the girls.

George Spache (1957)—Disabled Readers:

1. Showed more hostility and overt aggressiveness than normal readers.
2. Showed less ability to accept blame than normal readers.
3. Were poor in knowing how to handle conflict with adults.
4. Exhibited a passive but defensive attitude or negativism toward authority figures.

As you will note from these studies, several characteristics tend to appear with some regularity. On the other hand, some characteristics seem to be peculiar to each study, depending to some extent on the measuring instrument. Most researchers have been of the opinion that disabled readers as a whole possess personality characteristics somewhat different from those of normal readers. These same people, however, are quick to point out that within any group of disabled readers you are likely to find a great deal of variation in personality patterns.

The logical question for the educational diagnostician or remedial reading teacher to ask at this point might be, "Should I use personality inventories in the normal course of my diagnostic work with disabled readers?" As a rule we would suggest that your time could be better spent in other endeavors. Most group personality tests do not discriminate sufficiently between various levels of personality adjustment to allow one to accurately adjust the course of remediation to suit a particular individual. They would, however, in many cases allow you to distinguish between a student with serious personality problems from one who was relatively free of such problems. You should keep in mind, however, that the simple fact that a student is a disabled reader is quite likely to mean that personality problems will exist to some degree. And unless giving a personality test, or any other test, will alter the course of the remediation, there is nothing to be gained by giving the test.

Self-Concept

The self-concept is a personality factor and could have quite logically been discussed under the previous section. However, because of the extreme importance of the self-concept for students in remedial reading, it will be discussed here in a separate section. The important effect of the self-concept has been illustrated in numerous research studies such as those of Mary Lamy (1962), and William Wattenberg and Clifford Clare (1964). Lamy found that the self-concepts of kindergarten children correlated as highly with their success in beginning reading as did their IQ scores. Wattenberg and Clare found that measures of self-concept and of ego strength taken at the kindergarten level were predictive of reading achievement two and a half years later. Michael Thomson and Gill Hartley (1980) examined the other side of this "chicken and egg" issue. They concluded that a primary reading difficulty will often affect a child's social and emotional development. Thomson and Hartley urge teachers to recognize these problems early on and suggest that efforts be focused on areas such as teacher-pupil relations and support from the home. Clearly a strong relationship exists between self-concept and reading achievement. Therefore, we believe that when students with low self-esteem are identified, every effort should be made to improve these students' self-concepts.

A well-trained counselor or the school psychologist should, in most cases, be able to diagnose a student's self-concept with some degree of accuracy. If you refer students to them, you should make it a point to ask for a report on this aspect of the student's personality. However, there will be many students whom you will not be able to refer for a psychological evaluation. For these students you will need to make some sort of evaluation on your own. This can be done through observation and informal questioning and inventories. Although the psychologist has the advantage of formal training and more sophisticated instruments, the remedial reading teacher has the distinct advantage of being able to observe students over a longer period of time.

Students with low self-concepts are likely to give up easily and will often be inattentive. They may also be antagonistic and insecure and show signs of loneliness and indecision. Although they may at times present a braggadocio attitude, in the long run it will usually be apparent that this is simply a defensive mechanism.

One of the best ways of determining the type of self-concept a student may possess is simply to talk with the student. During the conversation ask questions such as, "Tell me about how you learn?" and "Why do you think you have had problems in learning how to read?" Sometimes students are hesitant to say things that they will quite readily put in writing. You can take advantage of this by having students write short essays with titles such as, "What I Think about Myself" or "My Ability to Learn." The use of incomplete sentences as explained under the section on projective techniques can also be helpful in assessing self-concept. In using this technique include incomplete sentences such as, "My ability to learn . . . ," and "Compared to other students. . . ."

Referrals

In making referrals to the school counselor or school psychologist you should consider several factors or questions. Some of these are as follows:

1. Is the student making satisfactory progress in the tutoring situation?
2. Does the student exhibit a cluster of abnormal behavioral symptoms?
3. What is the student's attitude toward me and toward remedial reading?

The student who is progressing well and who is not antagonistic toward remedial reading is not likely to need psychological help even though the student may possess a poor self-concept or appear to be slightly negative about certain aspects of school life. If you are somewhat familiar with general counseling techniques and attempt to provide materials and activities that foster improvement in students' self-concepts, you are quite likely to find a corresponding improvement in their attitudes. On the other hand, if the student does not appear to respond to your teaching after several weeks, then you should consider referring the student for further evaluation and counseling. Lastly, if after several weeks the student's overall attitude toward either you or the remedial reading program does not appear to have improved, a referral would again be in order.

IQ and Reading

It has been a fairly regular practice over the years to include an IQ test as part of the diagnostic procedure with disabled readers. To some extent this may have been justified, but in many cases it was probably wasted time and effort. As mentioned in Chapter 2, you should attempt to make the diagnosis as efficient as possible by eliminating any testing that will not ultimately affect the course of the remedial procedures. If this criterion were applied to the practice of IQ testing, there would be considerably fewer IQ tests given.

As a beginning point you should examine the reasons why IQ tests are often given. Probably the most often-stated reason for their administration in reading is to determine whether there is a match between the student's reading potential and reading achievement. Another often-stated reason for giving an IQ test is that it allows one to see how the student functions while taking the test and to examine the scores on various subtests. The thought behind this line of reasoning is that the student can then be helped by receiving remediation in areas where there are weaknesses and that this, in turn, should help the student's reading.

In examining the validity of these reasons we will first look at the relationship of reading and IQ. As stated in Chapter 1, there is a statistically significant relationship between IQ and reading, as shown from correlational studies. It appears, however, that the reason one tends to get significant relationships between the two is because the very high IQ students usually tend to read well and the very low IQ students tend to do poorly in reading. If one were to eliminate the high- and low-IQ students from the studies (perhaps above 115 and below 85), it is doubtful that the remaining group's IQ scores would then correlate significantly with their reading achievement scores. Yet approximately 70 percent of the students you will deal with would be likely to lie within the 85-115 IQ range. Furthermore, the innate abilities that are required for learning to read are evidently not completely the same innate abilities that are measured by IQ tests. This was illustrated in a study by Berj Harootunian (1966) who studied the relationship between reading achievement and various intelligence variables. Harootunian concluded, "The results suggest two conclusions: first, that several of the tests measure variables that are relevant in reading; second, that these variables are not being elicited by intelligence tests." (p. 391) Harootunian also stressed the fact that intelligence is composed of many factors and that you should not use a "single haphazardly composed score."

If the same innate abilities required for learning to read were measured by intelligence tests, it would certainly seem logical to use intelligence tests as a predictor of future reading ability. However, since studies such as those of Harootunian and others indicate that many of the abilities required for learning to read are not being measured by intelligence tests, it would appear that the argument for administering intelligence tests to measure students' reading potential loses a great deal of its validity.

The logical question at this point might be, How then do we measure a student's reading potential? Perhaps a more logical approach is to simply teach the student a sample of whatever must be learned about reading and see if the student is able to retain it. If the student can do this, do you really care whether the IQ is 80 or 150? You might also consider whether the actual course of instruction would be changed had the student's IQ been 150 versus 80. The answer to this in most cases might be *no*.

The second reason, as stated above, for giving IQ tests is to observe the way the student works and to observe and analyze performance on various subtests. There is certainly something to be gained by the reading diagnostician in analyzing the way the student works and in analyzing performance on various subtests. For example, it is helpful to know how well a student did on the subtest of vocabulary on the *Wechsler Adult Intelligence Scale (WAIS)*, the *Wechsler Intelligence Scale for Children—Revised (WISC-R)* or the *Stan-*

ford-Binet Intelligence Scale (S-B). This information can be especially beneficial in the diagnosis of comprehension difficulties as explained in Chapter 6. Scores achieved in the "Information" and "Comprehension" subtests of *WISC-R* and *WAIS* can also provide information on the student's awareness of his or her environment and ability to reason. You also gain information on how a student performs by watching him or her duplicate designs on the "Block Designs" subtest and by watching the student assemble the puzzles of the "Object Assembly" subtests.

Hubert Vance, Fred Wallbrown and John Blaha (1978) identified five meaningful *WISC-R* profiles, each of which was used to define a syndrome or cluster of behaviors related to disabled readers. However, the investigators pointed out that a substantial number of disabled readers have profiles that do not correspond to the five found in the study.

The question you must ultimately ask, then, is, Do you get enough worthwhile information to warrant giving the test? This, of course, must be answered by each diagnostician while working with students in various testing situations. From personal experience, after administering over 500 *WISC, WAIS,* and *S-B* tests to children and adults, our opinion is that seldom, if ever, is enough information obtained about the way the student worked or about the subtest scores to have justified taking the time to give the test. If the same type of information could not be obtained in any other way, perhaps this would not have been so, but this is not the case. There are short vocabulary tests available that will give you an estimate of the student's word knowledge. And, might it not be better to observe the way the student works and reacts in a reading task than in an intelligence-testing situation?

Psychological reports pertaining to students' performance often contain statements such as, "Juan seems to have difficulty integrating pieces into wholes," or "Frank has difficulty with eye-motor coordination." These kinds of statements may be quite true, but what do they tell us about how to teach Juan or Frank to read? Problems integrating pieces into wholes might show up in learning to sound words after learning phonemes, and problems with eye-motor coordination might show up in writing words. The problem you face, however, is that programs designed to teach part-to-whole integration and eye-motor coordination have not as a rule been successful in carrying over into reading instruction. What has generally been successful is a more direct attack on the problem, i.e., actual teaching of phonic blending or actual teaching of handwriting. Furthermore, problems with phonic blending can easily be located by giving a phonics test, and problems in handwriting can easily be spotted by having the student write.

As the preceding information indicates, teachers and diagnosticians probably tend to administer intelligence tests in many cases where it is really not necessary. In spite of this there are times when information from intelligence tests can be beneficial. For example, if the student does not improve after having received instruction for a period of time, an intelligence test might be beneficial to help you determine whether the student is an unusually slow learner as indicated by an extremely low IQ. Also, if intelligence test scores are already available to you when you receive a student in remedial reading, the subtest scores can provide information on his or her vocabulary, his or her ability to reason, etc., which may eliminate the need for certain reading tests. (See Chapter 17 for methods of interpreting scores made on the *WISC* and *WAIS*.)

You may also find yourself in a school system where intelligence test scores are used as a partial basis for accepting or rejecting students in a remedial reading program. Although we believe there are better ways of doing this (see Chapter 14), the practice still occurs; therefore, most remedial reading teachers should be familiar with the most commonly used intelligence tests.

One important point that should be stressed is that group intelligence tests that require reading (often referred to as verbal intelligence tests) are usually not suitable for use with disabled readers. For example, researchers such as Donald Neville (1961) have generally concluded that for children in the intermediate grades, a reading level of 4.0 is required for obtaining reasonably valid IQs on group tests that require any reading at all. Since many disabled readers do not read at, or even near, the 4.0 grade level, these tests would obviously not accurately measure these students' intelligence. There are other group intelligence tests that do not require reading, but these tests have an extremely low correlation with reading ability, or, in other words, do not measure reading potential to a degree that would make their administration worthwhile.

If intelligence tests are to be used as a measure of reading potential, obviously you must use individual-type tests in order to achieve any degree of accuracy. The most commonly used tests of this kind are the *Wechsler Intelligence Scale for Children—Revised* (*WISC-R*), the *Wechsler Adult Intelligence Scale* (*WAIS*), and the *Stanford-Binet Intelligence Scale* (*S-B*). The *Slosson Intelligence Test* (*SIT*) (Slosson, 1963), and the *Peabody Picture Vocabulary Test* (*PPVT*) (Dunn and Dunn, 1981), which take considerably less time to administer, have also been used for this purpose. As a remedial techer you are likely to find that many of the students referred for remediation have already been given an individual intelligence test; or as mentioned previously, there may be times when you would wish to request that one of these tests be given to a student with whom you have been working. In order to help you interpret the results of these tests a short description of each one follows.

WISC-R and WAIS

The *WISC-R* is designed for students from ages five to fifteen and must be given by a skilled examiner who has had special training in the administration and interpretation of this test. It contains a Verbal Scale with six subtests and a Performance Scale that also consists of six subtests. In most cases, however, only ten or eleven of the twelve subtests are used. In reporting intelligence, scores are given for the Verbal Scale, the Performance Scale, and a combined measure referred to as the Full Scale. The Verbal Scale consists of the following subtests:

"Information."   This subtest consists of thirty questions designed to measure subjects' general range of knowledge and information. It may be influenced to a small degree by culture and background; however, care was taken to include only questions that could normally be answered by anyone alert to their environment. One of the easier questions deals with the number of legs on a well-known animal and one of the more difficult questions deals with the use of a specific weather instrument.

"Comprehension."   This subtest consists of seventeen questions that Wechsler believes is a test of common sense that evaluates the subject's ability to use past information and to evaluate past experience. One of the easier questions deals with the student's knowledge of what to do when he or she has a certain type of injury, and one of the more difficult questions deals with the ethics of keeping a promise.

"Arithmetic."   This subtest of eighteen questions evaluates the subject's ability to solve arithmetical problems. All questions are to be answered orally, and the subject is not allowed to use paper and pencil.

"Similarities."   This subtest of seventeen questions measures the subject's ability to use logical reasoning processes to see similarities. One of the easier questions deals with the similarities between a wheel and a ball, and one of the more difficult questions deals with the similarities between two numbers.

"Vocabulary."   This subtest containing thirty-two words measures the student's knoweldge of the meaning of words. This type of subtest, although influenced to some extent by formal education, has traditionally been one of the best predictors of academic potential.

"Digit Span."   This is a measure of the subject's ability to recall a series of digits forward and backward. Wechsler does not maintain it is an especially good measure of intelligence at the higher levels, but he believes that the results of this subtest often have diagnostic value.

All of these subtests are administered verbally, and the subject has no visual stimulus and is, in no case, allowed to use paper and pencil.

The Performance Scale consists of the following subtests:

"Picture Completion."   This subtest consists of a series of twenty-six pictures each of which has something missing. The subject is required to indi-

cate, either by pointing or with a verbal answer, which part is missing. Wechsler states this test measures the subject's perceptual and conceptual abilities and the ability of the individual to differentiate essential from nonessential details.

"Picture Arrangement."   The subtest consists of twelve different series of pictures. Each series is placed in front of the subject in mixed order. The subject must place them in an order so as to make a sensible story. Wechsler believes this subtest measures the subject's ability to comprehend and assess a total situation.

"Block Design."   In this subtest the subject is given blocks with varying designs on them. The subject must arrange the blocks so as to match a pictured design shown by the examiner. Wechsler believes that this is a good test of overall intelligence, and he also believes that the way the subject goes about the task has considerable diagnostic significance.

"Object Assembly."   This subtest consists of four form boards that the subject is required to complete. Each is a timed exercise. Wechsler believes it measures the subject's ability to see whole-part relationships and tells something about the subject's thinking and working habits.

"Coding (Digit Symbol)."   In this subtest the subject is required to make associations between various symbols. This subtest gives some information about the subject's speed and accuracy of learning.

"Mazes."   This subtest is seldom used unless one of the other subtests is spoiled in the administration of the test. It consists of a series of eight pictured mazes that the subject is to find his or her way through.

The *WAIS* is very similar to the *WISC,* but it is designed for subjects of ages sixteen and older, and it does not include the "Mazes" subtest. Both tests tend to take from approximately forty-five minutes to two hours to administer, depending on the subject.

In scoring each subtest the examiner first determines the raw score. This raw score is transferred to a scaled score through the use of tables found in the manual. The scaled scores are easy to interpret since each has a mean of ten and a standard deviation of three. Knowing this it is also easy to find a percentile rating for each subtest using Figure 17–1, in Chapter 17. The scaled scores of each subtest are added and from these scores tables are provided for determining the subject's Verbal Scale, Performance Scale, and Full Scale intelligence quotients.

A number of studies have shown that disabled readers tend to have higher Performance Scale then Verbal Scale IQs. However, the Verbal Scale tends to have a higher correlation with the ability to read.

Stanford-Binet

The *Stanford-Binet Intelligence Scale* is designed to test subjects ranging from children of two years old through adults. Although it is an excellent all-around intelligence test, it has less diagnostic significance than the *WISC* and *WAIS* since most of the subtests are not scored separately. It is, however, possible to obtain a subtest score for the "Vocabulary" section, which, in most cases, would be of greatest concern to the reading specialist. The scoring manual gives standards for passing the "Vocabulary" section at various age levels. This information, of course, serves as a guide in judging the age level of a subject's vocabulary. You will find this information in the manual at the beginning of the section on the scoring of the "Vocabulary" subtest.

SIT

The *Slosson Intelligence Test* is a rather short test that takes from twenty to forty-five minutes to administer. Although a shorter time administration is listed in the manual, our experience has shown that the times that we have listed are more realistic. In devising this test the author adapted and used a number of items from the *S-B*. In most cases these were the items that are easy to administer. And, since many of the items are the same, the *SIT* naturally has a rather high validity when the *S-B* and/or *WISC* are used as the criterion for validity measurement. In spite of its brevity the research that has been reported on its use in reading diagnosis has been quite favorable. Furthermore, it is easy to administer and does not require extensive training. Although Slosson suggests that classroom teachers can easily learn to give it by reading the manual, we feel it is wise, if possible, to practice giving it under the supervision of someone who is trained in the administration of the *WISC, WAIS* and/or *S-B*. In a study by Robert Armstrong and Robert Mooney (1971) designed to study the implications of the *SIT* for the reading specialists, the authors concluded that it could be used by a test specialist or classroom teacher with as much confidence in the scores obtained as those of the *S-B* administered by a test specialist. It should be remembered that the *SIT* will only provide an overall intelligence quotient and that no subtest scores are reported in the scoring of the results. However, by examining the pattern of correct and incorrect responses, the diagnostician can estimate the student's relative strengths and weaknesses in such areas as general knowledge, vocabulary, computation ability, and auditory memory.

PPVT

The *Peabody Picture Vocabulary Test—Revised,* as its name implies, consists of a series of plates (pictures) that the subject is to identify as they are shown. The time for its administration may run from fifteen to twenty minutes. It can be somewhat useful to the reading specialist to simply determine the range of the subject's vocabulary and experiences as reflected by the subject's knowledge of pictures. Studies concerning its reliability and validity tend to vary a great deal depending on the type of students studied. Our own research in its administration and our examination of students' records in a large district where both the A and B forms are routinely given indicate that it is a highly unreliable measure of intelligence for individual students. The apparent reason for rather large discrepancies between its scores and those of the *WISC* and *S-B* is that the *PPVT* measures a much narrower spectrum of intelligence than either the *WISC* or *S-B*. The reading specialist should keep this in mind while working with it and in most cases merely interpret the score as a measure of vocabulary and experience and not as an overall measure of intelligence.

Cultural Influences

Although it is often difficult to diagnose cultural factors per se, there are some cultural and/or socioeconomic factors that research has shown to have a relation to, or to contribute to, reading difficulties. As a reading specialist you should be aware that these relationships exist.

The studies of M. Deutsh as reported by Edith Grotberg (1970) illustrate some of the problems that are often common to students who come from impoverished backgrounds. Deutsh found that impoverished children have inferior visual and auditory discrimination and inferior time and number concepts. No specific physical defects of the eyes, ears, or brain could be found in these children that would contribute to these problems. Grotberg suggested that impoverishment might create conditions of sensory deprivation, language restrictions, and low motivation for achievement and that all of these conditions acting together may then produce a child with the same characteristics as those referred to as learning disabilities.

Cultural and socioeconomic level also tend to influence overall attitudes toward the school situation. James Stedman and Richard McKenzie (1971) found that middle-class Mexican-American attitudes were similar to those of Anglo middle-class Americans, but Mexican-Americans of lower-class backgrounds tended to place a lack of emphasis on formal education.

A multitude of cultural and/or socioeconomic factors apparently tend to work together to produce disabled versus normal readers. This is well illustrated in a study by Catherine Thurston et al. (1969), who studied the differences between able and disabled black readers. The following differences were found:

1. The able readers came from families with more than one car.
2. More able than disabled readers liked to read poetry.
3. More able than disabled readers received money for working.
4. More able than disabled readers felt close to their friends.
5. More able than disabled readers had fathers who worked.
6. More able than disabled readers had mothers who worked away from home.
7. More able than disabled readers got a daily newspaper other than the local paper.
8. More able than disabled readers had an encyclopedia set in their home.
9. More able than disabled readers had taken a bus trip on a bus other than a school bus.
10. More able than disabled readers had been to a county fair.
11. More able than disabled readers had ridden in an elevator.
12. More able than disabled readers had been hiking through the woods and hills.
13. More able than disabled readers played a musical instrument.
14. More able than disabled readers had been to more than one town to do their shopping.

Thurston and her group also studied a group of white able and disabled readers. In that group they found the following differences:

1. More disabled than able readers had only one car in the family.
2. More disabled readers had their own room. (This was a rather surprising finding.)
3. More able than disabled readers had parents who attended PTA meetings.
4. More able than disabled readers had been to a music recital.
5. More able than disabled readers got a daily newspaper other than the local paper.
6. More able than disabled readers had taken a trip on a train.

7.   More able than disabled readers had been in a building higher than eight stories.
8.   More able than disabled readers had parents who visited their classrooms.
9.   More able than disabled readers received the local newspaper.

It is evident from the foregoing information that various cultural and socioeconomic factors tend to influence students' reading ability as well as their academic functioning in general. However, it is also evident that seldom, if ever, could any one variable be identified as the primary cause of reading disability in a specific student. The reading specialist should be aware of the many variables that evidently contribute to reading difficulties. And, at times, reading procedures will need to be modified to fit the special needs of students from impoverished backgrounds.

Language Factors

Many experts now consider reading to be a language-related or language-centered process. Kenneth Goodman (1967) presented a model of reading based on psycholinguistic theory. Indeed, Goodman suggested that reading is a "psycholinguistic guessing game," wherein the reader relies on three types of information when confronting the reading task. The first two are semantic (meaning) and syntactic (sentence sense) clues, which the reader uses to anticipate the content of the material. The third type is graphic (sound-symbol, or instant word recognition) clues, which the reader uses when necessary. The reader continually checks the accuracy of the reading based on the sense of the passage. If necessary, the reader will reread the material in search of clear meaning. (You may have just demonstrated this theory if you reread the last few sentences.) According to Goodman the reader comprehends by using only as many of the semantic, syntactic, and graphic cues as required. As the reader's skill improves, less reliance is placed on graphic cues. Since semantic and syntactic cues are dependent on the reader's linguistic competence, the development of language skills is crucial to successful reading.

John Downing (1971–1972) used the term *cognitive clarity* to refer to the young reader's search for an understanding of the written code based on what is already known about the oral language system. Barbara Fox (1976), in a review of research, found that many beginning readers do not understand the terms *word*, *sound*, and *letter* and thus are unable to separate spoken and written language into units. Albert Harris (1979) added to the list the following words: *page*, *sentence*, *line*, *first*, *last*, *middle*, *before*, *after*, *above, below.* Harris also indicated that beginning readers may fail to understand that printed words are arranged sequentially from left to right and lines from top to bottom on a page of print.

To further complicate matters, Susan Glazer and Lesley Morrow (1978) found that written materials prepared for six, seven, and eight year olds were more complex syntactically than the oral language of the children for whom the materials were intended.

As noted in Chapter 1, useful tests for diagnosing language disabilities are not presently available. However, Martha Evans, Nancy Taylor, and Irene Blum (1979) described the development of an instrument that identifies and measures certain aspects of written language awareness that are related to beginning reading achievement. They found that the best predictors of future reading ability were those tasks which stressed the *relationship* between oral and written language codes, rather than those that evaluated characteristics specific to the writing system.

For the present the diagnostician can best evaluate children's language abilities through careful observation and an awareness of how individual students compare with their peers with respect to (1) vocabulary range, (2) knowledge of sentence structure, (3) clarity of pronunciation, and (4) listening comprehension.

SOME IMPORTANT CAUTIONS FOR THE REMEDIAL READING TEACHER IN THE DIAGNOSIS AND REMEDIATION OF PSYCHOSOCIAL PROBLEMS

Studies such as those that show that children who have come from a low socioeconomic level tend to read more poorly than children who come from homes of a higher socioeconomic level should be interpreted with a great amount of care—so should such factors as those mentioned above. For example, the fact that more able readers had parents who had visited their classroom may mean that the parents took an active interest in their children and thus created an overall environment that was conducive to reading. On the other hand, the fact that more able than disabled readers had visited a building of eight stories or higher probably has very little practical value for the remedial reading teacher. Many disabled readers are simply lacking in the experience background that is necessary to learn to comprehend as well as those children who come from homes where they have been provided with richer backgrounds of experience. For example, a student's reading ability will not be improved by a visit to a building of eight stories or higher. However, providing a rich background of experiences through audiovisual materials, field trips, discussion, etc., may in time develop the student's background of experiences sufficiently to affect reading comprehension.

Part B: REMEDIATION

TECHNIQUES FOR REMEDIATION OF PSYCHOSOCIAL PROBLEMS

General Techniques

Most of the techniques generally suggested for working with disabled readers with psychosocial problems are simply good overall teaching procedures that would prove effective with any student. However, because of the high teacher-pupil ratio in many classrooms and because of the tendency of some teachers to become overly occupied with the subject matter being taught, some of these techniques are often overlooked.

Set Appropriately High Expectations for Students. Regrettably, teachers sometimes contribute to students' poor self-concepts by expecting too little of them. Many remedial students have been for years the designated plant waterers in their classrooms. Instead of receiving challenging and rewarding instruction they are given custodial tasks to complete. Every remedial teacher should seek to provide the maximum amount of *purposeful* and *meaningful* instruction that requires students to work to the limits of their ability. All students, especially remedial readers, deserve the opportunity to experience the special satisfaction that comes from a job well done. A number of research studies, reviewed elsewhere in this chapter and in Chapter 1, have shown that the teacher's expectations are a critical determinant of students' achievement.

Certainly it takes time and experience for the remedial teacher to know just how much to expect or demand of a student at a particular point in time. However, we urge you not to fall into the trap of expecting too little of students simply because they have experienced failure in the past. The situation is not unlike that faced by the teacher of children who are physically handicapped. It is difficult, in some cases, not to feel sorry for the children. Yet their improvement depends, to some extent, on their teacher's ability to overcome feelings of pity and to set high expectations within the limits of the students' capability.

We have observed remedial students in classrooms, special programs, and clinical settings and have noticed that they often balk at high expectations, exhibiting any number of behaviors designed to reduce the teacher's demands. At the Elementary Reading Clinic at California State University, Hayward, the following procedure has proven effective:

1.   Inform the student that you are sure that he or she is not "dumb," that you are positive that the student will learn, that some effort will be required, and that most of the activities will be enjoyable.

2. Show the student the daily lesson plan and ask the student to assist you by checking off each activity as it is completed. Point out that a number of particularly enjoyable activities will occur along the way, but that other, more rigorous activities must also be completed.
3. Keep the student actively involved, maintain a brisk pace, and do everything possible to keep the student on-task at all times.
4. Praise the student's efforts when warranted after each activity and at the end of the session.
5. Communicate with the student's parents, preferably in writing, indicating what the student accomplished, your pride in the student's efforts, and the specifics about the "homework" assignment.

These procedures can, of course, be utilized effectively with groups of students in classrooms or school remedial programs.

While setting high expectations is essential, you must be careful not to make unreasonable demands of students. Psychologists have known for years that some students become the class clown because it provides a justification for other students laughing at them. Students soon realize that in certain classes they are likely to be called on to perform tasks such as working a difficult math problem or reading a difficult passage and that they are likely to be laughed at when and if they fail to do a good job. Students who feel assured that they will have no unreasonable demands made of them are much less likely to feel a need to anticipate others' laughter by trying to provoke it. You can help assure students that unreasonable demands will not be made of them by letting them know that you are aware of their abilities and weaknesses and that in no case will you embarrass them or ask them to perform tasks for which they are not ready.

A number of the principles alluded to in this section will be repeated for emphasis in the discussion of the other general techniques that follow.

It Is Important That the Student Participate in Planning the Remedial Program.   One of the important steps in a good counseling procedure is to encourage students to verbalize their educational problems and to discuss the kinds of activities that would probably prove helpful in remediating these problems. Students who have had a hand in planning their remedial program are more likely to see a need for each day's activities and become more enthusiastic about them. For example, students often fail to see that an activity as crucial as practice in the act of reading is relevant to their problem. The remedial teacher should help students understand how essential this practice is by pointing out that all complex skills, such as playing a musical instrument, swimming, or even riding a bicycle, require substantial practice for improvement. The teacher might then present the student with a wide selection of books and other materials written at the student's independent level. From these materials the student may then choose those that he or she prefers and plan with the teacher specific times for practice during and after remedial sessions.

In cooperative planning you should not leave the student with the impression that you are not sure what should be done. Be positive, confident, and persuasive in discussing the student's diagnosed needs, but work cooperatively to help the student understand why certain activities are necessary.

Cooperative planning sessions with students can also do much to improve their self-concept. Many students come to view themselves negatively because they believe they are a part of an overall curriculum in which they have consistently failed. This, of course, leads them to believe they are not as intelligent as other members of their class. However, when a student sees that the teacher is willing to take time to discuss what needs to be done and the student then begins to experience consistent success, the student's overall self-concept is likely to improve.

Students Need To Be Constantly Aware of Their Improvement.   In a general classroom environment it is difficult for remedial students to really know whether they are learning or improving in various skills. In fact, disabled readers are quite likely to believe that they are getting worse since their faster-achieving classmates constantly seem to be doing everything faster and better than they are. It is also difficult for disabled readers to achieve success because they have no measure with which to compare their progress. For example, most disabled readers are not aware of the scores they achieve on standardized tests, and even if they were, their progress as indicated by these scores would not be meaningful to them.

In remedial reading you can make students aware of their progress in many ways. For example, a basic sight word test administered to a student at the beginning of a remedial program can be used as the basis for cooperative program planning. This test can then be filed in the student's record folder. After a number of words have been learned, the student can again be given the original test and shown the results of his or her progress. The same sort of thing can be done with phonic elements. Student progress can also be shown by tape recording a somewhat difficult reading passage at the beginning of a remedial period and then tape recording it a second time after the student's reading has improved. Students are often startled at hearing their improvement. Another method of showing improvement is to simply point out things the student has learned on a daily basis, e.g., making comments as, "Look, Sam, you knew the 'fl' sound today. Do you remember you didn't know it yesterday?" Or, "Did you notice you have learned the two hard words that you didn't know last week?" It is not only important to talk about these indicators of improvement but also to get students to verbalize the fact that they too notice this improvement. Another effective technique is to use charts or graphs of the student's progress and to display them prominently in the instructional area. We have found this technique to be as effective with older students as with elementary-age pupils.

The Student Needs To Learn By Methods That Are Enjoyable.   Many students in remedial reading come to view school, and especially reading, as drudgery. Most adults as well as children will not seek activities that they do not perceive as somewhat pleasurable, let alone those that they perceive as drudgery. One of the best methods of determining the type of activities students enjoy is to simply ask them. It is also a good idea to occasionally provide several alternatives, if possible, and let the students decide which alternative to choose. Many reading activities, for example, can be taught by games. Although at times games may be a less-efficient method of learning than teacher-directed activities, the change of attitudes that students experience in learning may more than make them worthwhile.

Avoid Unfavorable Comparisons With Other Students.   These comparisons should be avoided whether it be on the basis of academic achievement, behavior, or other social or ethnic factors. Most experienced teachers have found that comparisons really never serve to improve the student being compared but more than likely make the student antagonistic. If comparisons are made they should be done on the basis of present behavior versus previous work or behavior. This gives the student no reason to become antagonistic.

Provide the Student With As Much Success As Possible.   Although this may sound like an old cliché, it is an important technique in working with disabled readers. As stated earlier, a number of studies have shown that a large percentage of disabled readers possess a low self-concept. The reason for this low self-concept is in many cases due to repeated failures in reading and other reading-related activities. For many students this then means that they must constantly experience success until they come to see themselves as successful. Other studies have shown that as children grow older their self-concepts become more stable and resistant to change. This, of course, means that older students must receive large dosages of success over a long period of time if their self-concepts are really going to change.

You can provide success for your students in a number of ways. One of these is to apply the IRI criteria to books students choose to read so as to insure that they are at their free or independent reading level (see Chapter 11 for a thorough explanation of this procedure). You should also make sure that most seatwork lessons are comparatively short and well understood before students attempt to do them. One of the most successful methods of providing success for students is to let them read to students in the lower grades or, if their home situation permits, to let them read to a preschool-age brother or sister. Students who are not disabled in a particular area of reading can also achieve a measure of success by helping other students who are disabled in that area. This also frees the teacher to do more individualized instruction.

Provide a Friendly Atmosphere in Which Students Feel Free to Express Their Opinions.   Many students perceive their teachers as authority figures with whom they are not free to discuss their likes and dislikes and opinions in general. You can easily let students know they are free to discuss their opinions without the necessity of receiving your stamp of approval or without being criticized for opinions that happen to be contrary to yours. As a remedial reading teacher you should also attempt to ignore antagonistic attitudes or at least not take them too seriously. Some disabled readers will be extremely antagonistic about reading, and this antagonism will often appear to be directed toward you. However, most teachers find that, as disabled readers begin to improve and perceive the teacher as being directly responsible for much of this improvement, their antagonistic attitudes also improve.

Be Consistent in Your Behavior Toward Students.   Many students come from homes where they may receive verbal or physical punishment one day for behavior that would be accepted or tolerated on another day. You should attempt, as nearly as possible, to set up standards for behavior and expectations for completion of assignments in the beginning and then be consistent in these behaviors and expectations. Few things bother students (regardless of age) more than not knowing what to expect from their behavior. When students do not know what to expect, they are also more likely to experiment to determine what behavior on their part is likely to bring about a change of behavior on the part of their teacher. All students, and especially disabled readers, need the security of consistent behavior patterns from their teacher.

Attempt to Improve Students' Relationships With Their Peers.   Studies such as that of Deon Stevens (1971) have shown that disabled readers are not as sociably accepted as their normal-achieving peers. To some extent this can be altered by arranging for disabled readers to demonstrate their strengths in other areas. If remedial activities are conducted outside of the student's classroom situation, the remedial reading teacher may need to work in conjunction with the student's homeroom teacher to arrange for this type of success experience. These experiences might include such things as the demonstration of hobbies or of reading material practiced in remedial reading.

Counseling Disabled Readers

Most disabled readers can be expected to possess some degree of emotional maladjustment even though it is not always apparent. For this reason an integral part of the remedial reading program should provide for counseling. Contrary to the beliefs of some people effective counseling can be done by the remedial reading teacher with brief training in a few specific techniques. This point has been emphasized by Lawrence and others who have carried on extremely effective counseling programs for disabled readers. The technique described by Lawrence is a nine-step procedure, as follows:

1. The counselor introduced himself or herself as a person who was interested in students and concerned about their happiness in school.
2. The counselor attempted to establish an atmosphere in which he or she was uncritical, friendly, and accepting of the student's personality.
3. The counselor attempted to provide a sounding board for the student's feelings. No attempt was made to interpret these feelings.
4. The interviews were student centered.
5. In most cases direct questioning was avoided. Any questions that were asked were done so in a general way.
6. In the beginning stages discussion was only possible through the use of drawings and pictures done by the student. In the later stages other pictures were used as a stimulus such as those of the *Children's Apperception Test.*
7. The student was asked for three main wishes, and these wishes were discussed fully.
8. During the interviews the counselor attempted to find opportunities to praise the student's personality (not skills). In doing this the counselor attempted to build the student's self-image.
9. Various areas of the student's life were covered. These included the following: "relationship with parents; relationship with siblings; relationship with peers; relationship with other relatives; hobbies and interests; aspirations immediate and long-term; worries, fears, anxieties; attitude toward school; and attitude toward self."   (p. 120)

A counseling technique that has been used effectively for some time in the Reading Center at the University of Texas at El Paso is one described by James Gardner and Grayce Ransom (1968). It is a rather comprehensive eight-step procedure that can rather easily be adapted to the needs of specific individuals. This procedure can easily be learned by teachers with only a minimum amount of study. Following is a description of this procedure:

1. *Provide the subject with an adequate rationale for his or her learning problem.*   In this step the counselor (C) attempts to determine why the subject (S) believes he or she has failed to some degree in reading. As Gardner and Ransom point out, many students manifest a strong underlying fear that they are mentally retarded or have serious brain dysfunction although the subject may mask this belief to some extent. C then attempts to help S realize that S does not fit the pattern of a mentally retarded or brain-injured student. In doing this C can point out that S is not in any of the special classes that exist for this type of student. S

is also made aware of his or her intelligent behaviors, such as knowing the rules of complicated games such as Monopoly, baseball, and football and/or competencies that C and S may find to discuss. S's background is then discussed in terms of possible reasons for failure. These might include such things as prolonged absence from school in the beginning years, or lack of continuity of instruction because of family moves or because of perceptual immaturity. C should fully explain to S how these factors can impede learning progress so that S can accept one or more of these reasons as an explanation or rationale for the learning problem.

2. *Provide social reinforcement for S's positive statements about school.* Whenever S makes a positive statement about school, a teacher, or school-related activity, C smiles and shows heightened or overall interest. The theory behind these actions on the part of C is that changing the verbal responses of S may lead to a corresponding change in behavior.

3. *Help the subject learn basic discriminations about his or her own behavior.* In doing this C attempts to discover circumstances that lead to S's failure to complete assignments or S's failure to act in a manner in keeping with a healthy academic orientation. This is done by asking S to discuss the circumstances that lead to failure. After C discovers these circumstances, S is helped to become aware of his or her undesirable behavior. This can be done by role playing in which S assumes the role of a student in the classroom and C assumes the role of the teacher. Gardner and Ransom emphasize that C must attempt to get an exact conception of precisely what S does.

4. *Teach the subject the aversive consequences involved in the continued use of avoidance patterns.* In this step C attempts to show S the immediate consequences, rather than delayed consequences of avoidance patterns. As Gardner and Ransom aptly point out, we often tell students that they are likely to be unable to obtain a certain job or they will be unable to accomplish some other long-term goal. In most cases these long-term goals are unrealistic as far as children are concerned. In this step, however, the authors suggest showing short-term consequences such as those of the S who daydreams. C might say,

> You look out of the window because you feel you are not a good reader. But now you are in a practice situation, with reading material that you know you can handle. But you have the *habit* of looking out the window. You must break that habit. It will cause nothing but trouble, for you look out the window and you miss the word. When you miss the word, you fall behind and lose your place. When this happens, you start foundering around, getting scared, thinking you are stupid, and getting mad at yourself and the teacher and the book. These are the things that happen when you start to look out the window. (p. 533)

5. *Help the subject to develop alternative modes of responding.*   In this process C may help S to develop alternative modes by assuming the role of S and demonstrating S's avoidance behaviors. S may then be asked to suggest alternative modes of responding or C and S may both discuss alternative modes. Gardner and Ransom also emphasize the importance of maintaining communication with other teachers of S so that they can be alerted to the types of behavior being developed. The responses can then be reinforced as other teachers note them.

6. *Help the subject label his or her feelings.*   As Gardner and Ransom point out, most students are not able to discriminate among their moods or feelings. In this step C should attempt to explain concepts such as avoidance and anger. In doing this the authors suggest stopping the student as he or she is reading something that appears to be difficult and asking how S is feeling *right now.* Although, as the authors state, many S's will report feeling "funny," later discussion will often prove that S is angry or disgusted at not being an able reader. Do not force S to admit to feelings S does not possess; however, you may find that suggesting possibilities such as "afraid," "angry," "wanting to stop," "angry at the teacher," "angry with myself," or "tired" often helps S to discover how he or she really feels.

7. *Maintain a positive attitude toward the personality and academic potentiality of the subject.*   This is often a quality that requires some reorientation on the part of the teacher doing the counseling. However, knowing that most studies show that all but about 2 percent of the school population *can* learn to read should help C maintain a positive attitude. C must show his or her belief in the worth of S by everything C says and does.

8. *Maintain communication with the subject's teachers.*   Be sure that S's other teachers know what goals you are attempting to achieve and what responses are currently being developed so that they can reinforce these responses when they occur.

This procedure can easily be adapted to the particular needs of each student. Some students, for example, may display considerably less avoidance behavior than others. When this is the case, less time would naturally be spent in steps 3, 4, and 5. You should be careful, however, not to overlook less apparent, yet important, avoidance behaviors.

Another important step in the counseling process with disabled readers is to make sure they understand and verbalize their diagnosed reading problems. Perhaps there is an appropriate analogy between remedial reading and Alcoholics Anonymous. Spokespersons for AA say that there is little hope in rehabilitating people who do not first *admit* that they are alcoholics. Likewise, in remedial reading, it is important that students recognize and verbalize their problems. An initial interview with the student can readily reveal whether the student is aware of the problem. This can be done by asking such questions as, "What do you think about your reading?" or "Now that you have told me you do not read very well, can you tell me why you say that?" Students often respond to questions such as these with statements such as, "Well, I don't seem to understand what I read," or "I can't seem to figure out new words."

Some students with apparent problems will insist that they really have no difficulty in reading. For this type of student it is often helpful to tape record their oral reading and let them listen to it as it is replayed. While listening they can be asked to circle any words missed, repeated, or substituted. When doing this you should, of course, avoid argument with the students, and you should not appear to be trying to "prove that the student has a reading problem."

After students recognize their problem, they should be encouraged to talk about it. You can show them the kinds of things you plan to do to remediate the difficulty.

A new form of psychological therapy reported by Albert Harris (1981) is worth mentioning. The method is called *suggestopedia,* and it is a system that emphasizes the use of positive suggestion, relaxation, and visualization. Proponents believe that most students have much greater potential for learning than is presently being realized. The system appears to be based on sound psychological principles. Harris states: "Suggestopedia is a new development in the application of psychological techniques to education, and one worth watching." (p. 408)

It is important to note that the procedures outlined here for counseling disabled readers are by no means meant to supplant the normal cognitive or academic aspects of the program. Rather, they should serve as a most important supplement to these activities.

Counseling Parents of Disabled Readers

Because of the close relationships that exist between inability to read and emotional problems connected with the home environment, parent counseling can be an important part of the remedial reading program. Although concrete research tends to be lacking on the effectiveness of large-scale or intensive programs, there is some evidence to indicate that parent counseling can improve student achievement as well as parental attitudes. For example, Janice Studholms (1964) studied the results of group guidance with mothers of disabled readers. She found that the group guidance sessions not only improved the attitudes of the mothers, but that the attitudes of the students towards their lessons also became more positive. The students who developed the greatest positive change in attitudes also made greater achievement. Studholms noted, however, that the attitudes of the students tended to regress after the termination of the counseling sessions.

The type of counseling program instituted tends to vary a great deal depending on the orientation of the counselor. It is not advisable for a remedial reading teacher who is not highly trained in counseling techniques to attempt to provide parents with anything more than a general orientation to the remedial reading program. This orientation might include the following types of activities:

1. A discussion of the basis for students' acceptance to the program with an emphasis on the fact that students in remedial reading are not mentally retarded but disabled readers who usually have considerably more potential than is being demonstrated.
2. Discussion of the fact that pressuring disabled readers to achieve usually results in more harm than good.
3. Coordinating activities of home and school.

At the Elementary Reading Clinic at California State University, Hayward, parents participate in a number of activities designed to ease their feelings of guilt, improve their effectiveness in helping their children with the reading problems, and enhance their communication with the clinic staff and other educational agencies. These activities include:

1. An initial meeting to discuss the clinic experience, to provide an overview of the program, to meet the staff, to become aware of the facilities and resources, to discuss remedial reading problems generally, and to discuss expectations for parents, children, clinicians, and the clinic director.
2. A home visit by the clinician to learn about the child from the parents in the home environment, to discuss the specifics of the initial diagnosis and remediation plans, to clarify how the parents may assist with home assignments, and to answer questions.
3. An evening program for parents at the clinic site to describe coming events in clinic; to allow for questions, answers, and discussion; to share materials and techniques that parents may use to assist their children at home; and to provide for a private conference between parents and clinicians for discussing the pupil's progress and scheduling the clinic visit.
4. A clinic visit in which the parents spend a morning with their child in the clinic program. At their discretion, the clinicians may have the parents assist with some of the activities to determine which, if any, of the instructional procedures can be utilized effectively by the parents at

home. The parents also have an opportunity from this direct participation to become more aware of the clinic program and the needs and progress of their children.

5. The Clinic Fair, a culminating day of reading games, activities, and an awards presentation (for all participating children) to which all family members are invited.

6. An optional final conference to discuss the final report (a copy of which is sent to the child's school), to review specific recommendations, and to advise the parents about future educational options. When this conference is not held, the reports are mailed to the parents.

7. A written evaluation form sent to all parents seeking feedback on various aspects of the clinic program. Interestingly, many parents report that their participation in the above activities, in addition to the time they spent with their children in transporting them daily, had a strong positive impact on their relationship with their children.

Many of these activities have been adapted by reading specialists for use in their school programs. Although the activities require much time to plan and conduct, the reading specialists insist that they are a valuable part of the remedial services.

If the parent counseling is to be done by an expert counselor experienced in group techniques, the sessions should include activities such as those mentioned above but might also include information such as that used in a counseling program described by Patricia Bricklin (1970):

1. Information to "help parents understand their child's behavior as it refers to typical child development and to sort out those behaviors growing out of his learning disability. And . . . learn to recognize and accept their own feelings as well as those of the child." (p. 338)

2. ". . . Help parents set more effective limits, accept and acknowledge feelings and develop appropriate independence in the child." (p. 338)

3. Help parents learn to cope with their own feelings about their child's problems.

Improving the Disabled Reader's Self-Concept

During the past two decades many studies have been done to study the relationship between students' self-concepts and reading ability. Following are a few important generalizations that could be derived from these studies:

1. There is a fairly high correlation between the self-concept of beginning readers and their achievement in reading in the elementary grades.

2. The self-concept is learned and is amenable to change.
3. The self-concept of a first grader seems to be easier to change than the self-concept of upper elementary school or junior or senior high school students.
4. There is a fairly high degree of relationship between teachers' and parents' expectations and students' self-concepts.

These generalizations have some important implications for remedial reading teachers. One important implication is that the remedial reading program should have built-in provisions for the improvement of students' self-concepts as well as for the improvement of students' cognitive skills. This means that the remedial reading teacher should be constantly alert to capitalize on any opportunity to build the student's self-image. Some ways of doing this are as follows:

1. Accept the student as a worthy individual who is capable of learning.
2. Constantly look for things in which the student *is* successful and point these out.
3. If possible, arrange for older disabled readers to help beginning readers by reading to them or by helping them with other tasks.
4. Keep careful records of progress and share these with students.
5. Make sure disabled readers do not attempt to read materials at their frustration level. Before checking books out to them to take home to read for pleasure, apply the IRI criteria as explained in Chapter 11. Or if you know the free or independent reading level of the student, make sure that any books the student chooses to read for pleasure are not written above that level, as measured by one of the better-known readability formulas.
6. Make certain that assignments are understood and can be done without a great deal of difficulty.
7. Encourage students to bring their hobbies to class, and show materials relating to these hobbies to other members of the class.
8. Encourage students to think about and constantly imagine themselves being excellent readers.

Another implication from the generalizations mentioned earlier is that students with mild reading disabilities should be located, and corrective work should begin as soon as possible. Because of the inability of many classroom teachers to spot incipient reading problems some students' reading problems do not receive attention until they become severe enough to make them clearly noticeable. If a student does not receive remediation until the reading disability becomes clearly apparent, the remedial reading teacher is likely to have to deal with a student with a negative self-concept that will be much less amenable to change than it would have been during the student's earlier years in school.

Improving Language Skills

Socioeconomic factors frequently cause or contribute to students' language difficulties. Therefore, a discussion of appropriate procedures is included here, even though language development might properly be considered within the realm of cognitive skills.

Guy Bond, Miles Tinker, and Barbara Wasson (1979) discuss the reading problems of children who are learning to speak English as a second language. Their recommendations have equal relevance for native English speakers who have difficulty in understanding or speaking English. The authors state:

> The procedures ordinarily used in teaching beginning reading in our schools assume that each child already has learned to understand and speak the language. Language-handicapped children first need a program to improve their English. A preparatory instructional period ordinarily should have three simultaneous activities: first, building up a basic vocabulary for understanding and speaking; second, improvement of facility in oral communication; and third, providing a background of meaningful experiences. Words and concepts associated with experiences must be in English. Thus the child learns to speak and understand a vocabulary before he encounters it in reading. (p. 105)

Psycholinguists such as Kenneth Goodman (1967) and Frank Smith (1971, 1977) believe that once oral language facility has developed reading should occur as a natural outgrowth of the child's language. These writers believe that teachers should deemphasize instruction in specific decoding skills and should instead present reading as a contextual activity. For applications of language-centered reading models, the reader may also refer to David Pearson (1978), and Carol Chomsky (1972, 1979).

MaryAnne Hall (1979) recommends five language-centered approaches for pre- and beginning readers. A discussion of each of these follows below. Other resources for specific language development activities include books by Doris Lee and Joseph Rubin (1979) and Walter Petty and others (1976).

1. *Provide exposure to written language in prereading.* Reading readiness activities should focus on experiences with the printed word rather than pictures and other nonprint materials. Children can best learn the specific prereading skills, such as visual discrimination, left to right progression, the important terms (word, sound, letter, etc.), and

letter knowledge through lessons that rely on actual word forms. A critical concept for children to learn at the beginning stage is that writing represents "talk written down"; that is, the written language is a code for meaning.

2. *Use the language-experience approach for beginning reading.*   A variety of language-experience techniques were discussed in Chapter 4 for the purpose of building students' general sight vocabulary. We strongly endorse this approach as a vehicle for helping children to bridge the gap between oral and written language forms. Research and experience have shown that this is a particularly motivating and satisfying approach for both children and teachers.

3. *Make reading comprehension-centered.*   Every effort should be made to teach reading as a meaning-getting activity. This does not mean, in our opinion, that there is no place for instruction in phonics or basic sight vocabulary in the reading program. Rather, the teacher must relate this instruction to the goal of reading comprehension. The best way to do this is to teach specific decoding skills in the more meaningful context of phrases, sentences, and stories whenever possible. Also, the teacher should make frequent checks to be sure that pupils understand what they are decoding, and the teacher should take time to *discuss* with children the meaning of what the children have read.

4. *Correlate reading and writing.*   This is easy to do if the language-experience approach is used. Evidence suggests that writing activities not only improve children's reading comprehension but also serve to reinforce the learning of decoding skills.

5. *Immerse children in an environment of language and literature.*   One of the most fundamental, important, and enjoyable teaching activities is to read to children of all ages. Children who have been read to extensively prior to school are generally at an advantage. Teachers must provide for those children who have not had this experience. Immersion in language is also reflected in the classroom environment. Objects should be labeled. Books and other printed materials, such as children's language-experience stories, should be attractively displayed and available. Time must be provided for children to express themselves verbally and to look at, read, discuss, and enjoy their written materials.

Improving Teacher Expectations

A number of studies done during the 1960s have shown that teacher expectation can have a strong influence on the achievement of students. There also seems to be a never-ending circular pattern between teacher expectation and students' self-concepts. For example, a teacher who has low expectations for a student is likely to relay those feelings to the student in one way or another without openly admitting it. The student sensing this feeling will tend to develop a poor self-concept and will consequently be likely to achieve less, which, in turn, will verify the teacher's expectations for the student and make the teacher even more likely to have lower expectations for the student.

Through a series of studies Robert Rosenthal (1968) and other researchers have found that teachers are able to communicate their expectations to students, whether these expectations are high or low, without even being aware of doing so. For example, Rosenthal found that when the interactions between experimenters and subjects were recorded on film and then reviewed, only 12 percent of the examiners ever smiled at their male subjects, while 70 percent smiled at their female subjects. In another study examiners were to examine subjects who were behind a screen out of their sight. The examiners were told that one group of subjects was brighter than another group. It was found that the examiners tended to obtain greater success from the so-called bright group even without being able to see them. Evidently verbal clues are relayed to the subject even when the examiner is not aware of doing so.

Perhaps the most heartening thing about some of these experiments, however, is that some researchers have shown that many teachers are not influenced by information on students' achievement and IQs. The type of phenomenon mentioned earlier often need not happen if teachers are aware that their low expectations can influence students' self-concepts and achievement. For example, a study conducted by David Elijah (1980) found that first-grade teachers' expectations were not altered by falsified scores on reading readiness tests. The results also indicated that the teachers' rankings of students' readiness were as reliable as rankings obtained using a popular reading readiness test. In a somewhat related study, Hilary Schofield (1980) found a correlation between the attitude and achievement of teachers and pupils. Findings indicated that high achievement and high attitude in teachers were positively associated with high achievement and high attitudes in students.

This type of information has a great deal of relevance for the remedial reading teacher. Some specific suggestions for dealing with the influence of teacher expectation are as follows:

1. Read the research of Robert Rosenthal and Lenore Jacobson (1968) and others and become aware of the ways in which teacher expectations are relayed to students. Simply knowing of this phenomenon is much more likely to prevent you from forming and thus relaying low expectations to your students.

2. Realize that every student is a worthy human being and that every student is capable of learning.

3. Look for the strengths that students possess and focus on these rather than dwelling on reasons for their inability to learn.
4. Do not be unduly influenced by IQ scores. Remember that many students with high IQ scores have reading problems and that many students with comparatively low IQ scores become excellent readers.

SUMMARY

Psychological and sociological problems are often less visible in disabled readers. For this reason they are often likely to receive less attention in the overall remediation planned for disabled readers. Studies have shown, however, that remedial programs that incorporated counseling, along with teaching of the cognitive skills of reading, have been considerably more successful than those that omit these aspects of the overall remedial reading program.

Methods of diagnosing psychosocial problems are not as exacting as the methods used for diagnosing the cognitive skills of reading. However, certain observation procedures and informal assessment techniques can be useful in gaining insight into students' problems in these areas.

Counseling procedures have been developed that can quite easily be learned by the remedial reading teacher. There are also some important procedures developed from psychological theories that can rather easily be learned and applied by remedial reading teachers.

Language factors and their relation to reading disability were discussed, and some techniques for improving students' language abilities were presented.

REFERENCES

Armstrong, Robert J., and Mooney, Robert F. "The Slosson Intelligence Test: Implications for Reading Specialists," *Reading Teacher.* Vol. 24, (January, 1971), 336–340.

Bell, David Bruce. "The Motivational and Personality Factors in Reading Retardation among Two Racial Groups of Adolescent Males," Doctoral dissertation, Texas Tech University, 1969.

Bond, Guy L.; Tinker, Miles A.; and Wasson, Barbara B. *Reading Difficulties: Their Diagnosis and Correction.* 4th ed., Englewood Cliffs, N.J.: Prentice-Hall, 1979.

Brunken, R. J., and Shen, F. "Personality Characteristics of Ineffective, Effective, and Efficient Readers," *Personnel and Guidance Journal.* Vol. 44, (April, 1966), 837–843.

Buck, John N., and Jolles, Issac. *House-Tree-Person Projective Technique.* Los Angeles: Western Psychological Service, 1955.

Chomsky, Carol. "Stages in Language Development and Reading Exposure," *Harvard Educational Review.* Vol. 42, (February, 1972), 1–33.

Chomsky, Carol. "Language and Reading," *Applied Linguistics and Reading.* Edited by Robert E. Shafer. Newark, Del.: International Reading Association, 1979, pp. 112–128.

Chronister, Glen M. "Personality and Reading Achievement," *Elementary School Journal.* Vol. 64, (February, 1964), 253–260.

Downing, John. "Children's Developing Concept of Spoken and Written Language," *Journal of Reading Behavior.* Vol. 4, (1971–1972), 1–19.

Dunn, Lloyd M., and Dunn, Leota M. *Peabody Picture Vocabulary Test—Revised.* Circle Rines, Minn.: American Guidance Service, 1981.

Elijah, David. "Teacher Expectations: Determinants of Pupil's Reading Achievement," *Reading Improvement.* Vol. 17, (Summer, 1980), 117–121.

Evans, Martha; Taylor, Nancy; and Blum, Irene. "Children's Written Language Awareness and Its Relation to Reading Acquisition," *Journal of Reading Behavior.* Vol. 11, (Spring, 1979), 7–19.

Fotheringham, John B., and Creal, Dorothy. "Family Socioeconomic and Educational-Emotional Characteristics as Predictors of School Achievement," *Journal of Educational Research.* Vol. 73, (July–August, 1980), 311–317.

Fox, Barbara C. "How Children Analyze Language: Implications for Beginning Reading Instruction," *Reading Improvement.* Vol. 13, (Winter, 1976), 229–234.

Gardner, James, and Ransom, Grayce. "Academic Reorientation: A Counseling Approach to Remedial Readers," *Reading Teacher,* Vol. 21, (March, 1968), 529–536.

Gates, Arthur. "The Role of Personality Maladjustment and Remedial Reading," *Journal of Generic Psychology.* Vol. 59, (1941), 77–83.

Glazer, Susan M., and Morrow, Lesley M. "The Syntactic Complexity of Primary Grade Children's Oral Language and Primary Grade Reading Materials: A Comparative Analysis," *Journal of Reading Behavior.* Vol. 10, (Summer, 1978), 200–203.

Goodman, Kenneth S. "Reading: A Psycholinguistic Guessing Game," *Journal of the Reading Specialist.* Vol. 6, (May, 1967), 126–135.

Grotberg, Edith H. "Neurological Aspects of Learning Disabilities: A Case for the Disadvantaged," *Journal of Learning Disabilities.* Vol. 3, (June, 1970), 321–327.

Hall, MaryAnne. "Language-Centered Reading: Premises and Recommendations," *Language Arts.* Vol. 56, (September, 1979), 664–670.

Harootunian, Berj. "Intellectual Abilities and Reading Achievement," *Elementary School Journal.* Vol. 66, (April, 1966), 386–392.

Harris, Albert J. "Discussion: Linguistic Awareness and Cognitive Clarity in Learning to Read," *Reading Research: Studies and Applications.* Edited by M. L. Kamil and A. J. Moe. Twenty-eighth Yearbook of the National Reading Conference, 1979, pp. 295–296.

Harris, Albert J. "What Is New in Remedial Reading?" *Reading Teacher.* Vol. 34, (January, 1981), 405–410.

Krippner, Stanley. "Etiological Factors in Reading Disability of the Academically Talented in Comparison to Pupils of Average and Slow-Learning Ability," *Journal of Educational Research.* Vol. 61, (February, 1968), 275–279.

Lamy, Mary. "Relationship of Self-Perception of Early Primary Children to Achievement in Reading," Doctoral dissertation, University of Florida, 1962.

Lawrence, D. "The Effects of Counseling on Retarded Readers," *Educational Research*. Vol. 13, (February, 1971), 119–124.

Lee, Doris, and Rubin, Joseph B. *Children and Language*. Belmont, Calif.: Wadsworth Publishing Co., 1979.

Murray, Henry A. *Thematic Apperception Test*. Los Angeles: Western Psychological Services, 1951.

Neville, Donald. "A Comparison of the WISC Patterns of Male Retarded and Non-Retarded Readers," *Journal of Educational Research*. Vol. 54, (January, 1961), 195–197.

Pearson, P. David. "Some Practical Applications of a Psycholinguistic Model of Reading," *What Research Has to Say about Reading Instruction*. Edited by S. Jay Samuels. Newark, Del.: International Reading Association, 1978, pp. 84–97.

Petty, Walter T., et al. *Experiences in Language: Tools and Techniques for Language Arts Methods*. Boston: Allyn and Bacon, 1976.

Robinson, Helen. *Why Pupils Fail in Reading*. Chicago: University of Chicago Press, 1946.

Rorschach, Hermann. *Rorschach Psychodiagnostic Plates*. Los Angeles: Western Psychological Services, 1960.

Rosenthal, Robert. "Self-Fulfilling Prophecies in Behavioral Research and Everyday Life," Claremont Reading Conference. *Reading Conference Yearbook*. Vol. 32, (1968), 15–33.

Rosenthal, Robert, and Jacobson, Lenore. *Pygmalion in the Classroom*. New York: Holt, Rinehart & Winston, 1968.

Schofield, Hilary L. "Reading Attitude and Achievement: Teacher-Pupil Relationships," *Journal of Educational Research*. Vol. 74, (November–December, 1980), 111–119.

Slosson, Richard L. *Slosson Intelligence Test*. East Aurora, N.Y.: Slosson Educational Publications, 1963.

Smith, Frank. *Understanding Reading: A Psycholinguistic Analysis of Reading and Learning to Read*. New York: Holt, Rinehart & Winston, 1971.

Smith, Frank. "Making Sense of Reading—And of Reading Instruction," *Harvard Educational Review*. Vol. 47, (August, 1977), 386–395.

Spache, George D. "Personality Problems of Retarded Readers." *Journal of Educational Research*. Vol. 50, (February, 1957), 461–469.

Stedman, James M., and McKenzie, Richard E. "Family Factors Related to Competence in Young Disadvantaged Mexican-American Children," *Child Development*. Vol. 42, (November, 1971), 1602–1607.

Stevens, Deon O. "Reading Difficulty and Classroom Acceptance," *Reading Teacher*. Vol. 25, (October, 1971), 52–55.

Strang, Ruth. *Diagnostic Teaching of Reading*. 2nd ed., New York: McGraw-Hill, 1969.

Studholms, Janice MacDonald." Group Guidance with Mothers of Retarded Readers," *Reading Teacher*. Vol. 17, (April, 1964), 528–530.

Thomson, Michael E., and Hartley, Gill M. "Self-Concept in Dyslexic Children," *Academic Therapy*. Vol. 16, (September, 1980), 19–36.

Thurston, Catherine, et al. "Cultural Background Study in Relation to Reading Ability," *Reading and Realism*. Edited by J. Allen Figurel. Newark, Del.: International Reading Association, 1969.

Vance, Hubert; Wallbrown, Fred H.; and Blaha, John. "Determining WISC-R Profiles for Reading Disabled Children," *Journal of Learning Disabilities.* Vol. 11, (December, 1978), 657–661.

Wagner, Mazie Earle, and Schubert, Herman J. P. *Draw-a-Person Quality Scale.* Los Angeles: Western Psychological Services, 1955.

Wattenberg, William W., and Clare, Clifford. "Relation of Self-Concepts to Beginning Achievement in Reading," *Child Development.* Vol. 35, (June, 1964), 461–467.

8

Diagnosis and Remediation of Physical Disabilities

The first part of this chapter contains a review of those physical disabilities that research and experience have indicated tend to affect reading ability. Following this discussion methods are presented for diagnosing disabilities serious enough to require referral or remediation. The last part of this chapter contains specific suggestions for the remediation of those disabilities that fall within the realm of the school.

Part A: DIAGNOSIS

As indicated in Chapter 1 most of the physical disabilities with which you are concerned in reading could be classified under the headings of problems of the eye, problems of the ear, problems with speech, neurologically impaired functions, and problems of general health. Because of the difficulties you will encounter in dealing with problems of neurological disabilities, the information on this subject is omitted from this chapter and will be discussed in more detail in Chapter 9. As so often happens in the business of the remediation of reading disabilities, you will find that many of these areas tend to overlap so that it becomes difficult, if not impossible, to determine which factors are actively contributing to a student's reading disability and which factors, although not functioning normally, are merely concomitant.

In the diagnosis of educational problems you also face a number of problems that may not be of great concern to the medical doctor concerned with the problems of a student's physical health. For example, in dealing with problems of the ear, the physician may find that a student's ear appears healthy and that the student's auditory acuity is normal. From an educational standpoint, however, you could not assume that this same student would not experience problems in listening. Even with normal auditory acuity, the student's auditory discrimination may still not be adequate to learn without experiencing difficulties with certain phonemes. In addition to possible problems with auditory acuity and auditory discrimination the student may also experience difficulty with auditory memory. Problems with auditory memory will be discussed later; however, it should be remembered that only rarely would difficulties with anything but auditory acuity be discovered in a routine physical examination.

The diagnosis of reading difficulties as related to physical disabilities obviously requires much more than a report from the family physician. This chapter deals not only with those problems of the eye, ear, speech, and general health that are likely to become apparent in a physical examination, but also with some of the less visible problems that are likely to surface only through diagnostic teaching and careful observation. In addition to testing and diagnostic teaching you should also keep in mind that a parent interview can yield valuable information concerning possible physical disabilities that may have contributed, or are contributing, to the student's reading problem.

DIAGNOSIS OF PROBLEMS OF THE EYE

To properly understand a discussion of seeing as it relates to reading and learning it is important to understand the terms. It has become popular for many authors to create their own terms and definitions. This, of course, causes much confusion when trying to read material written by different authors. Terms here will be as common and as obvious as this complex subject will allow.

Seeing

This is a general and all-inclusive term.

Sight Versus Vision

It is imperative that teachers and all others concerned with diagnosis of problems of the eye realize that, in reading, we are concerned with more than sight. Although the exact terms may vary slightly, the term *sight* is often referred to as the ability to see, or the eye's responses to light, whereas *vision* refers to the student's ability to interpret information that comes through the eyes. Obviously then, a student without proper sight, unless corrected, can never have adequate vision. On the other hand, a student who has adequate sight may lack the vision or perceptual ability to correctly interpret various symbols.

Sight concerns the ability of the eye to resolve detail. This is a mechanical or physical process. The measurement of this ability to resolve detail is called *acuity*. Sight, then, is defined as the production of acuity. Sight can be likened to a snapshot camera and drugstore prints. Sight includes the snapping of the shutter; that is, the making of the optical image or picture in the back of the eye. This back part, called the *retina*, is like the film in the camera. Sight would include sending the image to the brain; that is, taking the film to be developed. Good sight means good acuity. The Snellen measure of acuity is 20/20 for good acuity. The larger the denominator, the lesser the acuity. That is, the person with 20/80 acuity would need to be four times as close to an object as a person with 20/20 acuity to see it as well. Acuity has no relationship to how the student understands or perceives the detail or how efficiently the student can read. Poor readers, in fact, often have good sight.

Vision is the processing of sight to give location, memory, and intersensory relationships. Vision is a mental process. It cannot be compared to the camera. Vision might be thought of as the work of a skilled darkroom artist which consists of not just developing film but retouching the negative, deciding the portion of the negative to use, and getting the right shade of color to the picture.

Proper processing of sight should tell the student where the object is in space as well as its orientation. This processing should also give the student memory of similar past experiences to compare, and it should evaluate this with the other senses such as hearing and touch.

Perception is the end result of sight and vision. This is the output. Reading ability seems to be dependent not only on visual perception, but also on auditory perception and tactual perception. If the student cannot differentiate *b* from *d*, the processing of sight for location is not good (visual-spacial perception). If the student draws a triangle after being shown a square, the student's processing to give memory is not adequate (visual memory). If the student cannot visualize the sequence of the letters *c-h-a-l-k* when the word *chalk* is spoken, or if the student cannot relate visual stimulus to touch stimulus, then there is a deficiency in intersensory processing.

Vision is also often used as an all-inclusive term to designate several aspects of the use of the eye. Stanley Krippner (1971) cites the writing of N. Flax as having developed a definition that should help clarify the definition for all professions. Flax refers to disorders of the peripheral nervous system (PNS) and the central nervous system (CNS). Krippner states,

> To Flax, PNS disorders refer to deficiencies of the end-organ system of vision (i.e., the eye); they include visual acuity, refractive error, fusion, convergence, and accommodation, all of which involve the eye mechanism and which are re-

sponsible for producing clear, single, binocular vision. CNS disorders involve deficiencies in organizing and interpreting images received by the eyes and sent to the brain. In CNS disorders, a clear, single visual image may be present but the child cannot decode the printed word because of problems in organization and interpretation of what is seen. (p. 74)

In reading, the CNS problems described here are usually referred to as visual perceptual problems.

The incidence of eye disorders often varies considerably depending on whether the research is discussing what Flax referred to as possessing problems of the PNS category, or both. These differences are often evidenced in the writings of ophthalmologists versus optometrists on the subject of vision.

The ophthalmologist (also called an oculist) is a physician or medical doctor (M.D.) who has taken specialized medical training in the care of the eye after receiving an M.D. degree. The ophthalmologist is licensed to prescribe glasses and other medication and to perform surgery to correct visual problems. The optometrist, on the other hand, receives a Doctor of Optometry degree (O.D.) in a college of optometry. The optometrist is a specialist in sight and vision. As Krippner points out, many optometrists also take more advanced study in developmental vision and become proficient in visual training that is concerned with the CNS aspects of vision. Because of the nature of their training there is a tendency for ophthalmologists to concern themselves more with the PNS aspects of the eyes and for optometrists to be more concerned with both the PNS and CNS aspects. This, of course, is a rather broad generalization, but it accounts, to a large extent, for the large differences often reported on visual problems as causative factors in reading disability.

Regardless of the type of doctor doing the testing it is generally agreed that certain types of disorders of the eye do contribute to, or may be causal factors in, cases of reading disability. The following are eye and sight skills and anomalies that are involved with seeing and reading.

Accommodation.   This is commonly called focusing. Like a camera, the eye must adjust the optics to make a clear picture. In the eye this adjusting of focus is called accommodation. The eye must accommodate for the printed words in a book at twelve inches or for the words on the chalkboard at fifteen feet. As the student's book gets closer, the amount of accommodation must be increased. There is a neurological connection between this center and the center that causes the eyes to turn in. When the student increases accommodation, this other center causes the eyes to turn in. A student can have inaccurate accommodation or spasm (hypertonicity) of the muscles (ciliary muscles) controlling accommodation.

Convergence.   This is the turning in of the eyes. As a single point moves closer to the two eyes, they must converge to insure that the image in each eye is centered. Convergence is accomplished in two different ways. It is accomplished first by the neurological connection with accommodation. The more stimulus to accommodate, the more stimulus is put into convergence. This convergence is called *accommodative convergence.* This can be thought of as automatic convergence as a result of increased accommodation. This accommodative convergence does not perfectly align the eyes on a point at the distance for which they are accommodated. Therefore, manual convergence (turning the eyes in or out to complete the alignment after automatic or accommodative convergence has occurred) must now be used to obtain perfect centering of the image in each eye. This centering is called *fusion,* and the manual convergence is *fusional convergence.* A student can have insufficient accommodative convergence, thus requiring more manual convergence. The student can also have excessive accommodative convergence, which means the student must manually diverge the eyes to get fusion. The student can also have a limited ability to manually converge the eyes for a very near point. This would mean that converging to the normal reading distance requires a high percentage of the student's total ability to converge.

Fusion.   This refers to the aligning of each eye so that the image in each is centered. They center in identical places on the retinas (back of the eye) where each eye has maximum acuity. The point in the back of the eye with maximum acuity is called the *macula.* If the images are not properly centered, the student will see double.

Hyperopia.   This is commonly called *farsightedness.* It is congenital and anatomical. Among the various refractive errors listed as causing reading disabilities this is perhaps listed most often. Hyperopia causes the student both excessive accommodation and convergence. Therefore, when it is present two of the ocular motor skills function improperly. This will result in blurring, eye fatigue, headache, and loss of interest in close work.

Myopia.   The common name for this is *nearsightedness.* It is a refractive error, and the symptoms are the reverse of hyperopia. There is a great deal of evidence that most myopia is developmental. Myopia does not interfere with reading; in fact, this is a common condition with good readers. Since the myopic eye is focused for a near point, this eye will require less accommodation. Uncorrected myopia will, however, cause the student to have problems with board work or other tasks requiring seeing at a distance.

Astigmatism.   This condition, like hyperopia and myopia, is an optical or refractive one. Astigmatism can exist with hyperopia and with myopia. In fact, it is not usually a condition by itself and when it is, the eye is partly myopic and partly hyperopic. To understand astigmatism, consider the power of the optics of a narrow vertical section through the eye, and the power of a narrow horizontal section. If the power in the vertical is different than the power in the horizontal, the optical system has astigmatism.

Astigmatism causes the print to be blurred and causes eye fatigue. Since there are different focuses in the eye, the eye will do more changing focus trying to make the image clear. This can also cause headaches and interfere with reading efficiency.

Both hyperopia and astigmatism can cause suppression and strabismus. High amounts of hyperopia frequently cause crossed eyes due to the excessive accommodative convergence. If these children are properly fitted with lenses at an early age, the excessive convergence will usually be relieved and the eyes will straighten.

Aniseikonia.   This is a condition in which there is a different size and/or shape of the image of each eye. When there is no difference in refractive error of the two eyes, a difference in image size is due to a different physical size of the eye ball. A student with this condition would have difficulty fusing. Therefore, it would contribute to reading disability.

Anisomatropia.   This is a condition in which there is a different refractive power in each eye. This is almost always accompanied by aniseikonia.

Heterophoria.   This refers to the basic position of the eyes at rest as they relate to each other. The eyes assume this position of rest when one or both eyes are closed. This would remove any need to converge or align one eye with the other. There would be no stimulus to fusion. The eyes would be disassociated. When there is no stimulus to fusion and the eyes are outward from each other, the condition is *exophoria*. When there is no stimulus to fusion and the eyes deviate inward, it is known as *esophoria*. When disassociated (no stimulus to fusion) and one is turned above the other, it is termed *hyperphoria* (up) or *hypophoria* (down). Heterophoria means that any one of these conditions exist. The student can overcome heterophoria and obtain fusion without treatment. However, when the condition becomes severe, it is known as heterotropia and cannot be overcome without treatment.

Suppression.   This is a neurological block of the picture stimulus from the macula so that the picture in that eye is not seen. This is done at the brain. Any time the student has difficulty with fusion, one eye may become suppressed. This relieves the need to fuse and there is no longer a fusion problem. Suppression works to block out the picture only in the central area. This is the point at which the student is looking—the fixation target. The suppressor does not suppress the sight to the sides. If a student develops suppression at an early age, *amblyopia* almost always results.

Amblyopia.   This is commonly called *lazy eye*. It is lowered acuity in the suppressed eye. This is true even when the other eye (the good eye) cannot see. When suppression is not developed until school age, there is usually less loss of acuity.

Heterotropia.   When a heterophoria (tendency of one eye to deviate in one or another direction) is great and cannot be overcome, the eyes will not be fused. One might say a heterotropia is a heterophoria that cannot be overcome. Deviation outward is *exotropia*, inward is *esotropia*, and vertical is *hypo-* or *hypertropia*. If the student is able to hold the eyes in alignment, part of the time it is termed *intermittent tropia*. When one eye deviates at one time and the other eye deviates at other times, it is an *alternating tropia*. The student with a tropic condition either sees double or suppresses the deviating eye when the eyes are not fused (one deviated).

Hysteria.   This is a condition in which emotional upsets frequently cause lowered acuity, reduced sight to the sides, and difficulty in accommodation. There are usually no other signs of the hysteria.

Fixation (Ocular Fixation).   This is the ability to precisely hold fusion on a given target.

Pursuit.   This is the ability to maintain fixation on a moving target.

Saccadic Skills.   This is the ability to fixate on a sequence of different targets. This may be back and forth on targets, to the left and to the right, several in a row left to right, or from far to near and back.

Ocular Motor Skills.   This refers to the movement skills of the eyes. This would include heterophorias, convergence, accommodation, pursuit, fixation, and saccadics.

Instruments for Checking Vision

The Snellen Chart.   For years the most popular instrument for testing sight has been the Snellen Chart, which originated in 1862. The fact that it is used so widely is unfortunate since there is an overwhelming amount of evidence to indicate that it is inadequate as a screening device for testing vision in schools. One of the earlier studies criticizing its use was by George Spache

(1939), who listed a number of reasons why it was inadequate for use in schools. Among the reasons listed by Spache were the following:

1. It does not measure the efficiency of the eyes at reading distance.
2. "Only 20–40 percent of all the children are identified who really need the help of an eye specialist." (p. 623)
3. It does not measure the coordination of the eyes (phoria tests).
4. It does not detect astigmatism.
5. If it is used with a group of children, some of the group who take the test last are likely to have memorized the letters. Spache also stated that some of the lines were especially difficult or easy to read because of the groupings of certain configurations of letters.

Somewhat later the Snellen type of instrument testing was criticized in a study by Malmquist (1965), who stated that the instruments of the Snellen type did not take into account vision defects at normal reading distance. Malmquist also mentioned that a number of other defects of vision were found to remain undetected when instruments of the Snellen type for measuring vision were used. On the other hand, the Keystone Telebinocular (another type of eye-testing instrument) succeeded in identifying all the cases of visual difficulties, given the criteria of the visual examinations made by a group of medical eye specialists. A strong indictment of the use of the Snellen Chart also came from Gordon Bixel (1966), who stated that although it was a valid test in itself, its use was often detrimental. Bixel believed its use was detrimental because the results of its interpretation could ruin a child's future. Bixel points out that when children pass the Snellen test they are expected to perform tasks that many simply cannot see to do. They are then considered to be lazy or stupid. Bixel says,

> No one would consider putting a thermometer in a child's mouth and, when the temperature registered normal, proclaim good health. But that is just what is being done visually. Letters are placed on the wall and if the child can read standard size letters, he is told he needs no glasses, his eyes are all right. (p. 181)

Other vision testers that have proven satisfactory for testing of disabled readers are the Bausch & Lomb Vision Tester (and School Vision Tester), and the Keystone Visual Survey Telebinocular. A description and illustration of each of these follow:

The Bausch & Lomb Vision Tester and the Bausch & Lomb School Vision Tester.   These are essentially the same instrument; however, a different set of slides is used for school vision testing. The School Vision Tester (see Figure

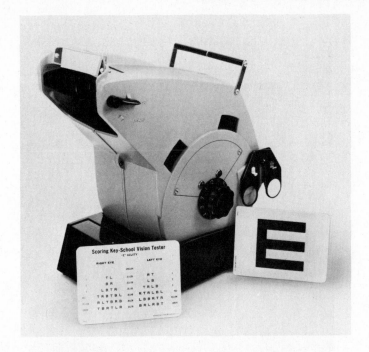

FIGURE 8-1.   The Bausch & Lomb School Vision Tester.
Reproduced by permission of Bausch & Lomb, Rochester, New York 14802.

8-1) includes the following tests: Acuity Far (right eye), Acuity Far (left eye), Far Sightedness (right eye), Far Sightedness (left eye), Phoria Far, and Phoria Near. All tests can be completed in approximately two minutes. The Bausch & Lomb Vision Tester is used more frequently in industry. In addition to the tests listed for the School Vision Tester it also includes tests for depth perception and color blindness.

The Keystone Visual Survey Telebinocular Instrument.   This instrument is used for the following tests: Simultaneous Perception, Vertical Imbalance, Lateral Posture at Far Point, Fusion at Far Point, Usable Vision of Both Eyes at Far Point, Usable Vision of Right Eye at Far Point, Usable Vision of Left Eye at Far Point, Stereopsis, Color Blindness, Lateral Posture at Near Point, Fusion at Near Point, Visual Acuity of Both Eyes at Near Point, Visual Acuity of Right Eye at Near Point, and Visual Acuity of Left Eye at Near Point. (See Figure 8-2.)

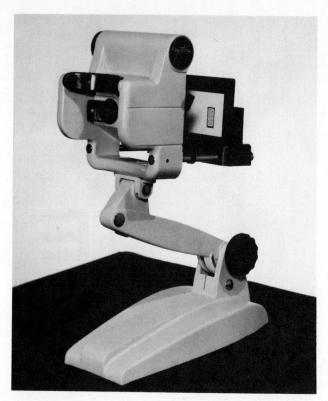

FIGURE 8-2.   The Keystone Visual Survey Telebinocular.
Reproduced by permission of Keystone View Company, 2212 E. 12th St.,
Davenport, Iowa 52803.

Vision Screening

Although research information definitely indicates a need for near-point vision testing, it does present some problems for younger children. For example, Arthur Keeney (1969), an ophthalmologist, stated that visual screening at far point is more reliable than visual screening at near point or reading range and that near-point range is influenced by age, refractive error, light, accommodative effort, pupillary diameter, and convergence stability. He stated that the coefficient of reliability in near-point acuity is approximately .75 to .78 and the reliability coefficient for far-point acuity is approximately .95 to .97. He also emphasized that the plus-lens screening procedure often used for farsightedness is somewhat unreliable, and that any screening instrument does not take the place of professional eye care but should be thought of as an assisting device used to identify individuals needing care on the basis of a few salient points.

Gail Weber (1980), in a study of fifty elementary age pupils, found that children with deficient visual skills may experience greater problems academically. Weber found that two simple vision tests used in her study could be more useful than customary screening in identifying vision problems. The first test was the Pursuit, Centering, and Alignment Test, which identifies a child who cannot track a moving target. The Convergence Test identifies children who have difficulty converging the eyes toward each other to look at a near object. This test purports to measure fusion, fixation, and binocular vision ability.

All students in remedial reading should be given a visual screening test as part of their initial testing upon entering the program. But, as William Smith (1969), an optometrist, points out,

> Even the most sophisticated and carefully performed tests are neither final nor absolutely conclusive. In doubtful cases, it is my practice to repeat tests on different instruments and at different times. It is not unusual to obtain variable findings when performed in such a manner. However, when results are repeatedly and relatively compatible, it is safe to draw conclusions as to probable complicity. (p. 148)

In discussing a group of students with whom he had worked, Smith said, "Again using experience as the basis for evidence, I can add that many of the children in the group reported and in others (before and since), whose reading became markedly improved with orthoptic treatment, were, according to earlier reports, supposed to have had normally functioning, blameless visual systems." (p. 148)

During a four-year period in which accurate records were kept on the visual problems of students in the Reading Center at the University of Texas at El Paso, it was found that approximately 50 percent of the students, all of whom were disabled readers, had visual problems that had been undetected through normal school screening procedures. It is also interesting to note that the results in testing substantiate the statement made by Smith that tests made at different times produce differing results. Referrals to eye doctors are only made after at least two visual screening tests in which *both* indicate that a referral is called for.

The problem encountered in obtaining differing results in visual screening lies not so much with the screening device but with students themselves. For example, a student's eye muscles may be able to compensate for a slight muscle imbalance on one day, whereas, on another day the problem may appear somewhat more severe. Because of this problem it is imperative that the remedial reading teacher, as well as students' other teachers know something about the observable symptoms of visual difficulties. A checklist to guide your observations is shown in Figure 8–3. In using such a device it should be emphasized that referrals should not usually be made on the basis of one symptom, but rather on the basis of the observation of the presence of a cluster of these symptoms.

FIGURE 8-3.   Educator's Checklist

Observable Clues to Classroom Vision Problems

Student's
name_____ Date_____

1.   Appearance of Eyes:
    One eye turns in or out at any time   _____
    Reddened eyes or lids   _____
    Eyes tear excessively   _____
    Encrusted eyelids   _____
    Frequent styes on lids   _____

2.   Complaints When Using Eyes at Desk:
    Headaches in forehead or temples   _____
    Burning or itching after reading or desk work   _____
    Nausea or dizziness   _____
    Print blurs after reading a short time   _____

3.   Behavioral Signs of Visual Problems:
    A.   *Eye Movement Abilities (Ocular Motility)*
        Head turns as reads across page   _____
        Loses place often during reading   _____
        Needs finger or marker to keep place   _____
        Displays short attention span in reading or copying   _____
        Too frequently omits words   _____
        Repeatedly omits "small" words   _____
        Writes up or down hill on paper   _____
        Rereads or skips lines unknowingly   _____
        Orients drawings poorly on page   _____
    B.   *Eye Teaming Abilities (Binocularity)*
        Complains of seeing double (diplopia)   _____
        Repeats letters within words   _____
        Omits letters, numbers or phrases   _____
        Misaligns digits in number columns   _____
        Squints, closes or covers one eye   _____
        Tilts head extremely while working at desk   _____
        Consistently shows gross postural deviations at all desk
            activities   _____
    C.   *Eye-Hand Coordination Abilities*
        Must feel things to assist in any interpretation required   _____
        Eyes not used to "steer" hand movements (extreme lack of
            orientation, placement of words or drawings on page)   _____
        Writes crookedly, poorly spaced: cannot stay on ruled lines   _____
        Misaligns both horizontal and vertical series of numbers   _____
        Uses his hand or fingers to keep his place on the page   _____
        Uses other hand as "spacer" to control spacing and align-
            ment on page   _____
        Repeatedly confuses left-right directions   _____
    D.   *Visual Form Perception (Visual Comparison, Visual Imagery,*
        Visualization)
        Mistakes words with same or similar beginnings   _____
        Fails to recognize same word in next sentence   _____

        Reverses letters and/or words in writing and copying   _____

        Confuses likenesses and minor differences   _____

        Confuses same word in same sentence   _____

        Repeatedly confuses similar beginnings and endings of
            words   _____

        Fails to visualize what is read either silently or orally   _____

        Whispers to self for reinforcement while reading silently   _____

        Returns to "drawing with fingers" to decide likes and differ-
            ences   _____

E.   *Refractive Status (Nearsightedness, Farsightedness Focus
        Problems, etc.)*

        Comprehension reduces as reading continues; loses interest
            too quickly   _____

        Mispronounces similar words as continues reading

        Blinks excessively at desk tasks and/or reading; not else-
            where   _____

        Holds book too closely; face too close to desk surface   _____

        Avoids all possible near-centered tasks   _____

        Complains of discomfort in tasks that demand visual inter-
            pretation   _____

        Closes or covers one eye when reading or doing desk work   _____

        Makes errors in copying from chalkboard to paper on desk   _____

        Makes errors in copying from reference book to notebook   _____

        Squints to see chalkboard, or requests to move nearer   _____

        Rubs eyes during or after short periods of visual activity   _____

        Fatigues easily; blinks to make chalkboard clear up after
            desk task   _____

Observer's Suggestions:

Signed_____

        (Encircle): Teacher; Nurse; Remedial Teacher; Psychologist; Vision Consultant;
        Other.

Address_____

        _____

Visual Discrimination

Research by Raj Gupta, Stephen Ceci, and Alan Slater (1978) and by Rose-marie Park (1978–1979) has shown that students' abilities to discriminate letters and words are the most reliable of the many visual perception tasks insofar as predicting later reading achievement. Hal Seaton (1977) and other researchers have found that there is little or no benefit from visual discrimination training with pictures or geometric shapes. William Rupley, Michael Ashe, and Pearl Buckland (1979) found that even utilizing forms that looked like letters, but were not, did not yield positive results.

Thus it would appear to be most helpful for visual discrimination activities to focus on the recognition of letters and words. Diagnosis is generally accomplished by having students select from a row of letters or words those items that exactly match the stimulus letter or word. It is not necessary for the student to name the letter(s) or pronounce the word(s) in such a test, but rather to identify the appropriate item(s) through visual discrimination. Research by Edward Paradis (1974) among others has shown that most students have mastered this ability by the time they enter school.

Eye Movements and Reading Speed

Contrary to the belief of many people unfamiliar with the work of the eye in reading, the eye does not sweep smoothly across the page in reading. As we read, the eye stops and starts, making a series of short, quick movements. These are often referred to as *saccadic movements*. We do not see clearly as the eye moves; therefore, in order to see a word or group of words, our eyes must stop and fixate, move to the next word or small group of words, fixate again, etc.

The time it takes to fixate varies, according to our research studies, between one-fourth and one-sixth of a second, with the average time for a good reader running between one-fifth and one-sixth of a second. Most researchers also agree that it takes from 1/25 to 1/30 of a second for the eye to move from one fixation to the next, and it also takes from 1/25 to 1/30 of a second for the eye to sweep from the end of one line of print to the beginning of the next. According to Albert Harris and Edward Sipay (1980) the average span of recognition of words or the average number of words it is possible to see clearly during each fixation runs from .45 for an average first grader to 1.11 for an average college student. One would naturally be able to see something to the right and left of each word or group of words as one fixates using peripheral vision. However, most researchers agree that, even for the very best reader, it would be impossible to see an average of more than three words clearly enough to read them. In reading, then, one would show a pattern similar to Figure 8–4.

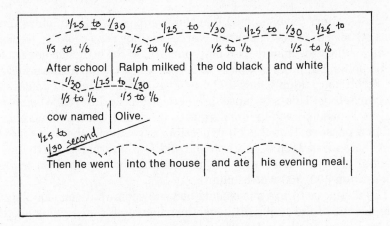

FIGURE 8-4.   Eye Movements and Reading Speed.

If you were to check the reading (or word seeing) speed of someone, assuming this person had the widest span of recognition (three words), the fastest fixation time (1/6 second), the fastest sweep time from one fixation to another (1/30 second), the fastest return sweep from one line to the next (1/30 second), the greatest number of words that could be read (or seen) per minute might be computed as follows:

6 fixations/second multiplied by 3 words/fixation
$6 \times 3 = 18$ words/second

18 words/second multiplied by 60 seconds
1080 words/minute

However, for every six fixations you would have five movements from one fixation to the next ($1/30 \times 5 = 5/30$ seconds.) If you assume that for every six fixations you also have one return sweep, that adds another 1/30 of a second. Therefore, for every six fixations you have $5/30 + 1/30$ or $6/30 = 1/5$ second lost in sweep time. Roughly, then, you would have to subtract one-fifth of the 1080 words/minute you had previously calculated since that time would be lost to sweep time. Therefore, the total number of words this reader could read (or see) would be as follows:

$1/5 \times 1080 = 217$
$1080 - 217 = 864$

It would then appear that even under ideal conditions this reader could not *see* more than 864 words/minute.

Some writers have claimed that the reader gets enough clues through peripheral vision, even though all words are not seen clearly, to read as many as 3500 words/minute. It is our opinion that the evidence does not support this belief, but there is a possibility that a few people do have this capability. Note in our calculations that we have differentiated between *reading* and *seeing* words. This is because there is a semantic difference between the two. If we consider *reading* to mean getting a general idea of what is contained in a passage, then it is often possible to read only the first few words or first sentence of each paragraph and still *read* the material. On the other hand, as stated earlier, it is probably not possible for even the best readers to *see* more than 800–900 words/minute.

The diagnosis of eye movements became somewhat commonplace during the decade of the 1960s. Although instruments for measuring eye movements had been available for doing this since the late 1800s, the influx of federal money through ESEA Title I Programs enabled many schools to buy devices for recording eye movements. One such device is the Reading Eye Camera[1] which makes a recording of students' eye movements as they read. The older models recorded eye movements on film that had to be developed after the student had completed reading. A newer model records the student's eye movements directly on paper similar to a graph. These recordings can be analyzed to discover the number of fixations and regressions that a student makes while reading.

Studies such as those of Miles Tinker (1958) have shown that undesirable eye movements are usually only symptomatic of various reading problems such as lack of word recognition. And when the word-recognition problem is remediated, the student's eye-movement pattern would become normal. More recent research has sometimes relied on modern technology. This includes studies by R. D. Elterman and others (1980), who used an infrared recording technique, and Ruby Den Buurman, Theo Roersema, and Jack Gerrissen (1981), who used a display system controlled by the reader's eye movements. Lester Lefton, Richard Nagle, and Gwendolyn Johnson (1979) compared the eye movements of good- and poor-reading third graders, fifth graders, and adults. The authors concluded that the eye movements of poor readers were quantitatively and qualitatively different from those of normal readers. The poor readers' eye movements were chaotic, frequent, of longer duration, and generally unsystematic. In another study, Lefton, Benjamin Lahey, and David Stagg (1978) reached similar conclusions and found that disabled readers' problems resulted not from an inability to discriminate letters, but rather from an unsystematic search strategy.

Further research in this area may lead to specific procedures to be used in remediating reading difficulties. However, at present it would appear

[1]Manufactured and distributed by Educational Development Laboratories, Huntington, New York.

to be a misuse of time and money for the classroom teacher, reading specialist, or reading clinician to bother to diagnose eye movements as a part of normal remedial procedures.

DIAGNOSIS OF PROBLEMS OF THE EAR

Classification of Auditory Problems

Auditory problems that are of concern to reading specialists could be classified under three categories. These categories are "auditory discrimination,"
"auditory acuity," and "auditory memory." Studies of the auditory abilities
of advanced and disabled readers such as that of Pauline Flynn and Margaret Byrne (1970) have sometimes shown that disabled readers, as a group,
have inferior auditory abilities as compared with average or advanced readers. Other studies report conflicting results to those of the Flynn and Byrne
study. The correlation between auditory disabilities and reading disabilities
is often low or insignificant. In other words, there are likely to be a few severe cases of auditory disabilities within a group of disabled readers; however, the most disabled readers are not necessarily the same students with
serious auditory disabilities. Guy Bond, Miles Tinker, and Barbara Wasson
(1979) suggest that both research and clinical experience provide evidence
that some children overcome auditory difficulties while others do not. Various factors affect the outcome, according to Bond, Tinker, and Wasson, including the severity and type of auditory disability, the amount of time that
passes before remediation is begun, the quality of the treatment, the desire of
the student to read, and the coordination of the efforts of the parents, specialists, and others.

Auditory Discrimination and Auditory Perception.   Auditory discrimination
is generally considered to be the ability to discriminate between various combinations of sounds. In reading, of course, you are usually concerned with the
ability to discriminate between or among similar sounding phonemes. You
are also concerned with a student's ability to *mask,* which is the ability to
hear a certain sound when interfering sounds or noises are present.

It is reasonable to assume that auditory discrimination is important to
learning to read, since the student must hear the difference between similar
sounds in order to accurately reproduce these sounds. It is also important
that a student has the ability to mask other extraneous noises so that what
the teacher or another student is saying can be heard.

However, controversy exists regarding the role of auditory discrimination in learning to read. Many practitioners assume that skill in this area is
essential for later reading success, even though much of the research does

not show a significant relationship between performance on tests of auditory discrimination and reading tests.

Some earlier research, such as that reported by Jerome Rosner (1973) and Gerald Strag and Bert Richmond (1973) did show a positive relationship between auditory discrimination and reading.

Patrick Groff (1975) reviewed the results of relevant empirical research on this issue and concluded that "there is enough negative evidence as to the causal effect of auditory discrimination on reading success to warrant further examination on this supposed relationship." (p. 746) Groff suggested that "a cautious, skeptical outlook to the importance of auditory discrimination on reading ability is needed." (p. 746)

In a response to Groff, Shirley Finnegan (1979) suggested that problems of definition and testing clouded the data that Groff analyzed. Finnegan asserted that adequately defining the term *auditory discrimination* and conducting a proper study show a relationship between auditory skills and word calling.

Nonetheless, recent research has borne out Groff's skepticism. Susan Neuman (1981) conducted a study in which first-grade children were taught various auditory perceptual skills, including auditory attention, auditory discrimination, auditory blending and closure, and auditory memory and comprehension. She found that although the auditory training did produce superior growth in auditory skills, these gains did not transfer to reading achievement among the experimental group. Indeed, the control group, which had been involved in individual activities such as reading and math games and special art projects, showed a slightly greater increase in tested reading ability.

Barbara Matthews and Charlena Seymour (1981) found that tests of auditory discrimination were not likely to differentiate between learning-disabled children and nonlearning-disabled children, unless both groups also had difficulties in speech articulation.

Karl Koenke (1978) compared three of the most frequently used tests of auditory discrimination—Wepman's *Auditory Discrimination Test,* the Goldman-Fristoe-Woodcock *Test of Auditory Discrimination,* and the Kimmell-Wahl *Screening Test of Auditory Perception.* Fifty-two third-grade students were evaluated on all three tests, using different random sequences to control for testing effects. Koenke found that when the cutoff scores recommended by the various authors were used as the criterion, the numbers of students passing or failing the three tests were significantly different from each other. Of the fifty-two students, only two passed all three tests and only twelve failed all three tests. Thirty-eight of the students (or 73 percent) passed on one or two of the tests and failed on the others. Understandably, Koenke woefully concluded that "auditory discrimination is that which auditory discrimination tests measure." Mary Ann Geissal and June Knafle (1977) pointed out that auditory discrimination tests and exercises are complicated by such factors as dialect differences, vocabulary range, previous experience, differing views on the nature of the task, examiner bias, and the lack of visual cues.

After reviewing the literature concerned with the relationship of auditory-perceptual skills to reading ability, Reid Lyon (1977) concluded that there was insufficient evidence to support the view that intact auditory-perceptual skills are necessary for the adequate development of reading ability:

> Although many of the investigations cited indicate that poor readers do manifest difficulties in auditory perception, an equal number of studies found good readers who demonstrated deficits in auditory skills and poor readers who demonstrated adequate auditory-perceptual abilities. (p. 570)

Lyon also points out that correlational studies must be interpreted with caution. A correlation between two factors may be the result of a causal effect preceding in either direction, or both factors may be related to a third, unknown factor that is the causative source. This fact notwithstanding, Lyon states, "Evidence indicates that the relationships obtained between auditory-perceptual ability and reading skills reach a higher correlational value when the samples selected for study consist of younger children rather than older children." (p. 569)

Clearly, the practitioner faces a dilemma. In light of the evidence presented above, perhaps it would be best to ignore problems of auditory perception when completing the diagnosis and carrying out remediation procedures. On the other hand, some studies have shown positive correlations between auditory-perceptual abilities in the prereading period and future success in reading. In addition, many teachers and reading specialists report that auditory discrimination training is successful with kindergarten and first-grade children who lack that ability.

Unfortunately, the research evidence does not tell us whether auditory discrimination should or should not be taught. We believe the practitioner should take a cautious approach. The procedures for diagnosing and remediating auditory discrimination problems are relatively simple and need not be too time consuming. We recommend that teachers and reading specialists test and teach auditory discrimination skills to young children (ages five to seven) when such an approach appears to be warranted. All children in a particular class will not require this instruction, and for those who do the amount of time spent should not be so great as to detract from other, more important reading-skill areas.

Students with auditory discrimination problems may exhibit certain difficulties. Following is a list of some of these. It should, however, be stressed that any student may exhibit one or more of these symptoms from time to time and still not have problems with auditory discrimination. This list should serve only to alert you to the possibility that the problem might exist:

1. Phonics knowledge inadequate
2. Frequent requests for a repeat of oral material presented by the teacher
3. Difficulty in understanding what was said by the teacher or another student
4. Pronunciation of certain words unclear
5. Tendency to hold mouth open while listening
6. Tilting of head while listening

The best-known and most-used test for auditory discrimination is *The Auditory Discrimination Test* (Wepman, 1973). This is an individual test in which the examiner pronounces a number of pairs of words that are either alike, or alike except for one phoneme, e.g., *lack-lack*, and *tub-tug*. The student is to respond by telling whether the two words are the same or different.

When giving *The Auditory Discrimination Test* it is important that the student understand that "same" and "different" refer to the *sounds* of the words and not to the *meaning* of the words. If a student does poorly, it is also a good idea to wait several days and give the same test or an alternate form to insure that the results of the first administration were valid. If in giving the test you find that a great many students fail, you should consider having a sample of that group tested by another person to insure that your pronunciation is not at fault.

It is important to note that *The Auditory Discrimination Test* is only a test for "minimal pairs" and does not test other auditory discrimination skills such as the ability to mask sounds. If you suspect a student is having difficulty with masking, the best way to confirm your suspicions is to ask the student to respond in writing to various questions in a normal classroom setting. For example, pronounce words and ask the student to write the initial consonant sounds, ending sounds, or medial vowel sounds. When doing this, however, it is important that the student know the sound-symbol relationships involved.

Auditory Acuity.   This simply refers to the ability to hear sounds of varying pitch (frequencies or vibrations) heard at different degrees of loudness (measured in decibels). Normal speech frequency tends to run from 125 up to as high as 8000 cycles per second with more in the 130-to-4000 range. It has been noted that students with hearing loss in the higher frequency ranges (500 +) often tend to have difficulties in school because they are often taught by female teachers whose voices tend to be of higher frequency than those of male teachers. It is also important to note that certain consonant sounds such as "s," "z," and "t" are of higher frequencies than the vowel sounds. Students also experience hearing loss in terms of loudness. A loss of up to five decibels is considered near normal or would probably cause the student very little difficulty. A loss of six to ten decibels may cause slight difficulty, and a loss above ten to fifteen decibels would normally cause difficulty, especially if the student was not seated near the front of the room or did not wear some corrective hearing device. Students with a hearing loss in any of two frequencies in one ear or the other at a decibel level are considered to have a problem serious enough to be referred for clinical evaluation.

Auditory acuity is measured by using an audiometer such as the MA-19 manufactured by Maico Hearing Instruments, shown in Figure 8-5. This portable instrument can be used for conducting tests for either individuals or groups.

Other manufacturers of audiometers are as follows:

Maico Hearing Instruments
7375 Bush Lake Road
Minneapolis, Minnesota 55435

Royal Industries
Audiotone Division
P.O. Box 2905
Phoenix, Arizona 85036

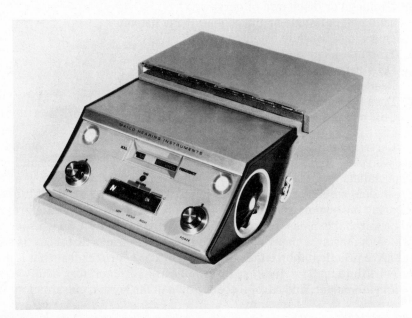

FIGURE 8-5.   The Maico Model MA-19.

Reproduced by permission of Maico Hearing Instruments, 7573 Bush Lake Road, Minneapolis, Minnesota 55435.

Auditory Instrument Division
Zenith Radio Corporation
6501 W. Grand Ave.
Chicago, Illinois 60635

Precision Acoustics Corporation
55 W. 42 Street
New York, New York 10036

Beltone Electronics Corporation
Hearing Test Instruments
   Division
4201 W. Victoria Street
Chicago, Illinois 60646

Many remedial reading teachers will not have an audiometer available for their use; however, in many cases audiometric testing is available through the school nurse. In some remedial reading programs audiometric testing is done as a matter of course for all students. Where a school nurse is available and willing to do this testing, we recommend that it be done. On the other hand, routine audiometric testing is often not necessary unless it is indicated because of a student's failure on an auditory discrimination test or because of noted symptoms of hearing loss. These symptoms are as follows:

1.   Cupping hand behind the ear.
2.   Complaints of buzzing or ringing noises in the ear.
3.   Gives the appearance of being lazy or of not paying attention.
4.   Drainage or discharge of ears.
5.   Tilts head at angle or turns head while listening.
6.   Opens mouth while listening.
7.   Frequent head colds.
8.   Does not respond well to oral directions.
9.   Reads in unnatural voice tones.
10. Does not enunciate clearly.
11. Stiff or strained posture while listening.

Certain other informal tests—such as the "watch tick," "coin click," and "whisper" tests—have also been used by classroom teachers and reading specialists for many years. You should keep in mind, however, that testing a student's ability to hear a watch tick or two coins click is not the same as hearing the human voice in the classroom. These tests are, therefore, likely to be unreliable measures of a student's hearing ability. The whisper test, in which the tester whispers a word or phrase at various distances, is somewhat more practical than either the watch tick or coin click tests but is still a poor substitute for *The Auditory Discrimination Test,* auditory acuity testing with an audiometer, and careful observation in the normal classroom setting.

Auditory Memory.   This refers to the ability to listen to, and then remember or repeat, a series of words, digits, a sentence, nonsense symbols, etc. This ability is, of course, important in learning to read. For example, in sounding a three-letter word the student must hold the first two sounds in memory to put them with the third letter in order to analyze the word. As word analysis becomes more difficult, e.g., in applying various syllabication principles, vowel rules, and individual grapheme sounds, the student is faced with a great deal of both visual and auditory memory. Comprehension of oral, and to some extent silent, reading also depends on the student's auditory memory. Interestingly, a recent study by Cermak and others (1980) found that learning-disabled children were not at a significant disadvantage on a short-term retention assessment task. Three groups of learning-disabled children and one control group of normal readers were required to remember verbal information over intervals of up to eighteen seconds while being distracted. All of the learning-disabled groups performed at least as well as the normal controls.

Although auditory memory is an important skill for reading, and the measurement of the skill is not difficult, there is some doubt about the importance of measuring it. The problem lies in the fact that few research studies have shown that training in the improvement of auditory memory skills results in an increase in reading ability, although auditory memory per se can be improved. Part of the problem in the past, however, may have been in training students in the memory of digits and nonsense or nonreading-related sentences rather than in training them in materials directly related to reading. For example, research at the Reading Center at the University of Texas at El Paso has shown that students who cannot remember and repeat at least a five-word sentence benefit from auditory memory training that deals directly with listening to and repeating sentences. You should also remember that many exercises in phonics and structural analysis actually train students in auditory memory skills.

If you wanted a standardized test for auditory memory of digits, you could either administer the "Digit Span" subtest of the *WISC-R* or the *WAIS*. You should note, however, that remembering a series of digits is not necessarily parallel to the auditory memory abilities required for reading. Memory for sentences can be assessed to some extent by using the "memory for sentence" items on either the *Stanford-Binet Intelligence Scale* or the *Slosson Intelligence Test*. It is also easy to develop your own test of sentence memory by simply writing several four-word sentences, several five-word sentences, etc., until you reach a point where few or no students can repeat the sentences. This can then be standardized by giving it to normal students at each grade level to determine the average sentence length remembered at each grade level.

From a practical standpoint, however, most remedial reading teachers can best diagnose auditory memory by careful diagnostic teaching, i.e., noting whether students can remember such things as a five- to eight-word sentence, a series of directions, or four to five letters in a word.

DIAGNOSIS OF SPEECH PROBLEMS

There is some disagreement concerning the relationships between various speech disorders and reading disability. Some studies have found the incidence of speech disorders among disabled readers to be no higher than among normal readers, while others have reported that 20 to 35 percent of groups of disabled readers have speech disorders. One of the major reasons for these discrepancies is probably the fact that in some studies reading ability was assessed with an oral reading test and in others it was assessed with silent reading tests. There is also considerable evidence that many speech disorders, even though present, cannot easily be recognized by a lay person. Also, when certain speech disorders are in evidence, it is sometimes difficult to determine whether they are a hindering factor in reading.

There is often a relationship between problems of auditory acuity and/or auditory discrimination and speech disorders. If a student shows evidence of either of these auditory difficulties, you should note whether the student also shows evidence of a speech problem.

Most speech disorders, and especially those of an organic nature, should be diagnosed and treated by a speech specialist. The remedial reading teacher, however, should be aware of the symptoms of speech disorders, and whenever a cluster of these symptoms appears, or when one or more appear to a serious degree, the student should be referred to a speech specialist. Some of these symptoms are as follows:

1. Inability to clearly produce the phonic elements shown on the test in Appendix A.
2. Inability to reproduce certain phonic elements after hearing them (closely related to auditory acuity and/or auditory discrimination).
3. Peculiar movements of the head and/or mouth on phonic elements or words mispronounced. Also watch for difficulty in forming lips to make certain sounds.
4. Too much or too little volume (closely related to auditory acuity).
5. Long pauses before certain phonemes or phonograms.
6. Refusal (or resistance) to talk.
7. Use of improper tonal quality (closely related to auditory difficulties).
8. Skipping or slurring certain words, phonemes, or phonograms.
9. Stuttering.

DIAGNOSIS OF GENERAL HEALTH PROBLEMS

In most cases the educator is neither trained nor equipped to diagnose problems of general health. For this reason the remedial reading teacher will need to rely on information gained from the student's past health history and from careful observation. The parent interview can be an important source of information concerning general health. In interviewing the parents of disabled readers check into health background concerning any chronic illnesses or allergies, any medication taken for allergies or other illnesses, childhood injuries or diseases that kept the student out of school for extended periods of time, eating habits, general stamina as evidenced by outside activity, and sleep habits. Information from parents can be especially helpful, since they know the student and have, in most cases, had an opportunity to observe the student longer than anyone else. We have found information gained from parents to be especially helpful where there are other children in the family with whom they can compare a certain child. On the other hand, information coming from parents of an only child is often less objective, since they have no norm with which to compare that child.

Some health problems will not be apparent even with careful observation; however, some health problems do manifest certain observable symptoms. Some of these symptoms that may have relevance to a reading disability are as follows:

1. Lack of energy, listlessness, or general fatigue (including falling asleep).
2. Poor eating habits.
3. Susceptibility to colds.
4. Labored breathing.
5. Complaints of dizziness and/or headaches.
6. Inability to concentrate for sustained periods of time.
7. Irritability, especially after physical exercise or near end of the day.
8. Evidence of much better work at the beginning of the day.
9. Complaints of stomach ache or nausea.
10. Considerably overweight or underweight.
11. Unsteadiness in writing or small motor activities.
12. Chronic absenteeism.

When a cluster of these symptoms appears, or when any one symptom appears to a strong degree, the student should be referred to the school nurse; or the student's parents should be contacted concerning referral to a medical doctor.

Part B: REMEDIATION

REMEDIATION OF PROBLEMS OF THE EYE

In many situations the responsibilities of the teacher in eye treatment cease once a referral has been made to an optometrist or ophthalmologist. The only problem with which the teacher is then concerned is that of the remediation of educational disabilities that may have been caused by eye problems. There are also many instances in which the teacher should work in cooperation with the eye doctor to carry out a total program adapted to the special needs of visually handicapped students. For this reason a clear channel of communication needs to exist between the teacher and the student's doctor. Generally teachers are not concerned with disorders of the eye involving the peripheral nervous system, i.e., visual acuity, refractive error, fusion, convergence, and accommodation, after an eye doctor has examined the student and prescribed accordingly.

It should be noted that there is considerable disagreement among various optometrists and ophthalmologists as well as some disagreement among the members of each group concerning the value of orthoptic training and school-related visual perceptual training. For example, a rather typical statement concerning the beliefs of many ophthalmologists comes from Harold Martin (1971) in describing the beliefs of Dr. George Campian, a clinical professor of ophthalmology. Martin says,

> He feels that if an orthoptic program aimed at muscle balance and convergence is associated with any improvement in reading, the reading improvement must result from the patient's increased concentration rather than from the exercises themselves. He also points out that refractive errors are of negligible importance in reading disorders. (p. 470)

The opposite viewpoint, perhaps more typical of the beliefs of many optometrists, is expressed by William Swanson (1972) in describing the results of his study of the effectiveness of optometric vision therapy. Swanson states,

> Study of 100 consecutive cases of learning disorders revealed that optometric vision therapy was successful in 93 percent of the cases. The accuracy of this figure was verified by a registered psychologist. The criterion for success was a definite indication of improvement in the person's learning ability, as verified by subsequent tests, by report of the parent, the patient, or the teacher. Fifty-seven parents reported improvement in their child. The teachers reported improvement in 48 percent, and retesting showed improvement in 82 percent. (p. 42)

Because of the apparent disagreement among various eye doctors it seems best to again recommend that a clear channel of communication be established between remedial teachers and optometrists or ophthalmologists and that suggestions for teacher work with specific students come directly from the examining doctor.

REMEDIATION OF PROBLEMS OF THE EAR

As stated in the section on diagnosis, problems of the ear could be divided into three categories in dealing with reading disabilities. These categories are auditory discrimination, auditory acuity, and auditory memory. Although all three areas are of importance to teachers who deal with students' auditory deficiencies, remediation of problems in auditory acuity is usually not within the realm of the remedial reading teacher.

Auditory Discrimination

Although practice in auditory discrimination, in general, may be somewhat beneficial, it is usually only necessary to provide remediation in those combinations with which the student has particular difficulty. These can, of course, easily be located by giving *The Auditory Discrimination Test*. For example, a student who cannot hear the difference between *vow* and *thou* will need practice in discriminating between the "v" and "th" phonemes. There are also certain combinations that cause difficulty for specific ethnic groups. For example, native Spanish speakers often have difficulty with the short "i" and short "e" sounds and with the *ch* and *sh* digraphs. You should be especially aware of these difficulties. It should be noted, however, that many children, as in the case of blacks from certain areas, can hear these differences in others' speech, and seem to be aware of them in reading, yet they do not pronounce them correctly in their own speech. In some black dialects, for example, the *s* is often omitted in speaking, yet many of these same students seem to have no difficulty in answering questions concerning comprehension of singular and plural concepts. Where these problems appear only in students' speech and do not appear to be detrimental to their reading, it is probably best to ignore them.

Remedial exercises for auditory discrimination may be done orally, but putting them on audio tape will save much time in the long run. These can be categorized and retrieved when needed. (It should be stressed that teacher-made tapes should not be used unless the reproduction quality is very good.)

Practice exercises for various pairs may be done as follows:

A.   (Beginning level) Hearing likenesses and differences—"*v*" and "*th*."
      (Try to avoid using the same combinations as those on the test so that it
      will not be repetitious for later use.)
      Tape Script: "Listen to each pair of words I pronounce and decide
      whether they are the same or different. If they are the same, circle the
      word *same* on your answer sheet. If they are different, circle the word
      different on your answer sheet. Number one is *van* and *than*. Number
      two is *then* and *then*." etc.
      The answer sheet would appear as follows:
      1. Same–Different
      2. Same–Different
      etc.
      The answer part of the script would be as follows:
      "The first two words were different. They were *van* and *than*. Circle
      different if you did not do so before. The next words were the same.
      They were *then* and *then*. Circle *same* if you did not do so before." etc.

B.   (Second level) Hearing beginning sounds—*v* and *th*. (This requires a
      knowledge of phonics.)
      Tape Script: "Look at row one on your answer sheet. Circle the word
      that begins the same as *very*. Now look at row two. Circle the word that
      begins the same as *though*. "
      The answer sheet would appear as follows:
      1. th   v   b   c
      2. v   b   th   f
      etc.
      In making exercises of this nature it is important to also give the an-
      swers on the same script. This will teach and reinforce the concept and
      will also conserve the teacher's time. The correction part of the script
      for the examples would be as follows:
      "Now we will check the answers. Number one was *very*; the answer
      should have been *v*, the second letter in the row. Circle it now if you did
      not get it right. Number two was *th*; these letters are third in the row.
      Circle them now if you did not get them right." etc.

C.   (Third level) Writing beginning sounds—"*v*" and "*th*." (This also re-
      quires a knowledge of phonics.)
      Tape Script: "Listen to the words I pronounce. They all begin with
      either *v* or *th*. After you hear each word I pronounce, write the begin-
      ning sound you hear in the blank by the number. Number one is *van*.
      Number two is *than*." etc.
      The answer sheet would appear as follows:
      1. _____
      2. _____
      etc.

The answer part of the script would be as follows: "The first word was *van*. It begins with *v*. You should have written a *v* by number one. The second word was *than*. It begins with *th*. You should have written *th* by number two." etc.

As you will note, this type of exercise takes the beginning reader from simple discrimination of similar sounds to the more difficult process of writing sounds when they are heard. When developing exercises of this nature you should also keep in mind that some students have difficulty with medial and ending sounds. Exercises for the remediation of these types of auditory discrimination problems can easily be devised with slight changes in the tape scripts.

Commercial materials are also available for the remediation of problems of auditory discrimination. These materials are listed in Appendix C. You should remember, however, in using most commercial materials that it is usually very difficult to select lessons to remediate a specific problem without requiring the student to go through a considerable amount of other material that in many cases would be of little value. Reid Lyon (1977) adds the following observation:

> Although programs, methods, and techniques designed to enhance auditory-perceptual skills continue to be manufactured and sold commercially, their value in facilitating reading achievement remains doubtful. . . . A major problem impeding endorsement of auditory-perceptual training programs is that the developers of these methods and materials do not usually provide research evidence that their products are actually effective in improving the auditory skills they purport to train. Moreover, even if such training were found to increase selected auditory abilities, the effect of this improvement on subsequent reading achievement is rarely documented. (p. 570)

Auditory Acuity

Auditory acuity difficulties should normally be treated by a medical doctor. However, in some cases the doctor is not likely to feel that the student's hearing is impaired enough to treat from a medical standpoint. The physician may recommend that allowance be made, within the school setting, for the student's auditory acuity problem. When such is the case, you should, if possible, consult directly with the child's physician concerning suggested measures for dealing with the problem. In most cases recommendations would be somewhat as follows:

1. Place the student near the front of the room for any instruction in which the teacher or other students speak from the front of the room.
2. Try to remember to face the student when talking to him or her, and speak slowly and clearly.

3. If outside noises interfere through windows, seat the student as far away from these as possible.
4. Teach the student to use a visual mode for learning the spelling of words and word attack whenever possible.
5. To make sure the student is correctly receiving instructions and/or directions, have the student write them from time to time. Also check immediately, once the student has begun to work, to make sure the directions were heard properly.
6. Use programmed materials if they are available for teaching certain concepts.
7. Try to use written directions along with oral directions.
8. Have the student use headphones when listening to recorded material.

Auditory Memory

This is an important skill for reading; however, studies have tended to show that although certain memory factors can be improved, a corresponding increase in reading ability does not necessarily follow. Perhaps one of the major problems in the past has been in training areas not necessarily related to reading. For example, a student who cannot remember a series of digits forward or backward is also somewhat likely to experience reading problems in remembering a sequence of events. However, we know that remediation that focuses on practice in remembering a series of digits is not likely to result in a corresponding increase in remembering details or a series of events in reading.

Although research on the effectiveness of specific kinds of auditory memory training directly related to reading is lacking, a more logical approach would seem to be through exercises such as giving practice in having the student listen to and repeat sentences. Start with sentences containing as many words as the student can remember and work up to sentences equivalent to those remembered by other students of the same age group. Another approach is to attempt to associate auditory sequences with visualization of the process. For example, have the student attempt to "see in the mind's eye" what is read or heard. This, in our experience, aids in recall.

REMEDIATION OF SPEECH PROBLEMS

Students who have any speech defects should be referred to a speech therapist for an evaluation. Following the evaluation the remedial reading teacher should make it a point to personally consult with the speech therapist concerning any special treatment that should be afforded the student. In some cases the recommendations of the speech therapist may require that certain precautions be taken in teaching the student, e.g., teaching the student in a one-to-one situation without the necessity of performing before a group. In other cases the therapist may feel that exposure to group situations may be appropriate and even desirable. Because speech problems are so diverse and the problem of any one student may be entirely unique, general recommendations for the treatment of speech problems would be inappropriate.

In spite of the fact that general recommendations for the handling of students with speech problems are not practical, it should be stressed that the speech therapist should be informed about the nature of the remedial reading program. For example, the speech therapist should have a knowledge of such factors as the amount of time the student spends in remedial reading, the amount of individual versus group work, possible reasons for the student's reading disability, and the degree of the reading disability. Armed with this information the speech therapist and remedial reading teacher can combine their efforts to plan a dual program of remediation.

REMEDIATION OF GENERAL HEALTH PROBLEMS

Once a student has been referred to a medical doctor for various problems of general health, there is usually little or nothing that can be done by the remedial reading teacher. However, the remedial reading teacher should attempt to stay alert to the symptoms mentioned in the section "Diagnosis of General Health Problems" and consult with the student's parents concerning any recommendations made by the student's physician for maximizing learning conditions. For example, some students may require more breaks for rest and relaxation, provision for mid-morning and/or mid-afternoon snacks, etc. The problem, however, as with dealing with other specialists, is to insure that channels of communication are always open.

SUMMARY

The physical problems with which the remedial reading teacher is usually concerned might be classified as problems of the eye, problems of the ear, problems with speech, neurologically impaired functions, and problems of general health. Because of the complexity of neurological problems they have not been discussed in this chapter, but they are thoroughly covered in Chapter 9. Problems of the eye are prevalent in a number of cases of students with reading disability. The remedial reading teacher should become familiar with instruments for vision screening and should learn to recognize symptoms of visual difficulties. The remedial reading teacher should also learn to administer tests for auditory discrimination and should learn to give auditory acuity tests or should refer to the school nurse or a hearing specialist those students who have inadequate auditory discrimination. Auditory memory is also an important skill required for reading. However, definitive research is lacking that would clearly indicate that training in auditory memory will, in turn, improve students' ability to read.

There is some disagreement as to whether speech difficulties actually contribute to reading disability. In reality, a common factor such as inadequate hearing is probably more responsible for difficulties in speech as well as reading.

The remedial reading teacher should be familiar with symptoms of students who possess problems with their general health. When a cluster of these symptoms appears in a student, or when any one symptom appears to a strong degree, then that student should be referred to the school nurse, or the parents should be contacted so that the student can receive attention from a medical doctor.

The remedial reading teacher is usually not concerned with the treatment of physical disabilities but should learn to recognize various symptoms when they occur so that a proper referral can be made. However, some types of exercises can be done to improve auditory discrimination.

REFERENCES

Bixel, Gordon. "Vision—Key to Learning or Not Learning," *Education*. Vol. 87, (November, 1966), 180–184.

Bond, Guy L.; Tinker, Miles A.; and Wasson, Barbara B. *Reading Difficulties—Their Diagnosis and Correction*, 4th ed., Englewood Cliffs, N.J.: Prentice-Hall, 1979.

Cermak, Laird S.; Goldberg, Judith; Cermak, Sharon; and Drake, Charles. "The Short-Term Memory Ability of Children with Learning Disabilities," *Journal of Learning Disabilities*. Vol. 13, (January, 1980), 25–29.

Den Buurman, Rudy; Roersema, Theo; and Gerrissen, Jack F. "Eye Movements and the Perceptual Span in Reading," *Reading Research Quarterly*. Vol. 16, (1981), 227–235.

Elterman, R. D.; Abel, L. A.; Daroff, R. B.; Del'Osso, L. F.; and Bornstein, J. L. "Eye Movement Patterns in Dyslexic Children," *Journal of Learning Disabilities*. Vol. 13, (January, 1980), 16–21.

Finnegan, Shirley D. "Auditory Skills and Word Calling Ability," *Academic Therapy*. Vol. 14, (January, 1979), 299–309.

Flynn, Pauline T., and Byrne, Margaret. "Relationship Between Reading and Selected Auditory Abilities of Third-Grade Children," *Journal of Speech and Hearing Research*. Vol. 13, (December, 1970), 731–740.

Geissal, Mary Ann, and Knafle, June. "A Linguistic View of Auditory Discrimination Tests and Exercises," *Reading Teacher*. Vol. 31, (November, 1977), 134–140.

Groff, Patrick. "Reading Ability and Auditory Discrimination: Are They Related?" *Reading Teacher*. Vol. 28, (May, 1975), 742–747.

Gupta, Raj; Ceci, Stephen; and Slater, Alan. "Visual Discrimination in Good and Poor Readers," *Journal of Special Education*. Vol. 72, (1978), 409–416.

Harris, Albert J., and Sipay, Edward R. *How to Increase Reading Ability*. 7th ed., New York: Longman, 1980.

Keeney, Arthur H. "Vision and Learning Disabilities," Paper presented at the Annual Conference of the National Society for the Prevention of Blindness, Milwaukee, Wisconsin, 1969.

Koenke, Karl. "A Comparison of Three Auditory Discrimination-Perception Tests," *Academic Therapy*. Vol. 13, (March, 1978), 463–468.

Krippner, Stanley. "On Research in Visual Training and Reading Disability," *Journal of Learning Disabilities*. Vol. 4, (February, 1971), 66–76.

Lefton, Lester A.; Lahey, Benjamin B.; and Stagg, David I. "Eye Movements in Reading Disabled and Normal Children: A Study of Systems and Strategies," *Journal of Learning Disabilities*. Vol. 11, (November, 1978), 549–558.

Lefton, Lester A.; Nagle, Richard J.; and Johnson, Gwendolyn. "Eye Movement Dynamics of Good and Poor Readers: Then and Now," *Journal of Reading Behavior*. Vol. 11, (Winter, 1979), 319–328.

Lyon, Reid. "Auditory-Perceptual Training: The State of the Art," *Journal of Learning Disabilities*. Vol. 10, (November, 1977), 564–572.

Malmquist, Eve. "A Study of Vision Defects in Relation to Reading Disabilities and a Test of the Validity of Certain Vision Screening Programmes in Elementary School," *Slow Learning Child*. Vol. 12, (July, 1965), 38–48.

Martin, Harold. "Vision and Its Role in Reading Disability and Dyslexia," *Journal of School Health*. Vol. 41, (November, 1971), 468–472.

Matthews, Barbara A. J., and Seymour, Charlena M. "The Performance of Learning Disabled Children on Tests of Auditory Discrimination," *Journal of Learning Disabilities*. Vol. 14, (January, 1981), 9–12.

Neuman, Susan B. "Effect of Teaching Auditory Perceptual Skills on Reading Achievement in First Grade," *Reading Teacher*. Vol. 34, (January, 1981), 422–426.

Paradis, Edward. "The Appropriateness of Visual Readiness Materials," *Journal of Educational Research*. Vol. 67, (February, 1974), 276–278.

Park, Rosemarie. "Performance on Geometric Figure Copying Tests as Predictors of Types of Errors in Decoding," *Reading Research Quarterly*. Vol. 14, (1978–1979), 100–118.

Rosner, Jerome. "Language Arts and Arithmetic Achievement and Specifically Related Perceptual Skills," *American Educational Research Journal*. Vol. 10, (Winter, 1973), 59–68.

Rupley, William; Ashe, Michael; and Buckland, Pearl. "The Relations Between the Discrimination and Letter-Like Forms and Word Recognition," *Reading World*. Vol. 19, (December, 1979), 113–123.

Seaton, Hal. "The Effects of a Visual Perception Training Program and Reading Achievement," *Journal of Reading Behavior*. Vol. 9, (Summer, 1977), 188–192.

Smith, William. "The Visual System in Reading and Learning Disabilities," *Journal of School Health*. Vol. 39, (February, 1969), 144–150.

Spache, George. "Testing Vision," *Education*. Vol. 59, (June, 1939), 623–626.

Strag, Gerald A., and Richmond, Bert O. "Auditory Discrimination Techniques for Young Children," *Elementary School Journal*. Vol. 73, (May, 1973), 447–454.

Swanson, William. "Optometric Vision Therapy—How Successful Is It in the Treatment of Learning Disorders?" *Journal of Learning Disabilities.* Vol. 5, (May, 1972), 37–42.

Tinker, Miles. "Recent Studies of Eye Movements in Reading," *Psychological Bulletin.* Vol. 54, (July, 1958), 215–231.

Weber, Gail Yerby. "Visual Disabilities—Their Identification and Relationship with Academic Achievement," *Journal of Learning Disabilities.* Vol. 13, (June–July, 1980), 301–305.

Wepman, Joseph M. *The Auditory Discrimination Test.* Chicago: Language Research Associates, 1973.

9

Diagnosis and Remediation of Severe Reading Disabilities[1]

The first part of this chapter presents a discussion of the dilemma of the reading specialist in dealing with severe reading disabilities. As you will note, even the terminology presents a problem. Information is then presented on the history of diagnosis and modern-day diagnostic aspects including typical symptoms and precautions to be observed. The last part of the chapter deals with prior theories of remediation and their success, followed by present-day theory and its implementation.

THE DILEMMA OF THE HARD-TO-TEACH CHILD

Most problem readers encountered during a teaching career have clearcut, easily diagnosed reasons for their failure to learn. Such students do respond to remediation efforts, which can vary from mild to prolonged.

But what about the student who underachieves in reading, writing, math, and other cognitive tasks, for whom ordinary remedial methods are of limited success? Both the classroom teacher and the remedial reading specialist experience the frustration and challenge of such a student. "This student seems capable, but just doesn't catch on to what we're doing" is a common observation. And not infrequently such students are characterized by normal to high intelligence, appear to be free of emotional problems, have adequate vision and hearing, and present no obvious health problems —thereby adding to the dilemma.

Many labels and descriptive terms have been applied to these children

[1]Chapter 9 was written by Wilson Wayne Grant, M.D., Fellow, American Academy of Pediatrics; Assistant Clinical Professor, Texas Tech School of Medicine.

over the years. Around the turn of the century, they were labeled *problem children* and were described as lazy or unmotivated. But educators, physicians, and psychologists began to sense that these were, in fact, *children with a problem*, who for some reason were unable to process information as other children were able to.

Today, the accepted term for these children is *learning disabled*. In this chapter we will be addressing two general classes of disorders, or learning disabilities, that commonly interfere with the learning process. The first is the broad spectrum of disorders commonly called specific learning disabilities, and the second is attentional deficit disorders, also known as hyperactivity.

Part A: Diagnosis

SPECIFIC LEARNING DISABILITIES

One of the first reports of a child with a learning disability to appear in the literature was authored by a British general practitioner, W. Pringle Morgan (1896). In his case report Morgan wrote:

> Percy F.—a well-grown lad, aged 14 . . . is the eldest son of intelligent parents, the second child in a family of seven. He has always been a bright and intelligent boy, quick at games and in no way inferior to others of his age. His greatest difficulty . . . his inability to learn to read . . . is remarkable, and is pronounced, and I have no doubt it is due to some congenital defect. He has been at school or under tutors since he was seven years old, and the greatest efforts have been made to teach him to read, but in spite of this laborious and persistent training, he can only with difficulty spell words of one syllable. . . . The schoolmaster who has taught him for some years says that he would be the smartest lad in the school if the instruction were entirely oral. . . .

Many teachers will recognize this boy; he has been in their class at one time or another.

During the first quarter of the twentieth century, interest in reading and learning problems grew. Other case reports appeared in the literature, especially those made by ophthalmologists, who were often the first physicians consulted about failure to read.

J. A. Fisher (1910), an ophthalmologist and early observer of reading problems, felt that such disabilities were due to structural damage of the brain. For others, functional neuromaturational delays rather than anatomical abnormalities were more likely causes. Out of this debate Samuel Orton expanded the neurological model and developed one of the first comprehensive theories of learning disabilities in children. Based on his work in the

1930s, Orton (1937) coined the term *strephosymbolia* meaning "twisted symbols" and postulated that mixed or incomplete dominance was the underlying reason for the learning (reading) difficulties. He based these views on his observations of frequent left-handedness or ambidexterity and the tendency toward reversals in writing and reading among the reading-disabled children. Orton believed that this abnormality of brain development was genetically determined given its increased incidence in certain families. With his assistant, Ann Gillingham, he developed a variety of teaching strategies and remediation techniques. Many of Orton's theories have not stood the test of time, but as pointed out by developmental pediatrician, Melvin Levine (1980), Orton's pioneering work encouraged further research.

In the 1940s and 1950s, research from educational, psychological, and medical disciplines attempted to establish causative factors and remedial techniques. *Dyslexia* was one of the earliest labels used to define a child such as was described by Dr. Morgan in 1896.

From the beginning researchers had difficulty defining dyslexia, which literally means "inability to recognize words." The term has come to mean such different things to different people that it has limited value today. During the 1950s and 1960s a number of terms were coined that derived from the belief that learning disabilities were due to anatomic damage to the brain. These were replaced by the term *minimal brain dysfunction* when no *apparent* brain injury could be found in most learning-disabled children.

By the late 1960s it was the general consensus that these previous labels were too emotionally charged as well as inadequate; professionals moved increasingly toward more functional classifications, finally arriving at the term *specific learning disabilities*. Perhaps due in part to its incorporation into federal legislation, this new classification has persisted in the language of most disciplines.

In April of 1967 the Council for Exceptional Children during a meeting in St. Louis prepared a definition of *learning disabilities*. N. Dale Bryant (1972) states their conclusions:

> A child with learning disabilities is one with adequate mental abilities, sensory processes, and emotional stability, who has a limited number of specific deficits in perceptive, integrative, or expressive processes which severely impair learning efficiency. This includes children who have a central nervous system dysfunction, which is expressed primarily in impaired learning efficiency.

Bryant also noted that another definition emphasizing the basic nature of the language process was adopted by the National Advisory Committee on Handicapped Children in January of 1968. This definition follows:

> Children with special learning disabilities exhibit a disorder in one or more of the basic psychological processes involved in understanding or in using spoken or written languages. These may be manifested in disorders of listening, think-

ing, talking, reading, writing, spelling, or arithmetic. They include conditions which have been referred to as perceptual handicaps, brain injury, minimal brain dysfunction, dyslexia, developmental aphasia, and so on. They do not include learning problems which are due primarily to visual, hearing, or motor handicaps, to mental retardation, emotional disturbance, or environmental disadvantages.

This definition was incorporated into the landmark federal legislation of 1975 concerning education of the handicapped (P.L. 94, 1975, p. 142).

You may still find the term *dyslexia* used by some professionals. Developmental dyslexia is today defined as "a constitutional and often genetically determined deficit in written language skills such as reading, writing, and spelling." It may or may not be associated with difficulty in symbol recognition, disordered development of time concepts, or disordered concepts of space. Al Benton (1975) has specified that dyslexia implies a constitutional, neurological basis for reading and learning failure. More often than not, however, you'll find *dyslexia* being used interchangeably with *reading and learning disability*.

Characteristics of Learning Disabilities

To understand the learning-disabled child, it would help to briefly review the steps in the learning process. These steps are outlined in Figure 9.1 and discussed below.

Learning begins with a stimulus; that is, a particular piece of information to be processed such as the alphabet or a series of words. The learner must *attend to* the stimulus for a sufficient length of time for it to be fixed in the mind. The learner having attended to the information, the sense organs then register the information, transmitting it via nerves to the brain for processing. Of course, for normal processing to occur the brain must *perceive accurate information*. That means, for example, words of proper shape and orientation are received, not upside-down or mishapen versions.

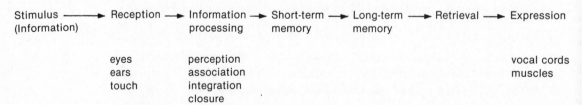

FIGURE 9-1.   The Process of Learning.

With the stimulus accurately received in the brain, a complex *processing of information* occurs. This information is stored in the *short-term memory*. Information is stored in the short-term memory for a limited period. Depending on the degree of relevance of the stimulus to the learner and its association with existing stored knowledge, it may be transferred to *long-term memory*. Only as information is firmly fixed in the long-term memory is it really learned. The learner should then be able to *retrieve* the information when needed and *express* it in a meaningful way.

Blocks to learning can occur at any point in the learning cycle. Initially the child must attend to the stimulus long enough to latch onto, or learn, it. Failure to concentrate results in inefficient, inconsistent learning. This brings us to disorders of attention and their effect on learning, which will be discussed later in this chapter. Sensory disorders that interfere with information reception were discussed in Chapter 8.

Careful observation during the teaching-learning process is most helpful in identifying students with severe reading disability. But you must know what to look for to make meaningful observations. A number of symptoms are typical of the learning-disabled child. Note, however, that these symptoms can be present in any student. Also, most severely disabled readers exhibit a number of symptoms, since one problem interacts with another to produce varying degrees of disability and thus varying symptoms.

What follows is a list of symptoms associated with cases of severe reading disability; these symptoms are common to learning disability cases in general.

1. *Reversals of letters or words.* In the case of letters, the student may reverse *b*'s and *d*'s, *p*'s and *q*'s, or less commonly *n*'s and *u*'s, thus making *bad* read *dab* or *baby* read *dady*; in the case of words, parts of words may be reversed as in *ant* to *nat*, or entire words may be reversed as in *saw* to *was* or *on* to *no*.

2. *Short or erratic memory for words.* Words that a normal reader would learn in teaching-learning situations may require many more exposures for the disabled reader. Also, a word could be remembered and spoken correctly one time and not recognized the next time. This failure to recognize may occur within a period of minutes.

3. *Oral rereading not improved following silent reading or a first oral reading.*

4. *Inability to hold information in memory until needed.* Memory problems are exhibited in the use of context clues; that is, the student cannot remember what has just been read and so cannot derive a new word from context. Problems are also exhibited in use of phonics or structural analysis for word attack. In sounding a word with three phonemes the student may forget the first one or two by the time the third appears.

5. *Difficulty with concentration.* Some students simply cannot attend to a paragraph or story as it is being read or cannot listen for periods beyond a half minute. This problem becomes apparent when dealing with abstract relationships such as sound-symbol correspondence. Students with subtle difficulty in concentrating may not have obvious hyperactivity or other behavior problems.

6. *Inability to see whole relationships or form a gestalt.* This difficulty is illustrated by the phonetic speller who is unable to form a mental image of a word. Also, words are often spelled exactly as they sound, e.g., *liks* for *likes* or *hav* for *have.*

7. *Emotional instability.* Most students become irritated when they fail to experience some success. Students with severe reading disability, however, have a tendency to become extremely irritable on meeting a task at which they are not immediately successful. Their moods may also change rapidly.

8. *Impulsiveness.* This problem is illustrated by the student who guesses at words rather than working them out using word-attack skills. Impulsiveness is best demonstrated when pictures are represented on a page. The student may say "bunny" for "rabbit" when the word *rabbit* is accompanied by an illustration of a rabbit.

9. *Poor eye-motor coordination.* This problem can be measured using tests. It can also be noted by observing the student write or engage in motor activities such as cutting with scissors or coloring. Tests have the advantage of providing scoring criteria or norms from which to judge the student's performance. However, the eye of an experienced teacher may be just as capable in identifying eye-motor coordination problems.

10. *Difficulty with sequencing.* This problem arises in poor spelling but may be more common in reading when the student has difficulty remembering the specific order of words in a sentence, events in a paragraph, days in a week, or months in a year.

11. *Inability to work rapidly.* This problem arises in in reading assignments but is equally common in written work. The student is always behind the pace set by others and gets irritable if rushed. There is also a tendency to perseverate, or dwell on a particular point for an extra long time.

12. *Omissions of words and phrases.* It should be emphasized that many students omit an occasional word, but some severely disabled readers consistently omit words, especially unknown words. There is also a tendency to skip whole phrases or lines and to constantly lose place.

13. *Directional confusion.* This may show up, as mentioned before, in lack of ability to distinguish *b* and *d*, and so forth. Confusion can extend, however, to inability to distinguish left and right, front and back, before and after.

14. *Poor auditory discrimination.* This condition may be present even when the student's auditory acuity is excellent. Again, many students have

difficulty with auditory discrimination, but the severely disabled reader has trouble learning minute differences in words such as *pen* and *pin* or even *him* and *hen*. Disabled readers are also erratic in their ability to discriminate sounds.

15.   *Hyperactivity.* The hyperactive student frequently has a short attention span and is wiggling and squirming, tapping fingers, etc. These signs are more apparent when the student is under stress such as when completing an assignment. (See the next section for additional description of hyperactivity.)

16.   *Poor syntax, stuttering, and halting speech.* The student who exhibits speech problems seems to need to think ahead when talking; that is, words do not flow smoothly, or when they do the order of the words is illogical.

17.   *Achievement in arithmetic considerably higher than in reading and spelling.* Perhaps there is a physiological explanation for this. Some people who have suffered strokes have been left unable to read but still able to solve difficult math problems.

Causes of Learning Disabilities

With specific learning disabilities, dysfunction of the central nervous system interferes with the learning process, specifically the *perception, organization, storage, retrieval, and expression of information.* This process is quite complex and not fully understood. At one time most reading and learning difficulties were commonly attributed to disorders of visual perception. This assumption derived from the difficulty observed in the disabled learner with reversals of letters and words as well as difficulty with space orientation and figure-ground pattern. Such aberrations being fairly obvious and readily observed, it is understandable that they received considerable attention. Many and varied remedial techniques grew out of this theoretical position. Prominent among these were the teaching methods of Marianne Frostig (1973).

Recent evidence suggests that perceptual dysfunction may not be as significant as once thought. According to F. R. Vellutino (1977), remedial programs based on perceptual techniques alone have had limited effectiveness in teaching children to read. The problem shared by most disabled readers is not perception of letters and words but association of symbols with their spoken counterparts. Vellutino (1977) illustrated this distinction in two separate experiments involving carefully selected samples of school children in grades two through eight (ages seven to fifteen). His findings suggest that verbal rather than visual information is lacking with poor readers, thereby limiting the utility of visual discrimination exercises.

Ronald MacKeith (1977), in a review of reading disability research, concluded that remedial measures for reading readiness derived from theories of visual deficits have no usefulness in correcting reading problems. In his view most learning disabilities are related to dysfunction of information processing, such as the association, integration, memory, and expression of information.

Our ability to definitively test these intricate steps in the learning process is unfortunately limited. As this text points out, more is to be gained from evaluating the child from a functional standpoint; in other words, posing questions such as, How does this child read? In what skills is the child deficient? How are learning tasks approached? (Diagnosis of information-processing skills is discussed in detail in Chapter 10.)

In reaction to theoretical positions emphasizing neurological factors in the cause of learning disabilities, other professionals turned to environmental and emotional factors. Bruce Balow (1971) expressed this view:

> Obviously some few cases arise from an unusual neurological switchboard, scrambled circuitry, crossed wires or blown fuses, but the large mass of learning disabled are far more likely to derive from an innate or acquired vulnerability coupled with an environment in home and school that is inhospitable or downright hostile to learning in the basic skills. (p. 513)

Most experts today subscribe to the concept that multiple factors—genetic, neurological, and environmental—interplay to produce a learning-disabled child (Levine, 1980). Most experts would agree with Kinsbourne (1979): "We know in principle that a lag in cognitive development can derive either from an individual variation in genetic programming or from early damage to an area of the brain destined to control the behavior in question." The child's ability to cope with this developmental lag certainly is influenced by the emotional and educational environment. Nevertheless, those of us who spend time working with these children recognize the child who comes from one of the best families, has the best educational opportunities, and yet still is unable to learn.

It is clear from this discussion that we have much to learn about the causes of learning disabilities. But caution is in order about too much emphasis on causation. The important task is to teach the child how to read, count, and spell, and that can be done without a detailed knowledge of causative factors.

Tests Used in the Evaluation of Specific Learning Disabilities

Teachers and diagnosticians will be confronted with a variety of tests and test scores in the evaluation of children with learning disabilities. Each test has a purpose and a varying degree of usefulness to the teacher in planning a remedial program. In evaluating tests, it is helpful to consider what information a test is designed to give and what use that information has. For example, some tests give information that is of practical value in determining the cause and expected natural course of the child's disability but that may be of limited value in planning a remedial program. Neurological tests (those of handedness, dominance, soft signs, etc.) fall into this category. On the other hand, a neurological test may document that a student has a physical, developmental reason for clumsiness indicating that messy writing or disorganized approach to tasks is not due to laziness or poor habits. Other neurological tests are designed to provide specific data about information processing and, therefore, may be of more practical help in planning a remedial program.

The following list of tests is not exhaustive. It only gives a sample of the more widely accepted tests available.

1.   *The WISC-R and WAIS.* These tests have been used extensively in reading diagnosis and are discussed in other chapters in this text. It is possible for a psychologist trained in learning and reading diagnosis to gain some evaluation of a student's information-processing capabilities from performance on the *WAIS* or *WISC-R.* Too often, however, these are not as helpful as they should be considering the time required to administer them.

2.   *Tests for handedness, dominance, and knowledge of left and right.* These tests have been used and researched extensively in the diagnosis of severe as well as mild reading disabilities. One such battery is the *Harris Tests of Lateral Dominance* (Harris, 1958). It tests such factors as knowledge of left and right, hand preferences, eye dominance, and foot dominance. Other researchers and diagnosticians have used similar but unpublished testing instruments. It should be noted that at certain age-grade levels significantly more children who are severely disabled may, as Harris points out (1958, p. 20), show more confusion in identifying left and right and mixed hand dominance, or at other age-grade levels show strong left preferences. However, this does not mean that a student who exhibits these symptoms is disabled in reading, nor does this knowledge provide us with any information of significant value in planning a program of remediation for a severely disabled reader. In most cases, based on what is now known about severe reading disability, there is little to be gained from tests for handedness, dominance, or knowledge of left and right.

3.   *Other tests used in diagnosis of disabled readers.* The *Bender Visual-Motor Gestalt Test (BVMG)* (Bender, 1958) and the *Developmental Test of Visual Perception (DTVP)* (Frostig, 1964) have been used in the diagnosis of severely disabled readers. However, as in the case above, the fact that a student does poorly on the *BVMG* is not conclusive evidence of a disability; or, if a disability is present, the information derived from the test scores is of little use in prescribing meaningful remedial activities. The *DTVP* attempts to identify students who have problems with perception in space and eye-motor coordination. Many

studies indicate, however, that the type of activities prescribed for the remediation of weaknesses found on this test are of little or no value in the remediation of concomitant difficulties in reading. (For a review of such studies, see Hammill, Goodman, and Wiederholt, 1974).

The *Illinois Test of Psycholinguistic Abilities (ITPA)* (Kirk, McCarthy, and Kirk, 1968) attempts to measure what you do need to know about the seriously disabled reader. That is, it tends to indicate weaknesses in such areas as auditory decoding, visual decoding, and auditory association. However, the reliability and validity of the subtests have not been clearly established. Furthermore, it is somewhat difficult and time consuming to administer. And, since no clearcut information exists concerning the relationship of subtest weaknesses to reading disabilities, the information derived from it is not worth the time and effort required for its administration in most cases.

The causes of cases of severe learning disabilities cannot be easily discovered by any of our most commonly used diagnostic tests as the above discussion illustrates. In an article on the study of pyschoeducational assessment of learning disabilities, David Sabatino, William Wickham, and Calvin Burnett (1968) indicated that global measures, such as IQ, are of little value in assessing severe reading and learning disability. What they believe is needed is "specific information processing behaviors"; that is, information on how the student learns so that you may capitalize on strong modes of learning and strengthen weaker modes. Gathering information on specific processing behaviors may enable you to modify the classroom environment to achieve the best results with this type of student (Sabatino, Wickham, and Burnett, 1968).

The information-processing behaviors can, to some extent, be assessed by a psychologist or a diagnostician using information derived from the tests discussed here as well as other commonly used tests. However, the classroom teacher or the remedial reading teacher can in most cases gain a working knowledge of a student's information-processing behaviors by careful observation and diagnostic teaching. (The diagnosis of information-processing behaviors and teaching techniques are covered in detail in Chapter 10.)

HYPERACTIVITY AND ATTENTIONAL DEFICIT DISORDER

Few subjects in child development have received as much attention in recent years as hyperactivity. Despite the attention, confusion and misunderstanding surround this subject. Yet there is little need for confusion. In the past decade more precise information has clarified many of the issues.

Prominent among the reasons for confusion about this topic is the term *hyperactivity* itself. To begin with, not all that is active is hyperactive. A variety of factors can cause a normal child to appear more active than the child's peers. Preschoolers and toddlers by nature are active. Nervous, anxious children may appear more active than other children. And some children by nature are more active, alert, and inquisitive but still learn in a normal way. They exhibit problem behaviors when bored or understimulated.

Characteristics of Hyperactivity

The truly hyperactive (or hyperkinetic) child with an attentional deficit disorder has a set of characteristics that in combination impair learning and social adjustment to a significant degree. According to Marcel Kinsbourne and Paula Caplan (1979) such attentional deficits, alone or in combination with learning disabilities, are common precursors to underachievement in the classroom.

While the appearance of increased body activity is often the most noticeable symptom in a child with hyperactivity, this is not necessarily the most significant symptom. These children present a cluster of disruptive characteristics that when seen together are easily recognized. These typical characteristics are:

1. *Disordered activity.* One of the most prominent characteristics of hyperactive children is a quality of physical activity that is disruptive. They do appear more active than most normal children of their age and maturity. In the extreme they are restless, incessantly moving from one activity to another. At play they tend to be loud and boisterous, constantly changing activity and disrupting the play of other children. In the classroom they are restless, frequently getting out of their seats. They run when they should walk and invariably talk when they should listen. They crave attention and praise, but seem to always act in ways that get them into trouble.

Thus, these children do appear *hyperactive*—that is, to have increased activity—but in reality they may not be. Researchers have placed a modified pedometer, a watchlike instrument that measures body movement, on normal children and children with hyperkinetic syndrome. Surprisingly, in such experiments children with the hyperkinetic syndrome do not always have a greatly increased rate of activity. But the *nature* of the activity in the hyperkinetic child differs vastly. Behaviors tend to be random, disorganized, and nongoal directed. It is the *quality*, not necessarily the *quantity*, of activity that is abnormal. The random and disorganized nature of their movements does, however, give the appearance of increased activity.

2. *Disordered attention.* Parents and teachers of hyperactive children frequently complain that the child won't pay attention to anything. The teacher says, "He has a short attention span," or "she can't concentrate on her work." However it is expressed, hyperkinetic children are unable to control and modulate their attention. They are unable to focus on one task or

activity for any length of time. When one observes them, their minds appear to be bouncing from one interest to another with rapidity and lack of order.

Concentration is the ability to focus one's mind on a limited number of activities and stimuli for a given period of time while simultaneously screening out all other unrelated stimuli. The hyperactive child cannot do this and is therefore not consistently productive; the hyperactive child is *stimulus bound*. This means that all stimuli that bombard the senses are attended to, and sometimes simultaneously. Only a very strong stimulus can override all others and capture the hyperactive child's undivided attention. More often than not the child does not pay effective attention to instructions or material being presented. When an assignment is begun, the child is often distracted before completing the task. Decisions are made before all the data are in, and all too often the child stops listening before hearing all the questions. Choices are thus made impulsively.

3. *Disordered impulse control.* The ability of hyperactive children to control their impulses is impaired, so they literally act before they think. To a greater or lesser degree they are unable to stop, look, and listen. Strong impulse control is a sign of maturity that gradually develops through childhood. The hyperkinetic child, fails to do this as well as other children. In class the child repeatedly speaks without being called on. Another perplexing symptom related to impulsiveness is disordered emotional control: "One moment she is happy and the next she's crying." Just as hyperkinetic children have trouble controlling and organizing their activity, attention, and impulses, so they cannot organize and control their emotions well either. At one moment they may change from a happy and peaceful mood to crying and frustration.

As mentioned earlier, the term *hyperactive child* is confusing. One reasons is that the physical hyperactivity, while at times disruptive, has the least effect on the child's ability to learn. The destructive factor is the disorganized, unstructured attention. In fact the physical hyperactivity is largely a by-product of the attentional deficit. It is the body following the distractible, disorganized mind.

Recognizing this, the latest edition of *Diagnostic and Statistical Manual of Mental Disorders* (DSM III) of the American Psychiatric Association has introduced a new term, *attentional deficit disorder*. This is a much better diagnostic term because it focuses the emphasis on the most relevant problem. For the remainder of this chapter this term will be used in place of, or interchangeably with, *hyperactivity*.

Causes of Hyperactivity, or Attentional Deficit Disorder

As with specific learning disability, many causative factors have been proposed for hyperactivity, or attentional deficit. The linkage of hyperactive, impulsive, and attentional deficit behaviors with organic brain lesions has a long history with reports occurring as early as 1900. The consequences of a major encephalitis epidemic in 1918 further linked behavior changes with organic brain damage. Survivors of encephalitis were found to have significant behavior changes, including persistent hyperactivity, distractibility, irritability, and impulsivity. In 1937 Charles Bradley published a study on the use of stimulant drugs in the treatment of children in a residential center. Previously hyperactive, distractible children showed improvement in schoolwork and social adjustment.

Some interesting circumstantial evidence exists to suggest that genetics may play a role in producing attentional deficit disorders. For a long time it has been known that both hyperactivity and learning disorders are more common in males, suggesting genetic factors. Those working with children are struck by the frequency of a father or mother remarking that "I was just like him when I was a child. I almost didn't finish school." And it is not uncommon to have two or more siblings in the family with similar problems. But, of course, there are many other children whose families have no history of learning problems. It seems then that genetics may play a role in some cases, but the extent or nature of the role is still undefined.

There are some professionals, albeit a small group, who claim that hyperkinesis and learning disabilities are not due to physical factors at all but to emotional stresses and poor environment. An unsuitable emotional environment can produce unhealthy mental and emotional development, and this in turn can affect the child's school performance. However, the emotionally disturbed child and the hyperactive child differ on several counts, and it is very important that a proper distinction be made between the two during the diagnostic and treatment process.

Children from an economically and socially deprived environment may underachieve in school and may not behave in the way middle-class teachers expect. But this does not make them hyperactive or learning disabled. It is important when forming judgments about a particular child to consider all possible factors before applying labels, particularly where disorders are concerned.

As with specific learning disabilities, attentional deficit disorders are most likely caused by several factors working conjointly. The right constitutional background (neurological and genetic) acted on by certain environmental factors facilitates the expression of the attentional deficit.

Evaluation of the Child with Hyperactivity,
or Attentional Deficit

Although either may occur alone in a given student, hyperactivity will occur with some frequency in conjunction with specific learning disability and delayed motor development. Figure 9.2 illustrates the various combinations.

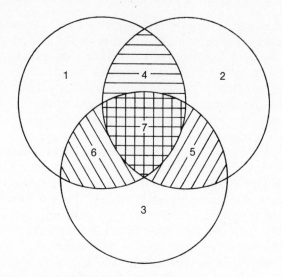

1. Attentional deficit (hyperactivity) alone
2. Specific learning disability alone
3. Motor coordination deficit alone
4. Attentional deficit + specific learning disability
5. Specific learning disability + motor coordination deficit
6. Attentional deficit + motor coordination deficit
7. Attentional deficit + specific learning disability +
   coordination deficit

FIGURE 9-2.   The Spectrum of Learning Disability.

Each child is unique and has a particular combination of strengths and weaknesses. If a teacher suspects a student's learning difficulties are complicated by attentional problems, referral is in order. Evaluation of such children requires the cooperation of many people: teacher, parents, psychologists, and physicians. There is no one test that will discriminate the attentional deficit disorder from other conditions. The teacher's observations of the quality of the child's performance in the classroom are one of the most important diagnostic measures.

Part B: REMEDIATION

SPECIFIC LEARNING DISABILITIES

Most of the early theories of severe reading disabilities and their con-comitant remedial techniques have met with little success. Since reading is a field in which new programs and materials constantly appear, it is important for the remedial reading teacher to know what programs have been unsuc-cessful in the past to avoid unfruitful duplication of efforts.

Probably the best known of the early theories was proposed by the neuropathologist Samuel Orton (1928), who believed that the two halves of the brain were alike in size and design and reversed in pattern. That is, the left hemisphere would bear the same relation to the right hemisphere that the left hand bears to the right hand. Orton concluded that records, or *engrams* as they were called, of one hemisphere would be mirror copies of the other. If a student failed to establish the normal physiological habit of using exclusively those engrams of one hemisphere, a confusion in orienta-tion would result causing a student to be unable to recognize differences between pairs of words that could be spelled backwards. Orton and his asso-ciates reported considerable success in the use of certain physical exercises, along with intensive remediation in reading, in overcoming the reading diffi-culties of a number of children. It is somewhat difficult now to assess the significance of the physical therapy in relation to the direct remediation in reading. Orton was not given to making idle claims, and his work has been of considerable value in furthering an understanding of possible causes of severe reading disabilities. In interpreting his work one must keep in mind that even if his explanation was correct, or partially correct, one should not automatically assume that a physical training program could correct damage already done.

Carl Delacato, working on Orton's theory that severe reading disability was often caused by failure to develop proper neurological organization, developed a program designed to overcome these difficulties. Delacato (1959) suggested physical exercises and remedial procedures dealing with sleep patterns, tonality, handedness, visual control, and so forth. Most medical and educational professionals find little evidence in the literature for the general application of Delacato's or other motor training programs in the treatment of learning problems. The use of various types of perceptual training pro-grams at one time appeared to hold great promise. Present evidence, how-ever, indicates that this area too shows limited success. Many disabled stu-dents do have various kinds and degrees of perceptual handicaps as measured by perceptual tests. In simple terms, however, the remediation of perceptual handicaps does not improve the ability to read or even the potential for reading. In a very thorough review of the literature on perceptual training programs, Hammill, Goodman, and Wiederholt (1974) concluded that "the results of attempts to implement the Frostig-Horne materials and Kephart-Getman techniques in the schools have for the most part been unrewarding." (p. 476)

Bruce Balow (1971) had a similar assessment in an earlier review. He concludes:

> . . . While motor and perceptual skill weaknesses are frequently found in learning disabled pupils, there is great likelihood that these are most often simply concomitants without causal relevance; thus the argument cannot depend upon assumed etiologies for learning disabilities. (p. 523)

Despite his conclusions, Balow cites six reasons why one might consider the addition of visual-motor activities to the curriculum for all primary-age students including students who suffer serious deficiencies in school skills. In summary, Balow's reasons address the importance of visual-motor skills in mastering schoolwork in general and the fact that such skills are "ordinarily left to develop incidentally." Similar reasoning is proposed by other authors who believe that such training will allow students to concentrate better after flexing their muscles and that the development of motor skills may simply contribute to the good mental health of students.

It is our view that these same benefits can be derived from activities more directly related to reading. Furthermore, personal observation suggests that teachers come to view such activities as ends in themselves. Perhaps most important, however, time spent in perceptual training usurps time for activities dealing more directly with reading disabilities.

Some Important Considerations in the Remediation of Severe Reading Disability

A few considerations are of special significance when dealing with severely disabled readers. One is an overall plan in dealing with these problems. Three steps of such a plan are:

1. Early identification of children who, although of normal intelligence, exhibit difficulty with reading and reading-related activities.
2. Formulation of an educational plan based on the student's specific strengths and weaknesses.
3. Continual assessment of the original plan as measured by diagnostic teaching.

Another important consideration in remediation is that severely disabled readers are more likely to benefit from a long-term intensive program than from the less intensive programs often found in the public schools. Jules Abrams and Herman Belmont (1969) found that full-time specialized reading instruction was superior to that usually carried on in most remedial programs. John Heckerl and Russell Sansbury (1968) also studied severely disabled readers and concluded that remedial therapy should be a daily occurrence. In their view an hour is the minimum time for each session, with the exception of sessions for younger children who cannot tolerate lengthy periods. They cautioned that long-term programs should be anticipated with little accomplished during the first six months or even the first year. They emphasized that provisions should be made for the severely disabled reader to receive intensive remediation for as long as profitable or until a functional reading level is achieved.

It is especially important to ensure that the program remains flexible. Once a program has been devised, tried, and evaluated, it should be re-evaluated in terms of its success. If little or no success results, another plan should be tried and again evaluated. This is an ongoing process in any remedial reading program, but it is of special significance to the severely disabled reader.

Techniques for Remediation of Specific Learning Disability

It should be emphasized that the techniques and materials recommended in this text for the mildly disabled reader are often successful for the learning-disabled child. It may be necessary at times, however, to modify techniques for more severely disabled children. For example, the methods for teaching basic sight words suggested in Chapter 4 can be used but will need to be repeated more often and used over a longer time period. Likewise, the methods suggested here are appropriate for the mildly disabled reader but are simply more time consuming and require individualized teaching.

The Fernald Approach.   The Fernald Approach is often referred to as the kinesthetic method. It was first described by Grace M. Fernald and Helen B. Keller in 1921. The following description of their approach with minor changes was taken from Fernald's book published in 1943.[2]

In the early stages of the Fernald Approach no commercially prepared materials are used. The teacher solicits words to be learned from the student. These words are taught until they are mastered. When a storehouse of words is acquired, the student is asked to compose a story. The story is written by the teacher, and any new words that appear are taught. The story is then typed by the teacher so that the student can read it the following day. You will note that this approach is essentially the language-experience method used so often in regular classrooms today.

[2]The Fernald Approach is reproduced here with minor changes by permission of McGraw-Hill Book Company.

Four stages are identified in teaching words. The stage used depends on the student's ability to learn. The stages follow:

Stage 1. Tracing. The word is first written for the student on the chalkboard or on a strip of paper or tagboard measuring approximatey 3″ × 9″ or 4″ × 10″. The word may be written in manuscript or cursive style depending on the type of writing used for the student's normal classroom activities. The student is asked to trace the word with the index finger or a combination of index and middle fingers and says each *word part* as it is being traced (not sounding the word letter by letter). This procedure is used until the word can be traced from memory. The student then writes the word from memory, again, saying each word part as it is written. The word is later typed and read in typed form. New words are filed in a box in alphabetical order.

In this stage certain points of technique are stressed:

1. The finger or fingers must contact the paper. Writing in the air is less successful.
2. The student should never copy a word but always write it from memory.
3. The whole word should be learned at once or as a unit.
4. Each word part should be said aloud as it is traced or written.
5. Whatever the student writes is typed by the teacher and read by the student before too long an interval has passed. This provides transfer from the written to the printed form.
6. The student should not be allowed to write a word incorrectly. If the student cannot remember a word, the session stops and initial tracing practice is resumed.

Stage 2. Writing Without Tracing. At some point words will not need to be traced. The student looks at the word in script, says it several times, and then writes it from memory. At this stage library cards are also substituted for the larger cards used initially. The words can be typed on one side of the card and written in manuscript or cursive on the other side. These cards are then filed alphabetically as were the cards in stage 1.

Stage 3. Recognition in Print. At this stage it is unnecessary to write each word in print. The student looks at the word and is told what it is. The word is pronounced once or twice and written from memory. Reading in books is usually started during this stage.

Stage 4. Word Analysis. The student is encouraged to look at new words and to try to identify familiar word parts (families or phonograms) and apply them to new words. Phonic sounding is discouraged, but the student is encouraged to develop the habit of looking for familiar parts of words.

In most cases the total nonreader would be started in stage 1 and students with partial disabilities started in stage 2. No special techniques are used to overcome word reversals, since the method teaches words in a left-to-right sequence.

Research on the effectiveness of the Fernald Approach shows little difference in its effectiveness compared to other approaches. This is probably due to the fact that students with very severe reading disabilities who are predisposed to learning by this method are simply not grouped together in the studies. It should be stressed, however, that this method is not for use with large groups of students; it is intended for use with the student who fails to learn by more commonly used methods.

Nonvisual Auditory-Kinesthetic-Tactile (AKT) Method.   Harold and Harriet Blau (1968) report that many children seem to learn well using the kinesthetic method just described. For other children there occurs a short circuiting between the eye and the brain; that is, something happens to the message the student sees before it reaches the brain causing words to come out scrambled. To remedy this the authors describe a method similar to the visual-auditory kinesthetic-tactile method but bypassing the visual channel.

Eldon E. Ekwall has used the nonvisual AKT approach in the El Paso Reading Center for several years. It has proven extremely successful with students who are unable to process information correctly when it comes through the visual channel. A description of this approach follows:

> Non-Visual AKT differs from VAKT in several ways, and variations of Non-VAKT are possible too. Primarily, however, the child is blindfolded or closes his eyes, and the word to be learned is traced on his back. As the teacher traces the word, she spells it aloud, letter by letter. Often, the second or third time around, the student can identify the letters being traced and he too spells out the word. Usually (until the student becomes too advanced for this) three-dimensional letters, arranged to spell out the word, are placed before the student and, still blindfolded, he traces these with his fingertips as he feels the letters being traced on his back. The letters are then scrambled, and still blindfolded, the student arranges the letters in the proper sequence. The blindfold is then removed, the student sees what he has done (often his first experience with coherent sequencing) and writes the word on paper, or at the board, and then on a file card for future review. (Blau and Blau, 1968, pp. 127–128)

Diagnosticians cannot be sure that the student's problem is a malfunction of the visual channel. It may simply be that blindfolding facilitates concentration in the auditory and kinesthetic aspects of the learning process.

General Teaching Procedures

Certain teaching procedures seem to be successful with many severely disabled readers, although in most cases these procedures are tedious and time consuming. For example, severely disabled readers require repetition and drill to a point often referred to as overlearning. This means that something has been learned so well that it evokes an automatic response. It is this automatic response level that is often successful with the severely disabled reader. Whether you are teaching word-attack skills or sight words, the automatic response level must be reached. For example, the sight word *no* should be presented enough times that the student automatically says "no" without any hesitation whatsoever when he or she sees the written word; this is the case regardless of the approach used.

With most severely disabled readers it is also helpful, if not absolutely necessary, to focus on one concept at a time. For example, do not try to teach the "d" sound with the "og" phonogram unless the phonogram has been previously learned. The need for a narrow focus makes the analytic system of teaching phonics often inappropriate with the severely disabled reader. The "d" sound may need to be learned in isolation until it evokes an automatic response.

A modified analytic approach may, however, be used. For example, after teaching the "d" and "l" sounds to the automatic level, you could then teach the "og" phonogram by using the words *dog* and *log*. Note, however, that no new concepts should be introduced until the prior concepts are automatic.

Many severely disabled readers can learn through the kinesthetic and tactile senses regardless of the degree of impairment of their auditory and visual channels. A number of learning activities utilizing this approach are available. The type will depend on the age-grade level of the student and the concept to be taught. Some examples of this approach are:

1.   Use of modeling clay to form letters and short words.
2.   Use of three-dimensional letters available commercially. (Some have magnetic backing to stick to a metal easel.)
3.   Use of salt or fine sand in a shallow box such as a shoe box lid in which the student can trace letters and words.
4.   Use of paper placed over screen wire (such as that used on screen doors) on which the student writes with a crayon. This leaves a raised surface on the paper, and the letters and words can be felt.

The use of immediate reinforcement in the accomplishment of goals is advised for all students, and it is especially helpful when working with the severely disabled reader. Reinforcement of short-term goals such as learning the "p" sound or the word *go* is more productive than attempting to reinforce longer-term goals such as "learning to read well enough so that you can read this book." The importance of reinforcement was illustrated by Barbara Batemen (1974). A young cerebral-palsied girl learned to type at a rate of two to three letters a minute with the aid of a stylus held in both hands. Her performance was praised and visitors were often "treated" to her typing demonstration. When the girl was given the opportunity to earn playing time with a prized magnetic board contingent on an increase in her typing rate, however, she soon increased to twenty-five to thirty words per minute.

Careful diagnostic teaching is probably the most important procedure to be followed in working with the severely disabled reader. Although this is not an easy procedure for the inexperienced teacher, it can be learned. For example, when working with a student on learning a new word be sure to note carefully any areas in which the student appears to experience difficulty. In teaching the word *man* consider carefully such questions as the following:

1. Were the *m* and *n* reversed?
2. Does the student seem to learn the word best as a gestalt (learning the whole word picture), or by concentrating on the phoneme-grapheme relationships?
3. Was there anything I did that made this word easier or more difficult to learn than others?
4. Does writing the word enable the student to learn it faster than previous words taught?
5. Does the student learn this and other words faster when they are used in a sentence?
6. Is the student, when working with the sounds, able to discriminate between the "m" and "n"?
7. What does the student think helps him or her learn best?
8. Does the student learn faster when the word is spoken aloud or when spelled aloud?
9. Did the student know all the phoneme-grapheme relationships before we started, or do I need to go back and teach those if this is the preferred method? Did the student even know the letter names?
10. After mastering the names and the letter sounds, did the student have trouble blending? Is blending a problem on other words as well?

Some commercial materials are designed specifically for the severely disabled reader. See Appendix C for a brief description of these materials.

Specific Teaching Procedures and Classroom Modifications

To list a specific set of procedures appropriate for all severely disabled readers would be futile since the symptoms of each student will differ. There are, however, some specific teaching procedures and classroom modifications that you may wish to consider depending on the particular diagnosed needs of any one student. Some of these specific procedures and modifications follow:

1.   Review materials previously learned as often as possible until responses are automatic.
2.   Illustrate new concepts with verbal explanations.
3.   Limit directions for oral and written assignments. For example, divide a three-part assignment into three parts and give directions for each part separately. (As with all suggestions in this section, procedures used depend on the capabilities of the student.)
4.   Provide a working environment that is as free of distractions as possible. Use study carrels or reading and study areas that are isolated from other students.
5.   Introduce new or distracting words with color cues such as a green letter at the beginning of a word and a red letter at the end of a word.
6.   Give the student sufficient time to respond to oral questions. One study showed that teachers allow on average about two to three seconds for a student to answer. Allow at least five to ten seconds if needed; in some cases a half minute may be more appropriate.
7.   Encourage the student to verbalize the response when writing something new.
8.   Encourage the student to use a finger, pencil, or underliner (piece of paper or ruler), or a piece of paper with a window cut in it when reading, if needed.
9.   Many experts have suggested permitting students to give oral answers to tests in their regular classroom if unable to produce adequate written responses. You should keep in mind, however, that this reinforces an undesirable habit. It is usually better to modify the time allowed for completion or to provide questions that require short answers.

Some Cautions in the Treatment of Severe Reading Disability

Regardless of the label attached to the condition, students still need to be taught. While labels have some validity with regard to causation, they are often of little help in designing a remedial program. Beyond using the term *learning disabled,* labeling is not only unnecessary; it is often damaging.

Several years ago a professor's son was brought to the El Paso Reading Center for help with his reading. The professor and his wife said their child had experienced a great deal of difficulty in learning to read because he was "dyslexic." When the boy was interviewed, (age fourteen) he said, "You know, I can't read because I have dyslexia." The clinic director and the teacher assured the boy that at his age most people automatically "get over" dyslexia (probably true to some extent). Within a period of six months the boy's grades in high school went from Ds and Fs to As and Bs, and he no longer had any trouble with reading.

A fairly normal or typical program of remediation was undertaken with this student focusing on his specific weaknesses in reading and especially in study skills. An important part of the remediation, however, involved enhancing this student's self-concept and getting him to realize that he was not saddled with some awesome disease from which he would never recover. The point of all this is, of course, that the use of the label *dyslexia* was in his case highly damaging.

If you are new to the field of reading, you may feel that very little was said here in terms of concrete procedures for identifying and working with severely disabled readers. This is quite true. The results of some of the most commonly used tests provide some help, but for all practical purposes the diagnosis and treatment of students with severe reading disability can best be handled by the teacher through careful, guided observation and diagnostic teaching.

ATTENTIONAL DEFICIT DISORDER, OR HYPERACTIVITY

Remediation of the attentional deficit child involves a three-pronged approach as follows:

1. Provide a proper environmental cocoon for the child that optimizes strengths and overcomes weaknesses.
2. Alleviate inciting factors.
3. Use medical therapy in a careful, considered way.

Providing an Environmental Cocoon

The goal of remediation of the attentional deficit child is breaking through the distractibility and impulsiveness to facilitate learning. Since the root of the problem is the child's unstructured and disorganized approach to most tasks, the first step is to provide a structured, well-organized, nondistracting environment. This involves the child's whole life—at home and at school. In this effort the teacher plays an important role. A regular schedule with minimum interruption is important, as is a consistent approach to learning tasks.

The demands of the classroom excite the major features of the attentional deficit disorder. In the classroom environment the child faces failure, punishment, demands for attention, and motor inhibition unparalleled in other spheres of the child's life. The child who is mildly disturbing at home can become a severe problem at school.

Techniques for Dealing with Attentional Deficit Disorder in the Classroom.

1. Seat the child near the teacher's desk in a reassuring, nonthreatening way.
2. Address the child by name before eliciting a response or calling attention to the child. It is helpful to stand near or touch the child when giving instructions to the class or eliciting a response.
3. Remember that physical features of the work environment influence the child's activity and distractibility levels. Consider these guidelines:
   a. Reduce stimuli in the child's visual field (place construction paper over windows, eliminate posters, pictures, etc.).
   b. Use lighting of medium intensity; no flickering or bright lights.
   c. Plan the schedule so that the child is not expected to concentrate when there is distracting noise in the hallway. Music set at a low volume can be helpful in masking continuous distractions.
   d. Create a private study office by screening off a work area for children with significant attentional deficits.
4. Give shorter assignments with immediate feedback on results. Stress quality not quantity. An attentional deficit child often has difficulty finishing work.
5. Use techniques that assist the short-term memory. Use a preprogrammed assignment card that is reviewed daily and kept at the student's desk.
   a. List each activity separately. If necessary, list specific steps separately.
   b. Require that the child have activities checked off as progress is made.
   c. Set approximate time limits for an activity. It may be helpful to provide a timer; note, however, that some children become more disorganized under time pressure.
   d. For maximum retention in short-term memory, use the following steps:
      Step 1. "Please pay attention. Tell me when you are ready." "Very good; now listen carefully to [these words]," etc.
      Step 2. Break the material to be retained into small units.
      Step 3. Use a multisensory approach to allow rehearsal of the material, i.e., speaking orally, writing down key words, drawing pictures, etc.
      Step 4. Have the child repeat orally the material to be committed to long-term memory.
      Step 5. Provide frequent rehearsals.
      Step 6. "Chunk" material; that is, combine it into meaningful units.

Step 7. Strongly reinforce any increment in amount of material remembered (with verbal praise and/or privileges).

6. Use techniques for dealing with impulsivity and what appears to be an increased activity level; confinement for long periods of time will be felt as pressure. The child should be given legitimate opportunities for physical movement.

   a. Lesson plans should include sorting, cutting, printing, and manipulating counters and gadgets.

   b. Allow the child to work standing or moving at times.

   c. Provide outlets for physical movements (running errands, sharpening pencils, etc.).

   d. Provide an adequate physical education program that allows for gross body movement without involving competitive team sports; this is essential.

Frequently you will find a student who shows symptoms of both attentional deficit and specific learning disability. With this student deal early with the learning impairment using whatever techniques are necessary to remediate the reading and learning problems. If the child senses pressure or failure in the learning area, attentional deficit and related behavior problems are likely to worsen; this would exacerbate learning difficulties and increase pressure and stress. Providing educational opportunities that complement the child's strengths and weaknesses is an important aspect of creating an environmental cocoon.

Alleviating Inciting Factors

The physician in evaluating a hyperactive child will look for factors that cause or aggravate the attentional deficit and related behavior problems. The child's emotional environment is of great importance here. Undue stress or pressure at home or at school worsens the attentional deficit. Efforts to reduce stress through counseling and instruction can be helpful. Recently Benjamin Feingold (1974) has popularized the use of special diets in the treatment of hyperactive and learning-disabled children. While this thesis has yet to be adequately tested, preliminary evidence suggests that behavior is aggravated by certain specific foods or additives for a minority of hyperactive children.

While the rare child may be helped by a restricted diet, no evidence supports the use of a special diet with most attentional deficit and learning-disabled children. The institution of such a diet is no simple matter—it takes much effort and can stigmatize the child, reinforcing a sense of inferiority. Diet therapy should be used only for carefully documented reasons and under the supervision of a knowledgeable physician.

Seeking Medical Treatment

A large body of evidence for the effectiveness of medical treatment of attentional deficit and related behavioral problems of hyperactivity and impulsiveness has been accumulated since Bradley's work in 1937, as Paul Wender (1971) points out. A variety of drugs has been used, but the most effective have been the stimulants (Ritalin and Dexedrine). Just how the stimulants work is unclear, although it is believed they affect the balance of neurotransmitters in the brain. (These neurotransmitters are chemicals, present in minute quantities, that participate in the transmission of impulses from one brain cell to another.)

Whatever the mechanism, proper medical therapy improves the attention span, decreases abnormal activity, increases frustration tolerance, and decreases impulsivity and emotional outbursts. Performance on psychological tests and in the classroom may be improved, but this is not due to any increase in actual intelligence. Rather, the medication allows the child to use native intelligence without interference. It does this primarily by improving the attention span and mental organization.

The use of medication does not reverse specific learning disabilities. This is important: simply because a child is underachieving in school is no reason to consider medical therapy. In fact, medical therapy should be undertaken only after a thorough evaluation and for specific indications. When given for the proper reasons and carefully supervised by a knowledgeable physician, medical therapy with stimulants is quite safe with minimal side effects.

The Importance of Communication Between Professionals

One of the most serious problems in effective use of combined educational and medical approaches has been the lack of communication between personnel in the two fields. Teachers, of course, cannot accurately diagnose which students may benefit from medical treatment. On the other hand, a student who literally "climbs the walls" in a normal classroom setting may be perfectly calm when visiting the doctor's office and thus appear normal. As a result, the doctor may believe that the teacher is overly concerned about a "few minor incidents" in the student's behavior. The teacher has no chance to describe the way the student reacts in the classroom and is told by the student's parents that the medical doctor believed nothing was wrong.

Teachers should remember that only a medical doctor can prescribe medication. But the medical doctor must remember that the student's classroom teacher or remedial reading teacher, having a chance to compare the student's behavior with that of many other students, is in a far better position to judge a student's behavior in relation to that of other students. A short standard teacher evaluation questionnaire summarizing the child's behavior in the classroom can be most effective in improving communication between physician and teacher.

A FINAL NOTE ON TEACHING TECHNIQUES FOR THE DISABLED CHILD

Dealing with the disabled child can be likened to finding a cure for cancer. Some medical researchers contend that there are so many different types of cancer that it is unrealistic to hope for a single cure. You, no doubt, face the same problem dealing with severely disabled readers. Most reading specialists now agree that the use of one term to describe problems of so varying a nature is unrealistic and makes the problem appear less complicated than it actually is.

It would be less than honest to leave the impression that magical techniques and procedures will work wonders for the learning-disabled child. More is known about it today than twenty years ago, but progress has been slow, and few, if any, miracle techniques have appeared. Luckily, most of the serious cases of reading disability, given intensive remediation over a long period of time, do show improvement.

It is important to remember that the learning-disabled child is a person whose problems often result in complete disequilibrium with the environment. Such a child is a unique combination of strengths and weaknesses and remains through it all an individual.

It would appear that, at present, very little is known about students who exhibit learning disabilities, including severe reading disability. For now, perhaps Harold Martin (1971) was correct in his assessment when he said:

> At present, it seems most prudent to try to understand how the child can best learn rather than only focusing on the reasons he doesn't learn when taught by traditional methods. If educators and other professional can recognize the factors and the environment in which the child will best learn—including motivation, perceptual strengths, style of learning—individualization of that child's teaching to capitalize on those strengths presently holds our most promising assistance to the handicapped child. (p. 471)

And, in summary, Balow's statement (1971) concerning learning disabilities seems especially relevant. He said, "Until experimentally proven otherwise, it may be that the simplest explanation of success obtained with any treatment for learning disabilities is the power and skill of the teacher who believes in it." (p. 519)

SUMMARY

Students with severe learning disabilities have presented a dilemma to teachers and other professionals in the past and, in many cases, this dilemma is still present today. Our diagnostic tools are limited, and pinpointing the nature and cause of a student's difficulties is not easy. There are, however, certain characteristics that cluster together and point to the appropriate diagnosis and treatment. Some students have disorders of information processing, others have disturbances in their style or approach to the learning situation, and some students have deficiencies in both areas.

Earlier programs for the remediation of severe reading disability have generally failed to prove their worth when thoroughly researched. However, some procedures are highly effective in specific cases. But what appears to work well with one student often fails to bring results with another.

There is a need for close cooperation among all professionals working with learning-disabled children, particularly teachers and physicians. Medical therapy is indicated for only a limited number of students—those with attentional deficit disorder, otherwise known as hyperactivity.

REFERENCES

Abrams, Jules C., and Belmont, Herman S. "Different Approaches to the Remediation of Severe Reading Disability in Children," *Journal of Learning Disabilities,* Vol. 2, (March, 1969), 136–140.

Adams, Richard B. "Dyslexia: A Discussion of Its Definition," *Journal of Learning Disabilities,* Vol. 2, (December, 1969), 616–626.

Balow, Bruce. "Perceptual-Motor Activities in the Treatment of Severe Reading Disability," *Reading Teacher,* Vol. 24, (March, 1971), 513–525 + .

Bateman, Barbara D. "Educational Implications of Minimal Brain Dysfunction," *Reading Teacher,* Vol. 27, (April, 1974), 662–668.

Bender, Lauretta. *Bender Visual-Motor Gestalt Test.* New York: Psychological Corporation, 1958.

Benton, Al. "Developmental Dyslexia: Neurological Aspects," in Friedlander, W. J., ed. *Advances in Neurology,* Vol. 7. New York: Raven Press, 1975.

Blau, Harold, and Blau, Harriet. "A Theory of Learning to Read," *Reading Teacher,* Vol. 22, (November, 1968), 126–129 + .

Bradley, Charles. "The Behavior of Children Receiving Benzedrine," *American Journal of Psychiatry,* Vol. 94, (1937), 577–584.

Bryant, N. Dale. "Learning Disabilities," *Instructor,* Vol. 81, (April, 1972), 49–56.

Delacato, Carl H. *The Treatment and Prevention of Reading Problems.* Springfield, Ill.: Charles C. Thomas, 1959.

Diagnostic and Statistical Manual of Mental Disorders, 3rd ed. Washington, D.C.: American Psychiatric Association, 1981.

Feingold, Benjamin. *Why Your Child Is Hyperactive.* New York: Random House, 1974.

Fernald, Grace M. *Remedial Techniques in Basic School Subjects*. New York: McGraw-Hill, 1943.

Fisher, J. A. "Congenital Word Blindness," trans. Opthalmological Society United Kingdom, Vol. 30, (1910), 216.

Frostig, Marianne. *Learning Problems in the Classroom*. New York: Grune & Stratton, 1973.

Hammill, Donald; Goodman, Libby; and Wiederholt, J. Lee. "Visual-Motor Processes: Can We Train Them?" *Reading Teacher*, Vol. 27, (February, 1974), 469–478.

Harris, Albert J. *Harris Tests of Lateral Dominance—Manual of Directions*. New York: Psychological Corporation, 1958.

Heckerl, John, and Sansbury, Russell. "A Study of Severe Reading Retardation," *Reading Teacher*, Vol. 21, (May, 1968), 724–729.

Kinsbourne, Marcel, and Caplan, Paula. *Children's Learning and Attention Problems*. Boston: Little, Brown, 1979.

Kirk, S. A.; McCarthy, J. J.; and Kirk, W. D. *The Illinois Test of Psycholinguistic Abilities*, revised edition. Urbana: University of Illinois Press, 1968.

Levine, Melvin. *A Pediatric Approach to Learning Disorders*. New York: Wiley, 1980.

MacKeith, Ronald. "Do Disorders of Perception Occur?" *Developmental Medicine and Child Neurology*, Vol. 19, (1977), 821.

Martin, Harold P. "Vision and Its Role in Reading Disability and Dyslexia," *Journal of School Health*, Vol. 41, (November, 1971), 468–472.

Orton, Samuel. "An Impediment to Learning to Read—A Neurological Explanation of the Reading Disability," *School and Society*, Vol. 28, (September, 1928), 286–290.

Orton, Samuel. *Reading, Writing and Speech Problems in Children*. New York: Norton, 1937.

Sabatino, David A.; Wickham, William, Jr.; and Burnett, Calvin. "The Psychoeducational Assessment of Learning Disabilities," *Catholic Education Review*, Vol. 66, (May, 1968), 327–341.

Vellutino, F. R. "Has the Perceptual Deficit Hypothesis Led Us Astray?" *Journal of Learning Disabilities*, Vol. 10, (1977), 375–385.

Wender, Paul. *Minimal Brain Dysfunction in Children*. New York: Wiley, 1971.

10

Diagnosing and Using Appropriate Teaching Techniques for the Disabled Reader

The first part of this chapter contains a discussion of the need for diagnosis beyond students' knowledge of skills. This is followed by a discussion of how humans learn and the theory of diagnosis for learning modalities. The last part of this chapter contains information on diagnosing and teaching to specific learning modalities, cognitive styles, and learning rates.

DIAGNOSIS BEYOND KNOWLEDGE OF SKILLS

In teaching disabled readers often little more is needed than a simple diagnosis of various skill deficiencies. With prescriptive teaching based on these skill deficiencies, success is often obtained in a matter of months. However, with the seriously disabled reader, as described in the previous chapter, it is not uncommon to work for one or two years with a student and still see very little progress. As Diane Sawyer (1974) points out, ". . . teaching to overcome specific skill deficiencies often results in teaching the same phonic generalizations or how to find the main idea over and over again." (p. 556) Sawyer also points out that with this type of student the only thing that is often different about the instruction from year to year is the teacher or the materials used. She further states that the research indicates a strong case for viewing the student as a problem solver or information processor and as an individual who reacts with his or her environment, rather than viewing the student simply as someone who is deficient in reading skills.

What we are implying is that the view of the severely disabled reader is often much too simplistic. As a result of this view teachers may use too simplistic a method of testing, which results in inefficient teaching. Edward Wolpert (1971) stresses the point that various ambiguities arise when the modality concept is applied to the process of learning rather than to the act of reading. He states, as we have stated throughout the sections in this book on testing, that the tests often used do not test in a situation that is analogous to what a student actually does in the act of reading. For example, a student may be given certain subtests of the *WISC,* which in reality may have little relationship to reading, and on the basis of these subtests be classified as poor in visual perceptual skills. Although the student may be poor in visual perceptual skills on the subtests of the *WISC,* this does not necessarily mean that he or she will not be a good visual learner in reading-type tasks. Wolpert also points out that to even divide tasks as indicated on most tests into "auditory" or "visual" is probably a false dichotomy, since most tasks call for the use of a combination of both auditory and visual modalities even when the task is labeled as one or the other.

Perhaps a more realistic view of the learning task for a severely disabled reader is one described by Jean Piaget as related by John Blackie (1968). Piaget portrayed learning as being composed of two processes. These processes are assimilation and accommodation. Blackie says, "Assimilation is what is done to what has to be learned so that it can be learned, and accommodation is what the learner has to do within himself in order to learn." (p. 40) In the diagnosis beyond the level of skills it is these processes of assimilation and accommodation with which you should concern yourselves.

When you face the dilemma of how to teach the severely disabled reader, it is easy to believe that there must be a miracle cure or magical approach that will solve the problem, if only you can identify it. Our experience as teachers and as supervisors of clinics that serve students with severe reading problems has led us to the following conclusions:

1.   Most disabled readers will learn successfully if sound diagnostic-remedial procedures (particularly those described in Chapters 4, 5, and 6) are employed over a period of time and the readers have sufficient opportunities to apply the skills in the act of reading.

2.   For those who still do not succeed, the best hope lies in providing "traditional" instructional procedures, but doing it better. *Better* may mean more instruction, with smaller increments of learning, over a longer period of time. It should be noted that traditional procedures encompass the wide range of approaches that have heretofore been described in this book.

3. For the *very few* students who still fail to read successfully after having received the best reading instruction that you can reasonably provide, it may make sense to try other approaches, even if there is a lack of sound research evidence to support these approaches.

4. Some of the approaches that do not appear to be justified at this time may, in the future, prove to be valuable as understanding of the reading process and how individual students learn expands. Also, new approaches to teaching the severely disabled reader will continue to emerge, and some of these may prove beneficial.

It is in this context that we present the information that follows in this chapter. We shall be discussing "theories" that have yet to be proven and critically examining some of the existing evidence that supports or fails to support these alternative approaches. A reading specialist may choose to reject a particular approach after becoming aware of the lack of evidence that supports this method. We would hope that no reading specialist would continue to embrace an approach *in spite* of all the evidence to the contrary. Instead, we would welcome future research that may modify what we presently know.

HOW HUMANS LEARN

An interesting study on how humans learn in terms of later retention was done by the Socony Vacuum Oil Company (Ekwall and Oswald), which has some important implications for diagnosis and remediation. In this study the following results were obtained:

Students' Power of Retention

1. 10% of what they read.
2. 20% of what they hear.
3. 30% of what they see.
4. 50% of what they see and hear.
5. 70% of what they say as they talk.
6. 90% of what they say as they do a thing.

It should be stressed that the information presented in this study is of a general nature and that the relative efficiency of one method of presentation over another often depends on several factors that will be discussed under the section entitled, "Research on Methods of Presentation of Modalities." However, from this study it is evident that some of the teaching procedures most often used are of little value in getting students to retain what you teach

them. For example, consider the value of simply "telling" students information (20 percent retention) versus getting them to say a thing as they do it (90
percent retention). From this it is also evident that even if you were able to
cover twice as much information in a lecture, it would be less efficient in the
end than if only half as much information was covered but in one of the more
efficient ways. Based on this type of information, in teaching you might then
use more of the following types of procedures:

1. Whenever teaching a new concept you should at least illustrate it using
    the chalkboard or overhead projector so that students can hear and see
    the information at the same time. This procedure alone brings the reten-
    tion percentage up to 50 percent versus 20 percent from an oral presen-
    tation alone.
2. Whenever possible you should also get students to voice a new
    principle, rule, word, etc., shortly after it has been taught (70 percent).
3. Whenever a new word, principle, rule, etc., is taught you should get
    students to "do" something with it. This might include such activities as
    writing or illustrating the rule, using a new word in a written sentence
    while they say the word and sentence, or getting them to act out action
    words as they say them. This can easily be done with some words such
    as *wash, throw, run,* etc., but would, of course, be more difficult with
    others.

From the kind of information presented above, it is also evident why the
kinesthetic-tactile or Fernald type of approach is often of considerable value
for some students. The procedure automatically incorporates the most effective techniques discussed in this study.

THE THEORY OF MODALITY DIAGNOSIS AND ITS IMPLICATIONS

There is controversy among reading and learning-disabilities specialists
about the value of modality-based diagnoses and instruction. The notion that
individual students possess varying strengths and weaknesses in their sensory modality capabilities is logical. Furthermore, it would seem reasonable
to believe that one could identify students' modality preferences and prescribe instruction accordingly. Modality-based teaching has strong intuitive
appeal.

In this section we will define the modality concept and describe the test
most often used for diagnosis in this area. Then we will examine the research
presently available to see if there is evidence to justify this approach. Later
in the chapter we will present methods for diagnosing and teaching to specific modalities.

The most commonly recognized and diagnosed learning modalities are auditory, visual, kinesthetic, and a combination of all of these. When the various learning modalities are referred to in the literature, however, they are usually listed as VAKT, or visual, auditory, kinesthetic, and tactile. The term *kinesthetic* is an adjective derived from the noun *kinesthesia* derived from *kinema*, or motion, and *aisthesis*, referring to perception. The term means sensation of position or movement through parts of the body such as nerve ends, tendons, muscles, and joints. The term tactile, of course, refers to the sense of touch. The term *VAKT* is also used, in some cases, to simply refer to a teaching method very similar to the Fernald Approach described in Chapter 9. Since it would be almost impossible to use a kinesthetic approach without using a tactile approach at the same time, the term *tactile* is often omitted when referring to the various testing and teaching modalities.

The Mills *Learning Methods Test* (1970) has become one of the best-known instruments for testing the various learning modalities. It is designed to determine whether a student learns words best by a "phonic or auditory," "visual," "kinesthetic," or "combination" method. The *Learning Methods Test* contains a series of words supposedly representing the primer, first-, second-, and third-grade levels. Each word is on a card that has the word printed on one side and the same word and a picture representing the word on the other side of the card. The student to be tested is given the lists of words to pronounce until the lowest level is found in which he or she misses forty words. These forty words are then divided into groups of ten. Each day ten words are taught in strict accordance with the directions given in the manual for one of the four methods. The time for teaching the words is also controlled so that fifteen minutes is spent on each group of words. The *Learning Methods Test* can be used quite successfully by someone who is adept in its use. However, it has a number of drawbacks that make its use impractical in many situations. For example, after ten words are taught by one method, the student is given an immediate recall test. The student then comes in the next day and takes a delayed recall test on the words learned the first day. After taking the delayed recall test the student is then taught ten words by another method and is then given another immediate recall test on the words just taught. The student comes in on the third day and takes a delayed recall test on the words taught on the second day and learns ten more words by another method, etc. It takes five days even though there are only four different methods, since one day must elapse before the student can be given the delayed recall test on the words taught on the fourth day by the fourth method. After the fifth day the clinician examines which method was most successful in getting the student to remember the most words on the delayed recall test, which is ultimately what one wants to accomplish. The fact that it takes five days or more is a drawback for many clinicians, since they simply do not see the student on a daily basis or do not have a five-day period in which to complete their testing. It also presents a problem when the testing is not begun on a Monday, since it would then be necessary to complete the testing during the following week, which does not allow equal time periods to elapse between the testing for the delayed recall periods.

The methodology used in several of the approaches has also been criticized to some extent. For example, as a part of the visual approach the student is presented the ten words with the picture side up. The student is told to look at the picture and then at the word. This practice is considered of dubious value in relation to actual reading. For example, S. Jay Samuels (1970) in a thorough review of the research on the use of pictures in reading quotes a number of studies that indicated that the use of pictures actually interfered with the reading act. However, perhaps the most serious problem is that, as Samuels states,

> Generally, concrete nouns and a limited number of adjectives and verbs can be illustrated. An additional shortcoming of pictures as cues is that they cannot reliably elicit the same response from all children; for instance, when shown a picture of a plane, one child may say "plane," another, "airplane," and a third, "jet." (p. 401)

It stands to reason that if one were to use the *Learning Methods Test* and determine that a student learned best by the visual approach in which pictures were presented, it would still not guarantee success for that student, since so many of the words he or she would normally be required to read would be words that could not be illustrated or would simply not be taught as they were presented in the test. In using the visual method Mills also suggests that a figure or outline of the shape or gestalt of each word be drawn on the board so that the student can match each word with this shape. This practice has also been questioned by a number of modern writers. The major problem, of course, is that many words have exactly the same shape, e.g.:

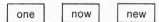

all have the same shape as do the following:

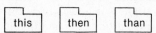

Therefore, the shape is really of little value in helping a student distinguish between words. A third major criticism of the *Learning Methods Test* is that the directions are in some cases somewhat unclear. We have used it for some time in our remedial reading classes and have found that one student who reads the directions does not interpret the methodology the same as another student or group of students who have read the same directions.

In spite of what may appear to be rather severe criticisms of the *Learning Methods Test,* it is a good training instrument for students who are learning about the concept of testing the various learning modalities, and we would recommend that it be used for this purpose, keeping the criticisms we have mentioned in mind. However, in a situation in which a reading clinician is able to see a student for only a short period of time, certain modifications need to be made in the Mills procedure. We would also suggest certain modifications even in a normal remedial situation because of the problems previously mentioned. These techniques will be discussed later in the chapter.

Unfortunately, the concept of testing for strong and weak modalities has little support in the research literature. On the positive side, Harold McGrady and Don Olson (1970) stress the fact that reading is a process that requires the integration of auditory and visual information. Since the English language is phonetic in nature, the letters represent sounds, and the written form (visual) of the language is symbolic and represents the spoken word (auditory). McGrady and Olson state, "Our clinical diagnostic studies of children with reading disabilities have revealed that many have problems with specific auditory or visual learning processes." (p. 582) These authors believe that these terms might best be termed psychosensory learning disorders. McGrady and Olson also state,

> Those who have psychosensory learning disorders cannot normally perceive and interpret sensation received through a particular sense channel. Similarly, they might not be able to relate sensory experience through a given sense modality to experience gained through another sense modality; for example, they might not be able to "auditorize" from what they see or "visualize" from what they hear. (p. 582)

In a review of the literature of modalities and reading, Bill Blanton (1971) indicated that it is virtually impossible to isolate any aspect of reading in which both the auditory and visual modalities are not involved to some degree. Blanton states,

> ... There are a number of studies suggesting that mode of presentation does not determine the modality by which material is learned. Rather, the mental image is determined by the ideational type of the individual. In other words, the visual learner may still visualize material to be learned despite the fact that it is presented auditorially. (p. 211)

This kind of information would tend to lessen our faith in the use of modalities tests such as the Mills *Learning Methods Test.*

More recent reviews of research studies conducted on modality approaches have cast grave doubt about the efficacy of this method. Sara Tarver and Margaret Dawson (1978) concluded, after reviewing fifteen research studies, that there was no evidence supporting an interaction between modality preference and method of teaching reading "when we are concerned with actual methods of teaching reading and measures of reading achievement rather than listening tasks and measures of recall or recognition." (p. 13) The authors concluded:

> It would seem efficacious at this time to devote more of our efforts to investigating the requirements of the reading task at the various stages of learning to read. . . . This information, in combination with assessment of each child's learning rate, may promote more effective individualization of reading instruction, individualization based on quantitative differences in rates of progression through an established sequence of reading skills rather than qualitative differences in perceptual functioning. (p. 16)

In Chapter 4 we quoted the opinion of Thomas Kampwirth and Marion Bates (1980), who reviewed twenty-two studies concerned with children under ten years of age that compared auditory and visual preferences to auditory and/or visual methods of teaching words. Kampwirth and Bates reported that twenty of the twenty-two studies indicated no significant interaction between matching modality preferences to teaching approaches. One study found that the auditory instructional approach was significantly more effective than the visual approach for both auditory and visual learners. One study found the visual approach to be most effective with both groups. Thus the reviewers concluded that there was little or no evidence to support the idea that remedial instruction should be based on modality preference.

In a response to Kampwirth and Bates, Walter Barbe, Raymond Swassing, and Michael Milone (1981) argued that modality-based instruction should not be rejected at the present time because:

1. the fact that "something has not been found does not mean it does not exist." (p. 263)
2. "the failure to discover significant aptitude-treatment interactions between modality strengths and reading instructional methods may reflect inadequacies of experimental design features rather than the lack of a relationship between the variables of interest." (p. 264)
3. "unless the variable of teacher modality strength is controlled, the study of pupil modality strengths and reading may be flawed." (p. 265)
4. "the criteria for determining who is visual, auditory, and kinesthetic in preference are not well established." (p. 265)
5. "modality is not a fixed characteristic." (p. 265)
6. 95 percent of the teachers of learning-disabled children believe that the research supports this approach.

Barbe, Swassing, and Milone concluded that: "Although no clear-cut evidence has been produced to support this practice, those who oppose it have not been able to muster proof that it is not useful." (p. 266)

Kampwirth (1981) responded to the response, in part, by writing:

> If we concluded . . . that we should recommend a certain procedure in spite of there being no evidence to support it, then it removes educational practice from the realm of science and relegates it to a set of notions one tries because they have intuitive appeal or face (faith?) validity. (p. 267)

and:

> The fact that 95 percent of these teachers believe in a concept does not make it true, it simply makes it popular. (p. 268)

There is also some indication that students' mode of learning may be cultural and experiential as well as constitutional. For example, Frank Riessmann (1962) indicated that culturally disadvantaged students are often oriented toward physical and visual learning rather than aural learning. The fact that culturally and/or economically deprived students are often poor in listening (aural) abilities has been demonstrated in a number of other studies. Typical of these studies was one by Ronald Linder and Henry Fillmer (1970), who studied the comparative effectiveness of auditory, visual, and a combination of auditory-visual presentations in second-grade Southern black male students who were disabled readers. Linder and Fillmer found the total auditory performance to be significantly poorer than the total visual and the total auditory-visual for the tasks performed. However, there were no significant differences between students' performance on the total visual and the auditory-visual results. In concluding their study Linder and Fillmer stated,

> As in all studies, individual children in this study did demonstrate a preference for one modality over another. The results reported have been group performances rather than individual. But there are several cases in which the results of the group study were contradicted by individuals, making the listing of generalizations a hazardous undertaking. Once again research indicates that not all pupils may be expected to learn more effectively from one single type of presentation. (p. 22)

Etta Miller (1979) further expanded on this point and offered a possible solution to the confusion:

> Research on modality preference does not account for the findings that under any method used some children with a particular modality preference learn to read easily while others with the same strength, receiving the same instruction and using the same materials fail. With little research to indicate the best procedures, teachers need to continue *to present words in a variety of ways* [emphasis ours]. This repetition of presentation may help children to build associations, to remember word forms, to make use of linguistic and syntactic clues,

and, perhaps, to attract and to hold the attention of boys and girls who have poor attending behavior. It may turn out that cognitive skills are more important to initial reading success than perceptual ones. (pp. 103–104)

We might conclude then, that the modality-preference approach can be justified only as a last resort or heroic approach, to be tried after other remedial techniques have failed. It is possible that in the future other evidence will suggest a broader application of this method. The diagnostic remedial procedures for discovering and teaching to dominant modalities that we shall present should be viewed in this light. Albert Harris and Edward Sipay (1980) agree. They state:

> Until more evidence is available, it seems that for most children a balanced eclectic approach that uses visual, auditory, touch, and kinesthetic cues in combination, and develops word identification and comprehension simultaneously, seems safer and less likely to produce difficulties than any method that relies primarily on one sensory avenue or stresses one important side of reading while neglecting another. When a child continues to fail in a given reading program, consideration should be given to employing a program that utilizes a different methodology. (pp. 70–71)

RESEARCH ON METHODS OF PRESENTATION OF MODALITIES

Some important generalizations on the kind of presentations that may be most effective for learning have been summarized by Sam Duker (1965). Some of these generalizations are as follows:

1. Combinations of visual and auditory presentations tend to be more efficient than presentations involving only auditory or visual presentations alone.
2. When the learner is familiar with the material, he or she is likely to retain more from an auditory presentation. If the material is unfamiliar, he or she is likely to retain more from a visual presentation.
3. Students with higher intelligence seem to benefit more from a visual presentation.
4. Students who read better seem to learn better through a visual presentation.
5. As students grow older they tend to learn better through a visual presentation. At the age of six they learn better as a group through an aural presentation; however, by the time they reach sixteen years of age they learn better as a group through a visual presentation.
6. More difficult material seems to be learned better through a visual presentation while easier material is learned better through an auditory presentation.

7. Students' immediate comprehension of information seems to favor a visual presentation, while their long-term comprehension seems to favor an auditory presentation.

8. The efficiency of a visual presentation seems to decrease as the interval of delayed recall increases.

9. One of the advantages of a visual presentation is the relative referability or opportunity for review of the material. When the material is of such a nature, or the teaching situation is of such a nature that less referability is possible, then the efficiency of a visual presentation is lessened.

10. Material that is well organized or follows some type of sequence such as factual information or prose is better understood with an auditory presentation. Material that is more discrete and unrelated is better understood with a visual presentation.

11. One might consider two factors in considering a visual versus an oral presentation. These factors are ease of learning and amount of retention. A visual presentation tends to favor ease of learning, while retention seems to favor an oral presentation.

Some interesting and pertinent generalizations have also been given by Robert Mills (1965) from a study done using his *Learning Methods Test* to evaluate various techniques of word recognition. Mills stressed that the information presented pertained to the learning of words only and did not necessarily pertain to the teaching of phonics or other reading skills. Mills studied a group of male and female subjects in grades two to four. His general conclusions were as follows:

1. The phonic method was least effective for the children with low intelligence (as a whole). The kinesthetic method was best for the same children with the greatest number of cases, but it was not statistically better than the visual or combinations methods.

2. For children with high intelligence the kinesthetic method was least effective.

3. The combination and visual methods were about equally good for children of average intelligence.

4. Children of high intelligence seemed to learn quite well by all methods; however, the visual method was superior to the kinesthetic method for this group.

5. For seven year olds the visual method appeared to be best, and the same group did poorest on the kinesthetic method. The phonic and combination methods did not appear to be especially effective nor ineffective with this group.

6. The eight year olds did better with the kinesthetic method. Mills believed that the fact that this group was just becoming proficient with handwriting tended to make some difference in this case.
7. For nine year olds no method was outstandingly effective nor ineffective; however, the visual method did tend to be better than the kinesthetic method for this group.
8. Mills found that children who had higher intelligence tended to learn words faster than those with lower intelligence; however, he found that there was no consistent relationship between age and a child's readiness to learn words.

In his conclusions Mills stated,

> Because different children learn to recognize words most efficiently by different teaching methods, the classroom teacher must be aware of these individual differences when he applies group-instruction techniques. Our research indicates the need for the teacher to familiarize himself with all the various techniques and to be versatile in the use of these if he is to teach all the children.
> In individual cases of failure to make the expected growth in word-recognition skills, our research indicates the need for a diagnostic study of the child to determine the most appropriate method for the particular individual. (p. 225)

The information presented above suggests that at least some students may have a preferred mode of learning. It is possible that some students become disabled readers because they are placed in a situation where they are exposed to teaching procedures that provide little opportunity for them to learn by a method that is best for them. To say that they do not learn because they are seldom or ever exposed to any portion of a certain method, however, would be an oversimplification since it is virtually impossible for any student to go through school without being exposed to a combination of the various methods discussed by Mills.

DIAGNOSTIC TECHNIQUES FOR DISCOVERING DOMINANT MODALITIES, COGNITIVE STYLES, AND LEARNING RATES

After a student has had an initial diagnosis and remediation is begun, three questions may arise in the mind of the teacher as he or she works with the student. These questions are: Is there a particular modality that seems most successful in getting the student to learn and retain information? Does the student seem to exhibit a particular cognitive style on which you can capitalize? How much instructional time is necessary, or how much repetition is necessary in order to get the student to learn and retain information? This section contains information designed to help you develop the skills to answer these questions about each of the students with whom you are working.

DIAGNOSTIC TECHNIQUES FOR DISCOVERING
DOMINANT MODALITIES

Before offering specific suggestions on the diagnosis of dominant learning modalities, we repeat that Mills's *Learning Methods Test* is an instrument designed to help you discover students' dominant modalities and, where time permits, it can be used successfully. On the other hand, there are certain features of Mills's test that make it difficult to use. Furthermore, it is our opinion that several of the techniques suggested by Mills have little or no value or practical application in the diagnostic-teaching process. What follows is a less formal technique for attempting to discover students' dominant modalities.

The Time Factor

Mills stresses, and we would agree, that when working with various modalities to discover which one seems best with a particular student it is important to control the amount of time spent on teaching by the use of each modality. Mills suggests a period of fifteen minutes for each modality with exactly ten words taught during this period of time. We would have had no argument with his time period nor the number of words that he suggests, except in many situations it is simply not practical to spend fifteen minutes per day on five successive days on each set of words. The essential point, however, is that approximately the same amount of time be spent in teaching using each modality. If your time is somewhat limited you may want to modify the time to five or ten minutes; however, the time period chosen should remain consistent for each modality tested.

Material to Be Taught

Students' preferences for certain modalities are likely to affect the way they learn many things; however, in reading it is usually diagnosed in their learning of words. This, in itself, presents some problems since some words can be illustrated with pictures while it is not practical to do so with others. Edward Wolpert (1972) studied the relationships of word recognition to word length, word shape, and word imagery. Wolpert was concerned with the ease with which forty-two first-grade children learned words varying in imagery value, length, and configuration. He found that his subjects learned a significantly greater number of shorter (three-letter) words than longer (five-letter) words. His students also learned a significantly greater number of high-imagery words (such as *nose*) than low-imagery words (such as *same*). On the other hand, word configuration did not seem to be as important as the other two factors. The important point, however, is that the results obtained in modality testing may to some extent depend on these extraneous factors, which may not always be apparent. For this reason results obtained from modality testing should be reconfirmed several times through careful diagnostic teaching as the student's remediation progresses.

From the foregoing discussion it is also apparent that the words chosen to be taught should, if possible, be of somewhat similar length and imagery value. Word length is quite easy to control, but imagery value, of course, presents a much more difficult problem. In our own reading centers we simply try to pick words that do not appear to have high imagery value but which would generally be in the speaking-listening vocabulary of the student to whom the words are to be taught.

In using the Mills *Learning Methods Test* it is often difficult to find forty words at any level that older students do not know. However, in a less formal setting you can pick words from the basic sight word list given in Chapter 4, or another good source, such as Fry's Instant Word List (Fry, 1972), which contains 600 words from levels one through six.

One point that also needs to be emphasized is that although words on lists may appear at preprimer, primer, first-, second-grade levels, etc., it does not really mean that the preprimer or primer words are easier to learn than the words on the second- or third-grade list. It only means that preprimer words are preprimer words because they have traditionally been preprimer words. They may, and usually are, of higher utility (or appear more often in print) than words at a higher grade level. However, if the student does not know the words to begin with, there is very little difference in the difficulty of the words. On the other hand, after a student begins to read he or she is more likely to encounter the preprimer or high-utility words more often, and simply because of multiple exposure to these words the student would be more likely to know them in a period of a month or two. But, for delayed recall of words (a day or two later) the imagery value of the word and its length are of more importance in determining how well it will be learned than the grade level from which it was derived. Therefore, if the words are in an older student's speaking-listening vocabulary, or in other words if the student can use them in a sentence, it really does not make any difference if words from several levels are mixed for modality-testing purposes.

There may be some situations in which it is not practical to teach ten words by each of the modalities to be tested. If your time is limited you may wish to cut the number to five or six and teach two sets on any one day. The essential point is that the same number of words be chosen to be presented using each learning modality.

The Teaching Procedure for Each Modality

It is important to keep in mind that whatever learning modality, if any, is found to produce the best test results in terms of delayed recall (which is the ultimate goal) it must be of a nature that would make its everyday use possible in a practical teaching situation. For example, as stated earlier, many words cannot be illustrated by the use of pictures, and, furthermore, many teachers are not artistic enough to illustrate them. For this reason it seems somewhat futile to concern yourself with whether a student can learn words when they are presented with a picture representing the word.

What follows then is a teaching procedure for four different modalities that can be modified slightly for some students yet should, in most cases, be practical for use on a daily basis.

A. Phonic or Auditory Modality Approach
    1. Print the words to be learned on cards (approximately $3\frac{1}{2}'' \times 8''$) before attempting to teach them to the student.
    2. Present the first card and pronounce it slowly while pointing to each phoneme. Do not try to pronounce it letter by letter if there are graphemes in the word that do not represent separate sounds. Do this a second time asking the student to pronounce each part after you.
    3. Say the word rapidly and ask the student to say it rapidly after you.
    4. Ask the student to use the word in a sentence. If the student cannot, use it in a sentence for him or her. Then ask the student to make up a sentence.

(All students can do these first three initial steps and should be required to follow them as outlined. Whether the following steps are done will depend on the phonics ability of the student. A sequence is suggested, but if the student cannot do some parts, do not waste time attempting them. Spend more time doing the parts with which the student is successful. In other words this approach may be modified, to some extent, from this point forward to fit the learning style of any one particular student.)

    5. Discuss the sounds in the word. If the student knows all of the sounds then simply go on to the next word. If the student does not know the sounds, then point to the first sound and ask the student to think of other words that begin with that sound. Do this same procedure with middle and ending sounds. Do not have the student look for little words in big words. If the student notes a little word in a larger word and its sound remains the same in the larger word, simply acknowledge that what he or she says is true, but do not encourage the practice. If the smaller word does not retain its

sound in the larger word, then explain that little words often change when they are a part of a longer word.

6. If time allows, you may wish to find and classify all words into piles that have the same beginning, middle, or ending sounds.

7. The time spent on discussion of other words that rhyme with the beginning sounds of words will vary with the time allowed for teaching and the number of words to be taught. Simply gauge your time accordingly. Be sure to allow time to review all words to be taught by this method during the last minute or so before stopping.

B. Sight or Visual Modality Approach

1. Print the words to be learned on cards (approximately 3½″ × 8″) before attempting to teach them to the student.

2. Point to the first word or simply sweep across it and pronounce it, e.g., say, "This word is *among*."

3. Ask the student to use the word in a sentence. If the student cannot, then use it in a sentence to demonstrate. Then ask the student to make up a sentence of his or her own.

4. Ask the student to look at the word and to look for anything about it that will help him or her to remember it, e.g., the double *e*'s in *seen* or the length of the word. If the student does not respond well to this, then repeat steps 1 through 3 with the next word and ask the student to tell you how the two words differ.

5. After all words have been taught, ask the student to make a sentence out of the words, adding any other words necessary to complete the sentence.

6. Have the student separate the words into categories that seem significant to him or her, e.g., all words with three letters and all words having no tall letters.

7. Allow time to review all words before stopping. This will again depend on the number of words to be taught and the time allowed to teach them.

C. Kinesthetic-Tactile Modality Approach

1. Begin this approach with nothing on the cards and with the specific words to be taught already selected, which may appear on a small list beside you.

2. Print the first word on a card saying the part of the word as you write it. Then say the word and have the student repeat it.

3. Have the student trace over the word several times using middle and index fingers. Be sure both fingers are in contact with the part being traced. Be sure the student says the word part while tracing it. Try to avoid emphasizing specific sounds.

4. As with the other methods have the student use the word in a sentence. If the student cannot do this, use it in a sentence yourself and then have the student use it in another sentence.

5. After the student has traced it several times, give the student a new card and have him or her attempt to write it from memory. If the student begins to make a mistake, simply stop the student, repeat steps 1 through 4 again, and have the student attempt it again. *Do not let the student write it wrong.*

6. Allow time to review all words before stopping. Again, this will depend on the number of words to be taught and the time allowed to teach them.

D. Combination Modality Approach

1. Begin with the words printed on the cards.

2. Tell the student the word and quickly trace over it pronouncing it as you do so. Then pronounce it quickly.

3. Have the student trace over it, again using middle and index fingers and saying the word parts as they are traced. Then have the student say the whole word quickly.

4. Have the student use the word in a sentence. As in the other approaches, if the student cannot use it in a sentence, then use it in a sentence yourself and have the student make up a sentence of his or her own.

5. Discuss any known sounds in the word and discuss the word length and any configuration that will help the student remember it.

6. Have the student classify words by stacking cards into piles with the same beginning, middle, or ending sounds and/or classify them by word length or specific configurations.

7. Allow time to review all words before stopping. As with the other approaches this will depend on the number of words to be taught and time allowed for teaching them.

In using the above modalities approaches, keep the following important points in mind:

1. Do not attempt to teach too many words in too short a period of time. It is better to learn fewer words and review them than to be so hurried on the last few words that they are not covered well.

2. It is delayed recall (at least a day or more) that really matters in terms of the best approach for a particular student. Keep this in mind even though immediate recall using a particular approach seems quite effective.

3. If certain parts of some modality approaches seem successful while others do not, do not hesitate to combine the approaches that seem to be most successful.

4. Remember that as students learn, their modality strengths may change somewhat; therefore, do not become permanently wedded to any one

approach, but constantly diagnose as you teach to determine whether the original modality diagnosis was correct or whether slight changes from time to time may be in order.

DIAGNOSING AND TEACHING TO SPECIFIC COGNITIVE STYLES

For many years teachers have noted characteristics of certain disabled readers that relate to their learning style. For example, most of you are familiar with students who hurriedly guess at words even though you are relatively sure they possess adequate word-attack skills. Other students continually make repetitions to correct omissions and/or insertions. And, some students, even though they can repeat numerous rules for word-attack skills, will seldom attempt to read an unfamiliar word. This style of thinking and reacting about known information is often referred to as cognition; and we refer to student's methods of thinking and reacting as their cognitive style.

In addition to the general observations mentioned above, a number of studies have been done that indicate that disabled readers, as a whole, may often differ in cognitive style from normal readers; yet recent research is heartening in that it indicates that certain undesirable cognitive styles can be changed. For example, Sawyer reviewed considerable research on the relationship between cognitive style and reading disability. She noted studies by George Spache that indicated that disabled readers at the primary level "exhibited less insight into the dynamics of a situation and exhibited less solution-seeking behavior." (p. 560) She also noted that Jules Abrams "found that nonreaders were more impulsive and less able to respond appropriately to environmental stimuli than good readers." (p. 560)

Although there are many degrees and types of cognitive styles, there has been a tendency recently to classify students as being either "impulsive" or "reflective." Although these terms probably oversimplify the situation, they do, at least, help us to understand something about the nature of the problem. For example, Lester Butler (1974) did a psycholinguistic analysis of the oral reading behavior of second-grade boys that he classified as either impulsive or reflective according to a test developed by Jerome Kagan (1965–1969). Butler found that the reflective subjects made more repetitions than the impulsive subjects. This was evidently because they corrected a greater number of their miscues through repetition. These results were in contrast to a study done by Kagan (1965–1966), who thought that reflective students tended to reflect more over their choices and would thus be likely to detect and correct more miscues than impulsive children. The difference evidently was in the fact that the errors that were made by Butler's group were corrected by repetitions rather than being noted before the error was made.

Alan Neal (1974) also did a study in which he studied reflectivity and impulsivity in fourth-grade students. He concluded that the impulsive student's behavior could be modified through the use of verbal exhortation, a finding that should hold a great deal of hope for the teacher attempting to help the student who makes errors caused from what is often termed "carelessness."

In the studies by Butler and Neal mentioned above, impulsive and reflective students were categorized using a matching figures test devised by Kagan. Eldon Ekwall and Judy English Solis (1971) also found different reading frustration levels of third-, fourth-, and fifth-grade students classified as "mixed cognitive style" versus "impulsive cognitive style" as measured by the polygraph. These students were classified on the basis of their scores on the *WISC, Bender-Visual Motor Gestalt, Rorschach,* and the *House-Tree-Person Test.* In all instances mentioned above, even though different instruments were used for the measurement of cognitive style, there is strong indication that various styles do exist and can be categorized.

As we noted in Chapter 2, Public Law 94–142 now mandates that an individual education plan (IEP) be prepared for each handicapped student. The IEP must include a "specific statement describing the child's learning style." To help meet this need Rita Dunn, Kenneth Dunn, and Gary Price (1977) have developed the Learning Style Inventory (LSI). The inventory was based on research data that yielded eighteen categories suggesting that learners were affected by (1) immediate environment, (2) emotionality, (3) sociological needs, and (4) physical needs. The LSI was administered to students, and the results were compared to teacher ratings on factors the teachers believed to be important in learning style. The study demonstrated that teachers were able to recognize certain learning-style factors with considerable accuracy. Marie Carbo (1980) subsequently developed the Reading Style Checklist, which is designed to aid the teacher's observations of students' responses to various reading methods.

Using Knowledge of Cognitive Style in the Classroom

From a practical standpoint, in dealing with cognitive styles, the remedial reading teacher can follow a diagnostic teaching procedure somewhat as follows:

1. Note whether the student systematically applies word-attack skills to words. If the student does not, teach the word-attack skills necessary for attacking similar words. Once the student has learned a few necessary rules, note whether he or she seems to be able to "think through" and apply these rules. If the student is able to learn rules for word attack and readily apply them, the more rule-oriented route may be a correct path to follow. On the other hand, if the student can learn

to give the rules verbally but does not seem to apply them, give him or her some practice in the application of the rules. If after considerable practice the student still does not seem to be able to apply the rules or generalizations, consider a more automatic or less rule-oriented approach to word attack. For example, one popular supplementary phonics series, during the course of about three years (one hour per day), teaches about 120 to 130 phonic generalizations. Many students seem to do well with this program, but regardless of the time spent in the program some students simply never seem to apply these rules. For students who cannot apply rules in word attack the automatic type of approach may be called for. In teaching the automatic approach you may wish to teach automatic recall of most phonemes as shown in the test in Appendix A when students see the written forms (graphemes). They can then learn phonograms or word families of high utility or compile lists of these on their own. By learning the phonemes of high utility plus a number of word families or phonograms a student will almost automatically be able to attack a great many words. Although this method of word attack may never become as systematic as it is for students who know and apply rules and generalizations, it will enable them to instantly attack a great many words without going through a long reasoning process of which many students seem almost incapable of doing.

2. Through oral diagnosis note whether the student reads very rapidly at the expense of errors that cause problems with comprehension. If so, discuss the need for more careful observation of word configuration and/or phonetic or structural analysis.[1]

3. Keep in mind that some students seem to possess a sort of "sixth sense" or innate psycholinguistic ability for learning the rules of the language. For this type of student an occasional error that does not change the meaning of a reading passage to any great extent or that does not generally hinder word-attack skills may not indicate the need for formal training in most word-attack skills. The student's time might better be spent in free reading or other worthy endeavors.

DIAGNOSING RATE OF LEARNING

Most classroom teachers get to know their students well enough to know that some learn faster than others. We often hear statements such as, "Denise just can't seem to learn no matter how hard I try to teach her," or "We must have gone over that word twenty times in class and Syril still doesn't know it." The first statement is quite unlikely to be true, but the second one might

[1] See Ekwall, Eldon E. *Locating and Correcting Reading Difficulties.* 3d ed., Columbus, Ohio: Charles E. Merrill, 1981, for a thorough analysis of the causes and remediation of specific types of errors.

very well be true and, in terms of research in learning, be nothing that should be considered extraordinary.

As stated in an earlier chapter most students require an average of at least twenty exposures to a word before it becomes a sight word for them. On the other hand, it is not uncommon for slower students to require over 100 exposures to a word before it is instantly known. Some may require as many as 200 exposures. Yet, many remedial reading teachers often feel that a student is almost incapable of learning if the student has not thoroughly learned a word exposed four or five times a day in a period of three or four days. If the word was taught in some manner in which the disabled reader encountered it five times per day for three successive periods, this would still be only fifteen exposures to the word, or less than the minimum amount of exposures required for a rapid learner in a developmental situation.

Marvin Wyne and Gary Stuck (1979) found that remedial students who received intervention to improve their time-on-task behavior achieved at a significantly higher level in reading than their counterparts who did not receive the treatment. The improved performance of the experimental group was maintained after their return to a regular classroom environment. Other recent research has confirmed the importance of pupils' on-task behavior as a critical factor in learning. Teachers should consider that one possible explanation for students' failure is that they do not always *attend* to material and information as it is being presented.

Most of us as adults have simply forgotten how difficult it was to learn to read. Albert Einstein, for example, was reported to have said that learning to read was the most difficult task that man has ever devised. What you must be cognizant of is just how difficult it is for some students to learn what you are teaching them so that you can develop an adequate perspective on how much time you must expect to spend with each student on learning a new word, a vowel sound, a vowel rule, a syllable principle, etc. When remedial reading teachers begin to do this on a somewhat scientific basis, they are often pleasantly surprised to find that many of their disabled readers are, in reality, not slow learners at all.

From a practical standpoint learning rate can be judged by using some of the following techniques:

1. Make note of one or two sight words that you wish to teach to a particular student. Then note on your daily record form (See Daily Lesson Plan Form in Chapter 15), as accurately as you can, how many times the word was taught and reviewed. You may also wish to ask the student to underline or count the number times he or she comes across the word in reading. After it is evident the student has mastered the word, check, as nearly as possible, the number of exposures or the amount of teaching it has taken to teach the student the word so that it is a thoroughly learned sight word.

2. Use the same recording procedure after teaching other concepts such as a vowel rule and syllabication principle. Then note whether the student can merely state the rule or whether he or she applies it regularly. If the student knows a rule or principle but does not apply it, note the number of worksheets or application lessons it has generally taken before the student was actually able to apply the rule. As mentioned previously some may never get to the point of actual application on a routine basis.

It would be unrealistic to do the sort of thing described above on a regular basis with nearly every word or concept taught. On the other hand, we have found that university students who are required to do this sort of exercise on a regular basis with disabled readers who appear to learn very slowly, often change their entire perception, in a positive direction, of a student's ability to learn. This, of course, affects teacher expectation, which, as previously stated, ultimately affects students' self-concepts.

SUMMARY

We are persuaded that most remedial readers will learn successfully if traditional diagnostic remedial procedures are employed over time. In rare cases it may be appropriate to try other, heroic approaches even if substantial research justification is lacking. In some cases it is desirable to diagnose for more than students' knowledge of the various reading skills. At the present time the notion that individual students possess different strengths and weaknesses in their sensory modality capabilities, while logical, has not been proved. The accumulating evidence suggests that this approach does not lead to improved student performance and that a combination method is most effective. Nonetheless, we have presented techniques for diagnosing and teaching to dominant modalities in this chapter in the hope that readers will have a better understanding of this controversial approach and consider it as a method for use when other approaches have failed.

There is also a growing body of research to indicate that students possess different cognitive styles of learning. It would appear feasible to note which cognitive style disabled readers possess so as to capitalize on a teaching method appropriate for each student's particular cognitive style.

The remedial reading teacher should also be aware of students' learning rates. Studies indicate that there is considerable variance in learning rates from individual to individual. By checking from time to time on the learning rates of individual students we are often pleasantly surprised to find that many disabled readers are, in reality, not slow learners. This can be beneficial in terms of teacher expectation, which will, in many cases, influence student achievement.

REFERENCES

Barbe, Walter B.; Swassing, Raymond H.; and Milone, Michael N. "Teaching to Modality Strengths: Don't Give Up Yet!" *Academic Therapy.* Vol. 16, (January, 1981), 262–266.

Blackie, John. "How Children Learn," *NEA Journal.* Vol. 57 (February, 1968), 40–42.

Blanton, Bill. "Review of ERIC/CRIER Research on Modalities and Reading," *Reading Teacher.* Vol. 25, (November, 1971), 210–211.

Butler, Lester G. "A Psycholinguistic Analysis of the Oral Reading Behavior of Selected Impulsive and Reflective Second Grade Boys," Paper presented at the International Reading Convention, New Orleans, 1974.

Carbo, Marie L. "Reading Style: Diagnosis, Evaluation, Prescription," *Academic Therapy.* Vol. 16, (September, 1980), 45–52.

Duker, Sam. "Listening and Reading," *Elementary School Journal.* Vol. 65, (March, 1965), 321–329.

Dunn, Rita; Dunn, Kenneth; and Price, Gary. "Diagnosing Learning Styles: A Prescription for Avoiding Malpractice Suits," *Phi Delta Kappan.* Vol. 58, (January, 1977), 418–420.

Ekwall, Eldon E., and Oswald, Lowell D. *Rx Reading Program—Teacher's Manual.* Glenview, Illinois: Psychotechnics, Inc., 1971, p. 1.

Ekwall, Eldon E., and Solis, Judy English. "Use of the Polygraph to Determine Elementary School Students' Frustration Reading Level," Final U.S.O.E. Report, 1971.

Fry, Edward. *Reading Instruction for Classroom and Clinic.* New York: McGraw-Hill, 1972, pp. 58–63.

Harris, Albert J., and Sipay, Edward R. *How to Increase Reading Ability.* 7th ed., New York: Longman, 1980. Copyright 1940, 1947, © 1956, 1961, 1970, 1975, and 1980 by Longman Inc. Copyright renewed 1968 and 1975 by Albert J. Harris. Reprinted by permission of Longman Inc., New York.

Kagan, Jerome. *Matching Familiar Figures Test.* Unpublished test devised by Jerome Kagan. Harvard University, 1965–1969.

Kagan, Jerome. "Reflection-Impulsivity and Reading Ability in Primary Grade Children," *Child Development.* Vol. 36, (September, 1965–1966), 609–628.

Kampwirth, Thomas J. "Not Just Another Fish Story: A Response to Barbe, Swassing and Milone," *Academic Therapy.* Vol. 16, (January, 1981), 267–269.

Kampwirth, Thomas J., and Bates, Marion. "Modality Preference and Teaching Method: A Review of the Research," *Academic Therapy.* Vol. 15, (May, 1980), 597–605.

Linder, Ronald, and Fillmer, Henry T. "Auditory and Visual Performance of Slow Readers," *Reading Teacher.* Vol. 24, (October, 1970), 17–22.

McGrady, Harold J., Jr., and Olson, Don A. "Visual and Auditory Learning Processes in Normal Children and Children with Specific Learning Disabilities," *Exceptional Children.* Vol. 36, (April, 1970), 581–589.

Miller, Etta. "First-Grade Reading Instruction and Modality Preference," *Elementary School Journal.* Vol. 80, (November, 1979), 99–104.

Mills, Robert E. "An Evaluation of Techniques for Teaching Word Recognition," *Elementary School Journal.* Vol. 56, (January, 1965), 221–225.

Mills, Robert E. *Learning Methods Test.* Rev. ed. Fort Lauderdale, Florida: The Mills School, 1970.

Neal, Alan J. "Reflectivity-Impulsivity in Grade Four Students and the Apprehension of Meanings of Unfamiliar Words. A Study Which Relates Cognitive Study and Reading Behavior," Paper presented at the International Reading Convention, New Orleans, 1974.

Riessman, Frank. *The Culturally Deprived Child.* New York: Harper & Brothers, 1962.

Samuels, S. Jay. "Effects of Pictures on Learning to Read, Comprehension and Attitudes," *Review of Educational Research.* Vol. 40, (June, 1970), 397–407.

Sawyer, Diane. "The Diagnostic Mystique—A Point of View," *Reading Teacher.* Vol. 27, (March, 1974), 555–561.

Tarver, Sara G., and Dawson, Margaret M. "Modality Preference and the Teaching of Reading: A Review," *Journal of Learning Disabilities.* Vol. 11, (January, 1978), 5–17.

Wolpert, Edward M. "Modality and Reading: A Perspective," *Reading Teacher.* Vol. 24, (April, 1971), 640–643.

Wolpert, Edward M. "Length, Imagery Values and Word Recognition," *Reading Teacher.* Vol. 26, (November, 1972), 180–186.

Wyne, Marvin D., and Stuck, Gary B. "Time-on-Task and Reading Performance in Underachieving Children," *Journal of Reading Behavior.* Vol. 11, (Summer, 1979), 119–128.

11

Using Informal Reading
Inventories, the Cloze
Procedure, and the Analysis
of Oral Reading Errors

The first part of this chapter deals with a general description of informal reading inventories and why they are used. Detailed descriptions are then given for their administration, scoring, and interpretation. Information on developing your own informal reading inventories is then provided as well as information on using the informal-reading-inventory criteria for matching students and instructional material. This is then followed by a section on the analysis of error patterns from oral reading errors. The cloze procedure is then explained along with information on developing, administering, and scoring cloze passages. Lastly, information is presented on techniques for using the cloze procedure to place students in graded materials, and on how to use the cloze procedure to select materials to meet the needs of students within a particular classroom.

THE INFORMAL READING INVENTORY

What Informal Reading Inventories Are and Why They Are Used

Informal reading inventories usually consist of a series of graded passages, usually from preprimer to at least the seventh- or eighth-grade level. From the first-grade level on there are usually two passages—one to be read orally and one to be read silently at each grade level. As the student reads orally, word-recognition errors are recorded, and from these a percentage of word recognition is computed. Following the reading of each passage (both silently and orally) the student is also asked a series of comprehension questions regarding the material. From these answers a percentage score is derived for reading comprehension. For older students the oral reading passages are sometimes omitted.

People who work with children on a day-to-day basis in reading often come to realize the inadequacy of many of the standard measures of reading achievement in terms of providing for the practical knowledge that is necessary for individualized instruction. Emmett Betts (1946) had this feeling when he described the criteria and idea of administering informal reading inventories (IRIs). Betts's feeling about the need for such an instrument has been demonstrated and written about many times since. For example, Frank Guszak (1970) refers to studies by P.A. Kilgallon and Robert McCracken pointing to the unreliable placement information received from standardized reading achievement tests. More recently Margaret Jones and Edna Pikulski (1974) have quoted various studies indicating that standardized reading achievement tests tend to overestimate children's instructional levels.

Jo Ellen Oliver and Richard D. Arnold (1979) compared the results of a standardized test, teacher judgments, and an informal reading inventory using third-grade subjects. They concluded:

> Based upon previous studies and the data gathered here, it would appear that scores from informal inventories place students in easier materials for instructional purposes than either standardized test scores or teacher judgement. Further, it would seem that as children proceed through the elementary grades, they are placed in increasingly more difficult and perhaps even frustrating materials. The data suggest one-half to one grade level in primary grades . . . with up to two full years in the fifth and sixth grades. . . . If this interpretation is accurate, it is understandable why students are frustrated by reading materials in many schools and why they have problems in the secondary schools, where reading is prerequisite to most learning. (p. 58)

The fact that overestimation of reading levels is a serious factor in reading becomes extremely important when one hears statements such as one made by Edwa Steirnagle (1974) that her experience and research led her to believe that 60 percent of reading failures are caused by the assignment of materials that are too difficult.

The Purpose of Informal Reading Inventories

In terms of the information presented above it is obvious that one of the main purposes in using informal reading inventories is to accurately place students in available reading materials or to provide for a proper "fit" between the two. Another important purpose of informal reading inventories is to determine students' free or independent, instructional, and frustration reading levels. In determining these levels an assessment must be made of students' reading comprehension when reading either orally or silently and of their word recognition when reading orally. A third important purpose of IRIs is to analyze the amount and type of students' word-recognition errors and to assess reading comprehension for diagnostic remedial purposes.

The Informal-Reading-Inventory Criteria and Levels

Reading is essentially a process of recognizing and understanding words and recognizing and understanding ideas. Or, said another way, in order to read efficiently one must reach a certain level of "word recognition" as well as a certain level of "comprehension." In reading these levels are normally designated as follows:

Free or Independent Level (Criteria to be met without examiner aid)

Word recognition—99 percent or better
Comprehension—90 percent or better

This is the level at which children should be reading when they are reading a library book or the level at which they should read their textbooks *after* the teacher has introduced them to the new vocabulary and built up a proper background of experiences for comprehending the concepts in the material. In general this is the level a student should be reading at when there is no one around to help. Although placement is normally based on the criteria mentioned above, teachers associate certain behavioral characteristics with this level of reading. These characteristics are described by Marjorie Johnson and Roy Kress (1965) as follows:

Rhythmetical, expressive oral reading
Accurate observation of punctuation

Acceptable reading posture
Silent reading more rapid than oral
Response to questions in language equivalent to author's
No evidence of lip movement, finger pointing, head movement, vocalization,
   sub-vocalization, or anxiety about performance. (p. 6)

Instructional Level (Criteria to be met without examiner aid)

Word recognition—95 percent
Comprehension—75 percent

This is the level at which children would normally be reading in their textbooks (social studies, science, basal reading) before the teacher has introduced them to the vocabulary and built up a background of experiences for
comprehending the concepts in the material. Again, placement is usually
based on the criteria mentioned above, but the related behavioral characteristics while reading should be the same as for the free or independent reading level.
   Everett E. Davis and Eldon E. Ekwall (1976) investigated some aspects of
the emotional state of frustration as related to reading in elementary school
children. They used a polygraph to assess certain physiological changes in
children while the children were reading and concluded that for most children, reading passages for instructional purposes must be no more difficult
than to allow for about 5 percent oral reading errors. Only a few children
have special protective devices that enable them to withstand greater
degrees of failure.

Frustration Level

Word recognition—90 percent or less
Comprehension—50 percent or less

This is the level at which the material is too difficult for sustained reading,
and it is a level to avoid if possible. Placement is again normally based on the
criteria mentioned above but related behavioral characteristics are as follows:

Abnormally loud or soft voice
Arhythmical or word-by-word oral reading
Lack of expression in oral reading
Inaccurate observation of punctuation
Finger pointing (at margin or every word)

Lip movement, head movement, sub-vocalization
Frequent requests for examiner help
Non-interest in the selection
Yawning or obvious fatigue
Refusal to continue. (p. 10)

Hearing Comprehension Level (Criteria to be met without examiner aid)

Comprehension—75 percent (The responses to questions should generally be
in language equivalent to the author's.)

The criteria given for the various levels mentioned above are from Kress and
Johnson, cited earlier. Although other slightly different criteria for some
reading levels are sometimes given by other authors, it should be emphasized
that these are usually based on "hunches." Research by Eldon E. Ekwall indicates that these criteria could probably be considered as correct providing
all repetitions are counted as errors. (See Ekwall and English, 1971; Ekwall,
Solis, and Solis, 1973.)

In order to determine the reading potential of disabled readers, examiners often begin to read passages at levels that are progressively higher
than the students' frustration level. Students listen as these are read to them
and the material is considered to be at their hearing comprehension level as
long as they meet the above-stated criteria, i.e., that they can answer 75 percent of the comprehension questions. The highest grade level at which they
can do this is their hearing comprehension level. For some disabled readers
this may be one or more grade levels above their frustration level. It should
be stressed, however, that using hearing comprehension as a guide to reading potential is only a rough estimate of this potential since some students
may possess less innate ability for listening than others. It has also been demonstrated that students from low socioeconomic levels often have listening
skills inferior to those of students from middle- or upper-income levels.
Therefore, misleading results can easily be obtained by putting too much
faith in the accuracy of the hearing comprehension level.

Administering Informal Reading Inventories

In administering an IRI the examiner normally sits across the table or preferably on one side of a table while the student sits facing the examiner to the
right or left side of the examiner. A right-handed examiner would place
the student to the left; a left-handed examiner would place the student to the
right. In this way the student is less able to see, and be distracted by, the
written notations the examiner makes. The student is given a booklet con-

taining a series of graded passages. The examiner usually has the student start at a level that the examiner believes will be rather easy for the student or that might be equivalent to the student's free or independent reading level. In order to determine the proper level to begin the IRI the examiner often administers a graded word list so that a more accurate determination of the free or independent level can readily be obtained. Several of the commercially available inventories contain their own graded word lists for this purpose. (These are discussed later in this chapter.) We have found the San Diego Quick Assessment List, listed in Chapter 4, to be quick and quite valid for easily determining the free or independent level at which to start and for estimating the instructional and frustration levels as well.

As the student is given the booklet of graded reading passages, the examiner usually gives directions somewhat as follows: "Here are some passages or stories I would like you to read. Please read them clearly and accurately and try to remember everything you read so that you can answer some questions about them when you are done. If you come across a hard word, try to read it as best as you can, but I may help you if you cannot get it at all." In introducing each passage the examiner often makes some comment about the content of the passage. For example, in having a student read a passage about an airplane ride the examiner may wish to say something such as, "This is a story about a boy who went on an airplane ride. Have you ever ridden in an airplane?" When doing this, however, be sure to avoid answering any questions that will later be asked about the story. Handing the student the first passage say, "Here is the first passage, read it aloud. Again, try to remember everything you read so you can answer some questions about it when you are through; go ahead and begin."

As the student reads, the examiner should have a copy of what the student is reading so that any word-recognition errors, hesitations, etc., can be recorded. It is better if the examiner's copy is double or triple spaced so that ample room is available for recording these errors. A code for marking oral reading errors is shown in the list that follows. Many people have learned another shorthand method of marking various kinds of word-recognition errors. We have found that students learn this code rather easily, but the important point is that you are able to look at the recorded errors and accurately interpret them immediately following the reading or even six months or a year later. For this reason you should become thoroughly familiar with either this or a modified version of this code. Although, when giving an informal reading inventory, it is necessary for the teacher to mark oral reading errors as the student proceeds through the reading material, it is usually a good idea for the teacher to tape the student's oral reading. This will enable the teacher to go back and check on the accuracy of the coding. This is especially important when major decisions are to be made about the placement of a student based on the student's performance on an informal reading inventory.

Code for Marking in Oral Diagnosis

To be scored as errors in marking informal reading inventories

1. Encircle omissions.
2. Insert with a caret (^) all insertions.
3. Draw a line through words for which substitutions or mispronunciations were made and write the substitution or mispronunciation above the word. Determine later whether the word missed was a substitution or mispronunciation.
4. If the student reads too fast to write in all mispronunciations, draw a line through the word and write a *P* for partial mispronunciation or a *G* for gross mispronunciation.
5. Mark inversions the same as substitutions and determine later whether the mistake was really an inversion or a substitution. Examples of inversions are *no* for *on, ont* for *not, saw* for *was,* etc.
6. Use parentheses ( ) to enclose words for which aid was given.
7. Underline repetitions with a wavy line.

Not to be scored as errors in marking informal reading inventories

8. Make a check (√) over words that were self-corrected.
9. Use an arced line to connect words where there was disregard for punctuation.
10. Make two vertical lines (‖) to indicate a pause before words.

Example of a coded passage

Dwight ~~was~~ saw going to visit ^with his Aunt ~~Nadine~~. He ~~packed~~ P his (suitcase). Then (his) mother took him to the ~~airport~~ P. Before he left he gave his mother a big ~~hug~~ bug.

After the student has finished reading the passage, the examiner should take it back (as casually as possible) and then ask the comprehension questions that have been prepared in advance. These questions should appear on the same sheet on which the student's word-recognition errors were recorded and can be marked with a "+" (plus) for correct answers or a "–" (minus) for wrong answers. If the student does not give a complete-enough answer to score it accurately, you should ask a neutral question to clarify the answer. Examples of neutral questions are, "Can you tell me a little more about that?" or "Can you explain that a little more?" On the other hand, try to avoid questions that give the student a 50–50 chance of getting it right. For example, in a question calling for specific details such as, "What color was the car?" you should not question further by saying something such as, "Was it blue or green?" There are also times when you may wish to record verbatim what the student says in order to take more time in scoring it later. On some answers half credit is sometimes given where even after neutral questioning the answer is still not clear-cut.

You are also likely to find some students who occasionally do not give any answer after a question has been asked. Remember that you should give ample time for the student to think about the question and try to answer it (usually five to ten seconds at least). If, however, after a period of time the student does not answer, you may wish to say, "Do you think you know that?" If the student does not know the answer, the student will usually say, "No." The point in doing this, of course, is to avoid wasting a great deal of time waiting for an answer from students who do not seem to take the initiative by simply saying, "I don't know."

After the student has read the first passage aloud and answered the questions, you will likely have the student read silently the alternate passage at the same grade level. You will give the student similar directions about remembering what is read. After the student has finished, you will again ask the comprehension questions. If, however, it is obvious that the first passage was too difficult for the student, you will continue *downward* one or more grade levels with oral reading until you have definitely established the student's free or independent level. Then you will continue upward again, alternating from oral to silent at each level. Have the student continue upward until the frustration level is determined for both oral and silent reading.

After the student's frustration levels are reached, you may wish to begin reading to the student to determine the hearing comprehension level. In doing this, however, you may wish to use another set of graded reading passages so as not to spoil the original set for an administration at a later date.

Scoring and Interpreting Informal Reading Inventories

In coding students' oral reading it often proves beneficial to code a passage exactly as a student reads it, although as you will note only the first seven types of errors (see the Code for Marking in Oral Diagnosis) are counted in computing the percentage of word-recognition errors. The coding symbols shown in 8 through 10 often provide information helpful in diagnosis of reading disability but are not used in computing the percentage of word-recognition errors. One of the main reasons that hesitations and lack of regard for punctuation are not counted as errors is that one could simply not be objective in scoring them. For example, two scorers would seldom reach perfect agreement on the exact number of times a student disregarded punctuation or hesitated too long. Therefore, if these things were counted as errors there would often be a low interscorer reliability (two or more people would not end up with the same number of errors) and the informal reading inventory would lose considerable validity. The items listed in items 1 through 7, however, are mistakes about which objective judgments can be made and, therefore, high interscorer reliability can be achieved, which can, in turn, make the IRI a valid instrument.

Most authorities have been in agreement (and we concur) that the types of errors shown in items 1 through 8 should be counted as errors. There are some authors, however, who feel that repetitions should not be counted as errors in marking IRIs. There are still other authors who believe that only repetitions of more than one word should be counted as errors. These people sometimes argue as Guszak does in quoting Kenneth Goodman's research. Guszak states, "In his research on oral reading Goodman has found that the repetition or regression is frequently the student's means of reprocessing a selective bit of data necessary to the emerging story line." (p. 667) They, therefore, feel that since the repetition was only made to correct an error, it should not be counted as an error. Ekwall and English (1971), however, used the polygraph (lie detector) to measure students' frustration reading level as they read progressively more difficult passages. Their findings were also reported by Ekwall, Solis, and Solis (1973), and Ekwall (1974). These studies showed that when *all* repetitions are not counted as errors, students actually become physiologically frustrated before they reach the percentage of errors normally recognized as being at the students' frustration level. That is, students become so concerned about their reading performance that their hearts beat faster, they begin to perspire, etc., just as one does when frightened or extremely nervous. With this sort of empirical research available it seems that there should be no doubt that, using the normally recognized criteria, *all* repetitions should be counted as errors.

It should also be kept in mind that although it may not seem "fair" to a student to count repetitions because the student ends up with more errors, it is in reality less fair not to count these errors. If the student appears to be a better reader than is actually the case, the student will be given reading material that is too difficult. On the other hand, seldom do you have to worry about students' reading material that is too easy for them as a result of this scoring.

One of the major problems that teachers have encountered in the past is that they were not really able to understand how to interpret the scoring criteria as it was originally outlined by Betts and later explained by Johnson and Kress. Briefly summarized, their scoring criteria are as follows:

Reading level	Word recognition	Comprehension
Free or independent	99% +	90% +
Instructional	95%	75%
Frustration	90% −	50% −

All of this seems easy enough until a teacher encounters several very confusing situations. First of all, note that in word recognition and comprehension the percentages for the free or independent reading levels are 99 percent "plus" and 90 percent "plus" respectively. On the other hand, the frustration reading levels for word recognition and comprehension are 90 percent "minus" and 50 percent "minus" respectively. The criteria for the instructional reading level for word recognition and comprehension are 95 percent and 75 percent respectively, and these are usually listed as "plus," which connotes that they are minimum levels. What you find then is a situation that might be graphically illustrated (using comprehension as an example) as in Figure 11-1.

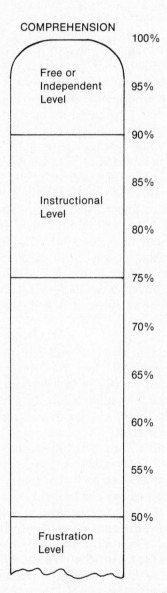

FIGURE 11-1.   Illustration of Various Levels of Comprehension.

It stands to reason then, that students scoring 90 percent or better are at their free or independent reading level, those between 75 percent and 89 percent are at their instructional reading level, and those students scoring below 50 percent are at their frustration reading level. However, the problem in interpretation often comes when the student scores above 50 percent or below 75 percent. We see then that by adding the "plus" and "minus" to our criteria we have created "four" categories while, in reality, we only have three levels. Although this is confusing to someone interpreting information derived from administering IRIs for the first few times, it really allows the teacher to make some subjective judgment based on the student's overall performance. The unmarked area (between 50 percent and 75 percent on comprehension) might essentially be counted as instructional reading level or frustration reading level based on how well the student performed on word recognition. Or, if you are dealing with silent reading, the decision as to which level a student is in might be based on how interested the student appeared to be in the subject or how much difficulty the student *appeared* to have with word recognition while reading the passage.

The same problem encountered with percentages of comprehension is also encountered with percentages of word recognition. In order to clarify how to make decisions for level placement based on both word recognition and comprehension we will look at some examples as shown in Figure 11–2.

In examining Figure 11–2 you will find the word recognition and comprehension levels of eight students (*a* through *h*). The exact percentages of word recognition and comprehension for each of these students on a particular reading passage are summarized below. Following this information an explanation is given of which overall reading level the students would normally be placed in when their word recognition and comprehension are both considered together.

Student A: This student is above the minimum levels in both categories (comprehension and word recognition); therefore, he is reading at his free or independent reading level.

Student B: This student is reading below the minimum levels in both categories, therefore, her overall reading is at her frustration level.

Student C: This student's word recognition score puts him in the high end of the questionable range where his overall reading could be considered as instructional or frustration level; however, since his comprehension is at the frustration level, his overall reading level is also at the frustration level. When either score (word recognition or comprehension) is in the frustration level, it would normally be impossible for the student to be at any other level regardless of how high the score was on the other factor involved.

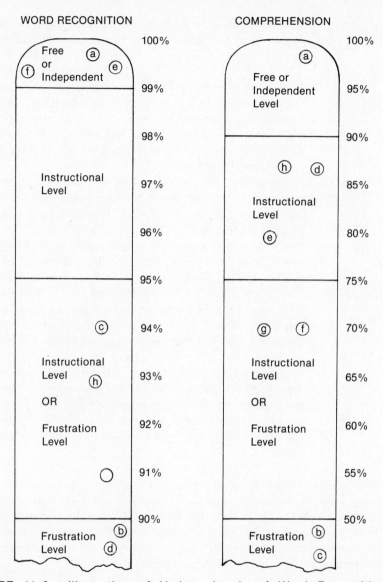

FIGURE 11–2.   Illustration of Various Levels of Word Recognition and Comprehension.

Student D: Again, this student has a word-recognition score that places him at frustration level, and, although his comprehension score was rather high (85 percent), he would still be considered at frustration level.

Student E: This student's score is in the free or independent level in word recognition and in the instructional level in comprehension. The overall score would not normally be any higher than the lower of the two scores. Therefore, her overall score would be considered at instructional level.

Student F: This student's score is also in the free or independent level in word recognition, but his score falls into the questionable range in the area of comprehension. Since his word-recognition score is so high and his comprehension score is in the high range of the questionable level (for either instructional or frustration), we would place him at the instructional level.

Student G: This student is in the low range of the questionable level for word recognition and in the high range of the questionable range for comprehension. We would not normally place a student in the instructional level unless one of her two scores was above the questionable level. Therefore, her overall level would probably be considered to be at the frustration level.

Student H: This student scored in about the middle of the questionable level for word recognition. He scored fairly high in the instructional range but not high enough to make us definitely feel that there is any reason to place him above his frustration level. In this case, however, if the student was extremely interested in what he was reading or seemed to possess a great deal of perseverance, it would perhaps be proper for him to read at this level for a short period of time. As a general rule, however, students should not read material that would be this difficult for them.

As you can see it is somewhat difficult to make decisions about the overall reading level of certain students even when given a certain amount of guidance (see Table 11–1). On the other hand, you should keep in mind that it is really only the teacher who knows the students, their interests, their ability to persevere, etc. And, the fact that the informal reading inventory criteria are somewhat flexible is often beneficial.

Developing Your Own Informal Reading Inventories and Using the IRI Criteria

As stated previously, one of the purposes of using IRIs is to determine students' free, instructional, and frustration reading levels. If this is your purpose, as it might be in an initial or final diagnosis done by a reading specialist or clinician, it would probably be much easier to simply use one of the com-

TABLE 11-1. Placement of Students Based on Word Recognition and Comprehension.

Student	Word recognition percentage	Comprehension percentage	Placement
a	99 or 100	100	Free or independent
b	Less than 90	Less than 50	Frustration
c	94	Less than 50	Frustration
d	Less than 90	85	Instructional
e	99 or 100	80	Instructional
f	99 or 100	70	Instructional
g	91	70	Frustration
h	93	85	Probably frustrational, but possibly instructional

mercially published reading inventories discussed later in this chapter. It takes many hours or even days to develop a good inventory of this nature, and there is little use in duplicating the efforts of experts who have devised good inventories for this purpose. In addition to considerations of time, teachers will find difficulty in selecting proper passages, establishing scoring procedures, assuring proper readability levels, and developing suitable comprehension questions. On the other hand, simply applying the IRI criteria to materials within your own school to determine proper balance between students and materials is one of the most valuable uses of the IRI criteria.

Whether you wish to make your own complete informal reading inventory or whether you merely wish to select passages from existing materials to determine whether a student is in accord with those materials, you will need certain guidelines. For lower level passages (preprimer through first grade) as few as twenty to forty words are often used. As the material increases in difficulty longer passages are usually selected (around 100–150 words at second- or third-grade level and up to 250–300 words at seventh- or eighth-grade level). Although research has shown that it is difficult to actually measure various comprehension skills, an attempt is usually made to devise comprehension questions over main ideas, important details, vocabulary, and inference. In order to insure a certain amount of validity, at least seven or eight questions are usually asked concerning each passage. One of the difficulties in constructing questions to accompany informal reading inventories is to be sure that the questions are passage-dependent. That is, you must try to eliminate questions that the student might answer correctly without even reading the passage. It has been commonly assumed that factual questions are less likely to be passage-dependent than inferential questions. However, research by Frederick Duffelmeyer (1980) found that approximately two-thirds of the factual questions on a popular informal reading inventory were passage-dependent and only about one-half of the inferential questions were passage-dependent. Duffelmeyer concluded that passage dependency is not a function of question type but rather a result of the item writer's ability to create good questions. William Valmont (1972) has provided some excellent guidelines for constructing questions for informal reading inventories. These are as follows:

1. Questions should be in the approximate order in which the information upon which they are based is presented in the passage.
2. It is generally preferable to place a main idea question first.
3. Ask the most important questions possible.
4. Check the sequence of questions to insure that a later question is not answered by an earlier one.
5. Check questions to insure that two or more questions do not call for the same response, fact, or inference.
6. A question that is so broad that any answer is acceptable is a poor question. If special questions to test divergent thinking are created, insure that reasonable, logical responses may be made.
7. A question that can be answered by someone who has not read the passage (except for vocabulary questions) is a poor question.
8. Avoid formulating questions whose answers call for knowledge based on something experienced by the pupil rather than from reading or application of information given in the story.
9. IRI questions are generally constructed to measure the student's comprehension of written matter. Therefore, insure that accompanying pictures do not aid the student in answering questions.
10. Keep your questions short and as simple as possible. Do not include irrelevant statements.
11. Generally, state questions so that they start with who, what, when, where, how, and why.
12. Do not let grammar or syntax unnecessarily complicate the questions.
13. Avoid stating questions in a negative manner.
14. Avoid overusing questions which require pupils to reconstruct lists, such as "list five ingredients" or "name four characters" or "tell six places." Anxiety or memory instead of comprehension may influence the pupil's performance.
15. Avoid writing questions with multiple answers which fail to establish specifications for the response.
    Poor: What happened after Susan heard the telephone?
    Better: What was the first thing that happened after Susan heard the telephone?
16. Do not mistake a question that calls for the reporting of several facts or details as an organization or sequence question.

17. To learn about a pupil's grasp of the vocabulary, ask the pupil to define the word, not to recall a word from the story.
    Poor: What word told you about the age of the man?
    Better: What does *old* mean?
18. Avoid stating a question as if to call for an opinion when asking the pupil to relate a fact.
    Poor: How do you think Skip got to the store?
    Better: How did Skip get to the store?
19. If a question is asking for a judgment, phrase it as "Why do you or don't you believe...." Do not reveal the information called for.
20. Avoid asking questions on which the child has a fifty-fifty chance of being correct: "yes/no" questions, or "either/or." (pp. 511–512)[1]

Thus far we have discussed using commercially published reading inventories or developing your own informal reading inventories. A third option may be available to you and have particular merit for placing students in basal materials. Here we refer to the informal reading inventories that may accompany the basal programs. We have found that the inventories prepared by the basal publishers are uneven. Some are quite thorough and helpful, and others appear to be hastily constructed. We would advise that teachers or reading specialists examine these inventories carefully according to the guidelines we have previously presented. You may find that the materials are adequate for your needs or that they may be modified slightly. In some cases you may find that the inventories that accompany basal readers are simply inadequate and should be discarded.

A Reading Level Guide to Calculate Reading Levels and to "Fit" Students and Materials

After working with beginning and practicing teachers for a number of years it is our feeling that few of these teachers really use reading inventories to advantage. For this reason Eldon E. Ekwall has created a "Reading Level Guide." There are several reasons why teachers have not used informal reading inventories or the criteria of the IRI for placing students in materials. These are as follows:

1. Most teachers have simply not had enough training in the field of reading to understand how to use the IRI criteria either for scoring informal reading inventories or for placing students at the right reading level.

[1]Valmont, William J. "Creating Questions for Informal Reading Inventories," *The Reading Teacher*. Vol. 25, (March, 1972), 509–512. (Reprinted with permission of the author and the International Reading Association.)

2. Those teachers who have studied the IRI criteria can usually interpret the results they obtain providing both comprehension and word recognition clearly fall into the "free" or "independent" reading level or the "frustration" reading level. However, when either word recognition or comprehension differ considerably, the obtained results become much more difficult to interpret. The Reading Level Calculator eliminates the problems usually encountered in interpreting obtained data.

3. Teachers are often hesitant to take the time to calculate the percentage of words recognized as well as the percentage of questions that were correct. The use of Tables 11–2 and 11–3 eliminates the need for calculating any percentages.

The Purpose of the Reading Level Guide. The purpose is to help beginning and practicing teachers, or the reading specialist, place students at the proper reading level. This information will enable you to quickly and effortlessly interpret information derived from informal reading inventories, and more importantly it will help you match the reading levels of children and books by applying the criteria for interpreting informal reading inventories.

The use of the criteria for scoring informal reading inventories eliminates the need for teachers to work somewhat complicated and time-consuming readability formulas on various classroom materials. It also eliminates the chore of attempting to assess the "reading level" of children. Furthermore, there is considerable chance that a book based on a reading level obtained by a readability formula will not be in accord with a teacher's assessed reading level. This is true for the two reasons that follow:

1. Readability formulas, at best, only produce a rough approximation of the level of difficulty of reading material.

2. Most tests only produce a rough approximation of a child's reading level. For example, a child whose reading level is based on a subject about which the child is thoroughly familiar is likely to score quite high because of the child's knowledge of the vocabulary and comprehension of the concepts. Because of this the child may be placed in materials that are too difficult. On the other hand, material written on subjects about which the child is unfamiliar may result in a placement that is too low. The important question, of course, is how well does a *certain* child read a *certain* set of materials.

The problem then is that every book or every different set of reading materials presents somewhat different problems for different readers depending on their background of experiences. The only practical solution is to ask a child to read the materials that you wish to use in instructing the child and see how well *that* child reads *those* materials. This applies whether you are a parent attempting to determine whether a certain library book is easy enough for your child to read or whether you are a teacher trying to find the right level of basal reader in which to place a student.

To determine whether a book or other reading material is at the proper reading level for a student, use the procedure that follows:

1. Have the student orally read a passage from the material. For younger students in grades one or two you will probably want to choose a passage of 25 to 100 words. For students at grade three or above you will probably want to use a passage of 100–200 words.
2. As the student reads, record the number of oral errors he or she makes using the Code for Marking in Oral Diagnosis. You may wish to have a copy of the material that the student is reading on which you can mark errors in word recognition. Or you may simply wish to make a fist and then hold up one finger (without the student noticing) each time an error is made in word recognition.

Coding the exact type of error will often enable you to locate certain reading difficulties that might not otherwise become apparent. If you are only interested in placement, you may wish to simply make a check for each oral error. If you do not mark each error, be sure that you jot down the total number of oral (word recognition) errors.

3. Ask the student questions concerning the material that the student has just read. You should usually try to ask at least four or more questions. Questions should preferably be prepared in advance and should sample the following kinds of comprehension:
   a. Knowledge of the main ideas
   b. Knowledge of important details
   c. Knowledge of vocabulary
   d. Ability to infer from material read
   Note the total number of questions that were asked and the total number of questions missed.
4. In Table 11–2 you will find numbers representing the total number of words in various passages in the left-hand column. Find the number or range that corresponds to the number of words in the passage just read. Place your left hand on this row. Look at the row of numbers across the top that represents the number of oral or word-recognition errors. Find the number of errors made by your student and place your right hand on this number. Now find the point at which the row that your left hand is pointing to intersects with the column at which your right hand is pointing. This number represents the percentage of word recognition (percentage correct).

TABLE 11-2.   Guide for Determining the Correct Percentage of Word Recognition.

Number of words missed

Number of words in reading passage	1	2	3	4	5	6	7	8	9	10	11	12	13	14	15	16	17	18	19	20
20–25	96	91	F	F	F	F	F	F	F	F	F	F	F	F	F	F	F	F	F	F
26–30	96	93	F	F	F	F	F	F	F	F	F	F	F	F	F	F	F	F	F	F
31–35	97	94	91	F	F	F	F	F	F	F	F	F	F	F	F	F	F	F	F	F
36–40	97	95	92	F	F	F	F	F	F	F	F	F	F	F	F	F	F	F	F	F
41–45	98	95	93	91	F	F	F	F	F	F	F	F	F	F	F	F	F	F	F	F
46–50	98	96	94	92	F	F	F	F	F	F	F	F	F	F	F	F	F	F	F	F
51–55	98	96	94	92	91	F	F	F	F	F	F	F	F	F	F	F	F	F	F	F
56–60	98	97	95	93	91	F	F	F	F	F	F	F	F	F	F	F	F	F	F	F
61–65	98	97	95	94	92	F	F	F	F	F	F	F	F	F	F	F	F	F	F	F
66–70	99	97	96	94	93	F	F	F	F	F	F	F	F	F	F	F	F	F	F	F
71–75	99	97	96	95	93	92	F	F	F	F	F	F	F	F	F	F	F	F	F	F
76–80	99	97	96	95	94	92	92	F	F	F	F	F	F	F	F	F	F	F	F	F
81–85	99	98	96	95	94	93	92	F	F	F	F	F	F	F	F	F	F	F	F	F
86–90	99	98	97	95	94	93	92	91	F	F	F	F	F	F	F	F	F	F	F	F
91–95	99	98	97	96	95	94	93	91	F	F	F	F	F	F	F	F	F	F	F	F
96–100	99	98	97	96	95	94	93	92	F	F	F	F	F	F	F	F	F	F	F	F
101–105	99	98	97	96	95	94	93	92	91	F	F	F	F	F	F	F	F	F	F	F
106–110	99	98	97	96	95	94	94	93	92	F	F	F	F	F	F	F	F	F	F	F
111–115	99	98	97	96	96	95	94	93	92	91	F	F	F	F	F	F	F	F	F	F
116–120	99	98	97	96	96	95	94	93	92	91	F	F	F	F	F	F	F	F	F	F
121–125	99	98	98	97	96	95	94	93	93	92	91	F	F	F	F	F	F	F	F	F
126–130	99	98	98	97	96	95	95	94	93	92	92	91	F	F	F	F	F	F	F	F
131–135	99	98	98	97	96	95	95	94	93	92	92	91	F	F	F	F	F	F	F	F
136–140	99	99	98	97	96	96	95	94	93	93	92	92	91	F	F	F	F	F	F	F
141–145	99	99	98	97	97	96	95	94	94	93	92	92	91	F	F	F	F	F	F	F

TABLE 11–2.   (cont.).

Number of words missed

Number of words in reading passage	1	2	3	4	5	6	7	8	9	10	11	12	13	14	15	16	17	18	19	20
146–150	99	99	98	97	97	96	95	95	94	93	93	92	92	91	F	F	F	F	F	F
151–155	99	99	98	97	97	96	95	95	94	93	93	92	92	91	F	F	F	F	F	F
156–160	99	99	98	97	97	96	96	95	94	94	93	92	92	91	91	F	F	F	F	F
161–165	99	99	98	98	97	96	96	95	94	94	93	93	92	91	91	F	F	F	F	F
166–170	99	99	98	98	97	96	96	95	95	94	93	93	92	92	91	F	F	F	F	F
171–175	99	99	98	98	97	97	96	95	95	94	94	93	92	92	91	91	F	F	F	F
176–180	99	99	98	98	97	97	96	95	95	94	94	93	93	92	92	91	F	F	F	F
181–185	99	99	98	98	97	97	96	96	95	95	94	93	93	92	92	91	91	F	F	F
186–190	99	99	98	98	97	97	96	96	95	95	94	94	93	93	92	91	91	F	F	F
191–195	99	99	98	98	97	97	96	96	95	95	94	94	93	93	92	92	91	91	F	F
196–200	99	99	98	98	97	97	96	96	95	95	94	94	93	93	92	92	91	91	F	F

5. Look in Table 11–3 and find the figure that corresponds to the number of questions asked and put your left hand on this figure. Then look across the top row of this table and find the figure that corresponds to the number of questions missed. Put your right hand on this figure. Find the point at which the row to which your left hand is pointing intersects with the column to which your right hand is pointing. This figure is the percent of comprehension questions that were correct.

6. Turn to the Reading Level Calculator (Table 11–4) and find the percentage of correct word recognition in one of the rows on the left-hand side and the percentage of correct comprehension in one of the columns on the top. Then find the point at which the row on the left intersects with the column on the top. If they intersect in one of the areas labeled *F*, the student is reading at the frustration level. If they intersect in the area marked *Inst.*, the student is reading at the instructional level. And, if they intersect in the area marked *Free*, then the student is reading at the free or independent level.

When using either Table 11–2 or Table 11–3 you will find that some rows and columns intersect in an area marked *F*. Whenever this occurs, it means that the child is reading at the frustration level regardless of other scores. Therefore, there would be no need to use the Reading Level Calculator because the student's reading level would have already been determined.

TABLE 11-3.   Guide for Determining the Correct Percentage of Comprehension.

Number of questions missed

		0	1	2	3	4	5	6	7	8	9	10
	10	100	90	80	70	60	F	F	F	F	F	F
	9	100	90	80	65	55	F	F	F	F	F	F
	8	100	90	75	65	F	F	F	F	F	F	F
Number of questions	7	100	85	70	60	F	F	F	F	F	F	F
	6	100	85	65	F	F	F	F	F	F	F	F
	5	100	80	60	F	F	F	F	F	F	F	F
	4	100	75	F	F	F	F	F	F	F	F	F
	3	100	65	F	F	F	F	F	F	F	F	F

In doing a quick check to determine whether certain materials are appropriate for a student you may often wish to omit the comprehension questions because of the time involved in both making up and asking these questions. Therefore, follow the same procedure previously described, but instead of asking questions simply consider the student's comprehension to be at the 100 percent level when using the Reading Level Calculator as described in step 6 above.

To determine the grade level at which a student is reading, use the procedure that follows. The procedure for using the Reading Level Guide for determining the grade level at which a student is reading is nearly the same as the previously described procedure with several exceptions. Before beginning this procedure you will need a series of reading passages of which the grade level of difficulty is already known. For example, you may have reading passages at the following levels:

Preprimer (PP)
Primer (P)
First Reader (F)
Second Reader, Book One (2-1)
Second Reader, Book Two (2-2)
Third Reader, Book One (3-1)
Third Reader, Book Two (3-2)
Fourth Reader (4)
Fifth Reader (5)
Sixth Reader (6)
Seventh Reader (7)
Eighth Reader (8)

TABLE 11-4.   Reading Level Calculator.

Percentage of comprehension

	55[a]	60	65	70	75	80	85	90	95	100
100	Inst.	Inst.	Inst.	Inst.	Inst.	Inst.	Inst.	Free	Free	Free
99	F	Inst.	Inst.	Inst.	Inst.	Inst.	Inst.	Free	Free	Free
98	F	F	Inst.	Inst.	Inst.	Inst.	Inst.	Inst.	Inst.	Inst.
97	F	F	F	Inst.	Inst.	Inst.	Inst.	Inst.	Inst.	Inst.
96	F	F	F	F	Inst.	Inst.	Inst.	Inst.	Inst.	Inst.
95	F	F	F	F	F	Inst.	Inst.	Inst.	Inst.	Inst.
94	F	F	F	F	F	F	Inst.	Inst.	Inst.	Inst.
93	F	F	F	F	F	F	F	Inst.	Inst.	Inst.
92	F	F	F	F	F	F	F	F	Inst.	Inst.
91	F	F	F	F	F	F	F	F	F	Inst.

Percent of word recognition (vertical axis label)

F = Frustration reading level
Inst. = Instructional reading level
Free = Free reading level

[a]You will note in using this Reading Level Calculator that the student is not considered to be at the frustration reading level below 75 percent if his or her word-recognition skills are still fairly high. The polygraph research referred to in this chapter indicated that if word recognition remains high, most students do not actually become frustrated until their comprehension level drops below the 50 percent level.

Have the student begin reading at a level that you think will be at the student's free or independent reading level and continue to read progressively harder passages. You may wish to determine this starting point by using the San Diego Quick Assessment List. Check the reading of each passage as described. In doing this, you would continue downward (if necessary) until the student's free or independent reading level is reached and then continue upward until the instructional and finally the frustration levels are reached.

In giving informal reading inventories you would normally wish to determine a student's free or independent, instructional, and frustration levels for both silent and oral reading. To do this you would need two written passages at each of the levels of difficulty mentioned above. Proceed the same as described before; however, this time alternate from oral to silent on each grade level, e.g., at second-grade level have the student read orally and then ask the comprehension questions. After doing this have the student read the other second-grade-level passage silently and again ask the student questions to determine the percentage of comprehension. To determine the proper level for passages that are read silently, simply find the percentage, derived from Table 11–3 for comprehension, across the top of the Reading Level Calculator, and consider the student's word recognition to be at the 100 percent level. Then determine the point at which these two figures intersect. As explained in step 6, the coded intersection point represents the level at which the student is reading.

Briefly then, use the Reading Level Guide as follows:

1.   Determine the number of oral (word recognition) errors.
2.   Convert this to a percentage by using Table 11–3.
3.   Determine the number of comprehension errors.
4.   Convert this to a percentage by using Table 11–3.
5.   Find the corresponding percentages derived on the Reading Level Calculator and determine the point at which these two percentages intersect. The coded intersection point represents the student's reading level.

Adapting Informal Reading Inventories for Use with Older Students

In most situations above grade six and even above the first and second grades a considerably larger amount of time is spent in having students read silently than orally. Some oral reading is done for practice in such areas as reading poetry and choral reading. In addition, many teachers find that oral reading practice may benefit older students by helping them to apply new skills or improve reading fluency. However, except for these reasons it is difficult to justify oral reading for other than diagnostic purposes. For this reason, in designing informal reading inventories to determine the grade level at which students are capable of functioning or in applying the IRI criteria to match students and materials, there is often little need to have students read orally.

When a student obviously reads very poorly, further diagnosis including oral reading may be called for. However, a study by Robert Pehrsson (1974) indicated that students read better when they are not interrupted during the reading process. When Pehrsson's students were told to read for meaning, their comprehension and rate of reading improved.

For these reasons we would suggest that in working with older students you first consider what you want to know about them. If your questions are those such as: Can Cindy read this social studies book at her instructional level? can Bill, who is in the ninth grade, read a particular trade book at his free reading level? Then you may wish to operate as described previously, but omit the oral reading, or word-recognition errors, as a factor in making these decisions.

Commercially Developed Informal Reading Inventories

In recent years a number of new, commercially developed informal reading inventories have become available. These inventories generally include a series of graded passages that may be used to assess the independent, instructional, and frustration levels of students for both oral and silent reading. Assessment includes both word recognition and comprehension. The inventories also contain graded word lists for placement in the passages and/or additional diagnosis of word recognition-skills.

In an excellent test review of commercial informal reading inventories, Kathleen S. Jongsma and Eugene A. Jongsma (1981) provided a table of descriptive information for the following inventories:

Analytical Reading Inventory (ARI) by Mary I. Woods and Alden J. Moe. Columbus, Ohio: Charles E. Merrill, 1977.

Basic Reading Inventory (BRI) by Jerry L. Johns. Dubuque, Iowa: Kendall/Hunt, 1978.

Classroom Reading Inventory (CRI) by Nicholas J. Silvaroli. Dubuque, Iowa: Wm. C. Brown, 1979 (3rd ed.).

The Contemporary Classroom Reading Inventory (CCRI) by Lee A. Rinsky and Esta de Fossard. Dubuque, Iowa: Gorsuch Scarisbrick, 1980.

Diagnostic Reading Inventory (DRI) by H. Donald Jacobs and Lyndon W. Searfoss. Dubuque, Iowa: Kendall/Hunt, 1979 (2nd ed.).

Diagnostic Reading Scales (DRS) by George D. Spache. Monterey, Calif.: CTB/McGraw-Hill, 1972.

Edwards' Reading Test (ERT) by Peter Edwards, Exeter, N.H.: Heinemann, 1980.

Ekwall Reading Inventory (ERI) by Eldon E. Ekwall. Boston, Mass.: Allyn and Bacon, 1979.

Informal Reading Assessment (IRA) by Paul C. Burns and Betty D. Roe. Chicago, Ill.: Rand McNally, 1980.

Standard Reading Inventory (SRI) by Robert A. McCracken. Klamath Falls, Ore.: Klamath Printing Co., 1966.

Sucher-Allred Reading Placement Inventory (SARPI) by Floyd Sucher and Ruel A. Allred. Oklahoma City, Okla.: Economy, 1973.

The reviewers' table is reproduced in Table 11–5. It summarizes the contents, passages, questions, administration, scoring, and interpretation of the inventories. This table should assist you in comparing the important features of these eleven inventories.

The advantages of using a commercially developed inventory were discussed earlier in this chapter. The main disadvantage is that the levels you establish may not match the levels designated in the specific instructional materials you use. Also, the Jongsmas have pointed out that there is great

TABLE 11-5. Informal Reading Inventories.

Features	ARI	BRI	CRI	CCRI	DRI	DRS	ERI	ERT	IRA	SARPI	SRI
Contents											
No. of forms	3	3	3	3	1	2	4	2	4	1	2
Range of passages	P-9	PP-8	PP-8	P-9	1-8	1-8	PP-9	6-13 yrs.	PP-12	P-9	PP-7
Graded word lists	P-6	PP-8	PP-6	P-7	1-8	1-6	PP-9	6-13 yrs.	PP-12	P-9	PP-7
Separate student passages	Yes	Yes	Yes	Yes	Yes	Yes	Yes	Yes	Yes	Yes	Yes
Student summary sheet	Yes	Yes	Yes	Yes	Yes	Yes	Yes	Yes	Yes	Yes	Yes
Class summary sheet	Yes	Yes	No	No	No	No	No	No	No	Yes	No
Pictures/illustrations	No	No	Yes	Yes	No	No	No	No	No	No	No
Motivation/purpose statement for each passage	Yes	No	Yes	Yes	Yes	No	No	No	Yes	Yes	Yes
Supplementary features[1]	B	B	ST	B, ST	ST	CL, ST	ST	B, ST	B	TT	CL, RS
Passages											
Length (words)	50-339	50-100	24-174	47-316	224-361	29-221	31-202	25-100	61-217	51-191	47-151
Content[2]	N, E	N, E	N, E	N, E	N	N, E	N, E	N, E	N, E	N, E	N, E
Readability estimates given	Yes	Yes	No	Yes	No	No	No	No	No	Yes	No
Readability formulas used[3]	HJ, SP	DC, FR, SP	DC, FL, SP	BG, DC, FR, HJ, SP	NI	DC, SP	DC, HJ	E, SM	FR, SP	DC, SP	DC, SP

(cont.)

Key:
NI = Not Indicated
[1]Supplementary Features: B, Bibliographies; CL, Checklists; CS, Case Studies; RS, Rating Scales; ST, Additional Student Tests; TT, Teacher Test.
[2]Content: N, Narration; E, Exposition.
[3]Readability Formulas: BG, Botel-Granowsky; DC, Dale-Chall; E, Edwards; FL, Flesch; FR, Fry; HJ, Harris-Jacobsen; SM, SMOG; SP, Spache.
Source: Jongsma, Kathleen S., and Jongsma, Eugene A. "Test Review: Commercial Informal Reading Inventories," *Reading Teacher.* Vol. 34, (March, 1981), 697-705. (Reprinted with permission of the authors and the International Reading Association.)

Same format student/teacher copies	No	Yes	No	No	No	No	No	Yes	No	No	Yes
Questions											
No. per passages	PP:2:6 3-9:8 3-9:8	PP:4 P-8:10	5	P-1:5 2:6 3:7 4-9:8	1-3:12 4-8:20	1-2:7 3-8:8	PP:5 1-9:10	4-10	PP:2:8 3-12:10	5	PP:5 P-7:13-15
Types of questions[4]	L,I, CE,MI, V	L,CE, MI,V	L,I,V	L,I, CE,MI, S,V	L,I, CE,V	NI	L,I,V	NI	L,I, CE,MI, S,V	L,I, CE,MI, V	L,I, CE,MI, V
Suggested answers given	Yes	Yes	Yes	Yes	No	Yes	Yes	Yes	Yes	Yes	Yes
Administering Require											
Oral	Yes	Yes	Yes	Yes	Yes	Yes	Yes	Yes	Yes	Yes	Yes
Silent	Optional	Optional	Optional	NI	Yes	Yes	Yes	Yes	Optional	No	Yes
Listening comprehension	Yes	Optional	Optional	Optional	Yes	Yes	Optional	Yes	Optional	No	Optional
Directions given for											
Starting/stopping	Yes	Yes	Yes	Yes	Yes	Yes	Yes	Yes	Yes	Yes	Yes
Marking miscues/errors	Yes	Yes	Yes	Yes	Yes	Yes	Yes	Yes	Yes	Yes	Yes
Aid given in oral reading	Yes	No	Yes	Yes	Yes	Yes	Yes	Yes	Yes	Yes	Yes
Probing of comprehension recommended	NI	Yes	NI	Yes	No	Yes	Yes	NI	Yes	NI	Yes
Timing of rate	NI	Optional	Optional	NI	NI	Yes	NI	Yes	Optional	NI	Yes

(cont.)

[4]Types of Questions: CE, Critical-Evaluative; I, Interpretive-Inferential; L, Literal-Factual; MI, Main Ideas; S, Sequence; V, Vocabulary.

TABLE 11-5. (cont.).

Features	ARI	BRI	CRI	CCRI	DRI	DRS	ERI	ERT	IRA	SARPI	SRI
Scoring											
Types of miscues/errors counted[5]	A, I, I/R, O, R, S	"Sig. Miscues"	A, I, O, R, S	A, I, I/R, M, O, R, S	A, I, O, S	A, I, I/R, M, O, R, S	A, I, I/R, M, O, R, S	I, O, S	A, I, I/R, M, O, R, S	A, I, M, O, R, S	A, I, M, O, P, R, S, SC
Partial credit for Comprehension questions	NI	Yes	Yes	Yes	No	Yes	Yes	Yes	NI	Yes	Yes
Criteria for levels independent											
WR	99/more	99/more		97/more	98/more	NI	99/more	95/more	99/more	97/more	
Comp.	90/more	90/more	NI	80/more	90/more	60/more	90/more	70/more	90/more	80/more	NI
Instructional											
WR	95/more	95/more	95/more	92/more	92/more	NI	95/more	90/more	85–95/more	92/more	92/more
Comp.	75/more	75/more	75/more	60/more	60/more	60/more	60/more	70/more	75/more	60/more	NI
Frustrational											
WR	90/less	90/less		91/less	90/less		90/less	90/less	90/less	92/less	
Comp.	50/less	50/less	NI	60/less	50/less	NI	50/less	70/less	50/less	60/less	NI
Listening comprehension	75/more	75/more	75/more	60–75/more	60/more	60/more	70/more	70/more	75/more	NI	40 unaided 70 aided
Interpreting											
Suggestions for diagnostic interpretation	No	Yes	Yes	Yes	Yes	Yes	Yes	No	Yes	No	Yes
Sample cases demonstrated	No	Yes	Yes	Yes	Yes	No	Yes	No	Yes	Yes	No
Teaching suggestions offered	No	Yes	No	No	No	No	No	No	No	No	No
Guidance for handling discrepancies in performance	Yes	Yes	Yes	Yes	Yes	Yes	Yes	No	Yes	Yes	Yes

[5]Types of Miscues/Errors: A, Aid; I, Insertions; I/R, Inversions/Reversals; M, Mispronunciations; O, Omissions; P, Punctuation; R, Repetitions; S, Substitutions; SC, Self-Corrections.

Jongsma, Kathleen S., and Jongsma, Eugene A. "Test Review: Commercial Informal Reading Inventories," *Reading Teacher.* Vol. 34, (March, 1981), 697–705. (Reprinted with permission of the authors and the International Reading Association.)

variability among the inventories with respect to the following: (1) content, style, and length of the passages; (2) directions for administration; (3) scoring methods; (4) comprehension questions; and (5) interpretation and use of results. Therefore, we suggest that you not only use Table 11–5 for a cursory comparison of the inventories but also carefully examine the specific inventory that you select to be sure that it meets your needs for student placement and diagnosis.

THE ANALYSIS OF ERROR PATTERNS FROM ORAL READING ERRORS

Although informal reading inventories can be a useful device for determining students' reading levels and for matching students and reading materials, one of their most important advantages is that they will allow you to diagnose specific reading difficulties from patterns of oral reading errors. We believe that this analysis is the single most important and revealing area of reading diagnosis. It is true that oral reading may present a slightly distorted view of a student's reading ability. Unfortunately, however, there is no way of analyzing directly a student's decoding skills when the student is reading silently. Therefore, we feel that closely observing oral reading behavior is the most accurate barometer of a student's ability *in the act of reading*.

A shorthand method of marking each specific type of oral reading error was described earlier in this chapter. Once you have become familiar with this marking system, you will find that almost every student presents a pattern of errors that then becomes a blueprint for instruction. This section is designed to help you analyze these patterns so as to provide more accurate and effective remediation.

You will recall that in the shorthand system presented previously it was suggested that you learn to mark several types of characteristics of students' reading that are not counted as errors in computing the percentage of word-recognition errors in informal reading inventories. Some of these characteristics, however, are important in the analysis of error patterns of disabled readers. In the section that follows a short description of each type of error, some possible reasons why students might make that particular type of error, and some remedial procedures for each error are presented.[2]

Omissions.   Students sometimes make omissions of parts of words (such as *s, ed,* or *ing* endings), whole words, phrases, or whole lines or sentences. Omissions are usually made either through carelessness or because a student lacks word-recognition or word-analysis skills. It should be emphasized, however, that the type of remediation would depend on the cause.

---

[2]For a more thorough analysis of oral reading errors and their diagnosis and correction see Eldon E. Ekwall, *Locating and Correcting Reading Difficulties,* 3rd ed. Charles E. Merrill, 1981.

Some students omit words simply because they are careless. If a student omits words at the free or instructional level as well as the frustration level, then it would be quite likely that the student's omissions were caused from carelessness. In such a case it should be called to the student's attention. This can be done by recording the student's reading and having the student listen and underline or circle words that were previously omitted. In some cases it is also beneficial to have students bring their finger down and point to each word as it is read. This is more effective than having them slide their finger along a line of print since they are often inclined to read ahead of, or behind, where they are pointing. Another technique that is helpful in overcoming carelessness is to have the student choral read along with another good reader or to read along with a tape recorder.

If a student makes omissions at the frustration level but does not make them at the free or independent level, then they are likely to be caused by difficulties in word recognition or word analysis. In such a case the omissions are only symptomatic of a larger problem. And, when the larger problem of word-recognition or word-analysis skills is remediated, the omission problem will in most cases disappear.

Methods of remediating difficulties in word recognition are given in Chapter 4; and methods of remediating difficulties in word-analysis skills are given in Chapter 5.

Insertions.   Students sometimes make insertions of word endings or insertions of extra words. Insertions may be caused from lack of comprehension, from carelessness, or when the student's oral language ability surpasses reading ability. If the insertions that the student makes are correct within the context of the sentence, it can usually be assumed that the student is comprehending the passage. In this case it might be assumed that these mistakes are a sign of carelessness, or the student's oral language ability may surpass the student's reading ability. When this is the case, you should call the student's attention to the mistakes. This may be done by simply telling the student or by having the student insert with a caret (⌃) all words on a reading passage that the student has read previously into a tape recorder. It is also helpful to ask questions that call for exact answers that can only be answered correctly without the insertions. As in the case of omissions, it is also helpful to have the student point to each word as it is read or to have the student choral read with one or more good readers or to read in conjunction with a tape recorder.

If the student's insertions do not make sense within the context of the sentence, the student is probably having difficulty with comprehension. In such a case the types of remedial exercises listed under the remediation section of Chapter 6 on comprehension development should prove helpful.

Substitutions and/or Partial Mispronunciations.   Substitutions usually differ from mispronunciations in that one complete (correct) word is substituted for another complete (correct) word such as *has* for *had*. This might also be termed a mispronunciation, i.e., mispronunciation of the last part of the word (*s* for *d*). We often classify the use of one "basic" sight word for another as a substitution. The use of one adjective for another is also classified as a substitution. On the other hand, the substitution of incorrect word endings or soft *c*'s and *g*'s for hard *c*'s and *g*'s or the wrong pronunciation of a letter or group of letters within a word is usually referred to as a partial mispronunciation.

A student who substitutes one word for another may be a careless reader or may lack word-recognition skills. The types of remediation for carelessness listed under omissions and insertions are also helpful in providing remediation for this problem. A student who mispronounces words because of poor word-recognition skills may need help with word recognition as listed in Chapter 4. The student who makes partial mispronunciations will, in most cases, also profit from work in word-analysis skills as listed in Chapter 5.

Substitutions or partial mispronunciations may result from the spoken dialect of the reader. In such a case the examiner must distinguish between "reading" errors and miscues that are a function of dialect rendering. A reading error would be a substitution or mispronunciation that results in a loss of meaning for the student. In some situations the reader may "translate" the written material into his or her own dialect. When this happens, the reader is not losing meaning. In fact, this process may reflect good comprehension on the part of the reader. For example, a black-dialect-speaking child may read the sentence, "Give me back my monkey," as, "Give me back my money." In this case the examiner should recognize that the reading error resulted in a loss of meaning. However, this same student may read the sentence, "Have they gone there?" as, "Is they gone there?" In this instance, although a substitution was made for the first word, the sentence was read in accord with the child's dialect and there was no meaning loss.

Patricia Cunningham (1976–1977) found that graduate students enrolled in reading courses at four state universities in different geographic regions corrected significantly more black-dialect-specific miscues than nondialect-specific miscues. Her research indicated that the teachers would correct 78 percent of the black-dialect-specific miscues and only 27 percent of the nondialect-specific miscues. Cunningham determined that ignorance rather than racism accounted for the differential correction rate and recommended that teacher training stress the meaning equivalence between standard English and black dialect, and the grammatical nature of black dialect. Larry Ditto (1974) found that teachers who were informed of the nature of linguistic differences perceived fewer dialect-related responses as reading errors than those who did not receive such information.

Teachers may unfairly penalize students for dialect rendering and place them in instructional materials that are too low. Therefore, we recommend that teachers who work with students who speak a nonstandard dialect become sufficiently familiar with the dialect to distinguish the errors that result in meaning loss from those that do not.

Gross Mispronunciations.   Gross mispronunciations refer to distorted pronunciation of words to the extent that the original pronunciation can hardly be recognized. Students who constantly make gross mispronunciations usually require help in any or all of the word-analysis skills but especially in phonics and structural analysis. They may also need help in the use of context clues. The student who grossly mispronounces words should be given a phonics test such as the one listed in Appendix A of this text and should be checked for knowledge of structural analysis and context clues. For some students it is also helpful to check on their vocabulary knowledge since students with a rich oral vocabulary are often hesitant to say grossly mispronounced or what, to them, would be nonsense words.

Inversions or Reversals.   Students sometimes make reversals of entire words (*was* for *saw* or *on* for *no*), partial reversals of words (*form* for *from*), or reversals or inversions of letters (*g* for *p, b* for *d, n* for *u*). Students make inversions or reversals for a number of reasons. For example, many younger students below the age of seven or eight tend to do so, but when they reach the age of seven and one-half to eight years, they almost magically seem to gain the perceptual maturity needed to overcome the problem. Some children simply never realize that English words are written from left to right and that English sentences are read the same way. Other more severely disabled readers seem to possess some sort of neurological dysfunction that causes the images of words and letters to reach the brain in a scrambled order.

It is commonly assumed that students who make persistent reversal errors will be either poor readers or nonreaders. Helen Kaufman and Phyllis Biren (1976–1977) undertook a study to determine whether children who made persistent spatial errors after age seven were poor readers, spellers, and writers. In their preliminary study the researchers found no correlation between the percentage of spatial errors and the students' reading grades. They did, however, find that a correlation may exist between spatial errors and poor spelling and handwriting.

Since it is difficult to determine why a certain student makes reversals or inversions of letters or words, the teacher will in most cases find it unprofitable to worry about the etiology of the problem but simply work on its remediation.

Bill Hardin and Bonnie Bernstein (1976) suggest that

The best way to deal with reversals is to initiate specific corrective exercises, emphasizing the following principles: habit formation; directionality (left to right); writing of letters; multi-modal approaches that give the child the advantages that go with seeing, saying and writing simultaneously; peer reinforcement. (p. 104)

Among their specific recommendations are the following:

1. Have the students trace letters or words while saying them to themselves.
2. Have the students copy words while pronouncing them.
3. Have the students write letters, then words, from dictation.
4. Work with a chalkboard.
5. Work with cursive writing as soon as interest develops.
6. Have the students count the number of *letters* in each word in a very short selection or the number of *words* in a short selection to develop a left-right habit pattern.
7. Have the students "read" short selections by naming the first letter of each word.
8. Emphasize left-right movement yourself when working at the chalkboard.
9. Have children work in pairs, dictating words, letters, or phrases to each other on a chalkboard, slate, or paper and correcting each others' errors. (This will involve children in proofreading their own work as well.)

Other remedial procedures that have often proven helpful are as follows:

1. Letting the student type words on a typewriter and see them take shape as they are typed.
2. Using a blue letter at the beginning of words and an orange letter at the end. These colors should, of course, be removed as soon as the word presenting difficulty has been mastered.
3. Using the nonvisual AKT approach as suggested in Chapter 9.
4. Using magnetic three-dimensional or felt or sandpaper letters and letting the student trace these as he or she says them.
5. Using the Fernald Approach as described in Chapter 9.
6. Uncovering words from left to right and reading them immediately after they are uncovered.
7. Explaining to the student that English words and sentences are to be read from left to right.

Throughout this book we have emphasized the importance of providing instruction that closely parallels the act of reading. The results of one study, which contradict this approach, merit mention. Jack McKiernan and Margo

Avakian (1980) reported on the effects of directional-awareness training on the remediation of receptive letter reversals. The researchers structured their study to maintain a distinction between directional awareness per se and letter recognition. The subjects received directional-awareness training *without* specific remediation on the letter-reversal problem. Using this approach, the researchers found significant improvement in the subjects' letter-reversal discrimination ability. The findings suggest that this may be one area where students' reading skills may be improved through training of a lower-level, nonreading skill.

Aid.   When a student lacks the ability to attack a strange word the student will usually ask for aid or simply wait until aid is given. Students who do this usually lack word-recognition and/or word-analysis skills and often lack self-confidence in their ability to attack strange words. When this happens, you should begin by testing the student's word-analysis skills as described in Chapter 5. In some cases you may find that the student is able to give various phonemes in isolation or may know certain rules but is unable to apply them in a practical situation. It would then be necessary to teach the student to *use* the word-attack skills. A strategy for doing this was presented in Chapter 5.

Repetitions.   Students may make repetitions because of poor word-recognition skills, poor word-analysis skills or because they have simply developed a bad habit. Before attempting to remediate the problem you should first determine the cause. This is, of course, necessary because the remediation given for repetitions caused from a bad habit would be considerably different from the remediation given for repetitions caused from poor word-recognition or word-analysis skills.

   If a student makes a number of repetitions in material written at the student's own grade level (for example fifth-grade level) you can usually determine the cause by having the student read material written at a grade level several grades below the point at which the student was making the repetitions. If the student continues to make as many repetitions in the material at a lower grade level, the problem is probably simply a bad habit. On the other hand, if the student makes considerably fewer repetitions in the easier material, then the student probably has a problem with word-recognition or word-analysis skills.

   Repetitions caused from a bad habit can be treated in much the same manner as described earlier for habitual omissions, i.e., having the student point to each word as it is read, having the student cover the material with a small card as it is read, having the student choral read with one or more good readers, or having the student read in conjunction with a tape recording. If it is determined that the problem of repetitions is not caused from a bad habit, then it would be necessary to determine whether the student is lacking in sight vocabulary (poor word-recognition skills) or whether the student is poor in word-analysis skills, or both. Procedures for making these decisions are described in Chapters 4 and 5.

It should be emphasized that many students make repetitions to correct errors that they discover as they continue to read. The errors are usually discovered from the context of the story line. Not all repetition errors are serious enough to interfere with comprehension or to seriously retard a student's reading ability. However, whether serious or not, they are usually indicative of some type of difficulty.

Disregard of Punctuation.   Students may disregard punctuation because they are simply not familiar with the meanings of various punctuation marks, because they lack comprehension, or because the reading becomes so difficult for them that they simply fail to attend to punctuation. One of the first steps in determining the cause of the problem is to give the student material to read that is written at a lower level of difficulty. If the student continues to disregard punctuation and appears to comprehend after being questioned concerning the material, the student may simply need to work on the meaning of various punctuation marks. If the student no longer disregards punctuation in the lower-level passage, then it can be assumed that the problem with punctuation is only symptomatic of a problem with comprehension or word recognition at higher levels. In this case it would be necessary to do further diagnosis to pinpoint the problem. However, punctuation per se could be ignored as a problem.

Pauses Before Words.   A student who pauses longer than is normal before words is usually either lacking in word-recognition or word-analysis skills or has formed a habit of word-by-word reading. If material written at a lower grade level can be located and given to a student who exhibits this problem, you can determine whether it is a habit of word-by-word reading or whether the student has a problem with word recognition and/or word analysis. If the student continues to pause before words in material written at a lower grade level, then you may wish to try putting some of the words that appear after the pauses onto flash cards. If the student seems to have almost instant recognition of the words on flash cards, you can feel fairly sure that the student has simply not learned to phrase properly or has developed the habit of word-by-word reading. In this case, activities such as drill with sight phrases using flash cards or a tachistoscope would probably prove helpful. The student may also profit from choral readings with one or more good readers or by reading in conjunction with a tape recording of a good reader. Simply discussing the problem with the student and letting the student hear his or her reading via a tape recording compared with that of a good reader will often prove successful.

If a student improves when given material at a lower level of difficulty, it can usually be assumed that the student was having problems with word recognition or word analysis (or both) at the higher reading level. If the student pauses before words and then says them correctly, it can usually be assumed that the student has good word-analysis skills but poor word-recognition skills or, in other words, does not possess a sight vocabulary equal to his or her grade level. In this case, activities such as those suggested in Chapter 4 would be appropriate. On the other hand, if the student pauses before words and is still unable to say them without aid, it can be assumed that the student needs help with word-analysis skills. In this case the type of remediation suggested in Chapter 5 would be helpful.

Analyses of Specific Passages

The coded passages that follow are typical of the oral reading errors made by many disabled readers. Following the passages are discussions of the types of errors and the kinds of remediation that would appear to be appropriate for these students. These are but brief samples of the oral reading behavior of these students. The analyses are presented to suggest some possibilities for remediation and to alert you to the value of diagnosing oral reading performance. You should not assume that a thorough diagnosis can be made from only one sample of oral reading.

John's First Airplane Ride

John's father and mother told him that he could go to/visit his grandmother and grandfather who\lived on a farm. They told him that he could ride on an airplane to go to visit them if he wanted to. John was very\thrilled and wanted to get started right away. When [Then] the time came to go John was very/excited. He packed his suitcase and got in the car long before his father was ready to take him to the airport.

When [Then] they got to the airport John saw many large airplanes waiting to leave and some that had just landed. When [Then] it came time to go John said goodbye to his father and mother. When [Then] he got on the airplane a lady told him to buckle his seatbelt. She told him that they would be leaving soon.

When [Then] the airplane started down the runway John was/afraid at first. But when they were in the air he was no longer afraid. The lady gave John something to drink and a sandwich to eat. John//enjoyed the airplane ride so much that he was sorry when it was over.

After studying the types of errors made by the student on the student's passage we are able to make certain assumptions about his reading. Some of these are as follows.

There were a number of words that were not in this student's sight vocabulary since he did not recognize them instantly as indicated by the pauses
before these words (*visit, lived, thrilled, excited, afraid,* and *enjoyed*). However, it is evident that he does possess good word-analysis skills since he was
able to read the words (in most cases) after pausing briefly. He made repetitions a number of times before words at which he had paused. He may have
been doing this to attempt to get partial clues from the context but may have
also done it simply to stall for time while he analyzed the word (knowing that
the teacher would be likely to tell him if he did not get the word in a reasonable amount of time). He seemed to have difficulty with the word *when,*
which he constantly called *then.* It should be noted, however, that when this
word appeared in a context that required it to be used instead of *then,* he
usually went back and corrected it, making a repetition to do so.

Knowing these things about this student's reading ability would provide
you with some valuable information for instruction, such as the following:

1. He needs to develop a larger sight vocabulary, which could best be done
   through wide reading. You know that a word becomes a permanent
   "sight word," or in other words is instantly recognized, after the student has encountered it from at least twenty up to as many as 140 times.
   Since he is, in most cases, able to get unknown words right because of
   his good use of word-analysis skills, it would be safe to assume that he
   would be saying these unknown words correctly and thus improve his
   word-recognition ability.
2. As just stated, he makes good use of word-analysis skills, including use
   of context; therefore, he would probably need very little more diagnosis
   or remediation in this area.
3. He should be given help with the word *when* so that he does not substitute it for *then.*
4. Although he has made a number of repetitions, it is evident that he did
   so only to use the context on an unknown word or to correct a word that
   was miscalled (in this case, *then* for *when*). For this reason it would
   probably not be necessary to work on the repetitions as errors; i.e., they
   are only symptomatic of other problems. And, when the other problems
   were cured, he would probably stop making repetitions automatically.
5. Although he did not know the words *visit* and *afraid* the first time he
   read them, he did know them when they were encountered the second
   time. Although most students need many repetitions of a word before it
   becomes a permanent sight word, it is evident that he learns new words
   very easily and at least temporarily retains them.
6. After pausing before *thrilled* he then said it with the accent on the
   wrong part of the word. If *thrilled* was in his listening-speaking vocabulary, he would have probably gotten it correct from having it in a usable
   context and by saying it correct except for improper accent. Therefore,

he would need to be given help with the meaning of this word. This might also indicate a need, depending on his grade level for more vocabulary (word meaning) development. A word-meaning test or vocabulary test such as the "Oral Vocabulary" subtest of the *Gates-McKillop Reading Diagnostic Test* would be useful in helping the examiner decide whether his oral vocabulary was equal to his grade level.

(Tuff) ~~was~~ is a big (brown) bear. He ~~lived in~~ lives on a big ~~park~~ p... . He ~~liked~~ likes to eat (honey) best of all. He also ~~liked~~ likes to eat bread. breakfast?

   Some people were in the park having a ~~picnic~~ party. They were ~~sitting by~~ setting on a big table. Tuff went to the ~~picnic~~ party too. (When) the (people) p... saw him they were (afraid.) a... They all jumped up and ran ~~away~~ around. ~~Then~~ The bear ate all of ~~their~~ the food.

This passage is drawn from the Ekwall Reading Inventory and is written at the first-grade level. The student who read it was clearly reading at the frustration level. Interestingly, she did quite well on the preprimer-level selection. Teachers should remember that the jump from a preprimer level to a first-grade level is much greater than the jump from say a fifth-grade level to a sixth-grade level.

   An examination of this passage reveals that a great deal of information can be gathered from an analysis of a student's oral reading, especially when the material is written at the student's frustration level. Obviously, the diagnostician must exercise caution and not ask the student to read numerous paragraphs at the frustration level. However, unless the student makes a significant number of errors or miscues, you will not have sufficient information on which to form an analysis.

   Some of the assumptions you can make about this student's reading are as follows:

   A number of basic sight words and other common words are not known, including *was, brown, lived, in, liked, by, when, away, then,* and *their.* These and others can be confirmed by the administration of a basic sight vocabulary test as described in Chapter 4. Fortunately, some basic sight words are known, and this may provide a foundation for future sight-word learning. Phonics skills also appear to be very weak, as this child was unable to unlock unknown words. On the other hand, there is evidence that this child has mastered the sound-symbol associations for most or all of the beginning single consonants. For example, even though this student was unable to correctly pronounce *park, bread,* and *picnic,* she did get the correct beginning sounds on these words. A thorough assessment of phonics skills as described in Chapter 5 would be in order. This student appears to have a good ability to use context clues. This is revealed by the fact that all substitutions are words that make some sense in the context of the passage, e.g., *is* for *was, lives on* for *lived in, likes* for *liked, breakfast* for *bread,* etc. This student most certainly lacks structural-analysis skills. This, of course, is to be expected of a student who struggles to read at such a low level.

On the basis of this one oral reading passage and presumably supported by additional testing of basic sight vocabulary and phonics skills, you can expect that instruction will be required in the following areas:

1. She needs to develop a larger basic sight vocabulary. Unfortunately, her low reading level will preclude wide reading as a vehicle for this improvement, except for carefully chosen materials (at the preprimer level) and perhaps language-experience stories. The specific procedures outlined in Chapter 4 should prove effective for increasing this student's instant recognition of basic sight words.
2. She needs to improve her phonics ability and learn how to attack unknown words. Procedures for doing this are outlined in Chapter 5.
3. Her ability to use context clues is a relative strength for this child. It is probable that this skill, when combined with word recognition and phonics skills, will enable this student to significantly improve in her reading ability.

Miscue Analysis

Kenneth Goodman (1969) and Yetta Goodman and Carolyn Burke (1972) have developed procedures for analyzing students' oral reading behavior based on Kenneth Goodman's psycholinguistic model of reading. These authors refer to students' errors as "miscues," based on the assumption that oral reading behavior arises from the student's underlying language competence.

Goodman and Burke's *Reading Miscue Inventory* is intended for use by teachers. The administration of this inventory is a time-consuming and complicated task. The examiner asks the student to read a complete passage that has not been previously seen by the student and that is written one grade level above the material that the student reads in class. The examiner may not aid the student in pronouncing unfamiliar words. After the passage is read, the student is required to retell the story. The examiner asks only general questions to guide the student's retelling. After careful analysis, the examiner is presumably able to determine the reading strategies employed by the student.

In our experience teachers have not found the *Reading Miscue Inventory* to be either practical or helpful in their work with remedial students. Some teachers do find, however, that this approach helps them to better understand the reading process. Eugene Jongsma (1978) found that teachers who were trained in miscue analysis became more aware of students' reading strengths as well as weaknesses.

George Spache (1981) summarized the criticisms of the *Reading Miscue Inventory* as follows:

> Reviewers of the Reading Miscue Inventory point out that the analysis of oral reading errors as suggested by its authors has not been shown to be related to the reading level for instruction. Much of the scoring of miscues is completely subjective, and there are no data regarding the expected frequency of these miscues at any age or grade level. Even the evaluation of the child's recall of the story under guiding or leading questions is completely subjective. The Inventory lacks standardized directions and reading selections, criteria for interpreting diagnostic patterns, norms for interpreting scores, reliability or validity data, and evidence for its prescribed reading strategies. (p. 142)

After a critical review of the research, Karen Wixson (1979) summarized both the strengths and weaknesses of miscue analysis:

> Recent promotion of miscue analysis has served the field of reading well. The popularization of miscue analysis has succeeded in bringing about an awareness of reading as a language process, and in sensitizing people to the necessity for a method of evaluation which will accurately reflect this process in operation. However, the exact nature of the relationship between oral reading errors, as analyzed by standard miscue analysis procedures, and the reading process remains unclear. Further, it is unknown whether miscue analysis succeeds in identifying the critical features of readers' oral reading performance which reveal their relative proficiency with the reading process. Accordingly, the current use of miscue analysis procedures as a basis for evaluation and planning in both research and instruction appears at best to be premature. (p. 172)

THE CLOZE PROCEDURE

The cloze procedure is another technique that is useful for placing students in graded materials or for selecting materials to meet the needs of a particular group of students. The procedure consists of deleting every nth word and replacing it with a blank line. Students are to then read the material and attempt to fill in the blanks using the correct word according to the proper context of the sentence. The percentages of correct answers are then calculated, and from these percentages free or independent, instructional and frustration reading levels are derived.

John Bormuth (1967, 1968) researched the use of the cloze procedure to derive the percentage of correct answers equivalent to the free or independent, instructional and frustration reading levels and to derive information on reliability. His studies were later duplicated and validated by Earl Rankin and Joseph Culhane (1969). Rankin and Culhane stated, "The results of this replication of two previous studies tend to corroborate the validity of the comparable cloze and multiple-choice percentage scores found by Bormuth. . . ." (p. 197) Rankin and Culhane also studied the validity of the cloze procedure and compared its use to that of multiple-choice tests.

> These substantial correlations indicate that the cloze procedure is a highly valid measure of reading comprehension. The average validity coefficient was .68. Since the multiple-choice tests took several weeks to construct, the cloze tests are preferable for measuring comprehension or readability, and they are measuring substantially the same thing. (p. 196)

Jones and Pikulski (1974) studied the use of the cloze procedures with a group of sixth-grade students. They pointed out the fact that their study concerned sixth graders only.

> Given this limitation, the data suggested that the cloze test gave a considerably more accurate reading level placement than did the standardized test. If the cloze test can approximate reading levels on an informal reading inventory as much as 70 to 80 percent of the time, its relatively brief administration time recommends its use to the classroom teacher. Not only does cloze procedure appear to provide a reasonably valid determiner of instructional reading level, but its very ease of construction and administration makes it a practical tool for teachers who have had no special training in test administration. (p. 437)

Developing, Administering, and Scoring Cloze Passages

In constructing cloze passages you could omit every third, fifth, tenth, etc., word. However, most of the research that has been done is based on the deletion of every fifth word. Blank lines of equal length are then used to replace each word that has been deleted. It should also be stressed that the commonly used percentages for determining students' free or independent, instructional and frustration reading levels are based on the deletion of every fifth word. If every eighth or tenth word were deleted, these commonly used percentages would not apply.

Passages may vary in length depending on the grade level of the students; however, for students of age levels equivalent to third- or fourth-grade level, or above, passages of about 250 words are often used. The entire first and last sentences are usually left intact. If passages of 250 words plus intact first and last sentences are used and if every fifth word is omitted, there would be fifty blanks, and every blank or answer would be equivalent to two percentage points.

Cloze passages may be administered in a group situation similar to the procedure with standardized reading tests. However, in administering cloze passages there are usually no specific time limits for completion of the work.

For passages in which every fifth word has been deleted the percentages of the various reading levels are as follows:

Free or independent level = 58 to 100 percent
Instructional level = 44 through 57 percent
Frustration level = 43 percent or below

In scoring the passages only the exact word omitted is usually counted as correct; i.e., synonyms are not counted as being correct. Bormuth's research has shown that the overall percentages change very little regardless of whether synonyms are counted as correct or incorrect. Furthermore, if words other than the exact word omitted were counted, it would make the passages much more difficult to score. That is, what one teacher might consider as an adequate answer another teacher may not. Thus you would tend to lose interscorer reliability. In scoring cloze passages, however, students are not usually penalized for incorrect spelling as long as there is little or no doubt about which word was meant to be used.

A plastic overlay such as an overhead projector transparency can be made of each cloze passage with the correct answers appearing on the plastic overlay. When this is superimposed on the student's copy you can readily check the number of right and wrong answers. These can, in turn, be converted to percentages.

Using the Cloze Procedure to Place Students in Graded Materials[3]

Often a teacher receives a new student and wishes to place the student in one of several different books that vary in difficulty or grade level. As an example, look at the case of a fifth-grade teacher. She teaches in a school where there are several sections of fifth graders but all are simply grouped heterogeneously so that each year she can expect to receive students reading from perhaps the first- or second-grade level through the sixth- or seventh-grade level. She has a number of basal textbooks available at various levels, but each time she receives a new student she is faced with the problem of which book to assign so that the student will be reading at his or her instructional level. The steps she could take to effectively use the cloze procedure to

[3]The explanation given in this section is based on Bormuth, John R. "The Cloze Readability Procedure," *Readability—1968*. Prepared by a committee of the National Conference on Research in English, National Council of Teachers of English.

help her develop testing materials for the various levels of books and then place students accordingly would be as follows:

1. Select a number of passages from various parts of each book (from six to twelve passages depending on the size of the book). Make sure each passage begins a new paragraph and is about 250 words in length.
2. Give the tests to a group of students (twenty-five to thirty) from classes in which the texts will commonly be used.
3. Determine the percentage of correct answers for each student on each passage. An example illustrating this is shown in Table 11–6. For illustrative purposes, however, only ten students have been shown as taking the cloze tests concerning each of eleven passages from a particular book. The mean score for each passage is then calculated and the mean of the mean scores is determined. The mean of the means is determined by adding all of the means and dividing by the number of means or the number of passages (in this case eleven).

$$\frac{65.4 + 48.1 + 74.0 + 39.8 + 60.4 + 42.4 + 42.4 + 25.6 + 41.2 + 73.0 + 52.0}{11} = 51.3$$

TABLE 11–6. Percentage Scores Made on Eleven Passages from a Book by Each of Ten Students.

	1	2	3	4	5	6	7	8	9	10	11
Don	66	60	72	28	62	44	28	54	52	64	42
Dwight	72	52	76	32	38	62	48	26	38	72	52
Denise	56	38	64	42	42	38	52	14	30	64	74
Syril	42	20	86	46	74	28	38	22	28	88	44
Ed	74	42	84	42	56	22	42	18	50	78	50
Rick	76	48	72	48	72	74	54	14	52	86	62
Judy	72	62	64	38	58	64	46	26	36	56	58
Jack	58	73	58	52	64	28	38	28	34	72	34
Cindy	64	38	82	38	62	42	40	26	42	84	44
Dennis	74	48	82	32	76	22	38	28	50	66	60
Totals	654	481	740	398	604	424	424	256	412	730	520

Mean score for each passage
(Total ÷ 10)   65.4   48.1   74.0   39.8   60.4   42.4   42.4   25.6   41.2   73.0   52.0

4. Select the passage score that is closest to the mean of the means. In this case the teacher would select passage number 11 since its mean score is 52.0 and the mean of the means is 51.3. In other words this passage is most representative of the book as a whole.

5. The procedure described above would be followed for each textbook that the teacher is likely to use. These cloze passages (one from each text) would then be duplicated and compiled into booklets. When a new student or group of students enters the teacher's room, each would be given a test booklet containing the cloze passages. When a student's score falls between 44 to 57 percent on one of these passages it should be at the instructional level. If it is above 57 percent, it should be at the free or independent level, and if it falls below 44 percent it would be at the frustration level.

The reliability of the procedure described above would depend on the following three factors:

1. Test length—Longer tests will be more reliable but will take longer to correct.

2. Number of passages used—If a larger number of passages are taken from each book, the one chosen is more likely to be representative of the book as a whole.

3. Variance in difficulty from page to page—Some materials vary unevenly in difficulty as they proceed. This is especially true of many textbooks other than basal readers.

Using the Cloze Procedure to Select Materials to Meet the Needs of the Students

In many states a state textbook committee selects approximately three to five basal textbooks from the many possible choices. These books may then be purchased using state funds. At this point, however, each school district often must select one textbook from the choice of three to five that best meets the needs of the students. In other instances a teacher may be given a choice of one or more of a number of books that best meet the needs of his or her students. Adequacy of teacher's manuals, supporting services and materials, and the format of the material itself are all important considerations in making such a choice. The most important factor, however, is whether the students with whom the material will be used can read the material. The following steps can be used to make this decision:

1. Select a number of random passages from each book or set of material. The same length of passages as described earlier can be used.

2. Select a random sample of the students with whom the book will be used.

3. Determine the mean of each passage from each set of materials or book.
4. Then determine the mean of the means from each set of materials or book as described earlier.
5. Any materials or books that fall within the range of 44 through 57 percent would be appropriate for use at the students' instructional level. Materials at 58 percent or above would be appropriate for use at the students' free or independent level, and materials below 44 percent would be inappropriate since they would be likely to be at students' frustration reading level.

In using the cloze procedure you should also exercise a certain amount of teacher judgment when making decisions concerning the difficulty of materials. For example, if a student is highly interested in a subject, or if the student has the ability to persevere, it would be permissible to consider material just below the 57 percent level as appropriate for the student to read independently. This would be especially true if several of the student's errors were correct synonyms.

The analysis of errors on the cloze procedure can also provide the teacher with useful information on the reading ability of the student. Although no specific procedures have been developed at this time, an informal survey of a student's answers will give practical information concerning the student's ability to read and write. For example a great deal of information can be derived about the student's ability to spell and about the student's overall comprehension and knowledge of the vocabulary in the passages by noting whether substitutions for the original words are meaningful synonyms or whether they are completely out of context. You can also tell whether the student has been able to remember details that were given earlier in the passage by noting whether the student uses these to answer questions later in the passage.

The cloze procedure has also been studied to determine its effectiveness as a teaching device. An excellent review of the cloze procedure research in this area was done by Eugene Jongsma (1971). Jongsma indicates that most teachers who simply used the cloze procedure as a teaching device without any follow-up activities or discussion found it of little or no value in "teaching" comprehension. However, he did find several studies in which students' comprehension was improved when students discussed their answers on cloze passages, i.e., why one answer was chosen over another or in the process of filling in the blanks why one blank was chosen over another.

SUMMARY

Information concerning the reading level and reading disabilities of individual students cannot be accurately derived using most group tests. For this reason teachers should learn to administer, score, and interpret informal reading inventories. Informal reading inventories can be useful in helping teachers determine students' free or independent, instructional, and frustration reading levels. The criteria used in scoring informal reading inventories are also useful in helping teachers find the "proper fit" between students and reading materials. And, by coding a student's oral reading errors teachers can often gain considerable insight into that particular student's reading disability.

The use of the cloze procedure is popular among specialists. It is valuable in determining students' free or independent, instructional, and frustration reading levels. It is also valuable for use in selecting materials to meet the needs of a particular group of students or in placing a student at the proper level in a set of graded materials. The cloze procedure has been well researched and has an advantage over informal reading inventories in that it can be administered as a group test.

REFERENCES

Betts, Emmett A. *Foundations of Reading Instruction.* New York: American Book Co., 1946.

Bormuth, John R. "Comparable Cloze and Multiple-Choice Comprehension Test Scores," *Journal of Reading.* Vol. 10, (February, 1967), 291–299.

Bormuth, John R. "Cloze Test Reliability: Criterion Reference Scores," *Journal of Educational Measurement.* Vol. 5, (Fall, 1968), 189–196.

Cunningham, Patricia M. "Teachers' Correction Responses to Black-Dialect Miscues Which Are Non-Meaning-Changing," *Reading Research Quarterly.* Vol. 12, (1976–1977), 637–653.

David, Everett E., and Ekwall, Eldon E. "Mode of Perception and Frustration in Reading," *Journal of Learning Disabilities.* Vol. 9, (August–September, 1976), 448–454.

Ditto, Larry D. "The Effects of Language Characteristics in Oral Reading," Doctoral dissertation, Michigan State University, 1974.

Duffelmeyer, Frederick A. "The Passage Independence of Factual and Inferential Questions," *Journal of Reading.* Vol. 23, (November, 1980), 131–134.

Ekwall, Eldon E. "Should Repetitions Be Counted as Errors," *Reading Teacher.* Vol. 27, (January, 1974), 365–367.

Ekwall, Eldon E., and Solis, Judy English. "Use of the Polygraph to Determine Elementary School Students' Frustration Reading Level," Final Report—U.S. Department of Health, Education, and Welfare, Project No. 0G078, 1971.

Ekwall, Eldon E.; Solis, Judy English; and Solis, Enrique, Jr. "Investigating Informal Reading Inventory Scoring Criteria," *Elementary English.* Vol. 50, (February, 1973), 271–274.

Goodman, Kenneth S. "Analyses of Reading Miscues: Applied Psycholinguistics," *Reading Research Quarterly.* Vol. 5, (Fall, 1969), 9–30.

Goodman, Yetta M., and Burke, Carolyn L. *Reading Miscue Inventory.* New York: Macmillan, 1972.

Guszak, Frank J. "Dilemmas in Informal Reading Assessments," *Elementary English.* Vol. 47, (May, 1970), 666–670.

Hardin, Bill, and Bernstein, Bonnie. "What about Reversals?" *Teacher.* Vol. 94, (October, 1976), 104, 108.

Johnson, Marjorie S., and Kress, Roy A. *Informal Reading Inventories.* Newark, Del.: International Reading Association, 1965.

Jones, Margaret B., and Pikulski, Edna C. "Cloze for the Classroom," *Reading Teacher.* Vol. 17, (March, 1974), 432–438.

Jongsma, Eugene A. *The Cloze Procedure as a Teaching Technique.* Newark, Del.: ERIC/CRIER and the International Reading Association, 1971.

Jongsma, Eugene A. "The Effect of Training in Miscue Analysis on Teacher's Perceptions of Oral Reading Behaviors," *Reading World.* Vol. 18, (October, 1978), 85–90.

Jongsma, Kathleen S., and Jongsma, Eugene A. "Test Review: Commercial Informal Reading Inventories," *Reading Teacher.* Vol. 34, (March, 1981), 697–705.

Kaufman, Helen S., and Biren, Phyllis L. "Persistent Reversers: Poor Readers, Writers, Spellers?" *Academic Therapy.* Vol. 12, (Winter, 1976–1977), 209–217.

McKiernan, Jack, and Avakian, Margo. "Directional Awareness Training: Remediation of Receptive Letter Reversals," *Academic Therapy.* Vol. 16, (November, 1980), 193–198.

Oliver, Jo Ellen, and Arnold, Richard D. "Comparing a Standardized Test, an Informal Reading Inventory and Teacher Judgment on Third Grade Reading," *Reading Improvement.* Vol. 15, (Spring, 1979), 56–59.

Pehrsson, Robert S. U. "How Much of a Helper Is Mr. Gelper," *Reading Teacher.* Vol. 17, (May, 1974), 617–621.

Rankin, Earl F., and Culhane, Joseph W. "Comparable Cloze and Multiple Choice Comprehension Scores," *Journal of Reading.* Vol. 13, (December, 1969), 193–198.

Spache, George D. *Diagnosing and Correcting Reading Disabilities.* 2nd ed., Boston: Allyn and Bacon, 1981.

Steirnagle, Edwa. From an address delivered to the El Paso County Council of the International Reading Association, April, 1974.

Valmont, William J. "Creating Questions for Informal Reading Inventories," *Reading Teacher.* Vol. 25, (March, 1972), 509–512.

Wixson, Karen L. "Miscue Analysis: A Critical Review," *Journal of Reading Behavior.* Vol. 11, (Summer, 1979), 163–175.

12

Diagnosis and Remediation
Through the Use of Interviews

The first part of this chapter contains a discussion of the interview as a source of information from parents and students. Specific techniques are then discussed, including the pros and cons of using a checklist to guide or structure the interview. A rather good parent interview and a rather good student interview are then illustrated and discussed in terms of technique and useful information derived. A rather poor student interview is then presented that illustrates some common errors to be avoided.

THE INTERVIEW AS A SOURCE OF INFORMATION

Interviews can be an important part of the diagnostic remedial process in some cases, especially in a clinical setting or in cases where it is evident that more information needs to be obtained concerning the home environment. Some types of information can often be obtained from an interview that will seldom become available elsewhere. It should be emphasized, however, that interviews are often time consuming, and unless the remedial reading teacher or reading clinician believes that further useful information will be revealed through the use of the interview then, in many cases, this step in the diagnostic process should simply be eliminated.

In some cases, however, a remark by the student or information gained from an initial application form (see Chapter 15) will indicate that information can be gained from parents or a guardian that would be of considerable value in working with a student. Although you will not be likely to interview the parents of every student or hold a lengthy interview with each disabled reader, there is still need for the remedial reading teacher or reading clinician to develop the ability to skillfully conduct an interview. Some types of information that can be derived from an initial parent interview that may or may not be available elsewhere are described as follows.

Information Gained from Parent Interviews

Parental Views of Student's Problems.   After having lived with a student for a number of years parents are in a unique situation to have gathered a great deal of information about a student's problems. This is especially true if the parents have other children who are not disabled readers so that they are able to make accurate comparisons. Parents are often able to accurately describe a student's problems, although they may not necessarily refer to them using the same terminology that the remedial reading teacher might use.

It is also important to determine whether parents understand the severity of the problem or whether they are overly concerned to the point of constantly badgering the student. On the other hand, they may lack the necessary understanding of the problem so that they may fail to provide a proper study environment, cooperation in library activities, motivation for improvement, etc.

One of the coauthors recently spent several hours one afternoon diagnosing the reading problems of a beginning second-grade student. This student was so hyperactive that it was nearly impossible to do the testing in a one-to-one situation. His teacher had told his mother that he "jumped around a lot and would not sit still." The mother, however, had no other children with which to compare the child and consequently believed that the teacher was overstating the seriousness of the problem. The child was referred to a pediatrician who prescribed medication to calm him down. Following this the child's performance immediately improved. The important point, however, was that through the interview the author could obtain the mother's views about the condition of the child and then provide immediate feedback in terms of suggestions for remediation of the child's problems.

Emotional Climate of the Home.   A great deal of information can be gained from parents about the emotional climate of the home by a skilled interviewer. This might include information on parental discord or sibling discord or rivalry that may be harmful to the well-being of the student.

Health Factors.   Although some information can be gained about a student's health from forms or applications, it is often desirable to elaborate on certain aspects of this information through the use of the interview. For example, we often find that in discussing eye examinations a parent is often led to believe that a student has had a thorough eye examination at his or her school when in reality all the student may have had was a rough screening test for far-point vision using the Snellen chart. Or, what may appear on a form to have been a minor ear infection during early childhood may, in fact, have been a chronic infection that has constantly contributed to a student's inability to use phonics because of inadequate auditory discrimination.

It is often difficult for a parent who is untrained in both health education and reading education to realize the important relationships that may exist between the two. For this reason a parent interview should usually cover various facets of a student's health in terms of those factors that contribute to reading retardation.

Reading Material Available at Home. Most homes contain some books, magazines, newspapers, etc., available for some members of the family to read. Many family libraries, in fact, contain fairly large quantities of books that parents may tend to perceive as good reading material for their children. In a few cases this may be true, but in most cases very little of the reading material available in the home library is of an appropriate nature for a disabled reader. Through the use of interviews the remedial reading teacher can thoroughly discuss the kinds of materials available in terms of reading level and interest and can advise parents of materials that may be more appropriate for disabled readers.

Library Habits and Time Spent in Reading. Through the use of interviews the remedial reading teacher can also obtain a much deeper insight into the actual amount of time a student spends reading, as well as the student's library habits. If a student is asked how much time is spent reading, the answer is quite likely to be somewhat meaningless since the student has little basis for "a lot" or "a little" in terms of comparison with other students. Furthermore, until students reach the age of eleven or twelve, they tend to have little or no accurate perception of time. Parents can, however, provide much more accurate information on such matters. Parents can also provide accurate information on students' use of the school and city library. During the interview the teacher can also provide helpful information on how parents can select books to meet the reading levels of their children.

Study Habits and Study Environment. The interview also provides an excellent opportunity to derive information concerning study habits and the study environment of a student. For example, questions such as, "Is a specific *amount* of time set aside each evening for study?" "Is a specific *time* set aside each evening for study?" "Does the student have a room of his or her own, or is it shared with another member of the family?" often reveal a great deal of useful information. Accurate information of this nature is difficult to derive from students because of their inadequate perception of time. It is also often difficult to derive from a parent through the use of forms or applications without further questioning.

Parental Expectation. Parental expectation, of course, varies a great deal depending on such factors as the educational level of the parents, the socioeconomic level of the parents, and to some extent the religious preference of the parents. Only through the use of the interview can the remedial reading teacher begin to determine whether the expectations a parent holds for a student are realistic in terms of that student's potential and achievement. The interview also provides an opportunity for the remedial reading teacher to counsel parents in terms of realistic expectations for the student in relationship to tests that have been administered for reading level and reading potential as indicated by IQ or, better yet, as measured by ability to learn reading-related tasks.

Social Adjustment. It would be difficult to derive information on a student's social adjustment as easily as it can be obtained from parent interviews by using such questions as, "Tell me about Erica's friends." "Tell me about how she gets along with her friends." "Does she have a lot of friends or does she prefer to play with one or two friends or play alone?" "Does she make friends easily?" or "Do other students seem to notice that she has a reading problem?" Information of this nature can be especially helpful if the parents have other children with which to compare the social adjustment of a specific child.

Independence and Self-Concept. The parent interview is also excellent for deriving information about the independent work habits and self-concept of a student. Questions that often elicit such information are those such as, "Can Jim seem to do work on his own or does he need someone to constantly urge him on?" Or, an open-ended statement that may tend to draw out the same or more information might be, "Tell me about Jim's work habits." Information can also be derived about a student's self-concept that may be much more difficult to obtain from the student by asking questions such as, "How does Jim feel about his reading?" "How does Jim feel about himself?" or more specifically, "What do you think about Jim's self-concept?"

Duties at Home. Students who have certain duties to perform at home are often more likely to be inclined to independently carry out work on school assignments. These duties may include such things as emptying the garbage, mowing the lawn, and washing and/or drying the dishes. Through the parent interview, information can be derived on how many of these duties a student is expected to perform as well as how well the student does those that are assigned. The parent interview is also a good opportunity to suggest the need for such duties to build independent work habits in the student.

Sleep Habits. A partial reason for the poor performance of many students is that they do not get the needed amount of sleep. Reading clinicians often find that information that appears on applications and forms filled out by parents is somewhat inaccurate. For example, a form to be filled out by parents may ask the question, "What time does the student normally go to bed?" Although a parent, in all honesty, may answer "9:00 PM," a careful interview will often reveal that this is, in reality, the time when parents would *like* the student to go to bed. In reality, the student may often be allowed to stay up much later to watch television programs, or the family may socialize a great deal, keeping the student up much later than the "desired" bedtime.

Successful Practices with the Student.   An interview with a student's parents is also often helpful in uncovering methods that the parents find successful in getting the best performance from the student. This might be a simple, "Please do this for me," to a small reward for successful completion of a task. A question that often elicits this information is to simply ask, "What do you find is successful in getting Dan to do things you want him to do?"

Previous Tutoring and Results.   Many students who come to reading clinics or to a remedial reading classroom have previously been tutored. The parent interview presents an excellent opportunity for the remedial reading teacher to discover the length, and to some extent, the success of past tutoring. For example, many parents will have some knowledge of the types and success of activities carried out in the past. Others may have records or examples of what has been taught that, in some cases, may provide helpful information on the types of materials and activities to use or to avoid in future work with the student.

Information Gained from Student Interviews

Information can also be gained through an initial interview with students that may be difficult to gain in other ways. Some examples of the kinds of useful information that may be derived from student interviews are as follows.

Self-Concept.   Studies quoted in Chapter 7 have shown the importance of a positive self-concept for success in reading. And, although inventories are available for measuring self-concept, a great deal can often be learned through an interview about how a student feels and about his or her ability to read. Statements or questions that often elicit this type of information are those such as, "Tell me about yourself," or, "How do you feel about yourself when you read?"

The Student's Perception of the Reading Problem.   Since it is difficult to provide help for someone with a problem who does not recognize that the problem exists, it is often beneficial to use questions such as, "How do you feel about your reading?" or, "Tell me about your reading," or even, "Do you think you have a problem with reading?" Many disabled readers, of course, recognize their problems immediately; however, a rather large percentage are either hesitant to admit to having a reading problem or simply do not recognize the fact that they are disabled readers. A student who does not admit to having a reading problem or who does not recognize the problem will often need to be diplomatically shown that, compared to other students of his or her age-grade level, the student does have a problem. This is an essential part of the eight-step counseling procedure described in Chapter 7.

Past Experiences in Reading. The interview also provides an opportunity to question students concerning their past experiences in reading. For example, students sometimes perceive themselves as having read a great deal when further questioning may reveal that, in reality, they have read almost nothing at all on their own. To the disabled reader, simply looking at pictures in magazines or looking at comic books may actually be perceived as reading. When this is the case, inaccurate answers will be given on inventories dealing with such questions. During an interview, however, the interviewer can readily tell whether the student really reads by asking such questions as, "Do you remember the name of the last book you read?" "Tell me about it," or, "Can you tell me the names of some books you have read this year?" One very common characteristic of severely disabled readers is that they have often really never read a book on their own.

Attitudes about Reading. The initial student interview also provides an excellent opportunity for the remedial reading teacher to learn more about student attitudes about reading, i.e., Does the student like to read? Has he or she had some extremely bad experiences with reading in the past? Questions that may be helpful in eliciting this type of information are those such as, "What do you think about reading?" "What are the good things you remember about reading?" "What are the bad or unpleasant things you remember about reading?" and, "Would you like to become a better reader?"

Reading Interests. Since the initial interview with a student would normally come during the first time you had a chance to meet alone, it is a good time to derive information on the student's interests and hobbies. In this way you will be able to help the student find materials to read that should be interesting. It should also be helpful in establishing initial rapport. The initial student interview can also provide information about interests in terms of future ambitions, vocational plans, etc., all of which can work to your advantage in establishing motivation for reading.

Reading Environment. It is a well-known fact that students tend to copy their peers' and parents' habits. The initial student interview usually provides an excellent opportunity for the remedial reading teacher to learn about the student's reading environment, i.e., Does the student have a quiet place to read at home? Does the student see various members of the family read a great deal? and, Does he or she generally come from an environment where reading is encouraged and rewarded?

Instructional Techniques and Materials That Have Been Used.   For most disabled readers who have experienced failure with a particular program or technique it is generally a good practice to change the technique as well as the materials. For example, we do not usually teach disabled readers using a hardbound basal reader since it might very well be negatively perceived. During the initial interview, the remedial reading teacher can often discover which materials have been previously used with the student. Although the student is not likely to remember the publisher of the materials, or in many cases the name of a particular book, the student is likely to remember the names of various characters in basal reader series he or she has used. In the El Paso Reading Center we use a sheet that lists the names of many of the characters in the most commonly used basal reading series. The interviewer can then simply ask questions such as, "Did you ever use a book about a little black dog named Tag?" or, "Did you use a book about Dot and Jim?" If the student answers yes to such a question, it is then easy to identify the type of program he or she has used in the past. In many cases the instructional program will also have generally utilized a particular technique. In order to make use of this type of information the teacher must be somewhat familiar with the most commonly used basal reading series.

If information on technique alone is desired, it can usually be obtained by using such questions as, "How did your teacher teach you words?" or, "What did your tutor do to teach you to sound out words?" Although in some cases answers to such questions may be rather vague, further questioning will usually clarify techniques that have been somewhat successful and unsuccessful in the past.

As in the case of parent interviews, the student interview can also provide useful information on such things as the amount of television the student watches each week, the student's duties at home, the time the student goes to bed, etc.

INTERVIEW TECHNIQUES

An interview can often be highly successful, or on the other hand, can be of little value depending on the skill of the interviewer. The skills needed for successful interviewing can quite easily be learned with a little experience and the mastery of a few important techniques. Some of the techniques that tend to help make interviews successful are as follows.

Make the Interviewee Comfortable

Whether it be an initial interview with a student or a parent, it is important to attempt to make the person being interviewed as comfortable as possible. Skilled counselors are usually masters at doing this from having had a great deal of practice.

In interviewing parents one of the best ways to make them feel comfortable is to get right down to business as soon as possible. They have usually come to the interview because they are concerned about their son's or daughter's reading disability. After an initial greeting and seating them in a comfortable chair, a statement such as, "Tell me about Don's reading" is often sufficient to break the ice and get them started talking.

In interviewing students the same situation exists. In this case, however, you may wish to simply say, "Tell me a little something about yourself." This leaves the student free to talk about anything he or she would like to. Sometimes, however, such a broad question is too open-ended for a student who may reply, "Like what?" In this case you may wish to prompt the student further by saying something such as, "Well, tell me about some of your hobbies, your pets, or what you like to do."

It also works well to seat the student or parent to the side of your desk facing you rather than behind it so that the desk does not form a barrier between the two of you.

Use Open-Ended Questions

Any experienced college professor or elementary or secondary school teacher knows that it is easy to set the tone of a class in the first few minutes. For example, if a professor begins the class with a lecture and then suddenly tries to hold an open discussion, the professor is likely to get little or no response for the first few minutes after the lecture session. The same principle holds true for interviewing. When only questions are asked by the interviewer that call for one- or two-word answers, a tone or mood is often set that is difficult to change. On the other hand, when the interviewer begins the interview with open-ended questions he or she usually sets a tone or mood in which the interviewee does much of the talking. All that is often needed is a nod of the head, an occasional "Yes" or "I see" or perhaps another open-ended question to redirect a response that has gone off in an undesired direction.

Some good examples of open-ended questions or statements for parents are, "Tell me about Susie's reading," "Why do you think she developed the problem?" or, "How does she feel about her ability to read?" Some good examples of open-ended questions or statements for students are, "Tell me about your reading," "Why do you think you have this problem?" or "Tell me about what you like to read about."

Give the Interviewee Time to Think

Since most of us are used to talking with various people on a daily basis, it may, at first, seem almost foolish to emphasize the fact that we often do not give the interviewee time to respond. For the untrained interviewer, however, there is often a tendency to feel the need for a constant or unbroken chain of verbal exchanges. You should remember, however, that in an interview the interviewee is often asked to recall information and/or to gather thoughts and express opinions about matters to which he or she might not have given much thought in the past.

In interviewing parents of disabled readers there is seldom any difficulty eliciting information since they have, in most cases, pondered many of the questions that you are likely to ask. On the other hand, in the initial interview with students it is often more difficult to get them to "open up" and begin talking. During this time inexperienced interviewers often feel ill at ease and feel compelled to keep a constant conversation going. It is often helpful to ask an open-ended question or to make an open-ended statement such as, "What do you think about your reading?" or, "Tell me about a book you have read," and then give the interviewee ample time to speak, which in some cases may be as long as fifteen to thirty minutes.

Ruth Strang, who was a world-renowned authority in counseling and reading, once interviewed a group of high school students in front of a graduate class that one of the co-authors was taking. In the beginning she asked a few questions, and there were several rather long periods of silence. A little later every one of the high school students began to open up and became extremely talkative. After the interview Dr. Strang left and invited students in her graduate course to continue interviewing the high school students. One of the first questions asked of the students was why they suddenly became so talkative after being so quiet at first. They all agreed that Dr. Strang (whom they, of course, did not realize was an expert in interview technique) seemed so helpless in her quest for information that they all felt a compassionate need to help her out by talking! We can all learn a lot from Dr. Strang's technique when we find a rather shy student.

Refrain from Expressing Negative Judgment or Attitudes

Whether you are interviewing a parent or a student, you are not likely to agree with everything the interviewee says. In the beginning stages of your work in counseling either students or parents, it is often wise to refrain from expressing negative judgment or attitudes about opinions that they may express. This is not to say that as an interviewer you should not be honest in your approach, but that you may need to temporarily hold back some rather strong convictions you may possess about certain subjects. For example, many parents berate comic books and tend to express the opinion that they would really prefer that their children did not read them. On the other hand, most reading specialists would probably tend to feel that if a student has not developed the reading habit, then even the reading of comic books would be a positive step in the process of improving his or her reading. During the initial interview, however, it is often wise to refrain from strongly disagreeing with the interviewee, who will soon begin to sense this disapproval and will, in turn, tend to attempt to terminate the interview. There will usually be ample time at a slightly later date to counsel either the student or parent about reading habits, etc., about which you believe a change in attitude is essential.

Avoid the Use of Technical Terms

Most of you have been in a situation where someone used a term that you were not familiar with when they spoke to you. You are then faced with the sometimes embarrassing situation of either having to ask what the term means, or of trying to "bluff" your way through the situation until the subject is changed. This sort of situation should be avoided when interviewing students and especially parents. Those of you who have been working in education for a number of years often find yourselves asking questions in which terms somewhat unfamiliar to parents are often used. For example, you might ask questions such as, "How does Rose-Marie get along with her siblings?" Has she had any traumatic experiences during the past year?" or, "Do you perceive her as an introvert?" Some people may not know what *siblings, traumatic, perceive,* and *introvert* mean. This would, of course, cause a great deal of embarrassment for the person being interviewed.

Promise Only What You Know You Can Accomplish

If you were told by a medical doctor that you had cancer, you would immediately ask such questions as, "What are my chances for recovery?" "How long will it take to recover if I do recover at all?" and, "How much is it likely to cost?" Parents who have either known for some time or have recently discovered that their child has a reading problem are also naturally concerned about the remedial reading teacher's prognosis for success. This is quite natural. However, there is a natural tendency to tell parents that everything will probably be all right in a short amount of time. A number of research studies have demonstrated the effectiveness of remedial reading, but most of these same studies have also demonstrated that for most disabled readers, and especially those that are severely disabled, regaining the ability to read at grade level is a long-term process.

Although parents should not be discouraged from seeking remediation for a disabled reader, they should be made to understand that most disabled readers need to learn what normal-achieving students are learning in addition to making up for material they have already missed. And, in most cases, this is likely to be a rather long process. A fairly good rule of thumb, although with many exceptions, is that with good tutoring a student may take nearly as long to recover from a reading disability as he or she took to develop it.

It is easy to explain to parents that their child made more rapid progress than you expected. On the other hand, it is much more difficult to explain to parents that after a long period of tutoring their child has made little or no progress. For this reason parents should be reassured that progress from tutoring is usually forthcoming, but that the rate of achievement is likely to vary a great deal depending on such factors as potential for learning and the severity of the problem.

Do Not Undersell Your Own Knowledge and Abilities

People, of course, vary a great deal in their self-concept as well as in their innate and acquired abilities. However, to some extent society demands that one display a certain amount of modesty in dealings with other people. The display of a certain amount of modesty in some areas is only natural; however, the remedial reading teacher should not be so modest in dealing with parents that the parents, in turn, lose faith in the ability of the teacher. Most well-trained reading teachers realize that very little is really known about certain types of severe reading disability. When students appear to exhibit the symptoms of what is often termed *dyslexia*, or severe reading disability, it is usually wise to tell parents that progress in remediation with this type of student is often very slow and that educators as well as people in other professions know very little about the exact type of remediation for these kinds of problems. However, if you are well-trained and realize these limitations exist, you should also convey to parents that you are as capable of dealing with the problem as any other "expert" in the field. You may also wish to convey to parents that if symptoms appear that you are not qualified to deal with, you will recommend someone who is more qualified in a certain area.

The essential point, however, is that you do not sell yourself short. People do not want to think they are taking their car to a second-rate mechanic, let alone placing their child with a second-rate remedial reading teacher.

Avoid the Use of Words That May Offend Older Students

Every family appears to use various titles in referring to members of the family. When dealing with students of any age and especially older students it is usually a good practice to refer to parents as "your mother and/or father" since these are terms that are not cold and yet do not appear childish to some students.

Avoid the Use of Overly Personal Questions

In interviewing parents you are likely to find a great deal of difference in their willingness to discuss certain factors that may affect the well-being of a child. It is usually a good idea to avoid the use of personal questions such as, "Do you have a happy marriage?" or, "Is there a great deal of conflict in the home?" If a parent feels such matters are important, the same information can usually be elicited by open-ended, less personal questions such as, "Can you tell me something about the emotional climate of your home?"

Refer to Yourself in the First Person

Most experienced interviewers and teachers of older students refer to themselves in the first person. However, there is a tendency for inexperienced interviewers and/or teachers of very young children to refer to themselves as "Mrs. Smith" or "your teacher." This is often quite offensive to middle-grade and older students and should simply be avoided.

Ask Only One Question at a Time

A common mistake of inexperienced interviewers is asking several questions at one time. This reminds us of a presidential press conference where an overzealous reporter asks the president a whole series of questions to which the president may reply, "Now which question do you want me to answer?" or if he chooses to be less sarcastic he may attempt to answer the first one or two questions, but then finds himself asking, "Now what were the other questions?" Parents or students, being even less adept at remembering a series of questions or in even remembering that more than one was asked, usually answer the first question or the one they feel is most important anyway.

Remember That Children Usually Have an Inaccurate
Perception of Time and Numbers

Teachers who are accustomed to working with older students (especially past the age of twelve), unless they have younger children of their own, often fail to realize that younger children have a very inaccurate perception of time and numbers. For example, in interviewing eight- or nine-year-old students about how much time they spend watching television, there would be very little use in simply asking a question such as, "About how much television do you watch each week?" If you really wanted to get a much more meaningful answer to such a question, you should ask specific questions such as, "What programs did you watch last night?" or you can go through the *T.V. Guide* with them and have them tell you specifically which programs they have watched.

The same procedure should be used when dealing with numbers in asking questions such as, "About how many books have you read this year?" It would be much more meaningful to attempt to make a list of some of the titles that the student remembers.

THE USE OF INTERVIEW GUIDES
AND/OR CHECKLISTS

The use of an interview guide or checklist may be advantageous or detrimental depending on the skill with which they are used. The interviewer who uses a very detailed checklist has the advantage of being reminded to cover all of the information on the checklist. However, the use of a detailed checklist often has the disadvantage of structuring the interview to the point that it is likely to prevent the interviewer from carefully listening to the responses of the interviewee. When this happens, the interviewer may fail to capitalize on certain significant remarks made by the interviewee.

Personal experience indicates that the use of a broad outline of points to be covered in an interview is often helpful but that when the outline or checklist becomes too detailed the spontaneity of the conversation is too often lost. For this reason we would suggest that a broad outline similar to the following be used when interviewing students.

1. Interests
    1.1. Clubs—church
    1.2. Hobbies
    1.3. Friends
    1.4. How is spare time spent?

2. Student's Attitudes
    2.1. Toward family
    2.2. Toward school
        2.1.1. Favorite subjects and least-liked subjects
    2.3. Teachers
    2.4. Friends
    2.5. The reading problem
        2.5.1. Is the student aware of the problem?
        2.5.2. What does the student think the problem is?
        2.5.3. How much trouble has the student had?
        2.5.4. Why does the student have this difficulty?
        2.5.5. What are the student's suggestions for solutions?
        2.5.6. Does the student enjoy reading?
        2.5.7. What does the student read?
        2.5.8. Does the student go to the library or own books of his or her own?
    2.6. The student
        2.6.1 How does the student feel about himself or herself in relation to other students?

A similar broad outline may be developed for use in interviewing parents; however, in many situations parents will have filled out a form or application before meeting with the teacher. If such a form or application exists, it may, to some extent, serve as a guide to the interview, i.e., for clarifying information on the student's health history, the onset of the reading problem, etc. The outline used with parents will also vary depending on whether it is used in the public schools, a university clinical situation, etc. For these reasons you should develop an outline that is meaningful to you in your own particular setting.

EXAMPLES OF INTERVIEWS

The first interview is one that took place between a university student (I) who was meeting the mother (M) of a ten-year-old boy (Tim) for the first time. During this interview the boy was not present. After interviewing the mother, the university student asked the mother to wait in the reading center while the interviewer held a short interview with Tim (T).

    As you read these two interviews, try to note any techniques used by the interviewer that seemed to work especially well. Secondly, note whether any information was gained that would have been helpful in working with the boy. Also note any techniques that could be improved on.

Initial Interview with Tim's Mother

1.   I: Who recommended Tim for the reading center?

2.   M: Mrs. Jones had a friend who came here, so several of the teachers and I came up here last spring. She thought it would be good for Tim because they tried numerous things to pinpoint the problem.

3.   I: It is difficult to pinpoint the problem, especially if you don't have the right tools. What seems to be his main problem?

4.   M: I don't really know. I can't put my finger on it. He has difficulty, or maybe he doesn't even try to attack the words. I suppose he has the tools for them because he was tutored by the reading resource teacher.

5.   I: Oh yes!

6.   M: For a while she felt that he was not happy because there were too many other children and she was afraid that he felt he was being categorized as being not too bright. He has the tools for breaking the words down so let's take him out of the tutoring and see how he does. He comprehends well, and if you read the material to him, he gets it.

7.   I: He understands what is read to him?

8.   M: He doesn't. Usually I read the whole chapter for him but I don't do his reading for him because they do this at school but say he doesn't really want to read. He doesn't take books. We belong to one of the Weekly Reader Book Clubs because he wanted to, and those books just sit on the shelf. They are only third-grade books, but he doesn't even try to read any of them. They are pretty long, and he really wants something quick so that he can read.

9.   I: He wants something that's real quick to read?

10.   M: He doesn't attempt words that he could sound out if he tried. He just guesses at them, and it's frustrating for me because I think that he can do better. Sometimes I wonder if his memory needs training because he can look at those vowels and he can't tell you what they should say. I think by now he has had it every year.

11.   I: You say he has a hard time with the vowel sounds, what about the consonant sounds?

12.   M: Well when he first went to the second school, which was in the second grade, the teacher that tested him said that he had trouble with consonant blends and things like this, but she could not find anything like dyslexia.

13.   I: This is something that I will not categorize Tim with. Teachers are getting away from this kind of thing.

14.   M: Well he can't read fast enough, which makes all his achievement tests low because he doesn't get through with them. He does have a good attitude about school. I think the teachers say he does.

15.   I: What kind of work does he do in his other subjects?

16.   M: Well he doesn't . . . I don't know. He doesn't knock himself out studying, but he does try.

17.   I: He tries?

18.   M: Yes, he really puts forth lots of effort in everything he tries to do. My helping him at home is not good because I get frustrated, and he is in tears. When he was in the second grade I really tried hard to work with him, and it just made both of us nervous wrecks, and so in the third grade my husband said just let him go. Either he makes it or doesn't. You're not doing him any good by yelling.

19.   I: I see. When did you notice that he had a specific reading problem?

20.   M: Well, after first grade and he came out with a "C" in reading, but he couldn't read.

21.   I: He couldn't read at all?

22.   M: Really! Like nothing could he read, and he was not happy.

23.   I: I imagine that this upset him.

24.   M: I think that he felt kids would make fun of him and that stuff. They did this usually coming home because he couldn't keep up in reading with the rest of them, so we put him in another school and Mrs. Jones was his teacher. She would work with him on Saturdays. At the end of the year she realized how little he had to work with. She said that he had a poor foundation, or just had not retained what was given him. There was talk of holding him back, but they said he had the ability to do the work and that he would be bored with doing the same things. She said he was just like being in a cage and couldn't get through to the material. So he doesn't mind school. He gets upset if he gets too much homework and stuff, but he is eager to learn. He was just beside himself to come here. Tim said that he could not wait until he could read better.

25.   I: Yes. That's a good sign. I'm glad he wants to come to the center. Now tell me, how does he get along with his peers?

26.   M: He gets along with them all right, but since he goes to the new school, he doesn't know too many children in the immediate neighborhood. He goes out and rides with them sometimes. I somehow think that he is a little immature because . . . I don't know. I used to think that he was.

27.   I: He just turned ten?

28.   M: Yes, just in August. I think maybe he depended on everybody because he is the third child and close to the others. The daughter just older than him took care of him. She did things for him. He didn't have to talk as early as everybody because we were always handing him things. Of course, he had the hearing problem also.

29.   I: Yes.

30. M: So I thought maybe he couldn't hear all of these sounds or distinguish them when writing and spelling. But supposedly his hearing is in normal limits now. The loss that he does have would be with the female voice range, which could have given him lots of trouble earlier in his schooling.

31. I: Yes, in the first grade when he was being taught to read. When did this problem get cleared up completely?

32. M: About two years ago. Whenever he gets a cold, his hearing level goes down. But he is not taking allergy shots now. We just give him an antihistamine when his nose starts running and this does all right. He hasn't had too many ear infections, but there is scarring in the ears. But anyway, the hearing tests indicate that his hearing is within the normal range.

33. I: I noticed this on the application. The previous hearing difficulties could have been a problem.

34. M: But in two years he should have been able to pick up all of the sounds.

35. I: He might have missed something important at the beginning that could be the cause of his reading problem. I hope to find out what it is. Do you read to Tim?

36. M: Well, we used to. My daughter used to read to him quite a bit. Nobody has read to him in the past year or so, and I'm sure he had less read to him than the older ones because I haven't had the time with the other children, you know. This isn't the right thing to do. Maybe there was too much television. So he didn't bother to read or listen.

37. I: Are his study habits good at home?

38. M: Oh no! I don't think they are particularly good. When I ask him what homework he has, he says none. They work individually at school, so most things he finishes there, unless he really goofs something up. Then he brings it home. Since he started this year, I haven't had to push him. I think he has kept up. Of course, he hasn't been in school very long. And he seems happy and content. Interested, at least. He comes home with tales on what has gone on. So I think he is enjoying school. The other night he said that he surely will be glad to read better, so he can read the instructions on model airplanes.

39. I: That is interesting. Does he like most models?

40. M: Yes, and he likes animals and stuff like that. He liked to read about them, but most of the books that have the information he wants are a little beyond him.

41. I: Books that are more scientific?

42. M: He just can't break down the words. They are just too much. He is unfamiliar with the words so they don't mean anything to him. His

vocabulary is not very big. I am sure that is why he can't read very well. I feel his vocabulary is not as good as most children his age. He seems to understand anything we say . . . all of us talking. He doesn't act like he can't understand.

43. I: That's good. Besides his ear problem, has he had any other serious illness?

44. M: No. Just the normal things.

45. I: Does Tim do much reading at home?

46. M: Not much. He joined the book club, but this lasted only a year. He would never finish a book. I tried to encourage him to go to the shelf and read these books, but he wasn't too interested.

47. I: Is he interested in the comics?

48. M: Oh yes. Peanuts he always reads. Of course they don't have very much writing on them.

49. I: But it is still reading!

50. M: But he doesn't have much interest in books. If there's nothing good on television, he might sit down and read. He reads comic books like Archie once in a while. I think they're really trash.

51. I: What are his favorite television programs?

52. M: The cartoons of course. (laugh)

53. I: Does he spend much time watching them?

54. M: Yes.

55. I: Does Tim like sports?

56. M: He is not very well coordinated. He can't catch a ball well or anything like that. I'm sure that's partly our fault. We're not very athletic. His older brother gets very put out with him because he can't catch anything. So he doesn't want to bother. I think Tim would like to except he doesn't do as well as the others and this discourages him. The kids always make comments, you know.

57. I: Kids are sometimes cruel to each other.

58. M: Yes, they are. But Tim still tries. He goes to the "Y" three times a week. . . . He took a physical fitness test, but did not do very well. He clobbered himself on the chin-ups and other things. He doesn't do them at home. He did not ride a bicycle as soon as most children do. There are a lot of hills . . . but he rode a lot this summer with a friend.

59. I: Does he make friends easily?

60. M: He doesn't go seeking new friends. Of course, not going to the same school as the other kids in the neighborhood is probably bad. On the weekends he stays at home or tries to get a friend from his school to play with that lives near us. Or he plays with his younger sister.

61. I: I see. Well, would it be all right to get Tim's record from the school?

62.   M: Yes. They said they would be glad to send the center anything that could be of help.

63.   I: That is good. You've been very helpful. I appreciate the time you have given me very much. Thank you.

Initial Interview with Tim

1.   I: Is there anything you want to start off telling me, Tim?

2.   T: Well, I'm in the fifth grade and ten years old.

3.   I: What do you like to do?

4.   T: I like to draw and I like to do drama at school, and paint and do papier-mâché, and all kinds of art.

5.   I: What kind of drawing do you like to do the best?

6.   T: Of people.

7.   I: Of people?

8.   T: No, I don't really draw them. I just make them up.

9.   I: So you just make them up. That's fine. What about your paintings?

10.   T: On my paintings, I paint like pictures of the sun, or the grass or something like that.

11.   I: I see. Getting back to people, what kind of people do you like to draw?

12.   T: Well some of the time I draw them with glasses and big ears, and big chins and things like that. . . .

13.   I: Funny things? They call them caricatures.

14.   T: Yes, that's right.

15.   I: What about the drama? Do you like to act?

16.   T: Yes.

17.   I: In plays?

18.   T: Well, in school the teacher would give us . . . well, like make up a pantomime for this week. So we would go home and practice and think of a pantomime and practice it, and the next time we had drama we'd do it. And we'd talk about it and make criticisms about it. So the next time we could do better.

19.   I: What do you like to pantomime?

20.   T: Well, really it depends . . . like in a . . . like something sad, well not sad, but something unusual . . . that doesn't happen very often or . . .

21.   I: Something out of the ordinary. Something that doesn't happen every day. What are some of the things you have done?

22.   T: Well, today, I don't know if this is very unusual, but I took a chair, put a table in front of me, act like the chair was a car and the table was a car and it was in the middle of the road, and I tried to get it out of the way. . . .

23. I: Did they guess what you were doing?
24. T: Yes.
25. I: What do you think about the way you read?
26. T: Well, I don't know. I guess I'm not too good.
27. I: What do you mean by that?
28. T: Like when I read, I don't know some of the words.
29. I: What do you do when you come to a word you don't know?
30. T: Sometimes I try to sound it out, but I can't do that most of the time.
31. I: Do you think we should try to help you with that?
32. T: Yeah, that would be alright.
33. I: Do you think you usually understand what you read?
34. T: Yeah, if I know all the words.
35. I: Well, tell me something, Tim. Do you like to read?
36. T: Yes.
37. I: What's your favorite story? Or books?
38. T: Well, there's not many books about monkeys, but I'd like to read about monkeys.
39. I: What about the other animals?
40. T: Well, I like them, too. Dogs, cats, yes, I like them, too, and I like to read about them too—and Vikings.
41. I: And Vikings. You must like the seamen. What do you like about the Vikings?
42. T: Well, I'm not sure. They just seem brave and all this, and they only liked to live in the cold, and I also like things about the cold, like walruses, Eskimos, and things like this.
43. I: That's good. That's real good. That's interesting. I imagine you know a lot of things about these subjects.
44. T: Well, not a lot. But some.
45. I: You said you liked the Vikings. The Vikings were seamen. Do you like the sea?
46. T: Yes.
47. I: Have you ever seen the ocean?
48. T: Not in true life. In pictures and movies. But that's all.
49. I: That's good. Tim, how do you do your homework?
50. T: We don't have very much homework. We most of the time just do it at school.
51. I: What are you reading about in geography?
52. T: Well, we don't have geography. It's social science.
53. I: I see.
54. T: We talk about people and things. In the fifth chapter they talk about prehistoric things. They told us in the first of it that this railroad company was digging . . . well, making a path and came across this great, big, old rock; tried to move it aside, and when they did, there were five skeletons there. And skulls. And this guy . . . I

       forget what they called them . . . well, dug farther down and found their bodies . . . and this guy thinks they were prehistoric men.

55.   I: That's kind of in line with your animals. You know they find a lot of prehistoric animals. Maybe we can find you some good books and stories about these.

56.   T: Yes, that would be alright.

57.   I: How much time, Tim, do you spend reading outside of school time?

58.   T: Not much. Well, most of the time after school, I want to read but most of the books are too easy for me, or they're just . . . There's this one book that I was starting a long time ago. I stopped that one cause I was reading this other book, and another book, and finally I just read the same one to where I was before and quit.

59.   I: And you quit at the same place?

60.   T: Yes. That's all I read.

61.   I: Well, maybe one of these days you can go back and finish it. Can you tell me the names of any of the books you have read this year?

62.   T: Well, let's see. (pause) I guess I just can't remember any. There was this other book I told you about; but I guess I really don't read very much.

63.   I: Do you think you would like to read if we could find something about monkeys or other animals?

64.   T: Sure.

65.   I: How much time do you spend watching television?

66.   T: Well, let's see. On school days not much. Well, maybe a little, but most of the time I'm wrestling with my brother. Or I'm drawing pictures.

67.   I: So you don't spend too much time watching television during the weekdays. How much do you watch during the weekends?

68.   T: On Saturdays I watch quite a little bit. I like to watch Disney and things like that. I watch the cartoons.

69.   I: Who do you watch them with?

70.   T: If Sarah's awake, I take her down with me on Saturday. I put her by the door where all of the toys are. She plays and I watch her and the T.V. She's my baby sister.

71.   I: Tim, how do you get along with your brothers and sisters?

72.   T: O.K. most of the time.

73.   I: Who do you play with most of the time?

74.   T: My brother.

75.   I: How old is he?

76.   T: He's fourteen.

77.   I: What are some of the things you do?

78.   T: Sometimes we make up things. Like I made a model of this mummy and we decided like it was the year 2000 or something and I'd look

at the mummy and say some mumble jumble, and say, Mummy, come alive. And really, most of the time we pretend that a lot of things are real. And my brother likes to read also.

79. I: Does your brother read to you?
80. T: Well, he used to. But now he doesn't.
81. I: Tim, I think that's about all for now. I want you to know that we're going to help you as much as possible during the coming weeks. You certainly have been helpful to me and I thank you.

In the preceding interviews you will note that each statement made by either the interviewer or interviewee is numbered. These numbers are used in the following discussion in directing your attention to specific techniques and/or information derived from the interviews.

Techniques Used and Information Gained from
Initial Interview with Tim's Mother

Note the following techniques used by the interviewer:

3. Use of open-ended question to elicit what Tim's mother believed was his most important problem.
5. Use of simple statement, "Oh yes!" to get her to continue talking.
7. Question to clarify whether the mother believed Tim had a problem with comprehension.
9. Repetition of enough of the mother's statement to clarify what she meant *and* to let her know the interviewer was listening very carefully.
11. Further questioning to clarify the problem.
13. The interviewer diplomatically tells the mother that no one really knows what dyslexia is and the term should probably not be used.
17. Very short repetition (in question format) to encourage the mother to continue.
21. Clarification of what the mother meant by "couldn't read."
23. Neutral statement that encouraged the mother to continue.
29. Again, the use of a simple "Yes" to get her to continue.
31. Clarifying the question.
41. Again, simple statement that encourages her to continue.
49. Interviewer does not disagree but lets her know that reading comic books is still reading, which indicates the interviewer's approval.
57. Encouraging, reassuring remark.
63. Expression of appreciation for mother's help.

Now note the following useful information derived from the interview:

4.   Mother indicates that Tim probably has problems with word-attack skills.

4.   He has been tutored before.

6.   Indication of a possible problem with low self-concept.

6,8.   There is some confusion about whether he comprehends well.

8.   Tim does not read much, if any, on his own.

8.   There is some indication that he might be encouraged to read if the interviewer could find something short that Tim could finish in a small amount of time.

10,12.   Indication of difficulty with consonants, consonant blends, and vowels.

14.   Mother perceives Tim's reading speed as too slow.

14.   Tim has evidently maintained a good attitude towards school.

18.   As with many parents, mother cannot work well with her son on his reading problem.

20,21.   Indication of a problem from the very beginning of school.

24.   More indication that Tim may have a low self-concept.

26.   Mother believes he may be immature.

28.   Some indication that he may lack initiative and/or self-confidence.

30,32,   Possible explanation for Tim's poor start in school and a possible
34.   problem at the time he was interviewed. (Tests performed at the reading center indicated that he still had a severe hearing loss. When this was corrected he improved very rapidly.)

36,38.   Some indication of poor study habits.

38.   An indication of Tim's desire to learn to read better.

38,40.   Information on what might motivate him to read.

42.   His mother believes his vocabulary is low.

46.   Indication that Tim does very little reading at home.

48.   An indication that he does like comic books.

50.   Mother has a negative attitude about comic books.

56.   More indication of the possibility that Tim has a low self-concept.

60.   Some indication that he does not have many friends his own age to play with at home.

Techniques Used and Information Gained from Initial Interview with Tim

Note the following techniques used by the interviewer:

1.   Use of open-ended question to let Tim talk about anything he wished to talk about.

3.   Another open-ended question to draw the student out.

5–23.   Interviewer indicated deep interest in Tim's interests and thus helped establish rapport.

25.   Open-ended question to uncover Tim's perception of his reading problem.

27.   Further pursuit of Tim's perception of his reading problem.

29.   Question to verify Tim's perception of his reading problem.

31.   Solicitation of Tim's commitment that he needs help.

33.   Diagnosis of Tim's perception of whether he has a comprehension problem.

35–47   Eliciting of information on reading interests.

55.   Solicitation of Tim's commitment to read about things he is interested in.

57–61. Questioning to find out whether Tim really reads on his own. Note that in number 61 the interviewer "pins him down," so to speak, and discovers that Tim really doesn't read any books at all.

81.   Assurance is offered that the interviewer will help him as much as possible, but no promises are made that cannot be kept.

Now note the following useful information derived from the interview:

4–24.   Considerable information is obtained about what Tim likes to do in his spare time.

26.   Information is obtained on Tim's perception of his ability to read.

28–34. Information is obtained on Tim's perception of his reading problem.

34–48. Information is obtained that should be helpful in locating materials that Tim should be interested in reading.

50.   Information is obtained on the amount of homework required by the teachers in the school he attends.

58–62. Student does not read anything that is not required.

66–70. Information on how free time is spent.

72–80. Information on relationship with siblings.

Initial Interview with Danny

Although psychologists often tell teachers not to teach by showing examples of what not to do, we have chosen to use one more example of an initial student interview, this one to illustrate some of the problems beginning teachers encounter in learning proper interview techniques. As with the case of the two preceding interviews, it will be discussed more thoroughly at the end. However, as you read it, be sure to note the tremendous difference between this interview and the preceding student interview, due to the fact that this student did not practice the interview techniques discussed earlier in this chapter.

In this case the interviewer was also meeting this nine-year-old student, Danny, for the first time. An interview had already been conducted with his mother.

1. I: Hi, Danny. I'm Mrs. Stevens. How old are you?
2. D: Nine.
3. I: Nine years old, boy, that's getting up there, huh? What grade are you in?
4. D: Fourth.
5. I: Fourth grade. Did you have any trouble finding UTEP?
6. D: Ummm, yeah.
7. I: Did you help your mother?
8. D: Nope.
9. I: You didn't.
10. D: Nope.
11. I: She didn't know the way and I told her you probably could help her. Is this your first time here?
12. D: Uh huh.
13. I: It's kind of big, huh?
14. D: Uh huh.
15. I: Think you'd like to come here someday?
16. D: Uh huh.
17. I: Go to school when you're all grown up and out of high school.
18. D: Uh huh.
19. I: Think you might, huh?
20. D: Uh huh.
21. I: Well, where do you go to school?
22. D: Edwards.
23. I: Edwards, where is that—at Biggs Field?
24. D: Uh huh.
25. I: Do you live on post?
26. D: Nope.
27. I: You don't? Where do you live?
28. D: Biggs Field.
29. I: Biggs Field. I know where that is. We used to live at Ft. Bliss. Do you know where Ft. Bliss is?
30. D: Uh huh.
31. I: Do you go there often?
32. D: Uh huh.
33. I: Just to the P.X., huh.

34. D: Uh huh.
35. I: That's a fun trip, huh? Do you participate in sports, play football, baseball?
36. D: Used to.
37. I: Which one—football or baseball?
38. D: Football and baseball.
39. I: You are not playing football this fall, huh?
40. D: Uh huh.
41. I: I understand your brother is playing and you wanted to go to the game tonight.
42. D: Uh huh.
43. I: That's just a practice one though, isn't it?
44. D: Uh huh.
45. I: So that's not too great, just to miss the practice one.
46. D: I don't know.
47. I: Do they play their games on Saturdays?
48. D: Uh huh.
49. I: Bet you won't miss many of them, huh? You won't miss any of them.
50. D: Maybe, I got to go to catechism.
51. I: Oh, you have to go to catechism on Saturdays. Well, what else do you do?
52. D: Nothing.
53. I: Nothing? Do you know why you came here?
54. D: Nope!
55. I: You don't know. Mother didn't tell you.
56. D: Nope!
57. I: Well, this is the reading center. Do you have any trouble with reading?
58. D: Uh huh.
59. I: Maybe you can tell me about it. What trouble do you have with it?
60. D: Hard words.
61. I: Hard words—when you say hard words, are they little words or big words?
62. D: Big words.
63. I: Big words, and why do they give you do much trouble?
64. D: (*cannot be understood*) They all have twenty letters.
65. I: They all have what?
66. D: Around twenty or fifteen letters in them.
67. I: They all have too many letters. Oh boy, you didn't learn how to break them down into syllables?
68. D: Yep.
69. I: Oh, you do know how.
70. D: Uh huh.

71. I: And they still give you trouble, huh?
72. D: Uh huh.
73. I: Anything else about them that causes trouble?
74. D: Nope!
75. I: Nothing else. How about little words, do you have any trouble with them?
76. D: Sometimes.
77. I: Sometimes. Do you know when?
78. D: Once in a while.
79. I: Once in a while. Umm. Can you tell me one little word that gives you trouble? (*Long pause*) Can't think of any?
80. D: Nope!
81. I: Maybe there aren't too many that's giving you trouble, huh, just a few.
82. D: Uh huh.
83. I: How long have you had trouble with reading? Do you know?
84. D: About a year.
85. I: About a year. Do you have trouble talking about what you've read?
86. D: Nope!
87. I: When you read, you can tell the teacher what you have read, what it was all about.
88. D: Uh huh.
89. I: O.K. Does your teacher give you any special help with your reading?
90. D: Nope!
91. I: Do you have any trouble when you are in the reading group?
92. D: Nope.
93. I: You don't. Do you have any special friends?
94. D: Yeah.
95. I: How many?
96. D: Five.
97. I: Boys or girls?
98. D: Boys.
99. I: All boys.
100. D: Uh huh.
101. I: Does the teacher help you with your reading if you have trouble?
102. D: Sometimes.
103. I: Sometimes. Well, what does she do when she doesn't help you? What do you do? Well, what does the teacher do?
104. D: She just sits around.
105. I: She just sits around.
106. D: Uh huh.
107. I: Does she let you figure the word out on your own or does she help you?

108. D: She helps me.
109. I: She helps you with it. What do you like to read, Tom? I'm sorry, I called you Tom. That's my little boy's name. Dan, what do you like to read?
110. D: Books
111. I: Any special kind of books?
112. D: Nope!
113. I: No special kind?
114. D: Nope!
115. I: Do you like comic books?
116. D: Yep!
117. I: How about books on sports, football players?
118. D: Yeah! (*Appears to be excited*)
119. I: Can you tell me one that you have about a football player maybe.
120. I: (*long pause*) You don't know, huh?
121. D: I know one but I can't . . . I don't know his name.
122. I: Who is it about—Oh, you don't know the football player's name.
123. D: Uh huh.
124. I: Ummm, it wouldn't be Roger Staubach would it?
125. D: (*Negative headshake*)
126. I: No
127. D: Nope.
128. I: Ah, is he an offensive player or a defensive player?
129. D: Defense.
130. I: Do you know which team?
131. D: Yep.
132. I: Dallas.
133. D: Nope!
134. I: Which one?
135. D: Minnesota.
136. I: Minnesota. Oh, boy I can't, I don't know many on the Minnesota team. O.K. Tom, I keep saying Tom. That's not great. O.K. Dan, can you tell me anything else about reading that bothers you?
137. D: Nope!
138. I: No! Can you tell me anything else that you like to do?
139. D: Nope!
140. I: Well, do you particularly like coming out here to the reading center?
141. D: Yeah.
142. I: Did you know I was a teacher?
143. D: Nope!
144. I: I am. Your mother said she thought you knew. I teach first grade. What do you think about that? (*Pause*) They're all the little ones, huh?

145. D: Uh huh.
146. I: Is Mrs. James your friend?
147. D: I don't know. (*very low*)
148. I: Huh?
149. D: I don't know.
150. I: Did you like going to the special reading classes?
151. D: Uh huh.
152. I: You did. Did they help you?
153. D: Yeah.
154. I: How about Mrs. Edwards? Is that her name?
155. D: Used to be.
156. I: What's her name now?
157. D: Her name is—(*unfinished*) She was it after school was out. Let's see, I'd go every Saturday.
158. I: You would go every Saturday to her.
159. D: Uh huh.
160. I: And she would help you with reading.
161. D: Yep.
162. I: At her house.
163. D: Yep!
164. I: Did you like that?
165. D: Yep!
166. I: What did she help you with? Do you remember? What did she have you do?
167. D: She'd write cards and write words on them and then I have to read it.
168. I: Read the word—she would write words on the card and you would have to read it.
169. D: Uh huh.
170. I: Did you ever read any stories?
171. D: Nope!
172. I: Did you ever learn any sounds? Did she just write letters and have you say the sounds?
173. D: Uh huh.
174. I: Were you pretty good at that?
175. D: Yeah!
176. I: How about ending sounds?
177. D: Nope!
178. I: You weren't good at those?
179. D: Nope!
180. I: Oh, well, we'll have to work on the ending sounds then, huh?
181. D: Uh huh.

182. I: Right! Can you think of anything else that we'll have to work with? Can you think of anything that Mrs. Edwards did with you that you didn't get too good at that maybe I can help you with?
183. D: Nope!
184. I: You can't? O.K. Do you think that maybe the next time we talk you'll be able to think of something else I can help you with other than ending sounds? O.K.?
185. D: O.K.
186. I: Can you think of anything else I need to know?
187. D: Nope.
188. I: O.K.

Problems in Technique in Danny's Interview

As you have, no doubt, realized, this interviewer fell into the trap of dominating the conversation and failed, in most cases, to use open-ended questions. This resulted in a setting in which most of the student responses were one-word utterances such as "Uh huh" or "Nope." Other problems encountered were as follows:

3. Failure to use open-ended questions and allow student time to think.
17. Interviewer talks down to student.
35. More than one question at once.
45. Argumentative statement that the student doesn't really believe.
55. Interviewer again talks down to student as she might to a preschool child.
59. This is a good open-ended question, but when the student said, "Hard words," the interviewer, instead of saying, "Tell me more," actually took away the incentive of the student to give more thought and his own explanation of his problem.
67. The interviewer expresses an assumption that may or may not be valid.
81. The interviewer again puts words in the mouth of the student.
83. This statement should have been pursued in terms of the student's perception of why _he_ thought he had had trouble with reading for just "one year."
103. Three questions at once!
109. The interviewer not only forgets the student's name but implies that he reminds her of her "little boy."
136. The interviewer again forgets the student's name.
144. Although there is nothing wrong with being a first-grade teacher, it is not necessary, or probably wise, to emphasize this fact when working

with a fifth grader who may tend to think that a first-grade teacher can only teach "little boys and girls."

172. In this statement, as in a number of other instances, the interviewer practically tells the student how to respond.

188. The interview is ended very abruptly.

SUMMARY

Learning good techniques to use in interviewing students as well as parents is an important skill that should be practiced and developed by the remedial reading teacher. The interview can not only supplement the use of applications and questionnaires but can, in many cases, bring out information that may not readily become apparent. There are a number of techniques, which if successfully applied, can help the interviewer obtain useful information by making the interviewee feel at ease, and thus enhance his or her responsiveness to the questions of the interviewer.

13

A More Efficient Path
to Diagnosis

The purpose of this chapter is to allow the reading specialist, classroom teacher, education diagnostician, psychologist, or any others who are somewhat familiar with the diagnostic process to complete a diagnosis in the most efficient manner possible. The diagnostic flowchart will be presented and described along with specific examples of tests to use in completing the reading diagnosis.

USING THE DIAGNOSTIC FLOWCHART

There is all too often a temptation to simply "give every test you have to a disabled reader." Much of the diagnostic process can be eliminated if the diagnosis is done in the most efficient way. All too often we have seen diagnostic report after diagnostic report (especially by psychologists testing in the field of reading) in which many tests administered did not provide information of any kind that would have been useful in planning a program of remediation. Although the flowchart that appears in Figure 13–1 appears rather complicated, you will find that it can easily be understood as you read the explanations of each section in this chapter. You will note that all tests and/or survey instruments referred to in the flowchart have a direct bearing on the reading problems faced by children. Thus information obtained in giving the tests and/or survey instruments will always be of value in planning a program of remediation.

In explaining the flowchart found in Figure 13–1 we will refer you to the particular part being discussed by the use of the numbered signs that appear beside the shapes—circles, rectangles, and so on—in the figure. Figures

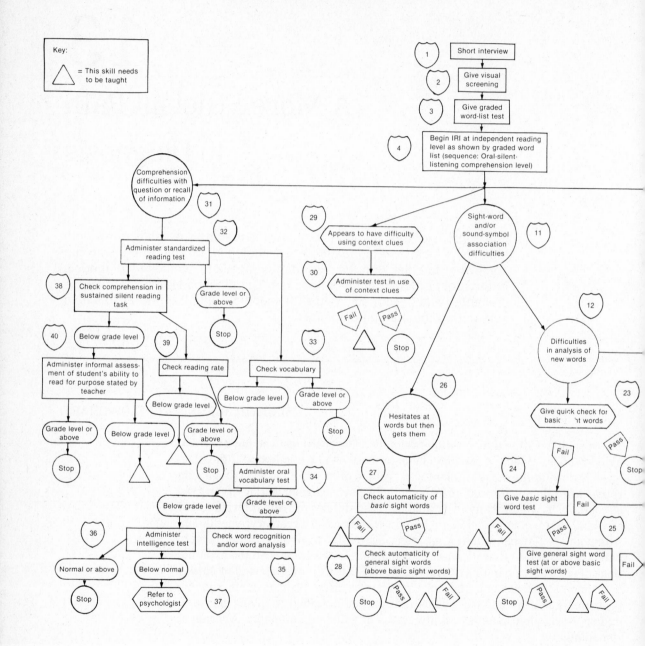

FIGURE 13-1. Diagnostic Sequence.

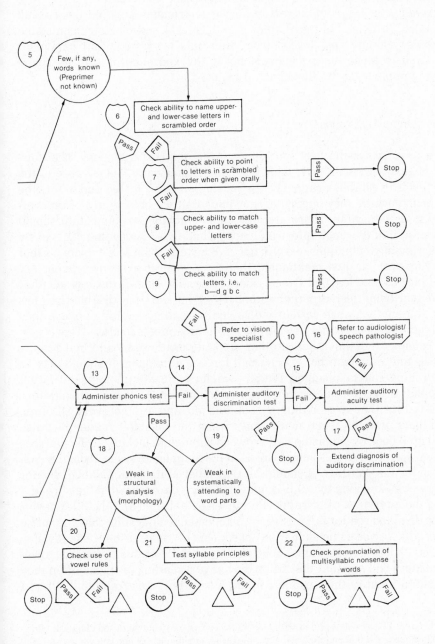

13-2 through 13-6 show portions of the flowchart of Figure 13-1, and will be referred to as we discuss the steps in diagnosis.[1]

Whenever a particular test or survey instrument is called for, consult the section at the end of the chapter that lists tests, survey instruments, and sources explaining how to construct materials for testing that particular skill. Each of these testing instruments is indexed according to its corresponding number on the flowchart in Figure 13-1.

The First Four Steps of the Diagnostic Process

Figure 13-2 shows the first four steps of the diagnostic process. The flowchart begins with number 1, which is a short interview. The purpose of the interview is to establish rapport with the student being tested and to find the answer to several very important questions that we believe are often overlooked in an interview. There are, of course, a number of things that should be covered in a thorough interview. Since Chapter 12 is devoted exclusively to interviewing techniques, we will not elaborate here on this subject a great deal. However, as just mentioned, there are several extremely important things that can be learned from a short interview. One of these is whether the student being tested perceives himself or herself as a disabled reader. Many students who are seriously disabled in reading actually believe they are about as good a reader as many of the other students in class. This is perhaps because they have heard other students orally read and make many mistakes and thus feel that it is normal for this to happen. It should also be kept in mind that a disabled reader watching other students read is not aware that they are really reading as they should be. All the disabled reader knows is that they are holding a book and turning a page every so often. There have probably been many times when the disabled reader has also picked up a book or magazine and browsed through it, looking at the pictures and perhaps picking up some of words in the main headings or from the captions under the pictures. It should be remembered that the disabled reader has no way of knowing that this is not what *everyone* does when they "read." During the interview, after rapport has been established and the interviewer has the disabled reader talking freely, an open-ended question that cannot be answered with yes or no should be asked. One of the coauthors usually simply says, "What do you think about your reading?" At this point some disabled readers will say that they think they have a reading problem; often they are able to identify their problem quite accurately, for example, "When I

---

[1]Eldon E. Ekwall collaborated with Lois Bader on the construction of the diagnostic flowchart that appears in this chapter. We wish to express our thanks for her knowledge and contributions, although we accept responsibility for the sequence and explanations presented in this chapter.

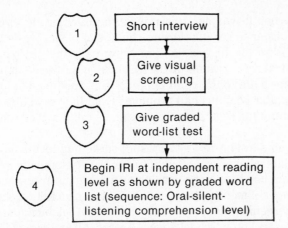

FIGURE 13–2.   The First Four Steps of the Diagnostic Process.

read I don't seem to remember what I read," or, "When I read I don't know many of the words." However, many readers will reply something along the lines of "Oh, I guess it's O.K." When disabled readers say this, it is often helpful to ask them to tell the interviewer about some of the books they have read lately.

When asked about some of the books they have read lately most disabled readers will still not readily admit that they have not read any. They will usually reply that they have checked some out of the school library. The coauthor then asks the disabled reader to tell him about some of the books. Many disabled readers will be able to give the interviewer the names of one or two books that have been checked out. The coauthor then asks the student to tell him about a particular book he or she has mentioned. At this point it becomes very obvious that the disabled reader has only checked the book out and perhaps, at most, looked at the pictures but has no knowledge whatsoever of the subject matter contained in any of the books.

The type of reader described above is often more difficult to teach since he or she does not really perceive a reading problem. Therefore, it is often necessary to counsel (very diplomatically) such disabled readers to convince them that they *do* have a problem. We feel that it is extremely important in the first few sessions that the students not only *admit* there is a problem but also *verbalize* it themselves. At this point they are much more likely to respond to instruction and take an active part in correcting it themselves.

Other things the interviewer will want to know is if the disabled reader has a quiet place to read, if a specific time is set aside to read, if he or she comes from a reading environment, if the mother and father read, and if the student is encouraged to go to, or is taken to, the public library to check out books on a periodic basis. It is also helpful to know when the reading problem started. For example, if a student started having a reading problem in the fourth grade when it was not apparent in the third grade, then the student may be much easier to remediate since he or she obviously had the potential to learn to read in the first place. In such a case the disabled reader may have experienced some traumatic event, such as a divorce in the family that upset the reader's life to the point of hampering reading. On the other hand, the disabled reader who has had problems from the very start of school may have less potential for reading (not necessarily intelligence) than many other students.

You will note in Figure 13–2 a visual screening test is next. During the interview the interviewer would want to ask the student how long it has been since the student has been to an eye doctor to have his or her eyes checked. If it has been over six months to a year, then it is probably worth the time to give a visual screening test such as the Keystone Telebinocular, the Titmus, or the Bausch and Lomb School Vision Tester. Of course, if the student already wears glasses and has gotten them recently, it would not be necessary to do this part of the diagnosis. It should, however, be emphasized that the interviewer should differentiate between whether the student has had his or her eyes checked or whether the student has been to see an eye doctor. If the interviewer simply asks whether the student has had an eye check, the student may think the interviewer means being checked by the school nurse, who often uses nothing but the Snellin Chart, which has proven to be of *absolutely no value* in testing farsightedness or near-point vision (see Chapter 8 for more information on this point).

Another reason for giving an eye test now is that it helps put the student at ease in the diagnostic process, since in most cases there is no reason for the disabled reader to be threatened by a reading-type situation. Therefore, it helps establish stronger rapport with the student being tested. You might ask, "Why is an ear examination not given at this time too?" Research by Helen Robinson (as discussed in Chapter 1) has shown that a large percentage of disabled readers have some type of eye problem, whereas problems with the ear occur less often. Possible problems with the ear are in Figure 13–4.

We now go to number 3 in Figure 13–2. This is the use of a graded word list. The graded word list is usually used to determine the point at which to start the informal reading inventory (which will be discussed in number 4). The graded word list is usually a series of ten to twenty words ranging from preprimer to sometimes as high a level as the twelfth grade. Depending on which list you are using, criteria will be given for finding a student's independent, instructional, and frustration reading levels. The student is handed a list of words beginning approximately at the point where the tester thinks the student might be reading at his or her independent level. If in doing so the tester finds that the words first given are at the student's instructional level, then the tester will have the student read the next lower grade level of words until the student's independent reading level is obtained. The tester may wish then to proceed upward by one grade at a time until the student's frustration level is found. The idea behind the use of the graded word list is to save time in administering the informal reading inventory. It should, however, be remembered that a graded word list gives no indication of the student's ability to comprehend and thus cannot ever be trusted as an accurate measure of the student's actual independent reading level. One coauthor, using the *San Diego Quick Assessment Test* to find the independent or entry level of the *Ekwall Reading Inventory* and using a sample of forty students from grades one through nine, found the exact level 18 percent of the time, within one grade level 28 percent of the time, and within two grades levels 72 percent of the time.

As you can see, the use of that particular list is not especially exact. If the teacher knew the student being tested, then the teacher might want to omit the use of the graded list. On the other hand, if the tester is completely unfamiliar with the reading level of the student about to be tested, then in most cases the use of a graded word list would probably save time in administering the informal reading inventory.

We now go to number 4 in Figure 13–2, which is the administration of an informal reading inventory. As with many instruments the informal reading inventory has its shortcomings; however, it is probably the single most valuable instrument the tester could use near the beginning of a complete diagnosis in reading. When using the informal reading inventory the student is asked to read passages at each grade level going as low as is needed to find the student's independent reading level and then continuing upward grade by grade until the instructional and frustration reading levels are found. The student usually reads two passages at each grade level and the tester then asks a series of questions on the subject matter of the material read. One of the passages at each grade level is usually read aloud by the student and the other is read silently.

The informal reading inventory will provide information on the student's knowledge of basic sight words, instant knowledge of words above the basic sight word level, use of context clues, ability to attack words that are not in the student's sight vocabulary, and the student's ability to comprehend.

Testing for Letter Knowledge

After examining the results of the informal reading inventory the tester will then know in which direction or directions to proceed.

For example, if the student did not know many of the basic sight words and was reading at a very low level, the tester would probably move to number 5 as shown in Figure 13–3. The tester would want to know if the student knew all of the letters of the alphabet. The most difficult task in knowing the letters of the alphabet would be to simply show the student a card with all of the letters of the alphabet in lower case in scrambled order and then in upper case in scrambled order and ask the student to read them (as referred to in number 6). If the student could do this, then it would be safe to assume that the student knew this skill, and the tester would simply stop at this point. On the other hand, if the student was unable to name all of the letters of the alphabet in scrambled order, the tester would move on to number 7 to determine if the student could point to the letters in scrambled order as they were pronounced by the tester. If the student could at least do this, then testing would stop at this point. If the student could not do this, then the tester would move on to number 8 and determine whether the student could match upper-case letters with lower-case letters. For example, the tester would show the student a card with a complete set of both upper- and lower-case letters. The tester might point to an upper-case T and ask the student to point to the lower-case t, and so forth. If the student could do this, then the alpha-

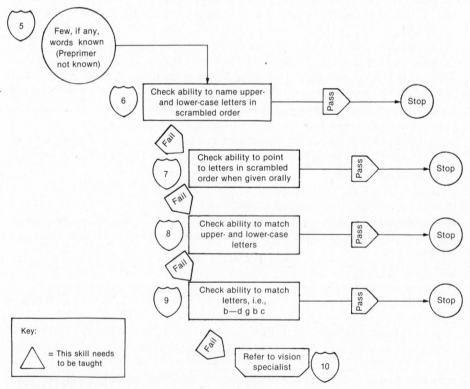

FIGURE 13–3.   Testing for Letter Knowledge.

bet testing would stop at this point. If the student could not do the task just mentioned, the tester would move on to number 9 and write in manuscript form several letters in scrambled order. For example, there would be two lower case e's, two lower case a's, etc. The student would then be asked to match each of the two letters that look alike. If the student was successful at this task, then the teacher would probably have to teach the student the letters of the alphabet. On the other hand, if the student could not even do this task, then the student should probably be referred to a vision specialist (as indicated in number 10).

Testing for Word-Recognition and Word-Analysis Skills

After administering an informal reading inventory the tester would, of course, know whether the student had problems with basic sight words or with sound-symbol (phoneme-grapheme) relationships, as shown in number 11 in Figure 13–4. If the student seemed to have trouble in attacking or in analyzing new words (number 12), the tester would then administer a phonics test (number 13). It should be stated at this point that if the tester has some doubts about the word-analysis skills of the student being tested and the student is at or above the age-grade level where these skills should have been mastered, then a phonics test might not be necessary. Any student at grade level 4.0 or above should have mastered these skills. If there is some doubt in the mind of the tester as to whether time should be taken to administer a phonics test, then the tester might want to have the student attempt to read a list of long nonsense words, such as those shown in Ekwall (1981, pp. 176–177), Ekwall (1979, pp. 20–21), or Appendix A. These are a group of long nonsense words that incorporate many of the most-used vowel digraphs, diphthongs, r-controlled vowels, and rules for soft and hard c and g. If the student about to be given tests for word-attack skills can readily read all of these words, then it would not be necessary to give a phonics test or to test for structural analysis. It should, however, be pointed out that if this list is used and the student cannot readily read all of the words, then testing with these words should stop immediately. In other words, if the student begins to falter on any of the first few words, then, rather than embarrass the student, the tester should say something to the student such as, "These are not real words; they are very difficult to read. The fact that you cannot read them is no problem. We will start with some testing that I am sure will be easier for you." The tester might then administer a phonics test. Although there are a number of phonics tests on the market, we suggest the use of the *El Paso Phonics Survey* as the phonics test to test phoneme-grapheme relationships. The reasons for using this particular type of test are listed in Chapter 5, and the test itself may be found in Appendix A. If the student missed many of the items on the *El Paso Phonics Survey*, then the tester may wish to proceed to

FIGURE 13–4. Testing for Word-Recognition and Word-Analysis Skills.

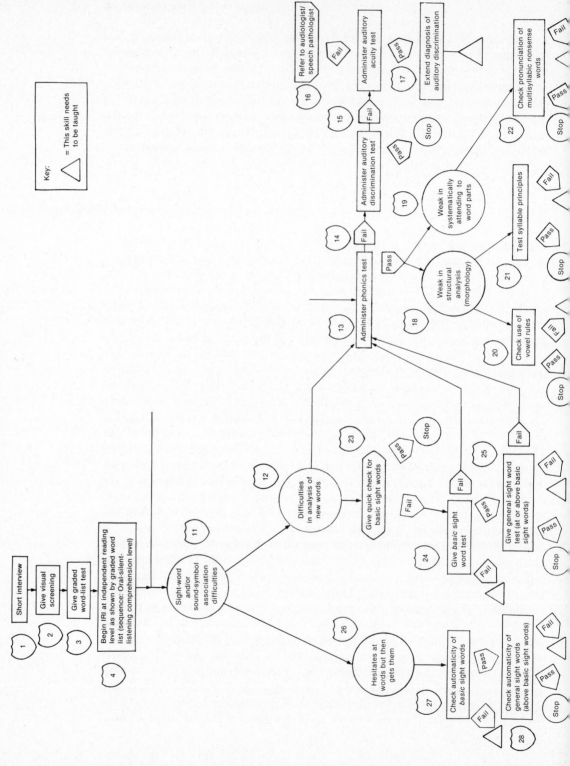

number 14 and administer an auditory discrimination test since there is a possibility that the student may not be able to distinguish the difference between or among certain sounds. We doubt, however, in most cases whether it is worth the tester's time to administer an auditory discrimination test. We are each directors of the reading center or reading clinic at our respective universities. We have found that quite a number of children fail this type of test; yet if administered again, most students after having been given proper directions again, do much better or get every item right. There are, however, a few students who really have a serious problem with auditory discrimination. Adults who have learned or attempted to learn a foreign language, no doubt, have found that, at first, they could barely tell the differences between certain sounds in the new language. Yet after hearing these sounds a number of times language learners find it becomes almost no problem at all to distinguish between sounds that, at first, presented rather serious problems. Knowing this one cannot say that, in some cases, auditory discrimination training is not necessary. An auditory discrimination test is also often helpful in discovering students who have auditory acuity problems. A student who fails an auditory discrimination test should be given another form of the same test perhaps a day or more later. If the student again fails the auditory discrimination test, it would be wise to administer an auditory acuity test (number 15). If the student is found to have a problem with auditory acuity then the student should be referred to an audiologist or speech pathologist (number 16). If the student found to have problems with auditory acuity is part of the caseload of the person doing the original testing, then the original tester should stay in close contact with the audiologist or speech pathologist, who can then advise the teacher about teaching children with this type of problem. If auditory acuity is not a problem, then further testing of auditory discrimination may be required (number 17).

If the student passes the phonics test or does reasonably well and knows nearly every phoneme-grapheme combination, yet has trouble in the analysis of new words, then you would probably want to move to number 18 to check the student's knowledge of structural analysis or morphology. However, if the student is very weak in knowledge of phoneme-grapheme relationships, there would be very little use in testing in this area for such things as the vowel rules and syllable principles (numbers 20 and 21) until the information covered on the *El Paso Phonics Survey* has been taught.

A number of the most important vowel rules will already have been tested after having given the *El Paso Phonics Survey*. For example, students knowledge of the vce and cvc vowel rules are actually tested in the vowel section of this test. Knowledge of regular vowel pairs and r-controlled vowels, as well as students' knowledge of the two most common sounds of *ow, oo,* and *ea,* are also tested. In our opinion it is so easy to assemble your own tests for knowledge of the other most common vowel rules and syllable principles that it is not worth purchasing any of the existing commercial tests designed for the purpose. Suggestions for procedures for testing for vowel rules, syllable principles and other structural analysis skills are presented in Chapter 5 of this book or Ekwall (1981, Appendix K).

As shown in number 19, occasionally a student is found who knows the information on the *El Paso Phonics Survey,* as well as the vowel rules and syllable principles. In this case you might want to give the student a list such as the *Quick Survey Word List* found in Ekwall (1981, Appendix I). If you prefer, you can simply make up some two-, three-, and four-syllable words that are phonetically regular to see if the student is simply careless in systematically working through words (number 22). Or you may follow the specific procedures for evaluating structural analysis skills that are presented in Chapter 5.

After having given the student an informal reading inventory, you may have some doubt as to whether the student knows all of the most commonly used basic sight words as shown in number 11. In this case the tester would want to move on to number 23. One of the coauthors has devised a quick check for basic sight word knowledge. This is a list of thirty-six basic sight words ranging from those that are the easiest to those most often missed by students. In constructing this quick check test this coauthor, with help from teachers in the Darlington area schools in Darlington, South Carolina, administered the Ekwall Basic Sight Word List to 500 students in each of grades two through six. The test was administered on an individual basis using a filmstrip developed for Tachomatic 500 by Psychotechnics, Inc. This had the advantage of using flash cards, but the length of time exposure to the students could be controlled somewhat better. A computer analysis was then done to indicate which words were missed, from least to the most often in ascending order. Then approximately every seventh word was used, from the easiest to the most difficult. We have found that if students are able to pronounce every word on this list given in a flash presentation, the students are likely to know almost every, or every, basic sight word, thus eliminating the need for giving an entire basic sight word test. This quick test may be found in Chapter 4 in this book or in Ekwall (1981, Appendix M).

When giving the informal reading inventory it may be quite obvious that the student has missed a number of basic sight words. In this case it would be better to simply move to number 24 and administer an entire basic sight word test. If the student fails to know a number of words on this test, then these words would have to be taught. On the other hand, if the student does very well on the entire basic word test as well as on the test for basic sight word phrases, then the tester might wish to give the student a graded sight-word test (number 25).

A graded sight-word list may be constructed from the vocabulary used in the set of basal readers the student is using. If the student knows almost all of the basic sight words but does poorly on a graded sight-word list consisting of words below his or her grade level, then it would indicate that the student simply needs to read much more to come into contact with words at a higher level more often in order to develop a larger sight vocabulary.

When you give an informal reading inventory, the student may hesitate at a number of words and then get them correct (number 26). If some of the words at which the student hesitates are basic sight words, then it would be well to give the student a flash presentation of the basic sight words to check for instant knowledge of each of these high-utility words (number 27). On the other hand, if the student has almost instant knowledge of the basic sight words, then you would want to move to number 28 to test for instant knowledge of words that the student should have developed by the grade level he or she is in. If the student hesitates at these words but then gets them, as mentioned above, then it would again indicate that the student simply needs to do more reading to come into contact with these words enough times that they become instantly known. This is the only way the student will become a fluent reader.

Testing for Context Clues

When giving the informal reading inventory you will probably be able to tell to some extent whether the student is having trouble using context clues. If this appears to be the case as shown in number 29 in Figure 13–5, then a more formal test should be given for the student's ability to use context clues (number 30). When testing a student for ability to use context clues it is extremely important not to require the student to read material at the difficult instructional level or at the frustration level.

It is quite simple to devise your own test for context clues. We suggest that you either write or find material at each grade level from grades one through at least six. Leave out certain words that are rather obvious and can be gotten from the context if the student is capable of this skill. This test differs from the cloze procedure in that it does not matter whether every fifth or every nth word is omitted. What is important is that the words left out can easily be gotten from the context. Depending on the age and grade of the student, you may want to leave out words and simply replace them with blanks, each blank having the same length. We believe a test for the use of context clues is more accurate, however, if the words omitted are replaced with Xs, with one X for every letter of the omitted word.

In most cases tests for context clues are interpreted on an informal basis; i.e., we simply say the student is pretty good, good, very poor, etc., at using context clues. One of the coauthors has written a test for context clues in which there are six reading passages written at levels from one through six. This test appears in Ekwall (1981, Appendix J). This test is designed so that the tester can tear out the page from the book and cut it in half. One half of the page is cemented to a 5" × 8" card, and the other is cemented to the other side of the card. The part the student sees contains a reading passage with about six words left out and replaced with Xs. On the other side (the side at which the tester looks) the words left out are simply underlined. A stu-

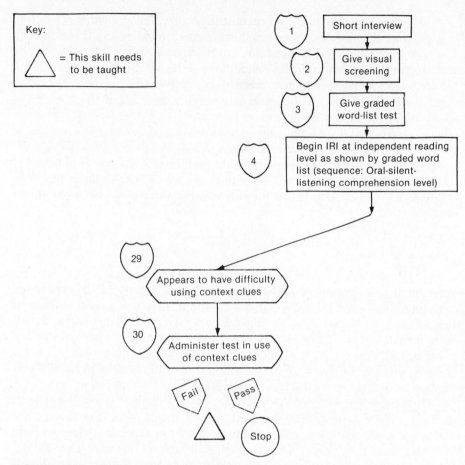

FIGURE 13–5.   Testing for Context Clues.

dent who makes no errors is considered excellent, one who makes one error is considered good, one who makes two errors is considered fair, and one who makes three or more errors is considered poor.

Testing for Comprehension and Vocabulary Skills

After having given an informal reading inventory it will, of course, be quite simple to determine if the student is having problems in the area of comprehension. If this is the case, then the tester would move to number 31, as shown in Figure 13–6. You might find that the student has recently (usually at the end of each school year) been given a standardized reading test. If one is

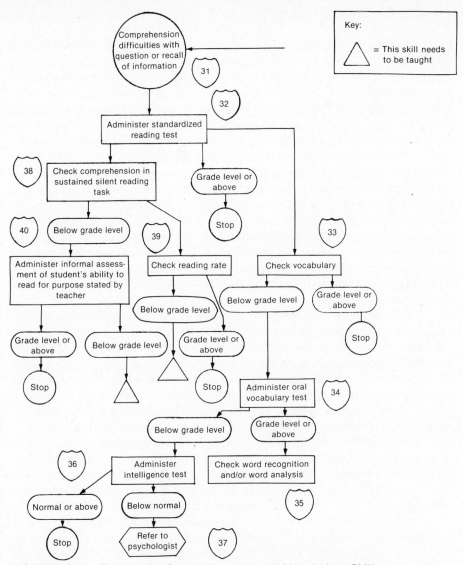

FIGURE 13-6. Testing for Comprehension and Vocabulary Skills.

not available we suggest that one be administered for the appropriate grade level (number 32). Most standardized reading tests are divided into two main sections: vocabulary and comprehension. Perhaps this terminology is incorrect since we believe vocabulary to be a subcategory of overall comprehension.

As shown in number 33, the tester would want to examine the grade-level equivalent at which the student has scored on the vocabulary section. If the student was at grade level or above, then a problem with vocabulary could be discounted and you could move on to number 38. However, if the student is below grade level on vocabulary, he or she should probably be given an oral vocabulary test (number 34). If the student scores at grade level or above then either the student has poor word-attack skills or the student read slowly enough when taking the written test to do very poorly (number 35). If this is the case, then the tester would want to check the student's ability in word attack if this had not already been done. On the other hand, if the student scored low on the oral vocabulary test too, then the tester may wish to administer, or ask a qualified psychologist to administer, an intelligence test (number 36) to test to see if the student was below normal in intelligence or at least was deprived in his or her ability to learn. If the results showed that the student was near normal or above normal in intelligence, then the tester would simply recommend that the student be given help in the development of vocabulary. If the student was considerably below normal in intelligence, the student should be referred to a psychologist for further testing (number 37) with the possibility of putting the student in a special program for students of very low intelligence.

If the student scored low in overall comprehension as shown in number 38, then it would probably be wise to check the student's reading rate (number 39). If the student's reading rate was extremely slow for grade level, then this would naturally account for part of the problem with comprehension since most standardized reading tests are timed. In this case the tester would probably want to recommend that the student be given some training in learning how to speed up his or her reading. If the student's reading rate was near normal or above, then the tester would want to discount this factor.

After checking the student's reading rate you would probably move on to number 40 to determine just where the student was having problems in overall comprehension. There are several things that could be checked here. The tester might try to determine if the student's comprehension seemed to break down at the sentence or paragraph level by having the student read and then asking a series of informal questions. The tester might also attempt to write specific kinds of questions covering written material such as those that check for the student's ability to get the main idea, important details, follow directions, and read critically. If the student did poorly in this area, then these skills would simply need to be taught.

TESTS, INSTRUMENTS, AND INFORMATION SOURCES TO APPLY TO THE DIAGNOSTIC SEQUENCE

Following is a partial list of tests, survey instruments, and sources of information on how to make your own tests or survey instruments for each of the subskills listed on the flowchart in Figure 13–1. Tests are listed in alphabetical order and only where noted do we recommend any one test or survey instrument over another. Further information on some of the tests may be found in Appendix B, such as number of forms, time for administration, grade level, subskills measured, etc. The name of the publisher is listed following each test. The complete address of each company may be found in Appendix D.

1. Further information on interviewing techniques may be found in Chapter 12 and at the beginning of this chapter.
2. *The Bausch & Lomb School Vision Tester*—Bausch & Lomb, Rochester, New York 14602;
   The Keystone Visual Survey Telebinocular—Keystone View Company, 2212 East 12th Street, Davenport, Iowa 52803;
   Titmus Vision Tester—Titmus Optical Company, Division of Applied Sciences, Petersberg, Virginia 23803.
3. *Analytical Reading Inventory*—Charles E. Merrill;
   Basic Reading Inventory—Kendall/Hunt Publishing Company;
   Classroom Reading Inventory—William C. Brown Company;
   The Contemporary Classroom Reading Inventory—Gorsuch Scarisbrick Publishers;
   Diagnostic Reading Inventory—Kendall/Hunt Publishing Company;
   Ekwall Reading Inventory—Charles E. Merrill;
   Slosson Oral Reading Test—Slosson Educational Publications;
   Wide Range Achievement Test—Stoelting Company.
4. *Analytical Reading Inventory*—Charles E. Merrill;
   Basic Reading Inventory—Kendall/Hunt Publishing Company;
   Classroom Reading Inventory—William C. Brown Company;
   The Contemporary Classroom Reading Inventory—Gorsuch Scarisbrick Publishers;
   Diagnostic Reading Inventory—Kendall/Hunt Publishing Company;
   Ekwall Reading Inventory—Allyn and Bacon.
5. Information on the student's sight vocabulary will be derived from the informal reading inventory; however, lists of basic sight words and phrases appear in Chapter 4.
6–9. For checking students' knowledge of the alphabet, we suggest that you construct a sheet as follows:

Lower Case

1. d   g   i   m   b
2. f   k   a   j   n
3. c   e   h   l   o
4. r   u   q   v   y
5. p   t   w   s   x   z

Upper Case

1. H   J   B   O   Z
2. C   I   X   R   U
3. A   G   L   S   V
4. E   M   Q   D   P
5. F   N   W   T   K   Z

Checking Ability to Match Letters

a   d   f   p   r   b
d   p   r   f   b   a

Your answer sheet may appear as follows: Mark with + for right and write in wrong answers as they are given.

1. d _____	6. f _____	11. c _____	16. r _____	21. p _____
2. g _____	7. k _____	12. e _____	17. u _____	22. t _____
3. i _____	8. a _____	13. h _____	18. q _____	23. w _____
4. m _____	9. j _____	14. l _____	19. v _____	24. s _____
5. b _____	10. n _____	15. o _____	20. y _____	25. x _____
				26. z _____

1. H _____	6. C _____	11. A _____	16. E _____	21. F _____
2. J _____	7. I _____	12. G _____	17. M _____	22. N _____
3. B _____	8. X _____	13. L _____	18. Q _____	23. W _____
4. O _____	9. R _____	14. S _____	19. D _____	24. T _____
5. Z _____	10. U _____	15. V _____	20. P _____	25. K _____
				26. Z _____

Student can match no letters_____.
Student can match some letters_____.
Student can match all letters_____.

10.   Refer to vision specialist. This referral should be to a qualified optometrist or ophthalmologist. Many school nurses still use the Snellen Chart, which is completely inadequate for measuring vision problems having to do with reading or any near-point work.

11.   As the student reads, it will become apparent whether he or she is having some problems with the analysis of new words (words that are apparently not recognized instantly and thus are not in the student's sight vocabulary). When giving an informal reading inventory the tester

usually tells the student any word at which the student pauses for more than five seconds. It will also become apparent whether the student lacks instant knowledge of some basic sight words that should have been mastered by the grade level he or she is in. For help with this analysis see the basic sight word lists in Chapter 4.

12. The student who appears to be having difficulties with the analysis of new words should be given a phonics test; however, it should be noted that a phonics test may be unnecessary for a student at a grade level where he or she should have mastered the basic skills of phonics and structural analysis (or morphology). Any student at the 4.0 grade level or above should have mastered these skills. If there is any doubt in the mind of the tester, then the tester might want to have the student attempt to read a list of long nonsense words such as shown in Ekwall (1981, pp. 176–177) or the same list as shown in Ekwall (1979, pp. 20–21) or as shown in this book in Appendix A. The use of this list was explained earlier in this chapter.

13. If the student is below the level where most of the skills of phonics and structural analysis should have been mastered, then he or she should be given a phoneme-grapheme (sound-symbol) test. We recommend the use of the *El Paso Phonics Survey* in making this assessment, for the reasons listed in Chapter 5. We urge the tester to be sure to consider the student's ability to apply phonics skills *in the act of reading* along with the results of the *El Paso Phonics Survey*.

14. *Auditory Discrimination in Depth*—Teaching Resources Corporation;
    The Auditory Discrimination Test—Language Research Associates;
    Goldman-Fristoe-Woodcock Test of Auditory Discrimination—American Guidance Service;
    Stanford Diagnostic Reading Test—Harcourt Brace Jovanovich;
    The Testing-Teaching Module of Auditory Discrimination—Pro-Ed.

15. Generally auditory acuity testing is left to the school nurse or the speech pathology department of larger universities. For the average remedial reading teacher it is probably better to refer the student with severe auditory discrimination problems to one of these people. On the other hand, it is not difficult to learn to use an instrument such as the Maico Model MA 39, MA 40, and MA 41—Maico Hearing Instruments, Inc., 7375 Bush Lake Road, Minneapolis, Minnesota 55435.

16. If the child is found to have an auditory acuity problem, he or she should be referred to an audiologist or speech pathologist.

17. If the child passes the auditory acuity test, then the diagnosis of auditory discrimination should be extended. Both of us have found in our respective clinics that students often fail an auditory discrimination test when given the first time but when given the second time, even though it is a different form, they perform quite satisfactorily. We often find that students who fail an auditory discrimination test do not understand the

directions; e.g., they think that they should respond with a statement of "same" when the words rhyme rather than call them "different" because they are not exactly alike. A more thorough discussion of auditory discrimination problems can be found in Chapter 8.

18. It should be kept in mind that a student who can use the vowel rules and syllable principles does not really need to know the rules per se. The learning of the syllable principles and vowel rules is a means to an end—and that end is being able to pronounce words that are not in the student's sight vocabulary. It is also important to note that one reason for teaching syllabication is so that the student knows the position of the vowel in a word; then, applying the proper vowel rule, the student is able to make a much more educated guess at the word than had the student simply tried every vowel combination possible.

The teacher should keep in mind that it is not necessarily knowledge of the rule in the sense of being able to state the rule that is important. What is important is that the student is able to use the rule. Many students can use rules, but if you asked them to recite the rule, they would be hard pressed to do so. Suggestions for constructing your own materials for testing students on vowel rules and syllable principles may be found in Ekwall (1981) or in this book in Chapter 5. A thorough description of alternative methods for testing for structural analysis skills is also presented in Chapter 5.

19. Some students are weak in systematically attacking words although they have the necessary skills to do so. Techniques for diagnosis in this area are presented in Chapter 5. You may also construct a list of two-, three-, and four-syllable words above the student's reading level or make nonsense words and give the student practice in working through these words.

20. Descriptions on how to make your own test on vowel rules are found in Chapter 5 and may also be found in Ekwall (1981).

21. Descriptions on how to make your own test on syllable principles may be found in Chapter 5, and in Ekwall (1981).

22. To see whether students can pronounce words systematically if given the time, make up two-, three-, and four-syllable words and nonsense words that are phonetically regular and see if, given encouragement and time, the students are able to use the word-attack skills that they should have learned. Description and examples are provided in Chapter 5.

23. If there is some doubt as to whether the student knows his or her basic sight words, we suggest that the student be given the Quick Check for Basic Word Knowledge found in Chapter 4. The student who misses any of these words should be given a check for an entire list of basic sight words. On the other hand, if the student does not miss any of these words, it can be taken for granted that the student knows all or nearly

all the basic sight words and would not need to be checked on an entire list of basic sight words.

24. *Basic Word Vocabulary Test*—Jamestown Publishers;
    Dolch Basic Sight Word Test—Garrard Publishing Company;
    Essential Sight Words Program—Teaching Resources Corporation;
    The Instant Words Criterion Test—Jamestown Publishers;
    Harris-Jacobson List—Harris, Albert J., and Sipay, Edward R. *How to Increase Reading Ability.* 7th ed., Longman: New York, 1980, pp. 372–373.

25. To test for knowledge of words that the student should have in his or her sight vocabulary, you can use the word lists found in basal readers. Students will probably not have quite all of these words in their sight vocabulary even if they are fair to good readers; however, it will enable you to get an idea whether the student is seriously deficient in words that are above those usually found on basic sight word lists but are above that level depending on the grade level of the basal reader to which the student is assigned.

26. When a student hesitates at words and then gets them correctly, this is usually a sign that the student has fair to good word-analysis or word-attack skills but that some words that the student should know by sight are not in that student's sight vocabulary.

27. The first step in determining whether a student is hesitating at words and getting them is to determine if the words are basic sight words or words above the level of those usually listed on basic sight word lists. The same procedure would be used here as in numbers 23, 24, and 25.

27,28. Follow the same procedure here as described in numbers 23, 24, and 25.

29. As the student reads, it will become apparent to some extent whether the student is able to effectively use context clues. It should be kept in mind that a student will not be able to use context clues effectively if he or she is reading at the frustration or near-frustration level. The student must be reading at an easy instructional level or at the independent level in order to make good use of context clues. The tester can easily make up tests for the use of context clues by using a set of graded passages in which some of the words are left out. When constructing these passages be sure that words omitted are those that could be gotten by using the context if the student understands what he or she is reading. The authors suggest making passages approximately thirty to forty words long leaving approximately six blanks. A student who makes no errors can be considered excellent at using context clues. A student who makes only one error can be considered good. A student who makes two errors can be considered fair, and a student who makes three or more errors can be considered poor. A test for the use of context clues can be found in Ekwall (1981, Appendix J).

30. Administer test as described in number 29.

31. When administering an informal reading inventory it will also become apparent to some extent whether the student is having problems with comprehension. However, some informal reading inventories do not contain enough questions for the tester to determine this. In this case the tester should administer a group achievement test such as one of those described in number 32. Since these are normally administered at either the beginning or end of the school year, it may not be necessary to take the time to administer a group achievement test, as it may already be in the student's record folder.

32. *California Achievement Tests*—CTB/McGraw-Hill;
    Gates-MacGinitie Reading Tests—Riverside Publishing Company;
    Iowa Tests of Basic Skills—Houghton Mifflin;
    Iowa Tests of Educational Development—SRA;
    Metropolitan Achievement Tests—Psychological Corporation;
    Monroe Standardized Silent Reading Tests—Bobbs-Merrill;
    Nelson Reading Skills Tests—Houghton Mifflin;
    Nelson Reading Tests—Riverside Publishing Company;
    Pressey Diagnostic Reading Tests—Bobbs-Merrill Educational
        Publishing;
    Reading Comprehension in Varied Subject Matter—Educators Publish-
        ing Service;
    SRA Achievement Series—SRA;
    Stanford Achievement Test—Psychological Corporation;
    Stanford Diagnostic Reading Test—Harcourt Brace Jovanovich;
    Sequential Tests of Educational Progress—Educational Testing Service;
    Test of Reading Comprehension—Pro-Ed;
    Woodcock Reading Mastery Tests—American Guidance Service.

33. Nearly all of the tests listed in number 32 have a reading vocabulary section that may be checked separately; however, all the tests in the following list have separate reading vocabulary sections:
    California Achievement Tests—CTB/McGraw-Hill;
    Iowa Tests of Educational Development—SRA;
    Metropolitan Achievement Tests—Psychological Corporation;
    Nelson Reading Skills Test—Houghton Mifflin;
    Pressey Diagnostic Reading Tests—Bobbs-Merrill Educational
        Publishing;
    School and College Ability Tests—Addison-Wesley Publishing Company;
    SRA Achievement Series—SRA;
    Stanford Achievement Test—Psychological Corporation;
    Test of Reading Comprehension—Pro-Ed;
    Vocabulary Comprehension Scale—Teaching Resources Corporation;
    Vocabulary Test for High School Students and College Students—
        Bobbs-Merrill Educational Publishing;
    Woodcock Reading Mastery Test—American Guidance Service.

34. *Gates-McKillop Reading Diagnostic Test*—Teachers College Press. (The 1962 edition contains an oral vocabulary test, but the newer version published in 1981 does not);

McCarthy Scales of Children's Abilities—Psychological Corporation (a short test meant only for ages 2½ to 8½);

Stanford-Binet Intelligence Scales—Houghton Mifflin;

Wechsler Adult Intelligence Scale (WAIS)—Psychological Corporation;

Wechsler Intelligence Scale for Children (WISC)—Psychological Corporation;

Wechsler Preschool and Primary Scale of Intelligence (WPPSI)—Psychological Corporation;

Woodcock Reading Mastery Tests—American Guidance Service.

35. If the student's oral vocabulary is near grade level or above, then a low score on the standardized reading vocabulary test would probably mean that the student had poor word-recognition or word-analysis skills. That is to say, the student simply could not read the words on the written test well enough to respond properly and thus achieved a low score. In this case one would want to go back to number 12 (difficulties in analysis of new words) if it had not already been done.

36. *Slosson Intelligence Test*—Slosson Educational Publications;

Stanford-Binet Intelligence Scales—Houghton Mifflin;

Wechsler Adult Intelligence Scale (WAIS)—Psychological Corporation;

Wechsler Intelligence Scale for Children (WISC)—Psychological Corporation;

Wechsler Preschool and Primary Scale of Intelligence (WPPSI)—Psychological Corporation.

37. A student with an extremely low IQ should be referred to a psychologist for further evaluation.

38. Check the comprehension scores from one of the tests listed in number 32.

39. Reading rate can be checked informally using materials of approximately the same reading level as those in the standardized reading test or at the grade level the student is in. Let the student read for approximately five minutes and then divide the total number of words read by five (if the student read for five minutes). An easier way of counting this many words is to count the words in three lines and divide by three to find the average number of words per line. Then take that number and multiply it by the number of lines read. This will usually give a figure nearly as accurate as counting every word, a very time-consuming job. A chart showing the number of words that a student should be able to read at each grade level may be found in the following source:

Harris, Albert J., and Sipay, Edward R. *How to Increase Reading Ability.* 7th ed., New York: Longman, 1980, pp. 556 and 560.

40. There is a great deal of controversy in the field of reading as to whether various reading subskills can be identified, e.g., reading for main ideas, important details, author's purpose, author's organization, following directions, etc. Most of the studies that have tried to identify specific skills have shown that a student who is good in one of these skills is likely to be good in all of them. The method of attempting to identify these specific skills is called *factor analysis.* This is a very difficult procedure and although it may appear to be an appropriate one for differentiating the subskills, it may still leave something to be desired. We would recommend the following source for information on informal diagnosis in the assessment of abilities in comprehension: Bader, Lois A. *Reading Diagnosis and Remediation in Classroom and Clinic.* New York: Macmillan, 1980, pp. 97–123.

SUMMARY

In this chapter we have described a step-by-step method of conducting the reading diagnosis, following the diagnostic flowchart that was also presented in this chapter. We have discussed how this approach can lead to more efficient use of time when completing the diagnosis and have provided a list of tests, survey instruments, and sources of information on how to prepare your own tests or survey instruments for each of the subskills listed on the flowchart.

REFERENCES

Ekwall, Eldon E. *Ekwall Reading Inventory.* Boston: Allyn and Bacon, 1979.
Ekwall, Eldon, E. *Locating and Correcting Reading Difficulties.* 3rd ed., Columbus, Ohio: Charles E. Merrill, 1981.

14

The Administration of the Remedial Reading Program

This chapter begins with a discussion of the roles and responsibilities of various types of reading specialists and the importance of two-way communication in defining these roles. This is followed by a discussion of ways in which the remedial reading teacher, the administrator, and parents can extend their help in the remedial reading program. Suggestions are then given for selecting and scheduling students. Following this, suggestions are given for developing facilities for and evaluating the remedial reading program. And, in conclusion, the International Reading Association's recommendations are presented as a code of ethics and qualifications for reading specialists.

THE ROLE OF THE READING SPECIALIST

A number of titles exist for various types of reading specialists depending on the role they are expected to serve. In 1979 the Evaluation Committee of the International Reading Association reported on a membership survey that identified the following official job titles: reading consultant, reading coordinator, reading diagnostician, reading specialist, reading supervisor, reading teacher, remedial reading teacher, and classroom teacher. In addition, more than 25 percent of the respondents had titles other than those mentioned above. The term *reading specialist* is considered the generic term. However, the International Reading Association suggests four main roles, or types, of reading specialists as follows:

A. *Special Teacher of Reading*
    A Special Teacher of Reading has major responsibility for remedial and corrective and/or developmental reading instruction.

B.   *Reading Clinician*
      A Reading Clinician provides diagnosis, remediation, or the planning of remediation for the more complex and severe reading disability cases.

C.   *Reading Consultant*
      A Reading Consultant works directly with teachers, administrators, and other professionals within a school to develop and implement the reading program under the direction of a supervisor with special training in reading.

D.   *Reading Supervisor*
      A Reading Supervisor provides leadership in all phases of the reading program in a school system.[1]

It should, of course, be remembered that in many schools and school systems any one reading specialist may take on a dual role and serve as both a special teacher of reading and as a reading consultant or as a combination of reading clinician and reading consultant, etc.

The Need for Clarification of the Role of Reading Personnel

Problems sometimes arise, especially in the case of newly assigned reading personnel, when their roles are not clearly defined. The defining of roles should also be a two-way process. That is, the reading specialist and the administrators and teachers with whom the reading specialist will be working should all perceive the reading specialist's job in the same way. As previously mentioned, however, problems are often created when there are diversified concepts of the role of reading personnel.

The problem of diversified concepts of the role of the reading consultant was illustrated by Richard Wylie (1969), who surveyed 100 classroom teachers and 100 reading consultants chosen randomly from four New England states. Wylie's questionnaire returns came from teachers in twenty-two communities and from consultants in sixty-three communities. Wylie asked several questions of consultants, but two which seem of importance in illustrating this problem were as follows:

Question 1:   "In what areas of reading instruction should the consultant give aid to the new teacher?" (p. 519)

The results of the teacher's and consultant's answers are shown in Table 14–1.

It is important to note that the teachers expected the consultant to come into their classroom or at least be invited to demonstrations on "how" to teach certain concepts or how to use new materials. On the other hand, the

[1]Reproduced by permission of the International Reading Association from a brochure entitled, *Roles, Responsibilities, and Qualifications—Reading Specialists.* Professional Standards and Ethics Committee of the International Reading Association, Newark, Delaware.

TABLE 14–1. Comparison of Teacher versus Consultant Views on Question 1.

Teacher	Frequency	Percent	Consultant	Frequency	Percent
Materials	66	85	Materials	72	86
Demonstrations	63	81	Time allotments	68	81
Diagnostic and corrective procedures	63	81	Grouping	64	76
Grouping	58	74	Scope of total program	63	75
Interpretation of test results	57	73	Interpretation of test results	63	75

reading consultants did not even consider this as a part of their job. The teachers also expected help with diagnostic and corrective procedures, but again, the consultants did not perceive this as a part of their job. It is also important to note that the consultants were concerned with time allotments and the scope of the program, whereas the reading teachers did not consider these factors in evaluating this phase of the reading consultant's job.

Question 2: "How should the consultant extend this aid?" (p. 519)

The results of the teacher's and consultant's answers to this question are shown in Table 14–2.

It should be noted that the teachers again believed that the consultant should do demonstration teaching and should free time for teachers to visit other classrooms within their school or other schools within the systems. Yet the consultants evidently believed that these two items were not a part of their role. It is interesting to note that the kinds of activities that the consultants believe they should perform would seldom take them out of their office and never take them into the classrooms to work with children.

Rita Bean (1979) studied teacher ratings of various reading specialist roles and analyzed the actual time spent by specialists in these roles. The study was conducted in a Right to Read Special Emphasis Project in Pittsburgh, Pennsylvania. The most valued and least valued roles of the reading specialists as perceived by teachers were as follows:

Most valued
In-service role
Developing materials (with teachers)
Conferring with teachers
Individual instruction (out of classroom)

TABLE 14–2.   Comparison of Teacher versus Consultant Views on Question 2.

Teacher	Frequency	Percent	Consultant	Frequency	Percent
In-service education; small groups, grade-level meetings	73	94	In-service education; grade-level meetings	79	94
Demonstration teaching	70	90	Orientation program early in year	74	88
			Bulletins or letters to teachers	70	83
Free time to visit other classrooms —schools	67	86	Suggestions of courses to take	61	73
Frequent meetings with reading specialists	62	79			
Workshops	44	56	Workshops	50	50

Least valued
Diagnosis—individual in the classroom
Diagnosis—group in the classroom
Group instruction in the classroom

The teachers rated the resource role as the most highly valued role. Yet an analysis of the actual time spent by the reading specialists revealed that this role is assumed only a small percentage of the time.

John Pikulski and Elliott Ross (1979) reported that reading specialists were seen as important and necessary personnel at all grade levels. The researchers also found that teachers wished to see reading specialists spend some time in a consulting role; however, the teachers preferred that reading specialists spend the vast majority of their time providing direct instruction to students. Pikulski and Ross also reported that classroom teachers expected reading specialists to be knowledgeable about reading instruction, to possess positive attitudes about people, and to respond well in interpersonal relationships.

John Mangieri and Mary Heimberger (1980) reported on the contrast in role expectations between reading specialists and school administrators. Questionnaires completed by 160 reading consultants and 156 administrators from five states are summarized in Table 14-3.

As the table indicates, the two roles that were most important to administrators were least important to reading consultants and vice versa. In this case the reading consultant's perceptions were consistent with those of the classroom teachers as reported by Bean, but somewhat in conflict with the teachers' perceptions reported by Pikulski and Ross.

The information presented above, as well as our own experience as consultants and in working with other consultants, leads us to conclude that before any new reading personnel begin their duties there should be a clear-cut understanding, in writing, of the role of various reading specialists. Further evidence of this problem was emphasized by Karl Hesse, Richard Smith, and Aileen Nettleton (1973), who studied content-area teachers' view of the role of the secondary reading consultant. They stated:

> There are differences in perceptions regarding the role of secondary school reading consultants among administrators, content area teachers, and reading consultants.
>
> Perceptions differ within content area departments as well as among content area departments.
>
> Because these differing perceptions do exist, for the sake of harmony and staff morale, it would probably be wise to assess the perceptions of all concerned personnel before the responsibilities of the consultant are decided. (p. 215)

Another problem has arisen from the implementation of P. L. 94-142 (discussed in Chapter 2) and the emergence of learning disabilities teachers. Many schools now employ both reading specialists and learning disabilities

TABLE 14-3.   Ranking of Reading Consultant's Roles (most important to least important).

By school administrators	By reading consultants
Instructor	In-service Leader
Diagnostician	Resource Person
Evaluator	Investigator
Adviser	Adviser
Investigator	Evaluator
In-service Leader	Instructor
Resource Person	Diagnostician

Reprinted with the permission of John Mangieri and the International Reading Association.

specialists. Since most of the students identified as learning disabled are primarily deficient in reading ability, the potential for conflict between the two types of specialists is great. Walter Sawyer and Bonnie Wilson (1979) suggest that learning disabilities teachers tend to use a medical model that focuses on the etiology (cause) of the problem, while reading specialists tend to evaluate the student's strengths and weaknesses along a "developmental skill hierarchy." These generalizations are broad and not accurate in all cases. However, there is a real possibility that students will suffer if one or the other specialists seeks to monopolize the remedial program, or worse, if both specialists work with students using drastically different approaches. Conflicting approaches may confuse students and negate the possibility for improvement. Sawyer and Wilson recommend that reading specialists focus on the acquisition and development of reading skills, while learning disabilities specialists assume primary responsibility for maintaining students in the "least restrictive environment." Both specialists have roles to play in the development of the IEP. In order to be of greatest assistance to students, the school administrator and classroom teachers should participate with the specialists in defining and clarifying the role expectations.

Problems are also likely to arise in terms of the school administrative structure when dealing with various reading specialists. For example, the elementary school principal usually knows exactly how he or she fits into the administrative structure of most school programs. This position might be illustrated as in Figure 14–1. Likewise the remedial reading teacher, or even

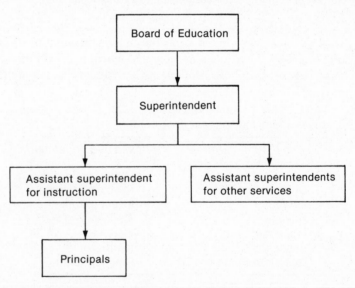

FIGURE 14–1.   Administrative Structure Showing the Position of the Principal.

the person who serves a dual role of part-time teacher and part-time consultant within one school, usually falls into a common administrative structure as in Figure 14–1 because they would simply extend below the principal, as shown in Figure 14–2.

However, the problem sometimes becomes more complicated when dealing with full-time supervisors or consultants who work in several schools. In these cases the administrative structure may be more like that shown in Figure 14–3.

In a situation as shown in Figure 14–3, problems are often encountered when teachers realize they really have more than one "boss." Further difficulties are often encountered in that there are no clear lines of authority between each school principal and various consultants and/or supervisors. Where the consultant and/or supervisor and principal are both congenial and diplomatic, this may matter very little. However, when the consultant and/or supervisor possess beliefs considerably different from those of the principal, it is often difficult for both to work harmoniously together.

The point of this, of course, is that before any reading position is filled, a needs assessment in reading should be conducted in the school or school district. In conducting this assessment participants should include all school administrators who are likely to be involved in working with the program, some classroom teachers, and, if possible, a competent consultant from a college or university who is familiar with the training of various reading specialists, their duties, titles, etc.

The duties and title of the reading specialist will depend on such factors as the size of the district, the number of schools with which the specialist will be expected to work, the competencies of teachers already within the school system, and other reading specialists already employed and their duties and titles. However, in order to clarify the roles of various types of reading personnel and the duties they may be expected to perform, the guidelines that follow should be helpful.

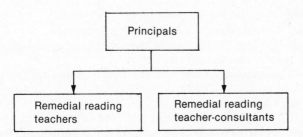

FIGURE 14–2.   Administrative Structure Showing the Position of the Remedial Reading Teacher or Teacher-Consultant Within Any One School.

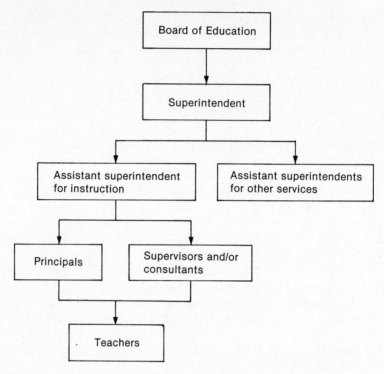

FIGURE 14-3.   A School Administrative Structure in Which There Are Supervisors and/or Consultants.

Responsibilities of Each Reading Specialist[2]

A. *Special Teacher of Reading*
Should identify students needing diagnosis and/or remediation.
Should plan a program of remediation from data gathered through diagnosis.
Should implement such a program of remediation.
Should evaluate student progress in remediation.
Should interpret student needs and progress in remediation to the classroom teacher and the parents.
Should plan and implement a developmental or advanced program as necessary.

B. *Reading Clinician*
Should demonstrate all the skills expected of the Special Teacher of Reading and, by virtue of additional training and experience, diagnose and treat the more complex and severe reading disability cases.

[2]Reproduced by permission of the International Reading Association.

Should demonstrate proficiency in providing internship training for prospective clinicians and/or Special Teachers of Reading.

C. *Reading Consultant*

Should survey and evaluate the ongoing program and make suggestions for needed changes.

Should translate the district philosophy of reading with the help of the principal of each school into a working program consistent with the needs of the students, the teachers, and the community.

Should work with classroom teachers and others in improving the developmental and corrective aspects of the reading program.

D. *Reading Supervisor*

Should develop a system-wide reading philosophy and curriculum, and interpret this to the school administration, staff, and public.

Should exercise leadership with all personnel in carrying out good reading practices.

Should evaluate reading personnel and personnel needs in all phases of a school-wide reading program.

Should make recommendations to the administration regarding the reading budget.

The Reading Specialist Position in Two School Districts

The guidelines shown above are those suggested by the International Reading Association. As stated previously, however, many school districts do not differentiate among the four specific titles as clearly as suggested here. For example, in the Parkway School District in Chesterfield, Missouri, and the Hayward School District in Hayward, California, much of the time of personnel working in reading is spent in teaching remedial reading. However, these reading specialists do not limit their time exclusively to the teaching of remedial reading. A description of the role of the reading specialist in both districts follows. In addition, information is provided on the development, recruitment, training, coordination, and resources for the Hayward program.

Role of the Reading Specialist, Parkway School District (1972)[3]

I. Remedial Reading

The primary role of the reading specialist in the Parkway School District is the instruction of pupils possessing deficient reading skills in relation to their reading potential.

A. Instruction

1. In the development of a caseload the following steps are taken:

a. A reading survey test is administered to these pupils to determine present reading ability.

[3]Reproduced by permission of the Parkway School District. Marti Sellinriek, Language Arts Coordinator, 1972.

    b. The reading specialist, working with the staff, will obtain referrals of pupils considered to be disabled readers.

    c. Guidance counselors will assist the reading specialists in administering individual intelligence tests to these pupils.

    d. A "potential caseload" consisting of no less than 50 pupils is developed according to state guidelines. Normally, a total of 30 to 40 pupils will receive instruction at any given period of time, beginning with top priority pupils.

    e. Pupils may be phased out of the program when it is felt that further remedial instruction is no longer considered beneficial.

    f. The required state forms are to be submitted to the State Department by October 15.

2. A course of study is prescribed for the pupils selected to receive remedial reading instruction in the following manner:

    a. A battery of diagnostic tests is administered to determine individual strengths and deficits.

    b. The reading specialist attempts to identify the pupil's preferred modality of learning.

    c. Awareness of pupil's attitudes and interests assists the specialist in motivating learners.

    d. Necessary data collected from the home, classroom, medical or other sources, as well as information used in the remedial process, will be placed in the folder required by the state for each child.

    e. A remedial reading program is planned for each student through the use of materials designed specifically to meet the needs of individual pupils.

    f. Cooperative planning by the reading specialist and the classroom teacher is necessary to provide methods and materials to be used in the classroom which correlate with the remedial reading program.

3. Schedules will be developed with the following consideration:

    a. A schedule is established for remedial classes on the basis of common needs for groups no larger than six students.

    b. Time will be allotted for staffing with teachers, clinic personnel, and other non-teaching responsibilities.

4. Instruction is conducted according to the following procedures:

    a. Parents are informed of pupil's inclusion in the remedial reading program.

    b. Instruction is given to remedial pupils, individually or in small groups.

    c. Evaluation is a continual process and the individual instructional program may be changed when necessary.

    d. During the process of remedial teaching, feedback and recommendations to the staff concerning the students should also be continuous.

    e. Pupil's progress will be reported to parents through conferences or other means of communication.

5. Referrals
   a. Referrals to the Parkway Right to Read Reading Clinic will be made when deemed advisable by the reading specialist.
   b. A reading specialist may initiate referrals to Special School District or other outside agencies according to Parkway guidelines.

B. Advisory and In-Service Education

The reading specialist serves as an advisor in the remedial area by working with administrators, teachers, guidance counselors, and the Parkway Right to Read Reading Clinic in the following ways:

1. To interpret the role of the reading specialist and the remedial program.
2. To help teachers administer diagnostic tests and interpret test results.
3. To assist the administration in planning the budget in the area of reading.
4. To help teachers understand materials used for remedial purposes.

C. Curriculum Development

In the area of Remedial Curriculum Development, the reading specialist has the following responsibilities:

1. To assist the district in development and/or location of materials for use by the disabled reader in the content areas.
2. To assist the district in development of programs for the early identification of student's potential learning style as it relates to the teaching of reading.
3. To provide orientation for new members of the reading specialist staff in the Parkway School system.
4. To participate in providing programs designed to improve the skills of the total reading staff. This may be done in cooperation with the staff of the Parkway Right to Read Reading Clinic.

The reading specialist will have a secondary role of assisting in the areas of corrective and developmental reading instruction.

II. Corrective Reading

A. Instruction

1. The reading specialist will introduce corrective materials for classroom instruction, upon teacher request.
2. Emphasis will be placed on the use of alternative methods of instruction as a means of preventing reading disabilities.
3. Follow-up and evaluation of materials introduced shall be conducted.

B. Advisory and In-Service

The reading specialist will serve as a resource teacher in the following activities:

1. Assists classroom teachers in initiating diagnosis of pupils and interpreting results of data collected.
2. Assists the teacher with classroom organization for corrective instruction.
3. Observes disabled readers in a classroom situation, upon teacher request.

    4. Evaluates pupil progress and performance in cooperation with the classroom teacher.

    5. Assists in the evaluation and selection of appropriate materials utilized by the classroom teacher for corrective instruction.

    6. Provides demonstration of new methods and materials.

C. Curriculum Development

    1. The reading specialist will evaluate programs presently in use for corrective instruction.

    2. New programs will be evaluated to assess their appropriateness for use in corrective instruction in Parkway.

    3. The reading specialist, in conjunction with the Parkway Right to Read Reading Clinic, will give assistance to teachers in developing corrective reading techniques.

III. Developmental Reading

A. Instruction

The role of the reading specialist is to become familiar with the developmental programs of each assigned school. This will allow the specialist to make suggestions for pupils' past reading experiences and present abilities.

B. Advisory and In-Service

In helping teachers, at their request, to initiate and develop reading programs in their class groups, assistance will be given in an advisory capacity toward a diagnostic approach to developmental reading instruction. This method would include the following activities:

    1. Reviews current information available from individual pupils.

    2. Obtains new information about the pupils.

    3. Selects a teaching approach (personalized, basal, etc.).

    4. Groups pupils for instruction.

    5. Selects appropriate materials.

    6. Plans periodic evaluation to assess the need for changes in materials or grouping.

    7. Assists teachers in developing goals and planning budgets in the area of developmental reading.

C. Curriculum Development

The reading specialist:

    1. Serves as a liaison between the classroom teacher and the language arts coordinator.

    2. Assists teachers to become familiar with new methods and materials.

    3. Plans and develops special reading projects.

    4. Interacts with the director of Research and Planning in those areas involving reading.

Role of the Reading Specialist
Priority Chart:
1. Primary responsibility
2. Secondary responsibility
3. Advisory responsibility

	Instruction	Advisory and in-service education (within each school)	Curriculum development
Remedial Reading	1	2	2
Corrective Reading	2	2	2
Developmental Reading	3	3	3

The position of reading specialist in the Parkway School District involves much more than simply being a teacher of reading. As outlined by the International Reading Association, in that district the reading specialist might be considered a "special teacher of reading," a "reading clinician" (since all teachers are highly trained in the clinical aspects of reading), or a "reading consultant," and in some ways these same people take on the duties of "reading supervisor."

Evidence on the importance of task competencies that count among reading specialists was presented by V.V. Garry (1974). Garry developed an extensive list of various competencies using a research of the literature, interviews with reading authorities, and interviews with advisors from the State Department of Education and reading specialist training institutions. Garry's list of task competencies was then presented to randomly chosen reading personnel, who were requested to assign a degree of importance to each task competency. Task competencies were rated on a scale of five through one. From a total of fifty competencies, twelve were rated in the highest quartile. These twelve were as follows:

1. "Helping teachers plan and provide corrective and remedial reading instruction and suggesting remedial techniques for disabled readers both in the classroom and special reading program."
2. "Teaching small groups of disabled readers."
3. "Assisting in interpretation of standardized and informal reading test results."
4. "Assisting classroom teachers in diagnosing and analyzing students' strengths and weaknesses in various skills areas."
5. "Diagnosing and recommending treatment for more complex and severe reading disability cases."
6. "Referring pupils with special problems to proper agencies such as guidance and psychological services."
7. "Providing guidance in determining extent of reading retardation by utilizing various procedures."
8. "Providing guidance in selecting and identifying candidates for remedial reading classes or a reading clinic."
9. "Providing guidelines and practical assistance for evaluating student progress in remediation."

10. "Suggesting and demonstrating use of instructional materials and procedures to teachers."
11. "Selecting and developing materials to promote higher level reading competency."
12. "Encouraging, helping, and stimulating teachers to use different strategies of teaching reading such as programmed reading, language-experience, individualized reading." (pp. 609–612)

It is important to note that in the Parkway School District, as well as in the study just quoted, the reading specialist is not expected to perform only one very specific role such as "remedial reading teacher." This is a healthy situation since it allows the reading specialist, regardless of title, to perform a role in which there is more communication between the classroom teacher and reading specialist. This communication, of course, provides an opportunity for the reading specialist to provide for more effective in-service education and inevitably to influence a school's reading program to a greater extent.

In the Hayward, California, Unified School District thirty-four reading specialists serve twenty-four elementary schools. Each of the schools has one reading specialist assigned to serve either kindergarten to grade three or grades four to six, depending on the needs of the school. Ten of the schools have a second reading specialist, so that in these schools all elementary students and teachers are served.[4]

The program is supported by a combination of special state funds and district resources. James Shanker was engaged by the Hayward district to serve as the district reading consultant. The primary emphasis was on the development of an elementary reading specialist program to assist administrators and teachers in promoting effective reading instruction.

The following beliefs guided the development of the Hayward program:

1. Leadership and support from the school board, the superintendent, and other district administrators are essential.
2. The principal, as key curriculum leader at the school site, should be involved in all efforts undertaken to improve reading instruction.
3. Only the most outstanding, fully qualified specialists should be hired.
4. The specialists must function as a coordinated group. It is the district's responsibility to provide leadership that will enable the reading specialists to clarify roles and responsibilities, define uniform procedures where needed, and develop essential materials and resources. Regular meetings of the group must occur.
5. The charge of the reading specialists must not be limited to remedial instruction. Their responsibilities should include assistance with all

[4]Some of the information in this section appeared in Shanker, James L. "The Reading Specialist Position: The Hayward Program," *Selected Proceedings from the Thirteenth Annual Conference of the California Reading Association,* San Diego, California, 1979.

facets of the school reading program, especially the improvement of classroom teaching practices.

6.   The reading specialists must receive ongoing supervision and assistance. They should be recognized for the outstanding work that they do and be provided with rewards and incentives to maintain their professional excellence.

Three steps were taken in the district to provide a framework for the effective implementation of the reading specialist program. These were as follows:

1.   A Reading Planning Committee was formed to respond to the need for a well-thought-out, coherent, and district-sanctioned reading curriculum. This committee was composed of elementary and secondary teachers, district administrators, and the reading consultant. A subcommittee of this group prepared a K–6 Reading Guide for use by all elementary teachers and administrators. The development of this guide served to clarify district expectations and to coordinate the school reading programs.

2.   The elementary schools adopted a new reading program, selected by teachers, to provide greater uniformity in the developmental reading curriculum.

3.   All district principals and selected central office administrators participated in an eleven-week refresher course that emphasized content and methods of reading instruction.

All available positions were advertised. Candidates were sought from both inside and outside the district and were selected after a thorough screening and interviewing procedure. This process was designed to determine the candidate's specific academic training, experience in both classroom and remedial reading instruction at the appropriate grade levels, ability to work effectively with classroom teachers and school administrators, and desire to serve children with special needs.

Each candidate was interviewed by a panel that included district administrators, reading specialists, and the district reading consultant. It should be noted that many of the specialists accepted positions on temporary contracts because enrollment had declined and because there could be no guarantee of continued state funding.

Under the direction of the reading consultant, intensive training workshops were held at the district office. All reading specialists participated in the development of a position description, a performance review (evaluation) instrument, forms and procedures for the identification and selection of students to be served, diagnostic and record-keeping materials, and forms and procedures for monitoring the school-wide reading program.

One goal of the training process was to establish uniformity in the materials and procedures for certain aspects of the job. The reading specialists recognized the advantages of a standardized position description, diagnostic battery, record-keeping forms, etc. Such an approach enabled the district to prepare a wealth of supplementary materials, provide central office support for curriculum change at the school sites, and minimize the confusion when students moved from school to school.

In addition to developing standard materials and procedures, the training sessions provided an opportunity for reading specialists to share with each other their special skills and experiences. A camaraderie developed that enhanced the professionalism and job satisfaction of members of the group.

Finally, the training sessions provided for the development of task committees for future projects including professional growth plans, newsletters, materials sharing, test interpretation, kindergarten program planning, and position papers.

The in-service meetings are held on a regular basis on Friday afternoons. In order to encourage the sharing of ideas and techniques, many of the meetings are held in individual reading specialists' resource rooms.

A variety of resources are available to the reading specialists, including a room in the district office for meetings that is convenient to duplication and laminating facilities. Another room houses materials and forms used by the reading specialists, which are printed in the nearby communications center. Numerous materials are also available at the district resource library, which is also located in the district office. These materials are delivered to the school site on request.

Local district funds are allocated to provide all reading specialists with essential materials and equipment at their school sites, including furniture, text materials, supplementary materials, audiovisual equipment, flash cards, stop watches, etc.

The reading specialists are primarily responsible to the building principals. They also receive regular supervision and assistance from the district reading consultant. The reading specialists complete an annual report which includes the contributions made by the specialists to the school program and data on the performance of all students directly served.

A description of the role of the reading specialist in the Hayward School District follows:

Role of the Reading Specialist, Hayward Unified School District (1980)[5]

I. Qualifications
Credential: Any teaching credential authorizing service in the grade level or specialty indicated, and possession of the Reading Specialist Certificate

[5]Reproduced by permission of the Hayward Unified School District, Hayward, California. Henry Nicolini, Administrative Director, Elementary Education.

or the Reading Specialist Credential issued by the California State Department of Education.

Provide evidence of adequate preparation, background, and experience for the position.

II. Conditions of Employment

A. Appointment and Term. The Reading Specialist shall be appointed by the Board of Education for a term of one year upon nomination and recommendation by the Superintendent.

B. Remuneration. Remuneration shall be determined by the official salary schedule for certificated personnel as adopted by the Board of Education. The salary paid shall include an additional sum above the official salary schedule of two hundred fifty dollars ($250) per teacher.

C. Work Year. The work year shall be the regular school year as established by the Board of Education for new and returning teachers.

D. Administrative Relationship. The Reading Specialist shall be responsible to the building principal. The central office staff shall assist the Reading Specialist in meeting the guidelines for the Reading Specialist program.

III. General Description of Position

A. Primary Duties and Responsibilities

1. Devotes time to pupils in either the primary grades or the intermediate grades to meet their reading needs commensurate with their potential. The Reading Specialist shall spend a minimum of 50 per cent of the work day in providing direct services to children. Other responsibilities shall be related directly to the program being served and shall not involve duties which are related to the general operation of the school.

2. Supplements the reading instruction otherwise provided in regular classes:

a. The specialist teacher may work directly with pupils within the regular classroom during reading or outside of the classroom at designated times; train instructional aides or volunteers to work with pupils; or train peer tutors. The teacher should use the variety of human resources available to work with pupils.

b. Guidelines suggest that group size should not exceed six; however, the teacher should use judgment in determining the most effective learning situation.

c. The first priority for primary Reading Specialists in providing service is to supplement instruction in grade one. Primary Reading Specialists will provide service to supplement instruction in grades two and three to pupils who have been determined to have reading difficulties. Kindergarten pupils may receive instruction if other children have been served. Intermediate Reading Specialists will provide service to supplement instruction in grades four through six.

3. Provides demonstration teaching where appropriate.

4. Assists in administering and analyzing group tests given to pupils.

5. Assists in reading assessment of pupils identified for participation in specially funded programs.

6. Diagnoses identified pupils in reading using appropriate formal and informal tests, interprets results, and assesses and evaluates the pupil's growth with other persons responsible for the learner.
7. Assists the classroom teacher in developing prescriptions to meet the needs of pupils and assists in planning appropriate lessons and supplemental reading experiences to meet the diverse needs of pupils.
8. Assists the classroom teacher in developing within the child a positive attitude toward learning to read and in referring pupils who need specialized remedial help to professional personnel for specialized services.
9. Disseminates current research in reading to teachers and parents.
10. Assists the building principal and cooperates with other support staff in developing, planning, and implementing inservice programs for staff members in the area of reading and language, and in interpreting specially funded programs to school staff, parents, and community.
11. Assists the principal and cooperates with other support staff in maintaining systems of record keeping in reading.
12. Attends conferences in reading at the district, county, and state levels and shares information with other staff members.
13. Assists auxiliary staff members in developing programs to meet the learner's needs.
14. Participates in faculty meetings, curriculum planning, selection of additional personnel, and other program-related activities.
15. Performs adjunct duties when mutually agreed upon between teachers and immediate supervisor.

How Should Help Be Extended by the Reading Specialist?

A traditional method in which remedial reading teachers have extended their help has been to simply "set up shop" in a room and schedule students to come to the room for a specified period of time, one or more days each week. Such an approach is often referred to as a *pull-out program*, since the students are pulled out of their regular classroom for special instruction. Although this particular mode of operation often works quite well, it does not lend itself to opening two-way channels of communication. For example, in this type of situation the remedial reading teacher often fails to visit the homeroom of many of the students being served and thus misses the opportunity to coordinate the work of the students with their homeroom teachers. In such a case there is also little opportunity for the teacher to provide the kind of information that classroom teachers need and want as indicated earlier in this chapter. One solution is for reading specialists to provide a broader range of services.

In the Hayward School District, reading specialists provide both direct and indirect services. *Direct services* refers to instructional efforts aimed at low-achieving students. *Indirect services* refers to other roles assumed by the reading specialists, such as resource person, staff development leader, and curriculum planner.

As noted in the position description above, the Hayward reading specialists devote at least 50 percent of their school day to providing direct services to students. The specialists are proscribed from supplanting the reading instruction of the classroom teacher. All direct services are provided over and above the regular classroom reading program. First priority is generally assigned to students in the lowest quartile, with second priority assigned to students placing in the second lowest quartile on standardized reading tests.

To provide direct instruction, the reading specialist may utilize the traditional *pull-out* format. Or the reading specialist may also work in the students' regular classrooms, either with small groups of students or, using a team approach, with the classroom teacher. When the specialist provides services in the regular classroom, this is often referred to as a *push-in program*. The push-in program may be temporary and is designed not only to provide additional direct instruction to remedial pupils, but also to model effective teaching methods and otherwise assist the regular classroom teacher. This approach enables the reading specialist to observe students in their own natural environment, facilitates the coordination of instruction and assignments, and promotes more effective communication with the classroom teacher. Carroll Green (1973) studied the attitude of teachers toward children. She found that both the behavior and attitudes of teachers improved when the reading specialists actually went into the classroom to work with children. She stated: "When teachers received help in improving their skill in working with the children in the classroom, three out of five demonstrated behavioral changes and four out of five improved their score on the attitude test." (p. 2) This type of operation, however, requires that the reading specialist be flexible and particularly skilled at human relations, since many teachers feel threatened by the presence of the reading specialist in the classroom. One very effective way to ease the concerns of the classroom teacher is to offer to teach a lesson to a group or, preferably, to the whole class of students, while the classroom teacher is present. If you indicate to the teacher that your purpose at this point is to get to know the children rather than to do a "demonstration lesson" for the teacher's benefit, your presence will likely be welcomed. Many reading specialists have found, for example, that a well-planned language-experience lesson with follow-up activities that can be displayed on a bulletin board serves not only to please the students but also to impress the teacher. Such an activity can be adapted for nearly any age level. It is also a good idea for the reading specialist to follow up the visit with a note to the teacher that emphasizes some of the positive aspects of the room or reflects appreciation of the job the teacher may be doing in working with the students. Many reading specialists have won over reluctant or even hostile teachers by demonstrating an ability to work successfully with students in a normal classroom setting.

There are some possible drawbacks to push-in instruction. Such an approach often requires the reading specialist to transport a considerable amount of materials from classroom to classroom. Also, the reading specialist may find it difficult to arrange for space that is both adequate and comfortable. Perhaps the greatest potential problem is coping with the stress that may result from working in a classroom where poor teaching practices occur. There is a tendency to assume that such teaching practices will cease to exist if you are not there to observe them on a regular basis. Or you might justifiably conclude that such problems are beyond the scope of the reading specialist's job and should be addressed only by the teacher's principal or other supervisor. However, our experience in working with reading specialists has shown that often the reading specialist is in a unique position to help teachers improve their teaching skills. This is precisely because the reading specialist's role is one of assistance and not evaluation. If you are a reading specialist working in a school where you observe one or more teachers who are having significant difficulties in teaching effectively, we urge you not to ignore the problem but rather to discuss the situation with the principal and seek to work cooperatively, diplomatically, patiently, and persistently with the teacher. Indeed, we believe that no form of in-service is more effective than direct one-to-one assistance. We are aware that the reading specialist who uses such an approach faces certain risks. However, if you have established credibility and can work effectively with people, these risks are minimized. Further, we believe that because good classroom instruction is crucial to the achievement of many students, some risk is worth taking.

Earlier we suggested that reading specialists may provide both direct and indirect services. The preceding paragraph illustrates a situation where direct services lead to indirect services. The two job descriptions previously presented include a number of indirect service responsibilities. These responsibilities may account for up to 50 percent of the Hayward reading specialists' time. What follows is a list that summarizes many of the possible indirect services that reading specialists may provide:

1. Working cooperatively with the school principal in developing, planning, and implementing the total school reading program.
2. Assisting classroom teachers in planning for and conducting classroom reading instruction. The reading specialist may assist the teacher in identifying individual student needs and planning appropriate lessons, or assist the teacher in the general organization and management of reading instruction.

3. Providing demonstration teaching lessons.
4. Providing a resource room for teachers, which includes instructional and supplementary materials, and information about current research and other professional matters.
5. Monitoring the progress of students in the basal program. The reading specialist may gather data at regular intervals that show the groups in which students are placed and the progress they are making in those groups.
6. Organizing and conducting local school reading in-service meetings and other staff development efforts.[6]
7. Training aides, volunteers, and cross-age tutors.
8. Conducting parent conferences.
9. Making presentations before parent or community groups.
10. Assisting in administering and analyzing group test data.
11. Assisting in the assessment of students for special programs or services, such as participating in the development of IEPs.
12. Testing and placement of students new to the school.
13. Assisting in the development of the reading budget, the evaluation of new materials, and the ordering of basic and supplementary materials.
14. Providing leadership for school-wide motivational reading activities.
15. Attending conferences, college courses, and meetings of professional groups and reporting back to the school faculty.

In a school system where reading specialists have specific titles, such as a reading supervisor who oversees or supervises the entire program or a reading consultant who provides in-classroom demonstrations and other kinds of help, it may be more practical to have special remedial reading teachers who spend the greater proportion of their time in simply working with disabled readers. In such cases the reading consultant may take on many of the responsibilities for in-service education and, in some cases, may serve as a liaison person between the remedial reading teacher and the classroom teachers.

Some school systems have also found it quite feasible to use mobile reading laboratories that can be moved from school to school. These laboratories are usually trailer houses or campermobiles that have been converted to reading laboratories by removing much of the original equipment and replacing it with bookshelves, study carrels, small tables and chairs, provisions for audiovisual equipment and viewing areas, etc. Where a reading specialist is expected to work in several schools on a rotating basis, the investment in a mobile laboratory often proves less costly on a long-term basis since

[6]For more information on this topic we refer you to: Shanker, James L. *Guidelines for Successful Reading Staff Development.* Newark, Del.: International Reading Association, 1982.

there is not the necessity to duplicate rooms and equipment in several different schools.

In such a case the mobile laboratory is simply moved to a new school two to three times weekly and all facilities become immediately available after a main power cord for electricity has been attached. This also allows the reading specialist to concentrate on providing only one attractive display of bulletin board materials and eliminates the upkeep and cleaning of two or more rooms. Most teachers working in such a situation also report a great deal of enthusiasm on the part of the students in being housed in this type of facility.

Still another method that is proving worthwhile is to allow classroom teachers free time to work in the school's reading center or reading clinic either during a particular part of the day or for a semester or more of time. School districts providing such opportunities for classroom teachers usually hire a permanent substitute teacher to take over the duties of the classroom teacher while the teacher is on extended leave in the reading clinic.

In a situation where the classroom teacher works in the reading clinic for one or more periods of the day, it allows for a great deal of coordination of the remedial program of the classroom teacher and the reading clinician. And, whether the classroom teacher is released for only one or two periods, or for an entire semester or year, it provides an excellent opportunity for the classroom teacher to learn a great deal about materials and techniques that can be useful in corrective teaching in the classroom setting.

The type of operation you choose will, of course, depend on the size of your school system and on the amount of materials, funds, and facilities available. Perhaps more important, however, it will depend on the present reading specialists and their willingness to work within a given situation.

THE ROLE OF THE PRINCIPAL AND OTHER ADMINISTRATIVE PERSONNEL

In an excellent article Sidney Rauch (1974) makes the point that the success of reading programs does not depend on any one special method, text, or type of organization within the classroom. Rauch lists basic characteristics of a successful administrator. These are as follows:

1.   The administrator should be knowledgeable about the reading process. His own experience as a classroom teacher, his observation of extremely competent teachers, enrollment in graduate courses in reading, attendance at conferences, or extensive reading in the field may contribute to his knowledge.

2.   He takes advantage of the training and expertise of reading specialists. He recognizes his own limitations in the reading area and knows that he and his staff can benefit from the knowledge and experience of special-

ists. Above all, there is a close relationship between the specialist and himself.

3. He consults with supervisory and teaching personnel before new programs are instituted or changes are made. Before new programs are put into operation, he makes sure that the necessary in-service training is provided.

4. He realizes that teachers are severely handicapped if materials are lacking. Therefore, he makes certain that the budget includes the basic instructional materials, as well as the needed supplementary texts and other aids.

5. He encourages and supports experimentation and innovation. He is never satisfied with the status quo. At the same time, he doesn't abandon a successful program because of publicity given a "new" reading method, or because some school board member confuses exploratory research with a definitive study.

6. He has the support and respect of the community as a person and as an educational leader. (pp. 298–299)[7]

In addition to those qualities listed above, other essential abilities or qualities that the administrator should possess are as follows:

1. The administrator should be thoroughly familiar with the state department of education's recommendations and/or requirements as well as those suggested by the International Reading Association for the training and background of various types of reading specialists.

2. The administrator should not only have the support and respect of the community for the reading program, as mentioned in number 6 above, but should consistently strive to make parents knowledgeable about the school's remedial reading program.

3. The administrator should schedule adequate time for remedial reading teachers for conferences with students, parents, classroom teachers, and all other staff personnel directly related to the reading program.

4. The administrator should encourage and provide for continual cooperative evaluation and take necessary steps to improve the program.

5. The administrator should take the initiative in developing a professional library accessible to all teachers.

Rauch also lists a number of excellent suggestions for administrators. We have paraphrased some of these and added others as follows:

1. Study and learn all that is possible about reading. Observe reading specialists in action and observe the classroom reading instruction of master teachers.

[7]From "Administrator's Guidelines for More Effective Reading Programs," by Sidney J. Rauch. *Journal of Reading*, January 1974. Reprinted with permission of the International Reading Association and the author.

2. As mentioned previously, Rauch makes the point that there is a specific need to clarify the role of various reading specialists. The various reading specialists should know exactly what is expected of them, and administrators and classroom teachers should view their roles in the same way. Rauch suggests that a job description for each type of reading specialist be developed similar to those shown previously for the Parkway School District and the Hayward School District.

3. Provide for continuous in-service training, not just in the form of lectures from "experts" or college professors but in the form of demonstrations and direct classroom assistance. The most successful in-service programs have been those that actively involved the teachers in the day-to-day experiences given in in-service training sessions over an extended period of time.

4. Provide for effective use of audiovisual materials and other facilities and/or materials needed by both classroom and remedial reading teachers.

5. Recognize that reading is a complex process and that what works with one student may or may not work with another. Provide an open environment where some structure is maintained, yet where experimentation based on research is encouraged.

In conclusion, we would strongly agree with Rauch, who states, "An administrator who knows about the reading process, who takes advantage of the training and expertise of reading personnel, and who recognizes the many factors that determine reading progress can mean the difference between the success or failure of a school reading program." (p. 300)

PARENTS' ROLE IN THE REMEDIAL READING PROGRAM

An area often neglected by the remedial reading teacher is the active involvement of parents in the remedial reading program. Some ways in which parents can and should help their children are as follows:

1. By creating within the home a reading atmosphere in which a time and a place for home reading is provided. This might be a time when every member of the household agrees that there will be no radio, television, or, if possible, no visiting friends. This would also include the responsibility of making sure that adequate reading material was provided.

2. By helping the child develop habits of regularity in eating, sleeping, studying, and attending school.

3. By encouraging home responsibilities to develop feelings of satisfaction from successful accomplishments.

4. By exhibiting a genuine interest in the school and in the child.

5. By maintaining a relaxed, cooperative attitude toward the child's reading without the exertion of undue pressure.
6. By developing experiential background by taking and discussing excursions, such as trips to the zoo, planetariums, plays, parades, and sporting events, which will assist in developing language facility and a background of experiences for comprehension.
7. By supporting students' interest in hobbies such as stamp collecting, model building, collecting matchbook covers, pamphlets, animal raising and care, etc., all of which require reading.
8. By reading to the child frequently and using simple language-experience approaches in the home.

There seems to be a great deal of controversy as to whether parents should actually attempt to teach their children at home. There is also considerable disagreement on whether disabled readers should be asked to read to their parents. There are, in reality, no pat answers to such questions. For example, some parents are able to work with their children and maintain a completely relaxed manner. Yet other parents, including some who are teachers, simply cannot work with their own children without creating a great deal of tension. One of the best ways to decide whether to recommend that parents work with their children is simply to ask the parents if they have the kind of working relationship that is conducive to parent tutoring. It is also a good practice to ask students how they feel about being tutored by one or both parents.

There is also no pat answer as to whether students should be asked to read to their parents. Again, however, if students wish to read to their parents and the parents are willing to be patient and calm, there is usually some benefit to this activity. Since many disabled readers have a low sight vocabulary caused from a lack of wide reading experience, multiple exposure to many words through oral reading is likely to be beneficial. One of the keys is to be sure to provide materials that are at or below the students' independent reading levels. Students can learn from material that is too easy but will only become frustrated when trying to read material that is too difficult. Parents should generally be advised simply to tell children words the children do not know rather than to tell them to "sound it out." In most cases, if the students know enough about word-attack skills to analyze new words, they will do so without being told.

In Chapter 7, in the section on counseling parents of disabled readers, we reviewed the procedures utilized at the Elementary Reading Clinic at California State University, Hayward, to acquaint parents with the clinic experience and to improve parents' effectiveness in assisting their own children. We pointed out that the activities suggested have been adapted by reading specialists for use in their school programs. Helen Esworthy (1979) reports on a similar summer reading clinic that sponsors weekly workshops to involve parents in their children's reading instruction. Esworthy reports success in (1) orienting the parents to the purposes of the program, (2) furthering the parents' knowledge about reading by offering workable ideas for home, and (3) teaching parents about instructional devices by having them make some for the clinic program.

Alvin Granowsky, Frances Middleton, and Janice Mumford (1979) reported their experiences in developing a program that involved parents as equal partners, sharing the responsibility for their children's education. Sadie Grimmett and Mae McCoy (1980) conducted a study in which written material sent by mail was used to train parents to assist their children in reading. They found that this communication stimulated parent involvement and resulted in accelerated reading achievement among third graders.

In the previous sections on the role of the reading specialist and the role of the principal and other administrative personnel, mention was made of the importance of effective communication and parent involvement. Enough evidence exists on the potential impact of parents on their children's reading achievement to warrant carefully planned, cooperative efforts on the part of administrators and reading specialists to address this critical area.

SELECTING STUDENTS FOR REMEDIAL READING

Although the selection of students for participation in the remedial reading program may appear to be an easy matter, there are, in reality, a number of problems involved in the process. For example, in the selection process you are likely to be confronted with the following questions: Who will make the initial recommendations and the final decision as to which students will actually be included in the program? Will number of years of reading achievement below grade level be used as a measurement of reading disability? Will reading potential or expectancy be considered? And, what types of tests will be used to determine the degree of reading impairment?

Problems in the Selection Process

One of the first steps in the initial selection process is to arrive at an acceptable definition of a disabled reader, or a reader who is a candidate for remedial reading. One approach to this problem in the past has been simply to use a specified number of years of reading achievement below grade level (in many cases two) as the lone criterion for placement in the remedial reading program.

A number of authors such as Charles Ullmann (1969) have pointed out that "years below normal grade for age" is a vague measure and is likely to result in a somewhat misleading picture of the prevalence of reading disability. Ullmann states:

> Whenever a fixed amount of grades or years below normal is set for defining reading disability, a progressively larger percentage of children, of each succeeding grade to which that standard amount is applied, will be defined as having a disability. This is due principally to deceleration in the average growth curve and the consequent reduction in the size of the steps from one grade to another. . . . It is no more appropriate to describe the gain between Grades 8 and 9 as equal to the gain between Grades 2 and 3, than it is to describe a 35-year-old man as 25 years taller than his 10-year-old son. (p. 557)

Another way of looking at this problem is on the basis of the percentage of knowledge lacking from normal, or 100 percent reading achievement. For example, a beginning third grader should have gained two years' reading knowledge, i.e., one year in going from the beginning to end of the first grade and another year in going from the beginning to end of the second grade. If this student is two years retarded in reading he or she would have an achievement level of 1.0 (not really 0.0), or in other words, a 0 (zero) percent reading knowledge. But a student at the beginning sixth-grade level should have gained five years of knowledge. If he is retarded two years from his expected level he is still five minus two $(5 - 2)$, or 3/5, or a 60 percent level of reading knowledge. Obviously then, the concept of a specified number of years of reading retardation is unfair and an inadequate measure.

Another method of measuring reading retardation is by use of some measure of a student's level of achievement versus some measure of potential. James Reed (1970) illustrates the great degree of variability in using such a method. For example, he quotes a study that indicated that an eighth-grade student with a measured IQ of 120 reading at a seventh-grade level would be judged to be two years, three years, or four and one-half years retarded in reading as judged by the Bond-Tinker, Tiegs and Clark, or Harris formulas respectively. As Reed aptly states, "Obviously, the amount of retardation is not an absolute but depends on the procedure used to measure it." (p. 347) In a concluding statement concerning his study of the use of *WISC* IQs to measure students' reading potential, Reed stated,

> Teachers and reading specialists should view with considerable skepticism any statement pertaining to the so-called intellectual, cognitive, or perceptual deficiencies of retarded readers. Many of the statements are interesting speculations, but nothing more. The particular pattern of deficits may represent only an artifact of the investigator's decision to use one measure of potential instead of another. A child's potential for reading is probably much more closely related to the materials and methods used for teaching than some arbitrary index of expectancy. (p. 352)

The problem of errors in measurement in identifying disabled readers was also studied by Robert Bruininks, Gertrude Glaman, and Charlotte Clark (1973), who compared the percentages of disabled readers identified by use of five achievement expectancy formulas. They stated,

> Analysis revealed that the prevalence of third-grade children exhibiting reading difficulties varied widely because of survey techniques and type of IQ test (verbal or nonverbal) used in the five achievement expectancy formulas. Using a nonverbal intelligence test score, the percentage of poor readers among third-grade children ranged from 16 percent with the Bond and Tinker formula to 54.6 percent for the formula using mental age alone. (p. 180)

These authors believed that rather than use an expectancy formula, it might be more realistic to use a criterion-referenced approach to test interpretation. In doing so one would measure a student's attainment of specific reading skills with a certain reading program rather than measure the student's achievement in relation to a group on a norm-referenced test. They also suggested that if reading retardation is measured according to the disparity between predicted and actual achievement, it should be done in relation to how long children have been exposed to systematic instruction (as in the Bond-Tinker Formula) and that they should have a larger disparity between predicted and actual achievement at higher grade levels.

The general philosophy of identifying students who are retarded in reading as soon as possible is strongly supported by research. For example, a PREP (Putting Research into Educational Practice) summary entitled *Treating Reading Disabilities* published by the Bureau of Research of the Office of Education stated:

> Early diagnosis is important, and the rule is "the earlier, the better." A four-year survey of some ten thousand children showed that when pupils with reading problems were identified by the second grade, they had a ten times greater chance for successful remediation than did those who were not identified until the ninth grade. (p. 5)

One of the major problems the remedial reading teacher has to deal with in working with older students is a low self-concept that is apparently much more difficult to change than a similar low self-concept of a younger student. This was illustrated by Erwin and Ralph Pearlman (1970), who studied the effect of remedial reading training in a private clinic. They concluded that children in grades one through three made greater gains during remediation than children in grades four through six. Children in grades one through three also maintained their gains better than the older students. The authors believed that this was because the children in grades one through three had faced fewer defeats and had maintained a greater degree of self-confidence.

A Suggested Procedure for Selecting Students for Remedial Reading

The six-step procedure, explained below, for selecting the final case load is illustrated in Figure 14-4. You will note that some of the procedures vary somewhat from those used in many schools today. You should keep in mind, however, that the procedures used in many schools today are simply based on precedent. The following procedure may, in many cases, not be the easiest way of developing the final case load, but if followed carefully it will usually result in a successful program.

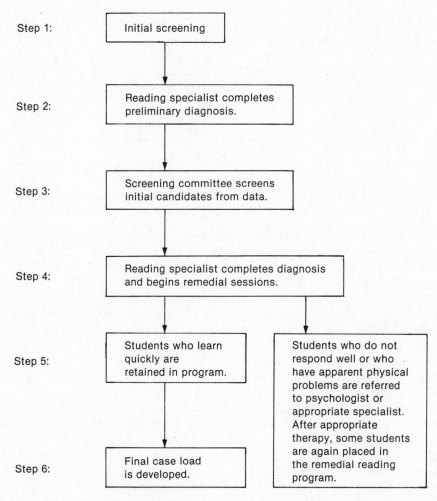

FIGURE 14-4.   A Suggested Sequence for Selection of the Final Case Load.

Step 1. The first step concerns the initiation of a procedure for receiving recommendations from teachers for those students whom the teachers believe might benefit from the remedial reading program. The successful operation of this procedure will, to a large extent, depend on the type and amount of orientation given to classroom teachers. Before attempting this step the remedial reading teacher, in conjunction with other reading and administrative personnel, must develop guidelines for the selection of students. The guidelines should include information on the degree of retardation considered minimal for selection, age-grade preferences, and methods of assessing retardation. These guidelines should then be communicated to all classroom teachers concerned with the program in an in-service meeting prior to their selection process.

As stated previously, the degree of retardation should vary according to the age-grade level of the student. Some general guidelines for selection of students might be as follows:

Grade level	Retardation for recommendation
1	2 to 3 months
2	4 to 6 months
3	6 to 8 months
4	1 to 1½ years
5	1½ to 2 years
6+	2 years or more

The reading specialist should be sure that classroom teachers feel that they are participating in the selection of students. Two different forms for teacher referral are included in the next chapter. Each of these forms requires the teacher to spend some time in completing the referral. We believe this is preferable to having teachers simply list the names of the students they wish to refer. By completing a referral form, teachers are less likely to refer students who are not in need of special assistance and more likely to make selections after careful thought.

At this stage the reading specialist should also examine the performance of referred students on group standardized achievement tests. In most schools such tests are given to all students on an annual basis. Although we know that group tests will simply not provide an accurate measure of the reading ability of all students, these data will generally reveal whether the student is performing at, above, or below grade level. The reading specialist can assume that most of the referrals will be for students who are reading below grade level. By looking at group test scores the specialist can determine if one or more teachers are referring pupils who do not have an apparent need for remedial instruction. Furthermore, many specially funded programs require that students be drawn from only the bottom two quartiles as measured by standardized tests.

To complete the initial screening the reading specialist selects a suitable number of students for preliminary diagnosis. In some situations this is not a difficult task, since the total number of students referred does not exceed the remedial reading teacher's potential case load. In many schools, however, the preliminary selection of students is a difficult and delicate matter. The reading specialist may know, for instance, that the total case load cannot exceed thirty-five pupils. However, classroom teachers may have referred seventy-five students, all but five of whom have scored below the fiftieth percentile on the standardized achievement test. In such a situation, it is obvious that some students who are in need of special assistance will not be able to receive it. The reading specialist, with the help and support of the principal, must communicate this problem to the teachers and seek to utilize an equitable approach. Often the reading specialist will choose first the students who appear to be most in need of remedial services; that is, those who have the lowest test scores. In some situations the specialist will select those students he or she believes will make the greatest gains from remedial instruction. Whichever approach is used, the faculty should understand the rationale and be willing to accept the decisions that are ultimately made. Also, the reading specialist should try to balance the initial screening decisions so that all teachers who referred students will have a similar number of students selected, if possible.

The reading specialist might screen approximately 20 percent more students at this stage than can be accommodated in the final program. In the subsequent steps in the selection procedure you will likely find that some of the initially screened students are not good candidates. Also, you will want to have extra students for a waiting list so that students can quickly be brought in to the program as vacancies arise.

Step 2. Once the preliminary screening is completed, the reading specialist can begin diagnosis on individual students. The preliminary diagnosis should be thorough enough to determine whether the student is a good candidate and to identify some of the specific reading strengths and weaknesses. At this stage the reading specialist will usually administer a pronunciation test, such as the San Diego Quick Assessment Test described in Chapter 4, a basic sight vocabulary test, also described in Chapter 4, and an informal reading inventory, described in Chapter 11. These tests will enable the remedial reading teacher to determine the degree of reading disability and also to evaluate some of the student's specific reading strengths and deficits. In some cases, depending on the number of students to be tested and the reading specialist's skill in administering tests efficiently, the specialist will also administer tests to determine students' abilities in phonics, structural analysis, context clues, and comprehension.

Many reading specialists find that they can complete the preliminary diagnoses (step 2) in about one week's time by testing, say, ten students per day. A rather thorough evaluation can be done in this period if the reading specialist is well organized and uses the assistance of trained aides or parent volunteers. Under the supervision of the remedial reading teacher, paraprofessionals can be trained to administer and score the pronunciation and basic sight vocabulary tests while the reading teacher administers the informal reading inventory and specific skills tests. With practice and expertise, many reading specialists find that the initial diagnosis can be completed in approximately thirty minutes per student. Since most classroom teachers are anxious for their remedial readers to begin receiving help immediately, it is important for the reading specialist to complete the testing as efficiently as possible.

Step 3.   In this step the reading specialist works with other members of a screening committee to select from the group diagnosed in step 2 those students who seem most likely to benefit from the remedial reading program based on the data gathered thus far. In many schools this screening is done by the remedial reading teacher without the aid of other school personnel. In some cases this works quite well, but the use of a committee for screening purposes can also be of great benefit to the remedial reading teacher. The use of a committee composed of the remedial reading teacher, the principal, at least one classroom teacher, and perhaps the guidance counselor can eliminate a number of problems that the remedial reading teacher is likely to encounter. For example, problems often arise when more pupils are taken from one teacher's room than from the room of another teacher. However, if a screening committee makes the decision, there is less likelihood that any one teacher will feel that his or her students are not receiving equal consideration. Similarly, a committee can provide support for the reading specialist in denying students who were referred on the basis of discipline problems rather than reading problems per se. The principal and guidance counselor can also add valuable input on such matters as scheduling and knowledge of students' home conditions. Earlier in the book we discussed P.L. 94–142 and the importance of role clarification among professionals and proper educational assessment for the student with learning difficulties. The screening committee described in this section may help to address both issues.

Steps 4 and 5.   In these steps, after the initial candidates have been selected, the reading specialist completes the administration of specific diagnostic tests and begins remedial sessions with individuals or small groups. At this point students might be tested for auditory discrimination and for vision. Those students with problems in either area would be referred to a specialist for further testing. For example, the student with auditory discrimination difficulties would be referred to an audiologist to determine whether the student had a hearing loss or whether the student simply needed training in discriminating sounds. And, the student who failed the vision screening tests would be sent to an optometrist or an ophthalmologist to determine whether vision correction was needed. During this period of time (perhaps two to four weeks) the remedial reading teacher might be working with a few more students than would be a normal case load for the entire year. This should be a period in which precise records are kept indicating exactly how fast each student learns. For example, a student who is weak in phonics would be given an individual phonics test during one of the first few sessions. After several weeks of work on specific phonemes missed or on unknown rules, the student would then be given another test for the purpose of determining exactly how much the student had learned and retained. At this point several alternatives might be open. If the student had made considerable progress during this period of time, the remedial reading teacher would probably wish to continue the remediation along the same general lines as before. On the other hand, if it was apparent that little or nothing had been learned or retained, the teacher would need to decide whether altering instructional strategy might be beneficial or whether referral to a psychologist or other specialists would be in order.

Step 6. Those students who seemed to learn rather quickly when taught would definitely be retained and made a part of the regular case load. Students who needed auditory or visual correction would also become a part of this final group. On the other hand, those students who did not seem to benefit from instruction, as indicated in step 5, would be referred to other specialists for help. For example, a child with severe emotional problems may need psychological help for an extended period of time. During this period the psychologist or psychiatrist may or may not recommend that the student come to remedial reading. However, many students would, sooner or later, again become a part of the final case load.

SCHEDULING CLASSES FOR REMEDIAL READING

One of the major problems faced by the remedial reading teacher and the principal is that of which classes to take students from for remedial reading training. We would suggest that, where it is possible, students be taken from either social studies or science classes to attend the remedial reading class. To begin with, much of the instruction in these classes is based on the reading of material from textbooks. Students who are candidates for remedial reading would, in most cases, not be able to benefit from that part of the instruction. Furthermore, there is no national science or social studies curriculum as there is in reading or mathematics. For this reason overall school achievement test results are not adversely affected to any great extent by having students miss a portion of these classes. In fact, most achievement tests only measure social studies and science vocabulary. And, studies by

Eldon E. Ekwall have shown that students who were encouraged to read books about social studies and science material in remedial reading gained as much, and in many cases more, in vocabulary knowledge as the students in regular classes.

If possible, students should not be taken from their regular reading classes or from physical education, art, or music classes. Much can be gained from their own reading classes if the teachers of these students understand their problems. And, in the case of classes such as physical education, art, and music the student is likely to miss a great opportunity to compete in a fun type of activity on an equal basis with other students.

THE NUMBER OF STUDENTS PER CLASS AND TOTAL CASE LOAD

The number of students in the remedial reading class will vary, to some extent, on the age-grade levels of the students and on the similarity of the problems of students who could be scheduled to work with the remedial reading teacher at the same time. A few students will need such intensive training that it will be imperative that they receive individual help, especially in the beginning stages of their remediation.

Many authorities in the field of reading and the research such as that of Edwa Steirnagle (1971) have indicated that classes ranging in size up to six can be beneficial without losing their effectiveness. In an evaluation of the El Paso Public Schools Title I Remedial Reading Program Steirnagle stated, "One surprising discovery was the fact that pupils who received one-to-one instruction from the teacher had not made the predicted progress. Classes consisting of five pupils who were instructed for a full hour, daily, produced the greatest gains." (p. 539) It should be pointed out, however, that later research by Steirnagle indicated that gains began to drop off rather sharply when the maximum number went beyond six to eight pupils.

Most reading authorities also agree that a teacher's total case load should not exceed forty pupils. In many cases, depending on the severity of the cases, and the amount of consulting the teacher is expected to do, the maximum case load might very well be thirty pupils or less. The length of the instructional period and the number of remedial sessions per week for each pupil will be discussed in the following section.

FREQUENCY AND LENGTH OF CLASS SESSIONS

Several research studies have been done in remedial and developmental reading classes to determine the effectiveness of differing lengths of class sessions as well as the effectiveness of the frequency of class sessions. As pointed out earlier in the chapter, younger students have a much better chance of recovering from reading disabilities and of then maintaining these gains. For example, Asher Cashdan and P. D. Pumfrey (1969) studied thirty-six junior high school students. They were placed in three groups. One group was given remedial training in groups of four to six for thirty to sixty minutes twice weekly. Another group was taught in the same size group for thirty to sixty minutes once weekly. Another group served as a control group and was given no remedial training at all. Twenty-two months later there were no significant differences in the achievement or attitudes of the three groups. The authors concluded that students of this age group needed a far more intensive and integrated program than the "two term" project that was conducted.

Robert Hicks et al. (1968) studied the gains made by third- and fourth-grade students. Their subjects were assigned to one of three experimental conditions. These conditions were half-hour remedial reading sessions, two, three, and four per week. At no time were any classes longer than five hours. The experiment lasted for approximately one school year. The authors found that the third-grade group that was instructed three times per week made significantly greater gains than the group that was instructed only two times per week. They also found that the third graders who were instructed four times per week made significantly greater gains than the groups that were instructed only two or three times per week. On the other hand, the data revealed that the number of sessions per week did not produce any significant differences at the fourth-grade level. These authors stated:

> The results of this study tend to indicate that time allotments are an important consideration in the development of a third-grade remedial reading curriculum, i.e., there is a direct and reliable relationship between the number of sessions and the amount of improvement in reading shown over the school year. No such relationship was demonstrated for the fourth-grade pupils who served as S's in this study. Two sessions per week seem to be as beneficial as three or four. (pp. 439 and 744)

Hicks et al. pointed out that their findings were consistent with those of Oscar Jarvis (1965), who found that lengthening the time per day for formal reading instruction over fifty minutes per day had no significant effect on the reading gain of fourth, fifth, and sixth graders in a developmental situation. Jarvis stated, "These data strongly suggest that we teach reading in the other curricular areas of the elementary school curriculum as well as in the formulized reading class." (p. 204) It should be emphasized, however, that the findings of Jarvis may not have been applicable to children in grades one, two, and three.

In summary, it again appears that at third grade, and probably below, students will benefit from two or three sessions per week, but they will gain and retain even more if they are given four to five sessions per week. On the other hand, students at the fourth-grade level and above are simply not likely to gain and retain progress in a short-term program (one year or less) regardless of the number of sessions. There would, of course, be many exceptions to this rule. For example, at the El Paso Reading Center, students at the fourth-grade level and above have improved by one to two grade levels in remedial sessions held once per week for a period of one semester. At the California State University, Hayward Reading Clinic, older elementary students have shown an average gain of two years after seven weeks of daily one-to-one instruction. In general, we might conclude that students in any grade can be helped, and the more frequently the sessions are held the greater the chance for success. However, for those students at fourth grade, or above, the remedial process is likely to take much longer.

The length of class sessions will, in many cases, depend on the administrative structure of the school. However, if possible, a remedial period of twenty to thirty minutes for second and third graders and forty to fifty minutes for fourth graders and above is usually adequate to teach a good lesson and yet keep them from becoming overly restless. If possible, these time periods should be broken up into several activities. Among these activities should be a time set aside for the selection of books for students to read on their own outside the classroom situation. Although students often require some assistance in book selection, this time period also allows time for record keeping by the teacher. Many reading specialists find it effective to "overlap" their schedules so that one group arrives five to ten minutes before the previous group is dismissed. When students in the arriving group enter the room, they know that they are to pick up a good book and enjoy some silent reading time. Thus, when the earlier group is dismissed, the teacher can expect that all of the members of the arriving group are present and in a good frame of mind for instruction.

TERMINATION OF STUDENTS FROM THE REMEDIAL READING PROGRAM

Ideally students should be terminated from the remedial reading program when they are again reading up to grade level. A number of studies have shown, however, that it is often necessary to continue remediation on a less intensive basis to enable formerly disabled readers to maintain reading skills already learned, as well as to keep up with their normally achieving peers. For example, Madeline Hardy (1968) studied the academic, vocational, and social adjustment of a group of young adults who had been disabled in reading and who had received clinical diagnosis and remedial treatment during their elementary school years. She concluded that it was possible to reduce reading retardation by a remedial reading program, but the amount of retardation tended to increase often at the end of the treatment. Gains made by the subjects were significant only during the periods of remedial work. Hardy also found that those students who displayed deficiencies in visual, perceptual, and motor skills at referral tended to retain these defects. She believed that because the disabled reader's problems tended to persist, remedial teachers should attempt to help the readers to understand, accept, and cope with their problems.

Bruce Balow (1965) studied three samples of boys and girls from the Psycho-Educational Clinic at the University of Minnesota. All were fifth and sixth graders who, according to tests, were bright enough to be reading at grade level or above, but who were reading three or more years below their expectancy level. Balow's subjects were mostly from a middle-class or lower-middle-class background. Prior to receiving remediation these students had been achieving at approximately one-half the rate of normal students. During their period of remediation, however, Samples I and II progressed at a rate of twelve and nine times their previous rates of achievement respectively. (There were no data available for Sample III.) Sample I did not receive any follow-up remedial assistance after being discharged from the clinic, while the students in Samples II and III were given far less intensive but nonetheless some supportive help following their remedial period. The students in Sample I did not lose the reading skills they had acquired during their period of remediation, but they did not continue to develop on their own. However, those students in Samples II and III continued to gain in reading skills more rapidly than they had prior to entering the program, although they did not gain as rapidly as normally achieving readers.

Balow concluded:

> The unfortunate but highly instructive element of these findings is that severe reading disability is not corrected by short-term intensive courses of treatment, even though it is ameliorated by such help. Neither, it would appear, is the cure to be found in intensive treatment followed by maintenance sessions of an hour or so per week, although again such a program is far superior to no special help at all. The implication which follows naturally from these conclusions is that severe reading disability is probably best considered a relatively chronic illness needing long-term treatment rather than the short course typically organized in current programs. (p. 586)

Benjamin Willis (1971) studied the growth curves of third-year students in a remedial program. He found that the greatest growth in reading skills appeared to take place during the fourth month of instruction. Growth increased each month, but seemed to level off by the fifth month. Although the results obtained by Willis were probably to some extent a function of the type of program provided and of the age of the students involved, there seems to be definite evidence that if other factors are not hindering students' progress, they should show some definite improvement after four months of instruction.

In summary one might conclude the following:

1.   The earlier disabled readers are identified (grades one to three) and placed in a remedial program, the more likely they are to gain the competence needed for achieving on a level with their normal-reading peers. Even then, some type of follow-up program should probably be provided for these students.

2.   Older students (grade four and above) who are severely disabled in reading should be considered as chronic cases who will not only need long-term treatment, but should also receive some follow-up help after being discharged from the full-time, intensive remedial reading program.

3.   Most students, and especially those at the third-grade level or below, should be referred to other specialists if they have not shown considerable gain after four to five months of instruction.

FACILITIES FOR REMEDIAL READING

As stated earlier there are several ways in which the remedial reading teacher may wish to operate: within the classroom of the teachers who have students in need to help, through the use of a mobile reading center, or in a more traditional setting of a classroom within the school in which students come to the remedial reading teacher. The importance of operating within a facility that is appealing to the eye cannot be overemphasized. Although students may not appear to mind coming to a room that is not brightly decorated and appealing, in reality most will probably be adversely affected by such an atmosphere. Although most students would not be likely to complain about their surroundings, they do make a major difference. This difference was pointed out to one of the coauthors when visiting a federal penitentiary to discuss their reading program with officials of that institution. Prior to the time that the writer had visited the institution, the reading classroom they used was in a basement. In that facility there was little or no sunlight, and there were a number of steam pipes running along the ceiling that tended to drip water from time to time. In general, it was a rather dreary atmosphere. The teacher of this class said that a day had seldom gone by that at least one physical fight did not break out between students in his classroom when the inmates were housed in this facility during the reading lessons. He stated, however, that after the reading class was moved into a sunny classroom that was brightly decorated there was not one instance in which inmates had even come near the point of physical violence.

Most elementary or secondary students would, no doubt, be considerably more inhibited than the inmates of this prison. But there is little doubt that students experience many of the same feelings caused by the influence of their surroundings as did the inmates of the federal penitentiary.

We have observed and taught in many remedial reading classrooms. What follows is a list of some of the positive things we have observed in these classrooms:

1. Individual folders and/or carriers for each student.
2. Evidence of individual students' progress displayed in rooms.
3. Students' work prominently displayed in rooms with decor that is bright and attractive.
4. Carpeted, comfortable area for free reading for early arrivals.
5. Lots of trade books properly displayed.
6. Numerous supplementary materials available, both commercial and homemade.
7. Use of materials to provide variety in directed instruction, such as chalkboard, chart rack, lap boards, pupil response devices, etc.
8. Various centers for variety in reinforcement, such as listening posts, record players, Language Masters, typewriters, recording studios, etc.
9. The reading specialist's room serving as a central depository for basal materials and other reading materials, and thus as a resource center for classroom teachers.

In addition to a pleasant classroom atmosphere there are a number of other facilities that are desirable. Some of these are as follows:

1. Office space for record keeping and conferencing with parents and students.
2. Adequate storage facilities for equipment, paper, books, and other materials.
3. Facilities for duplicating materials. These facilities may be housed within the classroom or out of the classroom; however, the remedial reading teacher usually needs to duplicate a great many materials and for this reason should have easy access to duplicating facilities.
4. Chalkboard space and bulletin board space.
5. Sufficient electrical outlets for use with overhead projectors, tape recorders, filmstrip projectors, etc.
6. Tables and chairs suitable for individual or small group work.
7. Individual study carrels with facilities for individual viewing of audiovisual materials and for individual study.
8. Filing cabinets.

The criteria for the selection of adequate books, programs, and materials in general for the teaching of reading are discussed in Chapter 16.

EVALUATING PROGRESS IN REMEDIAL READING AND MEASURING THE EFFECTIVENESS OF THE PROGRAM

Most remedial reading teachers are concerned with evaluating two aspects of the effectiveness of their program. One aspect is the effect of the program on individual students, and the other aspect is the effectiveness of the program as a whole.

Individual Evaluation

Individual evaluation can be carried out in a number of ways. One method of doing this is to simply keep very accurate records of pretest and posttest performance on individual diagnostic tests. For example, in giving a phonics test, the teacher will note exactly which phonemes were missed. After a period of teaching, the same test can again be given so that the exact amount of learning in this area can easily be evaluated. The same type of measurement can be done with knowledge of basic sight words, contractions, vowel rules and/or their application, etc. Many teachers are used to thinking about progress in terms of grade-level scores such as 3.4, 4.2, etc. As pointed out in an earlier chapter, however, most standardized achievement tests do not measure achievement for individual students accurately enough to be of any real value for remedial work. Therefore, although grade-level scores may give the appearance of being somewhat concrete measures, they are often misleading. And, in reality, criterion measures of gain in specific skills are much more meaningful in evaluating the effectiveness of a program for individual students.

Another useful method of measuring individual student gains is to use a checklist of the various characteristics and specific number of various types of errors when administering informal reading inventories. A checklist of this nature is shown in Chapter 2. In the first administration of the informal reading inventory each characteristic and specific number of each type of error (e.g., substitutions, insertions, etc.) can be noted. After a period of remediation the same passages can be given again. The second time, each characteristic and specific number of errors can again be noted. You can then figure the percentage of reduction in each type of error (hopefully) between the first and second administration of the test. If the overall grade level of the student has increased, however, it would be important that the percentages be computed only on the same passages that were given (up to frustration level) in the first administration of the test.

The informal reading inventory itself is also, of course, extremely useful as a measuring instrument for individual gains, i.e., in determining whether a student's overall free or independent, instructional, and frustration levels have risen during the period of instruction.

Individual gains that may not always be apparent as the teacher works with students on a daily basis can often become very apparent when tape recordings are made of students' oral reading. The initial reading of several passages can be recorded and after a period of remediation the same passages can be recorded following the first, on the same tape. Allowing students to hear their own progress in fluency and reduction in errors is also often highly motivating.

Group Evaluation

Group evaluation of remedial reading programs can also be somewhat difficult in some situations. For example, one method that has been used in researching the effectiveness of special or compensatory programs is use of a control group. This method, while offering a number of advantages, also has some disadvantages. One disadvantage is that there must be a control group at all. In a small school one may not wish to deprive the control group of the benefit of a promising new program simply for the sake of measuring any possible significant differences in posttest results between the two groups. Or, on the other hand, if students in another school are used as a control group, there is no assurance that students in the two schools are of equal ability; therefore, a comparison of the two would yield inaccurate results.

Another method for evaluating group gains is a comparison of pre- and posttest scores on standardized achievement tests. Students' growth can properly be reported in terms of grade equivalent units if you present a frequency distribution rather than attempt to average the students' gains. A hypothetical example of this type of report follows:

GE gain between pre- and posttesting	Number of students making this gain	Percent	Cumulative percent
1.5 and up	8	16%	100%
1.3–1.4	10	20%	84%
1.1–1.2	12	24%	64%
.9–1.0	10	20%	40%
.7– .8	5	10%	20%
.5– .6	3	6%	10%
less than .5	2	4%	04%
TOTAL	50		

Using the above example, you could make statements such as: "Sixty percent of all students seen by this reading specialist had gains of greater than 1.0 grade equivalents between pre- and posttesting."

The following is an explanation of a method of assessing gains that is relatively easy to interpret. This method deals with children's ratio-of-learning. Although the use of the concept of ratio-of-learning is not new, it is still unfamiliar to many people.[8]

The ratio-of-learning is a measurement of children's learning rate prior to entering a special program versus their learning rate while they are in the program. Because of the unreliability of group test scores for individual students, you should determine the ratio-of-learning for all students in a special program, rather than for individual students. The steps in using this method are as follows:

1. Determine the average number of years that all children in the special program have been in school at the beginning of the program. Remember that second graders have only been in school for one year as of the beginning of grade two, etc. Therefore, the number of years in school for most children equals their grade level minus one, unless they have failed a year. In that case the number of years in school would equal the grade level they should have been in, minus one.

    Example:

    | Sara | — | Grade 3 (never failed) | $3 - 1 = 2$ |
    | Blanca | — | Grade 5 (never failed) | $5 - 1 = 4$ |
    | Elaine | — | Grade 4 (failed one year) | $5 - 1 = 4$ |
    | Bill | — | Grade 3 (failed two years) | $5 - 1 = 4$ |
    | Jennifer | — | Grade 2 (never failed) | $2 - 1 = 1$ |

    Total number of years in school

    Number of students

    $\dfrac{15}{5} = 3$ years/ student

    Therefore, this group has been in school for an average of 3 years per student.

2. Determine the average number of years of achievement of the group when they enter the program. Remember that achievement of 1.0 actually means no achievement at all; therefore, the number of years of achievement for each student is equal to each student's grade level score on an achievement test, minus one.

    Example:

    | Sarah | — | Pretest achievement test score | $1.5 - 1 = .5$ |
    | Blanca | — | Pretest achievement test score | $3.5 - 1 = 2.5$ |

---

[8]The explanation for ratio-of-learning is largely adapted from an article by Eldon E. Ekwall entitled, "Measuring Gains in Remedial Reading," which appeared in the November 1972, *Reading Teacher*, Vol. 26, 138–141. Reproduced by permission of the International Reading Association.

Elaine — Pretest achievement test score 2.5 − 1 = 1.5
Bill — Pretest achievement test score 2.5 − 1 = 1.5
Jennifer — Pretest achievement test score 1.0 − 1 = 0.0

Total years on achievement test   11.0

$$\frac{\text{Total years of achievement}}{\text{Number of students}} \quad \frac{6.0}{5.0} = 1.2$$

Therefore, the average number of years of achievement for this group when they entered the program was 1.2 years.

3. Divide the average number of years of achievement by the average number of years that children have been in school. This will give you their average learning rate prior to entering the special program.

Example:

$$\frac{\text{Average number of years of achievement}}{\text{Average number of years in school}} \quad \frac{1.2}{3.0} = .40$$

The average learning rate for these children before entering the program was .40, or in other words, they had only learned four-tenths as much as they should have. Said another way, they were learning .40 month's knowledge, on the average for every month they had been in school.

4. Determine how long children were in the special program.

Example:

September 15th to May 15th = 8 months

5. Determine the average gain per pupil during the special program.

Example:

Sara — Posttest achievement test score 2.8
Blanca — Posttest achievement test score 4.8
Elaine — Posttest achievement test score 5.2
Bill — Posttest achievement test score 4.5
Jennifer — Posttest achievement test score 2.3

Total years on achievement test (posttest)   19.6
Total years on achievement test (pretest)   11.0

$$\frac{\text{Total years gained during the special program (difference between posttest and pretest)}}{\text{Number of students}} \quad \frac{8.6}{5} = 1.72 \text{ yrs/student}$$

The average amount of gain during the special program was 1.72 years per student. Note that it is not necessary to subtract one (1) from each student's score on the posttest and pretest since you are only finding the overall differences in the two scores. However, subtracting one (1) from each posttest score and each pretest score would give the same answer anyway.

6. Determine the average learning rate during the special program. The average learning rate during the special program is found by dividing the amount gained during the program by the number of years (or months) the students were in the program.

Example:

Number of years gained during the program $\dfrac{1.72}{.8} = 2.15$
Years in the program

The average learning rate during this special program was 2.15.

7. Compare students' average learning rate before entering the special program with their average learning rate while participating in the special program. It was .40, or they had been gaining .40 month's achievement for every month they were in school. While they were enrolled in this special program, their average learning rate was 2.15, or they gained 2.15 month's achievement for every month they were in the special program.

As one can see, students were learning 5.4 times as rapidly as they had been (2.15 ÷ .4 = 5.4), or simply stated, they were now learning at a rate of more than two times that of the average student. There would certainly be no doubt that this program was effective. Any learning rate in this case that was greater than .4 (the students' rate of learning prior to the special program) would have indicated an improvement in this group's rate of learning.

QUALIFICATIONS OF READING SPECIALISTS

The International Reading Association has taken the lead in developing recommendations for the qualifications of various classifications of reading specialists. Many states have now developed their own standards for reading specialists based on these recommendations. The IRA recommendations are as follows:[9]

Qualifications:

A. General (Applicable to all Reading Specialists)
    Demonstrate proficiency in evaluating and implementing research.
    Demonstrate a willingness to make a meaningful contribution to professional organizations related to reading.
    Demonstrate a willingness to assume leadership in improving the reading program.

[9]Reproduced by permission of the International Reading Association.

B. Special Teacher of Reading

Complete a minimum of three years of successful classroom teaching in which the teaching of reading is an important responsibility of the position.

Complete a planned program for a Master's Degree from an accredited institution, to include:

1. A minimum of 12 semester hours in graduate level reading courses with at least one course in each of the following:

    (a) Foundations or survey of reading.

    A basic course whose content is related exclusively to reading instruction or the psychology of reading. Such a course ordinarily would be first in a sequence of reading courses.

    (b) Diagnosis and correction of reading disabilities.

    The content of this course or courses includes the following: Causes of reading disabilities; observation and interview procedures; diagnostic instruments; standard and informal tests; report writing; materials and methods of instruction.

    (c) Clinical or laboratory practicum in reading.

    A clinical or laboratory experience which might be an integral part of a course or courses in the diagnosis and correction of reading disabilities. Students diagnose and treat reading disability cases under supervision.

2. Complete, at undergraduate or graduate level, study in each of the following areas:

    (a) Measurement and/or evaluation.

    (b) Child and/or adolescent psychology.

    (c) Psychology, including such aspects as personality, cognition, and learning behaviors.

    (d) Literature for children and/or adolescents.

3. Fulfill remaining portions of the program from related areas of study.

C. Reading Clinician

Meet the qualifications as stipulated for the Special Teacher of Reading. Complete, in addition to the above, a sixth year of graduate work, including:

1. An advanced course or courses in the diagnosis and remediation of reading and learning problems.

2. A course or courses in individual testing.

3. An advanced clinical or laboratory practicum in the diagnosis and remediation of reading difficulties.

4. Field experiences under the direction of a qualified Reading Clinician.

D. Reading Consultant

Meet the qualifications as stipulated for the Special Teacher of Reading. Complete, in addition to the above, a sixth year of graduate work including:

1. An advanced course in the remediation and diagnosis of reading and learning problems.

2. An advanced course in the developmental aspects of a reading program.

3. A course or courses in curriculum development and supervision.
4. A course and/or experience in public relations.
5. Field experiences under a qualified Reading Consultant or Supervisor in a school setting.

E.   Reading Supervisor
Meet the qualifications as stipulated for the Special Teacher of Reading. Complete, in addition to the above, a sixth year of graduate work including:
1. Courses listed as 1, 2, 3, and 4 under Reading Consultant.
2. A course or courses in administrative procedures.
3. Field experiences under a qualified Reading Supervisor.

CODE OF ETHICS

All reading personnel, as well as administrators, should be familiar with the International Reading Association's Code of Ethics, which follows:

The members of the International Reading Association who are concerned with the teaching of reading form a group of professional persons, obligated to society and devoted to the service and welfare of individuals through teaching, clinical services, research, and publication. The members of this group are committed to values which are the foundation of a democratic society—freedom to teach, write, and study in an atmosphere conducive to the best interests of the profession. The welfare of the public, the profession, and the individuals concerned should be of primary consideration in recommending candidates for degrees, positions, advancements, the recognition of professional activity, and for certification in those areas where certification exists.

Ethical Standards in Professional Relationships

1.   It is the obligation of all members of the International Reading Association to observe the Code of Ethics of the organization and to act accordingly so as to advance the status and prestige of the Association and of the profession as a whole. Members should assist in establishing the highest professional standards for reading programs and services, and should enlist support for these through dissemination of pertinent information to the public.
2.   It is the obligation of all members to maintain relationships with other professional persons, striving for harmony, avoiding personal controversy, encouraging cooperative effort, and making known the obligations and services rendered by the reading specialist.
3.   It is the obligation of members to report results of research and other developments in reading.
4.   Members should not claim nor advertise affiliation with the International Reading Association as evidence of their competence in reading.

Ethical Standards in Reading Services

1. Reading specialists must possess suitable qualifications . . . for engaging in consulting, clinical, or remedial work. Unqualified persons should not engage in such activities except under the direct supervision of one who is properly qualified. Professional intent and the welfare of the person seeking the services of the reading specialist should govern all consulting or clinical activities such as counseling, administering diagnostic tests, or providing remediation. It is the duty of the reading specialist to keep relationships with clients and interested persons on a professional level.

2. Information derived from consulting and/or clinical services should be regarded as confidential. Expressed consent of persons involved should be secured before releasing information to outside agencies.

3. Reading specialists should recognize the boundaries of their competence and should not offer services which fail to meet professional standards established by other disciplines. They should be free, however, to give assistance in other areas in which they are qualified.

4. Referral should be made to specialists in allied fields as needed. When such referral is made, pertinent information should be made available to consulting specialists.

5. Reading clinics and/or reading specialists offering professional services should refrain from guaranteeing easy solutions or favorable outcomes as a result of their work, and their advertising should be consistent with that of allied professions. They should not accept for remediation any persons who are unlikely to benefit from their instruction, and they should work to accomplish the greatest possible improvement in the shortest time. Fees, if charged, should be agreed on in advance and should be charged in accordance with an established set of rates commensurate with that of other professions.

Breaches of the Code of Ethics should be reported to IRA Headquarters for referral to the Committee on Professional Standards and Ethics for an impartial investigation.

SUMMARY

In initiating a remedial reading program it is especially important to develop a job description that the person or persons selected are expected to perform. There should be thorough communication among classroom teachers, administrative personnel, and reading personnel regarding both the title and duties that various reading specialists are expected to perform.

In each school, classroom teachers, administrators, reading specialists and parents all have special talents, in relation to their roles, that they can contribute to the remedial reading program. It is important that each of these groups becomes familiar with the program and that each learns about the unique contributions of the others.

Another important aspect of the remedial reading program is the selection of the type of student who is most likely to benefit from remedial instruction. It is also important to obtain and /or develop materials that are appropriate for the specific difficulties of students with whom the reading specialist will be working. Still another important aspect of the program is the development of facilities conducive of learning.

It is also important to develop methods of measuring the effectiveness of the program. Traditional methods of measurement in remedial reading are often inadequate. The methods suggested within this chapter may be found to be more appropriate.

Lastly, it is important to select reading personnel that are highly qualified and who will perform their duties in a professional manner.

REFERENCES

Balow, Bruce. "The Long-Term Effect of Remedial Reading Instruction," *Reading Teacher*. Vol. 18, (April, 1965), 581–586.

Bean, Rita M. "Role of the Reading Specialist: A Multifaceted Dilemma," *Reading Teacher*. Vol. 32, (January, 1979), 409–413.

Bruininks, Robert; Glaman, Gertrude; and Clark, Charlotte R. "Issues in Determining Prevalence of Reading Retardation," *Reading Teacher*. Vol. 27, (November, 1973), 177–185.

Cashdan, Asher, and Pumfrey, P. D. 'Some Effects of the Teaching of Remedial Reading," *Educational Research*. Vol. 11, (February, 1969), 138–142.

Esworthy, Helen F. "Parents Attend Reading Clinic, Too," *Reading Teacher*. Vol. 32, (April, 1979), 831–834.

Evaluation Committee of the International Reading Association. "What's in a Name: Reading Specialist?" *Journal of Reading*. Vol. 22, (April, 1979), 623–628.

Garry, V. V. "Competencies That Count among Reading Specialists," *Journal of Reading*. Vol. 17, (May, 1974), 608–613.

Granowsky, Alvin; Middleton, Frances R.; and Mumford, Janice H. "Parents as Partners in Education," *Reading Teacher*. Vol. 32, (April, 1979), 826–830.

Green, Carroll R. "Effects of Reading Supervisors on Teacher Attitudes Toward Children with Reading Problems." Abstract of unpublished doctoral dissertation, St. Louis University, 1973.

Grimmett, Sadie A., and McCoy, Mae. "Effects of Parental Communication on Reading Performance of Third Grade Children," *Reading Teacher*. Vol. 34, (December, 1980), 303–308.

Hardy, Madeline I. "Disabled Readers: What Happens to Them after Elementary School?" *Canadian Education and Research Digest*. Vol. 8, (December, 1968), 338–346.

Hesse, Karl D.; Smith, Richard J.; and Nettleton, Aileen. "Content Teachers Consider the Role of the Reading Consultant," *Journal of Reading*. Vol. 17, (December, 1973), 210–215.

Hicks, Robert A., et al. "Reading Gains and Instructional Sessions," *Reading Teacher*. Vol. 21, (May, 1968), 738-739.

Jarvis, Oscar T. "Time Allotment Relationships to Pupil Achievement," *Elementary English*. Vol. 42, (February, 1965), 201-204.

Mangieri, John N., and Heimberger, Mary J. "Perceptions of the Reading Consultant's Role," *Journal of Reading*. Vol. 23, (March, 1980), 527-530.

Pearlman, Erwin, and Pearlman, Ralph. "The Effect of Remedial Reading Training in a Private Clinic," *Academic Therapy*. Vol. 5, (Summer, 1970), 298-304.

Pikulski, John J., and Ross, Elliott. "Classroom Teachers' Perceptions of the Role of the Reading Specialist," *Journal of Reading*. Vol. 23, (November, 1979), 126-135.

Rauch, Sidney J. "Administrator's Guidelines for More Effective Reading Programs," *Journal of Reading*. Vol. 17, (January, 1974), 297-300.

Reed, James C. "The Deficits of Retarded Readers—Fact or Artifact?" *Reading Teacher*. Vol. 23, (January, 1970), 347-352.

Sawyer, Walter S., and Wilson, Bonnie A. "Role Clarification for Remedial Reading and Learning Disabilities Teachers," *Reading Teacher*. Vol. 33, (November, 1979), 162-166.

Steirnagle, Edwa. "A Five-Year Summary of a Remedial Reading Program," *Reading Teacher*. Vol. 24, (March, 1971), 537-542.

Ullmann, Charles A. "Prevalence of Reading Disability as a Function of the Measure Used," *Journal of Learning Disabilities*. Vol. 2, (November, 1969), 556-558.

Willis, Benjamin C. "Evaluation of the Reading Center's Remedial Program for the 1970-71 School Year." Paper presented at the Broward County School Board, Fort Lauderdale, Florida, December, 1971. Mimeographed.

Wylie, Richard. "Diversified Concepts of the Role of the Reading Consultant," *Reading Teacher*. Vol. 22, (March, 1969), 519-522.

15

Relaying Information, Record Keeping, and Writing Case Reports in Remedial Reading

This chapter contains a discussion of the necessity for accurately relaying information to and from individuals and agencies. A number of samples of forms for relaying this information are shown along with a short discussion of the use of each form. The latter part of the chapter contains a discussion of suggested techniques for writing case reports. This is then followed by an example of a final case report.

THE PURPOSE OF REPORTING AND RECORD KEEPING

There are a number of purposes for reporting and record keeping in remedial reading. One of the most important and obvious reasons is, of course, for the purpose of accurately transmitting information. Most people would not attempt to keep a record of a complex checking account in their head. Likewise, the information compiled on disabled readers becomes too complex for one person to remember. Furthermore, a number of people must often deal with the same student, and it, of course, becomes necessary to accurately relay this complex set of information from person to person without taking the chance of misinterpretation or loss along the way.

A second, similar reason for accurate record keeping is to provide proper guidance to the student. Most people have a tendency to think they can remember more than they actually can. At a meeting of psychologists a questionnaire was circulated about one week after a speech to those psychologists who attended and heard the speaker's presentation. Only about 8 percent of the material the speaker presented was remembered at all, and 50 percent of the 8 percent (or 4 percent) was misinterpreted or inaccurately understood. As the remedial reading teacher works with each student, implications for further work and diagnosis constantly appear. If these implications are not written down, they are usually forgotten.

Accurate record keeping and reporting also serves as a measure of progress of disabled readers. In working with a disabled reader on a daily basis it is often difficult to observe progress. This is analogous to the uncle or aunt who comes to visit and remarks on how the children have grown. Yet in being exposed to children on a day-to-day basis it is difficult to really observe any growth. For most disabled readers it is necessary to keep accurate records of progress to measure their growth in reading skills as well as to justify time spent in teaching them.

A third important purpose that reporting and record keeping serves is that of in-service education. As the remedial reading teacher makes diagnoses and reports findings in written form and as he or she works with disabled readers and makes suggestions to classroom teachers for assignments, a great deal of reading education often takes place. When the classroom teacher sees positive results from the work of the remedial reading teacher and from work suggested by the remedial reading teacher, changes in the methods of the classroom teacher are likely to follow.

Legal requirements also make certain record keeping and reporting necessary. For example, many remedial reading programs are federally funded. This funding usually requires some sort of proof of the effectiveness or success of the program for which the funds were expended. Depending on state and local district policies it is also sometimes necessary to obtain written permission from parents in order to enroll their children in remedial programs.

TYPES OF REPORTS AND RECORD KEEPING

The various communication lines necessary for a successful remedial reading program are illustrated below. In some cases the remedial reading teacher does all of the diagnosis; however, in some cases at least part of the work is done by a diagnostician. Therefore, in illustrating these lines of communication we have referred, in some cases, to the teacher and/or diagnostician who may or may not be the same person.

1. Diagnostician or remedial reading teacher — Classroom teacher and administrators
2. Diagnostician or remedial reading teacher — Parents
3. Diagnostician or remedial reading teacher — Other educational agencies

Reporting Information from the Classroom Teacher to the Diagnostician or Remedial Reading Teacher

The forms that follow are used by the classroom teacher to relay information concerning those students whom the teacher believes are good candidates for remedial reading. It should be emphasized, however, that before these forms are used it would, in most cases, be necessary for the remedial reading teacher to communicate information to the classroom teacher, which would provide guidance in selecting those students most in need of, and most likely to benefit from, remedial help. In most cases, the forms that follow would be distributed to the classroom teacher by the remedial reading teacher. If possible this should be done in an in-service meeting, at which time the use of the forms can be explained.

Form A is easy for the classroom teacher to use and yet can serve as a device for helping teachers become more aware of students' reading problems. Before using such a form, many teachers with little or no formal training in reading will need help in interpreting and using this form. However, this can also be used to advantage when the form serves as the subject of an in-service meeting at which time the remedial reading teacher can explain the various categories of the reading skills and how to identify problems in each category.

Form B is easy for most teachers to understand; however, it is more time consuming for the classroom teacher. But, since the classroom teacher is often in a position to observe students over a long period of time, this type of form can often provide information that is of considerable value in working with disabled readers.

Reporting Information from the Diagnostician or Remedial Reading Teacher to Classroom Teachers

Form C is one type of report that can be used by the diagnostician or remedial reading teacher in reporting information derived in the initial diagnosis. A form such as this is often helpful in providing guidance in placement of students at the proper reading levels and in pinpointing specific weaknesses, whether students appear to be proper candidates for remedial reading or not.

Forms D and E are to be used by the remedial reading teacher in reporting information back to the classroom teacher once a student has been accepted as a candidate for remedial reading. As you will note, Form D provides for continuous information on diagnostic information, work being carried on for correction of the student's problem, assignments for the student, and feedback from the classroom teacher. Form E is used for providing information on assignments either to the classroom teacher or to parents.

(Form A)

Remedial Reading Referral

Teacher:_____   School:_____

Grade:_____   Date:_____

Nothing is so valuable in determining which students need remedial help as the opinion of the classroom teacher. If you have, or have had, students whom you feel need special help in reading, would you please list them in the space provided.

Following is a partial list of common weaknesses. If you feel any of these apply to students you are referring, please list the corresponding numbers after their names. If there are other difficulties that you have noted, please explain these also.

1. POOR SIGHT VOCABULARY
2. INABILITY TO USE CONTEXT CLUES
3. POOR USE OF PHONIC ANALYSIS
4. POOR USE OF STRUCTURAL ANALYSIS
5. MAKES REVERSALS (*saw* for *was*, etc.)
6. CANNOT ADJUST SPEED TO DIFFICULTY OF MATERIAL

7. WORD-BY-WORD READS
8. MAKES INSERTIONS, OMISSIONS, ETC.
9. POOR WORK AND STUDY HABITS
10. POOR CONCENTRATION
11. LACKS CONFIDENCE
12. EXHIBITS POOR ATTITUDE
13. POOR COMPREHENSION
14. PHRASES POORLY
15. OTHER (please explain)

If you have additional information, please enter it in the *remarks* blank. Please keep this form and it will be collected in the near future.

Student:_____
Remarks:_____
Student:_____
Remarks:_____
Student:_____
Remarks:_____
Student:_____
Remarks:_____
Student:_____
Remarks:_____

If you have additional students, please list their names on the back of this sheet.

(Form B)

Teacher's Report for Remedial Reading Referral

Student's Name:_____ Teacher's Name:_____

1. What do you think is the student's main problem(s) in reading?_____
_____
_____
_____

2. What is the student's reading level or what book is he or she presently using?_____
_____

3. How is this student grouped for reading?_____
_____

4. How is this student grouped for other subjects, and what is provided for any special reading problems that he or she may have?_____
_____
_____

5. What are some other weak points that you have observed in this student? (Other than in reading.)_____
_____
_____
_____

6. What are some of the student's strong points?_____
_____

6. What are the student's reactions to reading? (Interests, attitude, etc.)__
_____
_____

7. What is the attitude of the student?
    Emotionally calm _____
    Apathetic _____
    Excitable _____
8. How does the student react to authority?
    Resistant _____
    Accepting _____
    Overly dependent _____
9. Describe the student's relationships to other students._____
_____

10. Have you noted any unusual emotional behavior by this student?_____
_____

11. How does this student react to a difficult task? Withdrawn:_____
Faces problem with little or no difficulty:_____
Acts impulsively:_____
12. How does the student act in the classroom? Calm and quiet: (If withdrawn please explain.)_____
Talkative:_____
Normal:_____
Other Information that you feel is important:_____
_____
_____

(Form C)

Individual Reading Diagnosis Report

Student:_____ Date tested:_____

School:_____ Teacher:_____

Student's age at time of testing:__ Student's grade at time of testing:__

In accordance with your referral the above-named student was tested and in my opinion does _____ does not _____ need to be in the remedial reading program.

COMPREHENSION (Combination of the *Gray Oral Reading Test* and an *Informal Reading Inventory*.)

```
                100 | +   +   +   +   +   +   +   +   +   +
Percent of       75 | +   +   +   +   +   +   +   +   +   +
comprehension    50 | +   +   +   +   +   +   +   +   +   +
                 25 | +   +   +   +   +   +   +   +   +   +
                  X |_____
                      1   2   3   4   5   6   7   8   9   10
                            Reading grade level
                             (comprehension)
```

    1. FREE READING LEVEL   Grade _____
    2. INSTRUCTIONAL GRADE LEVEL   Grade _____
    3. FRUSTRATION READING LEVEL   Grade _____
READING DIFFICULTIES:_____
_____
PHYSICAL OR OTHER DIFFICULTIES NOTED:_____
_____
TYPE OF HELP OR REMEDIATION RECOMMENDED:_____
_____
_____

1. FREE READING LEVEL: Reader level at which child can function adequately with no teacher help. Word recognition should be 99% accurate; comprehension of all types should average at least 90%.
2. INSTRUCTIONAL READING LEVEL: Reading level at which child can function adequately with teacher guidance and, at the same time, meet enough challenge to stimulate further growth. On a pretest at this level, word recognition should be 95% accurate and comprehension at least 75% accurate.
3. FRUSTRATION LEVEL: Reading level at which the child's abilities to function break down. Word recognition falls to 90% or below; comprehension, to 50% or below. May also be indicated by presence of symptoms of difficulty such as vocalization, tension movements, and so on. Serves as an indicator of rate of progress in that it shows how far above the instructional level learning can currently extend.

(Form D)

From:_____

To:_____

As you know, _____ is receiving help in reading. This time amounts to approximately thirty-five to forty-five minutes three times per week. That time is shared with from one to five other students. In order to make the most of that time, I hope we can work together with this student to his/her maximum benefit. I will try to give you a report from time to time on what I am working on with this particular student, and what I have asked the student to do between these sessions. If there is some question, please feel free to contact me or write a note at the bottom of this page and ask the student to return it to me.

Thank you.

Remedial reading teacher's diagnosis of the problem:_____
_____
_____

Work being carried on for correction of the above problem:_____
_____
_____
_____

Assignment for student:_____
_____

Comments from classroom teacher (to remedial reading teacher):_____
_____

(Form E)

ASSIGNMENT SHEET
Name:_____Date due:_____
Purpose of assignment:_____
_____

The following work has been assigned to be completed before the next meeting with the student's remedial reading instructor:

1._____
2._____
3._____
4._____
5._____
Remedial reading teacher_____

_____
(Signature of parent or teacher)

Reporting Information from the Diagnostician or
Remedial Reading Teacher to Parents

As stated previously, in some districts it is required that teachers and/or administrators obtain permission from parents before enrolling students in programs such as remedial reading or special education. Form F can be used for this purpose.

Form G can be used to report information from an initial diagnosis or from information derived from diagnostic teaching. As you will note, this form also provides a checklist of the types of activities that parents can do that are often beneficial to disabled readers.

(Form F)

Parental Permission Form for Remedial Reading

To:_____

From:_____

Date:_____

Your child, _____, has been given a series of reading and diagnostic tests, and it is my opinion that _____ should be given the help that we can provide in the remedial reading program. This is a class for children of normal intelligence who have some type of difficulty in reading.

I would like to extend the opportunity for you to visit with me concerning your child's reading problem and to visit the class in which we would like to enroll him/her. If you would like to visit this class, it meets on _____ from _____ to _____ in Room _____. Please feel free to visit at any time.

You have my permission to enroll _____ in the remedial reading program.

_____
(Signature of parent or guardian)

Note: Please ask your child to return this to me or send it to me at the following address:

_____

_____

_____

(Form G)

Progress Report to Parents

Date:_____

To:_____

From:_____(Remedial Reading Teacher)

     As you know, your child _____ has been receiving help in our remedial reading program. We feel that his/her primary need is:_____
_____
_____

     In addition to the help that your child has been getting at school, it would also be beneficial if he/she could receive help from you in the following areas:

1. ____ Show interest in homework assignments that have been given and check to see that these are completed on the date that they are due.
2. ____ Take your child to the public library and help him/her to find books that he/she would like to read.
3. ____ Help your child by being a good listener when he/she reads to you. Do not be overly concerned with the teaching of specific skills. We will try to do this in the remedial reading program.
4. ____ Try to set aside a certain period of time each day for pleasure reading. This seems to work better if a *specific time* is set aside rather than a certain *amount* of time. In other words the amount of time is also important, for example, thirty to forty minutes, but it is important that it be done at the same time each day if possible.
5. ____ Please comment in the *remarks* space below whether you believe your child has taken an increased interest in reading on his/her own.
6. ____ Other:_____
_____
_____

Remarks:_____
_____
_____

                                               _____
                                        (Remedial Reading Teacher—Signature)

Reporting Information from Parents to the Diagnostician
and/or Remedial Reading Teacher

Teachers who work in university or public school reading clinics, as opposed to a regular remedial reading classroom, often come in contact with a greater percentage of seriously disabled readers. Although ample background information is desirable for any disabled reader, it is often especially helpful in order to properly diagnose the problems of seriously disabled readers. Some of this background information is usually available in the cumulative folders kept by the public schools or from the records of other educational agencies. Form H may be adapted to your specific situation as a request form for obtaining students' records from these various educational agencies. Note

---

(Form H)

Date:_____

To:_____

_____

_____

_____

The following student _____, who lives at _____, is receiving remediation at the Reading Center at _____. In order to facilitate his/her remediation, we would appreciate any test results or records that you might have concerning this child.

Thank you.

_____, Director

Reading Center, _____

You have my permission to release any records concerning my daughter ☐ son☐

_____
                (student's name)

_____
                        Parent

Sent to:

---

that it contains space for a parent's signature. Many educational agencies require parental permission before they will release student records.

Form I is used at the El Paso Reading Center. As the title indicates, it is an application for admission of students to the Reading Center. Most of the information requested on this form is directly applicable to a thorough diagnosis of each student. However, a few items, such as information on handedness and birth history, are used for research information over a longer period of time. Reading personnel working in reading clinics may wish to use an adaptation of this form, or remedial reading teachers may wish to use a shortened version to obtain information considered pertinent for an immediate, thorough diagnosis.

(Form I)

Application for Admission to
Reading Center
(To be filled out by parents or guardians of student)

Name of student:_____
               (Last)   (First)   (Middle)

Address:_____Telephone_____
_____
       (City)   (County)   (State)

Student's birthdate:_____Age:_____Sex:_____

School:_____Grade level:_____
     (If not in school, indicate   (If not in school, last grade
     occupation of student)   level reached)

Name of parents or guardians:_____

Address of parents or guardians:_____

Telephone number of parents or guardians:_____

Occupations of parents or guardians:

(A) Father_____Employed by:_____
       (Be specific)

(B) Mother:_____Employed by:_____
       (Be specific)

Father's place of birth: _____Birthdate:_____Age:_____

Mother's place of birth:_____Birthdate:_____Age:_____

Father's educational level:_____Mother's educational level:_____

Is this student adopted?_____ If so, student's age when adopted:____

Does student know he/she is adopted?_____Father dead?_____

Mother dead?_____Cause of death?_____

Are parents separated?_____divorced?_____

Has either parent remarried?_____Has either parent
                          (Which one?)

been married before?_____

(Form I cont'd.)

With whom does student live?_____

Religious preference: Child_____Father_____Mother_____

READING PROBLEM

1. Why is student being referred to the reading center?_____
_____
_____
_____
_____
_____
_____
_____
_____

FAMILY HISTORY

1. List name, age, and sex of other children—oldest to youngest:_____
_____

2. Are the children all full brothers and/or sisters?
Yes_____ No_____
If the answer is no, then please explain._____
_____

3. Which of the above children are presently living at home?_____
_____

4. Has anyone else ever lived in the home?_____
_____

5. Has your family ever lived with anyone else?_____
_____

6. What languages are spoken in the home?_____
_____

7. Do any other members of the family have a reading problem?_____

8. Have there ever been any physical deformities on either side of the family, in any generation?_____
_____

9. Indicate general health of other members of the family:_____
_____

BIRTH HISTORY

1. Was child born premature?_____(If so, how much)_____

2. Was birth completely normal? (If not, please explain)_____
_____
_____

DEVELOPMENTAL HISTORY

1. At what age did child say first words?_____

2. At what age did child first walk?_____

3. Did this child walk and speak first words at an earlier or later date than other members of the family? (Please explain.)
_____
_____

(Form I cont'd.)

4. Has child ever had any serious illnesses?_____
_____
_____

5. Has child ever had any serious accidents?_____
_____
_____

6. Does student presently, or has child ever, worn glasses?_____
If Yes, who prescribed them?_____
7. When did student have last examination by an eye doctor? What were
the results?_____
_____
_____

8. Has student ever had any ear infections?_____If yes, please explain.
_____
_____

9. Has student's hearing ever been checked by a doctor?_____
_____

10. Do *you* think student hears well?_____

SOCIOEDUCATIONAL
1. Any special schools attended?_____
Name of school, type, where, when, and how long in attendance:
_____
_____

2. Has student ever had an intelligence or other mental test?_____
If so: what test(s), by whom given, where and when, and results?
_____
_____

3. Has child ever failed in school?_____What grades?_____
4. Has the student ever missed school for any long periods of time? (If so,
please explain.)
_____
_____

5. Usual scholastic rating:_____6. Best subjects?_____
7. Worst subjects?_____
8. How does student get along with siblings?_____
Other children?_____Parents?_____
9. Disposition? Happy?_____Affectionate?_____
Dependable?_____
Concentration?_____Temper?_____Fears?_____
(Other comments)_____
10. Does student fatigue easily?_____Symptoms observed:_____

(Form I cont'd.)

11. How does student sleep?_____At night?_____
Daytime nap?_____
12. Interests and abilities:_____
13. What does student like to do in spare time?_____
14. Does student like to compete with others? (Explain.)_____
_____

REFERRAL INFORMATION
  1. Who referred you to the reading center?
       Name:_____
       Address:_____
       _____
                    (City)   (State)
  2. Full name and address of family physician or student's physician:
       Name:_____
       Address:_____
       _____
                    (City)   (State)

CASE RECORD INFORMATION
Name of person who has completed this form:_____
_____
              (Signature)   (Date)

Form J is used for the initial case analysis of each student who enters the Reading Center. Note that space is provided for the number of reading errors and characteristics of the reader on an informal reading inventory on the first trial as the student enters the program. The same passages are again read at the end of the remedial period, and the percentage of increase or decrease is computed. This type of information is often more valuable than a simple grade-level designation, which may or may not be accurate. The rest of the form is used to help the remedial reading teacher synthesize various test results and other information collected in the initial diagnosis.

(Form J)

Initial Case Analysis

Name:_____

Sex:_____

Grade:_____

School:_____

Teacher:_____

I. Test Results—Tests Administered at Clinic
  A. Reading Status

1. Informal Reading Inventory	*Oral*	*Silent*
Independent level	_____	_____
Instructional level	_____	_____
Frustration level	_____	_____
Listening comprehension level	_____	_____

Types of Errors
(Indicate number of each type)

First trial		*Second trial*	*Percent of increase (+) or decrease (−)*
	Omissions		
	Insertions		
	Partial mispronunciations		
	Gross mispronunications		
	Substitutions		
	Repetitions		
	Inversions		
	Aid		
	Self-corrected errors		

(Form J cont'd.)

Characteristics of the Reader
(Indicate with check mark [√])

First trial		Second trial
	Poor word-analysis skills	
	Head movement	
	Finger pointing	
	Disregard for punctuation	
	Loss of place	
	Overuse of phonics	
	Does not read in natural voice tones	
	Poor enunciation	
	Word-by-word reading	
	Poor phrasing	
	Lack of expression	
	Pauses	

B. Intelligence
   1. *WISC*   3. *Stanford-Binet*
      a. Verbal_____
      b. Performance_____   IQ_____
      c. Full scale_____
   2. *Slosson Intelligence Test*
      IQ_____
C. Other (phonics, basic sight words). Be specific, i.e., exact words not
   known, which areas of phonics are weak, etc.

D. Summary of test results from student's school records

(Form J cont'd.)

II. Interpretation of Test Results
   A. Reading tests
      1. Phonics

      2. Structural analysis

      3. Comprehension

   B. Intelligence tests

   C. Other

   D. Physical
      1. Vision
         a. Presently wears
         glasses   _____ _____
                      yes   no
         b. Prescribed by whom_____
                  when_____
         c. Results of visual screening test_____
      2. Hearing
         a. Auditory discrimination test results
         b. History of hearing
           problems   _____ _____
                     yes   no
                 (explain)
      3. Present general health (level of energy, activity, sleep, diet)

      4. Health history (severe illnesses, operations, accidents, head and
         back injuries, allergies, etc.)

      5. Other

   E. Environmental and personality factors
      1. Home (parents, siblings, general environment)

      2. Home and family adjustment (security, dependence, indepen-
         dence, affection, warmth, etc.)

(Form J cont'd.)

3. Attitude toward school (rebellious, submissive, indifferent, relations with teachers, etc.)

4. Emotional adjustment

III. Summary of results and possible and/or probable causes of reading difficulty

IV. Recommendations
   A. Place of treatment

   B. Materials and approach

   C. Prediction or conclusion in regard to the course and termination of the reading problem

   D. Instructional period with student
      Days: (circle) Monday–Tuesday–Wednesday–Thursday–Friday

      Hours:_____to_____

Maintaining Student Records

As mentioned earlier in this chapter, one of the reasons for record keeping is to simply help the remedial reading teacher keep up to date on each student. When a remedial reading teacher acquires a case load of twenty-five or more students, the task of analyzing the diagnostic test results and progress is likely to become overwhelming without a certain amount of record keeping. It should be kept in mind, however, that the type of records kept will vary with such factors as the number of students with whom the remedial reading teacher is required to work, the degree of disability of the students, and the mode of operation of the teacher.

Most remedial reading programs use one of two common types of operation. In one type of operation the remedial reading teacher works with each student or with only two to three students at a time. In doing so, information is often gained on planning the next session from diagnostic teaching during the day's activities. Form K may be used for this purpose. Teachers who are either required to, or prefer to, work with a larger number of students during any one period usually find this type of record keeping to be somewhat burdensome. For this type of operation a daily worksheet such as that shown in Form L may be preferable. When using Form L the teacher would often plan the activities of students a week or more in advance. This sheet may be posted or duplicated and put in individual student folders in which the student, with some guidance, checks the plan and works on his or her own. This is, of

---

(Form K)

Meeting Number_____

Student_____

Date_____

Time_____

Relevant conditions (if any) of meeting_____
_____

Length of session_____

Summary of activities_____
_____
_____
_____
_____

Plan for next session_____
_____
_____
_____

Diagnostic implications of today's activities_____
_____
_____

Teacher comments_____
_____
_____
_____
_____

(Form L)

Daily Worksheet

Date_____to_____Period_____Grade_____

RFU—Reading for Understanding	RX —RX Reading Program
SRA—Reading lab	RFM—Reading for Meaning
LS —Literature Sampler	S —Story
PL —Pilot Library	O —Oral Reading
L —Listening	BBR—Be a Better Reader
T —Test	Mc —McCall Crabbs Tests
Ta —Tactics	PP —Programmed Phonics Books
SKS—Specific Skills Series	B —Boardwork or Overhead
SE —Self Expression	WS —Word Study

Name	Monday	Tuesday	Wednesday	Thursday	Friday

course, somewhat more like a conventional lesson plan for a class of developmental readers. It would also, in most cases, result in less individualization of instruction, which is highly important in remedial reading.

Reporting Information from Diagnostician or Remedial Reading Teacher to Other Educational Agencies

It is often necessary to send reports on students' progress to other educational agencies such as psychological evaluation centers, reading clinics, and/or private and public schools. In many cases the diagnostician and/or remedial reading teacher may simply reproduce and send copies of tests that have been administered. Although various test results often provide valuable information, they seldom contain the kind of information that the teacher can provide after having worked with a student for a period of time. For example, an intelligence test may show that a certain student's IQ is 120, but if the student is unable to learn when taught, then the fact that the student's IQ is 120 has very little meaning. It is much more meaningful, for example, to know that the student learns best by a specific procedure and/or that he or she responds well with a certain type of reward, or that the student is interested in, and will read, books on a subject in which he or she is especially interested.

In order to provide this type of information, the remedial reading teacher often needs to write a final case report on students' progress. The final case report can summarize test information that the teacher believes would be of help to another person who might continue working with a student, but more importantly, it can provide information on how rapidly the student learns and what procedures and materials have been especially helpful.

SUGGESTED PROCEDURES FOR WRITING CASE REPORTS AND RECORD KEEPING

The writing of case reports, although worthwhile, can be very time consuming. For this reason the remedial reading teacher should attempt to improve his or her ability to include all pertinent information while learning to exclude information that would be of little or no value to someone reading the report. In the section that follows, a number of suggestions are given on procedures that should generally be followed when writing case reports or in keeping records. Following these procedures is an example of a final case report.

1. *Use a type of outline form that will make sections and subsections clearly visible.* For example, each important section might be underlined and each subsection might then be indented under the main heading. This will enable the reader to quickly scan and spot specific information.

2. *Include important information but exclude any information that would be of no value in working with the student.* This might be illustrated in the case of a student who came to the teacher knowing only a few basic sight words. In the final case report it would be important to mention the total number of basic sight words not known when the student entered the remedial reading program. However, if the student had learned nearly all of the basic sight words during the course of remediation, there would be little or no value in actually listing which words were not known at the beginning of the remedial period. On the other hand, it would be important to make a statement concerning how the student seemed to learn the words in the easiest manner. It would also be helpful to actually list basic sight words still not known at the end of the remedial period. This would, of course, eliminate the need for further testing by the person receiving the report.

3. *Where "impressions" are stated, they should be identified as such.* This might be illustrated in the case of statements concerning a student's intelligence. For example, a statement such as, "Julie is highly intelligent because she seems to learn phonics rules rather quickly" would be inappropriate. It would be more appropriate to simply state, "Julie seems to possess the potential to learn phonics rules rather quickly." Some students seem to possess a high potential for learning some tasks; however, this would not necessarily mean that the student had a high intelligence quotient.

4. *List specific test scores and the source of each score.* It is important to state specific scores, but it is just as important to list the source of each score. For example, in discussing the reading level of a particular student as derived from several tests one might say, "Irma's instructional reading level would appear to be at the third-grade level as shown from her scores on the *San Diego Quick Assessment,* the *Classroom Reading Inventory* and the scores made this year on the *Iowa Test of Basic Skills.*"

5. *List specific skills needing remediation.* Some reports use vague statements such as "Martha seems to need help with word-attack skills." A statement such as this, however, is of little value since there are five main types of word-attack skills, and within each type there are a number of subcategories. It would be much more helpful to be more specific in stating this student's needs; e.g., "Martha would appear to benefit from instruction in the use of context clues. She also needs to learn all of the short vowel sounds and the following blends. . . ."

6. *Give a brief interpretation of the results of each test that may not be familiar to the person or persons reading the report.* An interpretation is especially necessary for some tests. For example, many people are not familiar with the norms of the *Wepman Auditory Discrimination Test.* To simply say "Jerry missed six items on this test" would not necessarily mean much to persons who were, or were not, familiar with the

test unless they looked at the norms provided in the instructions for administering this test. In interpreting these test results a statement such as the following would be more appropriate: "Jerry made six errors on this test. For a child of his age it would indicate that he has difficulty discriminating among certain phonemes." It would also be helpful to list which phonemes the student could not discriminate; however, that information would often be given in the results rather than in the interpretation.

7. *Keep sentence structure simple.* Make short, simple statements, as long complex sentences often become difficult to understand.

8. *Use third person when referring to yourself.* Rather than say "I think" or "It appears to me," it sounds more professional and perhaps less biased to say, "The clinician believes" or "The diagnostician would interpret this to mean. . . ."

9. *Make specific recommendations for the remediation of various difficulties noted.* As stated earlier, one of the purposes of writing case reports is that it serves as a vehicle for in-service education. For example, if it was noted that a student had a tendency to leave off or change endings such as *s, ed,* or *ing,* it would be beneficial to most teachers to list specific workbooks and the pages on which you might find exercises for the remediation of problems such as these. It would also help to simply list exercises that would help, such as the following:

    a. Have the student fill in blanks in sentences from several choices as shown in this example:

    Pat _____ when she saw the snake.
        (jumps, jumping, jumped)

    b. Give the student a reading passage from a newspaper story and have him or her look for, pronounce, and circle all *ing, ed,* and *s* endings.

10. *Give exact dates of the administration of each test.* Since students are constantly learning and changing, the exact dates of the administration of each test may be significant.

11. *Show summary of significant strengths and weaknesses.* Some people who read reports are not directly involved in the remediation of the student's problem. In other cases it is simply a fact that some people are not likely to read an entire case report with extreme care. Where this is the case, it is helpful to include a summary of the student's significant strengths and weaknesses. Furthermore, for the remedial reading teacher, clinician, or classroom teacher who will be charged with further remediation of the student, the summary will prove helpful in digesting the entire report.

12. *Include possible causal factors for weaknesses of the student.* In many cases it cannot be determined what caused a student to become a disabled reader. In other cases possible causes may be so complex that it would be extremely difficult to isolate any one factor or small group of

factors that were likely to have been causal factors in a student's reading disability. On the other hand, a teacher who has worked with a student for a period of time is likely to have gained a great deal of insight into the causal factors of a student's reading disability. When there are some definite signs that certain factors have contributed to a student's reading disability, these should be listed as "possible" factors. Knowing about such factors may prevent their reoccurrence.

THE FINAL CASE REPORT

The final case report that follows is somewhat longer than may be practical in many cases. It was chosen, however, because it illustrates most of the important points discussed in the previous section.

FINAL CASE REPORT

Name: Mark_____   Age: 9   Birthday: 11/12/__
School:_____   Grade: 4 (will be entering in
                             September)

Examiner:_____
Period of Diagnosis and Remediation: September 5, 19__ to May 26, 19__
Date of Report: June 3, 19__

General Background of Student

Home and Family Adjustment
Mark lives at home with his mother, stepfather, and five other children. Three of the children are his two sisters (10½ and 7) and a brother (9). The other two are half-brothers (6 and 4). After his mother's divorce from his father, Mark and his sisters and brother went to live with his grandmother. The four children lived with the grandmother approximately six years in Arizona. The parents feel that the adjustment of living with the grandmother to living with them was hard, but that he is fairly well adjusted now.

He reportedly gets along well with the other children in the family though he has an occasional fight with the older brother. He is generous and does not mind sharing. He has several close friends and bowls weekly in a league.

Health History
His general health is reportedly fine and there is no record of his having any major illnesses. However, his mother stated that when he was quite small he used to run straight into things. His eyes were checked by a specialist in Arizona when he was about six years old, but no vision problem was apparent at that time. He was given a complete hearing examination at about the same time and was found to have no problem.

Education

Mark did not attend kindergarten. He attended school (first and second grade) in Arizona. The school was apparently an "Open Concept" type school. According to his parents, the school personnel were aware of his reading problem, but he has never attended any sort of special reading classes. During the past year, in the third grade, he has been in a self-contained classroom. This teacher has worked very closely with the examiner in carrying out various assignments and remedial activities.

Results of Diagnostic Tests

Wepman Auditory Discrimination Test

This test was administered on September 12, 19____. The student made only one error on this test. He was not able to discriminate between the letters "t" and "p" in the words "cap" and "cat."

Interpretation: At the time the test was administered Mark was eight years old. A child of eight years old is not considered to have an auditory discrimination problem if he makes only one error on this test.

Keystone Visual Survey Test

This test was administered on September 12, 19____. Mark failed all of the subtests for near-point vision and the subtest for fusion at near point. He scored in the expected range on the remainder of the subtests. Mark was tested again on September 14, 19__ using the same test. The results were the same.

Interpretation: Since the results of this test indicated referral for further visual examination this was done. He was taken, by his mother, to an ophthalmologist on or about October 1, 19__. At that time he was given glasses to wear. He was told to wear them all of the time and has done so during the past school year.

San Diego Quick Assessment

This test was administered on September 13, 19__ and again on May 24, 19__. This is a word pronunciation test to estimate a student's Free or Independent, Instructional, and Frustration levels. The results were as follows:

>Date: September 13, 19__
>>Free or Independent Reading Level (Pre-Primer)
>>Instructional Reading Level (Primer)
>>Frustration Reading Level (First Grade)
>
>Date: May 24, 19__
>>Free or Independent Reading Level (First Grade)
>>Instructional Reading Level (Second and Third Grade)
>>Frustration Reading Level (Fourth Grade)

Interpretation: This is an indication that Mark's reading level (at least in terms of word knowledge) was no higher than First Grade Level at the time that he entered the remedial reading program. At the end of the program he had increased his word knowledge from two to three grade levels.

Diagnostic Reading Scales (Graded According to Informal Reading Inventory Criteria)
This test was administered on September 14, 19__ and again on May 25, 19__. Using the graded passages it enables one to obtain a student's Free or Independent, Instructional, and Frustration reading levels as the student reads both orally and silently. The results were as follows:

Date: September 14, 19__

	Oral Reading	Silent Reading
Free or Independent Reading Level	None	None
Instructional Reading Level	None	None
Frustration Reading Level	First Grade	First Grade
Listening Comprehension Level	Fourth Grade	

Date: May 25, 19__

	Oral Reading	Silent Reading
Free or Independent Reading Level	First Grade	Second Grade
Instructional Reading Level	Second Grade	Third Grade
Frustration Reading Level	Third Grade	Fourth Grade

Interpretation: This is an indication that Mark's reading level increased from one to three grade levels during the period of time that he spent in remedial reading. It should be noted that his silent reading tended to be about one level higher than his oral reading. This is because he still has some problems with certain word attack skills; however, his ability to attack words has shown considerable improvement during the past year.

CRS Basic Sight Word Inventory
This test was administered on September 14, 19__ and again on May 24, 19__. It is a test of 299 basic sight words. These words are graded at the Pre-Primer, Primer, First Grade, Second Grade (first half), Second Grade (second half), and Third Grade (first half) levels. The results were as follows:

Date: September 14, 19__

At this time Mark knew only eighteen of the words at the Pre-Primer level and twelve of the words at the Primer level. Only seven words were known at the First Grade level. The test was stopped at the end of the First Grade level. Some examples of the errors made on this inventory are as follows:

Word	Error	Analysis of Error(s)
big	bat	Medial vowel and ending consonant
him	his	Ending consonant
come	came	Medial vowel
three	their	Initial blend and ending sound
know	now	Vowel pair
your	yours	Insertion
play	pay	Substitution of initial consonant for blend

Date: May 24, 19__

At this time Mark knew all of the words on the *CRS Basic Sight Word Inventory.*

Interpretation: Mark seemed to learn basic sight words quite rapidly with very little difficulty.

Mills Learning Test
(Adapted form in which pictures were not used.) This test was given between September 19 and 22, 19_____. It is a test to determine by which (if any) method a student can best learn words.

Interpretation: It was found that Mark learned best by using a combination approach. During the past school year nearly all sight words were taught by this method.

RX Phonics Survey
This is a phonics survey that tests students' knowledge of the eighty most useful phonemes. It was administered on September 19, 19__ and again on May 26, 19__.

> Date: September 19, 19__
> At this time Mark knew only about twelve initial consonant sounds and about three initial consonant blends. He knew only one vowel sound.
> Date: May 26, 19__
> At this time he knew all of the initial consonant sounds, and all of the initial consonant blends and digraphs with the exception of the following:
> "sw" and "scr"
> He also knew all of the vowels (both long and short), vowel combinations, and special letter combinations with the exception of the following:
> "ow" (as in cow), "ew" (as in flew), "oi" (as in soil), and "aw" (as in paw)

Interpretation: At the beginning of the remedial period he knew very few phonic elements; however, he seemed to learn these quite rapidly. Much of the work in learning these was done using consonant substitution with known phonograms. The *Rx Reading Program* and *Webster Word Wheels* as well as the *Kenworthy Phonetic Drill Cards* were also very helpful in teaching phonics skills. Considerable teaching was also done using various commercial and homemade games.

No IQ tests were given since Mark seemed to learn nearly everything that was taught to him very rapidly.

Gates-McKillop Reading Diagnostic Tests—Oral Vocabulary VIII-2
This test was administered on September 15, 19__. It is a test to determine the grade level of a student's oral vocabulary. The results were as follows:

Date: September 15, 19__
Grade Level 4.7

Interpretation: At the time this was given it indicated that this student's oral vocabulary was considerably above both his oral and silent reading levels. It would indicate that any problems that he might have encountered in comprehension did not stem from a lack of oral vocabulary.

Summary of Diagnosis

Significant Weaknesses

1. At the beginning of the remedial period Mark had an extremely low basic sight word vocabulary.
2. Mark had a tendency to ignore medial and terminal sounds.
3. He did not know but a few of the initial consonant sounds and almost no consonant blends, consonant digraphs, vowel pairs, and special letter combinations.
4. Mark had a tendency to repeat a number of words and phrases. However, this tendency seemed to disappear almost as soon as he began to develop a larger basic sight word vocabulary. For this reason the problem of repetitions was assumed to be caused from a lack of knowledge of words rather than from a bad habit.
5. A number of omissions were also noted at the beginning of the remedial period. This problem also seems to have been overcome with the learning of a number of sight words and an improvement in his word attack skills.
6. At the beginning of the remedial period Mark showed definite signs of discomfort during testing. This problem also seems to have been overcome since he has come to know the examiner better and since he also seems to have gained some self-confidence.

Significant Strengths

1. Mark seems to learn almost any task rather quickly, especially when he receives tutoring in a rather small group or when he is tutored individually.
2. Although he seemed to have a rather low self-concept at the beginning of the remediation period, he now seems to have a rather good opinion of himself and believes that he can learn as well as anyone else.
3. He is rather large for his age and seems to excel in most sports. This seems to have been an important factor in building his self-confidence.
4. His ability to comprehend what he read was rather low in the beginning, but this was evidently caused from his lack of word knowledge. Now that he has enlarged his sight vocabulary he is able to comprehend quite well.
5. Mark seems to have an intensive interest in sports and is an avid reader of books on this subject.

Causal Factors in the Student's Reading Disability

One of the causal factors in Mark's reading disability may have been the social adjustment of first going through the period in which his parents were divorced and then again having to go through social adjustment of moving in with his mother and stepfather after a period of about six years. Another cause of his reading disability may have been his eyesight. The tests conducted by the examiner, as well as those conducted by the ophthalmologist, indicated that he had a rather serious visual problem. A third possible cause of his problem was the fact that he had attended a new "Open-Concept" school that was in its initial stages of operation and he received no corrective help as his disability in reading began to develop.

Summary of Instructional Program

During the past year a lot of instruction was given on learning basic sight words and on increasing his sight vocabulary in general. This was accomplished through the following methods:

1. The use of drill with phrase cards.
2. The use of a programmed textbook in phonics and structural analysis.
3. The use of the language-experience approach.
   In the beginning stages the student dictated stories which the examiner wrote down. These were then compiled into booklets and were later read back to the examiner by the student on a daily basis. Later the student wrote his own stories and illustrated them. These were also compiled into booklets which he practiced reading over and over again. This material was also sent home once he had mastered it to some extent. The stories were also cut up into sentences (or words) and again assembled in order to recreate the original story or to make up a new one.
4. Whenever possible, the examiner gave a great deal of praise to the student for his accomplishments.
5. The student was taught the most useful vowel rules and syllabication principles.
6. A number of exercises were used in which sentences appeared with one word left blank. This word was usually one which the student had previously missed. Wherever a blank appeared the student was given several choices of words to use in the blank. The word choices were normally those of similar configuration and would, in most cases, include the word that had been substituted by the student in place of the word missed.
7. Mark was encouraged to read a great deal on his own. At first he did very little of this, but after he had acquired a larger sight vocabulary he became an avid reader, especially of books concerning sports.

Prognosis for Success and Recommendations for Further Remediation
Prognosis
During the past year Mark has steadily improved in his reading ability. He appears to learn rapidly and there seems to be no physical or emotional problems that are now hindering his learning progress. At this point, however, he still needs to learn to use his newly acquired skills in vowel rules and syllabication principles. It would appear that he could profit from at least one more semester of remedial reading at which time another evaluation should be made. He has learned rapidly during the time that he spent in remedial reading this year and if the present rate of gain is maintained he should be reading up to grade level in a year or less.

Recommendations for Further Remediation

1. The student needs to do a great deal of free reading to increase his sight vocabulary through multiple exposure to many words.

2. Although he has become familiar with syllabication principles and vowel rules, he still needs more practice on using these skills.

3. Mark has been on a program of reading for approximately one hour per day during the past few months. His parents have set aside a certain time of day for him to read. This practice should be encouraged.

4. His parents should be encouraged to take him to the public library as often as possible.

5. It may be helpful to use some sort of reward system for a certain number of books read. He should, of course, be praised when he reads and should also be encouraged to try to find books that he would like to read on his own.

6. Mark still needs to learn the vowel pairs, "ow" (as in crow and cow), "ew," "oi," and "aw."

7. He seems to work best either by himself or in a small group. He seems to be highly distracted by large groups, especially when there is considerable noise in the room. Whenever possible, he should be taught either in a small group or individually.

SUMMARY

It is extremely important to develop a record-keeping system in teaching remedial reading to communicate important information derived from testing and teaching. The record-keeping system should be adequate but not burdensome, and should provide for communication among all the various people who are likely to come into professional contact with each disabled reader. Record keeping also serves the important purpose of measuring the progress of disabled readers and as a training technique, or as in-service education, for classroom teachers and parents. It is also extremely important that reading personnel familiarize themselves with techniques for the writing of case reports.

16
Evaluation and Use of Materials

The first part of this chapter deals with some important criteria to be considered in purchasing materials for teaching disabled readers. This is followed by a listing of some specific programs and books for use in remedial reading classes. The value and use of reading "machines" and/or mechanical devices is then discussed. The chapter ends with a discussion of the value and limitations of teacher-made materials and some specific ideas for creating these materials.

CRITERIA FOR EVALUATION

In purchasing materials for use in remedial reading there are certain criteria that these materials should meet that may not always be necessary when purchasing materials for developmental reading. Remedial reading deals with students who often possess weaknesses or gaps in learning in specific areas; whereas, in developmental reading the teacher is usually dealing with students who start from the beginning and need to learn the entire scope of reading skills. Following is a list of some of the important criteria that should be considered when purchasing materials for remedial reading.

Can Lessons Be Isolated for Teaching Specific Skills?

In most cases when teaching disabled readers it would not be necessary to have them go through an entire phonics program, learn *every* commonly taught vowel rule, learn all basic sight words, etc. For this reason materials and/or programs purchased for use in remedial reading should be of such a nature that various lessons can be pulled out for use in teaching specific skills without the necessity of the student going through the entire program. For example, if you were using a phonics program and knew the student was weak in only the *fl, bl*, and *gr* blends, you should be able to locate and use the parts of the program designed to teach these blends without having a student waste time in completing lessons that taught a number of other phonics skills that the student already knew.

Some materials and/or programs are such that a certain "level" of placement within the program is desirable. Where this is the case, the materials and/or program should contain a placement test for that purpose.

Is the Cost Reasonable in Relation to the Lifetime of the Materials?

Some materials, such as workbooks, may appear to be relatively inexpensive when they are purchased. However, if they are quickly used up by students, the per-pupil cost for their use may end up being considerably higher than nonexpendable materials that cost somewhat more. Therefore, when purchasing materials for use in remedial reading, consider the cost in relation to the total amount of usage available for each pupil.

Another important factor to consider is the amount of handling that materials are likely to receive. Materials that are likely to be handled a great deal should be of a heavy card stock and, if possible, should be laminated to protect them from heavy use. Cost, therefore, should also be considered in relation to the quality of the construction of reading materials.

How Many Students Can Be Serviced by the Material at One Time?

Some materials are of such a nature that only one student may use them at any one time, while others may be used by a number of students simultaneously. This is an extremely important factor to keep in mind when purchasing reading materials. For example, one new program requires the use of a rather expensive machine that will accommodate only one student at a time. Although each lesson is not high priced in relation to the total time it may last if handled carefully, the cost of the program then becomes extremely high priced in relation to the number of students that can be serviced during a specified period of time. On the other hand, many programs in kit form contain duplicate lessons on which several students can work at one time. Furthermore, since in many cases, students are not likely to be working on the same lesson at the same time, a small kit-type program may service a number of students at once.

Is the Cost Reasonable in Relation to the Spectrum of Skills Taught?

Some programs are extremely limited in relation to the number of reading skills taught, while others may cover a much greater spectrum of skills. If the lessons within a program can be used without the aid of some expensive mechanical device, then a program that covers a greater spectrum of skills is likely to service more students. On the other hand, it is often desirable in remedial reading to cover certain concepts in depth. Where this is the case, a program with a number of lessons reviewing difficult skills may be desirable.

Can Lessons Be Replaced Without Purchasing a Completely New Program?

Any experienced teacher is likely to know that certain cards, tapes, sheets, etc., that are a part of a reading program are likely to be lost, especially where the material receives heavy usage. In purchasing a program you should consider the possibility that this may happen, and give preference to materials and/or programs in which various components can be replaced.

Another important factor to consider is the ease of access to replacement parts. For example, is a local dealer available who can repair or replace broken and/or missing items? Is the program one that has established a good reputation, and is it manufactured by a large reputable company that is not likely to discontinue the item?

Is the Teacher's Manual Adequate or Burdensome?

We know that teachers are not likely to read a teacher's manual that is extremely long or burdensome. We have also found that many of the sales representatives who make a large part of their living selling these products have also not read the manuals. Therefore, from a practical standpoint, in purchasing a new program you should examine the teacher's manual to see if it covers the program adequately and yet is not so burdensome that it is unlikely to be read in its entirety.

Is the Format of the Material Different from That in Which Students Have Previously Experienced Failure?

It is common knowledge among personnel working in a reading setting that certain types of reading materials, such as hardbound books, have a tendency to be associated with failure for those students who are disabled readers. For this reason materials purchased for use in remedial reading should be of such a nature that they do not closely resemble materials with which students might already have experienced failure. For example, materials that seem to be extremely popular with disabled readers are softbound books, kits that contain easy, short lessons, programs with audio tapes, etc. One way to select materials of this nature is to ask the sales people to allow you to use samples of kits, etc., for a short period of time and then simply ask students their reactions to these materials.

Are Materials Highly Motivating?

In visiting a reading center it soon becomes evident which programs and/or materials are popular with the students. For the teacher who is unfamiliar with various types of material it is advisable to visit other reading centers or remedial reading classrooms and simply ask other more experienced teachers which programs and/or materials are most popular with students of various ages. If possible, it is also advisable to obtain samples of materials and try them out with students before buying them in larger quantities.

Are Books and Other Materials Graded According to a Well-Known Readability Formula or Are They Based on Publishers' Estimates?

Materials purchased for remedial reading instruction should generally have a high interest level and yet contain a low vocabulary load. Numerous studies have shown that it is not uncommon for science and social studies textbooks used by students at the seventh- or eighth-grade level to vary in difficulty from page to page from approximately the third- or fourth-grade level up to the eleventh- or twelfth-grade level. For example, many publishers advertise their trade books as having a certain interest level and as "being at an appropriate reading level for students from third through sixth grade." Any kind of books or material in which the readability level varies to such a large extent is inappropriate for use in remedial reading.

When possible you should attempt to purchase reading materials that have been written at specific grade levels on the basis of one of the better-known readability formulas such as the Spache Formula for grades one through three or the Dale-Chall Formula for grades four upward.

SOME RECOMMENDED BOOKS FOR USE IN TEACHING REMEDIAL READING

Any given list of books for use in teaching remedial reading is likely to become outdated to some extent with the passage of time. This is true especially because publishers tend to drop certain books and series of books from the market. In the list of recommended books that follows, however, are a number that have stood the test of time and have been highly successful in remedial reading programs. For this reason they are likely to be available for some time. This list is by no means complete, but it is representative of the types of books that meet the criteria previously outlined. In Appendix C you will also find a rather lengthy list of materials that also meet many of the criteria previously outlined.

Benefic Press, 1250 Sixth Avenue, San Diego, California 92101
Cowboy Sam Series, by Edna Walker Chandler. These exciting western-life adventures offer three levels of difficulty for each reading level. In each book, a section lists the reading skills covered.

Title	Reading Level	Interest Level
Cowboy Sam and Big Bill	pp[1]	pp–2
Cowboy Sam and Freckles	pp	pp–2
Cowboy Sam and Dandy	pp	pp–2
Cowboy Sam and Miss Lily	p[2]	p–3
Cowboy Sam and Porky	p	p–3
Cowboy Sam	p	p–3
Cowboy Sam and Flop	1	1–4
Cowboy Sam and Shorty	1	1–4
Cowboy Sam and Freddy	1	1–4
Cowboy Sam and Sally	2	2–5
Cowboy Sam and the Fair	2	2–5
Cowboy Sam and the Rodeo	2	2–5
Cowboy Sam and the Airplane	3	3–6
Cowboy Sam and the Indians	3	3–6
Cowboy Sam and the Rustlers	3	3–6
Teacher's Manual for Series		

Treat Truck Series, by Joy Treadway and Sandra Altheide. Stories in a modern environment provide humor and action. Vocabulary section lists words at and above reading level.

Title	Reading Level	Interest Level
Mike and the Treat Truck	pp	pp–2
Treat Truck and the Fire	pp	pp–2
Treat Truck and the Dog Show	p	p–2
Treat Truck and the Big Rain	p	p–2
Treat Truck and the Parade	1	1–2
Treat Truck and the Lucky Lion	1	1–2

[1] pp = preprimer.
[2] p = primer.

Treat Truck and the Storm	2	2–4
Treat Truck and the Bank Robbery	3	3–5

Moonbeam Series, by Selma and Jack Wassermann. These realistic space-age adventures afford reading practice to increase speed. They utilize the potential for critical thought.

Title	*Reading Level*	*Interest Level*
Moonbeam	pp	pp–3
Moonbeam Is Caught	pp	pp–3
Moonbeam and the Captain	pp	pp–3
Moonbeam Is Lost	p	p–3
Moonbeam and the Rocket Port	p	p–3
Moonbeam and the Big Jump	p	p–3
Moonbeam and the Rocket Ride	1	1–4
Moonbeam and the Dan Star	1	1–4
Moonbeam Finds a Moon Stone	2	2–5
Moonbeam and Sunny	3	3–6

Dan Frontier Series, by William J. Hurley. These adventure stories are about early frontier life in the Midwest. Dan, the main character, is a heroic frontiersman—not unlike Daniel Boone.

Title	*Reading Level*	*Interest Level*
Dan Frontier	pp	pp–2
Dan Frontier and the New House	pp	pp–2
Dan Frontier and the Big Cat	p	p–3
Dan Frontier Goes Hunting	p	p–3
Dan Frontier, Trapper	1	1–4
Dan Frontier with the Indians	1	1–4
Dan Frontier and the Wagon Train	2	2–5
Dan Frontier Scouts with the Army	2	2–5
Dan Frontier, Sheriff	3	3–6
Dan Frontier Goes Exploring	3	3–6
Dan Frontier Goes to Congress	4	4–7
Teacher's Manual for Series		

Tom Logan Series, by Edna Walker Chandler. Even slow readers are successful with the carefully controlled vocabulary in these stories about the Old West.

Title	*Reading Level*	*Interest Level*
Pony Rider	pp	pp–2
Talking Wire	pp	pp–2
Track Boss	p	p–3

Cattle Drive	p	p–3
Secret Tunnel	1	1–4
Gold Train	1	1–4
Gold Nugget	2	2–5
Cattle Cars	2	2–5
Stage Coach Driver	3	3–6
Circus Train	3	3–6

Butternut Bill Series, by Edith McCall. These high-interest, low-difficulty readers are about a boy named Butternut Bill and his life in the Ozark Mountain region.

Title	Reading Level	Interest Level
Butternut Bill	pp	pp–2
Butternut Bill and the Bee Tree	pp	pp–2
Butternut Bill and the Big Catfish	pp	pp–2
Butternut Bill and the Bear	p	p–3
Butternut Bill and the Little River	p	p–3
Butternut Bill and the Big Pumpkin	p	p–3
Butternut Bill and His Friends	1	1–3
Butternut Bill and the Train	1	1–4

Animal Adventure Readers, by Gene Darby. These are scientifically based animal adventure stories for primary children.

Title	Reading Level	Interest Level
Becky, the Rabbit	pp	1–3
Squeaky, the Squirrel	pp	1–3
Doc, the Dog	pp	1–3
Pat, the Parakeet	pp	1–3
Kate, the Cat	pp	1–3
Gomar, the Gosling	p	1–3
Skippy, the Skunk	p	1–3
Sandy, the Swallow	p	1–3
Sally, the Screech Owl	1	1–4
Pudgy, the Beaver	1	1–4
Hamilton, the Hamster	1	1–4
Horace, the Horse	1	1–4

Helicopter Adventure Series, by Selma and Jack Wassermann. This series features various ethnic groups and women in active roles. It offers controlled vocabulary and mature story content.

Title	Reading Level	Interest Level
Chopper Malone and the New Pilot	p	p–1
Chopper Malone and Susie	p	p–1

Chopper Malone and the Big Snow	1	1–2
Chopper Malone and Trouble at Sea	1	1–2
Chopper Malone and the Mountain Rescue	2	2–3
Chopper Malone and the Skylarks	3	3–4

Alley Alligator Series, by Athol B. Packer and Bill C. Cliett, Jr. These low-difficulty readers are about the adventures of three rangers and a baby alligator named Alley in the Florida Everglades.

Title	Reading Level	Interest Level
Alley Alligator	pp	1–3
Alley Alligator and the Fire	p	1–3
Alley Alligator and the Hurricane	1	1–4
Alley Alligator and the Big Race	2	2–5
Alley Alligator and the Hunters	3	3–6

Inner City Series, by Mike Neigoff. These stories deal with today's city life and how young people meet their problems with humor, imagination, and a determination to succeed.

Title	Reading Level	Interest Level
Beat the Gang	2	2–5
Tough Guy	3	3–6
Runaway	3	3–6
New in School	4	4–7
No Drop Out	4	4–7

Racing Wheel Readers, by Anabel Dean. Readers of this series are taken on the racing adventures of Woody Woods and his friends. Particularly appropriate for below-average readers, the stories are mature and contemporary, but they are written with a carefully controlled vocabulary.

Title	Reading Level	Interest Level
Hot Rod	2	4–12
Motorcycle Scramble	2	4–12
Motorcycle Racer	2	4–12
Drag Race	3	4–12
Destruction Derby	2	4–12
Stock Car Race	3	4–12
Baja 500	3	4–12
Safari Rally	3	4–12
Grand Prix Races	4	4–12
Le Mans Race	4	4–12
Road Race	4	4–12
Indy 500	4	4–12

Target Today Series, by Charles M. Brown, Dr. Helen Truher, and Dr. Phillip Weise. Each book in this series contains 100 short stories dealing with life today; the story characters are from many different ethnic and socio-economic backgrounds.

Title	Reading Level	Interest Level
Here It Is	2	4–12
Action Now	2–3	4–12
Move Ahead	3–4	5–12
Lead On	4–6	5–12

Horses and Heroines Series, by Anabel Dean. This series features high-interest content with controlled vocabulary. Although the leading character is a girl, both boys and girls will identify with Mary Major.

Title	Reading Level	Interest Level
Saddle Up	2	2–5
Junior Rodeo	2	2–5
High Jumper	3	3–6
Harness Race	3	3–6
Ride the Winner	4	4–7
Steeplechase	4	4–7

Sports Mystery Series, by Alan and Evelyn Lunemann. These readers would be very appropriate in remedial reading programs ranging from sixth to ninth grades. These are stories about teenagers, their problems and how they solve them, and the excitement they find in sports activities.

Title	Reading Level	Interest Level
Luck of the Runner	2	4–12
Ten Feet Tall	2	4–12
No Turning Back	2	4–12
Gymnast Girl	3	4–12
Ski Mountain Mystery	3	4–12
Fairway Danger	3	4–12
Tip Off	3	4–12
Pitcher's Choice	3	4–12
Scuba Diving Adventure	4	4–12
Face Off	4	4–12
Swimmer's Mark	4	4–12
Tennis Champ	4	4–12

World of Adventure Series, by Henry A. Bamman. Each adventure-filled book contains a vocabulary listing, a story map, a news article, and a tall tale.

Title	Reading Level	Interest Level
Lost Uranium Mine	2	4–9
Flight to the South Pole	2	4–9
Hunting Grizzly Bears	3	4–9
Fire on the Mountain	3	4–9
City Beneath the Sea	4	4–9
The Search for Piranha	4	4–9
Sacred Well of Sacrifice	5	4–9
Viking Treasure	6	4–9

Space Science Fiction Series, by Henry A. Bamman. People of the future face danger in outer space on trips of exploration and negotiation. There are extension sections for enrichment reading at the back of each book.

Title	Reading Level	Interest Level
Space Pirate	2	4–12
Milky Way	2	4–12
Bone People	3	4–12
Planet of the Whistlers	4	4–12
Inviso Man	5	4–12
Ice-Men of Rime	6	4–12

Mystery Adventure Series, by Henry A. Bamman. These mystery stories take teenage boys and girls into situations that test their determination, courage, and deductive reasoning. This series is for intermediate and junior high students who are reading below grade level.

Title	Reading Level	Interest Level
Mystery Adventure of the Talking Statues	2	4–12
Mystery Adventure of the Jeweled Bell	2	4–12
Mystery Adventure at Cave Four	3	4–12
Mystery Adventure of the Indian Burial Ground	4	4–12
Mystery Adventure at Longcliff Inn	5	4–12
Mystery Adventure of the Smuggled Treasure	6	4–12

Houses of Books Series. Two sets of clothbound books on high-interest subjects that let the child become involved in the book.

Title	Reading Level	Interest Level
House of Reading Fun	2–3	1–3
House of Challenge	4–8	4–6

Ranger Don Series, by Robert Whitehead. These books feature Don, a park ranger, his friends Mary Ash and Toni Green, and his dog Red. These books have high interest and controlled vocabulary.

Title	Reading Level	Interest Level
Ranger Don	pp	1–2
Ranger Don and the Forest Fire	pp	1–2
Ranger Don and the Wolverine	p	1–3
Ranger Don and the Indian Cave	p	1–3
Ranger Don and the Ghost Town	1	1–4
Ranger Don and the Tree Thief	1	1–4
Ranger Don and the Cougar	2	2–5
Ranger Don and the Mountain Trail	3	3–6

Cowboys of Many Races Series. This series presents life in the early West with the action, excitement, and adventure experienced by many people of different races and backgrounds.

Title	Reading Level	Interest Level
Cowboy Without a Horse	pp	pp–3
Cowboy on the Mountain	p	p–4
Cowboy Matt and Belleza	1	1–4
Adam Bradford, Cowboy	2	2–5
Cowboy on the Trail	3	3–6
Cowboy Soldier	4	4–6
Cowboy Marshall	5	5–7

Emergency Series. A series with high interest and controlled vocabulary based on the activities of a paramedic team.

Title	Reading Level	Interest Level
Emergency Squad	2.0	2–5
Emergency Ambulance #10	2.6	2–5
Emergency Life Support Unit	3.0	3–7
Emergency Air Ambulance	3.4	3–7
Emergency Firefighters	4.0	4–9
Emergency Rescue Team	4.3	4–9

Intrigue Series. Tales of mystery and intrigue to interest the most reluctant reader. High-interest, low-vocabulary stories emphasize vocabulary development and comprehension.

Title	Reading Level	Interest Level
Escape from Willing House	2.0	4–12
Pearls of Maslan	2.0	4–12
Danger in the Deep	3.0	4–12

The Jade Horse	3.0	4–12
Hidden Gold	4.0	4–12
Cave of the Dead	4.0	4–12

Bowmar-Noble Publishers, Inc., 4563 Colorado Boulevard, Los Angeles, California 90039
Reading Incentive Program, by Ed and Ruth Radlauer. This series is appropriate for students from grade three through high school. Action photographs are combined with idiomatic language and humor in twenty books. The reading range is grades three to five based on the Spache Readability Formula.

Motorcycles	VW Bugs
Horses	Dune Buggy Racing
Dune Buggies	The Mighty Midgets
Snowmobiles	Surfing
Custom Cars	Motorcycle Racing
Drag Racing	Drag Racing—Funny Cars
Karting	Hot Air Balloons
Minibikes	Bicycles
Slot Car Racing	Bicycle Racing
Teen Fair	Dogs

Starting Line Series, by Ed and Ruth Radlauer. This four-book collection focuses on high-interest content and a controlled-vocabulary format while reteaching basic reading skills. The interest level range is from grades four to six.

Title	Reading Level
Cats!	pp
Racing!	pp–1
Wheels!	pp–1.5
Kickoff!	2

Sports Reading Series. These kits are high-interest reading programs for students in grades four to eight. The reading level ranges from 2 to 4.5 on the Fry Readability Formula.

Big League Baseball Reading Kit
Pro Basketball Reading Kit
NFL Reading Kit

Gold Dust Books. This high-interest novelette series deals with mystery, adventure, sports, science fiction, and character development. Written at 2.0 to 2.9 reading level on the Fry Readability Formula, these twelve stories appeal to grades four to six children.

Library I	Library II
Mystery at Beach Bay	*Raging Rapids*
No Place to Hide	*The Full of the Moon*
The Big Find	*The Champion's Jacket*
Crazy Minnie	*Nightmare Nine*
Ride to Win	*Calling Earth*
Big Bad Ernie	*Escape from the Tower*

The Double Play Reading Series, for grades four to eight with a reading level of 2.5 to 5.9.

The Triple Play Reading Series, for grades seven to nine with a reading level of 2.0 to 7.0.

These series involve students in reading and acting out plays.

Kit 1: *Falling Star and Other Plays*
Kit 2: *A Light in the Window and Other Plays*
Kit 3: *The Motocross Trial and Other Plays*
Kit 4: *Purple Power and Other Plays*
Kit 5: *Second Stringer and Other Plays*

Crosswinds One and Two. This is a series designed for seventh and eighth graders whose reading levels range from 3 to 6 on the Fry Readability Formula. The texts cover a wide range of timely subjects.

The Reading Comprehension Series. This is a series of high-interest stories for students in grades four to eight printed on 8½″ × 14″ cards. On the back of each is a comprehension check. The reading level is from 3.0 to 4.4 on the Fry scale.

Dogs	*Crime Fighters*
Marguerite Henry's Horses	*Fads*
Aviation	*Special People*
Cars and Cycles	*Escape!*

Quicksilver Books. This is a collection of high-interest reading/writing books for use in grades four to eight. The reading level is from 3.0 to 4.5 on the Fry scale.

Childrens Press, 1224 West Van Buren Street, Chicago, Illinois 60607
Laura Brewster Mysteries, by Lisa Eisenberg. A series of exciting mysteries for reluctant readers. The series features insurance investigator Laura Brewster. Reading level is 3.0; interest level is grades four and up.

Falling Star	*House of Laughs*
Fast-Food King	*Killer Music*
Golden Idol	*Tiger Rose*

Space Police, by Leo P. Kelley. A series of action-packed stories of space-age cops and robbers. Reading level is 3.0; interest level is grades four and up.

Backward in Time	*Prison Satellite*
Death Sentence	*Sunworld*
Earth Two	*Worlds Apart*

Ready, Get Set, Go Books, by the Radlauers. A series of high-interest, low-vocabulary books presented on three levels of difficulty.

Ready Books: reading level is 1.1 to 1.5.

Shark Mania	*Dinosaur Mania*
Skateboard Mania	*Flying Mania*
Monster Mania	*Monkey Mania*
Roller Skate Mania	*Motorcycle Mania*

Get Set Books: reading level is 1.9 to 2.5.

Minibike Racing	*Fast, Faster, Fastest*
Trucks	*Model Trains*
Boats	*Racing Numbers*
CB Radio	*Wild Wheels*

Go Books: reading level is 2.5 to 3.0.

Dolls	*Model Cars*
Miniatures	*Ready, Get Set, Whoa!*
Bicycle Motocross	*Soap Box Racing*
Model Airplanes	*Soccer*

The Mania Books, by the Radlauers. A series of high-interest books written on the first-grade level. Contains many full-color photographs. Interest level is kindergarten to grade five.

Baseball Mania	*Hot Rod Mania*
Chopper Cycle Mania	*Pet Mania*

Gemini Books, by the Radlauers. These books are written on topics of high interest to today's readers. These contain many interesting facts and color photographs. Reading level is 2.5 to 4.0. Interest level is grades three to twelve.

Some Basics about Classic Cars	*Some Basics about Hang Gliding*
Some Basics about Windsurfing	*Some Basics about Motorcycles*
Some Basics about Waterskiing	*Some Basics about Running*

Some Basics about Women's
    Gymnastics
Some Basics about Bicycles

Some Basics about Skateboarding
Some Basics about Vans

Pacesetters. Through the controlled vocabulary of these books of fiction and fantasy, the reader can be successful. Reading level is 1.0 to 4.0; interest level is grades four and up.

Pacesetters 1—Ten titles
Pacesetters 2—Ten titles

Dell Publishing Company, Inc., Educational Department, 245 East 47th Street, New York, New York 10017
Hi/Lo Paperbacks. A series of paperback books designed to motivate reluctant readers. Interest level is for ages ten and up.

Title	Reading Level
Brainstorm	2.1
Great Unsolved Cases	2.6
The Hotshot	3.9
Pele: The King of Soccer	2.7
The Plant People	4.6
Run For Your Life	2.2
Tennis Rebel	2.3
Toni's Crowd	2.5
The Weekend	2.5
A Wild Heart	1.9
City Cop	3.8
Dracula Go Home	2.4
Frauds, Hoaxes and Swindles	2.9
A Test of Love	2.3
World War II Resistance Stories	3.5

Doubleday & Company, Garden City, New York 11530
Signal Books. These books are designed to stimulate, excite, and motivate reluctant readers. This series contains mysteries, tales of adventure, and biographies of people who have special meaning for today's young people. Reading level is grade four; interest level is grades seven to twelve.

The Economy Company, 1901 North Walnut, Oklahoma City, Oklahoma 73125
Guidebook to Better Reading Series. A series of high-interest, low-vocabulary materials for use in grades five to twelve. The reading levels range from grades two to six.

Follett Publishing Company, 1010 West Washington Boulevard, Chicago, Illinois 60607

Beginning-to-Read and Just Beginning-to-Read Books. These low-level, high-interest books with their simple sentence structure are great for independent reading by primary children—as well as older children with difficulties in reading.

Preprimer Level	*Level I*
The Birthday Car	Big New School
Cinderella at the Ball	Baby Bunny
Circus Fun	The Ball Book
Come Play with Me	Away Go the Boats
The Cookie House	City Fun
The Funny Baby	Four Good Friends
The Golden Goose	Follett Beginning-to-Read Picture
Happy Birthday, Dear Dragon	Dictionary
A House for Little Red	Jiffy, Miss Boo and Mr. Boo
Little Puff	Little Red Hen
The Little Runaway	Nobody Listens to Andrew
The Magic Beans	The Wee Little Man
Play Ball	Have You Seen My Brother?
The Snow Baby	You Are What You Are
The Three Bears	You Can Go Jump
The Three Goats	Funny Ride
The Three Little Pigs	I Love You, Dear Dragon
What Is It?	I Like Things
The Yellow Board	It's Halloween, Dear Dragon
	Happy Easter, Dear Dragon
	Know When to Stop
	Let's Go, Dear Dragon
	Let's Have a Play
	Little Red Riding Hood
	Magic Little Ones
	Magic Nutcracker

Level II	*Level III*
An Elephant in My Bed	Beginning-to-Read Poetry
The Boy Who Would Not Say His Name	Beginning-to-Read Riddles and Jokes
Mabel the Whale	Ride, Willy, Ride
Barefoot Boy	A Frog Sandwich: Riddles and Jokes
The Dog Who Came to Dinner	
One Day Everything Went Wrong	Gingerbread Children
Bears Who Went to the Seaside	The Ice Cream Cone

Beginning Crafts for Beginning
    Readers
The No-Bark Dog
Making Toys That Crawl and
    Slide
Making Toys That Swim and
    Float

Look Who's Cooking
Our Statue of Liberty
The Strange Hotel: Five Ghost
    Stories
Bear, Wolf and Mouse
The Cookie Cookbook
The Dog That Took the Train
The First Thanksgiving
When the Wild Ducks Come

Garrard Publishing Company, 1607 North Market Street, P. O. Box A, Champaign, Illinois 61820

The First Reading Books, by E. W. Dolch. Written with the very first sight words a reader learns, these books contain true and folklore tales about animals. These books are written on approximately a grade-one reading level; their interest level ranges from grades one to four.

Once There Was a Coyote
In the Woods
Monkey Friends
On the Farm
Tommy's Pets
Zoo Is Home
Once There was a Bear
Once There was a Cat

Once There was an Elephant
Once There was a Monkey
Once There was a Rabbit
Big, Bigger, Biggest
Dog Pals
Friendly Birds
I Like Cats
Some Are Small

The Basic Vocabulary Series, by E. W. Dolch. These true-life and folklore stories from all over the world are written almost entirely with the Dolch 220 Basic Sight Words and 95 Most Common Nouns. Their reading level is grade two, and their interest level ranges from grades one to six.

Folk Stories
Animal Stories
"Why" Stories
Pueblo Stories
Tepee Stories
Wigwam Stories
Lodge Stories
Horse Stories

Irish Stories
Navaho Stories
Dog Stories
More Dog Stories
Elephant Stories
Bear Stories
Lion and Tiger Stories
Circus Stories

Pleasure Reading Books, by E. W. Dolch. These old classics have been rewritten with a simple vocabulary so that even slow readers can derive pleasure from them. The reading level of these books is grade four; the interest level ranges from grades three and up.

Fairy Stories	*Old World Stories*
Andersen Stories	*Far East Stories*
Aesop's Stories	*Greek Stories*
Famous Stories	*Gospel Stories*
Robin Hood Stories	*Bible Stories*
Robinson Crusoe	*Gulliver's Stories*
Ivanhoe	

Target Books. Garrard's most popular *Discovery, Americans All,* and *Sports* books have been reset in a format that is mature in design and approach. These series were created for poor readers in high school and for less skilled readers in grades six to eight. However, their readability levels are grades three and four.

Adventures in Buckskin	*Big League Pitchers and*
Black Crusaders for Freedom	*Catchers*
The Founding Fathers	*Football Replay*
Heroes of the Home Run	*Four Women of Courage*
Indian Patriots of the Eastern	*Hockey Hotshots*
Woodlands	*Indian Patriots of the Great West*
Let's Hear It for America!	*Men of the Wild Frontier*
The Super Showmen	*They Loved the Land*
Three Jazz Greats	*Women in the White House*
Women Who Dared to Be	*Women with a Cause*
Different	*Pro Football's Greatest Upsets*
The Game of Football	*Lou Gehrig*
Susan B. Anthony	*William C. Handy*
Louis Armstrong	*Harry Houdini*
Nellie Bly	*Will Rogers*
Duke Ellington	*Sojourner Truth*
Walt Disney	*The Statue of Liberty Comes to*
America the Beautiful	*America*
The Story of the United States	
Flag	

Folklore of the World Books. These high-interest books are written with the storyteller's vocabulary. They retell stories from every corner of the world. The reading level is grade three; the interest level ranges from grades two to eight.

Animal Stories from Africa	*Stories from Africa*
Stories from Alaska	*Stories from Canada*
Stories from France	*Stories from Hawaii*
Stories from India	*Stories from Italy*
Stories from Japan	*Stories from Mexico*

Stories from Old China   *Stories from Old Egypt*
Stories from Old Russia   *Stories from Spain*

Young Animal Adventure Books. Easy reading books about baby animals. Reading level is grade two; interest level is grades one to four.

Doll: Bottle-Nosed Dolphin
Little Blue and Rusty: Red Kangaroos
Pen: Emperor Penguin

Globe Book Company, 50 West 23rd Street, New York, New York 10010
A Better Reading Workshop. A series of four text workbooks for use in intermediate and senior high. Includes many different kinds of reading material. Reading level is grades four to six.

The World of Vocabulary Series. A series of five workbooks each containing short, nonfiction selections for building vocabulary and other skills. For use in intermediate and senior high with students reading on grade levels two through seven.

Stories of Surprise and Wonder. Eighteen "thrillers" written on a third-grade level. Good for intermediate and senior high.

Beyond Time and Space. Twenty-two science-fiction stories to help interest intermediate and senior high students in reading. Reading level is grades three to five.

Weird and Mysterious. A series of twenty-seven nonfiction stories and exercises with an emphasis on word analysis, comprehension, vocabulary development, grammar, and usage. For use in intermediate and senior high. Reading level is grades two to three.

Ghosts and Spirits   *Adventures into the Unknown*
Creatures: Real and Imagined   *The Powers of Mind, Medicine*
                              and Magic

Holt, Rinehart & Winston, 383 Madison Avenue, New York, New York 10017
Impact on Reading. This series provides high-interest, high-quality literature for junior and senior high students. Each book contains literary selections in the different genres: short stories, poems, biographies, and novel excerpts.

Title	*Reading Level*
Circles	3.0–4.0
Mirrors and Windows	3.5–4.5

Blue Notes, Bright Notes	4.0–4.5
Searching	4.5–5.5
Conflict	5.0–6.0
Dreams and Dangers	5.5–6.9

Houghton Mifflin Company, One Beacon Street, Boston, Massachusetts 02107
Vistas. Stories for reluctant readers that were chosen for their high interest and appeal. Interest level is grades seven to twelve and reading level is grades four to six.

Horizons	*Paces*
Summits	*Networks*
Tempos	*Patterns*

Jamestown Publishers, P.O. Box 6743, Providence, Rhode Island 02940
The Adult Learner Series, by Judith Andrews Green. These books contain stories of very high interest to young adults. Yet they are written at the second-grade reading level, as established by the Fry Readability Formula.

Murder by Radio
The Man Who Stopped Time
The Man with the Scar

Attention Span Stories. These stories consist of one-page episodes with three cliff-hangers at the bottom of each page. The principal characters are in their teens and late teens, making the interest level ideal for students in middle school through early high school. The reading levels of the stories are grades two and three, as determined by the Fry Formula.

Time Trip	*Jungle Trip*
Survival Trip	*Star Trip*
Sports Trip	

Jamestown Classics. This program was developed by Walter Pauk. These classics are stories adapted from the world's greatest writers. Each forty-eight-page booklet contains an illustrated story written at grade five reading level. The interest level is from grades six to twelve.

From Jack London:

The Law of Life	*The Marriage of Lit-Lit*
Nam-Bok, the Liar	*Diablo, a Dog*

From Bret Harte:

Mliss	*The Outcasts of Poker Flat*
The Girl from Pike County	*The Luck of Roaring Camp*

From Arthur Conan Doyle's Sherlock Holmes:

The Musgrave Ritual	*The Red-Headed League*
The Case of the Six Napoleons	*The Case of the Five Orange Pips*

Leswing Press, P.O. Box 3577, San Rafael, California 94901
Star Knights Reading Series. This series is science fiction at its best with the Lambites, the Eaglepeople, and the Tortonians. The two vanguard books of this thirteen-book series are available now. The entire series is written at grades four to five reading level with an interest level geared all the way to young adults.

Star Magicians
Star Peril

Fast Wheels Reading Series, by Jerry Berg. Each book involves young people in fast-moving plots centered around cars, motorcycles, and the crucial problems that all young people face today—identity and social conflict. This series is designed for junior and senior high school students.

Title	Reading Level
Chevy V–8	3.4
Dirt-Track Racers	3.5
Camaro	3.6
Black-Powered Roadster	3.7

Learning to Read While Reading to Learn Series, by Dr. Jo Stanchfield and Dr. S. I. Hayakawa. Excitement, suspense, and action-filled experiences coupled with vivid photography and art work make older students want to read. Self-helps are included for decoding unknown words, for setting the stage, for motivation, and for analysis and interpretation.

Title	Reading Level
Set I	3.5–3.9
Behind the Scenes	3.5–3.9
A Place for Joe	3.5–3.9
Rescue on the Mountain	3.5–3.9
Dognappers	3.5–3.9
Viceroy's Daughter	3.5–3.9
Peculiar Lawn Mower	3.5–3.9
Operation Phoenix	3.5–3.9
Loud and Clear	3.5–3.9
Pedro's Secret	3.5–3.9
Set II	
The Big Break	3.9–4.3
Deadline for Tim	3.9–4.3

Chilling Escape	3.9–4.3
The Big Wild	3.9–4.3
The Vanishing Pirate	3.9–4.3
Hundred-Milers	3.9–4.3
Racing the Salt	3.9–4.3
Athlete, Artist—Jerry	3.9–4.3
Danger along the Trail	3.9–4.3

Your Own Thing Reading Series. These books have fast-moving stories about kids of the "now generation." The settings, urban in nature, provide for an honest approach to life in inner-city surroundings. The reading levels range from grades 4.1 to 5.8. However, the series will appeal to teenagers and young adults.

Turn On	*Go-Go Sawyer*
On the Run	*The Bad Scene*
Battle of Jericho	*Reach for the Sky*
Where the Action Is	*Out of Sight*
Tell It Like It Is	*High Octane*
Walk Like a Man	*El Rey*
Baby, That's Love	

Scholastic Book Services, 904 Sylvan Avenue, Englewood Cliffs, New Jersey 07632
Action and Double Action, developed by Mel Cebulash. These series are designed for students in grades seven to twelve. The programs develop basic word-attack, reading, and comprehension skills through reading, role playing, discussion, and writing.

Title	Reading Level
Action	2.0–4.0
Double Action	3.0–5.0
Action Library 1	2.0–2.4
Action Library 1A	2.0–2.4
Action Library 2	2.5–2.9
Action Library 2A	2.5–2.9
Action Library 3	3.0–3.4
Action Library 4	3.5–3.9

Scope Activity Kits. Written at grades four to six reading level for grades eight to twelve, the kits permit a student to explore a timeless theme at his or her own level of depth. They develop reading, reasoning, and language skills.

Human Behaviors	*Comedy*
Families	*Outsiders*

Science Fiction	*Poetry*
Do-It-Yourself Plays	*Monsters*
Survival	*Exploring the Unknown*
Advertising	*Television*
Radio	*The News*
Mystery	*Frauds and Hoaxes*
Sports	*Who Am I?*
Love	

SPRINT Libraries. Exciting, "grown-up" novels for students in grades four to six who have reading difficulties. These sets come in several ranges of difficulty.

Starter A, B	1.5–1.9
Library 1	2.0–2.4
Library 2	2.5–2.9
Library 3	3.0–3.4
Library 4	3.5–3.9

Reluctant Reader Libraries. Each library contains fifty paperbacks for use with children who read below grade level. All books are of high interest to young readers.

	Interest Level	Reading Level
Reluctant Reader	5	3, 4
	6	4, 5
	7	5, 6
	8	6, 7
	9	7, 8

Science Research Associates, Inc., 259 East Erie Street, Chicago, Illinois 60611

Science Research Associates Pilot Libraries. Pilot Library selections are unaltered excerpts from selected juvenile books. Each library contains seventy-two selections, from sixteen to thirty-two pages in length, of graded levels of difficulty. For each of the libraries the teacher is provided with a handbook that provides a synopsis of each book and questions for discussion. A student record book provides exercises for testing the student's comprehension.

Pilot Library Ic, Third Grade
Pilot Library IIa, Fourth Grade
Pilot Library IIb, Fifth Grade
Pilot Library IIc, Sixth Grade and Seventh Grade
Pilot Library IIIb, Eighth Grade

Super A, AA, B, and BB Kits. These kits are composed of comic book readers. They are high-interest stories with controlled vocabulary, based on the Harris-Jacobson word lists. They are suggested for grades four to eight, or even older.

Title	Reading Level
Kit A	2.0
Kit AA	3.0
Kit B	4.0
Kit BB	5.0

The Job Ahead: A Career Reading Series. This series contains high-interest stories at low reading levels that emphasize basic survival skills. The three texts have different reading levels (level 1: grade 3; level 2: grade 4; and level 3: grade 5), but look alike. Students in one class can read at different levels but share the same information. The Job Ahead is for grades seven to adult.

Getting It Together: 9–Adult. A series of books for use in remedial programs in grades nine through adult. These books contain the same material but are written on three levels of difficulty:

Level 1: grade three
Level 2: grade four
Level 3: grades five and six

A Mature Student's Guide to Reading and Composition. A series designed to help poor readers learn basic communications skills. The mature student is exposed to such everyday material as want ads, leases, contracts, and résumés written at a low reading level. Records and words cards are also available. Reading level is .0 to 4.0; interest level is grades seven to adult.

Sunburst Communications, Room G 232, 39 Washington Avenue, Pleasantville, New York 10570
Easy Reading Award Winners. Each of these titles is a proven winner with junior high school readers. The selection is broad enough to suit widely varied tastes and interests. Each paperback has been carefully checked in terms of reading level; they range from grades six to nine.

The Black Cauldron
The Contender
A Day No Pigs Would Die
Deathwatch
The Egypt Game
The House of Dies Drear
Hurry Home, Candy
Jazz Country

No Promises in the Wind
Old Yeller
Our Eddie
Quennie Peavy
Sing Down the Moon
Summer of my German Soldier
The Upstairs Room
To Be a Slave

The King's Fifth   *Where the Lilies Bloom*
My Side of the   *Zeely*
   Mountain

The Hi/Lo I, Hi/Lo II, and Hi/Lo High School have been carefully tested for readability with the Fry Readability Formula. Level 1 contains twenty-five titles with an average reading level of grade three. Level 2 averages grade four for its twenty-five titles. The high school program features twenty paperbacks, with reading levels grades four to six, that are popular with today's teens.

Reading for Every Day. This set of durable, colorfully illustrated cards helps the student learn and practice reading skills necessary for everyday life. It includes road maps, menus, and table of contents. Reading level is grade 4; interest level is grades four to seven.

Weekly Reader/Secondary Unit Books, 1250 Fairwood Avenue, P.O. Box 16618, Columbus, Ohio 43216
The Scrambler Series. This series provides short stories in comic book form on themes such as adventure, sports, wild tales, superstars and superheroes. The interest level spans grades five and six. The reading level increases from grade 2.5 to 4.0.

Cave-In and Other Stories about   *Shark and Stories about Fighting*
   Rescue   *to Win*
The Night Walker and More   *The Rubber Sole Kid and Other*
   Scary Tall Tales   *Funny Superstars*

Read It Right. Reading skills are strengthened through contact with materials used in real-life situations. These materials include newspapers, TV listings, menus, and train schedules. Reading level is 2.5–3.5; interest level is grades five to nine.

Reading Success Series. A high-interest series for problem readers ages ten to sixteen. Develops phonetic analysis, structural analysis, and word meaning skills. Reading level is 2.0 to 4.0; interest level is grades five to nine.

Reading All Around You. These three books are ideal for slow readers because of their real-life content. Reading level is 1.0 to 2.0; interest level is grades two to four.

READING MACHINES—THEIR VALUES AND LIMITATIONS IN REMEDIAL READING

Many people untrained in the teaching of reading would consider various machines or mechanical devices a necessary part of the remedial reading program. On the other hand, because they have read negative research information, remedial reading teachers often believe that most machines have little or no value in the teaching of reading. The truth about the value of the use of various machines and mechanical devices probably lies somewhere between these two opposing points of view.

Mechanical devices or machines most commonly used in teaching reading could generally be classified under one of two main categories. One category would be controlled reading or pacing devices, and the other would be tachistoscopic devices. Controlled reading devices are generally used for increasing speed, and tachistoscopic devices are used to present a timed exposure to a word, phrase, or group of numbers.

Since the remedial reading teacher is usually not concerned with increasing reading speed per se, the various devices for controlled reading have very little practical value in the remedial reading program. In developmental reading or in speed-reading classes controlled reading devices have proven helpful in increasing reading speed. But on the other hand, numerous studies have shown that when students simply pace their reading with their hand their gain in reading speed is usually equal to, or excels, gains made while using a controlled reading device. The Controlled Reader[3] can be set to show an entire line at a time or can also be set to use a guided slot that moves from left to right, thus preventing regressions and repetitions. It can be helpful to disabled readers who have developed the habit of making regressions or repetitions. It should be remembered, however, that regressions or repetitions are more often caused from lack of knowledge of sight words or difficulty with phonics or structural analysis or comprehension. When this is the case, the regressions or repetitions are only symptomatic of these causes and the use of a guided slot while reading would, in reality, be treating the symptom rather than the cause of the problem. Furthermore, a student can use a card to cover the line while reading, or can point to words as they are read, and accomplish essentially the same purpose.

Tachistoscopic devices were originally designed for several purposes. One of these purposes was to attempt to broaden students' visual span and thus enable them to see more numbers, letters, or words with each fixation of the eye. Some studies have indicated that students' visual span can be increased slightly by a tachistoscopic exposure to a progressively longer series of numbers of letters or words. However, it is somewhat difficult to tell whether the students were really increasing their vision span or their visual memory as they wrote down what they saw. The important point, however, is that tachistoscopic training of this nature seems to make little or no difference in reading speed.

Tachistoscopic training can be helpful for the purpose of increasing students' attention to word endings, medial vowels, etc., for those students who need training in this area. The tachistoscope can also be used to present sight words and sight phrases to groups of students. When doing this, stu-

---

[3]Controlled Reader, Educational Developmental Laboratories, Inc., McGraw-Hill Book Co., Huntington, New York.

dents can call out each word or phrase as it appears. For most students this is an extremely enjoyable activity and appears to be an effective learning technique.

TEACHER-MADE MATERIALS: THEIR VALUES AND LIMITATIONS

Almost any experienced remedial reading teacher has probably constructed a considerable amount of reading materials. These materials may include such things as flash cards, various types of games, and blending wheels. The teacher may also have students with specialized types of problems with word endings or medial vowels that require construction of specific types of exercises to meet the needs of these students. There is, therefore, little doubt that it is often necessary, as well as desirable, for the remedial reading teacher to construct materials.

Before constructing materials for use in remedial reading you should, however, ask yourself such questions as, considering time limitations and my salary on a per hour basis, can I make materials as cheaply as I can purchase them? When considered in this light the answer is often, definitely, no. For example, consider the time required to prepare a set of flash or phrase cards using basic sight words. When the cost of materials is considered plus the amount of teacher time required for such a project, the cost of simply purchasing commercially prepared materials would, no doubt, be considerably cheaper. This would also be true of such things as blending wheels and many other types of materials. Another important factor to consider is whether the time and effort involved in the construction of materials might be spent more profitably in other activities such as professional reading, test analysis, program planning, etc.

In summary, the real value in the use of teacher-made materials is that specific needs of individual students can often be met using materials that may not be available elsewhere. Also, time and/or budget limitations often do not allow the purchase of materials until a much later date.

EXAMPLES OF TEACHER-MADE MATERIALS

Following is a listing of some specific types of things the remedial reading teacher can do to lengthen the lifetime of commercially made materials or materials that can be constructed that are not likely to be available elsewhere.

Laminating Materials for Longer Use

When materials are laminated, they will last for a much longer period of time. Students can also write on laminated materials with an overhead projector pen or with a grease pencil used for overhead projector transparencies. The writing can readily be removed so that the materials can be used a number of times. For example, large flash cards can be laminated, and students can write over words using a kinesthetic approach and the students' writing can then be readily erased using a damp cloth for overhead projector pens or a soft dry cloth for overhead projector grease pencils.

Another good use of the laminating process is to take workbook pages from a student workbook and place these back to back with the same pages from the teacher's edition for the same workbook and then laminate both sides. Students can do the exercises on the student edition side of the page and then turn it over and check the accuracy of their work using the teacher's edition, which will have the correct answers on it.

There are three common ways to laminate materials. One way is to place laminating film over thin items that can easily be bent (such as a single sheet of paper). These are then run through a machine such as the 3–M Brand Thermofax "Secretary" Copier/Transparency Maker, shown in Figure 16–1. The machine then automatically seals the transparent film to the paper.

Another method of laminating is the use of the dry-mount press. The dry-mount press is a machine that applies heat to a piece of laminating film as it is placed over a piece of material to be laminated. One advantage of using the dry-mount press is that it can be used with thicker materials than can be run through a machine such as the 3-M Thermofax shown in Figure 16–1. It is, however, more time consuming to operate.

Perhaps one of the easiest and most economical methods of laminating materials now is to simply use laminate paper of the type that can be purchased in hardware stores. It comes in many colors, including woodgrain fin-

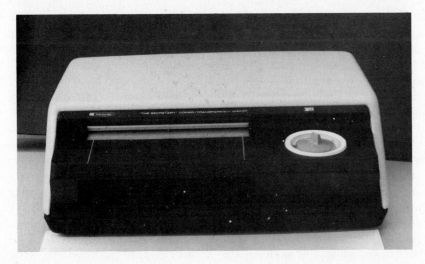

FIGURE 16-1. 3-M Brand Thermofax "Secretary" Copier/Transparency Maker.

ishes, etc.; however, it also comes in a clear plastic form. When the backing is peeled off of this material, you simply press it onto the material to be laminated and it forms its own bond without the aid of any heat or machine.

Teacher-Made Materials for Use with the Overhead Projector

The overhead projector has many uses in teaching remedial reading in ways that are commonly used by most teachers. However, it can readily be adapted as a tachistoscopic device. To do this you can simply take a piece of tagboard or cardboard and cut an opening in the center of it about the size of materials that you wish to present in a tachistoscopic manner. The tagboard or cardboard is then placed over the stage of the overhead projector where you would normally write so that light is emitted only through the cut-out square in the tagboard. Transparencies can then be placed over the square, and the transparency can be covered with an opaque object about the size of a package of cigarettes. When you wish to present a tachistoscopic exposure to a word or phrase you would simply uncover the hole in the cardboard momentarily so that the word or phrase is exposed for a very short period of time. This type of exercise is especially helpful in teaching students to attend to word middles and endings. If guides are placed above and below the cut-out square, a strip of plastic can be cut to fit into the guides. This makes it easy to center the words or phrases over the cut-out square when presenting words or phrases. (See Figure 16-2.)

Making Your Own Slides for Use with a 35 mm Projector

The Kodak Carousel projector and several other brands of 35 mm projectors can be moved from slide to slide by simply pressing a button, or on some models you can provide for a timed exposure by setting a timing mechanism on the projector. Projectors such as these work well for providing a tachistoscopic presentation of words and phrases. They can also be a helpful device for teaching phoneme-grapheme correspondence. You can easily make your own slides for use with a 35 mm projector by using overhead projector film. This is done by taking a common white piece of 8½″ × 11″ paper and dividing it into squares 36 mm in diameter. When this is finished, it will look like Figure 16-3.

In the upper left square the word *what* is printed with pencil. In the upper right the word *what* is typed with a typewriter. In the lower left a picture of a plate has been drawn or cut from a workbook and pasted on the paper, and the *pl* has either been typed or written in pencil below this picture. In the lower right square the phrase *in the house* has been typed. These four illustrations simply show what can be done in each of the many squares that would appear on an 8½″ × 11″ sheet of paper. After placing whatever you wish to have appear in each square, a xerox copy of the page can be made. This is in turn run through a machine such as the 3-M Thermofax copier,

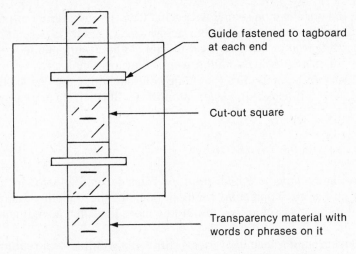

FIGURE 16-2. Using the Overhead Projector as a Tachistoscope.

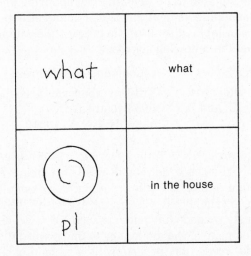

FIGURE 16-3.   Example of Four 35 mm Squares of an Overhead Projector Transparency.

and an overhead transparency is made that will have the same material on it as originally appeared on the completed 8½″ × 11″ sheet of paper. Each square is then cut along the lines so that you have squares approximately 35 mm in size. (The squares are drawn to approximately 36 mm initially because about one mm is lost in the cutting.) These 35 mm squares can then be mounted in slide mounts that can be purchased from photography stores or ordered through photography magazines. Most of the slide mounts that are available are heat sealed. Once the slide made from the transparency is mounted, the edge can be sealed with a hot iron. Heaters for mounting these heat sealing slides are available, but unless you intend to do a great many of them a regular iron of the type used to iron clothing works quite well. Slide mounts are also available that adhere once they are simply pressed together. These slides can be made for about one cent each plus the cost of the slide mounting, which if bought in larger quantities will run from one to two cents each.

Teacher-Made Materials for Use with the Tape Recorder

There are many ways in which the tape recorder can be used in teaching remedial and/or developmental reading. Some of these methods have been explained in previous chapters, but a few more ideas are listed below.

Adding Background Music to Stories.   Students will find oral reading much more enjoyable if they have written the material, if it is tape recorded, and if background music appropriate for the scene being described is dubbed in the tape recording. As students read, use an accompanying phonograph record with the proper sound effects to add music or sound effects. These sound effects records are available at some of the larger radio supply stores and are also available from the following source:

Item	Company and Address
Sound Effects Records, Volumes I, II, III, and IV	Ziff-Davis Service Division 595 Broadway New York, N. Y. 10012

Using the Tape Recorder as a Timing Device.   There are a number of instances in which the tape recorder can be used as a timing device in teaching either developmental and/or remedial reading. For example, in any kind of timed reading you can simply say, "Begin the exercise." Then after say thirty seconds, say, "Thirty seconds have now passed," etc. When teaching a skill such as looking on a page of the dictionary to find a word that should appear between two guide words, this procedure is also helpful. For example, the student can be given a list in which two guide words from the dictionary are shown at the top of the page. Following the guide words would appear a number of words. (The idea of using guide words, of course, is to be able to quickly decide whether a certain word would appear on the page between the two guide words shown at the top of the page.) The tape recorder would give directions such as the following:

At the top of the page are two guide words from a page in the dictionary. Following these words are a number of words that may or may not be on the page on which the two guide words appear. You will have five seconds to decide whether each of the words listed on this page would be found on the same page as the two guide words at the top of the page. When I say "begin," look at number one and mark a plus behind the word if it would be found on the same page as the two guide words at the top of the page. If it would not be found on that page, mark a minus after the word. We will now begin the exercise. Number one (*wait five seconds*), number two (*again wait five seconds*), etc.

After doing the exercise, the tape recorder can be used to check the accuracy of the student's work. In checking the work the tape recording would be as follows:

We will now check to see if you did each word correctly. I will say, "number one" and then "plus or minus" depending on which answer is correct. If your answer is correct, do not mark on your answer sheet. If your answer is not correct, circle the number by that word. Here are the answers: number one, plus, number two, minus, etc.

When the student has completed the work, you can instruct him or her to count the total number of correct answers and place that number at the top of the page.

Using the Tape Recorder to Pronounce Spelling Words. The tape recorder can also save the teacher valuable time in doing such things as pronouncing spelling words and then correcting students' papers when they have finished. In doing an exercise such as this the recording would be as follows:

Before you begin this exercise, number your paper from one to twenty-five. Turn the tape recorder off until you have done this. (*Allow a four-second pause.*) I will now pronounce each word and then use it in a sentence. When you hear each word, write it by the number I have just repeated. Number one is *rather*, I would rather go than stay home. *Rather*. Number two . . . , etc.

After you pronounce all of the words, they can then be checked with the tape recorder, which will also help the student learn words that were missed. In correcting this type of exercise the recording would be as follows:

Now we will check your paper. If you get a word correct, do not make any marks on your paper. If you do not get the word correct, write the word correctly behind the word that was not right. Here are the answers. Number one was *rather*. It is spelled r-a-t-h-e-r. Remember to write it correctly behind the word if you did not get it correct the first time. Again the word is spelled r-a-t-h-e-r. Number two is . . . , etc.

Using the Tape Recorder as a Self-Check Device. Many of the exercises that are commonly checked by the remedial reading teacher can easily be checked using the tape recorder and letting the student check his or her own work. This not only saves valuable teacher time, but also gives immediate feedback to the student on the accuracy of the work and will enable the student to learn more than he or she is likely to learn if a corrected paper is simply handed back.

Using the Tape Recorder for Book Reporting.   The tape recorder can also be used to enhance students' interest in reading. When students have read a book, let them go to the tape recorder and tell in their own words what they have read. These recordings can then be used by other students to decide if the books described are ones that they would like to read.

The teacher who is interested in furthering his or her knowledge of audiovisual techniques will find the following books to be helpful:

Drier, Harry N. *Career Development Resources: A Guide to Audiovisual and Printed Materials for Grades K–12.* Worthington, Ohio: C. A. Jones, 1973.
Hanley, John B. *Educational Media and the Teacher.* Dubuque, Iowa: William C. Brown Co., 1970.
Kinder, James S. *Using Instructional Media.* New York: Van Nostrand, 1973.
Murdock, Graham. *Mass Media and the Secondary School.* London: Macmillan, 1973.
Romiszowski, A. *The Selection and Use of Instructional Media.* New York: Wiley, 1974.

SUMMARY

Materials purchased for use in remedial reading should possess certain characteristics that may differ from those purchased for use in developmental reading. Remedial reading teachers and administrators should become familiar with these characteristics before they purchase these materials. The term *reading machines* has caused considerable confusion in and out of the field of reading. Reading specialists and administrators should also become familiar with various devices labeled *reading machines* and should also familiarize themselves with the research on the effectiveness of these devices.

There is now a wealth of materials available designed for both remedial and developmental reading. In spite of this, it is often necessary for remedial reading teachers to create their own materials. Techniques for creating these materials should be learned. However, before teachers spend considerable time in creating materials, they should be sure to investigate the possibility that similar materials are already available at a cost that would amount to less than the time and money spent on necessary raw materials.

17

Interpreting Test and Research Results in Reading

The first part of this chapter contains a discussion of the need for teachers to possess a basic understanding of some of the common terms needed in order to interpret and evaluate test and research results. The next part of the chapter contains an explanation of a number of terms necessary for interpretation of test evaluations and results. The final part of the chapter contains a discussion of the meaning of some common terms needed for the interpretation of research results in reading. This chapter was coauthored with Everett Davis.[1]

WHY TEACHERS NEED THE ABILITY TO
INTERPRET TEST AND RESEARCH RESULTS

Under the present standards for certification, in some states, teachers are not required to take a course in tests and measurements; and in most states teachers can begin teaching with little or no knowledge of basic statistical terms. However, teachers should possess a knowledge of a number of terms commonly used in describing test results, as well as those used in describing how accurately a test measures what it is supposed to measure. Without this basic knowledge it would be very difficult for a teacher to evaluate test reviews such as those found in Buros' *Mental Measurements Yearbook* (1972) or to even evaluate, in some cases, the descriptive information provided by the publisher.

[1]Dr. Davis is Associate Professor and Chairman of the Department of Educational Psychology and Guidance at the University of Texas at El Paso.

As the remedial reading teacher begins to work in the field, he or she is likely to find that knowledge gained in course work taken in college eventually becomes outdated and requires supplementation with material from professional books and periodicals. Much of the information found in these sources, and especially in professional periodicals, will present the results of research done by people working in the field of reading. In order to adequately understand much of this research at least some knowledge of statistical terms is needed.

The purpose of this chapter is only to provide the remedial reading teacher with knowledge of terms needed for interpreting test results and evaluations, and terms needed to interpret research results. It should be noted that an attempt is not made to provide teachers with a knowledge of how to do the problems involved in evaluating tests and test results or how to apply the statistical procedures discussed.

THE MEANING OF SOME COMMON TERMS NEEDED FOR TEST INTERPRETATION

Mean

The *mean* is simply the arithmetic average, as illustrated by the set of reading test scores shown below.

Julie	68
Syril	49
Enrique	38
Dennis	67
Judy	68
Denise	52
Total	342

The total (342) divided by the number of scores is 342/6 = 57. The symbol often used for the mean is $\bar{x}$. A symbol used for each of the raw scores, i.e., 68, 49, is x, and n represents the total number of scores. The Greek letter *sigma* (Σ) is usually used to represent the total sum, which in this case was 342. Therefore the formula for the mean would be

$$\bar{x} = \frac{\Sigma x}{n}.$$

The *median* is the point (not always the score) at which one-half of the ranked scores are above and one-half are below a midpoint. This is shown in the scores below.

Julie	68
Judy	68
Dennis	67
Denise	52
Syril	49
Enrique	38

One-half the scores are above a point one-half way between 67 and 52 and one-half of the scores are below this point. When there are an even number of ranked scores, as in this case, then the median is the midpoint of the two middle scores or $67 + 52 = 119 \div 2 = 59.5$. As stated above, 59.5 is not a "score" but simply represents a midpoint.

If there is an uneven number of scores, then the median is an exact score, as in the example below.

Julie	68
Judy	43
Luis	41
Bob	40
Dolly	32

In this case 41 is the score at midpoint, or the median.

In a set of scores the *mode* is that score that appears most often. It is possible to have more than one mode if a set of scores contains two or more raw scores that appear the most often an equal number of times. In the example shown below, 54 is the mode.

Raw scores = 22, 28, 34, 38, 42, 48, 54, 54, 57, 62

In the example that follows there are two modes (32 and 53).

Raw scores = 28, 32, 32, 38, 43, 48, 53, 53, 58, 62

Range

The *range* is a measure of variability that simply indicates the distance between the smallest and largest score. It is calculated by subtracting the smallest score from the largest score, as shown in the distribution of scores below.

$$18, 23, 26, 32, 33$$

If x_n = the highest score (33) and x_1 = the lowest score (18), the formula for finding the range is: range = $x_n - x_1$, or in this case the range = 33 − 18 = 15.

The Normal Curve

Figure 17–1 illustrates a *normal curve*. When many types of educational measurements such as intelligence, or even physical measurements such as height are taken, the largest number of scores falls at the mean with slightly fewer above and slightly fewer below the mean. When the distribution is "normal," i.e., with more scores at the median or mean and a gradually decreasing number at the extreme left (below the mean) and right (above the mean) in equal proportions, you get a smooth bell-shaped curve, as illustrated in Figure 17–1. It should also be noted that in a perfectly shaped bell or normal curve the mean, median, and mode would fall at the same point. This point is located at the center vertical line marked "0" at the bottom of the normal curve in Figure 17–1. The tallest or highest point on a bell curve or normal curve represents the highest score, or scores, or measurements, and the lowest point represents the lowest scores or measurements. It should also be stressed that you are not likely to obtain a smooth normal-shaped curve when measuring any characteristic unless you are dealing with large numbers of people from which that characteristic is measured.

Standard Deviation

Standard deviation (often designated by the Greek letter sigma "σ") is used to describe the variability of scores in relation to the mean. (The mean is a measure of central tendency.) You might think of standard deviation as a measure of the average distance of each of the scores, in a distribution, from the mean. Robert Koenker (1961) points out that standard deviation, quantile deviation, and range are the most commonly used measures of dispersion. He states,

> The purposes of measures of dispersion are as follows:
>
> 1. To find the spread or variability of a group of scores about the mean.
> 2. To compare the spread or variability of two or more groups.
> 3. To compare the spread or variability of one group on two different occasions. (p. 9)

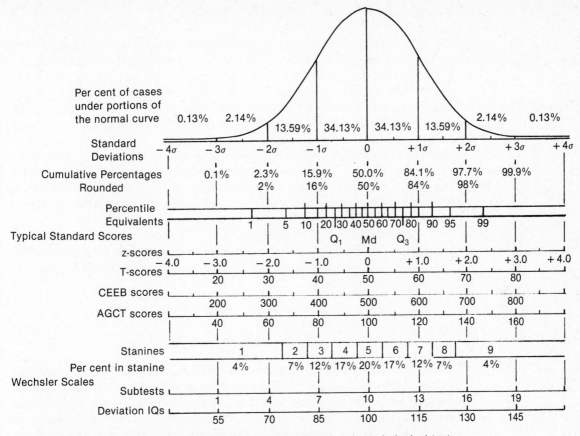

Per cent of cases under portions of the normal curve	0.13%	2.14%	13.59%	34.13%	34.13%	13.59%	2.14%	0.13%

Standard Deviations: -4σ -3σ -2σ -1σ 0 $+1\sigma$ $+2\sigma$ $+3\sigma$ $+4\sigma$

Cumulative Percentages Rounded: 0.1% 2.3% 15.9% 50.0% 84.1% 97.7% 99.9%
2% 16% 50% 84% 98%

Percentile Equivalents: 1 5 10 20 30 40 50 60 70 80 90 95 99

Typical Standard Scores: Q_1 Md Q_3

z-scores: -4.0 -3.0 -2.0 -1.0 0 $+1.0$ $+2.0$ $+3.0$ $+4.0$

T-scores: 20 30 40 50 60 70 80

CEEB scores: 200 300 400 500 600 700 800

AGCT scores: 40 60 80 100 120 140 160

Stanines: 1 2 3 4 5 6 7 8 9

Per cent in stanine: 4% 7% 12% 17% 20% 17% 12% 7% 4%

Wechsler Scales Subtests: 1 4 7 10 13 16 19

Deviation IQs: 55 70 85 100 115 130 145

Distributions of scores on many standardized educational and psychological tests approximate the form of the normal curve shown at the top of this chart. Below it are shown some of the systems that have been developed to facilitate the interpretation of scores by converting them into numbers that indicate the examinee's relative status in a group.

The zero (0) at the center of the baseline shows the location of the mean (average) raw score on a test, and the symbol σ (sigma) marks off the scale of raw scores in standard deviation units.

Cumulative percentages are the basis of the percentile equivalent scale.

Several systems are based on the standard deviation unit. Among these standard score scales, the *z-score*, the *T-score* and the *stanine* are general systems that have been applied to a variety of tests. The others are special variants used in connection with tests of the College Entrance Examination Board, the World War II Army General Classification test, and the Wechsler Intelligence Scales.

Tables of norms, whether in percentile or standard score form, have meaning only with reference to a specified test applied to a specified population. The chart does not permit one to conclude, for instance, that a percentile rank of 84 on one test necessarily is equivalent to a *z-score* of +1.0 on another; this is true only when each test yields essentially a normal distribution of scores and when both scales are based on identical or very similar groups of people.

FIGURE 17-1. The Normal Curve, Percentiles, and Standard Scores.

Courtesy of the Psychological Corporation. The scales on this chart are discussed in greater detail in *Test Service Bulletin No. 48.* The Psychological Corporation, New York, N.Y.

The standard deviation would vary with the range in a set of scores. That is, the greater the range in scores, the larger the standard deviation. In a *normally* distributed set of scores, however, 34.13 percent of the scores would fall one standard deviation above the mean and 34.13 percent would fall one standard deviation below the mean, as can be seen in Figure 17–1. Thus 68.26 (34.13 + 34.13) percent of the scores would fall within one standard deviation above or below the mean. It is fairly common to say that two-thirds (or 66⅔ percent) of the scores in a normal distribution fall within plus or minus one standard deviation (sigma σ) above or below the mean. Likewise, as can be seen in Figure 17–1, 95.44 percent of the scores in a normal distribution would fall within plus or minus two sigmas above or below the mean, etc.

Knowing the standard deviation of a set of scores can be useful in that it provides a standard index of measurement of any score from the mean. This can be useful to statisticians or to teachers in comparing individual scores on various types of data.

Percentiles or Centiles

When a teacher wishes to describe the relative standing of a particular individual in relation to other members of a group, the teacher often uses *percentiles*, or less often quartiles or deciles. A percentile score for an individual represents his or her score relative to the percentage of other individuals in a group falling below that score. Thus an individual falling at the sixty-fifth percentile would have done better on that particular test than 65 percent of the other people taking the test. It should be kept in mind, however, that the percentile score achieved by a student would be in relation to the group with which the student was compared. For example, a student in a school district with poor achievement may score at the eighty-sixth percentile as computed from local school norms. However, the same student may only score at the fifty-sixth percentile if the score is based on national norms.

It should also be stressed that percentiles scores are not evenly spaced along a baseline as can be seen from Figure 17–1. Since more scores tend to cluster around the mean, the number of raw score points between, for example, the fortieth to forty-fifth percentile may be considerably less than the number of points at the extreme ends or, for example, from the fifth to tenth percentile.

One of the advantages of using percentiles is that they are usually readily understood by anyone who understands percentages. On the other hand, they have one rather serious drawback. For example, in comparing students' percentile ratings near the center of a distribution you might see that John ranked in the fifty-sixth percentile and Mary ranked in the fiftieth percentile. Since it takes so few points to change percentile scores near the center of the distribution, a ranking of fiftieth versus a fifty-sixth percentile may make very little difference, or in other words, might easily have happened by chance.

It should be also pointed out that there is no one hundredth percentile since in reporting percentiles you are giving the percentage of cases that ranked below the number given. Therfore, a percentile rating of ninety-nine for a student means that 99 percent of the group ranked below that student. This, in turn, means that the student is in the top 1 percent.

Quartiles and Deciles

Quartiles and *deciles* also report an individual's relative standing in relation to other members of a group, just as in the case of percentiles. The twenty-fifth percentile is sometimes referred to as the first quartile and the seventy-fifth percentile is then referred to as the third quartile. In the case of deciles, the tenth percentile would be referred to as the first decile, the twentieth percentile would be the second decile, etc. It should be remembered that the first or third quartile or the first and second decile are *points* in the distribution of scores and do not represent proportions of the distribution. And percentiles of any kind are not equal units of measurement and, therefore, cannot be averaged or treated arithmetically.

Standard Scores

The use of standard scores enables one to interpret an individual's score in terms of the number of standard deviation units from the mean. Unlike percentiles, standard scores can be averaged and treated arithmetically. One of the most commonly used types of standard scores is the z-score. In some statistics books the lower case z is used to indicate scores derived from the following formula:

$$z = \frac{x - \bar{x}}{s}$$

In this case x represents a student's raw score, $\bar{x}$ represents the mean for that set of scores, and s represents the standard deviation of that set of scores. For example, if a student scored 120 on a test on which the mean was 112 and the standard deviation was 10, then you would have

$$z = \frac{x - \bar{x}}{s}, \quad \text{or} \quad z = \frac{120 - 112}{10} = \frac{8}{10} = .8$$

This tells us that the student's score was 8/10 or .8 standard deviation units above the mean.

In other books (and in Figure 17–1) z is transformed to a standard score in which the mean is 50 and the standard deviation is 10. These scores are referred to as T-scores or Z-scores. The advantage of using T scores is that they eliminate the use of decimals and negative numbers, as can be seen in Figure 17–1.

Some tests, such as the *College Entrance Examination Board (CEEB)*, and the old *Army General Classification Test (AGCT)* shown in Figure 17–1, are reported in transformed standard score form. For example, the *CEEB* has a mean of 500 with a standard deviation of 100. This allows someone knowledgeable about statistics and test scores to easily assess the value of a particular score. If a student received a score of 700 on the *CEEB* it is easy to see that this puts the student two standard deviation units above the mean. If you wished to interpret this score in terms of percentiles by following the vertical line in Figure 17–1 up to the cumulative percentages, you would see that a score of 700 on the *CEEB* places the student at the 97.7, or approximately at the ninety-eighth percentile.

Stanines

The *stanine* is another form of standard score with a mean of five and a standard deviation of approximately two. The term is derived from the words *standard* and *nine,* or *stanine.* Figure 17–1 will also enable you to see the approximate percentage of scores that would fall within each stanine. Note, for example, that only 4 percent of the scores fall within the first stanine, but 20 percent fall within the fifth stanine.

The terms *percentiles* and *stanines* are sometimes confusing to people who have not worked with statistical terms. It should be noted that percentiles and stanines are not equivalent. For example, note in Figure 17–1 that the beginning of the second stanine is approximately even with the fifth percentile and the beginning of the third stanine is approximately even with the twelfth and thirteenth percentile. The ninetieth percentile falls at approximately the beginning of the eighth stanine.

Standard Error

The term *standard error* is often used in describing tests. For example, a test author may report that the standard error for his test is five (5). The standard error may be thought of as an estimate of the reliability of this test score. The standard error is calculated by using both the test standard deviation and the test reliability coefficient. The use of the standard error enables you to estimate an interval of scores within which the individual's "true" score will fall. Thus, the test author who reports a standard error of five (5) is saying that there is a 68 percent chance that the "true" score, whatever it may be, will be within the interval from five points below to five points above the obtained score. For example, if an obtained score for an individual was ninety (90) and the standard error was five (5), you would be saying that you estimate that his "true" score will be in the interval from 85 to 95, and you expect that your estimation will be confirmed sixty-eight (68) times out of a hundred—provided you could ever determine the so-called true score.

Wechsler Scales

The subtests of the *Wechsler Intelligence Scale for Children—Revised* and the Wechsler IQs are both forms of standard scores. The Wechsler subtests have a mean of 10 with a standard deviation of 3. And the IQ Scale has a mean of 100 with a standard deviation of 15. The use of standard scores for both the subtest and IQ scales enables an experienced examiner to easily interpret the values of these scores. For example, if a student made a scaled score of 7 on the "Picture Completion" subtest, you would know it was one standard deviation below the mean. Likewise an overall Wechsler Full Scale IQ of 115 would be one standard deviation above the mean. Assuming all scores to be normalized (conforming to a standard normal curve), the student's "Picture Completion" subtest score would place him or her at the sixteenth percentile and the overall Full Scale IQ score would place him or her at the eighty-fourth percentile.

Reliability

Reliability is a term used in relation to testing to refer to the consistency with which a test agrees with itself. In using the phrase "agrees with itself" you might think in terms of its producing the same scores on several occasions when given to the same individual during a short period of time. It should be stressed, however, that high reliability in a test does not guarantee that a test is worthwhile. However, for a test to be valid (which is discussed next) it must be reliable.

Some tests used in reading tend to have a high intrascorer reliability but a poor interscorer reliability. That is, when the test is given by the same person, to the same students (intra), the same results are obtained. However, when the same students take the test from different examiners (inter), the results obtained are often different. This would probably mean that the examiners were scoring answers differently and thus the test could never be reliable when used by many different examiners.

Three methods of determining reliability are commonly used. One of these is to give the test and then repeat it at a later date (often called the *repeat* or *test-retest* method). If the students who performed high on it in the beginning perform high on it the second time and those who scored low on it the first time scored low on it the second time (or the students are generally in the same rank order on both administrations), the correlation will be high and it is considered to be reliable. Another method of measuring reliability is to take pupils' scores on the odd items and their scores on the even-numbered items (often called the *split-half technique*) and again see if the scores are in the same rank order or if they have a high correlation. A third method of measuring reliability is to compare one form of a test against another form of the test. This is often referred to as the *equivalent form* technique or method.

Validity

A test's validity is a measure of whether it really measures what it is designed to measure. It is quite possible for a test to be reliable without being valid. That is, one may be able to design a test that will give consistent scores for a student or a group of students, but it may not really measure what it purports to measure.

A number of reading tests may appear to measure what they purport to measure (or be valid) when, in reality, they do not. For example, one well-known basic sight word test that requires the student to circle on the answer sheet one of four choices when the examiner says a word purports to measure students' knowledge of basic sight words. It should be remembered, however, that it is considerably easier to get a certain word correct when it is called by a tester and the student is to circle one of four choices than it is to simply see the word and pronounce it. Since word attack in reading is a matter of seeing words and pronouncing them, a test that presents four choices is simply not valid. Research by Eldon E. Ekwall (Ekwall, 1973) has shown that this method of testing basic sight words is not valid because students then miss many words in actually reading that would appear to be known on the test. The same situation often exists in the area of phonics. That is, teachers do not test in a situation that is analogous to what the student actually does when he or she reads; therefore, the test results do not coincide with the student's ability to actually use phonic word attack.

Several methods are used to determine the validity of a test. One method is to correlate the results of a test with the results of another well-known test, i.e., determine whether those who score high on the new test also score high on the well-known test and whether those who score low on the new test also score low on the well-known test or, in other words, if the students are generally in the same rank order on both tests. This method would be fine if you actually *knew* that the well-known test was valid to begin with; however, the fact that a test is well-known and even that it is widely used does not make it valid. Another problem with this method of establishing validity is that the number of items missed by students on both tests may tend to correlate (be in the same rank order), but the students may miss different items on each of the tests. For overall achievement tests this would make very little difference, but on a diagnostic test that purports to diagnose specific blends, digraphs, etc., it would be very misleading.

Another method of establishing validity is to simply inspect the test or to send it to a group of specialists in the area for which it was designed. If the inspection or group consensus is that the test measures what it purports to measure, it is then considered to be valid. This is often called *content* or *face* validity.

A third method of measuring validity is to give a test to individuals (for example, a reading readiness test) and then measure their performance in reading at a later date. If the tests tend to correlate (the scores are generally in the same rank order) then we say the test has good *predictive* validity.

THE MEANING OF SOME COMMON NEEDED TERMS FOR INTERPRETING RESEARCH

Levels of Significance

In examining literature pertaining to research in reading as well as other fields, you will often encounter the use of various levels of significance. Levels of significance are used in a number of statistical procedures to determine whether the results obtained would have been likely to have happened by chance. For example, in giving a reading test to each of two groups of fifth-grade students, each of whom had been taught by different methods, you might find that one group had a mean grade-level achievement of 5.6 and the other group achieved a mean grade level of 5.9. With only this knowledge you would not really know if the scores of the group who had a mean achievement level of 5.9 merely happened by chance or whether the method of instruction used with them was so superior that these results could be expected nearly every year. In order to make meaningful comparisons between or among scores you should make use of the various levels of significance or what are sometimes referred to as *levels of confidence*.

If the proper statistical procedure was applied to the scores of the two fifth-grade students, you could determine whether a mean grade-level achievement of 5.9 was "significantly" better than the mean grade-level achievement of 5.6. If you discovered that the 5.9 mean grade-level achievement was significantly better than the 5.6 at the .05 level of significance (or confidence), you could conclude that these differences were, in fact, great enough that you would have expected these differences to have occurred by chance only five times out of 100. If you had found that the 5.9 mean grade level of achievement was significantly better than the 5.6 at the .01 level of significance or confidence, you could conclude that these differences were great enough that they would have happened by chance only one time out of 100.

In significance or confidence levels you will often see the .05, .01, or .001 levels reported. These may be shown as follows:

$p < .05$ This would mean that the probability of that event occurring would be less than five in 100. A researcher usually selects a confidence level as being significant or not significant before the statistical procedure is completed. If the .05 level had been selected, this $p < .05$ would be considered significant. This would, however, mean that there was a greater chance that the scores occurred by chance than if $p < .01$ or $p < .001$.

$p > .05$ This would mean that the probability of that event occurring would be greater than five in 100. Rather than show $p > .05$, researchers often simply label their results "NS" meaning "not significant" or, in other words, the chances of the event (that is, differences in test scores) are greater than we decided to risk.

$p < .01$ This would mean that the probability of that event occurring would be less than one in 100.

$p < .001$ This would mean that the probability of that event occurring would be less than one in 1000.

There is perhaps a growing tendency for researchers simply to report levels of significance as computed, e.g., the .02 level, and the .10 level. Some statisticians believe that when this is done, researchers are likely to claim that a level of say .10 or .15 is significant and, therefore, draw erroneous conclusions from their data.

Correlations

The term *correlation* is often used in a popular fashion to mean simply that there is some type of relationship or that two things have something in common. However, the term, when used in statistical research, usually refers to the coefficient of correlation (r) between two sets of variables. The most commonly used method of computing the coefficient of correlation is one devised by Pearson. It is often referred to as the Pearson Product Moment Correlation.

Correlations might be thought of as a measure of the rank order in distance from the mean or "going togetherness," of two sets of data or scores. Correlations may be highly positive or highly negative. A perfect positive correlation would be shown as 1.00 and a perfect negative correlation would be shown as -1.00. In order to compute a correlation coefficient (r) there must be two values or scores for each individual within a group. The correlation coefficient is then a measure of the rank order of scores on one test compared to the rank order of scores on the other test. The closer the rank order approaches 1.00, or a perfect positive correlation, the higher the chance that individuals who scored high on one test scored high on the other test and the individuals who scored low on one test scored low on the other test, or that all individuals within the group were in the same rank order on both tests. In negative correlation those individuals who tend to score high on the first test tend to score low on the second test, or, in other words, high scores on the first test are associated with low scores on the second test, and low scores on the first test tend to be associated with high scores on the second test.

Koenker (1961) states that there are a number of ways to interpret values in correlations. As an example he gives the following scale:

.84 to 1.00   highly dependable relationship
.60 to .79   moderate to marked relationship
.40 to .59   fair degree of relationship
.20 to .39   slight relationship
.00 to .19   negligible relationship (p. 52)

Koenker also points out that the same interpretation would apply to negative relationships. In that case, of course, the relationships between the scores would be in reverse.

It would be emphasized that the level of significance of a correlation should be reported in order to determine whether a high correlation between two variables might simply have happened by chance. For example, three students taking each of two tests could easily obtain the same rank order on the two tests simply by chance. However, 300 students taking each of the two tests would not be likely to obtain the same rank order simply by chance. In order to determine whether a given correlation is meaningful (highly significant), its level of significance is often reported.

It should also be pointed out that there is often a danger in drawing conclusions based on certain correlated data. For example, you might find that there was a high degree of relationship (or a high correlation) between reading ability in the first grade and the scores on a certain test for eye-motor coordination. This would not necessarily mean that training in exercises in eye-motor coordination would insure that students would improve in their ability to read. In fact, numerous research studies have shown that this does not occur. What evidently happens in cases such as this is that there is a common factor responsible, to some extent, for performance in both areas. However, that common factor, even though affecting both areas, may not be measured by either test.

t Tests and F tests

In researching various problems in reading, it is often necessary to determine whether the test performance of one group is significantly better or higher than the test performance of another group. In other cases it is necessary to determine whether the test performance of any one or more groups is significantly higher than the test performance of other groups. When researchers wish to make decisions of this nature the t test or F test is often used. Since the purpose of this chapter is only to acquaint you with enough information to understand research studies when you read them, the differences in these statistical procedures will not be discussed. What is important, however, is that you understand that with either the t or F tests you are concerned with whether measured differences between the means of two or more groups are significantly different. For example, assume a reading achievement test was given to each of two seventh-grade groups and the results showed an achievement level of 7.2 for one group and 7.4 for the other group. One would not really know whether these differences had occurred by chance or whether the differences were, in fact, great enough that you would not have expected them to have happened by chance more than five times in 100 ($p < .05$), one time in 100 ($p < .01$), etc. Whether these differences occurred by chance would depend on such factors as the number of students in each group and the standard deviation of the scores.

If the t or F test is used and the researcher reports significant differences between the means of the .05, .01, or .001 confidence levels, you would usually conclude that whatever was done with the group that achieved the higher means was superior, at least for those groups at that time, to what was done with the group that had the lower mean score.

Chi Square

The Chi Square Test (x^2) is used to test the distribution or ratio or frequency of a sample against another hypothetical or known distribution, ratio, or frequency. Or, as is often stated, it is used to test the difference between *expected* ratios, distributions, or frequencies and *observed* ratios, distributions, or frequencies.

An example of one use of the Chi Square Test in reading might be as follows: On a certain test, in previous research it was found that the expected distribution of mean scores for boys and girls was: boys 75, girls 75. However, in giving the test it is observed that the distribution or ratio of mean scores was: boys 85, girls 65. One would then tend to wonder if this observed distribution or ratio was different enough from the expected distribution to consider it significant. In order to determine the answer to that question, it would be necessary to use the Chi Square Test. After the Chi Square Test had been completed, you might find that this distribution or ratio was either not significant or significant at the .05, .01, or .001 levels. If it was not significant we would, of course, conclude that it could easily have happened by chance. If it was significant at the .05 level of confidence, we would conclude that the observed distribution or ratio was different enough from the expected distribution or ratio that we would not have expected it to have happened by chance more than five times out of 100, etc.

THE BUROS MENTAL MEASUREMENTS YEARBOOKS AND OTHER SOURCES OF TEST INFORMATION

Teachers and other personnel who find it necessary to use tests in their work should become acquainted with the Mental Measurements Yearbooks (MMYs). The MMYs are a series of books that have been published periodically (not yearly) since 1938. As stated by the editor, Oscar Buros (1968), the objectives of the test section of the MMYs are as follows:

a)   To provide comprehensive bibliographies of all standardized tests published in English-speaking countries.

b)   To provide frankly critical evaluations of tests, written by competent specialists representing a variety of viewpoints, to assist test users to choose the tests which will best meet their needs.

c)   To provide comprehensive bibliographies of articles, books, and theses dealing with the construction, validity, use, and limitations of specific tests.

d)   To impel test authors and publishers to place fewer but better tests on the market and to provide test users with detailed information on the validity and limitations of their tests at the time the tests are first published.

e)   To suggest to test users better methods of arriving at their own appraisals of both standardized and nonstandardized tests in light of their own particular values and needs.

f)   To stimulate contributing reviewers to reconsider and think through more carefully their own beliefs and values relevant to testing.

g)   To inculcate upon test users a keener awareness of both the values and dangers involved in the use and non-use of standardized tests.

h)   To impress test users with the desirability of suspecting all standardized tests—even though prepared by well-known authorities—accompanied by detailed data on their construction, validity, uses, and limitations. (pp. xv–xvi)

There are now eight yearbooks plus two *Tests In Print* (Buros, 1961, 1974). *Tests in Print* are a master index of the contents of the first seven yearbooks. They also contain a comprehensive bibliography of standard tests. These volumes indicate which of the first MMYs present the most recent information on various tests.

Of special interest to the reading specialist is an edition called *Reading Tests and Reviews*, (Buros, 1975) which is a smaller volume dealing principally with information pertaining to reading. This volume contains the following information pertaining to reading:

1. A comprehensive bibliography of tests in print.
2. A reprinting of the corresponding test reviews from the first six MMYs.
3. A classified index to the tests and reviews in the first six MMYs.
4. A directory of publishers.
5. Title and name indexes.

Another source of information on tests of reading is Roger Farr's (1971) annotated bibliography entitled *Measurement of Reading Achievement*. It contains information on the problems and procedures of assessing reading behavior.

Still another source of information on reading tests is a publication entitled, *Tests of Reading Readiness and Achievement: A Review and Evaluation* (Farr and Anistasiow, 1969). In this publication the authors present criteria for reviewing tests and information on various reading readiness tests and reading achievement tests.

SUMMARY

Remedial reading teachers are constantly faced with the task of reviewing descriptive information on new tests. They should also constantly review the professional literature in their field. Much of this literature is concerned with the results of research studies. In order to evaluate test reviews and research results at least some understanding of various statistical terms or procedures is required. The most commonly used of these terms or procedures are the *mean, median, mode, range, standard deviation*, characteristics of the normal curve, *percentiles* or *centiles, quartiles* and *deciles, stanines*, and various types of *standard scores*. The teacher should understand the characteristics of the normal curve and understand when it might be appropriate to use tests of significance such as the *t* and *F* tests. Remedial reading teachers should also understand the meaning of, and be able to interpret, studies dealing with reliability and validity. It is also highly important that reading personnel be familiar with, and understand, the values and limitations of correlations. Reading specialists should also be familiar with some of the publications designed to help them evaluate tests.

REFERENCES

Buros, Oscar K., ed. *Mental Measurements Yearbook.* Highland Park, N. J.: Gryphon Press, 1972.

Buros, Oscar K., ed. *Tests in Print: A Comprehensive Bibliography of Tests for Use in Educational Psychology and Industry.* Highland Park, N.J.: Gryphon Press, 1961 (Vol. 1), and 1974 (Vol. 2).

Buros, Oscar K., ed. *Reading Tests and Reviews.* Highland Park, N.J.: Gryphon Press, 1968.

Buros, Oscar K., ed. *Reading Tests and Reviews II.* Highland Park, N. J.: Gryphon Press, 1975.

Ekwall, Eldon E. *An Analysis of Children's Test Scores When Tested with Individually Administered Diagnostic Tests and When Tested with Group Administered Diagnostic Tests.* Final Research Report. University Research Institute, University of Texas at El Paso, El Paso, Texas, 1973.

Farr, Roger, ed. *Measurement of Reading Achievement.* Newark, Del.: ERIC/CRIER + IRA, 1971.

Farr, Roger, and Anistasiow, Nicholas. *Tests of Reading Readiness and Achievement: A Review and Evaluation.* Newark, Del.: International Reading Association, 1969.

Koenker, Robert H. *Simplified Statistics.* Bloomington, Illinois: McKnight & McKnight, 1961.

Appendix A: The *El Paso* Phonics Survey

THE *QUICK SURVEY WORD LIST* AND THE *EL PASO PHONICS SURVEY*

The *Quick Survey Word List* and the *El Paso Phonics Survey* are designed to test the student's knowledge of phonics word-attack skills. The *Quick Survey Word List* is also designed to test the student's knowledge of such word-attack skills as syllabication; vowel rules; rules for *C, G,* and *Y*; and accent generalizations. Directions for using each of these instruments follow.

DIRECTIONS FOR ADMINISTERING THE *QUICK SURVEY WORD LIST*

The *Quick Survey Word List* is designed to enable the tester to determine quickly if a student has the necessary word-attack skills to read successfully material written at an adult level. It may be given to the student at approximately fourth-grade level and above to determine whether it is necessary to administer the *El Paso Phonics Survey.* The student is simply given the word list to look at and is asked to pronounce each word. If the student can pronounce each of them correctly, it will not be necessary to administer the *El Paso Phonics Survey,* since the ultimate purpose of learning sound-symbol correspondence is to enable the student to attack new words.

If it becomes apparent after one or two words that the student is not able to pronounce the words on the *Quick Survey Word List,* then it should be discontinued and the *El Paso Phonics Survey* should be administered.

The correct pronunciations of the words on the *Quick Survey Word List* are shown on p. 597. This key shows the correct pronunciation as well as the part of each word that should be stressed. It should be remembered, however, that accent rules or generalizations pertaining to the English language are not consistent; therefore, if the words are pronounced correctly except for the accent or stress shown on certain syllables, they should be considered as correct.

Quick Survey Word List*

wratbeling	twayfrall
dawsnite	spreanplit
pramminciling	goanbate
whetsplitter	streegran
gincule	glammertickly
cringale	grantellean
slatrungle	aipcid

Pronunciation of Quick Survey Words

răt'-bĕl-ĭng	twā'-fräl
däs'-nĭt	sprēn'-plĭt
prăm'-mĭn-cĭl-ĭng	gōn'-bāt
hwĕt'-splĭt-tər	strē'-grăn
jĭn'-kyo͞ol	glăm'-mər-tĭck-ly
crĭn'-gāl	grăn'-tĕl-lēn
slăt'-rŭn-gəl	āp'-sĭd

Pronunciation Key

l — litt<u>l</u>e	ə — tamp<u>e</u>r
ə — <u>a</u>bout	hw — <u>wh</u>at
ä — f<u>a</u>ther	kyo͞o — <u>cu</u>te

EL PASO PHONICS SURVEY: GENERAL DIRECTIONS[†]

1. Before beginning the test, make sure the student has instant recognition of the test words that appear in the box at the top of the first page of the survey. These words should be known instantly by the student. If they are not, reschedule the test at a later date, after the words have been taught and the student has learned them.

*Ekwall, Eldon E., *Ekwall Reading Inventory*. Boston, Mass: Allyn and Bacon, 1979. Reproduced by permission of Allyn and Bacon, Inc.

†Reproduced by permission of Allyn and Bacon, Inc.

2. Give the student the El Paso Phonics Survey stimulus sheet pages.

3. Point to the letter in the first column and have the student say the name of that letter (not the sound it represents). Then point to the word in the middle column and have the student pronounce it. Then point to the nonsense word in the third column and have the student pronounce it.

4. If the student can give the name of the letter, the word in the middle column, and the nonsense word in the third column, mark the answer sheet with a plus (+). If the student cannot pronounce the nonsense word after giving the name of the letter and the word in the middle column, mark the answer sheet with a minus (–), or you may wish to write the word phonetically as the student pronounced it.

5. If the student can tell you the name of the letter and the small word in the middle column but cannot pronounce the nonsense word, you may wish to have him or her give the letter sound in isolation. If he or she can give the sound in isolation, either the student is unable to "blend" or does not know the letter well enough to give its sound and blend it at the same time.

6. Whenever a superior letter appears on the answer sheet, you may wish to refer to the Special Directions sheet.

7. To the right of each answer blank on the answer sheet, you will note a grade-level designation under the heading "PEK." This number represents the point at which most basal reading series would have already taught that sound. Therefore, at that point, you should expect it to be known. The designation 1.9 means the ninth month of the first year, and so forth.

8. When the student comes to two- or three-letter consonant digraphs or blends, as with *qu* in number 22, he or she is to say *"q-u"* as with the single letters. *Remember:* the student never gives letter sounds in isolation when engaged in actual reading.

9. When the student comes to the vowels (number 59), he or she is to say "short *a*," and so forth, and then the nonsense word in column two. If the student does not know that the breve (˘) over the vowels means short *a, e,* and so forth, then explain this. Do the same with the long vowels where the macron (—) appears.

10. All vowels and vowel combinations are put with only one or two of the first eight consonants. If any of these first eight consonants are not known, they should be taught before you attempt to test for vowel knowledge.

11. You will note that words appear to the right of some of the blanks on the answer sheet. These words illustrate the correct consonant or vowel sound that should be heard when the student responds.

12. Only phonic elements have been included that have a high enough utility to make them worthwhile learning. For example, the vowel pair *ui* appears very seldom, and when it does it may stand for the short *i*

sound as in "build," the long *oo* sound as in "fruit," or the short *u* sound as in "luck." Therefore, there is really no reason to teach it as a sound. However, some letters, such as *oe*, may stand for several sounds but most often stand for one particular sound. In the case of *oe*, the long *o* sound should be used. In cases such as this, the most common sound is illustrated by a word to the right of the blank on the answer sheet. If the student gives another correct sound for the letter(s) then say, "Yes, but what is another way that we could say this nonsense word?" The student must then say it as illustrated in the small word to the right of the blank on the answer sheet. Otherwise, count the answer as wrong.

13. Stop the test after five consecutive misses or if the student appears frustrated from missing a number of items even though he or she has not missed five consecutive items.

EL PASO PHONICS SURVEY: SPECIAL DIRECTIONS*

[a]3. If the student uses another *s* sound as in "sugar" (sh) in saying the nonsense word "sup," ask, "What is another *s* sound?" The student must use the *s* as in "sack."

[b]15. If the student uses the soft *c* sound as in "cigar" in saying the nonsense word "cam," ask, "What is another *c* sound?" The student must use the hard *c* sound as in "coat."

[c]16. If the student uses the soft *g* sound as in "gentle" in saying the nonsense word "gup," ask, "What is another *g* sound?" The student must use the hard *g* sound as in "gate."

[d]17. Ask, "What is the *y* sound when it comes at the beginning of a word?"

[e]23. The student must use the *ks* sound of *x*, and the nonsense word "mox" must rhyme with "box."

[f]33. If the student uses the *th* sound heard in "that," ask, "What is another *th* sound?" The student must use the *th* sound heard in "thing."

[g]34. If the student uses the *hoo* sound of *wh* in saying the nonsense word "whup," ask, "What is another *wh* sound?" The student must use the *wh* sound as in "when."

[h]69. The student may give either the *oo* sound heard in "moon" or the *oo* sound heard in "book." Be sure to note which one is used.

[i]70. If the same *oo* sound is given this time as was given for item 69, say, "Yes, that's right, but what is another way we could pronounce this nonsense word?" Whichever sound was *not* used in item 69 must be used here; otherwise, it is incorrect.

[j]71. The student may give either the *ea* sound heard in "head" or the *ea* sound heard in "meat." Be sure to note which one is used.

*Reproduced by permission of Allyn and Bacon, Inc.

^{k}72. If the same *ea* sound is given this time as was given for item 71, say, "Yes, that's right, but what is another way we could pronounce this nonsense word?" Whichever sound was *not* used in item 71 must be used here; otherwise, it is incorrect.

^{l}78. The student may give either the *ow* sound heard in "cow" or the *ow* sound heard in "crow." Be sure to note which one is used.

^{m}79. If the same *ow* sound is given this time as was given for item 78, say, "Yes, that's right, but what is another way we could pronounce this nonsense word?" Whichever sound was *not* used in item 78 must be used here; otherwise, it is incorrect.

EL PASO PHONICS SURVEY: ANSWER SHEET*

Name_____ Sex_____ Date_____

School_____ Examiner_____

Mark answers as follows
Pass +
Fail − (or write word as pronounced)

PEK
Point at which phonic element is expected to be known

		Answers	PEK				Answers	PEK
INITIAL CONSONANT SOUNDS					19.	z	zin _____	1.9
1.	p	pam _____	1.9		20.	c	cin _____	2.5 (sin)
2.	n	nup _____	1.9		21.	g	gin _____	2.9 (jin)
^{a}3.	s	sup _____	1.9		22.	qu	quam _____	1.9
4.	t	tup _____	1.9					
5.	r	rin _____	1.9					
6.	m	min _____	1.9		**ENDING CONSONANT X**			
7.	b	bup _____	1.9		^{e}23.	x	mox _____	1.9
8.	d	dup _____	1.9					
9.	w	wam _____	1.9		**INITIAL CONSONANT CLUSTERS**			
10.	h	hup _____	1.9		24.	pl	plup _____	1.9
11.	f	fin _____	1.9		25.	fr	frin _____	1.9
12.	j	jin _____	1.9		26.	fl	flam _____	1.9
13.	k	kam _____	1.9		27.	st	stup _____	1.9
14.	l	lin _____	1.9		28.	bl	blin _____	1.9
^{b}15.	c	cam _____	1.9		29.	tr	trin _____	1.9
^{c}16.	g	gup _____	1.9		30.	gr	grup _____	1.9
^{d}17.	y	yin _____	1.9		31.	br	brin _____	1.9
18.	v	vam _____	1.9		32.	sh	shup _____	1.9

*Superior letters indicate notes listed in El Paso Phonics Survey: Special Directions. Material reproduced by permission of Allyn and Bacon, Inc.

		Answers	PEK					Answers	PEK	
[f]33.	th	thup	_____ 1.9	(thing)	65.	ē	rete	_____ 2.5	
[g]34.	wh	whup	_____ 1.9	(when)	66.	ā	sape	_____ 2.5	
35.	ch	cham	_____ 2.	(church)	67.	ū	pune	_____ 2.5	
36.	dr	drup	_____ 2.5		68.	ō	sote	_____ 2.5	
37.	pr	pram	_____ 2.5		[h]69.	oo	oot	_____ 2.5	(moon
38.	sl	slup	_____ 2.5						or
39.	cl	clin	_____ 2.5						book)
40.	gl	glam	_____ 2.5		[i]70.	oo	oot	_____ 2.5	(moon
41.	sm	smin	_____ 2.5						or
42.	sk	skam	_____ 2.5						book)
43.	cr	crin	_____ 2.5		[j]71.	ea	eap	_____ 2.5	(head
44.	tw	twam	_____ 2.5						or
45.	sn	snup	_____ 2.5						meat)
46.	sch	scham	_____ 2.5		[k]72.	ea	eam	_____ 2.5	(head
47.	sp	spam	_____ 2.9						or
48.	sc	scup	_____ 2.9						meat)
49.	str	stram	_____ 2.9		73.	ai	ait	_____ 2.5	(ape)
50.	thr	thrup	_____ 2.9		74.	ay	tay	_____ 2.5	(hay)
51.	shr	shrup	_____ 2.9		75.	oe	poe	_____ 2.5	(hoe)
52.	squ	squam	_____ 2.9		76.	oa	oan	_____ 2.5	(soap)
53.	sw	swup	_____ 3.5		77.	ee	eem	_____ 2.5	(heed)
54.	spr	spram	_____ 3.5		[l]78.	ow	owd	_____ 2.5	(cow or
55.	spl	splin	_____ 3.5						crow)
56.	wr	wrin	_____ 4.5		[m]79.	ow	fow	_____ 2.5	(cow or
57.	dw	dwin	_____ 4.5						crow)
58.	scr	scrup	_____ 4.5		80.	or	orm	_____ 2.5	(corn)
					81.	ir	irt	_____ 2.5	(hurt)
					82.	ur	urd	_____ 2.5	(hurt)

VOWELS, VOWEL TEAMS, AND SPECIAL LETTER COMBINATIONS

		Answers	PEK				Answers	PEK	
59.	ă	pam	_____ 1.9	83.	aw	awp	_____ 2.9	(paw)
60.	ĭ	rit	_____ 1.9	84.	oi	doi	_____ 2.9	(boy)
61.	ĕ	nep	_____ 1.9	85.	ou	tou	_____ 2.9	(cow)
62.	ŏ	sot	_____ 1.9	86.	ar	arb	_____ 2.9	(harp)
63.	ŭ	tum	_____ 1.9	87.	oy	moy	_____ 2.9	(boy)
64.	ī	tipe	_____ 2.5	88.	er	ert	_____ 2.9	(her)
				89.	ew	bew	_____ 2.9	(few)
				90.	au	dau	_____ 2.9	(paw)

EL PASO PHONICS SURVEY*

Test Words

in	up	am

#				#			
1.	p	am	pam	38.	sl	up	slup
2.	n	up	nup	39.	cl	in	clin
3.	s	up	sup	40.	gl	am	glam
4.	t	up	tup	41.	sm	in	smin
5.	r	in	rin	42.	sk	am	skam
6.	m	in	min	43.	cr	in	crin
7.	b	up	bup	44.	tw	am	twam
8.	d	up	dup	45.	sn	up	snup
9.	w	am	wam	46.	sch	am	scham
10.	h	up	hup	47.	sp	am	spam
11.	f	in	fin	48.	sc	up	scup
12.	j	in	jin	49.	str	am	stram
13.	k	am	kam	50.	thr	up	thrup
14.	l	in	lin	51.	shr	up	shrup
15.	c	am	cam	52.	squ	am	squam
16.	g	up	gup	53.	sw	up	swup
17.	y	in	yin	54.	spr	am	spram
18.	v	am	vam	55.	spl	in	splin
19.	z	in	zin	56.	wr	in	wrin
20.	c	in	cin	57.	dw	in	dwin
21.	g	in	gin	58.	scr	up	scrup
22.	qu	am	quam	59.	ă		pam
23.	m	ox	mox	60.	ĭ		rit
24.	pl	up	plup	61.	ĕ		nep
25.	fr	in	frin	62.	ŏ		sot
26.	fl	am	flam	63.	ŭ		tum
27.	st	up	stup	64.	ī		tipe
28.	bl	in	blin	65.	ē		rete
29.	tr	in	trin	66.	ā		sape
30.	gr	up	grup	67.	ū		pune
31.	br	in	brin	68.	ō		sote
32.	sh	up	shup	69.	oo		oot
33.	th	up	thup	70.	oo		oot
34.	wh	up	whup	71.	ea		eap
35.	ch	am	cham	72.	ea		eam
36.	dr	up	drup	73.	ai		ait
37.	pr	am	pram	74.	ay		tay

75.	oe	poe		83.	aw	awp
76.	oa	oan		84.	oi	doi
77.	ee	eem		85.	ou	tou
78.	ow	owd		86.	ar	arb
79.	ow	fow		87.	oy	moy
80.	or	orm		88.	er	ert
81.	ir	irt		89.	ew	bew
82.	ur	urd		90.	au	dau

Appendix B: Reading and Reading-Related Tests and Inventories

Auditory Discrimination Tests

| Name and date of test | Skills or Areas Measured | | | | | | | | | | | Publisher |
	Vocabulary	Comprehension	Word attack	Speed	Listening	Other	Time for administration	Number of forms	Grade level	Group (G) or individual (I)	
Goldman-Fristoe-Woodcock Test of Auditory Discrimination (no date given)					X	Measures speech-sound discrimination	10–15 min.	1	Ages 4 and over	I	American Guidance Service
Wepman Auditory Discrimination Test (1973)					X	Recognize the sound differences between minimal pairs	15–20 min.	2	K–3	I	Language Research Associates

Basic Sight Word Inventories

Name and date of test	Skills or Areas Measured						Time for administration	Number of forms	Grade level	Group (G) or individual (I)	Publisher
	Vocabulary	Comprehension	Word attack	Speed	Listening	Other					
Dolch Basic Sight Word Test (1942)						Tests recognition of 220 high-utility words	Varies	1	All levels	G	Garrard Press
The Group Instant Words Recognition Test (no date given)						Sight recognition of 600 most common words	Varies	2	All levels	G&I	Jamestown Publishers
Harris-Jacobson List (1980)						Tests recognition of 335 high-utility words	Varies	1	All levels	I	Harris, Albert J., and Sipay, Edward R. How to Increase Reading Ability. New York: Longman, 1980, pp. 372–373.
The Instant Words Criterion Test (1981)						Sight recognition of 300 most common words	Varies	1	All levels	I	Jamestown Publishers
Johnson Basic Sight Vocabulary Test (1973)						Tests recognition of 300 high-utility words	Varies	2	1–3	I	Personal (University of Wisconsin, Madison, Wisconsin)

Commercial Informal Reading Inventories (see also Chapter 11, Commercially Developed Informal Reading Inventories)

Name and date of test	Skills or Areas Measured						Time for administration	Number of forms	Grade level	Group (G) or individual (I)	Publisher
	Vocabulary	Comprehension	Word attack	Speed	Listening	Other					
Analytical Reading Inventory (1981)	X	X			X	Graded word lists	Varies	3	2–9	I	Charles E. Merrill
Basic Reading Inventory (1978)	X	X				Graded word lists	Varies	3	Pre-primer–8	I	Kendall/Hunt
The Classroom Reading Inventory (1982)	X	X				Graded word lists, graded spelling survey	12 min.	4	All levels	I	William C. Brown
The Contemporary Classroom Reading Inventory (1980)	X	X				Group cloze tests, graded word lists	Varies	3	2–9	I	Gorsuch Scarisbrick
Diagnostic Reading Inventory (1979)	X	X			X	Graded word lists, phrase list	Varies	1	3–8	I	Kendall/Hunt
Ekwall Reading Inventory (1979)	X	X	X		X	Graded word lists, El Paso Phonics Survey	21–30 min. depending on level	4	Pre-primer–9	I	Allyn and Bacon
Informal Reading Assessment (1980)	X	X		X	X	Graded word lists		4	Pre-primer–12	I	Rand McNally
Sucher-Allred Reading Placement Inventory (1981)	X	X				Word recognition test, oral reading test	20 min.	1	Primer–9	I	Economy

Content-Area Inventories

Name and date of test	Vocabulary	Comprehension	Word attack	Speed	Listening	Other	Time for administration	Number of forms	Grade level	Group (G) or individual (I)	Publisher
					Skills or Areas Measured						
Content Inventories: English, Social Studies, Science (1979)	X	X				Cloze tests, study skills	Varies	1	4–12; English, 7–12	G	Kendall/Hunt

Decoding Inventories

Name and date of test	Vocabulary	Comprehension	Word attack	Speed	Listening	Other	Time for administration	Number of forms	Grade level	Group (G) or individual (I)	Publisher
					Skills or Areas Measured						
Decoding Inventory, 3 levels (1979)			X			Auditory and visual discrimination, context clues	Varies	1	Pre-primer–4 and above	I	Kendall/Hunt

Intelligence Tests

Name and date of test	Skills or Areas Measured						Time for administration	Number of forms	Grade level	Group (G) or individual (I)	Publisher
	Vocabulary	Comprehension	Word attack	Speed	Listening	Other					
McCarthy Scales of Children's Abilities (1972)						Assess motor and intellectual development	45 min. for age 5 and under; 1 hour for older children	1	Ages 2½–8½	I	Psychological Corporation
Peabody Picture Vocabulary Test–Revised (PPVT-R) (1981)						For testing verbal intelligence through pictures	15 min. or less	1	Ages 2½–40	I	American Guidance Service
Slosson Intelligence Test (1981)						A measure of intelligence	10–30 min.	1	Age 1–adult	I	Slosson Educational Publications
Stanford-Binet Intelligence Scale, Form LM (1972 Norms)	X	X				A measure of overall intelligence	45–90 min.	1	2–12 and sometimes older	I	Houghton Mifflin
Wechsler Adult Intelligence Scale—Revised (WAIS-R) (1980)	X	X				A measure of intelligence using subtests	1 hr.	1	Ages 16–74	I	Psychological Corporation
Wechsler Intelligence Scale for Children—Revised (WISC-R) (1974)	X	X				A measure of intelligence using subtests	1 hr.	1	Ages 6.0–16.11	I	Psychological Corporation
Wechsler Preschool and Primary Scale of Intelligence (WPPSI) (1967)	X	X				A measure of intelligence using subtests	50–70 min.	1	Ages 4–6½	I	Psychological Corporation

Language Dominance and/or Assessment Tests

Name and date of test	Skills or Areas Measured						Time for administration	Number of forms	Grade level	Group (G) or individual (I)	Publisher
	Vocabulary	Comprehension	Word attack	Speed	Listening	Other					
Ambiguous Word Language Dominance Test (1978)	X					Spanish/English language dominance	30 min.	1	Age 10 and above	I	Publishers Test Service, McGraw-Hill
Flexibility Language Dominance Test (1978)						Spanish/English language dominance	30 min.	1	Age 10 and above	G	Publishers Test Service, McGraw-Hill
Houston Test for Language Development (1978)	X	X	X		X	Also nonverbal communication	20–40 min. depending on age	2	Infancy– 6 yrs.	I	Stoelting
Language Assessment Battery (LAB) (1977) English Edition Spanish Edition					X	Subtests in reading, writing, speaking	41 min. 41 min.	1 1	K–12 K–12	K–2, I; 3–12, G&I	Riverside Publishing

Readiness Tests (Including Bilingual)

Name and date of test	Skills or Areas Measured						Time for administration	Number of forms	Grade level	Group (G) or individual (I)	Publisher
	Vocabulary	Comprehension	Word attack	Speed	Listening	Other					
Comprehensive Tests of Basic Skills, Readiness Test (1977)					X	Letter names, letter forms, phonics	2 hrs. 39 min.	1	K–1.3	G	CTB/McGraw-Hill
Cooperative Preschool Inventory						Knowledge of self, ability to follow directions, verbal expression, number concepts					Addison-Wesley
English Edition (1970)							Approx. 15 min.	1	Pre-school	I	
Spanish Edition (1974)							Approx. 30 min.	1	Pre-school	I	
Metropolitan Readiness Tests, 2 levels (1976)	X				X	Auditory and visual discrimination, phonics, math	Level 1, 90 min.; Level 2, 3 hrs.	2	K–1	G	Psychological Corporation

Reading Tests

Name and date of test	Vocabulary	Comprehension	Word attack	Speed	Listening	Other	Time for administration	Number of forms	Grade level	Group (G) or Individual (I)	Publisher
Skills or Areas Measured											
Assessment of Reading Growth (1981)											Jamestown Publishers
Level 9		X					50 min.	1	2–4	G	
Level 13		X					50 min.	1	6–8	G	
Level 17		X					42 min.	1	10–12	G	
Botel Reading Inventory (1978)						Used to find the student's highest instructional level	Varies		All levels	I	Follett
Spelling Placement Test								1			
Word Recognition Test	X					Estimate of oral reading fluency		2			
Word Opposites Test		X						2			
Decoding Test			X					1			
California Achievement Tests, C & D (Reading) (1977)	X	X					45–60 min.	2	K–12	G	CTB/McGraw-Hill

						Time	No.	Grade	G/I	Publisher
Comprehensive Tests of Basic Skills, *Español* (Reading) (1978)	X	X			Based on *CTBS S & T*	45–60 min.	1	K–8	G	CTB/McGraw-Hill
Comprehensive Tests of Basic Skills, *S & T* (Reading) (1973)	X	X				45–60 min.	2	K–12	G	CTB/McGraw-Hill
Comprehensive Tests of Basic Skills, *U & V* (Reading) (1981)	X	X		X		45–70 min.	2	K–12	G	CTB/McGraw-Hill
Diagnostic Reading Scales (1981)	X	X		X	Graded word lists, reading passages, word-analysis tests	Varies	1	1–8 and above	I	McGraw-Hill
Doren Diagnostic Test of Word Recognition Skills (1973)		X		X	Spelling and sight words	1–3 hrs.	1	1–6	G	American Guidance Service

(cont'd.)

Reading Tests

Name and date of test	Skills or Areas Measured						Time for administration	Number of forms	Grade level	Group (G) or Individual (I)	Publisher
	Vocabulary	Comprehension	Word attack	Speed	Listening	Other					
Durrell Analysis of Reading Diffi- culty—Revised (1980)	X	X	X	X	X	Spelling, visual, and auditory dis- crimination	Untimed: approx. 30–40 min.	1	1–6	I	Psychological Corporation
Gates- MacGinitie Reading Tests (1978) Basic R	X	X					65 min.	2	1.0–1.9	G	Riverside Publishing
A	X	X							1.5–1.9	G	
B	X	X							2	G	
C	X	X							3	G	
D	X	X							4–6	G	
E	X	X							7–9	G	
F	X	X							10–12	G	
Gates- McKillop- Horowitz (1981)	X		X			Spelling, audi- tory dis- crimination	Untimed	1	1–6	I	Teachers College Press
Iowa Silent Reading Tests, 3 levels (1973)	X	X		X		Study skills	56 min.– 1½ hrs. depending on level	2	6–12, college	G	Psychological Corporation

Test					Content/Notes	Time	No.	Grade	G/I	Publisher
Iowa Tests of Basic Skills (1982)										Riverside Publishing
Early Primary Battery	X	X		X	Also subtests in language, mathematics	2 hrs.–2 hrs. 40 min.	1	K–1.9	G	
Primary Battery	X	X		X	Same as above plus work-study skills	3 hrs. 55 min.	1	1.7–3.5	G	
Multilevel Battery	X	X			Language, math, work-study skills	4 hrs. 4 min.	2	3–8	G	
Iowa Tests of Educational Development (1978)	X	X			Language arts and mathematics	2¼ hrs.	2	9–12	G	SRA
McCarthy Individualized Diagnostic Reading Inventory (1976)	X	X			Study skills	Part 1, 35 min.–1 hr.; Part 2, 34 min.	1	2–12	I	Stoelting
Metropolitan Achievement Tests (Reading) (1978)		X				30–50 min. depending on level	2	K–12	G	Psychological Corporation
Nelson-Denny Reading Test (1981)	X	X	X			35 min.	2	9–12, college, adult	G	Riverside Publishing
Nelson Reading Skills Test (1977)	X	X			Word meaning	33 min.	2	3–9	G	Houghton Mifflin
Oral Reading Criterion Test (no date given)		X	X		To determine independent and instructional levels	Varies	1	1–7	I	Jamestown Publishers

(cont'd.)

Reading Tests

Skills or Areas Measured

Name and date of test	Vocabulary	Comprehension	Word attack	Speed	Listening	Other	Time for administration	Number of forms	Grade level	Group (G) or individual (I)	Publisher
Peabody Individual Achievement Test (no date given)		X	X			Spelling, math, general information	30–40 min.	1	K–adult	I	American Guidance Service
Performance Assessment in Reading (PAIR) (1978)	X	X				Study skills	Varies	1	Jr. high	G	CTB/McGraw-Hill
Pressey Diagnostic Reading Tests (no date given)	X	X		X			25 min. per section (3)	2	3–9	G	Bobbs-Merrill
School and College Ability Tests (SCAT), Series III (1979)	X	X					20 min.	2	3.5–12.9	G	Addison-Wesley
Sequential Tests of Educational Progress (STEP III) Primary Levels A–D (1974)		X	X		X		Untimed: 30–40 min. (approx.)	2	Pre-primary–3.5	G	Addison-Wesley
Intermediate and Advanced E–J (1979)	X	X			X		40 min.	2	3.5–12.9	G	

Test					Content	Time		Grade		Publisher
Sipay Word Analysis Test (SWAT) (1974)		X			Tests word analysis in detail	Varies	1	All levels	I	Stoelting
Skills Monitoring System —Reading (1977)	X	X				Untimed	1	3–5	—	Psychological Corporation
Slosson Oral Reading Test (1977)		X				3 min.	1	Pre-school–high school	—	Slosson Educational Publications
SRA Achievement Series (1978)					Reading, math, language arts					SRA
Primary Levels (Levels A–D)	X	X		X	Auditory Discrimination	2½–3 hrs. depending on level	2	K–3	G	
Upper Levels (3rd edition) (Levels E–H)	X	X				3 hrs.	2	4–12	G	
Stanford Achievement Test (1973)	X	X		X	Spelling	75–150 min. depending on level	2	1.5–9.9	G	Psychological Corporation
Stanford Diagnostic Reading Test (1978)	X	X	X		Auditory discrimination	96–145 min. depending on level	2	1.6–13	G	Harcourt Brace Jovanovich
Stanford Test of Academic Skills (TASK) (1973)	X	X				40 min.	2	8–13	G	Psychological Corporation

(cont'd.)

Reading Tests

Name and date of test	Skills or Areas Measured						Time for administration	Number of forms	Grade level	Group (G) or Individual (I)	Publisher
	Vocabulary	Comprehension	Word attack	Speed	Listening	Other					
Tests of Achievement and Proficiency (1982)		X				Subtests in study skills and other subject areas	4 hrs.	1	9–12	G	Riverside Publishing
Tests of Adult Basic Education, 3 levels of difficulty (1978)	X	X				Also language, math for vocational-bound persons	1½–2½ hrs. depending on level	1	Adult	G	CTB/McGraw-Hill
Test of Reading Comprehension (1978)	X	X					Varies	1	2–12	G	Pro-Ed
The 3-R's Test (1982)						Subtests in reading, math, language	130 min.	2	K–12	G	Riverside Publishing
Wide Range Achievement Tests (WRAT) (1978)			X			Also, spelling and math	15–30 min.	1	Ages 5–adult	I	Stoelting
Woodcock Reading Mastery Test (1974)	X	X	X			Letter identification	20–30 min.	2	K–12	I	American Guidance Service

Appendix C: Commercial Materials for Teaching Reading Skills in a Remedial Reading Center

Program	Reading skills	Level of difficulty
American Guidance Services, Inc. Department RT-L Circle Pines, Minnesota 55014		
GOLDMAN-LYNCH SOUNDS AND SYMBOLS DEVELOPMENT KIT There are sixty-four activities to stimulate production of the English speech sounds and recognition of their associated symbols. This kit contains puppet, tape cassettes, posters, picture cards, magnetic symbols and adventure story books.	Word-analysis skills (specifically phonetic analysis)	Primary–intermediate junior high
Barnell Loft, Ltd. 958 Church Street Baldwin, New York 11510		
AUDITORY READINESS SKILLS The *Auditory Readiness Series* offers instruction in the basic auditory skills. They are presented with an enjoyable gamelike technique that captures the students' interest. Suggested related classroom activities are included for reinforcement.	Auditory skills	Primary
CAPITALIZATION & PUNCTUATION This program develops ninety-four key capitalization and punctuation concepts. The program may be used for individual or group instruction. Duplicating masters are included.	Capitalization and punctuation	Grades 1–9

(continued)

(continued)

Program	Reading skills	Level of difficulty
INSTRUCTIONAL AID PACKS Each *Instructional Aid Pack* contains twenty-five to thirty-three cards, instructions to the teacher, a pretest, a posttest, and a class record. Each kit develops a specific skill. Examples are as follows:	Decoding skills Vocabulary development	Primary–junior high
Matching Letters and Words;		K–1
Matching Consonants;		K–1
Initial Blends;		Grade 2
Final Blends;		Grade 2
Vowels;		Grade 2
Compounds;		Grades 1–6
Prefixes;		Grades 4–9
Suffixes.		Grades 2–9
MULTIPLE SKILLS SERIES This is a comprehensive program designed to teach all of the basic reading skills from basic sight words to comprehension. Teachers may purchase these kits according to skills or grade level desired. Each multilevel set includes forty-eight booklets, a teacher's manual, duplicating masters for worksheets, and a class record sheet. This series also comes in a Spanish edition.	All	Primary–senior high
PICTO-CABULARY SERIES This program consists of two sets that are used to stimulate pupils' interest in words and to enlarge their own vocabularies. Each set is of equal difficulty. Each is made up of two copies of each of six different titles for a total of twelve booklets. Worksheets and teacher's manual are included with each set.	Vocabulary development (sight and meaning)	Intermediate–senior high
SPECIFIC SKILL SERIES This program gives students specific and concentrated experiences in reading for different purposes. It provides practice material for pupils on a number of different reading levels. It is a structured reading program with all the advantages of programmed learning. Learners get additional drill in areas of need. Each booklet is concerned with the development of one reading skill on one reading level.	Basic sight words Vocabulary development Word-analysis skills Dictionary skills Comprehension skills Study skills	Primary–adult

Program	Reading skills	Level of difficulty
SUPPORTIVE READING SKILLS This is a diagnostic and prescriptive reading program that supplements the *Specific Skills Series*.	All	Grades 1–9
WE STUDY WORD SHAPES These are reading readiness workbooks designed to help kindergartners and first graders make use of word shapes and word parts so that they will be prepared for the visual scrutiny necessary in the reading act. Children are taught to combine reliance on word shapes with letter clues at the beginning of words and to develop a sensitivity to specific visual qualities, such as shape, size, length, and peculiar characteristics.	Recognizing word shapes	Preschool–primary

Bell and Howell Company
7100 McCormick Road
Chicago, Illinois 60645

Program	Reading skills	Level of difficulty
LANGUAGE MASTER The language master is a card reader. The student inserts a card, watches and listens, records, and then immediately compares his or her responses to the information on the instructor track. The programs include a phonics program, alphabet mastery program, vocabulary-builder program, word-picture program, and a language-stimulation program. This program employs sight, speech, touch, and hearing in coordinated, effective instruction. The system includes a compact, portable unit that provides complete, self-contained dual track recording and playback capability. The unit is used with sets of cards containing visual material and a strip of magnetic recording tape.	Vocabulary development Word-analysis skills (specifically structural analysis and phonetic analysis)	Primary–adult
THE READING GAME	Sight-vocabulary program	Primary and elementary
VOCABULARY MASTERY PROGRAM	Vocabulary development	Level 5–7 (supplementary) Level 8–9 (remedial)
WORD-PICTURE PROGRAM	Vocabulary development	Grades1–6
STAR PROGRAM	Comprehension development	Grades 4–8

(continued)

(continued)

Program	Reading skills	Level of difficulty
Benefic Press 1250 Sixth Avenue San Diego, California 92101		
COMPREHENSION—CRITICAL READING KITS This kit is designed to develop reading comprehension skills. The high-interest reading selections include content in language arts, social studies, and science.	Comprehension	Primary–junior high
COMPREHENSION AND CRITICAL READING WORKBOOKS This workbook series is also designed to develop comprehension skills. These workbooks provide instruction and practice in four areas of reading comprehension: (1) Identifying main ideas, (2) Understanding details, (3) Seeing relationships, (4) Thinking critically.	Comprehension	3–8
VOCABULARY MASTERY The *Vocabulary Mastery Series* consists of duplicating master books designed to improve vocabulary. Activities include: (1) Matching word and meaning, (2) Word categories, (3) Dictionary use, (4) Meaning from context, (5) Games and puzzles.	Vocabulary development	3–8
Bowmar/Noble Publishers, Inc. 4563 Colorado Blvd. Los Angeles, California 90039		
BOMAR NOBLE SKILLS SERIES This is a workbook program designed to teach the skills shown.	Vocabulary development Dictionary skills Map-reading skills Spelling skills Library and reference skills	Grades 3–6
DOUBLE PLAY READING SERIES **TRIPLE PLAY SERIES** These kits are for motivating reluctant readers to read. Students listen and participate in plays of drama, comedy, and adventure. There are worksheets to evaluate comprehension. A teacher's guide is included.	Comprehension development	Grades 4–8

Program	Reading skills	Level of difficulty
LETTER SOUNDS ALL AROUND This is a program to teach beginning students the alphabet. Included are filmstrips, cassettes, workbooks and a teacher's guide.	Consonant and vowel recognition	Primary
PRIMARY READING SERIES This kit consists of high-interest story cards written at the interest level of younger readers. On the back of each card are questions to teach and evaluate basic comprehension skills. Also included is a teacher's guide.	Word recognition Comprehension development Vocabulary development	Interest: K–3 Reading: 1.3–2.5
READING COMPREHENSION SERIES This kit consists of high-interest story cards. On the back of each card are questions designed to teach and evaluate basic comprehension skills. Also included is a teacher's guide.	Comprehension development	Middle elementary–junior high
READING INCENTIVE PROGRAM—STARTING LINE This kit consists of high-interest filmstrips designed to motivate students to read. There are matching books. Included are workbooks to evaluate comprehension skills. Also included are duplicating masters and a teacher's guide.	Vocabulary development Comprehension development	Grades 3–12
READING ZINGO In this program the children listen to letters or words from a record, then mark the appropriate place on their cards, much like bingo.	Vocabulary development Word-recognition skills (specifically consonant blends and contractions)	Grades 3–6
SPORTS READING SERIES This kit consists of high-interest story cards about professional sports. On the back of each card are questions designed to teach and evaluate comprehension skills. Also included is a teacher's manual.	Comprehension development	Middle elementary–junior high

College Skills Center
1250 Broadway
New York, New York 10001

Program	Reading skills	Level of difficulty
88 PASSAGES TO DEVELOP READING COMPREHENSION These passages are to teach and evaluate comprehension skills. Selections range over the	Comprehension development	Intermediate–senior high

(continued)

(continued)

Program	Reading skills	Level of difficulty
fields of literature, sports, hobbies, mythology, historical oddities, the arts and sciences, and current-day happenings. Each passage has a comprehension check and can be graded on a progress chart for speed and comprehension.		
A PHONICS CHART FOR DECODING ENGLISH This chart organizes forty-four basic sounds into an easy-to-teach, easy-to-learn sequence. The chart features silent letters and common deviations from normal rules of phonics.	Decoding skills	Primary–intermediate
The Continental Press, Inc. Elizabethtown, Pennsylvania 17022		
CONTINENTAL PRESS MATERIALS Workbooks and liquid duplicating material to teach and emphasize fundamental and individualized instruction in reading skills.	Basic sight words Vocabulary development Word-analysis skills Dictionary skills Comprehension skills Study skills Oral reading skills	Primary–adult
The Economy Company P.O. Box 25308 1901 North Walnut Street Oklahoma City, Oklahoma 73125		
GUIDEBOOK TO BETTER READING SERIES This is a remedial reading program for students reading below grade level. All selections are written at a high-interest, low-vocabulary level. The program includes diagnostic exercises, evaluative exercises, review exercises, and recreational reading.	All	Grade 5–adult
READER'S THEATER This program is designed primarily to develop oral reading skills, build confidence, and encourage student participation. *Reader's Theater* offers students active involvement through reading scripts in a reader's-theater situation.	Oral reading skills Vocabulary development Comprehension development	Grades 1–6
EMC Corporation 180 East Sixth Street St. Paul, Minnesota 55101		

Program	Reading skills	Level of difficulty
PROGRAM BREAKAWAY This program consists of twelve readers, work-books, and teacher's editions, all of which are designed to teach comprehension skills in the content areas. Globe Book Company, Inc. 50 West 23rd Street New York, New York 10010	Comprehension development	Grades 1–6
A BETTER READING WORKSHOP This is a set of four workbooks.	Comprehension development Study skills	Intermediate–junior high
A NEED TO READ This is a flexible, multitext approach to teaching reading comprehension. It is a sequential pro-gram including seventy-two books and a teaching guide. The basic skill areas concen-trated on are: finding the main idea, building vocabulary, understanding details, and se-quence.	Comprehension development	Intermediate–junior high
READING POWER THROUGH CLOZE This is a set of workbooks that utilize the cloze procedure. Each lesson focuses on different kinds of words: verbs in one lesson; homo-phones in another; nouns, adjectives, ad-verbs, etc. There are follow-up activities and competency tests for each lesson. Harper & Row Publishers, Inc. Keystone Industrial Park Scranton, Pennsylvania 18512	Word analysis Vocabulary development Comprehension development	Intermediate–senior high
READING WITH PHONICS *Reading with Phonics* presents forty-four basic speech sounds in an organized, logical order. The program may be used either as a develop-mental or as a remedial program. Included are three texts/workbooks and a teacher's edition for each level.	Word-analysis skills (phonics)	Grades 1–4
SOUNDS AND SIGNALS A–E These five workbooks provide activities to re-teach or reinforce phonetic-analysis skills taught at the primary levels. There are mas-tery tests at the end of each book as well as an instructor's manual.	Word-analysis skills (phonics)	Grades 1–3

(continued)

(continued)

Program	Reading skills	Level of difficulty
Hayes School Publishing Co., Inc. 321 Pennwood Avenue Wilkinsburg, Pennsylvania 15221		
HAYES COMPANY MATERIALS Workbooks and liquid duplicating material to teach and emphasize fundamental and individualized instruction in all reading skills.	Word-analysis skills Dictionary skills Vocabulary development Study skills Oral reading skills	Primary–senior high
Incentives for Learning, Inc. 600 West Van Buren Chicago, Illinois 60607		
SPREAD READING PROGRAM This is an individualized, self-paced program designed to teach word-attack skills. Each lesson consists of task cards that stress different skills. In both programs (primary and intermediate) a mastery test is provided at the end of each section for review purposes.	Word-analysis skills	Primary–intermediate
Jamestown Publishers P.O. Box 6743 Providence, Rhode Island 02940		
COMPREHENSION CROSSROADS These are crossword puzzles designed to stimulate interest at the student's specific level. The puzzles are carefully restricted to the noted reading levels. Duplicating masters are included.	Vocabulary development Comprehension development	Reading: 3–12 Interest: 6–12
COMPREHENSION SKILLS SERIES Each booklet of this series is designed to develop a specific comprehension skill. There is a description of the skill, a lesson teaching the accurate use of the skill, and exercises to evaluate students' progress.	Comprehension development	Reading level: 4–12 Interest level: 6–adult
GRAPHICAL COMPREHENSION *Graphical Comprehension* is a text workbook designed to teach students how to read graphs as well as how to make their own graphs based on what they read. Each drill contains a lesson about one type of graph, followed by practical exercises that enable the student to practice the skill just learned.	How to read and make graphs	Reading level: 7–10 Instructional level: 9–college

Program	Reading skills	Level of difficulty
READING DRILLS These texts/workbooks contain thirty timed passages, each followed by comprehension questions, cloze tests, and a vocabulary exercise. The middle level is designed for students in elementary and junior high school. The advanced level is for high school and above.	Vocabulary development Comprehension development	Reading level: 4–10 Interest level: 4–adult
3000 INSTANT WORDS *3000 Instant Words* contains the most common words in the English language ranked in order of frequency. A diagnostic test is included for placement and measuring individual progress.	Vocabulary development	Primary–junior high

King Features
Education Division
Department 134
235 East 45th Street
New York, New York   10017

Program	Reading skills	Level of difficulty
BASIC SKILLS READING PROGRAM This is a self-checking program for teaching the basic reading skills. The heart of the program consists of card matching, which the student does according to cassette-tape stories.	Sequence Main idea Following directions Classification Noting details Word recognition	Lower elementary– intermediate
CAREER AWARENESS PROGRAM This is a thirty-two-book set that covers fifteen career clusters. Students learn about training and education requirements, job conditions, etc., in popular comic-book form.	Learning about various careers	Upper elementary– junior high
COMICS READING PROGRAM This program includes high-interest stories involving famous comic-strip characters, workbooks with puzzles and games, duplicating masters, and a teacher's guide. This program is intended to motivate young students to master basic reading skills.	All	Grades 3–6

Little Brown Bear Learning Associates, Inc.
P.O. Box 56116
Miami, Florida   33156

(continued)

(continued)

Program	Reading skills	Level of difficulty
PHONICS LEARNING GAMES This company markets many games for teaching phonics. Some games have specific series for remedial instruction. Some of the games are as follows: *Easy Word Puzzle, Easy Decoding for Vowels, Easy Decoding for Consonants,* and *Easy Decoding for Syllables.* The Macmillan Company 866 Third Avenue New York, New York 10022	Phonics	Primary–intermediate
MACMILLAN READING SPECTRUM This program consists of the spectrum of skills that are word-analysis level 1–6, vocabulary development level 1–6, comprehension level 1–6. The books are self-directing, self-correcting, and nonconsumable. There are eighteen booklets providing sequential instruction in word analysis, vocabulary development, and reading comprehension. The spectrum of books offers two classroom sets of children's books that have been carefully selected, a set A for grades 2–6, and a set B for grades 3–8. Each set contains many books so that every child can choose what he or she wants to read. In every book there is a synopsis, a cast of characters, excerpts for "flavor," and comprehension and interpretation questions.	Basic sight words Vocabulary development Word-analysis skills Dictionary skills Comprehension skills Study skills Oral reading skills	Intermediate–senior high
HIP READER PROGRAM This is a beginning reading program for teenage and adult nonreaders. The mature interest of these readers provides motivation to learn how to read. Mafex Associates, Inc. 90 Cherry Street P.O. Box 519 Johnstown, Pennsylvania 15907	Word-analysis skills	Grades 1–4
PHONIC WORD BUILDER This is a general word list arranged by phonic element in increasing order of conceptual difficulty. There are two sections. The first is composed of single vowels. The second is composed of vowel teams.	Word-analysis skills	All

Program	Reading skills	Level of difficulty
Charles E. Merrill 1300 Alum Creek Drive Columbus, Ohio 43216		
MERRILL READING SKILL TEXT SERIES This program is a logically planned, developmental reading-skills program designed to develop essential reading and learning skills through carefully devised sequential exercises. Some of the titles are *Bibs; Nicky; Uncle Bunny; Ben, the Traveler; Tom, the Reporter;* and *Pat, the Pilot*	Vocabulary development Word-analysis skills Comprehension skills Study skills	Primary–senior high
NEW PHONICS SKILL TEXT SERIES This program contains books A–D and teacher's editions for A–D. It is designed to teach accuracy and independence in word recognition and comprehension through recognition of the sound and structure of words. The series may be used independently or with any basal or individualized reading program.	Word-analysis skills (specifically phonetic analysis)	Primary–junior high
Milliken Publishing Company 1100 Research Blvd. St. Louis, Missouri 63132		
K-1 READING READINESS PROGRAM These are duplicating masters and task cards that teach word-analysis skills such as initial consonants, final consonants, long and short vowels, vowel teams, etc.	Word-analysis skills	Preschool–primary
Phonovisual Products, Inc. Box 5625 Washington, D.C. 20016		
PHONOVISUAL PHONICS PROGRAM This is a program for teaching phonics and structural analysis.	Word-analysis skills (specifically phonics and structural analysis)	Primary–junior high
READING TUTORIAL PROGRAM This is a sequential reading program. The kit contains nine readers, one teacher's manual, and award materials to help motivate the students.	All	Preprimer–grade 6

(continued)

(continued)

Program	Reading skills	Level of difficulty
VOWELS AND STORIES *Vowels and Stories* is a set of exercises designed to provide extensive practice in vowel sounds while building basic elementary reading skills. This is intended primarily as a remedial program for use with the reader above the first grade. The program consists of twenty-four units, each devoted to a particular vowel sound.	Word-analysis skills (specifically vowel sounds)	Grades 2–6

Rand-McNally & Company (School Dept.)
P.O. Box 7600
Chicago, Illinois   60680

Program	Reading skills	Level of difficulty
COMPREHENSION WE USE PROGRAM This is a basic workbook program for teaching and evaluating comprehension skills.	Comprehension development	Grades 1–6
DISCOVER PHONICS WE USE Appealing one-page lessons incorporate a variety of teaching strategies: letter substitution, rhyming words, riddles, crossword puzzles, and word games. There are optional filmstrip/cassette sets as well as various combinations of levels and materials for flexibility.	Word-analysis skills	Grades 1–6

Reader's Digest Services, Inc.
Educational Division
Pleasantville, New York 10570

Program	Reading skills	Level of difficulty
COMPREHENSION AUDIO LESSONS Each audio lesson helps to develop a specific reading skill—such as recognizing main ideas or noting sequence of events. Teachers can use this program with pupils on an individual, small group, or class basis. In each lesson a narrator first introduces the story; actors then portray roles in the dramatization while music and other sound effects heighten pupil interest, reinforce reading skills, improve aural comprehension and oral reading, help diagnose a pupil's ability to comprehend	Oral reading skills Comprehension skills	Primary–adult

Program	Reading skills	Level of difficulty
ideas, and demonstrate correct pronunciation and intonation, especially for bilingual students.		
NEW SERIES READING SKILL BUILDERS Each skill builder in the program helps to develop a specific reading skill, such as recognizing main ideas and noting sequence of events. There are cones with duplicating masters for each level and reading skill. Use it to spark the interest of both the good and reluctant readers, reinforce reading skills, improve aural comprehension and oral reading, help diagnose a pupil's ability to comprehend ideas, and demonstrate correct pronunciation and intonation. It may serve as a model for class dramatization.	Vocabulary development Comprehension development Study skills Oral reading skills	Primary–adult
ORIGINAL SERIES READING SKILL BUILDERS Each skill builder in the program helps to develop a specific reading skill such as recognizing main ideas, noting sequence of events, etc. This program is designed to spark the interest of both good and reluctant readers, reinforce reading skills, improve aural comprehension and oral reading, help diagnose a pupil's ability to comprehend ideas, demonstrate correct pronunciation and intonation, and serve as models for class dramatizations.	Vocabulary development Comprehension skills Study skills Oral reading skills	Primary–adult
RD 2000 LABS OR READING CENTER This is a comprehensive reading program in colorfully illustrated, high-interest magazine form. There are also accompanying audio lessons, activity books, and a teacher's edition. Each lesson highlights a specific reading skill.	Comprehension development Vocabulary development Word recognition Oral reading skills	Primary–junior high
READER'S DIGEST ADVANCED SKILL BUILDERS The advanced skill builders continue to refine the skills introduced in the original skill builders series. It is directed to the high school students who possess basic reading skills. Each kit contains readers, matching cassette tapes, workbooks, and a teacher's manual.	Vocabulary development Comprehension development Study skills Oral reading skills	Grades 7–9

(continued)

(continued)

Program	Reading skills	Level of difficulty
READER'S DIGEST READING SKILL PRACTICE PADS These are high-utility workbooks that extend basic reading, writing, vocabulary, and word-study skills.	Vocabulary development Word-analysis skills Comprehension development Study skills	Grades 1–6
READERS' WORKSHOP This is a program for all reading skills. The stories are of high interest, colorfully illustrated, and have easy-to-read type. It is an individually paced, self-checking program in which the student can monitor his or her own progress.	Vocabulary development Word-analysis skills Comprehension development Oral reading skills	Grades 3–9
READING SKILLS LIBRARY This is a reading and listening resource unit that will aid in building critical reading skills. It offers material to meet the reading needs of all the pupils in a class or school through use of books and cassettes.	Comprehension development Study skills	Primary–adult
READING TUTORS This program is a compact reading and listening comprehension unit that offers "private reading lessons" for pupils in a classroom. It offers self-contained learning materials. Pupils can learn at their own speed while the teacher moves from group to group or helps pupils with other activities.	Comprehension development Study skills	Primary–adult
VOCABULARY AUDIO SKILLS LESSON This program extends the audio program with dramatizations from thirty additional skill-builder stories. There are six vocabulary lessons on three cassettes at each level from 1–6. The program concentrates on developing word-study or word-analysis skills, such as mastering words by matching words and definitions, using key words correctly, identifying words with sensory appeal, identifying the correct word, using context clues to identify meanings, and using context clues to identify special meaning.	Vocabulary development Word-analysis skills	Primary–junior high

Program	Reading skills	Level of difficulty

Scholastic Book Service
904 Sylvan Avenue
Englewood Cliffs, New Jersey 07632

INDIVIDUALIZED READING FROM SCHOLASTIC This material helps a student to develop his or her own reading program by choosing what he or she wants to read from a wide range of children's literature in paperback. Students can progress at their own pace and sharpen important skills while becoming successful and independent readers. The titles of the program are: *Reaching Out, Reaching Up, Reaching Higher, Reaching Forward, Reaching Ahead,* and *Reaching Beyond.*	Basic sight words Vocabulary development Word-analysis skills Dictionary skills Comprehension development Study skills Oral reading skills	Primary–junior high
SCHOLASTIC LITERATURE UNITS This program contains titles such as *Animals, High Adventure, Small World, Courage, Family, Frontiers, Moments of Decision, Mirrors, The Lighter Side, Survival, Success,* and *Personal Code.* The students usually become interested when the subject matter of the course stems from their own most serious concerns. This program focuses on themes of vital interest, provides for individual differences, emphasizes major literary forms, integrates literature and reading skills, and develops good reading habits.	Vocabulary development Comprehension skills Study skills	Junior high–senior high

Science Research Associates, Inc.
155 North Wacker
Chicago, Illinois 60606

THE DIMENSIONS SERIES Each kit offers 120 reading selections in multi-level format, centered around a single broad theme. Skill cards provide comprehension checks and extension activities. *Our Story: Women of Today and Yesterday* (reading levels 3.0–8.9): selections illustrate accomplishments of women through the ages and their accomplishments. *We Are Black* (reading levels 2.0–6.0) fills a gap by portraying persons and events often neglected in traditional textbooks. *How America Began*	Comprehension development	Grades 4–12

(continued)

(continued)

Program	Reading skills	Level of difficulty
(reading level 3.0–8.9): American history from Columbus through the Civil War. *As America Grew* (reading level 3.0–8.9): American history from post–Civil War reconstruction to the Kennedy administration. *Countries and Cultures* (reading level: 4.5–9.5): fascinating glimpses of life as it is lived in foreign places.		
GETTING IT TOGETHER: A READING SERIES ABOUT PEOPLE This program consists of a text, a student re-source book, a student resource-book answer key, and a teacher's guide. The text contains stories about concerns of adolescents (family, school, dating, etc.). The student resource book has three sections. The first contains comprehension questions. The second contains information and exercises to help solve problems related to the story. The third section suggests additional projects and research.	Comprehension development	Grade 3–senior high
INDIVIDUALIZED READING SKILLS PROGRAM This program consists of four pupil books and a teacher's guide. Each book emphasizes a different vowel-skill program (short vowels, long vowels, variant vowels). The books are filled with high-interest reading selections and exercises to develop and evaluate new skills.	Phonics Structural analysis Vocabulary development	Grades 2–6
MARK II READING LABORATORY SERIES These kits each have ten levels. This allows the students to start at their present reading level and progress at their own rate, independent of the other students. Students check their own work and chart their own progress. Built-in mechanisms tell them when given skills need extra practice. Each kit contains 150 power-builder cards, 150 rate-builder cards, 150 skill-development cards—each with a key card. Teacher's handbook and duplicating masters included.	Word study Comprehension Study skills Vocabulary development Listening Rate improvement Dictionary skills Study skills	Kit 2A: reading 2.0–7.0 Kit 2B: reading 2.5–8.0 Kit 2C: reading 3.0–9.0

Program	Reading skills	Level of difficulty
THE MATURE STUDENT'S GUIDE TO READING AND COMPOSITION The 107 lessons use a phonics and sight-word approach. Students move through recognition of vowels into material written at a 4.0 reading level. Each lesson concentrates on the learning of a specific skill. After basic skills are properly developed, composition skills are introduced.	All	Grade 7–adult
THE PHONOGAMES SERIES This series contains three kits of phonics skill games. *The Readiness Stage* (grades K–1): this kit requires no reading. Thirty-six games on six levels help students discriminate and recognize initial and final sounds. Method of play involves two students in a simple form of tic-tac-toe. *The Phonics Explorer* (grades K–3): this kit emphasizes consonants, consonant blends, and consonant digraphs. Forty games and eighty stories provide practice with sounds and vocabulary. Reading activity sheets extend learning. *The Phonics Express* (grades 1–3): this kit emphasizes vowels and vowel digraphs. Thirty-six games and seventy-two stories provide practice with sounds, vocabulary, and reading. Activity sheets extend learning.	Word-analysis skills Phonics	K–3
READING LABORATORY I: WORD GAMES This kit includes phonics and structural analysis exercises for grades 1–3 and games that help students match their reading vocabulary to their listening vocabulary. This kit may be used independently or with reading laboratory kits IA, IB, and IC.	Phonics Structural analysis	Grades 1–3

(continued)

(continued)

Program	Reading skills	Level of difficulty
SCHOOLHOUSE READING KITS All three of these schoolhouse kits contain activity cards with duplicates, plastic response overlays, markers, pupil progress sheets, and teacher's guides. *Word Attack Skills Kit* (grades 1–3): this kit is organized into ten units, covering auditory discrimination; initial consonants; final, medial, and variant consonants; consonant combinations; vowels; compound words; contractions; variant endings; and affixes. *Word Attack 1-C* (grades 3–4): extends coverage of word-attack skills. Contains six units, covering phonics, structural analysis, syllables, word meanings, and dictionary skills. *Comprehension Patterns* (grades 3–8): this program focuses on the basic unit of comprehension, the sentence. Ten units include: simple sentence combining, rearranging sentence parts, modifiers of nouns, indirect objects, punctuation, pronouns and function words, ambiguity, and more.	Phonics Structural analysis Syllabication Word meaning Dictionary skills Sentence patterns Use of modifiers Punctuation Use of clauses	Grades 1–8
SRA BASIC READING SERIES This program contains an alphabet book for the readiness level, readers from A to F, workbooks from A to F, teacher's manual, teacher's handbook, test from A to F, cumulative tests from A to F, and teacher's test guide. This program concentrates on developing children's decoding skills through controlled exposure to sequenced sound-spelling patterns in stories, poems, and teacher-directed activities.	Basic sight words Vocabulary development Word-analysis skills Comprehension skills	Primary–junior high
SRA LUNCHBOX LIBRARIES This is a recreational reading series of short books to motivate young readers. Each kit contains two copies each of thirty-two selections. There are two levels in each kit, written a level *below* the level at which children are working in their basals to insure that beginners can succeed independently. Simple comprehension questions are at the end of each volume. *SRA Lunchbox Library: Preprimer*	Word recognition Vocabulary development Comprehension skills	Grades 1–3

Program	Reading skills	Level of difficulty
(grades K–1), *SRA Lunchbox Library 1A* (grades 1–2), and *SRA Lunchbox Library 1B* (grades 1–2).		
SRA PILOT LIBRARIES This program contains five levels of reading—1c, 2a, 2b, 2c, and 3b—with student record books, teacher's handbook, and key booklet. This program is designed to bridge the gap between reading training and independent reading by using short excerpts, complete in themselves, from full-length books. Each pilot library kit contains seventy-two selections called pilot books to whet a young reader's appetite and lead the reader to the original work. The books are sixteen to thirty-two pages long and are chosen for their interest, appeal, and reading level.	Comprehension skills	Grades 3–7
SRA READING FOR UNDERSTANDING This program is a set of four hundred reading comprehension exercises designed to aid each student in improving his or her ability to get meaning from reading.	Comprehension skills	R.F.U. 1: Grades 1–3 R.F.U. 2: Grade 3–adult
SRA READING LABORATORIES This program contains reading labs from 1a to 1c, 2a to 2c, 3a to 3b, and 4a, pupil booklets for labs, and is an individualized reading system based on the principle that learning is most effective if the student starts at his or her own level of reading, where the student is assured success. It allows the student to proceed as fast as his or her learning rate permits.	Basic sight words Vocabulary development Word-analysis skills Dictionary skills Comprehension skills Study skills	Grades 3–9
SRA SKILLS SERIES There are three basic skills sets to this series. Each kit contains forty-eight independent teaching units with instruction and practice for specific skills. A lesson plan for small group or class instruction and a casette tape for independent students are included in each kit. *Phonics Kit* (grades 1–3): this kit includes practice in initial consonants, final consonants, blends, consonant digraphs, vowel sounds, rhyming words, and other basic skills. *Structural Analysis Kit* (grades 3–7): this kit covers forty-eight essential skills, in-	Phonics Structural analysis Comprehension skills	Grades 1–8

(continued)

(continued)

Program	Reading skills	Level of difficulty
cluding prefixes, suffixes, possessives, contractions, syllabication, and stress. *Comprehension Skills Kit:* this kit covers forty-eight skills in three major comprehension areas: literal, inferential, and critical. This kit includes such skills as main idea, supporting details, cause and effect, fact vs. opinion, and more.		
SUPER KITS This is a high-interest, controlled-vocabulary comic-book series designed for reluctant readers with limited word-attack and comprehension skills. The series features well-known characters such as Batman, Superman, and Wonderwoman. Each kit contains ten readers, forty duplicator masters for activity sheets, forty-eight task cards, and a teacher's manual.	Vocabulary development Oral reading skills Phonics Comprehension skills	Grades 4–8
VOCABULARY 3 PROGRAM This kit contains twenty explora-wheels that show the elements of word structure such as prefixes, roots, and suffixes. Also included are 150 vocabulary builders that contain stories, articles, exercises, and activities in ten different interest areas.	Vocabulary development	Grade 5–junior college
Sunburst Communications RM U23 39 Washington Ave. Pleasantville, New York 10570		
HI-LO READING ACTIVITY CARD PROGRAMS This is a remedial reading program for improving reading comprehension. The program consists of high-interest books, activity cards for each book, and a teacher's guide for each set of activity cards.	Comprehension development	Both levels: 4–12 and 3–7
READING FOR EVERY DAY: SURVIVAL SKILLS Students develop reading competency by applying reading skills to everyday experiences. Examples include road maps, menus, and want ads.	Survival reading skills	Grades 4–7

Program	Reading skills	Level of difficulty
Teaching Resources Corporation 50 Pond Park Road Hingham, Massachusetts 02043		
GAMES This company markets many games useful for teaching the most basic reading skills. Some examples of games are: *Phonics Puzzles and Games, Phonics Wheel, Word Family Picture Cards, Pictures for Sound Posters, Sound Puzzles* (initial sounds, final sounds).	Word-analysis skills	Primary–intermediate
ESSENTIAL SIGHT WORDS PROGRAM This is a program to teach 200 basic sight words considered essential to mature reading. it contains many low-imagery words that may be difficult for students to learn. The program consists of two levels. Each level contains a pretest, worksheets, mastery sheets, books, and a posttest.	Basic sight words	Grades 1–3
Webster Division McGraw-Hill Book Company Manchester Road Manchester, Missouri 63011		
WEBSTER WORD WHEELS This program contains sixty-three wheels, seventeen beginning blends, twenty prefix wheels, eighteen suffix wheels, eight two-letter consonant wheels, and a file box. The purpose of this program is to teach students the basic phonetic and structural-analysis skills needed for reading readiness, vocabulary development, and basic sight word development on an individualized basis.	Word-analysis skills (specifically structural analysis and phonetic analysis)	Primary-senior high
Xerox Education Publications Education Center Columbus, Ohio 43216		
DICTIONARY SKILLS AND USING THE DIK*SHUH*NEHR*EE This program contains four books: book A is about a merry magician who teaches his tricks for alphabetizing; book B helps strengthen pronunciation and definition skills; book C works on root words, abbreviations, and parts of speech; book D reviews previous skills and stresses vowel and consonant sounds.	Dictionary skills	Primary–junior high

(continued)

(continued)

Program	Reading skills	Level of difficulty
FIRST STEP TO READING *First Step* teaches left-to-right progression by coloring, cutting, pasting, and painting. The pictures tell the youngsters which tools to use for each activity—such as pencil, crayon, scissors, paste, or paint.	Basic sight words Vocabulary development	Primary–intermediate
GRAPHS AND SURVEYS This program is an introduction to interpreting and preparing graphs and surveys and assembling, evaluating, organizing, and translating information into graphic form.	Study skills	Junior high–adult
LIBRARY SKILLS AND LEARNING TO USE THE LIBRARY This program contains four books: book A works with book parts; book B works with "cracking the code" of the Dewey decimal system; book C works with learning how to use the Reader's Guide; and book D works with using different reference books and using tools such as tapes, filmstrips, earphones, recordings, etc.	Study skills	Primary–senior high
MAP SKILLS FOR TODAY AND READINESS FOR MAP SKILLS This program consists of five books that help the students use maps as learning tools by providing a thorough guide in map terminology, symbols, and other map skills.	Study skills	Primary–senior high
PHONICS AND WORD POWER This program consists of books 1, 2, and 3; each book consists of three levels—A, B, and C—which help children review, maintain, and build the skills to turn printed symbols into units of meaning. Program 2 is for recognizing words, developing vocabulary and phonetic and structural-analysis skills. Program 3 is for multiple approaches to word-analysis skills.	Basic sight words Vocabulary development Word-analysis skills (specifically phonetic analysis)	Primary–junior high
READING SUCCESS SERIES This program uses a mature format, high-interest content, and stimulating illustrations. This series plots a sequence of skills based on what discouraged youngsters do know. There are six different thirty-two-page books, numbered by skill steps and sequenced.	Vocabulary development Word-analysis skills Dictionary skills	Primary–senior high

Program	Reading skills	Level of difficulty
READ-STUDY-THINK This is a series of practice books designed to improve reading comprehension. These skills are reading for literal and concrete facts, interpreting meaning and drawing generalizations, and organizing information.	Comprehension development	Primary–senior high
SPECTRUM OF SKILLS A series of books containing lessons and information designed to teach the skills noted.	Vocabulary development Comprehension development Word-attack skills	Intermediate and upper grades
TABLE AND GRAPH SKILLS This program contains four books. Book A teaches students to learn terms, symbols, and basic procedures that enable them to solve problems represented by tables and graphs. Book B introduces interpretive reading of tables and graphs. Books C and D introduce different kinds of graphs by pictures, box, bar, line, and circle, and emphasize critical and creative reading.	Study skills	Primary–junior high
SOME PUBLISHERS OF GAMES Barnell-Loft, Ltd. and Dexter and Westbrook, Ltd. 958 Church Street Baldwin, New York 11510 Garrard Publishing Company Champaign, Illinois 61820 Ideal School Supply Company Oak Lawn, Illinois 60453 Kenworthy Educational Service, Inc. 138 Allen Street Buffalo, New York 14205 Lyons and Carnahan Educational Publishers 407 East 25th Street Chicago, Illinois 60616 Science Research Associates, Inc. 259 East Erie Street Chicago, Illinois 60611	Basic sight words Vocabulary development (sight and meaning) Word-analysis skills Dictionary skills Comprehension skills Study skills Oral reading skills	Primary Intermediate Junior high Senior high Adult

(continued)

These are addresses of companies that have developed games such as Riddle Riddle Rhyme Time, Fun with Words, Pronoun Parade, One Too Many, Time for Sounds, Consonant Sounds, Vowel Sounds, Phonic Drill Cards, Phonic Word Builders, Dolch Games, Phonic Word Blend Flip Charts, Phonics We Use, Learning Game Kits, SRA Reading Laboratory I: Word Games, and others. These games are devised to help prepare children to read and teach children how to listen and follow directions, how to observe details, and how to express themselves by developing larger vocabularies. There are separate games to supplement phonics and reading instruction. Some games have directions for using the equipment to play additional games and word-building games that help students match their reading vocabulary to their listening vocabulary.

Appendix D: Names and Addresses of Companies That Publish Materials in Reading

Abingdon Press
201 Eighth Avenue South
Nashville, Tenn.   37202

Abrahams Magazine Service
56 East 13th Street
New York, N.Y.   10003

Academic Press
111 Fifth Avenue
New York, N.Y.   10003

Academic Therapy Publications
20 Commercial Blvd.
Novatio, Calif.   94947

Acropolis Books Ltd.
2400 17th Street N.W.
Washington, D.C.   20009

Addison-Wesley Publishing Company
Jacob Way
Reading, Mass.   01867

Addison-Wesley Testing Service
2725 Sand Hill Road
Menlo Park, Calif.   94025

Albert Whitman and Company
560 West Lake Street
Chicago, Ill.   60606

Allyn and Bacon
7 Wells Avenue
Newton, Mass.   02159

American Council on Education
1 Dupont Circle
Washington, D.C.   20036

American Guidance Service
Publishers' Building
Circle Pines, Minn.   55014

American Printing House for the Blind
P.O. Box 6085
Louisville, Ky.   40206

Association for Childhood Education
   International
3615 Wisconsin Avenue N.W.
Washington, D.C.   20016

Audio-Visual Research
1317 Eighth Street S.E.
Waseca, Minn.   56093

Baker and Taylor Company
1515 Broadway
New York, N.Y.   10036

Bantam Books
School and College Marketing Division
666 Fifth Avenue
New York, N.Y.   10019

Barnell Loft, Ltd.
958 Church Street
Baldwin, N.Y.   11510

Basic Skills Program
Office of Basic Skills Improvement
Room 1167—Donohoe Building
400 Maryland Avenue, S.W.
Washington, D.C.   20202

Bell and Howell
Audio-Visual Products Division
7100 N. McCormick Road
Chicago, Ill.   60645

Benefic Press
1250 Sixth Avenue
San Diego, Calif.   92101

Bobbs-Merrill Educational Publishing
4300 West 62nd Street
P.O. Box 7080
Indianapolis, Ind.   46206

Borg-Warner Educational Systems
600 West University Drive
Arlington Heights, Ill.   60004

R.R. Bowker Company
1180 Avenue of the Americas
New York, N.Y.   10036

Bowmar Noble Publishers
4563 Colorado Blvd.
Los Angeles, Calif.   90039

Burgless Publishing Company
7108 Ohms Lane
Minneapolis, Minn.   55435

C.C. Publications
P.O. Box 23699
Tigaro, Ore.   97223

Center for Applied Research in
    Education
P.O. Box 130
West Nyack, N.Y.   10995

Charles E. Merrill Publishing Company
1300 Alum Creek Drive
Columbus, Ohio   43216

The Children's Book Council
67 Irving Place
New York, N.Y.   10003

Children's Press
1224 West Van Buren Street
Chicago, Ill.   60607

Clarence L. Barnhart
Box 250
1 Stone Place
Bronxville, N.Y.   10708

College Skills Center
1250 Broadway at 32nd St.
New York, N.Y.   10001

Communacad
Box 541
Wilton, Conn.   06897

Consulting Psychologists Press
577 College Avenue
Palo Alto, Calif.   94306

Coronet
65 East South Water Street
Chicago, Ill.   60601

Council for Exceptional Children
1920 Association Drive
Reston, Va.   22091

Creative Curriculum
15681 Commerce Lane
Huntington Beach, Calif.   92649

Crown Publishers
1 Park Avenue
New York, N.Y.   10016

CTB/McGraw-Hill
Del Monte Research Park
Monterey, Calif.   93940

Curriculum Associates
5 Esquire Road
North Billerica, Mass.   01862

C. Lucas Dalton
5720 Caruth Haven
Suite 130
Dallas, Texas   75206

Dell Publishing Company
Education Dept.
245 East 47th St.
New York, N.Y.   10017

DES Educational Publications
25 South Fifth Avenue
P.O. Box 1291
Highland Park, N.J.   08904

Developmental Learning Materials
7440 Natchez Avenue
Niles, Ill.   60648

Dreier Educational Systems
25 South Fifth Avenue
P.O. Box 1291
Highland Park, N.J.   08904

A.B. Dick Company
5700 Touhy Avenue
Chicago, Ill.   60648

Dome Press
1169 Logan Avenue
Elgin, Ill.   60120

Doubleday & Company
501 Franklin Avenue
Garden City, N.Y.   11530

EBSCO Curriculum Materials
Box 11521
Birmingham, Ala.   35202

The Economy Company
Box 25308
1901 West Walnut Street
Oklahoma City, Okla.   73125

EDL/McGraw-Hill
1221 Avenue of the Americas
New York, N.Y.   10020

Educational Activities
P.O. Box 392
Freeport, N.Y.   11520

Educational Progress Division of Educational Development Corporation
P.O. Box 45663
Tulsa, Okla.   74145

Educational Service
P.O. Box 219
Stevensville, Mich.   49127

Educational Testing Service
Box 999
Princeton, N.J.   08540

Educators Publishing Service
75 Moulton Street
Cambridge, Mass.   02138

Encyclopedia Britannica Educational Corporation
425 North Michigan Avenue
Chicago, Ill.   60611

E & R Development Company
Vandalia Road
Jacksonville, Fla.   62650

ERIC Clearinghouse on Reading and Communication Skills
National Council of Teachers of English
1111 Kenyon Road
Urbana, Ill.   61801

Essay Press
P.O. Box 2323
La Jolla, Calif.   92037

Fawcett Books Group
Educational Marketing Dept.
1515 Broadway
New York, N.Y.   10036

Fearon-Pitman Publishers
6 Davis Drive
Belmont, Calif.   94002

Follett Publishing Company
Dept. D.M.
1010 West Washington Blvd.
Chicago, Ill.   60607

Franklin Watts
730 Fifth Avenue
New York, N.Y.   10019

Frohnhoefer's Books
R.D. 1, Route 9G
Tivoli, N.Y.   12583

Garrard Publishing Company
1607 North Market Street
Champaign, Ill.   61820

Ginn and Company
P.O. Box 2749
1250 Fairwood Avenue
Columbus, Ohio   43216

Globe Book Company
50 West 23rd Street
New York, N.Y.   10010

Gorsuch Scarisbrick Publishers
576 Central
Dubuque, Iowa   52001

Grossett & Dunlap
Education Division
51 Madison Avenue
New York, N.Y.   10010

Grove Press
196 West Houston Street
New York, N.Y.   10014

E.M. Hale and Company
Harvey House Publishers
128 West River Street
Chippewa Falls, Wis.   54729

Harcourt Brace Jovanovich
757 Third Avenue
New York, N.Y.   10017

Harper & Row
10 East 53rd Street
New York, N.Y.   10022

Hawthorn Books
260 Madison Avenue
New York, N.Y.   10016

Hayden Book Company
50 Essex Street
Rochelle Park, N.J. 07662

D.C. Heath
125 Spring Street
Lexington, Mass.   02173

Heinemann Educational Books
4 Front Street
Exeter, N.H.   03833

Hertzberg–New Method
Vandalia Road
Jacksonville, Ill.   62650

Holt, Rinehart & Winston
CBS Inc.
383 Madison Avenue
New York, N.Y.   10017

Houghton Mifflin
1 Beacon Street
Boston, Mass.   02107

Ideal School Supply Company
11000 South Lavergne Avenue
Oak Lawn, Ill.   60453

Imperial International Learning
Corporation
P.O. Box 548
Kankakee, Ill.   60901

Incentives for Learning
600 West Van Buren Street
Chicago, Ill.   60607

Instructional Fair
Box 1650
Grand Rapids, Mich.   49501

Instructor Publications
7 Bank Street
Dansville, N.Y.   14437

International Reading Association
800 Barksdale Road
Newark, Del.   19711

ITA, A Non-Profit Educational
Foundation
Hofstra University
Hempstead, N.Y.   11550

Jamestown Publishers
P.O. Box 6743
Providence, R.I.   02940

Kendall/Hunt Publishing Co.
2460 Kerper Blvd.
Dubuque, Iowa   52001

Kenworthy Educational Service
Box 60
138 Allen Street
Buffalo, N.Y.   14205

Keystone View
Division of Mast Development Company
2212 East 12th Street
Davenport, Iowa   52803

Kimbo Educational Publishers
P.O. Box 477
Long Branch, N.J.   07740

The Kingsbury Center
2138 Bancroft Place, N.W.
Washington, D.C.   20008

The Klamath Printery
628 Oak Street
Klamath Falls, Ore.   97601

Kraus-Thomson Organization, Ltd.
Rte. 100
Millwood, N.Y.   10546

Language Research Associates
P.O. Drawer 2085
Palm Springs, Calif.   92262

Lansford Publishing Company
1088 Lincoln Avenue
P.O. Box·8711
San Jose, Calif. 95155

Learning Arts
P.O. Box 179
Wichita, Kan.   67201

Learning Associates
P.O. Box 561167
Miami, Fla.   33156

The Learning Line
Box 577
Palo Alto, Calif.   94302

Learning Resources Corporation
8517 Production Avenue
San Diego, Calif.   92121

Leswing Press
P.O. Box 3577
San Rafael, Calif.   94901

Library of Congress
National Library Service for the Blind
   and Physically Handicapped
1291 Taylor Street N.W.
Washington, D.C.   20542

Listening Library
1 Park Avenue
Old Greenwich, Conn.   06870

Litton Educational Publishing
7625 Empire Drive
Florence, Ky.   41042

Longman
19 West 44th Street
New York, N.Y.   10036

The Macmillan Company
Front and Brown Streets
Riverside, N.J.   08370

McCormick-Mathers Publishing Company, A Division of Litton Educational Publishing
7625 Empire Drive
Florence, Ky.   41042

McDougal, Littell & Company
P.O. Box 1667-C
Evanston, Ill.   60204

McGraw-Hill Book Company
1221 Avenue of the Americas
New York, N.Y.   10020

McGraw-Hill Ryerson Ltd.
330 Progress Avenue
Scarborough, Ontario
Canada M1P   2Z5

Mast Development Company
2212 East 12th Street
Davenport, Iowa   52803

Media Materials
Department MDR
2936 Remington Avenue
Baltimore, Md.   21211

G. & C. Merriam Company
47 Federal Street
Springfield, Mass.   01101

Charles E. Merrill Publishing Company
1300 Alum Creek Drive
Columbus, Ohio   43216

Midwest Publications
P.O. Box 448
Pacific Grove, Calif.   93950

Milton Bradley Company
Springfield, Mass.   01101

Montana Reading Publications
517 Remrock Road
Billings, Mont.   59102

William Morrow & Company
105 Madison Avenue
New York, N.Y.   10016

National Association for the Deaf
814 Thayer Avenue
Silver Springs, Md.   20910

National Council of Teachers of English
1111 Kenyon Road
Urbana, Ill.   61801

National Public Radio
2025 M Street, N.W.
Washington, D.C.   20036

National Textbook Company
8259 Viles Center Road
Skokie, Ill.   60077

NCS/Educational Systems Division
4401 West 76th Street
Minneapolis, Minn.   55435

W.W. Norton & Company
500 Fifth Avenue
New York, N.Y.   10036

Open Court Publishing Company
Box 599
LaSalle, Ill.   61301

Phonovisual Products
12216 Parklawn Drive
P.O. Box 2007
Rockville, Md.   20852

Pitman Learning (formerly Fearon-
  Pitman Publishers)
6 Davis Drive
Belmont, Calif.   94002

Plays
8 Arlington Street
Boston, Mass.   02116

Prentice-Hall
Educational Book Division
Englewood Cliffs, N.J.   07632

Pro-Ed
5341 Industrial Oaks Blvd.
Austin, Texas   78735

Programs for Achievement in Readings
Abbott Park Place
Providence, R.I.   02903

Pruett Publishing Company
3235 Prairie Avenue
Boulder, Colo.   80301

The Psychological Corporation
757 Third Avenue
New York, N.Y.   10017

Psychological Test Specialists
Box 9229
Missoula, Mont.   59807

Publishers Test Service
2500 Garden Road
Monterey, Calif.   93940

G.P. Putnam's Sons
Coward McCann & Geoghegan
200 Madison Avenue
New York, N.Y.   10016

Rand McNally and Company
Box 7600
Chicago, Ill.   60680

Random House
201 East 50th Street
New York, N.Y.   10022

Reader's Digest Services
Educational Division
Pleasantville, N.Y.   10570

The Reading Laboratory
P.O. Box 681
South Norwalk, Conn.   06854

Resources
Instructional Communication
  Technology, Inc.
Huntington, Station, N.Y.   11746

Riverside Publishing Company
P.O. Box 1970
Iowa City, Iowa   52244

Santillana Publishing Company
575 Lexington Avenue
New York, N.Y.   10022

Scarecrow Press
52 Liberty Street
Box 656
Metuchen, N.J.   08840

Scholastic Book Service
904 Sylvan Avenue
Englewood Cliffs, N.J.   07632

Science Research Associates
155 North Wacker Drive
Chicago, Ill.   60606

Scott, Foresman and Company
1900 East Lake Avenue
Glenview, Ill.   60025

Simon & Schuster
Simon & Schuster Building
1230 Avenue of the Americas
New York, N.Y.   10020

Slosson Educational Publications
P.O. Box 280
East Aurora, N.Y. 14052

Smithsonian Institution
475 L'Enfant Plaza
Suite 4800
Washington, D.C. 20560

SRA
Science Research Associates
155 North Wacker Drive
Chicago, Ill. 60606

Steck-Vaughn Company
Box 2028
Austin, Texas 78767

Stoelting Company
1350 South Kostner Avenue
Chicago, Ill. 60623

Strine Publishing Company
P.O. Box 149
York, Pa. 17405

Sunburst Communications
Room U 23
39 Washington Avenue
Pleasantville, N.Y. 10570

SVE
Society for Visual Educational Inc.
1345 Diversey Parkway
Chicago, Ill. 60614

Teachers College Press
Teachers College
Columbia University
1234 Amsterdam Avenue
New York, N.Y. 10027

Teaching Resources Corporation
50 Pond Park Road
Hingham, Mass. 02043

University of Chicago Press
5801 South Ellis Avenue
Chicago, Ill. 60637

University of Illinois Press
54 E. Gregory Dr.
P.O. Box 5081
Sta. A
Champaign, Ill. 61820

University of Nebraska Press
318 Nebraska Hall
901 North 17th Street
Lincoln, Neb. 68588

The Viking Press
Viking Penguin, Inc.
625 Madison Avenue
New York, N.Y. 10022

J. Weston Walch, Publisher
321 Valley Street
Portland, Me. 04104

Webster Division of McGraw-Hill
    Book Company
1221 Avenue of the Americas
New York, N.Y. 10020

Weekly Reader
Long Hill Road
Middletown, Conn. 06457

Weekly Reader/Secondary Unit Books
1250 Fairwood Avenue
P.O. Box 16618
Columbus, Ohio 43216

Western Psychological Services
12031 Wilshire Blvd.
Los Angeles, Calif. 90025

Weston Woods Studios
Weston, Conn. 06883

William C. Brown Company, Publishers
2460 Kerper Blvd.
Dubuque, Iowa 52001

World Book-Childcraft International
Merchandise Mart Plaza
Chicago, Ill. 60654

The H.W. Wilson Company
950 University Avenue
Bronx, N.Y. 10452

Richard L. Zweig Associates
20800 Beach Blvd.
Huntington Beach, Calif. 92648

Index